T0183332

Lecture Notes in Business Information Processing 391

Series Editors

More information about this series at http://www.springer.com/series/7911

Boris Shishkov (Ed.)

Business Modeling and Software Design

10th International Symposium, BMSD 2020
Berlin, Germany, July 6–8, 2020
Proceedings

Editor
Boris Shishkov
Faculty of Information Sciences
University of Library Studies
and Information Technologies
Sofia, Bulgaria

Institute of Mathematics and Informatics
Bulgarian Academy of Sciences
Sofia, Bulgaria

Interdisciplinary Institute for Collaboration
and Research on Enterprise Systems
and Technology
Sofia, Bulgaria

ISSN 1865-1348 ISSN 1865-1356 (electronic)
Lecture Notes in Business Information Processing
ISBN 978-3-030-52305-3 ISBN 978-3-030-52306-0 (eBook)
https://doi.org/10.1007/978-3-030-52306-0

This Springer imprint is published by the registered company Springer Nature Switzerland AG
The registered company address is: Gewerbestrasse 11, 6330 Cham, Switzerland

Preface

BMSD (http://www.is-bmsd.org) is an annual international symposium on **Business Modeling and Software Design** that brings together researchers and practitioners interested in *enterprise modeling* and its relation to *software specification*. This book contains the **proceedings** of **BMSD 2020**, held in *Berlin, Germany*, on *6-8 July 2020*.

In the preface of the previous proceedings (*LNBIP 356*), we have referred to *Julian Lennon* - he had observed in 1991 that even though we had achieved *impressive* (*technical and technological*) *advances*, we were still *failing to adequately respond to some essential real life issues*. The good news is that now (nearly three decades later), we seem to be *benefitting more from technology*, including *ICT* – the *Information and Communication Technology*. Currently, it is easier and affordable for many people to gather information, to communicate, and to get things done from distance. With regard to this, **SOFTWARE** plays a crucial role. Nevertheless, many researchers and practitioners claim that *what we have today could have been even better*. Some of the key current software products have not evolved very much after the initial design, for example: [Microsoft] *Windows 10* and *Windows XP* do not differ that much, and the same holds for *Office 2003* and *Office 2016*; [Apple] The current *MacOS* looks nearly the same as the one from 10 years ago; [UNIX] *Linux* has been nearly the same for 30 years already; and so on. From one perspective, this is understandable because of companies' *competing for customers* most of whom would not want to learn a new and differently looking package. But from another perspective, *the societal context and customer needs* (and *preferences*) *are changing over time*; this means that some of the key "infrastructure"-level software products are becoming *less and less focused on the needs of customers*. Unfortunately, it is rarely the case that the software being developed is adapted to the user but just the opposite - the user needs to adapt his or her actions to the software environment at hand; otherwise, the value of using the software would be just partial. Good news here is that some *smaller-scale software applications* are trying to fill in that gap, by "acting on behalf of the user" in such environments. Anyway, we cannot and we should not differentiate between large-scale software and small-scale software. Software is about reflecting user needs in software specifications that are in turn realized, implemented, and deployed for the benefit of the **USER**. Hence, the **evolution challenge** is to be seriously taken into account when drawing visions for the *software of the next decade*. Next to that are two key desired features, namely **robustness** and **resilience**. In our view, during the *SARS-CoV-2 pandemic*, it showed up that there is much room for improvement, when it comes to robustness and resilience. Indeed, *ICT* helped a lot during the pandemic: *IT infrastructures and networks kept functioning* (for example, in hospitals, banks, and so on); employees were *working from home* and students were *studying from home*, supported by *ICT*; kids were able to *video-call* to their grandparents while in isolation; business people were able to *collaborate distantly*, supported by *videoconferencing*; and so on. But at the same time, some *weaknesses* popped up: *Enterprise information systems* featuring *supply chains* and/or *enterprise resource planning*, could have been more resilient - this would have facilitated supplies and decreased costs. Further, developing software that is adequate as it concerns **public values** and **regulations** is claimed to be a challenge as well: During the pandemic, we used to see IT systems that were often "wandering" between *regulations* (a number of countries across the world have declared a state of emergency, this leading to constantly changing regulations) and *public values* (they are "constant" but would often appear to be in conflict with some "fast written" new pandemic regulations). It is still an open question how to resolve such tensions. This is not trivial and goes beyond the technology itself; hence, it is not surprising that during the pandemic, key software development persons were stating social, even political attitudes. In this way, those persons had implicitly claimed an even bigger role for software, beyond the reflection of objectivized user needs in software specifications. What we observe today is that software is also "instrumental" as it concerns societal and even political issues, this going beyond servicing the user. Unfortunately, it seems to be insufficiently clear HOW it is established what a software system does with regard to *regulations* vs *public values*, for example. Finally, going back to the *evolution challenge*, we have observed during the pandemic that many software systems have failed to effectively adapt to the fast changing user needs. And what are the lessons learned after all? We argue that essentially, information systems and software applications are (and are to be) driven by the goal of BRINGING VALUE TO USERS, which makes them societally-relevant; but at the same time, developers should be careful when the "societal relevance" enters the territory of politics – in such cases, there should be *clear rules and criteria* as it concerns the conformance to *regulations*, *public values*, and so on. Next to that and beyond the above considerations, we argue that underestimating the crucial importance of *user needs* as THE inspiration when specifying software, is a key software failure over the last several decades. Improving this can only be achieved if methodologically aligning business (enterprise) modeling and software design – this brings the BMSD Community together. As mentioned in the *LNBIP 356* preface, **we are inspired to dream of better ways of developing (enterprise) information systems and software applications; we are active in proposing innovative ideas, encouraging open discussions, and stimulating community building, driven by the goal of contributing to the area of ENTERPRISE INFORMATION SYSTEMS**.

Since 2011, we have enjoyed **nine successful BMSD editions**. The first BMSD edition (**2011**) took place in **Sofia**, **Bulgaria**, and the theme of BMSD 2011 was: "Business Models and Advanced Software Systems." The second BMSD edition (**2012**) took place in **Geneva**, **Switzerland**, with the theme: "From Business Modeling to Service-Oriented Solutions." The third BMSD edition (**2013**) took place in **Noordwijkerhout**, **The Netherlands**, and the theme was: "Enterprise Engineering and Software Generation." The fourth BMSD edition (**2014**) took place in **Luxembourg**, **Grand Duchy of Luxembourg**, and the theme was: "Generic Business Modeling Patterns and Software Re-Use." The fifth BMSD edition (**2015**) took place in **Milan**, **Italy**, with the theme: "Toward Adaptable Information Systems." The sixth BMSD edition (**2016**) took place in **Rhodes**, **Greece**, and had as theme: "Integrating Data Analytics in Enterprise Modeling and Software Development." The seventh BMSD edition (**2017**) took place in **Barcelona**, **Spain**, and the theme was: "Modeling

Viewpoints and Overall Consistency." The eighth BMSD edition (**2018**) took place in **Vienna**, **Austria**, with the theme: "Enterprise Engineering and Software Engineering - Processes and Systems for the Future." The ninth BMSD edition (**2019**) took place in **Lisbon**, **Portugal**, and the theme of BMSD 2019 was: "Reflecting Human Authority and Responsibility in Enterprise Models and Software Specifications". The 2020 edition in Berlin marks the **TENTH EVENT**, with the theme: "Towards Knowledge-Driven Enterprise Information Systems."

We are proud to have attracted distinguished guests as keynote lecturers, who are renowned experts in their fields: **Jose Tribolet**, *IST - University of Lisbon*, Portugal (2019), **Jan Mendling**, *WU Vienna*, Austria (2018), **Roy Oberhauser**, *Aalen University*, Germany (2018), **Norbert Gronau**, *University of Potsdam*, Germany (2017), **Oscar Pastor**, *Polytechnic University of Valencia*, Spain (2017), **Alexander Verbraeck**, *Delft University of Technology*, The Netherlands (2017), **Paris Avgeriou**, *University of Groningen*, The Netherlands (2016), **Jan Juerjens**, *University of Koblenz-Landau*, Germany (2016), **Mathias Kirchmer**, *BPM-D*, USA (2016), **Marijn Janssen**, *Delft University of Technology*, The Netherlands (2015), **Barbara Pernici**, *Politecnico di Milano*, Italy (2015), **Hend*erik* Proper**, *Public Research Centre Henri Tudor*, Grand Duchy of Luxembourg (2014), **Roel Wieringa**, *University of Twente*, The Netherlands (2014), **Kecheng Liu**, *University of Reading*, UK (2013), **Marco Aiello**, *University of Groningen*, The Netherlands (2013), **Leszek Maciaszek**, *Wroclaw University of Economics*, Poland (2013), **Jan L. G. Dietz**, *Delft University of Technology*, The Netherlands (2012), **Ivan Ivanov**, *SUNY Empire State College*, USA (2012), **Dimitri Konstantas**, *University of Geneva*, Switzerland (2012), **Marten van Sinderen**, *University of Twente*, The Netherlands (2012), **Mehmet Aksit**, *University of Twente*, The Netherlands (2011), **Dimitar Christozov**, *American University in Bulgaria – Blagoevgrad*, Bulgaria (2011), **Bart Nieuwenhuis**, *University of Twente*, The Netherlands (2011), and **Hermann Maurer**, *Graz University of Technology*, Austria (2011).

The high quality of the BMSD 2020 technical program is enhanced by two keynote lectures delivered by outstanding guests: **Manfred Reichert**, *Ulm University*, Germany (the title of his lecture is: "Data-Centric, Large-Scale Process Management Software: Engineering, Technologies, Applications"); **Mathias Weske**, *HPI - University of Potsdam*, Germany (the title of his lecture is: "Business Processes: From Modeling to Mining and Back"). Also, the presence (physically or distantly) of former BMSD keynote lecturers is much appreciated: *Roy Oberhauser* (2018), *Norbert Gronau* (2017), and *Mathias Kirchmer* (2016). The technical program is further enriched by a panel discussion (featured by the participation of most of the abovementioned outstanding scientists) and also by other discussions stimulating *community building* and facilitating possible *R&D project acquisition initiatives*. Those special activities are definitely contributing to **maintaining the event's high quality and inspiring our steady and motivated Community**.

The BMSD'20 Technical Program Committee consists of a Chair and 109 Members from 37 countries (*Australia*, *Austria*, *Brazil*, *Bulgaria*, *Canada*, *China*, *Colombia*, *Czech Republic*, *Denmark*, *Egypt*, *Estonia*, *Finland*, *France*, *Germany*, *Greece*, *India*, *Indonesia*, *Italy*, *Lithuania*, *Grand Duchy of Luxembourg*, *Malaysia*, *Mexico*, *New Zealand*, *Palestine*, *Poland*, *Portugal*, *Russia*, *Singapore*, *Slovakia*, *Slovenia*, *Spain*,

Sweden, *Switzerland*, *Taiwan*, *The Netherlands*, *the UK*, and *the USA*, listed alphabetically) – all of them competent and enthusiastic representatives of prestigious organizations.

In organizing BMSD 2020, we have observed **highest ethical standards**: We guarantee *at least two reviews per submitted paper* (this assuming reviews of adequate quality), under the condition that the paper fulfills the BMSD'20 requirements. In assigning a paper for reviewing, it is our responsibility to *provide reviewers with relevant expertise*. Sticking to a **double-blind review process**, we guarantee that the reviewers would not know who the authors of the reviewed papers are (we send anonymized versions of the papers to the reviewers) and the authors would not know who has reviewed their papers. We require that reviewers *respect the content of the reviewed papers* and do not disclose (parts of) the content to third parties before the symposium (and also after the symposium in case the manuscript gets rejected). We *guarantee against conflict of interests*, by not assigning papers for reviewing by reviewers who are immediate colleagues of any of the paper's co-authors. In our decisions to accept / reject papers, we **guarantee against any discrimination based on age, gender, race, or religion**. As it concerns the EU data protection standards, **we stick to the GDPR requirements**.

We have demonstrated for a **TENTH CONSECUTIVE YEAR** a high quality of papers and as mentioned in the *LNBIP 356* preface, we are happy to have succeeded in establishing and maintaining (for many years already) a high scientific quality (as it concerns the symposium itself) and a stimulating collaborative atmosphere; also, our Community is inspired to share ideas and experiences.

As mentioned already, BMSD is essentially leaning toward **ENTERPRISE INFORMATION SYSTEMS (EIS)**, by considering the **MODELING OF ENTERPRISES AND BUSINESS PROCESSES** as a basis for **SPECIFYING SOFTWARE**. Further, in the broader EIS context, BMSD 2020 addresses a large number of research areas and topics, as follows:

› **BUSINESS PROCESSES AND ENTERPRISE ENGINEERING** - *enterprise systems; enterprise system environments and context; construction and function; actor roles; signs and affordances; transactions; business processes; business process coordination; business process optimization; business process management and strategy execution; production acts and coordination acts; regulations and business rules; enterprise (re-) engineering; enterprise interoperability; inter-enterprise coordination; enterprise engineering and architectural governance; enterprise engineering and software generation; enterprise innovation.*

› **BUSINESS MODELS AND REQUIREMENTS** - *essential business models; re-usable business models; business value models; business process models; business goal models; integrating data analytics in business modeling; semantics and business data modeling; pragmatics and business behavior modeling; business modeling viewpoints and overall consistency; business modeling landscapes; requirements elicitation; domain-imposed and user-defined requirements; requirements specification and modeling; requirements analysis and verification; requirements evolution; requirements traceability; usability and requirements elicitation.*

› **BUSINESS MODELS AND SERVICES** - *enterprise engineering and service science; service-oriented enterprises; from business modeling to service-oriented*

solutions; business modeling for software-based services; service engineering; business-goals-driven service discovery and modeling; technology-independent and platform-specific service modeling; re-usable service models; business-rules-driven service composition; web services; autonomic service behavior; context-aware service behavior; service interoperability; change impact analysis and service management; service monitoring and quality of service; services for IoT applications; service innovation.

› **BUSINESS MODELS AND SOFTWARE** - *enterprise engineering and software development; model-driven engineering; co-design of business and IT systems; business-IT alignment and traceability; alignment between IT architecture and business strategy; business strategy and technical debt; business-modeling-driven software generation; normalized systems and combinatorial effects; software generation and dependency analysis; component-based business-software alignment; objects, components, and modeling patterns; generic business modeling patterns and software re-use; business rules and software specification; business goals and software integration; business innovation and software evolution; software technology maturity models; domain-specific models; croscutting concerns - security, privacy, distribution, recoverability, logging, performance monitoring.*

› **INFORMATION SYSTEMS ARCHITECTURES AND PARADIGMS** - *enterprise architectures; service-oriented computing; software architectures; cloud computing; autonomic computing (and intelligent software behavior); context-aware computing (and adaptable software systems); affective computing (and user-aware software systems); aspect-oriented computing (and non-functional requirements); architectural styles; architectural viewpoints.*

› **DATA ASPECTS IN BUSINESS MODELING AND SOFTWARE DEVELOPMENT** - *data modeling in business processes; data flows and business modeling; databases, OLTP, and business processes; data warehouses, OLAP, and business analytics; data analysis, data semantics, redundancy, and quality-of-data; data mining, knowledge discovery, and knowledge management; information security and business process modeling; categorization, classification, regression, and clustering; cluster analysis and predictive analysis; ontologies and decision trees; decision tree induction and information gain; business processes and entropy; machine learning and deep learning - an enterprise perspective; uncertainty and context states; statistical data analysis and probabilistic business models.*

› **BLOCKCHAIN-BASED BUSINESS MODELS AND INFORMATION SYSTEMS** - *smart contracts; blockchains for business process management; blockchain schemes for decentralization; the blockchain architecture - implications for systems and business processes; blockchains and the future of enterprise information systems; blockchains and security / privacy / trust issues.*

› **IoT AND IMPLICATIONS FOR ENTERPRISE INFORMATION SYSTEMS** - *the IoT paradigm; IoT data collection and aggregation; business models and IoT; IoT-based software solutions; IoT and context-awareness; IoT and public values; IoT applications: smart cities, e-Health, smart manufacturing.*

BMSD 2020 received 65 paper submissions from which 28 papers were selected for publication in the symposium proceedings. Of these papers, 15 were selected for a 30-minute oral presentation (full papers), leading to a **full-paper acceptance ratio of**

23% (compared to 22% in 2019 and 19% in 2018) - an indication for our intention to preserve a high-quality forum for the next editions of the symposium. The BMSD 2020 keynote lecturers and authors come from: Algeria, Austria, Belgium, Bulgaria, Germany, Greece, Indonesia, Kazakhstan, Palestine, Portugal, Sweden, The Netherlands, Tunisia, Turkey, the UK, and the USA (listed alphabetically); that makes a total of 16 countries (compared to 10 in 2019, 15 in 2018, 20 in 2017, 16 in 2016, 21 in 2015, 21 in 2014, 14 in 2013, 11 in 2012, and 10 in 2011) to justify a strong international presence. Four countries have been represented at all ten BMSD editions so far – **Bulgaria**, **Germany**, **The Netherlands**, and the **UK** – indicating a strong European influence.

Clustering BMSD papers is always inspiring because this gives different perspectives with regard to the challenge of **adequately specifying software based on enterprise modeling**. Some BMSD'20 papers are leaning towards business processes: from more *philosophical considerations*, through *business rules / logic (declarative semantics)*, to *business process management*, and related *notations*; there are papers bringing this towards *organizational modeling* and *requirements*, considering relevant *modeling languages*, such as *UML* (the *Unified Modeling Language*), in general, and in particular -the *UML Use Case Diagram* and the *UML Sequence Diagram*; further, there are papers touching upon *product-line engineering*. Other papers are leaning towards information systems / software design, touching upon *IT architectures*, *service-level agreements*, *microservices*, and *resilience of EIS for large-scale disruptions*; further, there are papers considering *pattern recognition*, *executable protocols* as well as *IoT applications*. Still other papers are addressing data analytics and machine learning, as well as open data, in the perspective of *enterprise modeling* and/or *EIS specifications*. Finally, there are papers touching upon knowledge management and visualization tools as it concerns *enterprise architectures*. In this, the BMSD'20 papers are addressing many application domains of high societal relevance, such as *healthcare*, *education*, *transport*, *telecommunications*, and so on.

Fully respecting the desire of some participants not to travel abroad (because of the abovementioned pandemic), we have allowed, **as an exception**, distant participation for those Colleagues. Anyway, the unpleasant developments from the first half of this year did not bring us down! We are as successful as in previous years. We are as physical as we can be, inspired for collaboration, discussions, knowledge co-creation, and community building.

BMSD 2020 was organized and sponsored by the *Interdisciplinary Institute for Collaboration and Research on Enterprise Systems and Technology* (*IICREST*) and co-organized by the *University of Potsdam*, being technically co-sponsored by *BPM-D*. Cooperating organizations were *Aristotle University of Thessaloniki* (*AUTH*), *Delft University of Technology* (*TU Delft*), the UTwente *Digital Society Institute* (*DSI*), the *Dutch Research School for Information and Knowledge Systems* (*SIKS*), and *AMA-KOTA Ltd*.

Organizing this interesting and successful symposium required the dedicated efforts of many people. First, we thank the *authors*, whose research and development achievements are recorded here. Next, the *Program Committee members* each deserve credit for the diligent and rigorous peer reviewing. Further, we would like to mention the excellent organization provided by the *IICREST team* (supported by its *logistics partner, AMAKOTA Ltd.*) – the team (words of gratitude to *Aglika Bogomilova*!) did all the necessary work for delivering a stimulating and productive event, supported by our German Colleagues – *Prof. Norbert Gronau* and *Marcus Grum*. We are grateful to *Springer* for their willingness to publish the current proceedings and we would like to especially mention *Ralf Gerstner* and *Christine Reiss*, appreciating their professionalism and patience (regarding the preparation of the symposium proceedings). We are certainly grateful to our *keynote lecturers*, *Prof. Reichert* and *Prof. Weske*, for their invaluable contribution and for their taking the time to synthesize and deliver their talks. Last but not least, I take the opportunity to personally address my supervisor and Colleague from *Delft University of Technology*, and BMSD'17 keynote lecturer, *Prof. Alexander Verbraeck*, mentioning my gratitude and appreciation for all his valuable feedback concerning the BMSD'20 preparations; I benefited a lot from Alexander's help!

We wish you inspiring reading! We look forward to meeting you next year in *Sofia, Bulgaria*, for the *11th International Symposium on Business Modeling and Software Design* (*BMSD 2021*), details of which will be made available on: http://www.is-bmsd.org. In 2021, BMSD will get back to where it once started. We hope to see next year in Sofia very many of you, dear Colleagues from the BMSD Community!

June 2020 Boris Shishkov

Organization

Chair

Boris Shishkov	ULSIT/IMI-BAS/IICREST, Bulgaria

Program Committee

Hamideh Afsarmanesh	University of Amsterdam, The Netherlands
Marco Aiello	University of Stuttgart, Germany
Mehmet Aksit	University of Twente, The Netherlands
Amr Ali-Eldin	Mansoura University, Egypt
Apostolos Ampatzoglou	University of Macedonia, Greece
Paulo Anita	Delft University of Technology, The Netherlands
Juan Carlos Augusto	Middlesex University, UK
Paris Avgeriou	University of Groningen, The Netherlands
Saimir Bala	WU Vienna, Austria
Jose Borbinha	University of Lisbon, Portugal
Frances Brazier	Delft University of Technology, The Netherlands
Ruth Breu	University of Innsbruck, Austria
Bert de Brock	University of Groningen, The Netherlands
Barrett Bryant	University of North Texas, USA
Cinzia Cappiello	Politecnico di Milano, Italy
Kuo-Ming Chao	Coventry University, UK
Michel Chaudron	Chalmers University of Technology, Sweden
Samuel Chong	Fullerton Systems, Singapore
Dimitar Christozov	American University in Bulgaria - Blagoevgrad, Bulgaria
Jose Cordeiro	Polytechnic Institute of Setubal, Portugal
Robertas Damasevicius	Kaunas University of Technology, Lithuania
Ralph Deters	University of Saskatchewan, Canada
Claudio Di Ciccio	Sapienza University, Italy
Jan L. G. Dietz	Delft University of Technology, The Netherlands
Aleksandar Dimov	Sofia University St. Kliment Ohridski, Bulgaria
Teduh Dirgahayu	Universitas Islam Indonesia, Indonesia
Dirk Draheim	Tallinn University of Technology, Estonia
John Edwards	Aston University, UK
Hans-Georg Fill	University of Vienna, Austria / University of Bamberg, Germany
Chiara Francalanci	Politecnico di Milano, Italy
Veska Georgieva	Technical University – Sofia, Bulgaria
J. Paul Gibson	T&MSP - Telecom & Management SudParis, France
Rafael Gonzalez	Javeriana University, Colombia

Paul Grefen	Eindhoven University of Technology, The Netherlands
Norbert Gronau	University of Potsdam, Germany
Clever Ricardo Guareis de Farias	University of Sao Paulo, Brazil
Jens Gulden	University of Duisburg-Essen, Germany
Ilian Ilkov	IBM, The Netherlands
Ivan Ivanov	SUNY Empire State College, USA
Marijn Janssen	Delft University of Technology, The Netherlands
Gabriel Juhas	Slovak University of Technology, Slovak Republic
Dmitry Kan	AlphaSense Inc., Finland
Stefan Koch	Johannes Kepler University Linz, Austria
Michal Krcal	Masaryk University, Czech Republic
Vinay Kulkarni	Tata Consultancy Services, India
John Bruntse Larsen	Technical University of Denmark, Denmark
Peng Liang	Wuhan University, China
Kecheng Liu	University of Reading, UK
Claudia Loebbecke	University of Cologne, Germany
Leszek Maciaszek	Macquarie University, Australia / University of Economics, Poland
Somayeh Malakuti	ABB Corporate Research Center, Germany
Jelena Marincic	ASML, The Netherlands
Raimundas Matulevicius	University of Tartu, Estonia
Hermann Maurer	Graz University of Technology, Austria
Heinrich Mayr	Alpen-Adria-University Klagenfurt, Austria
Nikolay Mehandjiev	University of Manchester, UK
Jan Mendling	WU Vienna, Austria
Michele Missikoff	Institute for Systems Analysis and Computer Science, Italy
Dimitris Mitrakos	Aristotle University of Thessaloniki, Greece
Ricardo Neisse	European Commission Joint Research Center, Italy
Bart Nieuwenhuis	University of Twente, The Netherlands
Roy Oberhauser	Aalen University, Germany
Olga Ormandjieva	Concordia University, Canada
Paul Oude Luttighuis	Le Blanc Advies, The Netherlands
Mike Papazoglou	Tilburg University, The Netherlands
Marcin Paprzycki	Polish Academy of Sciences, Poland
Jeffrey Parsons	Memorial University of Newfoundland, Canada
Oscar Pastor	Universidad Politecnica de Valencia, Spain
Krassie Petrova	Auckland University of Technology, New Zealand
Prantosh K. Paul	Raiganj University, India
Barbara Pernici	Politecnico di Milano, Italy
Doncho Petkov	Eastern Connecticut State University, USA
Gregor Polancic	University of Maribor, Slovenia
Henderik Proper	Luxembourg Institute of Science and Technology, Grand Duchy of Luxembourg
Mirja Pulkkinen	University of Jyvaskyla, Finland

Ricardo Queiros	Polytechnic of Porto, Portugal
Jolita Ralyte	University of Geneva, Switzerland
Stefanie Rinderle-Ma	University of Vienna, Austria
Werner Retschitzegger	Johannes Kepler University Linz, Austria
Jose-Angel Rodriguez	Tecnologico de Monterrey, Mexico
Wenge Rong	Beihang University, China
Ella Roubtsova	Open University, The Netherlands
Irina Rychkova	University Paris 1 Pantheon Sorbonne, France
Shazia Sadiq	University of Queensland, Australia
Stefan Schoenig	University of Bayreuth, Germany
Andreas Sinnhofer	Graz University of Technology, Austria
Valery Sokolov	Yaroslavl State University, Russia
Richard Starmans	Utrecht University, The Netherlands
Hans-Peter Steinbacher	FH Kufstein Tirol University of Applied Sciences, Austria
Janis Stirna	Stockholm University, Sweden
Coen Suurmond	Cesuur B.V., The Netherlands
Adel Taweel	Birzeit University, Palestine
Bedir Tekinerdogan	Wageningen University, The Netherlands
Ramayah Thurasamy	Universiti Sains Malaysia, Malaysia
Jose Tribolet	IST - University of Lisbon, Portugal
Roumiana Tsankova	Technical University - Sofia, Bulgaria
Martin van den Berg	De Nederlandsche Bank, The Netherlands
Willem-Jan van den Heuvel	Tilburg University, The Netherlands
Han van der Aa	Humboldt University of Berlin, Germany
Marten van Sinderen	University of Twente, The Netherlands
Damjan Vavpotic	University of Ljubljana, Slovenia
Alexander Verbraeck	Delft University of Technology, The Netherlands
Barbara Weber	Technical University of Denmark, Denmark
Hans Weigand	Tilburg University, The Netherlands
Roel Wieringa	University of Twente, The Netherlands
Dietmar Winkler	Vienna University of Technology, Austria
Shin-Jer Yang	Soochow University, Taiwan
Benjamin Yen	University of Hong Kong, China
Fani Zlatarova	Elizabethtown College, USA

Invited Speakers

Manfred Reichert	Ulm University, Germany
Mathias Weske	HPI - University of Potsdam, Germany

Abstracts of Keynote Lectures

Data-Centric, Large-Scale Process Management Software: Engineering, Technologies, Applications

Manfred Reichert

Ulm University, Germany
manfred.reichert@uni-ulm.de

Abstract. The utmost importance of data for process-aware software systems has led to the emergence of data-centric process support paradigms, e.g., artifact-centric, object-aware, and data-driven approaches to BPM. By tightly integrating process and data, these approaches differ significantly from the widely used activity-centric process paradigm, aiming at the support of data-intensive business processes and offering by far the highest flexibility. In particular, the progress of a data-centric process depends on the availability of data rather than on the completion of activities. Moreover, the focus has shifted from large, monolithic activity-centric processes towards rather small data-driven processes (e.g., object lifecycles), which need to collaborate in order to reach a particular business goal. The keynote speech will provide profound insights into fundamental concepts, features, and enabling technologies of data-centric approaches to BPM. Moreover, it will discuss how this process support paradigm opens up new avenues with respect to the engineering, automation, and monitoring of large-scale business processes in the era of digitization and Industry 4.0.

Business Processes: From Modeling to Mining and Back

Mathias Weske

HPI - University of Potsdam, Germany
mathias.weske@hpi.de

Abstract. Business process management is a well-established discipline to improve working procedures in organizations. Traditionally, business process models are developed to capture the essence of these procedures. Based on process models, process analysis and improvement techniques are applied, processes are improved and automated using dedicated software systems. More recently the research focus has broadened to include process mining, which use process execution data to analyze processes. Currently there is massive interest in process mining, both in academia and industry. The talk will introduce some questions addressed and some solutions provided by process mining. Finally, we discuss the relationships between process modeling and process mining as well as potential applications of process mining to the area of digital health.

Contents

Full Papers

Full Papers

Organisations: Large Worlds or Small Worlds?

Coen Suurmond(✉)

Cesuur B.V., Velp, The Netherlands
coen@cesuur.info

Abstract. Approaches for the development of enterprise information systems based on social theories such as Habermas' theory of communicative action claim to facilitate the development of systems that support the organisational social life-world better than systems developed from a technical viewpoint. However, they will miss their target if the approach is leaning too much towards formalising repetitive and stable elements of the social patterns in an organisation, at the expense of the more informal and/or irregular events and processes. Such approaches run the danger that the open social organisational world is 'frozen' and moulded into a closed formal-rational system. This problem will be discussed in this paper as a contribution to the development of information systems for the social world of organisations.

Keywords: Organisation modelling · Theory of communicative action · LAP · DEMO

1 Introduction

Organisations are social entities, constituted by human action. Half a century ago, in the early days of the development of enterprise information systems, several researchers observed a problematic bias towards a technical point of view on organisations and a disregard for its social character. This led to the Language Action Perspective (LAP) approach, from which later DEMO evolved as a specific approach. LAP and DEMO both have their theoretical roots in Habermas' theory of communicative action. A major theme is Habermas' theory is the problem of colonisation of the lifeworld by systems (or: by system rationality). Therefore it is to be expected that these approaches will result in models of the organisation that support the lifeworld as an open social world, as opposed to the models of a closed formal-rational world that are the likely outcomes of a more technical orientation. The question to be investigated in this paper is, whether this is indeed the case. To generalise the question and to make it less dependent on Habermas' twin concepts of lifeworld/system, some variants of the opposing concepts of open social world/closed formal-rational world will be discussed.

For comparison Organisational Semiotics (OS) will be discussed as a third approach. OS has a similar origin and line of thinking as LAP but starts not from language and communication but from semiotics and social norms. Soft Systems Methodology (SSM) is selected for its contrast to the other three approaches. It originated in the same rejection

B. Shishkov (Ed.): BMSD 2020, LNBIP 391, pp. 3–19, 2020.
https://doi.org/10.1007/978-3-030-52306-0_1

of the one-sided technical view on organisations, it emphasises the role of communication in organisations, but it is founded on systems science. It leaves linguistic theories completely aside.

The research method is an analysis of texts from primary authors of the selected approaches in combination with an evaluation how the approaches would deal with an example conversation from business practice.

The first section of the paper deals with theories and concepts. Three variants of the opposing concepts of open social vs. formal-rational closed worlds will be introduced, followed by a short discussion of philosophical and linguistic concepts about pragmatism, pragmatics, speech acts and communicative action. In the next section the selected approaches will be analysed using texts from original primary authors, followed by the analysis of the possibilities and difficulties the approaches will have with a small but rich example of a business conversation, taken from real business practice. The last step is to draw conclusions from this and to formulate an answer to the research question.

2 Theory

2.1 Open Social World and Closed Formal-Rational World

In the theory of communicative action, the magnum opus of Habermas that provided the foundation of the approach of Language Action Perspective (LAP), Habermas analyses two parallel evolutionary processes that brought about our modern Western society [1, 2]. The first process is a process of rationalisation starting from mythical and hierarchical societies and culminating in the idea of communicative rationality. The latter is as guiding idea characteristic for our modern open society where ideally decisions are based on factual knowledge and open sincere discussion about social norms between equals. The second process is an inevitable and in essence beneficial process of evolving subsystems for fulfilling specific functions in a growing and increasingly complex society. Subsystems (or systems for short) in this theory have a limited function in a specific societal context and the mechanisms within the systems are tuned to its functions. Systems are governed by instrumental means-end rationality, decisions are made within the limited scope of achieving the functions of the system. Systems fulfil functions in society and should be governed by society by means of open discussion in society (communicative rationality). Habermas speaks of colonisation of the lifeworld by systems when systems are dictating society what to do, based on the instrumental rationality of the system.

The British economists Kay and King use the concepts of small worlds and large worlds in their recent book about decision making in organisations (the concepts originating from the American statistician Jimmy Savage) [3]. Models are used in decision making for understanding the situation and viewing possible futures. Small world models belong to processes that are more or less completely understood, remain constant over time, and that are independent of our actions and beliefs; they can accurately predict what will happen over time. The small world model represents reality accurately in the given context. The large world is the world where human action is based on incomplete information about the situation on hand and/or the possible course of events. The incompleteness of large world information is not accidental and reparable, but fundamental and irreparable, uncertainty is a fundamental property of the large world (therefore the title of their book: Radical Uncertainty). Large world models do not represent the essence of reality, but are helpful in understanding reality and in imagining what might happen under certain conditions. Where small world models enable accurate prediction, large world models enable understanding of possible future scenarios.

Large worlds can be considered to come close to Habermas' concept of communicative action, where small worlds can be viewed as comparable with Habermas' system concept. At the same time, it is important to keep in mind that (1) Habermas is analysing historical evolution of society, where systems are coming into existence to fulfil certain functions in society; (2) Kay & King are analysing the use of 'small world models' in prediction and decision making as contrasted with our human 'large world' where processes are not stationary and where off-model events happen; and (3) the approaches to ISD are partly about analysing organisational processes "as is", and partly about designing (or 'engineering') organisation processes "to be". In all three contexts, however, it is about the relation between the small world (to fulfil a certain function) and the large world (where people must make accountable decisions).

A third discipline contrasting a social and a formal view on the world can be found in contract law. In classical contract law, a contract is a mutual promise between two parties to exchange goods, services or money under specified conditions at a specified moment. Once the exchange is accepted to be fulfilled, the contract is over. As MacNeil defined the classical contract: "the discrete contract is one in which no relation exists between the parties apart from the simple exchange of goods" [4]. But "the discrete transaction is entirely fictional. There we postulate specialization and choice-determined projections of future exchange in the total absence of any society whatsoever. Even in the modern mythical world of neoclassical microeconomic theory such conditions do not exist" [4]. In social reality transactions and contracts are embedded in a wide network of social relations and conventions. In many cases, parties do engage more than once. The combination of general conventions, the common history and the expected future of the parties involved, and the specific situation provide the background against which parties are dealing with each other in preparing, fulfilling and concluding a contract. This is the reason why the legal scholar MacNeil wrote that "the core relational principle – analysis must always start with context – makes it possible to determine what circumstances should or should not be taken into account in dealing with transactions" [5].

In this subsection three twin concepts contrasting an open social worldview with a closed formal-rational worldview were presented. Habermas theory of communicative action with its opposition of lifeworld/system is the basis of the LAP and DEMO approaches, and the idea of the social lifeworld is used by both the OS and SSM approaches. The other two twin concepts from decision making (large world/small world) and from contract law (relational/classical contracts) represent the same opposing worldviews from different disciplines. In the next subsections the concepts of pragmatism, pragmatics, speech acts and communicative action will be discussed as being fundamental for the open social worldview.

2.2 Pragmatism and Pragmatics

The term pragmatism is derived from the Greek word πραγμα meaning deed or act. In pragmatism, "human cognition is placed in a naturalistic framework of behavioural responses to practical problems" [6] and is as such opposed to "spectator epistemology" or "mirror epistemology" according to which cognition is the representation of independent facts. The contrast is reflected in the early and later work of Wittgenstein. His Tractatus Logico-Philosophicus (1921) was about representation of the world as a collection of facts in propositional form [7]. In his posthumous work Philosophical Investigations (1953) he uses the concept of language games [8]. From the philosophical stance of pragmatism he takes human behaviour as the starting point for analysis of meaning. Language (and other kinds of social conventions) is learned by doing, by practicing competence in interpersonal interaction. Pragmatism approaches the world as a collection of (interacting) processes, as opposed to views that approach the world as a collection of 'things' and 'events' (representationalism). To give a stark example from the now raging corona-crisis: the primary meaning of "availability of PPE" (personal protective equipment) must be that front-line workers are actually protected in their work practices, meanings such as "stock level in warehouses" and "quantities ordered" might represent states of affair in supply chains but are meaningless as long as they cannot be translated into actual effective protection of workers.

The linguistic/semiotic concept of pragmatics is related but different. Pragmatics was introduced by Morris as part of the three branches of semiotics: "syntactics as the study of the syntactical relations of signs to one another in abstraction from the relation of signs to objects or to interpreters", "semantics deals with the relation of signs to their designate and so to the objects which they may or do denote" and "pragmatics [designates] the science of the relation of signs to their interpreters" [9]. The sequence of definition is interesting: first structure, then meaning, then usage. This is the way we would define a formal language. Carnap chooses the reverse sequence when he writes: "An investigation of a language belongs to *pragmatics* if explicit reference to a speaker is made; it belongs to *semantics* if designata but not speakers are referred to; it belongs to *syntax* if neither speaker nor designata but only expressions are dealt with" [10]. The latter sequence is the way we would learn a natural language: we start with linguistic utterances in context, then abstract from variable context to find more or less stable meaning, then abstract from context and meaning to find the rules of grammar about allowed structures of sentences. The latter sequence is the way a pragmatist such as Habermas or Wittgenstein would operate.

Habermas is investigating the requirements of linguistic competence of man in social interaction. The opening sentence of "What is Universal Pragmatics" is: "Universal pragmatics must identify and reconstruct the universal requirements for mutual understanding". It is about the dynamics of language used in interaction, rather than language 'frozen' in its representational function. Viewed from linguistics his concept is about pragmatics because it is about the usage aspect of language, viewed from philosophy his approach belongs to pragmatism because it takes meaningful human interaction in context as its starting point.

2.3 Speech Acts

In the first lecture of "How to do things with words" Austin wrote: "The phenomenon to be discussed is very widespread and obvious, and it cannot fail to have been already noticed, at least here and there, by others. Yet I have not found attention paid to it specifically" [11]. Austin recognises that using language is ipso facto a form of human action (the general point), and that some human acts such as declaring marriage or baptising a ship are constituted by language alone (a more specific point). Austin observed "philosophers have assumed that the only things they are interested in are utterances which report facts or which describe situations truly or falsely", and that there are many other sorts of use of language. Austin introduces the term performative utterances ("rather an ugly word, and a new word, but there seems to be no word already in existence to do the job") for utterances that are actions: "When I say 'I name this ship the Queen Elisabeth' I do not describe the christening ceremony, I actually perform the christening; and when I say 'I do' (sc. Take this woman to be my lawful wedded wife), I am not reporting on a marriage, I am indulging in it.". Austin emphasises that using so-called performative verbs is not an essential condition for a performative utterance: 'I order you to shut the door', 'Shut the door', or just 'Door' can be variant utterances for the same performative act. In How To Do Things with Words, Austin connects the illocutionary act with the intention of the speaker, expressed by means of a convention (without some background convention, the intention would not be recognized – uptake is the word used by Austin – and the utterance would be just an exclamation by the utterer), where "perlocutionary act always includes some consequences". Along this line of thinking, an utterance like "I see what you mean" as reaction to an earlier utterance in a conversation can perform the perlocutionary act of social bonding in a conversation, where the utterance "I have heard you!" can bring about the opposite. Perlocutionary effects are dependent on both the illocutionary force of the speaker and the uptake thereof by the hearer.

For Habermas, Austin's insight is one of the pillars of his philosophy, speech acts "have a constitutive meaning … for communicative action" [1]. Habermas summarises the locutionary, illocutionary and perlocutionary act as: "Thus the three acts that Austin distinguishes can be characterized in the following catchphrases: to say *something*, to act *in* saying something, to bring about something *through* acting in saying something". Habermas adds two fundamental aspects to the speech act theory in order to integrate this theory into his wider theory of communicative action. The first addition is a further specification under which conditions a speech act is 'felicitous' (Austin's term). It postulates that a speech act refers simultaneously to the relation of the speaker to the objective outer world, to the social intersubjective world and to his own subjective world. In communicative action, the speaker claims his utterance to be truthful in the outer world, valid in the social world, and a sincere expression of his personal world.

The second addition concerns the classification of speech acts. Austin was clear in his analysis that although at first sight it seems easy to classify illocutionary verbs, in practice natural language allows for many ways to express illocution using social context. Think of that notorious utterance of the president of the US towards the head of the FBI "I hope you can let this go": is the president expressing here his hope, or is he telling the head of the FBI what he must do? This classification issue is not only about types of illocution, but also about 'illocutionary strength' such as the difference between a strong wish and a weak desire (and whether a strong wish of a superior in an organisation is in fact a command depends on organisational culture and the personalities involved). Habermas does not try to find a classification of speech acts by analysing practical usage of language (empirical-pragmatic approach), he conceives a formal-pragmatic classification based on the prevailing aspect of the mode of communication: cognitive, interactive, or expressive [12]. In the first mode the prevailing goal is the establishing of facts about the outer world, in the second mode the establishing of legitimate interpersonal relations, and in the third mode the disclosure of the speaker's subjective attitudes and feelings. But, to repeat, in each and every speech act the speaker relates to all three worlds (objective, social, personal), the mode of communication only determines which actor-world relation is primary.

2.4 Communicative Action

"In contexts of communicative action, we call someone rational not only if he is able to put forward an assertion and, when criticized, to provide grounds for it by pointing to appropriate evidence, but also if he is following an established norm and is able, if criticized, to justify his action by explicating the given situation in the light of legitimate expectations" [1]. In this quote Habermas integrates the concepts of rationality (being able to give grounds for an utterance), speech acts (as social action) and pragmatism (meanings and norms are established and evolving by their application in social groups). Communicative action is oriented towards a mutual understanding of the participants in the conversation (remark: reaching an understanding does not necessarily imply reaching consensus, although Habermas sometimes seems to imply the latter). In practice, of course, people may misrepresent their feelings, their intentions, or the facts. If a speaker wilfully misrepresents in order to get some result out of the hearer, Habermas speaks of (hidden) strategic action.

2.5 Recapitulation

In this section the oppositional concepts of the open social world and the closed formal-rational world were discussed, along with the concepts of pragmatism, pragmatics, speech acts and communicative action. An essential characteristic of the oppositional concepts is the role of context and intentionality. The open social worldview is based on (1) human action (2) under given circumstances (3) oriented towards some future state, (4) not necessarily fully specified; (5) people are expected to be able to justify their actions by giving reasons that are valid in the given circumstances. Natural language furnishes a very flexible instrument for both preparing and accounting for actions, using language in an innovative way should the need arise. The closed formal-rational world on the other hand is perhaps best characterised by the event-process-chain concept: the system being in a given state, an event triggers a formally specified chain of transformations to new states. Circumstances are either a codified part of the state definition, or out of scope. The events are driven by codified rules, not by the intention to a given situation. The intention to get to a given state was part of the development process, when the rules were specified, and subsequently codified in rules. In organisational theory the old example of a closed formal-rational system would be the Weberian bureaucracy, in modern times it is a software system. However, in a bureaucracy the rules are still interpreted by humans, in a software system it is a machine.

3 Approaches to Information System Development

3.1 Language Action Perspective

In a contribution to a task force meeting in June 1980 about decision support systems, Flores and Ludlow discussed systems for more general support of the activities of management and office workers [13]. They contrast their analysis to "the current tradition in which communication is analysed in terms of the transfer of information and management is equated with the making of decisions". Their main observations about work in the office are that (1) people are continuously making conversations, and conversations generate commitments, (2) speech acts are about expressing what is not obvious against a background of obviousness and relevance; and (3) "managers seem to be absorbed in many short interactions … managers manifest a great preference for oral communication". Their answer to the question of the activities of managers is that they "create commitments in their world, take care of commitments, and initiate commitments within the organization. … world is also what is brought forth through language as a commitment established by an utterance". Incidentally, this focus on the role of conversations in organisations has been taken up recently by LAP author Goldkuhl, as witnessed by a recent paper where Goldkuhl writes "In summary, social relations can be instated concerning future states and actions as expectations and commitments" [14].

The second seminal text of the language-focused approach is the 1982 paper by Goldkuhl and Lyytinen entitled "A Language Action View of Information Systems" [15]. In this paper an organisation is defined as essentially a social system based on interpersonal communication, where people act by communicating. The approach is based on the theory of speech acts that was originated by Austin, further developed by Searle [16] and developed further still and applied in his wider social theory by Habermas: "To perform a communicative act is to … predicate and refer (propositional content), to … establish interpersonal relations, and to intentionally try to influence the listener/reader" [15]. The authors contrast their language action view where social interaction is at the core and the technical system is considered an instrument facilitating formalised social communication patterns with the traditional view on information system development, focusing on the technical aspects of the system and considering the social environment of the system as peripheral. In the view of Goldkuhl and Lyytinen, system development is concerned with developing a formalised professional language based on existing user communication. User participation is necessary for achieving intersubjectivity in the resulting description of the user world and the formalised language operating on that world.

A third text that is often cited in publications about Language Action Perspective is the book Understanding and Cognition by Winograd and Flores, published in 1986 [17]. The paper by Flores and Ludlow mentioned above was about communicative behaviour related to decision making in organisations, the Winograd-Flores book was focused on the more general question about computer capabilities in relation to the nature of human society. The first part of the book uses Heidegger to analyse human beings, communication and language. It is not possible for a human being to view the world from the standpoint of an external and objective observer, "Heidegger insists that it is meaningless to talk about the existence of objects and their properties in the absence of concernful activity". Later on, in the chapter about language, the authors emphasise that "meaning arises in listening to the commitment expressed in speech acts" and "the articulation of content – how we talk about the world – emerges in recurrent patterns of breakdown and the potential for discourse about grounding", and they state as a consequence from these points: "Nothing exists except through language".

The developments and achievements of the LAP approach were discussed by Lyytinen in 2004 in his contribution to the 9th LAP conference, entitled "The Struggle with the Language in the IT – Why is LAP not in the Mainstream?" [18]. He describes LAP as "based on a set of heterogeneous theoretical foundations that ranged from non-monotonic and non-traditional logics (deontic, illocutionary, possible world semantics), theories of language (hermeneutics, speech act theory, discourse theory) and social behaviours (ethnomethodology, symbolic interactionism) to overarching philosophies of social action (theory of communicative action, autopoiesis)". LAP was different from other approaches in (1) challenging "widely held beliefs about data and the nature of computing" and (2) challenging "the dominant functional and realist view of the language … that was cherished in AI and database communities". However, and in spite of academic success of LAP induced thinking, LAP was "not widely known nor practiced outside the narrow borders of the LAP community". At the 10th and last LAP conference in 2005, Weigand agrees with Lyytinen's observation that LAP is not in the mainstream, and asks whether belonging to the mainstream is something to be pursued "as long as this mainstream is dominated by the same rationalistic motives as it was 20 years ago" [19]. Further, Weigand reflects on the complexity of communication and postulates that "much more than simplified speech act theory is needed to do justice to all the subtleties and dynamics of communication". He also mentions the inherent dialectics of communication. Arguing against using simplified speech act theory, Weigand argues that "communicative form (the running practices in the organization) cannot be reduced to essential communication models".

A decade later, in 2017, Goldkuhl wrote "LAP revisited: Articulating information as social relation" as an invited paper for a LAP workshop trying to revive the LAP research community [20]. In this paper Goldkuhl took stock of the earlier LAP theoretical foundations in general, and the different ways to come from the concept of speech acts (speaker perspective only) to a concept of conversation. Goldkuhl observed that one research strand was based on patterned exchange of speech acts (e.g.: the action workflow defined concept proposal/agreement/performance/satisfaction as stages in the dialogue), another strand was based on a dialogue without restriction to certain fixed speech acts. The first strand is recognisable in the DEMO approach (see below), Goldkuhl's research is based on free form exchange of information between an initiator and an addressee. Such an exchange constitutes a social relation between the communication partners. This aspect was already present in the three seminal LAP papers mentioned above, but Goldkuhl in 2017 makes this point an explicit point of his theory. The earlier search in LAP to find a meaningful classification of speech acts is replaced by Goldkuhl with a search for a meaningful classification of social relationships established by reciprocal communicative acts. Goldkuhl observes that in the context of information, communication and language use oriented on IS practices information may be digitised, and he defines his scope as digitisation in professional-institutional settings. At the same time, he recognises "that there is an interest for how digitized information sets are elements of broader communication patterns in social settings", and "in IS we have thus an interest for digital artefacts in use contexts.". In the example case in this paper (about social welfare allowance), however, all communication acts are by digitized exchanges between client, social welfare officer, and back-office systems. All decisions are based on information in the system. The observation in the Goldkuhl & Lyytinen paper "the formal and closed nature of information systems implies a need for information channels side by side the formalized information systems" seems to be forgotten, which is especially notable in a social welfare case.

3.2 DEMO – Design and Engineering Methodology for Organisations

In 2020 Dietz and Mulder published Enterprise Ontology [21], a complete overhaul of the earlier book with the same title published by Dietz in 2006 [22]. All current theories (now 11 different theories) are systematically presented in this new book. For the purpose of this paper I will focus on the ontological PSI theory about the operation of organisations. In the Enterprise Engineering Manifesto, edited by Dietz, the second postulate is: "Enterprises are essentially social systems, of which the elements are human beings in their role of social individuals, bestowed with appropriate authority and bearing the corresponding responsibility. The operating principle of enterprises is that these human beings enter into and comply with commitments regarding the products (services) that they create (deliver). Commitments are the results of coordination acts, which occur in universal patterns, called transactions" [23]. The PSI theory is about business conversations and business transactions. The notion of business conversation is founded on Habermas' theory of communicative action with its claims to truth, rightness and sincerity (terms used by Dietz and Mulder). The communicative act is presented as constituted by four elements: performer, intention, addressee, proposition (in a formal specification of DEMO a limited set of 11 allowable intentions are codified). The universal transaction patterns is constructed involving two actors, the initiator and the executor. The organisation is a network of actors and transactions. A transaction T is started by an actor A requesting something and an actor B accepting (promising) or declining. When transaction T is finished actor B declares that fact upon delivery, and actor A is accepting (or rejecting) the fulfilment of the transaction. The transaction-in-progress can be cancelled or aborted if requested by the initiator, the executor can allow or refuse. A transaction can be composed of derived transactions, each derived transaction having the same universal transaction structure as the initial transaction (but in most cases with different initiators and executors).

DEMO distinguishes between actors, subjects and actor roles: an actor is a subject (human being) in an actor role. The diagrammatic presentation of the standard transaction pattern suggests that the same actor that requests the transaction will later on accept the delivery (this actor role is called the initiator); and the same actor that promises the transaction will later on deliver (this actor role is called the executor). In case of a transaction between two businesses, it is more likely company A (as a legal person) is initiator, company B (as a legal person) is executor; different natural persons will engage on behalf of their company in the initiating and concluding transaction conversations. As far as I can see DEMO assumes not the same legal person but the same natural person here.

3.3 Organisational Semiotics

The first major publication on what was to become organisational semiotics was the book Information, published by Stamper in 1973. He wrote in the opening pages of his book: "Information is a word used very loosely, especially in the context of business studies, to identify a mixed bundle of concepts. The time has come for us to use these concepts with greater precision" [24]. He identified the sign as carrier of information in formal systems, informal systems, communication networks and computers. Semiotics being the science that studies signs, Stamper uses the subdivision of semiotics by Morris into pragmatics, semantics and syntax as a basis for analysing information. Later, Stamper extended this to his semiotic ladder with six levels: physical world, empirics, syntactics, semantics, pragmatics, social world. The first three levels are in the realm of computer science, the latter three belong to the realm of information science. With the exception of the physical world this semiotic ladder in DEMO is mapped to its performa level (social world; social correspondence), informa level (pragmatics and semantics; cognitive correspondence) and forma level (syntax and empirics; notational correspondence).

Stamper described in his 1973 book the difference and the tension between formal and informal systems: "Formal systems are intended to operate in a uniform way, throughout time and over the whole of the wide territory across which the organisation may be spread. Formal systems are insensitive to local problems which are the major concerns of the informal systems" [24]. However, Stamper does not differentiate here between two senses of 'formal'. The first sense is about having a generalised and meaningful form, to be interpreted by humans in a given context. The second sense is about being subjected to formal logical rules, devoid of meaning. The essential difference here is that humans are capable to recognise the general form and the specific (iconic) situation at the same time. Human semiosis is about dealing with this kind of tension between the general and the particular, while automata are just following formal logical rules and nothing more [25]. In the 1996 chapter mentioned above Stamper describes the organisational onion as consisting of three levels: an outer layer of an informal information system, ("a sub-culture where meanings are established, intentions are understood, beliefs are formed and commitments with responsibilities are made, altered and discharged"), a middle layer of an formal information system ("bureaucracy where form and rule replace meaning and intention"), and an inner layer with IT system(s) ("mechanisms to automate part of the formal system") [26]. Later, Liu and Wi formulated three essential conditions for processing information in the IT system: (1) well-defined work processes, (2) clearly defined human responsibility, and (3) explicitly specified rules for operations [27]. In my view, the ambiguity of the term 'formal system' is not solved here. Although the pejorative view of bureaucracy is indeed that "form and rule have replaced meaning and intention", I do not think that you can maintain the position that workers in a bureaucracy are equal to automata.

Stamper later developed the MEASUR methodology, which has as unifying principle "the idea that an information system is a system of social norms through which responsible agents collaborate". In requirements analysis, "conventional analysis seeks the truth, MEASUR aims to locate responsibility". Stamper reminds us that "most norms by which business operates are never made explicit … at best they are made explicit in the form of rules which people have to interpret". According to Stamper, every norm has the form "*if* <condition> *then* <some agent> *is permitted/forbidden/obliged to do* <action>" [26]. In my view, however, this canonical form makes either a norm applicable regardless of the situation where the norm is applied, or the condition clause must account for all kinds of situations, which is unworkable. Here we meet again the problem of formulating rules for human use and formulating rules for automatic processes.

3.4 Soft Systems Methodology

Checkland differentiates between natural systems and human activity systems. Natural systems "are systems which could not be other than they are, given a universe whose patterns and laws are not erratic" [28]. For human activity systems, Checkland firstly argues that "the observer and *the point of view from which his observations are made*" is important to investigate such a human activity system, where for a natural system the system is 'out there' and the observer is external to it. A second essential difference is that "the irreducible freedom … of a human actor means that there can never be accounts of human activity systems similar to, and having the same logical status as accounts of natural systems".

Checkland further distinguishes between systems that are the result of 'blind' evolutionary processes and designed systems. The latter systems are created by purposeful human activity because there is a need for them. Checkland writes: "Man as designer is able to create physical artefacts to fulfil particular defined purposes. And similarly he may create structured sets of thoughts, the so-called 'designed abstract systems". In the conclusion of this chapter Checkland writes: "The systems map suggests that the absolute minimum of systems classes needed to describe the whole of reality is four: natural, designed physical, designed abstract, and human activity systems". It is noteworthy that Checkland considers a social system as a kind of system that "should be placed astride the boundary between human activity and natural systems", exhibiting both "properties due to the natural characteristics of man the social animal" and activities due to rational behaviour. In 'SSM: a 30 year retrospective' Checkland confirmed this when he wrote "This led to the idea of modelling purposeful 'human activity systems' as sets of linked activities which together could exhibit the emergent property of purposefulness" [29]. In my view, this dichotomy of purposeful human behaviour and human behaviour as a social animal is troubling when looking at actual human behaviour. While Checkland differentiates between goals and purposes (a goal will be either achieved or not, a purpose is "an end which can be pursued but never finally achieved" [28]), I wonder whether the term 'purposeful behaviour' would not be better replaced by 'intentional behaviour'. The latter term would not suggest to dichotomise human behaviour in either 'animal-like' or instrumental.

Reflecting on his action research program, developed in practice, Checkland found parallel lines of thought in the work of Churchman and that of Vickers. Churchman developed the concept of 'inquiring systems' dealing with "designing systems for finding things out", and about the dialectics of alternating model building with confronting models with realty. Vickers analysed how norms and behaviour can evolve in discussion. He studied the work of a Royal Commission: "The commissioners used the norms which they brought with them to the conference table; but these norms were changed and developed by the very process of applying them; by the impact of the reality judgment which they focused; by the impact, attrition and stimulus of each commissioner on the others; and by the exercise of their own minds as they applied them in one way or another, in the search of a better 'fit'" [30]. Checkland's action research program is co-founded on these two notions of building models as an instrument of inquiry, and of working in a social world that changes as a result of doing the analysis.

In 2006 Checkland and Poulter published the book Learning for Action, subtitled "a short definitive account of SSM and its use for practitioners, teachers and students" [31]. The authors emphasise in answering Frequently Asked Questions that SSM is more about principles than about rules: "SSM's basic principle is to think separately about, and then relate, two different elements: perceptions people have of a complex human situation, and constructed conceptualizations aimed at gaining insights into that situation" and "Both the logical/analytical mode of thinking (as in model building) and the slower sense-making mode – as you allow the situation to 'speak to you'". Also interesting as representation is their answer to a FAQ about using of hand-drawn diagrams in SSM. They explain: "… diagrams dominated by straight lines, right angles and rectangular boxes … convey the impression: this is the case, full stop! The hand-drawn diagrams … underline that absolute certainty is forever elusive in human affairs; they are working diagrams, part of the learning process". In anticipation of the paragraph about speech act theory, this it is quite a good example for the difference between locution and illocution: the two ways for diagrammatically representing a certain structure (using very clean straight elements, or using more irregular and messy hand-drawn elements) have the same locution (the structure represented in the diagram) but have a different illocutionary force: definitive and certain vs. tentative and uncertain.

4 Example Case

Some time ago I was in a meeting at a meat processing company with a production manager. During the meeting we were interrupted by Peter. He opened the door and asked the production manager: "Did you hear from customer C?", answered by "No, but do 2 × 2". The follow-up by Peter was the statement/question: "I'll prepare 2 bins 1600 kg, OK then?" answered by "Fine, I hope to hear from C early afternoon". Some clear facts can be distilled from this very short conversation. Firstly, the conversation is constituted of speech acts based on social norms and related to transactions. Secondly, someone needs information how to proceed, but not all relevant information is available yet. Thirdly, the interlocutors have different social roles.

The conversation can be analysed on several levels. On the surface level it is a clean exchange of question and answer: "What should I do?" "Prepare 2 bins with 1600 kg". The latter speech act is a directive for doing something in production. Also on the surface level, the outcome of the conversation could be seen as the production manager initiating a transaction to be executed by Peter (but to describe the conversation as initiated by the executor Peter would be apt). Organisational hierarchy and informal social norms determine who initiates the transaction, and who executes. Both production manager and Peter are committed, the first by his request of the transaction, the latter by acceptance of the request. On a second level, however, the situation is less clear-cut. The conversation is an implicit shared appraisal of the situation between two experienced colleagues on an equal footing. What do we know? What do we expect? What are our possibilities? What are the risks? What are we going to do? This is quite different from a simple request to execute a transaction. It is more like "we (production manager and Peter) think that it is wise and safe to prepare 2 bins of 1600 kg, in anticipation of an expected customer order". At the same time, there is no complete symmetry between the two colleagues. His organisational position and his informal contacts with sales and planning (mutual adjustment) give greater authority to the production manager; his better view of the actual production situation and possible scenario's on the shopfloor gives a greater authority to Peter. It might well be that a pattern has evolved that the actual decisions are made by Peter because of his experience and capabilities, and that Peter only consults the production manager in order to give him an opportunity to comment and/or to get some commitment (possibly to cover his back).

The example exhibits a fair degree of incompleteness compared to the standard specification of an order. The interesting thing is that the incompleteness is of two kinds: resolvable and irresolvable. Some lacking incomplete elements are vague because they are implicit and part of background knowledge (1) "2 bins with 1600 kg" suggests a weight of 1600 kg in each bin, but "everyone" knows that the capacity per bin is about 750–950 kg, so the 1600 kg is about total weight; (2) the organisational role of Peter is left blank partly because his informal position is not clearly defined; (3) the product involved is not specified at all. The other kind of incompleteness is about the uncertainty that is inherent in the situation: a customer order is expected but not placed yet, but production must decide how to proceed. Conflicting social norms involved are about satisfying the customer (what does he expect, how will he react → aspects of relational contracts!), efficiency of the production process, and responsibilities of the persons involved (both formal and informal). It is a typical example of communicative action and open discussion between knowledgeable colleagues.

The conversation is an illustration of everyday pragmatism. Not, as some would have it, pragmatism as "whatever works is true" (this is not pragmatism but opportunism, alas also a fact of life), but pragmatism as taking circumstances into account in meaningful conversation. Facts and values are weighed in context in order to determine a sound way to proceed. The speech acts are elliptical (incomplete sentences, leaving words out), and express a specific mix of uncertainty, doubt, and beliefs (illocutionary aspect). The subject of the conversation is to assess this "uncertainty mix" between the colleagues, not to eliminate uncertainty and doubt. The perlocutionary effect of the conversation is some shared knowledge and belief of the colleagues that will coordinate their further action that day. It is an example of communicative action where the colleagues reason about the situation on hand. The outcome is not necessarily consensus, an alternative outcome could have been: "I don't think you are right, but proceed as you proposed and deal with the consequences". The crux is that under given circumstances with irresolvable uncertainty a decision is needed and the two colleagues have an open conversation with a clear outcome. The commitment of the colleagues is expressed in the concrete speech acts (which allow subtle shades of commitment by the combination of the utterances and the specific way they are uttered).

The origins of the LAP, DEMO and OS approaches suggest they are well placed to deal with the analysis of cases such as the above. It is indeed about communication, transactions, speech acts, norms and commitments. Both LAP and OS aim for formalisation of communication and social norms. While formalisation can be very useful to elicit what is going on in an actual organisation, it would be wrong to reduce the communication to mere formalised and digitised facts, rules, and processes. A social norm is never absolute and always susceptible to interpretation in context. Social norms are weighed in context when they are contradictory. One of the fundamental social norms is about commitment, and could be formulated as: "to be as good as one's word". With natural language having so many words and combinations of words to express valid and sincere commitment, there are equally many degrees of commitment. In many cases people do not ask for certainty or unconditional commitment, but enough to proceed in a proper way (a colleague who demands certainty where none could reasonably be given, will breach a basic norm of communicative action). A one-sided emphasis on the formalisation of communication and social norms of LAP and OS will lead to closed formal-rational models of the organisation and its processes.

DEMO will have similar problems. It gives communication a place at initiating and concluding transactions, and seems to grant a lot of discussion freedom to the communication partners (initiator and executor). However, the result of the communication is moulded in a formal standard with 11 permitted intentions. This is a strongly formalised and reduced representation of possible commitments. It is a reduction of transactions to the form of classical contracts as discussed by MacNeil, and does not do justice to the relational aspects of transactions. There seems to be something paradoxical in DEMO, emphasising the importance of the human factor in organisations (reflected in the notion of communicative action) and at the same time grossly reducing human intentions and commitments to a very limited set without gradation.

SSM would not have the problems mentioned above. It is really a contrast with the other three approaches, using models to gain understanding. Models in SSM are not meant to represent the 'real' organisation and its processes. At the same time, it is not very specific about the underlying mechanisms in organisations. It provides a general framework and guiding principles, but offers no specific theories about the inner workings of an organisation. SSM could profit here from the theories behind LAP, DEMO and OS. To some people it might seem that SSM is pragmatic in the opportunistic sense: find a way to produce something workable, do not bother with underlying theories. However, the guideline "let the situation speak to you" in order to get a grip on what is going on in an organisation is far from opportunistic. It is a stimulus to come to a real understanding of the ineffable lifeworld of the organisation.

5 Conclusion

The evaluation above indicates that the theories behind each of the approaches of OS, LAP and DEMO highlights important social aspects of organisational behaviour: the role of norms in OS, the role of speech acts in LAP, and the open conversations of initiator and executor of a transaction in DEMO. The approaches are in this respect oriented towards pragmatism (organisation-in-action), towards speech acts (language-in-action), and disputable social norms (actors-in-action). But, and that is a big caveat, each of these three approaches is reductionist in more than one sense. The first sense is the reduction to one or a few basic principles. The second is a reduction to a formalised hierarchical systematic view of social reality. An extra problem is that both OS and LAP do not differentiate between formalisation in the sense of bureaucratic rules, based on natural language and human interpretation (natural language being a social sign system), and formalisation in the sense of using a formal language and interpretation by computers (using a formal sign system). All three approaches aspire to model the organisation as a preparatory step towards digitisation and automation. An important difference between DEMO on the one hand and LAP and OS on the other is that DEMO explicitly grants business conversations full communicative freedom where LAP and OS seem to mould conversations into formalised patterns. The outcome of a free-form DEMO conversation, however, is codified in a predefined set of intentions.

Judged by the intended outcome, LAP, DEMO and OS all seem to view the organisation as essentially a small world. Although analysis is started from the lifeworld as an open social world, the approaches work towards formalised models of organisational structure and organisational communication processes and closed formal-rational systems. The social welfare case by Goldkuhl (discussed at the end of Sect. 3.1) with its emphasis on fully digitised information exchange is an illustration of this point. The non-transactional view on communication of Flores and Ludlow [13], which is illustrated by the business example, seems to have been forgotten in LAP (and DEMO), as well as the discussion by Winograd and Flores of the role of natural language (with all its subtleties in use) in the constitution and evolution of the lifeworld [17]. Probably Weigand was right with 2005 in his remark that LAP was simplifying communication too much.

SSM offers a contrast in adhering to a large world view on the organisation. Although the approach does not use theory about communicative action, in practice the ideas behind this theory have a much better chance to be recognised when applying this approach (but that is up to the individual consultant). Only this approach recognises explicitly that organisations will change as a by-product of human action, one of the characteristics of the large world as defined by Kay & King.

With regard to the research question, the most important difference between LAP, DEMO and OS on the one hand and SSM on the other hand is the role of models. Where the first three treat models as representing the organisation and its processes “in a real sense”, SSM treats models as practical instruments for understanding, not necessarily reflecting “the real organisation”. The first three approaches view the social world as being represented “in the model”, while SSM views the social world as “beyond the model”. To answer the research question: in LAP, DEMO and OS there is a real risk that the formal-rational models (and systems based on the models) will get prominence in the social lifeworld of the organisation, thereby facilitating the colonisation of the lifeworld by systems. The SSM view of the organisational social world as beyond the model views systems as instruments to support, but not rule, the lifeworld. It acknowledges the organisational lifeworld as a large world with irresolvable uncertainties to be encountered by responsible human action, thereby supporting the relational view on transactions.

For further research, it should be useful to integrate the analytical insights of LAP, DEMO and OS into the SSM approach. For the design of ICT systems it should be interesting to look at systems that are tolerant for (temporary) inconsistencies. When the social world decides to proceed in a way that is not compatible with the logic programmed into the IT system, it should be possible to allow inconsistent states in an IT system. The issues to be resolved are then: How to program for allowable inconsistencies? How to report/account for inconsistencies? How to recover from inconsistencies?

References

1. Habermas, J.: The Theory of Communicative Action, vol. 1. Polity Press, Cambridge (1984)
2. Habermas, J.: The Theory of Communicative Action, vol. 2. Polity Press, Cambridge (1987)
3. Kay, J., King, M.: Radical Uncertainty. The Bridge Street Press, London (2020)
4. MacNeil, I.R.: The New Social Contract. Yale University Press, New Haven (1980)
5. MacNeil, I.R.: Reflections on relational contract theory after a neo-classical seminar. In: Campbell, D., Collins, H., Wightman, J. (eds.) Implicit Dimensions of Contract. Hart Publishing, Portland (2003)
6. Koopman, C.: Pragmatism. In: Allen, A., Mendieta, E. (eds.) The Cambridge Habermas Lexicon. Cambridge University Press, Cambridge (2019)
7. Wittgenstein, L.: Tractatus Logico-Philosophicus. Routledge, Abingdon (2005). Translated by C.K. Ogden
8. Wittgenstein, L.: Philosophical Investigations, 4th edn. Wiley-Blackwell, Chichester (2009). Translated by G.E.M. Anscombe, P.M.S. Hacker, J. Schulte
9. Morris, C.: Writings on the General Theory of Signs. Mouton, The Hague (1971)
10. Carnap, R.: Introduction to Semantics and Formalization of Logic, 3rd edn. Harvard University Press, Cambridge (1968)
11. Austin, J.L.: How to Do Things with Words, 2nd edn. Harvard University Press, Cambridge (1978)
12. Habermas, J.: What is Universal Pragmatics? In: Cooke, M. (ed.) On the Pragmatics of Communication. MIT Press, Cambridge (1998)
13. Flores, F., Ludlow, J.J.: Doing and speaking in the office. In: Fick, G., Sprague, R.H. (eds.) Decision Support Systems: Issues and Challenges, pp. 95–118. Pergamon Press, Oxford (1980)
14. Goldkuhl, G.: LAP revisited: articulating information as social relation. http://www.vits.org/publikationer/dokument/805.pdf. Accessed 15 Dec 2019
15. Goldkuhl, G., Lyytinen, K.: A language action view of information systems. In: Ginzberg, M., Ross, C.A. (eds.) Proceedings of the 3rd International Conference on Information Systems, pp 13–29. TIMS/SMIS/ACM (1982)
16. Searle, J.R.: Speech Acts. Cambridge University Press, Cambridge (1969)
17. Winograd, T., Flores, F.: Understanding Computers and Cognition. Ablex Corporation, Norwood (1986)
18. Lyytinen, K.: The struggle with the language in the IT – why is LAP not in the mainstream? In: Proceedings LAP 2004 (2004). https://pdfs.semanticscholar.org/bec5/672f846c1e819f7519b7ca161a6648f2ad33.pdf. Accessed 20 Jan 2020
19. Weigand, H.: LAP: 10 years in retrospect. In: Proceedings LAP 2005 (2005). http://www.vits.org/konferenser/lap2005/Paper%201-LAP.pdf. Accessed 20 Jan 2020
20. Goldkuhl, G.: LAP revisited: articulating information as social relation. http://www.vits.org/publikationer/dokument/805.pdf. Accessed 20 Jan 2020
21. Dietz, J.L.G., Mulder, H.B.F.: Enterprise Ontology. Springer, Berlin (2020)
22. Dietz, J.L.G.: Enterprise Ontology. Springer, Berlin (2006). https://doi.org/10.1007/3-540-33149-2

23. Dietz, J.L.G. (ed.): EE Manifesto. http://www.ee-institute.org/en/ee-manifesto. Accessed 18 May 2020
24. Stamper, R.: Information in Business and Administrative Systems. Wiley, New York (1973)
25. Van Heusden, B.P.: The Trias Semiotica (2020, in press)
26. Stamper, R.: Signs, information, norms and systems. In: Holmqvist, B., Andersen, P.B., Klein, H., Posner, R. (eds.) Signs of Work – Semiosis and Information Processing in Organisations, pp 349–379. De Gruyter, Berlin (1996)
27. Liu, K., Li, W.: Organisational Semiotics for Business Informatics. Routledge, Abingdon (2015)
28. Checkland, P.B.: Systems Thinking, Systems Practice. Wiley, Chichester (1999)
29. Checkland, P.B.: Soft systems methodology: a 30-year retrospective. In: Checkland, P.B. (ed.) Systems Thinking, Systems Practice, pp. A1–A66. Wiley, Chichester (1999)
30. Vickers, G.: Appreciative behaviour. In: The Open System Group (ed.) The Vickers Papers, pp. 152–167. Harper & Row, London (1984)
31. Checkland, P.B., Poulter, J.: Learning for Action – A Short Definitive Account of Soft Systems Methodology and Its Use for Practitioners, Teachers and Students. Wiley, Chichester (2006)

Process Reference Models: Accelerator for Digital Transformation

Mathias Kirchmer[1,2(✉)] and Peter Franz[3]

[1] BPM-D, West Chester, USA
Mathias.Kirchmer@bpm-d.com
[2] University of Pennsylvania, Philadelphia, USA
[3] BPM-D, Kingston upon Thames, Surrey, UK
Peter.Franz@bpm-d.com

Abstract. For most organizations digital transformation has become a key topic. Organizations have to deal with new digital tools and its business impact on a daily basis. Hyper-Automation has become a reality. However, only a small number of organizations have their business processes sufficiently under control to realize the full value of digital technologies. Process reference models can be developed as a way to address that challenge. Those digitalization process reference models enable and accelerate a process-led approach to digital transformation and prepare an effective value realization. The models formalize and structure the knowledge about a digital business process and help to re-use it efficiently. Process reference models make the business impact of digital technologies transparent and manageable. This accelerates the design and evaluation of new digital processes as well as the roll-out across the organization. This article defines process reference models and discusses the different types of such models. It describes which special characteristics process reference models need to be applied successfully in digital transformations. Then it explains how to use those reference models in the context of digital transformations. The following case study illustrates the impact of the digitalization reference models and its importance in practice.

Keywords: BPM · Business process management · Digitalization · Digital transformation · Process design · Process improvement · Process modelling · Reference models · Value realization

1 Why Re-examining Process Reference Models, Now

Digital transformation has become a key topic in most organization (Kirchmer et al. 2016). New digital tools are available with increasing regularity – and many of them have the potential for a major business impact. Hyper-Automation has become a reality (Stoudt-Hansen et al. 2019). However, only a small number of those organizations have their business processes sufficiently under control to realize the full value of new digital technologies and the related transformation (Kirchmer 2019; Cantara 2015). Process reference models (PRM) help to address that challenge by accelerating the analysis and design of business processes (Kirchmer 2017). They enable an efficient process-led

B. Shishkov (Ed.): BMSD 2020, LNBIP 391, pp. 20–37, 2020.
https://doi.org/10.1007/978-3-030-52306-0_2

approach to digital transformation which realizes the anticipated value. PRM support the transfer of digital business models into appropriately automated digital processes (Scheer 2018).

Process reference models formalize and structure the knowledge about a business process and help to re-use it efficiently. PRM make the business impact of digital technologies transparent, tangible and with that manageable. They allow to plan for the business results of a digital transformation. PRM support the implementation of new digital processes as well as the roll-out across the organization. After the transformation PRM help keep processes on track and benefit from new technology developments.

The effective use of process reference in digital transformations requires a new form of reference models as well as an appropriate approach for its application. This article examines both aspects.

The article defines and segments process reference models. It explains which characteristics PRM need to be suited as accelerator in digital transformations. This descriptive part of the article is followed by a prescriptive section discussing how to use PRM in transformation initiatives. A case study illustrates the findings and shows the relevance of PRM in practice. The article ends with an outlook to related future research.

2 Definition and Value of Process Reference Models

The definition and value proposition of reference models in general and process reference models in specific is followed by a discussion of different types of such models and their characteristics. This lays the basis for further examination of specific characteristics of reference models necessary for an effective use in digital transformation initiatives.

2.1 Definition and Value of Process Reference Models

Reference models are defined as generic conceptual information models that formalize recommended practices for a special domain (Kirchmer 2017; Fettke and Loos 2007a, b; Scheer 1994). Those models have the following main characteristics:

- Representation of common or even best practices: Reference models provide the necessary knowledge for conducting business activities in a specific domain at a common or best performance level.
- Universal applicability: Reference models deliver business content that can be used well beyond an individual specific situation.
- Reusability and Adaptability: Reference models are conceptual frameworks that can be easily re-used in many related projects. They are structured for easy adaptability to specific situations.

Therefore, reference models deliver common or best practice information that can be used many times, for example in multiple organizations, business units or for different projects. The format allows easy adaptability to specific situations. That's why they are, in general, available in digital form, in most cases as files of process modeling and repository tools (Kirchmer 2017). Although the currently available reference models often do not completely fulfill all those characteristics (Fettke and Loos 2007b), they at least come close to it.

Process reference models (PRM) are reference models that consist of "conceptual models" that describe business processes in form of process models, using standard modelling approaches such as BPMN (Fisher 2012). Those can be complemented by models for other views on processes, like functions, data, organizational structure or deliverables of the process (Scheer 1998). Processes describe how an organization creates value. This is why PRM are the most important reference models needed to enable and accelerate value-driven transformation initiatives. In the following we focus the analysis on PRM. The definition of PRM is visualized in Fig. 1.

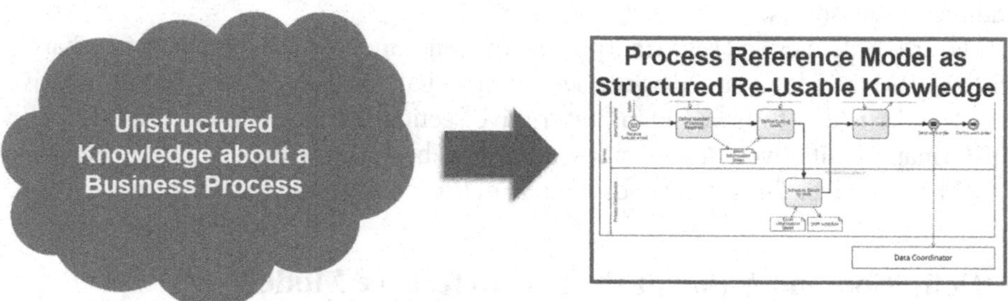

Fig. 1. Definition of process reference models

The use of PRM provides business benefits in the design, implementation, execution, and controlling of new business processes or the adjustment of existing ones. The major impact lies in the design phase of the process lifecycle management. PRM are accelerators of process improvement and transformation initiatives. Here some typical examples of the provided value (Kirchmer 2017):

- Cost reduction
- Time reduction
- Quality improvement
- Risk reduction
- Transparency over new or common practices
- Common language – supporting effective communication
- Preparation for benchmarking
- Enabling of standardization
- Innovation through transfer of practices between domains

It is much more efficient to modify an existing PRM in order to adapt it to a specific context than to develop the entire process model from scratch. The result is a significant reduction of design time and with that related cost. Experience has shown that the design time for processes can be reduced by up to 70% (Kirchmer 2017). The required high-quality modeling of PRM can be transferred and used in enterprise-specific process-modeling activities. This is true for syntactic, as well as, for semantic aspects. The content of PRM is already validated. Hence, its application leads to risk reduction.

The structure of a PRM includes the thinking of various experts and experience from different organizations. The syntax and formal structure can be used as a solid starting point and "best practice" for company specific process initiatives. This is especially helpful in determining the different levels of detail that an enterprise modelling approach should cover: the levels can be defined in relation to the levels used in the PRM. A knowledge domain described by PRM becomes transparent through the clear and easy-to-read structure of the PRM. Hence, it is easier to scope projects based on such reference models. A PRM defines the terms used in the model, for example functions or data objects. Hence those definitions can be the basis for a common language for all people involved in related process management initiatives. This simplifies the communication between different people involved, such as members from business and technology or external project collaborators. If several enterprises or divisions of a large organization use the same PRM as a basis to design their business processes, this facilitates the benchmarking of those processes later since it is easier to compare "apples with apples" due to the use of the same or similar terms and structure of the processes. The result is also a standardization of business processes though re-use of PRM process components. PRM can be leveraged to transfer practices from one industry to another, enabling process innovation. For example, a bio-technology company may use the configuration process of a machinery company by applying a machinery industry reference model.

PRM accelerate and simplify the design of business processes while ensuring a high quality of the results. This increases efficiency and effectiveness of process improvements and accelerates process transformation initiatives.

2.2 Types of Process Reference Models

Process reference models represent knowledge of various business domains. According to those domains, different types of PRM can be distinguished (Kirchmer 2017). The distinction of those reference model types supports an examination of characteristics of reference models to be used in digital transformation initiatives. Here the most common types of reference models:

- Industry PRM: These represent common or best practices of a specific industry sector, like banking, insurance, telecommunication, technology, pharmaceutical or machinery industry.
- Technology PRM: These describe common practice processes on the basis of a specific technology, in most cases a software application, for example enterprise resource planning (ERP) systems.
- Procedural PRM: These show best practices of non-industry specific domains or of domains that are not part of the daily operational business of an organization, for example a reference model for project management, process improvement or functional areas such as Human Resources or Finance to illustrate common practices.
- Company PRM: These models represent common practices within a larger organization or a company group, for example, a common practice for organizing maintenance processes, call center operations or underwriter processes - in the specific context. These PRM do not fully meet the criteria of universal applicability. But, in large organizations these models can be of high importance, for example for standardization

initiatives or the rapid roll out of process improvements. These are "universally used" within the larger company group.

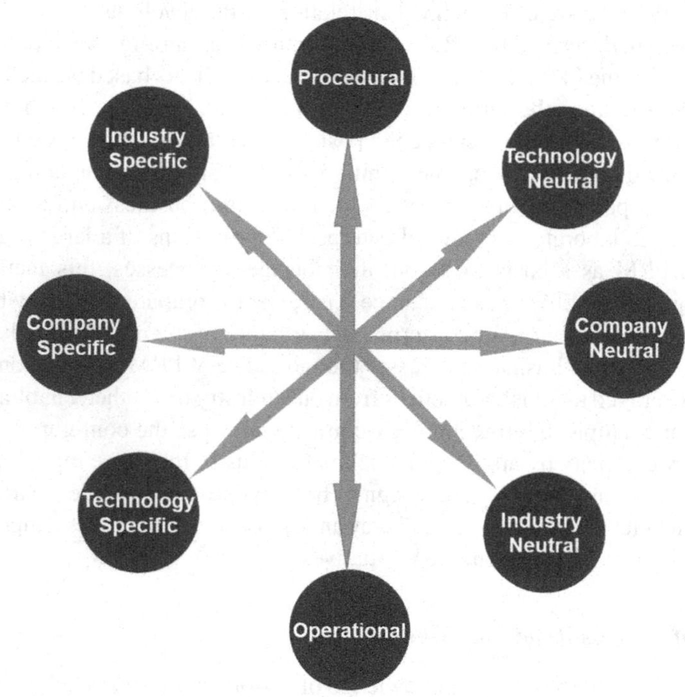

Fig. 2. Types of process reference models

PRM often represent a combination of two or more model types. For example, the PRM could be a technology-based reference model for a specific industry, explaining how industry specific processes are leveraging specific technologies, such as an ERP system, to achieve best process performance.

The presented types of reference models are illustrated in Fig. 2. They are leveraged now to identify specifics for the characteristics and use of reference models in digital transformations.

3 Characteristics of Digitalization Process Reference Models

Digital transformations leverage internet-based digital technologies to integrate physical products and people to enable new high-performance business processes (Kirchmer 2017). This specific context shapes the characteristics reference models need to be successfully used as accelerators. These characteristics are identified and described below. PRM with those characteristics are referred to as digitalization process reference models (DPRM) Fig. 3 illustrates the definition of digital transformation to set the context.

Software-based process reference models to accelerate automation initiatives have been developed and used for over 20 years. Initially they have been created to make the business content of complex application systems, such as ERP systems, transparent (Curran and Keller 1999; Kirchmer 1999). Also, the use of technology-based reference models for specific functional areas has been explored for quite some time (Kirchmer et al. 2002).

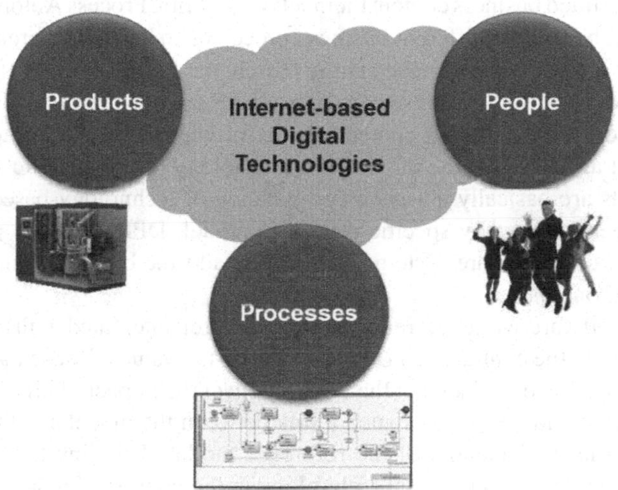

Fig. 3. Digital transformation

However, requirements to describe processes enabled through digital technology solutions have evolved. While ERP systems and similar applications focus on relatively stable back office processes, such as finance, human resources or warehouse management, today's business environment requires support of front office, market-facing business processes that are built to change. The same way, technologies have become more flexible and universally usable, such as no-code digital platforms. DPRM must incorporate those trends and reflect the potential of the right flexible combination of different digital technologies to support new digital business processes. Only then those reference models become real accelerators for digital transformation.

The requirements for new characteristics of DPRM are examined using the ARIS architecture as the guiding framework (Scheer 1998). We identify technology driven and business driven requirements. On the business level, organizational, functional, data, control and deliverable related aspects are distinguished.

3.1 Technology-Driven Requirements for Process Reference Models

In the traditional support of back-office areas, most business processes have been supported through one or a very limited number of applications, such as a finance system, human resources module or asset management application. Processes reflecting market facing activities which drive ongoing change, are often supported through a combination of digital technologies, for example a digital integration and development platform, combined with several application components, enterprise integration applications (EAI), a workflow engine and robotic process automation (RPA). DPRM need to reflect this combination and provide guidance for the appropriate combination of technology components. This significant extension to traditional software reference models is visualized in Fig. 4.

Most of the new digital technologies can be used in a very flexible way, they don't have much pre-defined business content themselves. Robotic Process Automation (RPA), for example, can be used in different business processes to handle different documents, such as supplier invoices or insurance claims (Kirchmer and Franks 2019). This is a big difference to traditional software systems, such as ERP systems, where process reference models just describe the business content of the software. DPRM have to provide the business context and describe the impact of a technology in this specific situation. The reference models are basically always a combination of technology-based models and functional or even a company specific reference model. DPRM do not just make the business content of a software system visible, they add the business dimension to the technology components.

Traditional software-based reference models are often integrated with the underlying application to guide the configuration. This increases the value of those models (Curran and Keller 1999). Due to the fact that the DPRM reflect the impact of different technologies, it is more demanding to create such a link between the model and the technology itself to realize the full potential of the reference model. This link has to be defined individually for each involved digital technology in the context of a business scenario. This could, for example, require the inclusion of additional components into the DPRM, such as configuration tables or rule definitions relating to a specific configuration of a digital platform.

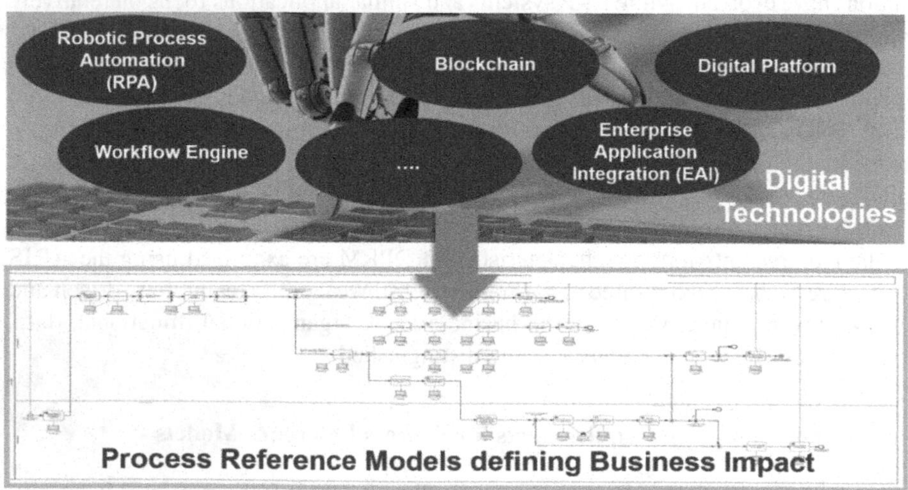

Fig. 4. Reference models reflect the support through multiple digital technologies

3.2 Business-Driven Requirements for Process Reference Models

In order to use DPRM as accelerators for digital transformations various business-related requirements need to be fulfilled. This leads to an enrichment of the content of those models.

Many digital transformation initiatives require the creation of new roles in an organization and the modification or elimination of existing roles. Organizations tend to struggle with this dimension of digital transformations (Kirchmer and Franz 2019). They save, for example, through RPA a few hours of time for people in different roles, however, this does not enable major improvements since no role can be fully eliminated. A real redefinition of roles and responsibilities is often key for realizing the full potential of a digital transformation. The reflection of those organizational aspects is important for DPRM. The role definitions are reflected in the process models, but also in complementing organizational role models.

DPRM provide the business content reflecting a combination of digital technologies applied in a specific business context. The description of the relation between functions and enabling technology components is therefore a key component of those reference models. Attributes describing the functions may include specific technology requirements that help identifying new emerging technologies during a transformation initiative.

Directly related to this aspect is the general need to include data elements into the DPRM. The combination of different technologies to support end-to-end processes requires the handling of the data and related documents through different systems while avoiding manual transactional activities. The handling of data aspects has to be made transparent through the DPRM to accelerate the integration of the different technologies during the implementation of the digital process. The data objects in the process models may have to be complemented with appropriate data models.

The development of a solid business case for digital transformations, agreed upon by business and IT, is for many organizations challenging and time consuming. DPRM have to support and accelerate this aspect of the transformation. DPRM need to include relevant information, such as typical time and cost attributes as well as common probabilities at decision points, to enable transparency over the expected performance of a process and rapid creation of the business case. Since the DPRM reflects, in general, a highly automated process, transaction times can be determined relatively easy by the involved technologies. Average industry-specific cost rates and distribution of probabilities complement this business content. DPRM can then be used to enable simple simulations to achieve quantifiable benefit estimations for cycle times, cost, scalability or potential effort for exception handling.

3.3 Use of a Dynamic Process Repository

The integration of business and technology aspects in DPRM makes their availability in a dynamic digital process repository even more important. This simplifies the ongoing update of the reference models when new technology capabilities emerge, or better business practices become available. The frequency of changes to the DPRM used in digital transformations is higher than the more traditional reference model, such as industry models or even traditional software reference models. Housing the DPRM in a digital repository is basically mandatory to enable accelerated digital transformations.

Figure 5 illustrates the use of an integrated process repository to represent all information relevant for the DPRM. The development of the DPRM in the repository follows the general guidelines for process repository management (Franz and Kirchmer 2012).

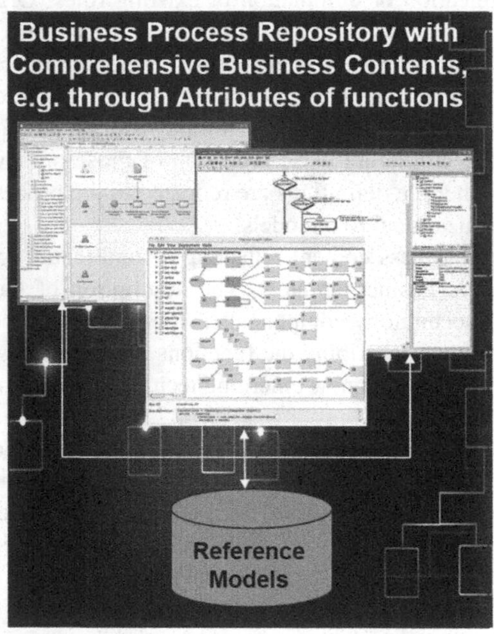

Fig. 5. Reference models combine comprehensive business content in a process repository

4 Using Digitalization Process Reference Models

Digitalization process reference models are purchased or developed in the initial planning phase of a digital transformation. They are then leveraged as accelerators during the transformation. Once improved or new digital business processes are in place, reference models continue to add value for the ongoing process improvement and controlling. The reference models can support the entire process lifecycle, enabling an ongoing digitalization journey.

4.1 Acquiring Digitalization Process Reference Models

Reference models are knowledge products that can, in principle, be acquired on the market, either as independent products or components of larger offerings, for example as part of a software licensing or a consulting agreement. They can today be acquired at software or technology companies, consulting firms, industry organizations or academic institutions (Kirchmer 2017). However, this is mainly valid for traditional reference models.

DPRM with the characteristics described above, optimized to accelerate digital transformations, are still in an emerging state, hence, there is no real market for those products. Therefore, such reference models have in most cases to be developed as part of a digital transformation. This requires the collaborations of functional experts, information technology experts of the organization who conducts the transformation and technology vendors.

DPRM can be developed as part of a pilot initiative, for example in a specific product area of an organization. The to-be process models reflecting the business impact of the relevant digital technologies are used as a starting point for the DPRM. Product or business area specifics are removed from the process models, attributes, such as cost or time attributes of functions, are generalized, for example through average values, or replaced through industry standards. The resulting DPRM can then be used across all remaining business units – or even in other organizations. Every use case is an opportunity for the continuous improvement of the models. Business and technology developments should be briefly evaluated before re-using the reference model.

4.2 Applying Digitalization Process Reference Models

The use of DPRM in digital transformations is consistent with the application of reference models in general to support the rapid and effective design of business processes. Components of the DPRM that are not relevant for a specific business context are removed and the process logic is adjusted wherever necessary. If the DPRM is missing certain process components, for example a sub-process needed in a specific business unit, those elements are added to the model. The result is a business-unit-specific process model, reflecting the design necessary to achieve defined goals, leveraging the identified digital technologies (Kirchmer 2017). Changes to the reference model can lead to additional requirements for supporting technologies or to the elimination of technology components. Technology information in the DPRM supports the identification of such scope changes and guides the appropriate modelling of the additional process components. It is effective when the transformation plan needs to be adjusted accordingly.

The approach to use digitalization reference models is illustrated in Fig. 6.

If the digital transformation does not just establish new processes, but replaces and adjusts existing ones, the DPRM can already be used to identify relevant processes for the as-is analysis. Weak points and improvement potentials of those as-is processes can be determined through comparison of as-is process models with the reference models. The impact of the introduction of new digital technologies and related business content can be made transparent by visualizing where the as-is processes will change once it transitions to the DPRM-based to-be situation.

DPRM simplify the definition of intermediate realization scenarios as they are required by agile transformation approaches (Kirchmer and Franz 2019). These scenarios represent process minimum viable products (MVP). This is achieved in a combined top-down and bottom up approach. The expected business value helps to identify the high-level structure of the first intermediate to-be process scenario to be realized as an excerpt of the DPRM. The agile configuration and development approach (Sutherland 2014) to the underlying technologies determines the detailed design of the digital business processes in each intermediate scenario. The consideration of relevant data aspects

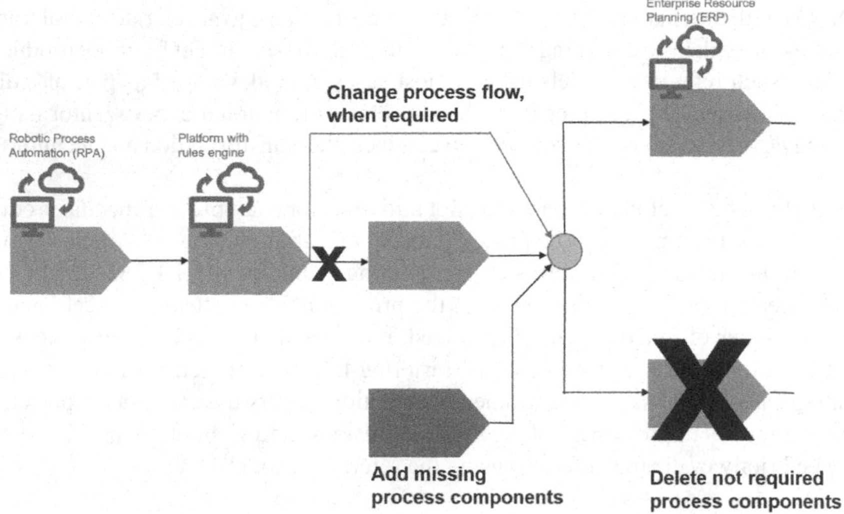

Fig. 6. General use of process reference models

plays an integral role in the definition of these MVP process scenarios. Since these are included in the DPRM the model can again be leveraged.

The business case is developed and refined using an appropriate process simulation approach. To-be process models, built based on the DPRM, can be simulated delivering specific cost, cycle time, resource needs and show the scalability of the transformed processes. This is the foundation for a solid business case, including and aligning business and IT views. Transparency over the quantitative business impact of the digital processes accelerates decisions and simplifies a value-driven implementation of the transformed processes.

The flexibility of digital technologies often encourages the creation of process variants leading to negative ongoing cost effects and reduced agility. Therefore, process standardization is an important topic in digital transformations. The use of DPRM supports the standardization of business processes across different business units while facilitating a systematic efficient roll out of digital technologies. Since many digital technologies, like RPA, are easy to use, there is a high risk that different business units acquire those technologies and use them in their own way. Results are process variants that lead to ongoing management challenges, for example in the roll out of new advanced processes or the rapid reaction to change. Guidance through the DPRM avoids this situation. The right degree of standardization is supported by defining which components of the reference model can be modified without special approval, for example because they are product specific. Other model components may be considered as company standard that can only be changed in exceptional cases after a thorough approval procedure. The integrated business and technology view in the DPRM simplifies the definition of appropriate guidance for the transformation initiatives.

The use of DPRM to simplify and accelerate standardization of digital processes is a key benefit. This is illustrated in Fig. 7.

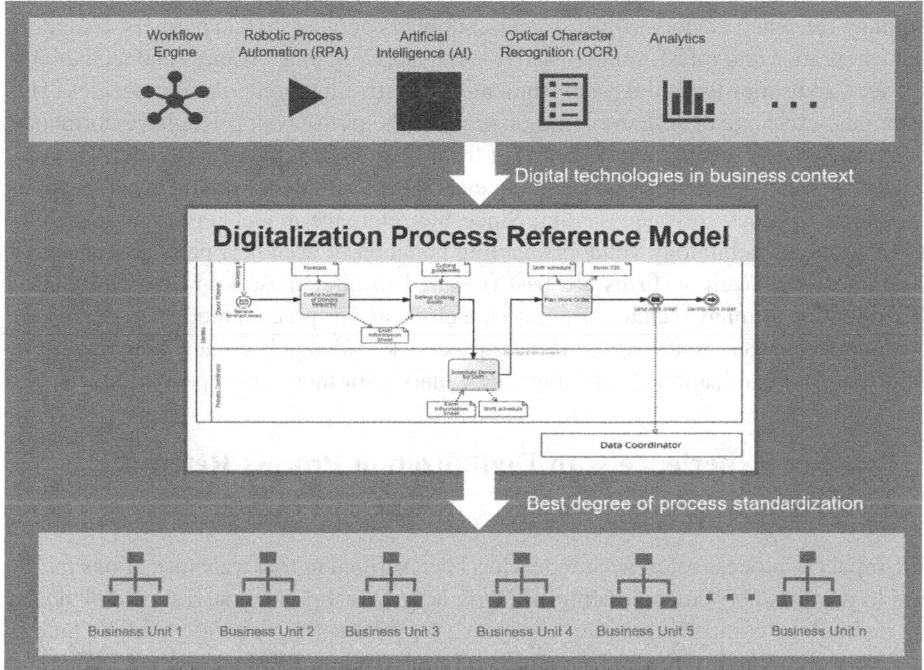

Fig. 7. Using a process reference model to standardize digital business processes

4.3 Continuous Use of Digitalization Process Reference Models After Transformation Initiative

After the digital transformation of a business process, the process reference models continue to provide value to an organization. It can be used to identify opportunities for future process improvements that are relevant across various business units. The availability of new or enhanced digital technologies can be evaluated based on updated DPRM. This allows business-driven decisions on guidelines for the roll out of new technology releases and new investments.

DPRM are used to identify further requirements for new and enhanced digital technologies. The structured description of process enhancements based on the DPRM explains new requirements to technology vendors. Hence the models can become a communication tool between an organization and its external suppliers. DPRM also support the alignment of different technology vendors to enable the desired digital process. Technology vendors use the same approach to suggest upgrades and changes to their clients – in the context of their larger use of digital technologies in processes across the organization.

DPRM can be leveraged as global design model to simplify the integration and alignment of new business units, for example in a merger or acquisition situation. The reference models accelerate the use of new business practices and technologies. The application of the models can be even expanded across company boundaries by sharing company reference models with customers, suppliers or other market partners to support their integration and transformation activities. It helps aligning business and technology practices and simplifying the establishment of effective inter-enterprise processes. The systematic exchange of best and common practices helps to develop a high- performance company network where members benefit from each other's digital experiences.

The internally developed DPRM may even be converted into products and become the source of a new revenue stream. Since the reference model represents capabilities of multiple technology vendors enabling common or even best practices, end-user companies or consulting firms are best prepared to offer those knowledge products. The transition of many technologies into the cloud makes process models key assets of an organization (Kirchmer 2015). Hence, process knowledge becomes more and more important for organizations, justifying a new market for those knowledge products.

5 Practice Experience with Digitalization Process Reference Models

The impact of process reference models has been verified in four transformations initiatives in practice: new customer onboarding in a credit union, integrated supply planning in a technology company, procure-to-pay in a logistics service provider and the underwriter process of an insurance company. In all projects the DPRM were developed in the context of the initiative as company-specific reference models based on a combination of digital technologies. All cases showed reduction in design time of 40% or more as well as efficiency effects in other phases of the transformation, for example the development of business cases. All initiatives delivered significant business value through the transformation initiatives enabled through the reference models.

The effects of the DRPM is explained using the case example of a major North American insurance company. We have selected this case since it uses a typical digital technology environment and rolls out processes into multiple business units. Scope is the transformation of the underwriter processes in more than 10 product areas. Goal is a significant cost reduction, better scalability as well as an improved broker experience. The transformation is enabled through the emerging digital no-code platform Unqork (Unqork 2020), which is integrated with various other technologies, including a new document management system and major existing applications. Unqork delivers application functionality, a flexible workflow engine, a portal as well as various analytics capabilities.

The reference models were developed in the context of a pilot initiative in one specific product area and then re-used for over 10 product units. It has been a joint development effort with members of the insurance company and the technology supplier.

The models describe how an underwriter process can be moved to the next level, leveraging the described technologies. The DPRM consists of 28 individual process models with 345 tasks. It was develop using the Signavio Process Manager as modelling and repository tool as well as for process simulation (Signavio 2020). The reference model includes all characteristics described above. However, detailed technology-based data models will only be added in a later step once we have experience with at least two to three live Unqork-based processes. This avoids too frequent adjustments.

The structure of reference model is illustrated in Fig. 8. It currently consists of two levels of detail to describe the overall flow as well as the detailed tasks. The modelling method is BPMN. Level one in the figure is just illustrative (and therefore not readable), level two gives an idea about the level of detail used to describe the digitalized tasks.

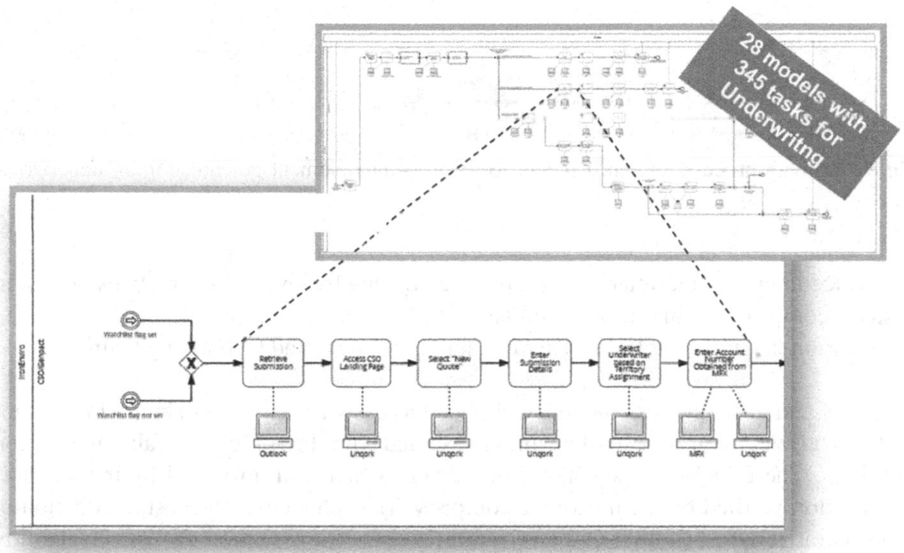

Fig. 8. Process reference models for underwriter processes in an insurance company

The reference model was first used to identify improvement opportunities of existing processes. It was determined, which steps could be completely automated or avoided. Roles that could be eliminated entirely were identified as a result of the analysis. Compared to traditional approaches to analysis, we recognized a reduction of time of about 30%. Figure 9 shows an example of an as-is process with symbols that indicate were the new digital process described in the reference model has an impact on the desired performance of the underwriter processes. Hence, for every step of the as-is process it is defined how it will be affected through the digital transformation.

The to-be processes were developed using the DPRM as a basis, as described before. This brought significant benefits. Here the main impacts:

- Accelerated processes design: time reduction of over 50% compared to other similar traditional initiatives
- Transparency over business impacts of new Unqork platform in combination with other digital components minimized time required for discussions of expected process changes

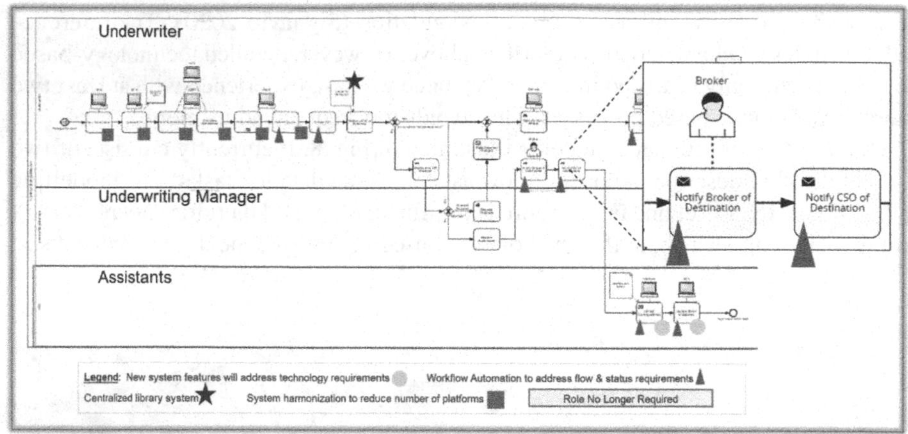

Fig. 9. Using a process reference model to identify improvement potentials in an underwriter process

- Reduced implementation risk and improved quality by leveraging practices proven in same company in other product units
- Common language for transformation across business and technology teams

As-is and to-be process models were used as basis for a process simulation to support the development of a solid business case and align the following value realization activities. The DPRM already had time attributes included, provided by the technology vendor, verified by the insurance company. This allowed to forecast a reduction of administrative effort of 88% and an overall process cost reduction of 49%. Scalability is expected to increase by a factor of 9. This information led to a reduction of time to develop an agreed upon business case by at least 70%. Previous efforts to get a consensus of expected benefits of this digital transformation were not successful since business and information technology (IT) people had different opinions regarding potential benefits. The use of the DPRM to develop comprehensive to-be models in a short time brought all involved parties to the same page and simplified decision. The use of the simulation approach leveraging DPRM-based to-be models is visualized in Fig. 10.

The reference models were also used to prepare the people change management. New and modified roles were identified. The tasks per role were exported from the DPRM for early preparation and from the DPRM-based to-be processes models to support specific training, information and communication initiatives (Kirchmer 2017). This information could be delivered as a side product without any additional preparation time. Hence, an almost 100%-time reduction.

The analysis and design effort for this underwriter transformation was reduced by over 60% after the DPRM was available. This confirmed role of the reference model as accelerator of the transformation initiative. In a next step, it is planned to include detailed configuration data of the Unqork platform to leverage the reference model as accelerator of the technical software configuration and implementation.

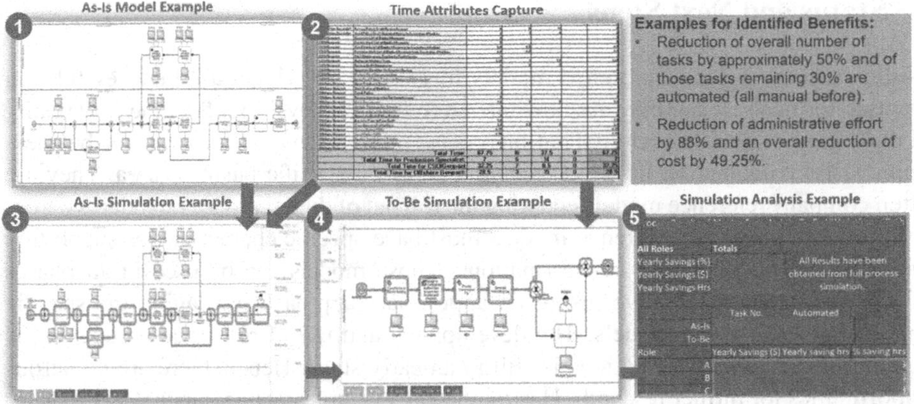

Fig. 10. Simulation approach using a digital process reference model to quantify identified improvements

To support the roll-out of the approach across different profit centers and product areas, the use and maintenance of the reference model has been described in a "reference model playbook". The table of content of the playbook is shown in Fig. 11.

Contents

Fig. 11. Table of content of the playbook for the use of the digitalization process reference model

The use of process reference models as accelerators of digital transformation has been successful and well accepted by the involved organizations. Biggest challenge was to convince transformation leaders to consider the development and use of those models. Once they decided to go this way, transformation teams recognized quickly the benefits and encouraged the further use of the DPRM-based approach.

6 Status and Next Steps

While business process reference models in general have been used successfully in practice for many years, they are now moved to the next level to reflect the new reality of the digital world. Those digitalization process reference models describe the business impact of a combination of digital technologies in a specific business area. They are often company reference models enabling the roll out of digital process standards across an organization. Those reference models must have specific characteristics supporting the requirements of digital transformations. Those models can be used in all phases of a transformation initiative, using an appropriate approach leveraging the specific characteristics of those models. The development and use of reference models in the context of digital transformations is still in an early stage. Hence, there are numerous opportunities for further research. Here some key examples:

- Identify process scenarios and suited combination of supporting digital technologies as basis to develop more general digitalization process reference models
- Simulations approach and reporting of results to support business case development, change management and technology configuration
- Establish a close integration of the models with the enabling digital technologies to expand the use of the modeling during the technology configuration and development
- Develop a business model for the productization of digitalization reference models

The use and management of process reference models has become an important component of the discipline of business process management in the digital age. These digitalization models are impactful accelerators for digital transformations. Practice results have confirmed significant benefits of those knowledge assets.

References

Cantara, M.: Start up your business process competency center. In: Documentation of The Gartner Business Process Management Summit, National Harbour (2015)

Curran, T.A., Keller, G.: SAP R/3 Business Blueprint: Business Engineering mit den R/3-Referenzprozessen. Addison-Wesley, Bonn (1999)

Fettke, P., Loos, P.: Classification of reference models: a methodology and its application. Inf. Syst. E-Bus. Manag. **1**(1), 35–53 (2007a)

Fettke, P., Loos, P.: Perspectives on reference modelling. In: Fettke, P, Loos, P (eds.) Reference Modelling for Business Systems Analysis, pp. 1–20. Hershey, London (2007b)

Fisher, L.: BPMN 2.0 handbook – methods, concepts, case studies and standards in business process modelling notation (BPMN). Lighthouse Point (2012)

Franz, P., Kirchmer, M.: Value-Driven Business Process Management: The Value-Switch for Lasting Competitive Advantage, 1st edn. McGraw-Hill, New York (2012)

Kirchmer, M.: Business Process Oriented Implementation of Standard Software – How to Achieve Competitive Advantage Efficiently and Effectively, 2nd edn. Springer, Berlin (1999). https://doi.org/10.1007/978-3-642-58428-2

Kirchmer, M.: The process of process management – mastering the new normal in a digital world. In: BMSD Proceedings, July 2015

Kirchmer, M.: High Performance through Business Process Management –Strategy Execution in a Digital World. Springer, 3rd edn. Springer, New York, Berlin (2017). https://doi.org/10.1007/978-3-319-51259-4

Kirchmer, M.: Value-driven digital transformation: performance through process. In: IM+io, Best and Next Practices aus Digitalisierung | Management | Wissenschaft, Heft 2, Juni 2019

Kirchmer, M., Franz, P.: Value-driven robotic process automation (RPA) – a process-led approach for fast results at minimal risk. In: Shishkov, B. (ed.) BMSD 2019. LNBIP, vol. 356, pp. 31–46. Springer, Cham (2019). https://doi.org/10.1007/978-3-030-24854-3_3

Kirchmer, M., Franz, P., Lotterer, A., Antonucci, Y., Laengle, S.: The value-switch for digitalisation initiatives: business process management. BPM-D Whitepaper, Philadelphia, London (2016)

Kirchmer, M., Brown, G., Heinzel, H.: Using SCOR and other reference models for E-Business process networks. In: Scheer, A.W., Abolhassan, F., Jost, W., Kirchmer, M. (eds.) Business Process Excellence – ARIS in Practice, pp. 45–64. Springer, Heidelberg (2002). https://doi.org/10.1007/978-3-540-24705-0_4

Scheer, A.W.: Unternehmung 4.0 – Von disruptiven Geschaeftsmodell zur Automatisierung von Geschaeftsprozessen, 1st edn. AWSi Publishing, Saarbrucken (2018)

Scheer, A.W.: ARIS – Business Process Frameworks, 2nd edn. Springer, Berlin (1998). https://doi.org/10.1007/978-3-642-58529-6

Scheer, A.W.: Business Process Engineering – Reference Models of Industrial Enterprises, 2nd edn. Springer, Berlin (1994). https://doi.org/10.1007/978-3-642-79142-0

Signavio: Signavio Process Manager (2020). https://www.signavio.com/products/process-manager/

Stoudt-Hansen, S., et al.: Predicts 2020: barriers fall as technology adoption grows. A Gartner Trend Insight Report, Boston (2019)

Sutherland, J.: SCRUM – The Art of doing Twice the Work in Half the Time. Penguin Random House, New York (2014)

Unqork: Unqork Insurance Software (2020) https://www.unqork.com/solutions/insurance

Making Enterprise Information Systems Resilient Against Disruptive Events: A Conceptual View

Boris Shishkov[1,2,3](✉) and Alexander Verbraeck[4]

[1] Faculty of Information Sciences, University of Library Studies and Information Technologies, Sofia, Bulgaria
[2] Institute of Mathematics and Informatics, Bulgarian Academy of Sciences, Sofia, Bulgaria
[3] Institute IICREST, Sofia, Bulgaria
b.b.shishkov@iicrest.org
[4] Faculty of Technology, Policy, and Management, Delft University of Technology, Delft, The Netherlands
a.verbraeck@tudelft.nl

Abstract. *Enterprise Information Systems* (*EIS*) are designed to deal with *normal variability* in their inputs and data. Empowered by CONTEXT-AWARENESS, some *EIS* even count on *sensors* and/or *data analytics* for capturing changes outside of the system. Nevertheless, *context-awareness* would often fail when *EIS* are affected by (large-scale) *disruptive events*, such as disasters, virus outbreaks, or military conflicts. Hence, in the current paper, we take a step forward, by considering *context-awareness* for *disruptive events*. We combine *context-awareness* with *risk management* techniques, such as FMECA and FTA, that are useful for defining and mitigating risk events. To avoid having to define the likelihood for such very-low-probability disruptive risks, we use CONSEQUENCE-BASED RISK MANAGEMENT rather than traditional *risk management*. We augment this approach with the *context-awareness* paradigm, delivering a contribution that is two-fold: (i) We propose *context-awareness-related measures* and *consequence-based-risk-management-related measures*, to address *disruptive events*; (ii) We reflect this in a *method featuring the application of context-awareness and risk management for designing robust and resilient EIS*.

Keywords: Enterprise information system · Resilience · Context-awareness · Risk management

1 Introduction

Larger organizations are essentially supported by *Enterprise Information Systems – EIS* [1, 2], such as *Enterprise Resource Planning* systems (*ERP*), *Customer Relationship Management* systems (*CRM*), and *Supply Chain Management* systems (*SCM*). Such systems help organizations' *business processes* to run smoothly and to be of full value [3]. Their correct working assumes an adequate alignment between the *EIS* and the enterprise *environment* [4].

B. Shishkov (Ed.): BMSD 2020, LNBIP 391, pp. 38–54, 2020.
https://doi.org/10.1007/978-3-030-52306-0_3

As the environment of organizations is continuously changing, such an alignment can only be achieved if the *EIS* is situation-aware – this means sensitive to environmental changes [5]. *Sensors* [6] and *data analytics* [7] provide information about the state of the system and its environment, and *EIS* can adapt to perceived changes using *run-time behavior algorithms* [5].

Under regular business uncertainty, this is supposed to work. Nevertheless, when *large-scale disruptive events* occur, adaptive algorithms stop working. For example: (i) A virus outbreak or a large-scale strike in a country may effectively "shut down" businesses, public services, and logistics [8]; (ii) A disaster may physically destroy computer assets of partner organizations such as suppliers and customers [9, 10]; (iii) A cyber-attack may cause huge disruptions in the technology that supports business processes [15].

As a result, organizations that run an *EIS* and cannot adapt sufficiently, would essentially stop functioning. This is because of the dependence on their *EIS* that cannot deal with the exceptional changes in the current situation, providing sub-optimal support to corresponding business processes. It seems that businesses are not prepared to act in such situations [8] and have to fall back to manual interventions for which the IT-supported business processes are not designed.

We argue that what is needed during disruptive events is a "*resilient mode*" for *EIS*, building on the following four characteristics:

- The *EIS* determines when the data is out of bounds by setting boundaries for parameters in the environment and scanning the environment for parameters that don't fall into the boundaries (context awareness);
- The *EIS* has ways to fall back to atomic processes that are less integrated than the processes that are normally carried out, and that can temporarily deal with missing or incomplete data, or data that is inconsistent with other data in the system (fault tolerance);
- The *EIS* has alternative implementations of essential processes that can be run manually. Additionally, data that normally enters the *EIS* in an automated way, can also be provided by hand. (fallback options);
- The *EIS* has ways to get back to normal mode when the large-scale disruption is over. This means that data that has been handled in manual mode or by atomic processes rather than by integrated processes can be merged with existing data to provide a consistent, but not necessarily complete, picture of the disrupted period (recoverability).

We consider *Context-Awareness* (*CA*) and *Risk Management* (*RM*) as key underlying paradigms in this regard. *CA* relates to the ability to sense that the *EIS* is operating out of bounds with respect to the set of acceptable values of the environmental parameters. The field of *RM* can provide practices for fault tolerance, fallback options, and recoverability.

As it concerns *CA*, Alferez and Pelechano [11] claim that it may be useful to translate the ideas of adaptation in the natural world to software, assuming that such adaptations are carried out in response to changing conditions in the surrounding physical environment and/or in the supporting computing infrastructure; this is referred to as *CA*, especially as far as *EIS* are concerned [11]. Even though the system would not be expected to reconfigure itself for an unknown situation, it could at least sense that it is in such a situation. This is in line with the views of Dey et al., who already suggested in 2001 that context-aware *ICT* (*Information and Communication Technology*) applications should make use of the context that is relevant for the interaction with users; by "context" they mean information that concerns the state of people, places, and objects [12]. In further studies, Dey and Newberger argue that context information is typically gathered in an automated fashion [13, 14].

The *RM* field has traditionally dealt with making systems more robust against outside risks. This is being achieved by assessing potential risks on beforehand, classifying their likelihood and impact, and (based on the severity of the risk) providing mitigation measures to deal with the risk [16]. The *RM* field deals with disruptive events rather than with normal variability. *RM* thinking in general can be very useful for *EIS* robustness improvement. Several *RM* techniques such as *Failure Mode Effect and Criticality Analysis* (*FMECA*) and *Fault Tree Analysis* (*FTA*), are typically used for mechanical systems. We argue that *FMECA* and *FTA* could also be useful for the many interdependent components of an *EIS*.

This paper proposes innovative directions for more robust *EIS*, inspired by insights from *CA* and *RM*, while acknowledging the "emerging" nature of such research, characterized by insufficient existing experience on (and validation of) the feasibility of such "disaster-proof" *EIS*.

The remaining of this paper is structured as follows: A problem elaboration follows in Sect. 2. Related work analysis and corresponding conceptualization (featuring *CA* and *RM*) are presented in Sect. 3 and Sect. 4, respectively. Section 5 shows the possible application of *CA* and *RM* to disruptive events. Section 6 is proposing a corresponding method. Finally, Sect. 7 concludes the paper.

2 Problem Elaboration

This section elaborates the problem, by highlighting the difference between (i) normal variability and (ii) disruptive events:

(i) is about the regular variability in business processes and easy-to-predict situations, for example: "Supplies are delivered late and production processes need to be rescheduled based on the late supply", "Information provided by a business partner is incorrect and needs to be corrected", "There is shortage of a product and an alternative supplier needs to be selected to deliver the missing supply", "The agreed payment date is not met by a customer and a reminder needs to be sent", and so on. This is all well-manageable, by just assuming different possible situation variants and preparing (at design time) corresponding *EIS* variant actions. In these straightforward cases, situation awareness can be a solution: data indicates that the system is in an unwanted or inconsistent state (but a state that has been foreseen). The business logic in the *EIS* can choose the pre-defined rules to deal with the system state accordingly.

(ii) is about things that are not predictable at design time or where the likelihood of the occurrence of the event is considered to be so low that implementing variant actions in the *EIS* is seen as too costly for something that may never happen. For example: one would not know at design time what disruptions in the business processes could be caused by an earthquake, a virus outbreak, or a military conflict.

In this work, we do not address (i) where there is already much knowledge and experience [17]. As it concerns (ii) however, we observe insufficient knowledge and lack of exhaustive experience. Hence, we explore the handling of disruptive events by *EIS* in the current paper.

In this regard, we firstly define the four essential (in our view) aspects of any *EIS*, namely: data, operation, quality of service, and public values – see Fig. 1.

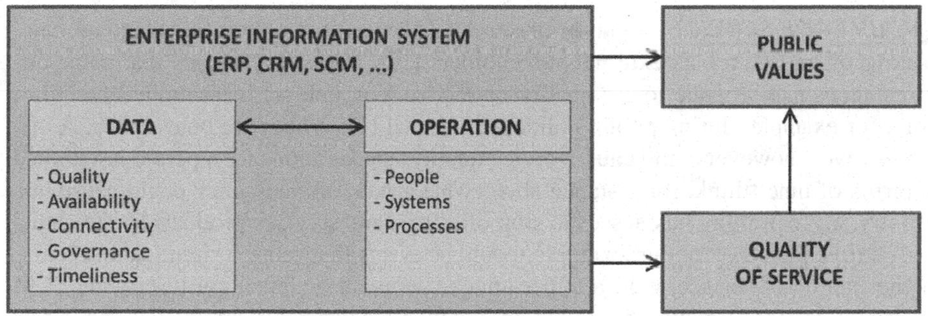

Fig. 1. The essential aspects of an *EIS*

As the figure suggests, there are several key issues that are fundamentally underlying the functioning of any *EIS*, namely: DATA (any *EIS* is about gathering, processing, and exchanging data, and for this reason the data availability, quality, timeliness, and so on are considered essential), OPERATION (one fundamental thing about an *EIS* is certainly its operation – what it does, how it does it, how different business processes are synchronized, and so on), QUALITY OF SERVICE (the quality of the services delivered by an *EIS* is the reason for its existence – going below a quality "threshold" would be considered as a failure), and PUBLIC VALUES (it is of crucial importance that in its operation, an *EIS* is not violating public values, such as privacy, accountability, and so on [31]). With these four aspects, we do not claim exhaustiveness and we only argue that they are essential for maintaining the overall value of an *EIS*. We briefly discuss each of the aspects below:

[*DATA*]. As suggested above and in line with [2], *EIS*' dealing with data is a matter of the timely availability of data, its quality, and the way it is transferred and governed. Any *EIS* can deal with data variability, such as data entry errors, formatting errors, brief connectivity interrupts, or late availability of data. Dealing with disruptive events is much harder. Think, for instance about: encrypted information that cannot be decrypted anymore (quality); a natural event wiping out a key supplier of data where the data is lost forever (availability); damaged Internet cables to islands leading to a disconnect of weeks or months (connectivity); a request to immediately provide information stored in the *EIS* to the Police after a terrorist attack (governance); receiving an invoice more than a year late after the annual budget has closed (timeliness).

[*OPERATION*]. The correct functioning of an *EIS* assumes the availability of a certain number of people to operate it on a day-to-day basis [18], as well as availability of hard- and software and clear processes. Organizations have catered for normal variance such as people leaving the organization, for hardware crashes and software maintenance, and for people not always following procedures. Nevertheless, a disruptive event could cause the available operating staff to be reduced below a level where the system can still function (think, for instance about the effects of a virus pandemic, or a long-term strike of key personnel). Disruptions could also cause massive hardware or software unavailability, or breaching procedures on a large scale.

[*QUALITY OF SERVICE*]. Quality-of-service is key as it concerns the adequate functioning of an *EIS* for its external stakeholders [19]. Variability means that some circumstances may assume lower quality-of-service (e.g. delays) for a limited period of time, for example: during public holidays, financial IT services are unavailable. A disruptive event however could cause service quality deteriorations for a period not limited in terms of time (think, for instance about what a state of emergency could cause in a country, e.g. enforcing businesses to stop offering some services/products for an undisclosed time period). Another example would be events that cause a significant decrease in the quality-of-service: e.g., a cyber-attack causes an organization to provide SCM track-and-trace information by phone on a daily basis instead of automated and in real time.

[*PUBLIC VALUES*]. Public values, such as privacy and accountability, are always part of what is demanded from *EIS* [20, 21]. Variability means that even though most public values are addressed in a way considered to be widely accepted in Society (for example, respecting privacy), those same values may be considered differently in some situations, again stemming from a wide public consensus (for example, disclosing privacy-related details of a criminal). A disruptive event nevertheless may lead to a definitive violation of public values (think, for instance about the possibility that a government declares a state of emergency and enforces an organization to disclose personal data stored in its *EIS*).

We obviously cannot design an *EIS* for every situation that may occur, so the operation of the *EIS* is usually limited to situations that stay within certain bounds, which typically do not include the effects of disruptive events. We suggest to expand the functionality of an *EIS* (and therewith the organization) with the following three functions, so it can keep functioning in the case of a disruptive event:

- Firstly, we need to **detect that an anomaly has occurred**. Many *EIS* do not specifically define, measure and guard the acceptable boundaries for variables in the environment that allow it to function properly. This makes it impossible to automatically detect that the state of the environment is out-of-bounds. As we will see later, *CA* is of use here.
- Secondly, the *EIS* should **continue to function** as much as possible in spite of the state of the environment being anomalous. This asks for a *Risk-Based, Robust Design*

of the *EIS*, where critical parts can independently keep functioning when other parts of the system fail as a result of the event, and where inconsistent components can either be switched off, switched to manual operation, or by-passed.

- Thirdly, when the event is over, and the environment (slowly) returns to normal, the *EIS* would usually still have gaps in its data, internal inconsistencies, and procedure violations. *Resilience* therefore needs to be built-in to the *EIS* to allow the *EIS* to **return to its normal state** again.

As mentioned in the Introduction, we will identify opportunities and propose solution directions with regard to those challenges, inspired by studies touching upon CA and RM – this follows in Sects. 3 and 4, respectively.

3 Context-Awareness: Related Work and Conceptualization

This section covers related work, both from ourselves and from others, leading to a conceptualization for *CA*.

3.1 Analysis

We analyze firstly our previous work followed by relevant work of others.

As it concerns our previous work: In [22], we have analyzed different ways (in particular based on Bayesian Modeling and Semiotic Norms) of achieving application behavior adjustment, based on context data and assuming states that are foreseen at design time. Related to this, we have considered in [23] the application specification itself, making it explicit that following context changes, the application behavior is to be updated accordingly. In [2], we have taken a systemics [24] perspective for *CA*, addressing the environment and its changes, to which the system should adapt. In [4], we have considered three system adaptation perspectives with regard to context-aware systems, namely: (a) driven by the goal of optimizing the system-internal processes; (b) driven by the goal of maximizing the user-perceived effectiveness; (c) driven by the goal of achieving sensitivity to public values. Further, we have explicitly established that in each of those cases we have a different perspective of the context – as the context can relate to what is happening inside the system; to the user, or to public values. Nevertheless, we have only considered states that are foreseen at design time. Finally, in [25], we have studied business process modeling from the perspective of *CA*, addressing in particular business process variants – different business process variants could be relevant to corresponding context situations. Hence, our earlier research only relates to the “normal variability perspective” but not to the “disruptive events perspective”.

As it concerns related work: Anind Dey is among the most recognized researchers addressing *CA* [12, 13]. He has improved our understanding of the notion of context and made serious progress in the development of context-aware applications. We argue nevertheless that he has not explicitly considered the challenge of tackling disruptive events, when system states cannot be foreseen at design time. The same holds for many R&D *CA* projects, such as AWARENESS [5]. Bosems and Van Sinderen have considered “context-aware computing” as the combination of sensor, reasoning, and other technology that provides systems with real-time awareness [26] but the "reasoning" has not been explicitly addressed and is mainly related to Event-Condition-Action (ECA) rules [27]. In our view, ECA-rules are only limited to situations that are known at design time. The useful survey of Alegre et al. [28] is mainly focused on the development of context-aware applications as well as on the consideration of public values but not on the "disruptive events perspective". The same holds for the works of Alférez and Pelechano [11] – they consider the dynamic evolution of context-aware systems, the development itself, and the relation to web services, still not explicitly distinguishing between the "normal variability perspective" and the "disruptive events perspective". And the same holds for the service-orientation perspective as proposed by Abeywickrama [29].

Even though we do not claim exhaustiveness with regard to the related work analysis, we are convinced that it covers some of the most representative researchers and works relevant to the problem considered in this paper.

Hence, we argue that it is still an open question how to effectively extend context-aware systems, such that the "disruptive events perspective" is adequately covered.

For this reason, the conceptualization presented below (that is actually inspired by the works mentioned above) is only providing a general basis. It will subsequently be used in the following sections featuring proposed solution directions.

3.2 Conceptualization

Inspired by previous work [2, 4, 22], we essentially refer to concepts as presented in the meta-model for context-awareness (see Fig. 2 – left), which is built using the notations of the UML Class Diagram [30]:

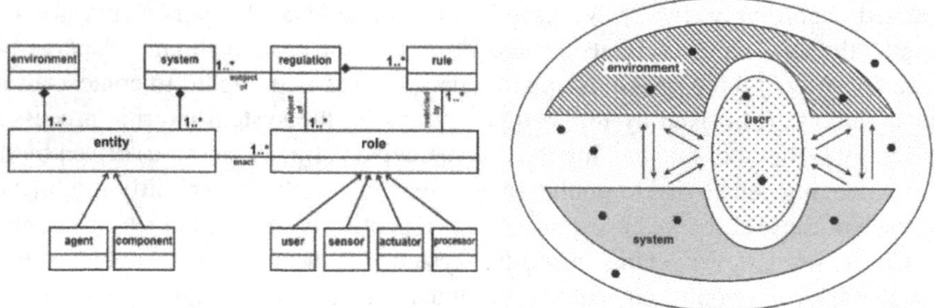

Fig. 2. Left: Considered meta-model for context-awareness (Source: [4], p. 197); Right: Considering the notions of *system*, *environment*, and *user* (Source: [2], p. 140)

Looking at the meta-model, we consider a *system* and its *environment*. Both are composed of numerous *entities* which in turn can be *components* (not pro-active) or *agents* (pro-active and intelligent). One *entity* (an *agent*, for example) can enact many different *roles* (and in the current paper, we limit ourselves to four role categories, namely: *user*, *sensor*, *actuator*, and *processor*) that are restricted by corresponding *rules* and are subject to *regulations*. A regulation in turn is composed of *rules* and is affecting not only the *roles* but also the *system* as a whole.

It is always a question whether we consider the *user* to belong to the *system* or to the *environment*. From one point of view, the *system* is driven by the goal of delivering something to the *user* and hence, the user is to be considered part of the *system*; nevertheless, from another point of view, the *user* is not among the entities that are delivering the product/service because the *user* is consuming it and hence the *user* is not to be considered part of the *system* (and is thus part of the *environment*) [2]. It is therefore not surprising that a lack of consensus is observed about how the *user* is to be considered. Hence, we clearly distinguish between: (i) what belongs to the *system*; (ii) what belongs to the *environment*; (iii) what belongs to the *user* (see Fig. 2 – right).

Further, in line with what was stated above: there are items that neither belong to the *system*, nor to the *environment*, nor to the *user*.

Finally, those "items" (visualized in Fig. 2 (right) as small black hexagons) actually reflect ENTITIES from the meta-model – see Fig. 2 (left) and they in turn fulfill actor-roles (ROLES, for short), for example: if a manager analyzes sales information, then (s)he is fulfilling the *role* "data analyst".

In summary, there is interaction among entities (fulfilling corresponding roles) in several perspectives: between system and environment; between system and user; between environment and user. Other entities are not involved in interactions, at least as it concerns the system under consideration.

For achieving *CA*, **sensors** that provide context information upfront are considered to be an instrumental enabler for adapting the system behavior. Bare sensor data is useless for this purpose. It has to be combined with rules for establishing the context state and changes in the context state. **Data analytics** can be used to further analyze the context state over time. Learning algorithms can provide us with expected behavior of the environment in the future, based on analyzing the trends from the past, and can, for example, predict the expected behavior of a stakeholder [7, 46]. Even though we are using historical data for this, we can use this data through learning and prediction algorithms for getting insight in what is most likely to happen in the future. Nevertheless, for the sake of brevity, we are only addressing sensor-driven CA in the current paper and do not elaborate on the data analytics techniques.

It is important to note that the current section is featuring the adaptation of the system behavior as it concerns *CA* Applications; this is driven by changes in the environment, in system-internal processes, and/or in processes that connect the system and its environment. But all those changes have been envisioned at design time; hence, when an unforeseen change would occur, not considered at design time, the system would be driven by algorithms that are nevertheless only considering expected changes. Thus, we argue that such a "prescribed" behavior would be of limited use in the case of a disruptive event – in such a situation, the environment would have changed to a "level" not expected at design time. For this reason, it is not surprising that in most *CA*-related literature, the perspective of an unexpected state of the system or the environment is missing.

4 Risk Management: Related Work and Conceptualization

For *RM,* we again cover the analysis first and then the conceptualization.

4.1 Analysis

Although there are many papers about information systems for *RM*, the number of papers on *RM* for *(E)IS* is comparatively small. González-Rojas and Ochoa-Venegas [32] show a decision model for the purchase or development and implementation of *EIS*, and indicate that most approaches do not consider risk attributes. Scott & Vessey [33] discuss risks in *EIS* implementation. Their risk factors focus mainly on the internal organizational risks for successful implementation. Their paper does, however, briefly mention the ability to withstand environmental change but only focuses on reactive measures from a management perspective to deal with external change. Broad [34] shows how a risk mindset can be an integral part of the systems development life cycle, and explicitly mentions risk assessment as a key ingredient for the development of information systems. The *RM* Framework (*RMF*) on which it is based, was developed by NIST [35]. The focus of the *RMF* is just on privacy and security, concerning the public values aspect in Fig. 1. O'Donnel [36] touches upon an important aspect of *RM*: the event identification phase, that links closely to the notion of *CA* in the previous section. This phase is one of the eight phases [37] from the Enterprise *RM* (*ERM*) field. ERM focuses on external events that can disrupt the enterprise's goals, but not particularly the *EIS*. In that sense, it is close to the ISO 31000 standard [38] that also focuses on enterprise risk rather than on external risks for the correct functioning of the *EIS* within the enterprise.

An *EIS* is a system. Therefore, another source of information for designing robustness into *EIS* is the systems engineering literature. Technical systems are designed in such a way that disruptive effects on the system are minimized. Still, not all methods for systems engineering explicitly address risk as part of the design methodology. The systems engineering sources that do, such as [39], still focus on risk analysis to study the potential failure of the system itself, rather than the system failing due to extreme events from the outside. The techniques that are discussed can, however, still be used to study external events. Important examples are Failure Mode Effects and Criticality Analysis (FMECA) as well as Fault Tree Analysis (FTA) [39]. The NASA Systems Engineering Handbook [40] looks at the design of mission critical systems, where the *RM* is further specified [41]. Here, continuous *RM* and risk-informed decision making are the basis of the design of complex systems. These sources, and the systems engineering sources in general, are focusing on how to design a system, and how to manage the design or construction of the system (project risk). Therefore, they mainly focus on *known risks* rather than on the *unknown threats* that we consider in the current paper.

4.2 Conceptualization

ISO 31000 [38] defines **risk** in a rather broad way: "the effect of uncertainty on objectives", where "risk is often expressed in terms of a combination of the consequences of an event and the associated likelihood of occurrence". This follows a broad set of literature that defines the *expected value* of the risk as *likelihood x consequence*, where "likelihood" is the chance of the risk event occurring and "consequence" is some expression of an objective that can be hurt (e.g., safety, throughput, cost, customer satisfaction). Given the fact that the types of risks we are looking at all very-low-probability, very-high-impact risks (often termed *black swan risks* [42]), this is a fallacy. When the risk event fires (with a very low probability), we have to deal with the major consequence. When it doesn't, nothing happens. The expected value does not represent this in any useful way. Because many of these risks exist, it is on the one hand impossible to list all risks, while on the other hand some of these highly improbable risk events will actually fire. Since we are looking at *rare events* where the likelihood of occurrence of the event is extremely low, there is so little data available that the actual probability is often completely unknown, making it even harder to use the "likelihood x consequence" formula to decide on the relative importance of a risk. As the *Handbook of Systems Engineering and Management* [43] states (p. 180): "Risk of extreme events is misinterpreted when it is solely measured by the expected value of risk".

Therefore, we have to use a completely different approach. Instead of looking at the likelihood and consequence, we only look at the consequence. The fact that *something* could render our *EIS* useless for several months is what counts, not the calculation how often this would occur on average. We call this approach **Consequence-Based Risk Management** (*CBRM*). The *CBRM* approach stems from natural hazard research and climate change research where the most vulnerable locations are studied first. Taking this approach to *EIS*, we can define the following important terms:

- A **risk event** is an uncertain discrete occurrence that, if it occurs, would have a positive or negative effect on achievement of one or more objectives [44]. We focus mostly on the negative consequences in this paper.
- A **consequence** is the possible outcome of a risk if it occurs [44]. In our case, this relates to the intended functions of the *EIS* that need to be fulfilled. The consequence can be measured as the reduction in the agreed *EIS* service level.
- **Criticality** is defined as the importance of a component in the *EIS* to be able to fulfill the *EIS* functions.
- **Vulnerability** is defined as the (qualitatively or quantitatively assessed) likelihood that an *EIS* component will be exploited by the occurrence of a risk event.
- **Recoverability** is defined as the time it takes after the risk occurred to bring back the normal service level of the *EIS*.
- **Robustness** relates to decreasing the consequences for a wide set of risk events. This can, e.g., be done by decreasing the vulnerability of critical *EIS* components, by increasing the *EIS* recoverability or by decreasing the criticality of the involved components.
- **Enterprise *RM* (ERM)** is the integrated application of *RM* across the entire business, addressing all levels of risk, including strategic, business, corporate, reputation, portfolio, program, project, technical, safety, etc. [44].

Given the discussion about the inapplicability of the concept of expected value, and the fact we are dealing with rare events, the focus on any method trying to improve the robustness should start with identifying unwanted **consequences** for **critical components** in the *EIS*. In case there is information about the vulnerability of such components, the most vulnerable component can be addressed first. Several methods to deal with vulnerable critical *EIS* components exist, as we will see in Sect. 5.2.

5 The Disruptive Events Focus

5.1 Context-Awareness

At the end of Sect. 3, we have concluded that most current *CA* solutions consider expected changes, which makes *CA* to be of limited use when it comes to disruptive events. In this section we therefore focus specifically on situations assuming unexpected changes and go beyond what is predicted/expected at design time. Several examples:

- A factory of a supplier is completely shut down (e.g., during a pandemic) but the *EIS* would only start finding this out and alert the organization when the first shipments would not arrive on time.
- A user is physically unable to connect to an *EIS* (e.g., during a disaster) but business processes of this user are fully dependent on the ability to use the *EIS*.
- Critical infrastructure is down for a long period (e.g., during an outage) and as a result of this, key *EIS* components are unable to operate, restricting the overall performance of the *EIS*.

As can be seen from the above examples, the types of disruption and their effects are different from normal variant situations. As a first measure in addressing such cases, we could aim at **sensing** what is going on, where the *EIS* is able to sense the occurrence of a disruptive event. In this regard, we count on KPI (Key Performance Indicators), which means that the designer should be able to identify outlier situations in each of the key modules of the *EIS*. Here, sensors and data feeds that are normally not considered for the day-to-day operation of the *EIS* would play an important role.

As a second measure, we could look into the **problem localization**. The *EIS* itself should always be capable of establishing which of its key modules is down or in an inconsistent state. This measure certainly relates to the first one as it also involves sensing, but this time for the *internal* state.

As a third measure, we could look into ways to **bypass the inoperative module**. This is a serious design challenge assuming "emergency *EIS* behaviors" – the designer should have established all possible scenarios featuring *EIS* "running with less engines". For example, if an *EIS* has 4 key modules: M1, M2, M3, and M4, then it should be known whether it can run without one of M1, M2, M3 or M4 (or even without a combination of several of the modules), and if yes – how. Then, if in the case of a disruptive event a problem localization has been established, the affected module is to be excluded from the system, where other modules are informed to ignore or bypass this inconsistent or faulty one. This would allow the damage to remain mainly local while many other (essential) system functions would stay available.

As a fourth measure, we consider **recoverability** – the *EIS'* ability to re-establish normal functioning, after the inoperative module(s) go back to normal.

5.2 Risk Management

From a *RM* perspective, several measures can help to deal with large-scale, unexpected changes. We provide three possible measures below:

As a first measure, we advise to make the *EIS* component **less vulnerable**. Example strategies for the data and operation aspects of Fig. 1 are to store data in human readable formats so humans can take over some processing functions if the *EIS* does not operate anymore. AI (Artificial Intelligence) techniques and business process automation can be used in case the operators are unavailable and the system needs to continue operating. In a sense, components become less vulnerable if fallback options for the operation of the component exist (note that the criticality of the component did not change: components are still critical for obtaining the agreed *EIS* service level).

As a second measure, we advise to make the *EIS* components **less critical**. Example strategies for the data and operation aspects of Fig. 1 are to duplicate data to multiple locations for the data aspect, and to have sufficient extra staff in multiple locations - for the operations aspect. Reliability analysis teaches us that criticality of a components goes down if we **duplicate** that component [39]. If one has many copies of something, it does not matter so much if one of the copies gets lost. *Blockchain* [45], for instance, explicitly uses duplication of records over so many servers that integrity of the data can be guaranteed because the system continuously checks if all copies are the same, and it is almost impossible to change the value in all servers at once to make an undetected change to the data.

As a third measure, we advise to make the *EIS* components **more resilient**. One of the biggest problems is starting up an information system that has been in an unplanned state. Internal data is inconsistent due to the risk event happening and starting up is hampered by the system wanting to maintain consistency all the time. Under normal variability, the consistency checks are a good thing: they guarantee that every time a small variation occurs, it does not go undetected and corrective actions can be performed. When there are thousands or millions of inconsistencies, this is not an option. Rather than trying to stubbornly maintain consistency, the system should be able to move to a more lenient state where most inconsistencies are tolerated (but can still be reported). This helps the system to go back to a working state after the disruption has passed, and thereby it makes the *EIS* more resilient, since resilience was defined as the ability for the *EIS* to return to its normal state again.

6 Application of Context-Awareness and CBRM for Robust and Resilient Enterprise Information Systems

There are several steps in designing a robust *EIS* that roughly follow the steps in any *RM* method [34, 35, 41, 43, 44]. We adapted the *RM* method by starting with the consequences of the risk event rather than the causes or risk events themselves. *CA* is used in several of the phases to enable *CBRM*.

Phase 1. Risk Identification and Analysis

Step 1. Identify the objectives of the EIS. The **Quality of Service** and the **Public Values** aspects at the right of Fig. 1 are the starting points for defining the objectives of the

EIS. As long as the system stays within the defined levels of service and adheres to the defined public values such as safety and privacy, the system is operating normally. These objectives should be identified and related to the **components** of the system. Which component or chain of components in the operations or data aspect of Fig. 1 is directly or indirectly responsible for reaching each business objective? Of course, the objectives might be taken from a design document of the *EIS*, but there could be a difference between the intended use of the *EIS* at design time, and the actual use when carrying out the CBRM study.

Step 2. Identify the critical components of the EIS. Based on the analysis of step 1, we can see which components are responsible for fulfilling many of the objectives, and which components are responsible for fewer objectives or even just one objective. Combined with a **usage analysis** (how often is each function of the system used) and a **business analysis** (how much money, long-term customer relations, or corporate responsibility is involved in the (in)ability to use such a component), the components of the EIS can be ranked in terms of their criticality.

Step 3. Identify the vulnerability of the components of the EIS. For some of the components, it may be known that vulnerabilities exist. A *worst-case analysis*, for instance, can be based on a long list of consequences consisting of natural disasters (e.g., pandemic, flooding, earthquake) and man-made disasters (e.g., regional war, cyber-attack, ransomware) on the system. Rather than trying to study the likelihood of each event, it is sufficient to see which components of the system would be impacted by such events. The result of this step is a list of **components** that can be ranked from components showing up often in the analyses (**vulnerable**) to components showing up less often (not so vulnerable).

Step 4. Combine criticality and vulnerability. Our priority should be based on those components that are critical and vulnerable. From this analysis, an **overall ranking** can be made to show which components decrease the **robustness** of the system most. Personal preferences of the IT managers and overall enterprise management can also be taken into account into the selection of the most vulnerable components. Qualitative assessment and experience can be an important addition to the priority ranking shown above, since it may be hard to take into account non-quantifiable factors in the priority ranking. From a CBRM perspective, we have now identified those components for which the consequences of risks would be most devastating on being able to maintain the agreed service level of the *EIS*.

Phasc 2. Mitigation Planning

For each of the identified critical and vulnerable components, a risk mitigation strategy should be designed, in line with *RM* practices. This mitigation strategy can be one of [44]:

Strategy 1: **Accept** the risk. It is possible that the organization is not able to adapt the component that is critical and vulnerable. Still, there is now awareness that this component is a risk for the enterprise, and monitoring can be put in place to sense that the conditions in which the component can function are violated (see Phase 3).

Strategy 2: **Reduce** the risk. One of the strategies from Sect. 5.2 can be used to make the component less vulnerable, less critical, or more resilient. Often this involves sensing as well, e.g., to see when a fallback option needs to be switched on (see Phase 3).

Other Strategies: Risks can also be Transferred (e.g., insured) or Avoided (e.g., by removing vulnerable components) [44]. These strategies can be applied but since they do not consider *CBRM* and *CA*, they are not covered further in this paper.

Phase 3. Monitoring

Although one might think that it is possible to make the system totally fail-safe by reducing all risks to zero, in practice this is undoable due to time and budget constraints. Therefore, many of the solutions will be implemented partially, where an effort can be made to switch the system manually to another state when needed, or to reduce the risk only when the consequence actually occurs. A strategy where repairs are not immediately made but we make a plan for dealing with the consequence when it happens, is called a **contingency strategy**. The "Accept" strategy from Phase 2 above is an example of using contingency. In order to be able to apply such a strategy, constant monitoring of the **context** of the system needs to take place to assess that the system gets into a state that is conflicting with the assumptions of the critical modules of the system. It is important for *CA* to distinguish between normal variability and consequences of disruptive events. Thresholds for different contextual variables need to be set for the *CA* algorithms, based on the boundaries within which the critical modules function correctly.

Note that one of the requirements of the above method is that the *EIS* consists of **components**, each with a clear **function**, that can be distinguished and for which the interfaces are known. When the *EIS* is monolithic, the above strategies cannot work, and neither the provides solutions from CBRM, nor the provided insights from CA will have added value.

7 Conclusions

Even though most current Enterprise Information Systems (*EIS*) appear to be adequately dealing with variability, they would often fail when affected by a (large-scale) disruptive event. As we have studied in the current paper, Context-Awareness (*CA*) is a useful paradigm as it concerns the capturing of changes occurring in the *EIS* environment, including changes that lead to unplanned states. *CA* can be accomplished by adding an extra function for monitoring the environment, aiming at establishing whether or not the *EIS* needs to adapt accordingly. As mentioned above, we have been inspired by the strengths of this paradigm as it concerns variability, and we propose extending the use of *CA* towards disruptive events, by considering three measures, namely the capturing/sensing of an unexpected environmental state, the localization of the problem (in terms of affected *EIS* modules), and bypassing (if possible) of inoperative modules. Further, we have studied the relevant strengths of Risk Management (*RM*), considering relevant techniques, such as FMECA and FTA, in the light of a particular approach, namely Consequence-Based Risk Management (CBRM). On that basis, we have proposed three corresponding measures, namely: to make *EIS* components less vulnerable, to make them less critical (e.g., by duplicating them), and to increase their resilience.

Finally, we have proposed an integrated method featuring the application of *CA* and CBRM for robust *EIS*.

The combination of *RM* and *CA* to deal with disruptive events for *EIS* is a conceptual solution. For validation of its usefulness and applicability, it has to be tested in either a simulation or a real application. Disruptive events luckily do not happen every day. Further research will therefore focus on testing the method on a simulated *ERP*, *SCM* or *CRM*, and seeing whether the *RM* methods can be applied and whether the *CA* functions can be automated to flag the disruptive events correctly, and trigger the right corrective action that was defined as a result of applying consequence-based risk management and reliability engineering in the *EIS*.

Future work will focus on elaborating the proposed CA and CBRM methods and on testing the approach on a simulated or real case.

References

1. Snoeck, M.: Enterprise Information Systems Engineering, the MERODE Approach. Springer, Cham (2014). https://doi.org/10.1007/978-3-319-10145-3
2. Shishkov, B.: Designing Enterprise Information Systems, Merging Enterprise Modeling and Software Specification. Springer, Cham (2020). https://doi.org/10.1007/978-3-030-22441-7
3. Shishkov, B., van Sinderen, M., Verbraeck, A.: Towards flexible inter-enterprise collaboration: a supply chain perspective. In: Filipe, J., Cordeiro, J. (eds.) ICEIS 2009. LNBIP, vol. 24, pp. 513–527. Springer, Heidelberg (2009). https://doi.org/10.1007/978-3-642-01347-8_43
4. Shishkov, B., Larsen, J.B., Warnier, M., Janssen, M.: Three categories of context-aware systems. In: Shishkov, B. (ed.) BMSD 2018. LNBIP, vol. 319, pp. 185–202. Springer, Cham (2018). https://doi.org/10.1007/978-3-319-94214-8_12
5. Wegdam, M.: AWARENESS: a project on context AWARE mobile NEtworks and ServiceS. In: Proceedings of 14th Mobile and Wireless Communications Summit. EURASIP (2005)
6. Kopják, J., Sebestyén, G.: Comparison of data collecting methods in wireless mesh sensor networks. In: IEEE 16th World Symposium on Applied Machine Intelligence and Informatics (SAMI), Kosice and Her-lany, Slovakia (2018)
7. Han, J., Kamber, M., Pei, J.: Data Mining: Concepts and Techniques, 3rd edn. Morgan Kaufmann Publ. Inc., San Francisco (2011)
8. Reuters: Italian PM Orders Businesses to Close All Operations. In: The Guardian - International Edition, London (2020)
9. Takizawa, K.: Resilience of communities affected by the great east japan earthquake and restoration of their local festivals. In: Bouterey, S., Marceau, L. (eds.) Crisis and Disaster in Japan and New Zealand. Palgrave Macmillan, Singapore (2019)
10. Shibata, Y.: Writing Shanghai, the atomic bomb, and incest: homelessness and stigmatized womanhood of Hayashi Kyōko. In: Bouterey, S., Marceau, L. (eds.) Crisis and Disaster in Japan and New Zealand. Palgrave Macmillan, Singapore (2019)
11. Alférez, G.H., Pelechano, V.: Context-aware autonomous web services in software product lines. In: Proceedings of 15th International SPLC Conference. IEEE, CA, USA (2011)
12. Dey, A.K., Abowd, G.D., Salber, D.: A conceptual framework and a toolkit for supporting the rapid prototyping of context-aware applications. Hum.-Comput. Interact. **16**(2), 97–166 (2001)
13. Dey, A.K., Newberger, A.: Support for context-aware intelligibility and control. In: Proceedings of SIGCHI Conference on Human Factors in Computing Systems. ACM, USA (2009)

14. Papadimitriou G.: Future Internet: The Cross-ETP (2011). http://www.future-internet.eu/fileadmin/documents/reports/Cross-ETPs_FI_Vision_Document_v1_0.pdf. Accessed December 2011
15. Choraś, M., Kozik, R.: Machine learning techniques applied to detect cyber attacks on web applications. Log. J. IGPL **23**(1), 45–56 (2015)
16. Hopkins, P.: Fundamentals of Risk Management - Understanding, Evaluating, and Implementing Effective Risk Management. IRM (2012)
17. La Rosa, M., Van Der Aalst, W.M.P., Dumas, M., Milani, F.P.: Business process variability modeling: a survey. ACM Comput. Surv. **50**(1), Article 2 (2017)
18. Dietz, J.L.G.: Enterprise Ontology, Theory and Methodology. Springer, Heidelberg (2006)
19. Abeywickrama, D.B.: Context-aware services engineering for service-oriented architectures. In: Bouguettaya, A., Sheng, Q., Daniel, F. (eds.) Web Services Foundations. Springer, New York (2014). https://doi.org/10.1007/978-1-4614-7518-7_12
20. Friedman, B., Hendry, D.G., Borning, A.: A survey of salue sensitive design methods. In: A Survey of Value Sensitive Design Methods, vol. 1. Now Foundations and Trends (2017)
21. Van den Hoven, J.: Value sensitive design and responsible innovation. In: Owen, R., Bessant, J., Heintz, M. (eds.) Responsible Innovation: Managing the Responsible Emergence of Science and Innovation in Society. Wiley, Hoboken (2013)
22. Shishkov, B.: Tuning the Behavior of context-aware applications. In: Shishkov, B. (ed.) BMSD 2019. LNBIP, vol. 356, pp. 134–152. Springer, Cham (2019). https://doi.org/10.1007/978-3-030-24854-3_9
23. Shishkov, B., van Sinderen, M.: From user context states to context-aware applications. In: Filipe, J., Cordeiro, J., Cardoso, J. (eds.) ICEIS 2007. LNBIP, vol. 12, pp. 225–239. Springer, Heidelberg (2008). https://doi.org/10.1007/978-3-540-88710-2_18
24. Bunge, M.A.: Treatise on Basic Philosophy. A World of Systems, vol. 4. D. Reidel Publishing Company, Dordrecht (1979)
25. Shishkov, B., Mendling, J.: Business process variability and public values. In: Shishkov, B. (ed.) BMSD 2018. LNBIP, vol. 319, pp. 401–411. Springer, Cham (2018). https://doi.org/10.1007/978-3-319-94214-8_31
26. Bosems, S., van Sinderen, M.: Models in the design of context aware well being applications. In: Meersman, R., et al. (eds.) OTM 2014. LNCS, vol. 8842, pp. 37–42. Springer, Heidelberg (2014). https://doi.org/10.1007/978-3-662-45550-0_6
27. Cano, J., Delaval, G., Rutten, E.: Coordination of ECA rules by verification and control. In: Kühn, E., Pugliese, R. (eds.) COORDINATION 2014. LNCS, vol. 8459, pp. 33–48. Springer, Heidelberg (2014). https://doi.org/10.1007/978-3-662-43376-8_3
28. Alegre, U., Augusto, J.C., Clark, T.: Engineering context-aware systems and applications. J. Syst. Softw. **117**(1), 55–83 (2016)
29. Abeywickrama, D.B., Ramakrishnan, S.: Context-aware services engineering: models, transformations, and verification. ACM Trans. Internet Technol. J. **11**(3), Article 1 (2012)
30. UML: The website of the Unified Modeling Language (2020). http://www.uml.org
31. Shishkov, B., Janssen, M.: Enforcing context-awareness and privacy-by-design in the specification of information systems. In: Shishkov, B. (ed.) BMSD 2017. LNBIP, vol. 309, pp. 87–111. Springer, Cham (2018). https://doi.org/10.1007/978-3-319-78428-1_5
32. González-Rojas, O., Ochoa-Venegas, L.: A decision model and system for planning and adapting the configuration of enterprise information systems. Comput. Ind. **92–93**, 161–177 (2017)
33. Scott, J.E., Vessey, I.: Managing risks in enterprise systems implementations. Commun. ACM **45**(4), 74–81 (2002)
34. Broad, J.: Risk Management Framework. A Lab-Based Approach to Securing Information Systems. Elsevier, Amsterdam (2013)

35. NIST: NIST Special Publication (SP) 800-37 Revision 2, Risk Management Framework for Information Systems and Organizations: A System Life Cycle Approach for Security and Privacy. NIST, December 2018. https://csrc.nist.gov/publications/detail/sp/800-37/rev-2/final
36. O'Donnel, E.: Enterprise risk management: a systems-thinking framework for the event identification phase. Int. J. Acc. Inf. Syst. **6**, 177–195 (2005)
37. COSO: Enterprise Risk Management - Integrating with Strategy and Performance. Committee of Sponsoring Organization of the Treadway Committee (COSO) (2017)
38. ISO: ISO 31000 - Risk Management. International Organization for Standardization (ISO), Geneva (2018)
39. Blanchard, B.S., Fabrycky, W.J.: Systems Engineering and Analysis, 4th edn. Prentice-Hall, Upper Saddle River (2006)
40. NASA: NASA SP-2016-6105 Rev2: NASA Systems Engineering Handbook. NASA (2016). https://www.nasa.gov/connect/ebooks/nasa-systems-engineering-handbook
41. NASA: NASA/SP-2011-3422: NASA Risk Management Handbook (2011). https://sma.nasa.gov/sma-disciplines/risk-management
42. Taleb, N.N.: The Black Swan - The Impact of the Highly Improbable, 2nd edn. Random House, New York (2010)
43. Haimes, Y.Y.: Chapter 3: risk management. In: Sage, A.P., Rouse, W.B. (eds.) Handbook of Systems Engineering and Management, 2nd edn, pp. 155–204. Wiley, Hoboken (2009)
44. Hillson, D., Simon, P.: Practical Project Risk Management: The ATOM Methodology, 2nd edn. Management Concepts Press, Tysons Corner (2012)
45. Underwood, S.: Blockchain Beyond Bitcoin. Commun. ACM **59**, 15–17 (2016)
46. Borissova, D., Cvetkova, P., Garvanov, I., Garvanova, M.: A framework of business intelligence system for decision making in efficiency management. In: Saeed, K., Dvorský, J. (eds.) CISIM 2020. LNCS, vol. 12133, pp. 111–121. Springer, Cham (2020). https://doi.org/10.1007/978-3-030-47679-3_10

A Reference Model for a Service Level Agreement

In Domain of Information Sharing Services

C. Hofman[1] and E. Roubtsova[2(✉)]

[1] Graduated Master of Science Student of the Open University, Heerlen, The Netherlands
cor.hofman@gmail.com

[2] Open University, Heerlen, The Netherlands
ella.roubtsova@ou.nl

Abstract. Information sharing between government organizations is regulated by Service Level Agreements (SLA's). Design and implementation of an SLA demands involvement representatives of several organizations. They need to communicate with the same concepts and validate the requirements for the service and quality indicators. In order to support the design of an SLA and its monitoring, we propose related concept, goal and protocol reference models. The first conceptual model view is built using a literature review. The next model views include the details found by analysis of existing SLA's. The novelty of our models is that they compose an SLA from service level objectives (SLO's), explain the meaning of SLO's monitoring, support execution of an SLA and expose the monitoring logics.

Keywords: Service Level Agreement (SLA) · SLA modelling · SLA monitoring · Service Level Objective (SLO) · Goal model · Conceptual model · Executable protocol model

1 Introduction

In order to serve citizens, government organizations provide informational services to each other and rely on each other. For example, they share information about income of citizens. Government organizations formulate collaborative requirements for information sharing including timeliness and reliability. All these, mostly non-functional, requirements for the information sharing services are combined into a Service Level Agreement (SLA).

"A service-level agreement (SLA) sets the expectations between the service provider and the customer and describes the products or services to be delivered, the single point of contact for end-user problems, and the metrics by which the effectiveness of the process is monitored and approved" [3].

Representatives of different organizations should agree on an SLA. For communication, for understanding each other, the professionals need a shared conceptual model of the service and shared understating of its monitoring. As the

B. Shishkov (Ed.): BMSD 2020, LNBIP 391, pp. 55–68, 2020.
https://doi.org/10.1007/978-3-030-52306-0_4

requirements in an SLA are mostly non-functional, their monitoring and validation is only possible with specially designed indicators assessing data collected from a running service process. Because an SLA-contract development process has so many points of attention from the partners of the contract and an SLA contains requirements for potential implementation automatic measurements, this process needs systematic modelling and a supportive system of a SLA life cycle. Supportive systems for SLA-contract development may share a reference model.

In this paper, we propose a reference model for a system that supports an SLA life cycle. It consists of three consistent views: a conceptual, a goal, and an executable protocol models. It supports an SLA preparation, agreement and monitoring. Our reference model contains points of changes and can be used for collecting the variable parts of SLA-contracts.

In order to guarantee methodological triangulation, we use more than one method [13] for gathering concepts and their relations and understanding of an SLA.

- Section 2 presents the results of a literature review used to built a first conceptual reference model of an SLA.
- Section 3 discusses the analysis of existing SLA documents and identification of different types of some concepts of the conceptual reference model.
- Section 4 validates the relations of the conceptual reference model by the strategic goal model of an SLA.
- Section 5 validates the relations of the conceptual reference model by the executable protocol model showing SLA development, acceptance and monitoring.
- Section 6 discusses the variation points of the reference models.
- Section 7 concludes the paper and proposes future work.

2 Literature Review for Building the First Conceptual Model of an SLA

The presented literature review has been aimed to identify the concepts used for description of an SLA and relations of these concepts. We discuss the concepts and relations named in literature. We cover the works on SLA reported in journals "Decision support systems", "Future Generation Computer Systems" and "Performance evaluation" by Elsevier, "Journal of Network and Systems Management" and "Distributed and Parallel Databases" by Springer, IEEE Software journal and the Proceedings of the 16th ACM SIGSOFT International Symposium on Foundations of Software Engineering. In the following text, the concepts and their relations found in literature are presented in italic and shown in Fig. 1.

The definitions of an *SLA* found in literature can be classified as external and internal.

External definitions specify the essential condition for an *SLA* to exist. External definitions see an *SLA* as a technical contract that *legally binds* two *parties* being *providers* and *consumers* [1,5].

Internal definitions define the content of an *SLA* in form of *producer requirements* and *consumer requirements* [11], explicitly distinguishing between a *Service*, its *functional* and *non-functional requirements*, where the latter are *expressed as Service Level Objectives (SLO's)*.

The functional part of a *Service* (Fig. 1) consists of a *Consumer process (request)* and a *Producer process (reply)* [9,16]. The consumer sends one or more key values identifying the data of interest. The producer then sends a reply containing the requested data or an indication that the data is not available. The *non-functional requirements* of the *Consumer* and *Provider* are grouped in Service Level Objectives *SLO's* [5]. Each *SLO* is refined to a set of *Quality Of Service (QoS)* with an associated *QoS Level constraining* the *QoS* [4]. For example, a consumer can demand a maximum response time, where a producer might want to limit the maximum number of service requests per time interval to a maximum (i.e. maximum throughput). Both of these *SLO's* define performance constraints that are included into an SLA. For monitoring of quality, the performance of the real service should be compared with these constraints.

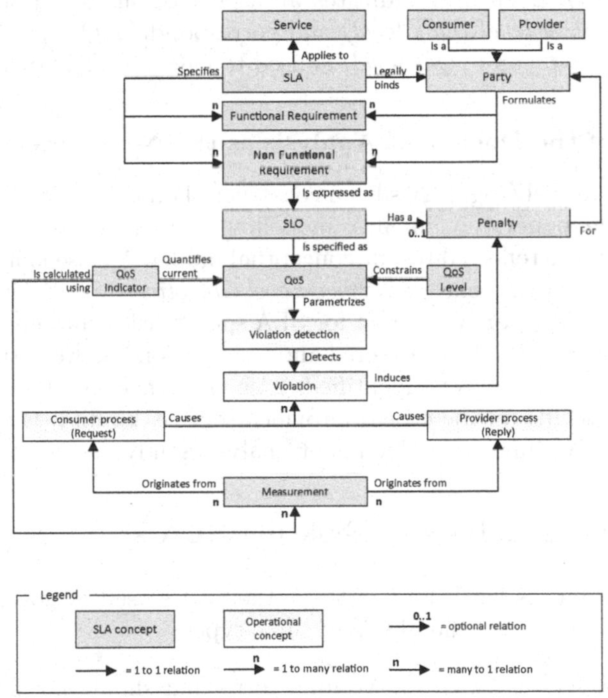

Fig. 1. Concepts defining an SLA in literature

The inability to meet specified *SLO's* are the reasons for *Penalties*, which can be *induced* on *Consumer* and *Provider* if a *Violation* is caused [10]. *Penalties* are seen as an essential part of an *SLA*, since they add a stimuli avoiding extra costs if an *SLO* is not met [11]. A *violation* can also have a resolution, used to neutralize the *violation.* A violation can be sent to "the single point of contact for end-user problems"[3]. The resolution is not included into our conceptual model as it often demands investigation and such help desk issues are out of the scope of an SLA life cycle.

For monitoring of an *SLA* on a *producer process* and a *consumer process, QoS indicators* are specified. The literature does not differentiate the indicators. It is mentioned that some process specific *measurements* are needed to calculate the indicators, which can originate from producer and consumer process characteristics [10]. *Violation detection* is conceptually based on rules, which are decision functions, parameterized with *QoS Indicators* and *QoS levels* for the consumer and producer related *QoS.* It signals the current existence of *Violations.*

Each *QoS indicator* corresponds to the *QoS* specified for an *SLO* and uses specified *QoS level* acceptable for the consumer and the producer.

From our conceptual model (Fig. 1), an SLA can be defined as a *legal binding* between a *producer* and a *consumer* specifying agreed service functionality (*functional requirements*) and *non-functional requirements* split into *service level objectives (SLO's).* Each SLO indicates an aspect of quality of *service (QoS),* has specified *quality level (Qos level)* and corresponding *QoS indicators.* Each pair of *QoS indicator* and *(Qos level)* is used to calculate a *penalty.*

2.1 Choice of the Document Analysis as the Next Research Method

The conceptual model (Fig. 1) has been constructed on the basis of the literature analysis. All the papers on an SLA modelling remain abstract about SLO's [2,4,5,10] and this is reflected by our conceptual model. A close look at the found definition shows that the concept *Service Level Objectives (SLO's)* is not ready to be included into a supportive system for SLA specification and implementation. The types of SLO need to be discovered and the relations between the SLO types and QoS Indicators need to be identified. Also the functional requirements can be made more specific for the type of provided service. To find the types of SLO used in practice, we initiated a document analysis study.

3 Document Analysis of Existing SLA's

The document analysis has been fulfilled in the SLA's used by government organizations[1]. We have found the SLO's of three types:

1. SLO Volume per year with the Volume norm that should not be exceeded;
2. SLO Response Time in hours with
   (a) Percentage of the on-time responses per year;
   (b) Percentage of the late responses per year;
   (c) Percentage of the too-late responses per year;

[1] We are not allowed to name the organizations, however we have the documents for revision.

3. SLO Data quality with the norm of data with faults;

Each of these norms-constraints has similar structure: a name, a norm and a period of measurement. An SLO presents an aspect of monitoring, i.e. the QoS-norm. For example, the "Response Time" is specified as one working day (8 h). It is accepted if the 92% of responses per year are on-time, 7% of late responses are within five days and 1% of too-late responses are within 10 days.

The SLA's define also the data formats in requests and replies that can be controlled both on the provider and on the consumer sides.

The document analysis of existing SLA's shows that an SLA is related with three aspects of service support: (1) security, (2) data controls, and (3) monitoring of Quality of Service (QoS).

The security deals with concept *Request*. Data controls are related to one pair of concepts *Request-Reply*. The security and data format controls are internal for the service producer. The consumer recognizes them as delays and delays are included into QoS of an SLA.

The monitoring of SLOs with QoS concerns both the producer and the consumer, it should be understood by both parties.

3.1 Choice of Goal and Protocol Modeling as the Next Research Method

The logic of QoS measurement cannot be exposed in a reference model. The logic of QoS measurement combines the strategic agreements, operations of measurement and monitoring and decision about penalties.

In order to combine the strategic agreements, operations of measurement and monitoring and decision about penalties, we define a pair of corresponding goal and executable protocol models. Both models use the concepts of the conceptual reference model of an SLA (Fig. 1). The choice of the modelling techniques is motivated by the observed resemblance between the monitoring KPI's and SLO's with QoS. The KPI's have been already successfully modelled with pairs of semantically related goal and executable protocol models [12, 14]. We use this experience for modelling of monitors for SLO's with QoS.

4 Goal Model of an SLA Life Cycle

Any service based business needs a supportive system for an SLA preparation and monitoring. This is the main goal of the goal model. *G1.Support system for a Service Level Agreement (SLA) preparation and monitoring.*

Now we present a description of the goal model depicted in Fig. 2.

G1 is refined by the following sub-goals:

- *G1.1. Support of an SLA preparation;*
- *G1.2. Support of a service with an SLA instance generation*
- *G1.3. Support of an SLA instance monitoring a calculation of penalties*

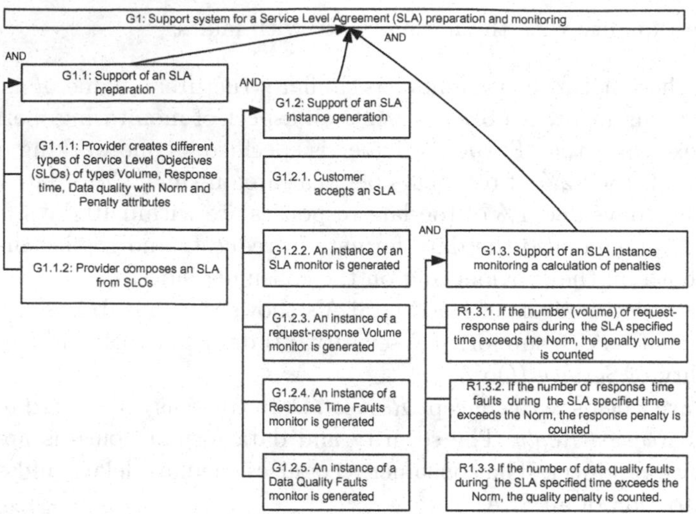

Fig. 2. Goal model of an SLA life cycle

G1.1 is refined with sub-goals

- *G1.1.1. Provider creates different types of Service Level Objectives (SLOs) of types Volume, Response time, Data quality with Norm and Penalty attributes*;
- *G1.1.2. Provider composes an SLA from SLOs.*

G1.2. is refined with

- *G1.2.1. Customer accepts an SLA*;
- *G1.2.2. An instance of an SLA monitor is generated;*
- *G1.2.3. An instance of a request-response Volume monitor is generated;*
- *G1.2.4. An instance of a Response Time Faults monitor is generated;*
- *G1.2.5. An instance of a Data Quality Faults monitor is generated.*

G1.3. is refined with requirements for the monitoring

- *R1.3.1. If the number (volume) of request-response pairs during the SLA specified time exceeds the Norm, the penalty volume is counted;*
  R1.3.2. If the number of response time faults during the SLA specified time exceeds the Norm, the response penalty is counted;
- *R1.3.3. If the number of response time faults during the SLA specified time exceeds the Norm, the response penalty is counted.*

All concepts in requirements are countable and comparable, the norms can be built into the SLA monitors in correspondence with the SLA.

5 Protocol Model of an SLA

5.1 The Behaviour of the Information Sharing Service

The behaviour of the information sharing service is a request and the corresponding reply, where both the request and reply are specified with a data structure.

- Each request structure contains *request identifier, request time stamp, key field name for information search* and *name of requested data item.* For example, *(request identifier, day-month-year, identification number of a citizen, citizen related data (year-1)).*
- Each reply structure contains *reply identifier, initiated request identifier, request time stamp, reply time stamp, key field for information search from the request name of data item in the request* and *value of the requested data item.*
- The attributes of these data structures are used to measure the data quality, data volume and response time. Each field of a request and a reply has type quality borders and the quality checks are implemented in the service.
  - The number of faults of quality checks of replies indicates *Data Quality* of the service.
  - The number of requests in a given time period is called *Volume* of the service.
  - For each reply, the difference between the "reply time stamp" and the "request time stamp" is called *Response Time.*

5.2 What Is a Protocol Model?

The executable form of a protocol model is textual [15]. It specifies concepts as protocol machines presenting OBJECTS (concepts) and BEHAVIOURS (constraints) with their attributes, states, recognised events, transitions and callbacks for updates of attributes and derived states. Because a protocol model is an executable model of an information exchange service behaviour with data, it is a suitable model to illustrate and demonstrate the monitoring logic of quality indicators.

The graphical form of a protocol model is used for communication and model explanation. It illustrates the protocol machines (concepts and constraints), recognised events, states and transitions. It does not show the data structures of protocol machines and events.

A protocol machines are composed using the CSP composition for machines with data defined in [6,8]. The CSP composition means that all protocol machines are synchronised, i.e. an event is accepted by a protocol model only if all protocol machines recognizing this event are in the state to accept it. The state of each protocol machine is a data structure. Any event in a protocol model is another data structure. The data from the event-instance is used to update the state of protocol machines accepting this event.

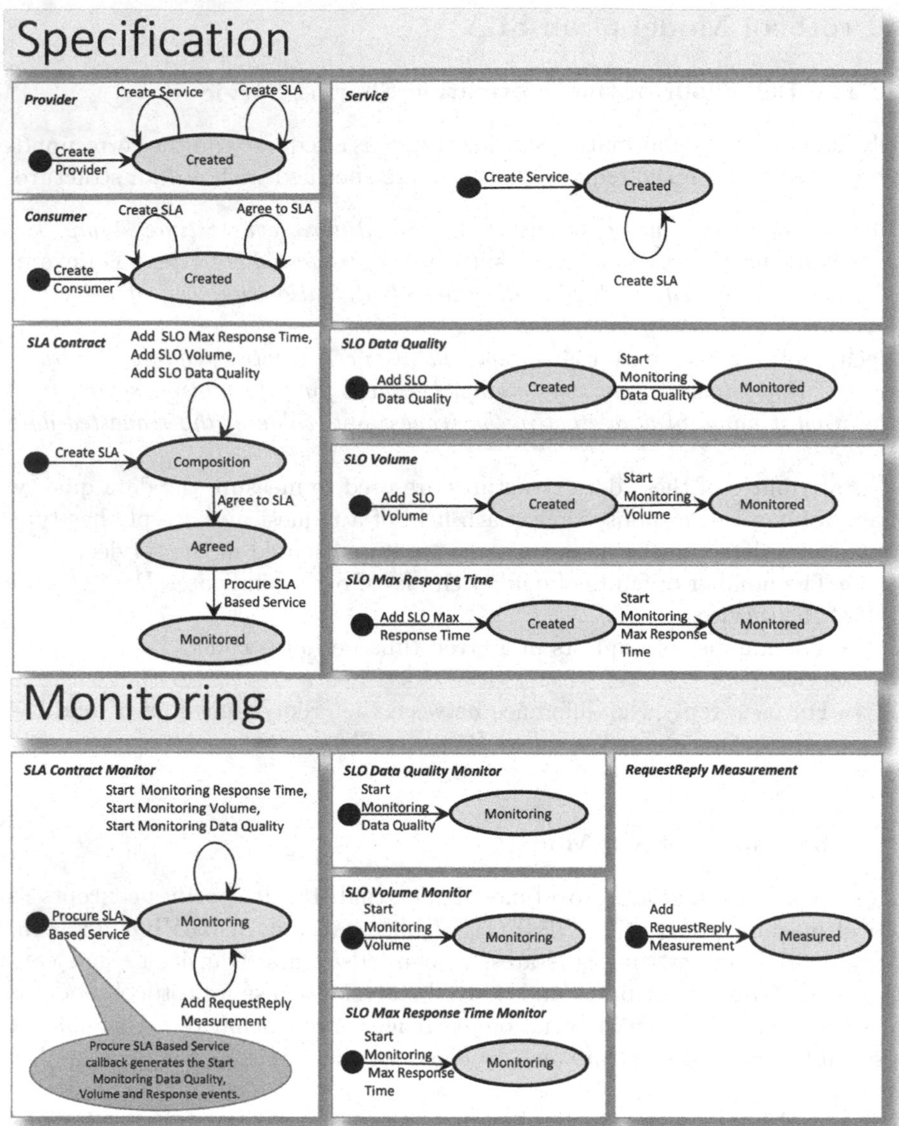

Fig. 3. Protocol model of SLA life cycle

5.3 Protocol Model of an SLA

In Fig. 3, the reader can see the graphical presentation of protocol machines *Provider*, *Consumer* and *Service* corresponding the concepts of the conceptual model (Fig. 1) and presenting behaviour of objects of those concepts. All these concepts should be in state *Created* to enable event *Create SLA* contract.

The protocol machine *SLA Contract* in state *Composition* allows one to *Add SLO Volume*, *Add SLO Max Response Time* and *Add SLO Data Quality*. Each SLO is a protocol machine that can be in the state *"does not exist"* (depicted as a small black circle), in state *Created* or in state *Monitored*.

When a *Provider* and a *Consumer* accept event *Agree to SLA*, the *SLA contract* goes to state *Agreed*. State *Agreed* reflects the agreement and fixes the *SLA Contract* preventing further SLO's to be added. In the state *Agreed*, event *Procure SLA Based Service* is enabled. This event transits the *SLA Contract* to state *Monitored*.

An *SLA Contract Monitor* is automatically created by the event *Procure SLA Based Service*. The *SLA Contract Monitor* delegates SLO specific monitoring to several SLO specific monitors. This event also triggers submitting event instances *Start Monitoring Data Quality*, *Start Monitoring Volume* and *Start Monitoring Max Response Time*. These events create the specialised SLO monitors. To simulate service utilisation, the object instances of *RequestReply Measurement* are created with events *Add RequestReply Measurement*.

Providers and *Customers* should implement monitors of SLO's. We model the executable monitors of SLO's to show them to *Producers* and *Customers* before actual implementation. This helps to prevent unexpected penalties and misunderstandings. Each SLO is monitored by successively calculating an *Indicator Value*, the occurrence of a *Violation* and a *Payable Penalty*.

The executable textual form of the protocol model is available to be downloaded from [15], be executed in the Modelscope tool available online and the monitors are generated from the model. We show the three types of monitors and the callbacks code used by monitors to update data.

5.1 Monitoring SLO Max Response Time

The values to monitor the *SLO Max Response Time* are shown in Fig. 4. It is monitoring the last measured response time, the maximum response time is 1 day and the penalty of 3, 000, 00, if violated.

The monitoring logic for the *SLO Max Response Time* is shown in the code fragment below. Function *SLA Contract Monitor.getIndicatorValue()* returns the *Response Time* attribute specified by the youngest *RequestReply Measurement* instance. Function *getViolation()*evaluates the relation *Response Time* > *Norm Value*. Function *getPayablePenalty()* calculates the *Payable Penalty*.

```
public class SLOMaxResponseTime extends Behaviour {
public int getPayablePenalty(){
// If no violation return no Penalty, i.e. zero
   if (! this.getBoolean("Violation")) return 0;
// Return penalty specified by SLO
   return this.getInstance("SLO").getCurrency("Penalty Value");
}
public boolean getViolation(){
// Get the last response time
   String duration = this.getString("Indicator Value");
// No last measurement, no violation
   if (duration == null) return false;
// Create classifier: > response norm and classify the current response time
```

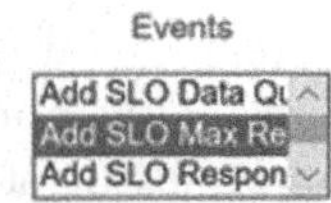

Fig. 4. Adding the SLO Max Response. Generated from the protocol model [15] in Modelscope tool [7].

```
return new ClassifierDurationFromSLO( this.getInstance("SLO"), ">").classifies(duration);
}
public String getIndicatorValue(){
// Get the last request/reply measurement
    Instance measurement =
        this.getLastMeasurement(this.getInstance("SLA Contract Monitor"));
// Return the response time, formatted as: days (HH:mm:ss.sss)?
    if (measurement == null) return null;
    return measurement.getString("Response Time");
}}
```

5.5 Monitoring SLO Volume

Figure 5 shows a monitor for the *SLO Volume.* It evaluates the number of requests over the last 365 days. During this period a maximum of 12,500 data items may be requested. As long as

$$(Indicator\,Value <= Norm\,Value)\,is\,true,$$

no violation exists. If violated, an extra 100.00 is paid as a *Penalty* for every excess data item requested.

Function *getIndicatorValue()* calculates the cumulative number of data items requested during a period defined by the *Period Value* attribute of the SLO. This is calculated as the sum of the *RequestReply Measurement*, found in its *Volume* attribute. Only request volumes are cumulated that fall within the specified period. Function *getPayablePenalty()* identifies every excess data over the *Norm* and calculates *Payable Penalty*, proportional to the excess volume measured for the period.

```
public class SLOVolume Time extends Behaviour {
  public int getPayablePenalty() {
 // If no violation, then no Penalty
```

SLO Name	Volume For C	String
Period Value	365	String
Norm Criteria	<=	String
Norm Value	12500	Integer
Norm Unit	Data items	String
Penalty Value	100.00	Currency
SLO Volume	(new SLO Volume)	SLO Volume

Add SLO Volume

reset form

Fig. 5. Adding the SLO Volume. Generated from the protocol model [15] in Modelscope tool [7].

```
    if (! this.getBoolean("Violation")) return 0;
// Get the associated SLO specification and
// Calculate excess volume and proportional penalty
    Instance slo  = this.getInstance("SLO");
    return (this.getInteger("Indicator Value") - slo.getInteger("Norm Value"))
    * slo.getCurrency("Penalty Value");
  }
public int getIndicatorValue() {
// Get only measurement for a specific SLA within the period and sum the measured volumes.
    return sum( this.getInstance("SLA Contract Monitor"),
this.getInstance("SLO").getString("Period Value"),"Volume");
  ]
protected int sum(Instance slaMonitor, String period, String
  measurementObjectName, String measurementAttributeName) {
      //    The every individual attribute value to the totalValue.
    int totalValue = 0;
    for (Instance measurement: this.getMeasurementsInPeriod(slaMonitor,
 period, measurementObjectName))
    totalValue += measurement.getInteger(measurementAttributeName);
//    Return the sum calculated in totalValue
    return totalValue;
  }
//
protected List<Instance> getMeasurementsInPeriod(Instance slaMonitor,
   String period, String measurementObjectName) {
    //    For every measurement that matches the SLA Contract Monitor
    long periodStart = System.currentTimeMillis() - new Duration(period).getTime();
    List <Instance>measurements = new ArrayList<Instance>();
for (Instance measurement:
        slaMonitor.selectByRef(measurementObjectName,"SLA Contract Monitor")){
//    If the measurement is within the period add it to the list
      if (periodStart <= AbstractMeasurement.getTimeMillis(
                  measurement.getString("Time Stamp"))) measurements.add(measurement);
    }
//    Return the list of measurements for the SLA Contract monitor within the period
    return measurements;
  }}
```

5.6 Monitoring SLO Data Quality

Figure 6 shows the example SLO Data Quality specification. A monitor instance for an SLO Data Quality is calculated over a period of 365 days. A maximum of 1% data quality issues are allowed for the data items delivered by the provider. The SLO is violated if the percentage of data quality issues exceeds 1% during the period. If violated, a Penalty of 1, 000.00 has to be paid once.

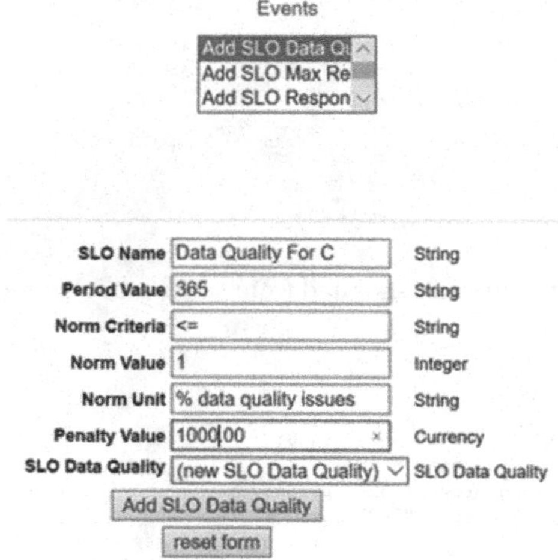

Fig. 6. Adding the SLO Data Quality. Generated from the protocol model [15] in Modelscope tool [7].

Function *getIndicatorValue()* in this monitor calculates the percentage of data quality issues during the monitoring period. The data quality issues and the entire data population are cumulated a to calculate this percentage.

```
public class SLODataQuality extends Behaviour {
  public int getIndicatorValue() {
// Get the related SLO specification, Get the SLA that is being monitored and
// get the period that is monitored
    Instance slo      = this.getInstance("SLO");
    Instance sla      = monitor.getInstance("SLA Contract Monitor");
    String period     = slo.getString("Period Value");
// Get the measurements for the SLA within the period and
// sum the value of attribute Data Quality Issues
    int value          = sum(sla, slo.getString("Period Value"), "Data Quality Issues");
// Sum the total volume of data items requested
    if (value == 0) return 0;
    int total          = sum(sla, period, "Volume");
// Calculate percentage of data quality issues
    return Math.round( 100f * (float)value / (float)total );
  }}
```

6 SLO-Concept as a Model Variation Point

In Sect. 3 we mentioned our study of existing SLA's and their SLO's. Almost all SLO's fit in three types *SLO Response Time*, *SLO Data Quality* and *SLO Volume*. Some of them can be seen as composition of several SLO's of a given type. For example, we have found *SLO Classified Response Time*, which is composed from four *SLOs Response time*. Response times in this SLO are classified into four categories: *on time*, *late*, *too late*, and *far too late*. Response times of requests are collected over a period of time and a category are expressed as a percentage of responses. We have used this compositional SLO to validate our reference model. The reference model with this SLO remains the same, but the monitoring logic is specified for each category of response times.

We also have found one SLA that includes an *SLO Mean Time To Repair* used to monitor resolving service disturbances reported by the consumer to the single point of contact of the service. The concept *disturbance* is outside of our reference model. This SLO can be included into an SLA only if the service provider is able to repair disturbances.

7 Conclusion

The information exchange services are often used by non-technical businesses and they need a reference model for preparation, monitoring and reviewing. In this paper, we have presented a version of a reference model that shows the concepts, the goals and the executable protocol of an SLA monitoring. The reference concepts, goals and an executable model contribute to the understanding of the designed SLA.

The concepts and their relations have been found via a literature review. The concepts of Service Level Objectives (SLO's) have been refined using the document analysis of the existing SLA's in domain of information exchange services. In the domain of Information Sharing Services, three main types of SLO's (Volume, Response Time and Data Quality) have been identified. These types of SLO's are used to structure the process of SLA preparation and monitoring. The logic of SLO's indicators, violation and penalty calculation can be reused and composed for different SLO's.

Keeping an SLA alive is considered as one of the issues in organizations. The goal and protocol models can be used for demonstration of an SLA for the customers and providers both before their agreement, and during the service utilizing. The models show the logic of the SLO measures, indicators and penalty calculation. An executable protocol model transforms an SLA documentation into a part of management process and, therefore, contributes to active use of the SLA for reviews, assessment of targets and planning.

In the future work, our reference model, built for the information exchange services, can be validated in different service domains. The reference model can be also useful in context of help desk processes in organizations, as SLA's are often guaranteed by several departments and the customer expects the declared quality of service provided by several departments.

References

1. Blake, M.B., Cummings, D.J., Bansal, A., Bansal, S.K.: Workflow composition of service level agreements for web services. Decis. Support Syst. **53**(1), 234–244 (2012)
2. Emeakaroha, V.C., et al.: Towards autonomic detection of SLA violations in Cloud infrastructures. Future Gener. Comput. Syst. **28**(7), 1017–1029 (2012)
3. Gartner Glossary: Gartner (2019). https://www.gartner.com/en/information-technolog/glossary/sla-service-level-agreement
4. Keller, A., Ludwig, H.: The WSLA framework: specifying and monitoring service level agreements for web services. J. Netw. Syst. Manage. **11**(1), 57–81 (2003)
5. Leitner, P., Ferner, J., Hummer, W., Dustdar, S.: Data-driven and automated prediction of service level agreement violations in service compositions. Distrib. Parallel Databases **31**(3), 447–470 (2013)
6. McNeile, A., Roubtsova, E.: CSP parallel composition of aspect models. In: AOM 2008, pp. 13–18 (2008)
7. McNeile, A., Simons, N.: (2011). http://www.metamaxim.com/
8. McNeile, A.T., Simons, N.: State machines as mixins. J. Obj. Technol. **2**(6), 85–101 (2003)
9. Menascé, D.A., Ruan, H., Gomaa, H.: QoS management in service-oriented architectures. Perform. Eval. **64**(7–8), 646–663 (2007)
10. Paschke, A., Bichler, M.: Knowledge representation concepts for automated SLA management. Decis. Support Syst. **46**(1), 187–205 (2008)
11. Raimondi, F., Skene, J., Emmerich, W.: Efficient online monitoring of web-service SLAs. In: Proceedings of the 16th ACM SIGSOFT International Symposium on Foundations of software engineering, pp. 170–180. ACM (2008)
12. Roubtsova, E.: Interactive Modeling and Simulation in Business System Design. Springer, Heidelberg (2016). https://doi.org/10.1007/978-3-319-15102-1
13. Roubtsova, E.: Categories of research methods and types of research results illustrated with a continuous project. In: 21st International Conference on Enterprise Information Systems, pp. 634–641 (2019)
14. Roubtsova, E., Michell, V.: KPIs and their properties defined with the EXTREME method. In: Shishkov, B. (ed.) BMSD 2013. LNBIP, vol. 173, pp. 128–149. Springer, Heidelberg (2013). https://doi.org/10.1007/978-3-319-06671-4_7
15. SLA protocol model: Protocol Modelling (2019). https://newprotocolmodelling.weebly.com/uploads/2/8/7/6/28769871/sla4_20191010.zip
16. Zimmermann, O.: Architectural decisions as reusable design assets. IEEE Softw. **28**(1), 64–69 (2011)

Graph-based Multi-Criteria Optimization for Business Processes

Frank Nordemann[1(✉)], Ralf Tönjes[1], Elke Pulvermüller[2], and Heiko Tapken[1]

[1] Faculty of Engineering and Computer Science,
Osnabrück University of Applied Sciences,
Albrechtstr. 30, 49076 Osnabrück, Germany
{f.nordemann,r.toenjes,h.tapken}@hs-osnabrueck.de

[2] Institute of Computer Science, University of Osnabrück,
Wachsbleiche 27, 49090 Osnabrück, Germany
elke.pulvermueller@informatik.uni-osnabrueck.de

Abstract. A process usually includes several different criteria to determine the quality of its operation. Criteria represent characteristics such as robustness, accuracy, cost and time of the complete process and of its different elements. Since there is rarely a single dominant criterion, optimization needs to evaluate multiple criteria against each other to find the most appropriate process configuration.

This paper introduces a graph-based approach for the multi-criteria optimization of business processes. Based on the introduction of multi-criteria process to graph transitions and use-case-driven evaluation metrics, criteria graphs are created in a discrete or joint manner. Two graph evaluation types allow addressing the demands of various use cases by following an automated, priority-based iterative analysis or by analyzing in a non-strict, more comprehensive way. Originally being designed to decide on one of multiple robust process paths, the approach proves to be highly flexible for many different application areas.

Keywords: Business processes · Multi-criteria-analysis · Unreliable communication environments · PML · BPMN · *rBPMN* · KPI · DAG.

1 Introduction

A business process can be defined as a composition of several different operations. A composition may include various ways to traverse from start to end, also called process paths. A path is determined by process variables, getting evaluated at decision points part of the composition and defining the process configuration. Process Modeling Languages (PMLs) may be used for its technical representation. Examples include traditional flow charts, Petri Nets [13], UML Activity diagrams [20] and Event-driven Process Chains (EPCs) from ARIS [10]. However, one of the most widely applied PMLs is the Business Process Model and Notation 2.0 (BPMN, [19]). BPMN is used as an exemplary PML in this paper.

B. Shishkov (Ed.): BMSD 2020, LNBIP 391, pp. 69–83, 2020.
https://doi.org/10.1007/978-3-030-52306-0_5

Usually, the evaluation of a process includes many criteria. Criteria are process characteristics such as accuracy, error ratio, volume of data, self-sufficiency level, performance requirements, robustness, calculation time, failure probability and cost. Especially in the field of business administration, sets of crucial process criteria are also known as Key Performance Indicators (KPIs). Most process evaluations use a diverse set of criteria, often defined in a prioritized order. For instance, if several paths in a process meet the required robustness, other criteria may be used to distinguish relevant paths.

This paper introduces a graph-based multi-criteria optimization approach for business processes. The approach may be used to configure process operation at design time and to optimize execution at runtime. The main research contributions of the paper include:

1. A real-world example for the multi-criteria process-to-graph transition,
2. methods for the discrete and joint definition of criteria graphs including metrics for graph analysis,
3. (automated) graph analysis procedures based on priorities, the comparison of all options/alternatives, and a combination of both.

The approach has been developed as part of *resilient BPMN* (*rBPMN*), a BPMN extension for unreliable communication environments [17]. While being applied to distinguish several robust process paths, the approach proved to be applicable for use cases of different application areas.

The remainder of the paper is organized as follows: Related work (Sect. 2) and a brief introduction into *rBPMN* (Sect. 3) are presented first, followed by the creation of criteria graphs (Sect. 4) and the multi-criteria analysis (Sect. 5). Finally, the approach is discussed (Sect. 6) before a summary concludes the paper (Sect. 7).

2 Related Work

Literature lists several publications addressing criteria optimization for business processes and for BPMN-based processes in particular. Significant publications related to the approach presented in this paper are outlined subsequently.

A comprehensive survey of business process performance analysis is provided by [1]. Different approaches and PMLs are discussed. Three dimensions of performance attributes (time, cost, quality) are identified, integration of non-performance related criteria is not addressed.

The addition of reliability and performance criteria to BPMN processes is illustrated in [3]. [4] uses metadata to simulate process reliability. Reliability analysis of BPMN processes is the focus of [15] and [21], while [8] studies effects of human and non-human resources on reliability. Literature introduces concepts for the integration of Quality of Information (QoI) criteria, such as the reliability of devices and resources [5,9,14] in the Internet of Things (IoT).

In [6], an algorithm for the multi-criteria-based selection of web services is introduced. The authors of [16] present an approach for the optimization of Quality of Service (QoS) aspects in cloud-driven process execution environments.

Being motivated by optimization techniques for data-intensive queries and flows in data management, [12] illustrates a concept for automated performance optimization of BPMN processes. A minimization of performance cost is intended by reordering and paralyzing process tasks. While the concept also uses Directed Acyclic Graphs (DAGs, [11]) as the approach described in this paper does, the process-to-graph transition and the optimization analysis show significant differences due to the different strategies and objectives of the procedures. Not addressing process optimization, graphs have been used in [7] describing a method to rate the similarity of different processes concerning tasks and their control-flow relations.

Enhancement of business processes is an important aspect of process mining. The topic combines process modeling and analysis with computational intelligence and data mining techniques [23,24]. However, process mining requires to have past process data (event logs) on-hand for analysis. While this may help to identify appropriate criteria edge weights, it is not required by the approach presented in this paper.

Many of the listed publications focus on adding and/or optimizing a single selected criterion (e.g. reliability) or a related criteria set (e.g. quality, cost and time). Some of the approaches are bound to specific use cases, missing customizability for other application areas. To the best of the authors' knowledge, none of the available publications presents a flexible approach for the graph-based multi-criteria optimization of BPMN business processes. No literature contribution outlines a use-case-driven multi-criteria graph creation and analysis procedure that may be applied at process design time and at runtime.

3 Resilient BPMN (*r*BPMN)

BPMN is used increasingly in domains besides the classical business process modeling. Examples are areas such as Cyber-Physical Systems (CPS) and IoT as well as scenarios taking place in rural environments (e.g. agriculture, road-side-construction, wildlife observation), undeveloped or disaster-affected regions. While all of these use cases may benefit from BPMN and its collaborative features, they are exposed to intermittent and failing connectivity. However, processes should not interrupt or break because of failing communication.

Resilient BPMN (*rBPMN*) is a BPMN extension to support robust process modeling and execution for unreliable communication environments [17]. Its features allow to model and verify robust communication at process design time and to dynamically optimize operation at runtime. *rBPMN* enables robust processes by *i)* adding alternatives for possibly failing message flows, by *ii)* moveable process elements between participants (e.g. moveable service functionality) and by *iii)* the dynamic identification and usage of service offering participants. *rBPMNs* extensions include new graphical elements and annotating metadata, designed to be used by experts of the applied domain.

Figure 1 presents a subset of message flow types relevant for this paper. In contrast to BPMN message flows, *Opportunistic Message Flows* (abbreviated: *OppMessageFlows*) of *rBPMN* include a scenario-based description of communication requirements and expected connectivity to verify robustness at design time. While this information is also part of *Opportunistic Decision Flows (OppDecisionFlows)*, these message flows define sets of alternatives in case of connectivity failures. Such a set of *OppDecisionFlows* is grouped by non-graphical *Opportunistic Message Groups (OppMessageGroups)*, and each *OppDecisionFlow* is labeled with an alphabetic character to express its belonging to a certain *OppMessageGroup* (e.g. *OppMessageGroups a/b* in Fig. 1). The style of the circle within an *OppDecisionFlow* determines whether at least one (solid line) or none (dashed line) of the *OppMessageGroup* alternatives needs working connectivity for process robustness.

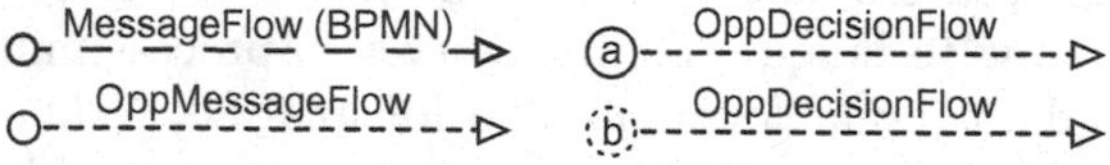

Fig. 1. Selected message flow elements of BPMN and *rBPMN*.

An approach using DAGs to identify robust process paths has been introduced in [18]. Robustness is a crucial, but not the only criterion for most processes. Other criteria may be taken into consideration for a requirements fulfilling process configuration. For this reason, this paper is motivated to demonstrate a graph-based multi-criteria optimization approach for BPMN business processes.

4 Criteria Graphs

This section illustrates the procedure to create criteria graphs based on BPMN/*rBPMN* business processes. For reasons of comprehensibility, graph creation is explained using a real-world example of an agricultural slurry application. Guidelines and methods may be applied to other use cases.

After describing the slurry scenario, relevant process criteria are identified and a graph is created. The section concludes by presenting two different ways to apply multiple criteria to the created graph, used as a foundation for the graph analysis in Sect. 5.

4.1 Example Slurry Process Scenario

The example slurry process S is depicted by the *rBPMN* diagram of Fig. 2. S features advanced Precision Farming techniques to apply slurry onto fields in an environmental-friendly way. The process uses services of different participants for its realization. *OppDecisionFlows* grouped by the *OppMessageGroups a, b, c* indicate that not all of the involved message flows need to be executed for robust

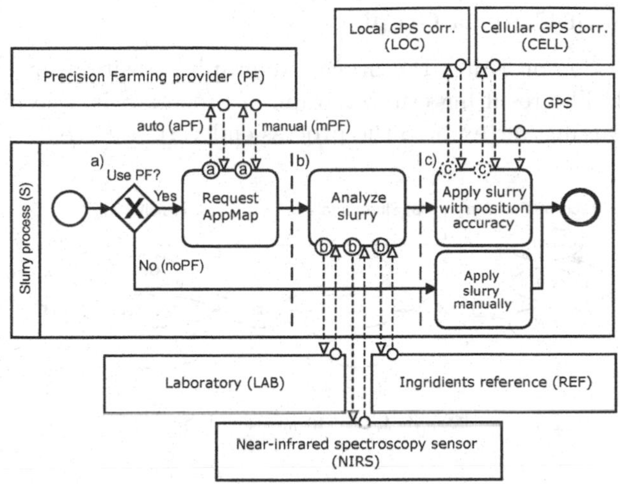

Fig. 2. Process example S showing an agricultural slurry application interacting with services offered by different participants.

process operation. Instead, at least one message flow (for a, b) or none (for c) need to be executed. However, message flow decisions affect process criteria such as robustness, accuracy, cost and time.

S is split into the three segments S_a, S_b and S_c. In S_a, the user decides if Precision Farming shall be used and if a subsection-based slurry application map (AppMap) shall be created automatically (*aPF*) or manually (*mPF*) with increased accuracy. Following in S_b, an analysis method for the slurry's ingredients (such as nitrogen and phosphor) is chosen. Options with diverse precision are a laboratory analysis (*LAB*), usage of a near-infrared spectroscopy sensor (*NIRS*) and data of an ingredients reference table (*REF*). Lastly, three options for the slurry spreader's positioning precision during application are provided in S_c, an important aspect to comply with official regulations: *GPS* only with basic precision and *GPS* with a correcting offset signal based on a cellular service (*CELL*) or based on a local correction station (*LOC*) in the field's proximity.

The scenario of Fig. 2 serves as a foundation for subsequent explanations.

4.2 Identification of Optimization Criteria

Process optimization starts with the definition of process criteria that need to be optimized. The criteria set chosen for example process S includes typical parameters also relevant for other application domains. The set includes the process criteria:

- **Robustness** (Robust.): Stability of process communication.
- **Accuracy** (Accur.): Precision of the result calculated by an activity.
- **Cost:** Monetary value required to run/execute an activity.
- **Time:** Time frame required by an activity to finish its operation.

4.3 Creation of Criteria Graph

This subsection demonstrates the process-to-graph transition for example process S of Fig. 2. The resulting criteria graph of process S is presented in Fig. 3, from process starting vertex S to the process end vertex S' ($S \rightarrow S'$).

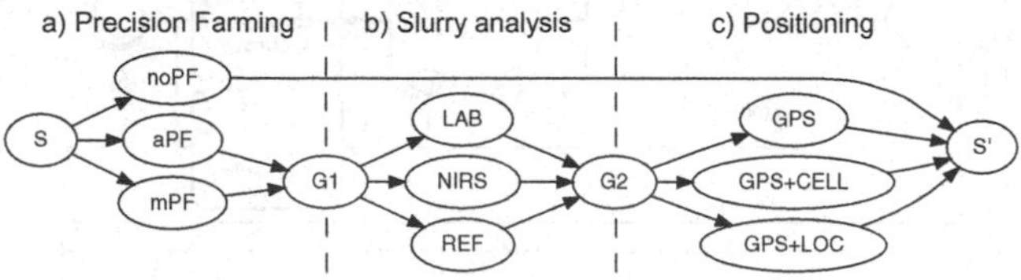

Fig. 3. Criteria graph of S.

Part S_a of the slurry application consists of three choices: At first, a decision is made whether or not Precision Farming features should be used. If so, the second decision determines if the subsection-based AppMap should be created automatically (*aPF*), or manually (*mPF*) by a Precision Farming expert resulting in advanced accuracy. The criteria graph reflects this by three separate path options for *noPF, aPF* and *mPF* in Fig. 3a. While the two process paths using AppMaps join at vertex *G1*, this is not the case for *noPF*. Since the path of *noPF* includes no more choices, it is directly connected to end vertex *S'*. *G1* is a glue vertex combining different process paths, used due to the absence of a merging BPMN element.

Process part S_b defines the type of analysis applied to identify slurry ingredients. Again, three choices are available: Ingredients may be identified by a precise laboratory analysis (LAB), approximated by an infrared sensor (NIRS), or roughly estimated by looking up typical slurry ingredient values for the current slurry type (e.g. cattle, pig) in a reference table (REF). The criteria graph integrates a separate path for every choice, joining all together at glue vertex *G2* in Fig. 3b.

In the final process part S_c, the geographical precision of the slurry application is determined. The process is operable using plain *GPS* with basic precision, which might not be precise enough to comply with official regulations in all areas and countries. Precision may be optimized by adding a GPS correction offset using *CELL* or *LOC*.

S_c is reflected by three separate paths in the criteria graph. *GPS* is part of every path since it is mandatory for process operation. One path is extended by *CELL*, another by *LOC* respectively (cf. Fig. 4). There is no need to explicitly include the *CELL/LOC* extensions by own vertices. Instead, vertices for GPS and *CELL/LOC* may be combined, leading to a more compact graph as illustrated in Fig. 3c. In this aspect, combining vertices also requires to combine belonging edge weights.

In general, the creation of criteria graphs is about separating graph paths for independent process parts and extending graph paths for combined/coherent

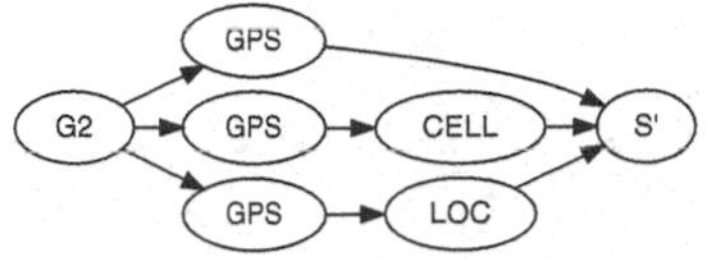

Fig. 4. Criteria graph of S_c with explicit vertices for the combination of GPS with *CELL* and *LOC* respectively.

process parts. A detailed list of process-to-graph transition rules for BPMN and *rBPMN* process elements may be found in [17]. Since the rules have been created for the criteria of robustness, additional rules may be necessary depending on the chosen set of criteria.

4.4 Application of Criteria-Based Graph Weights

The next step after creating the criteria graph is to add criteria-based graph weights. A weight is used to express how well a criterion is met by the related process element. Normalization of real-world criteria values is useful to enhance comparability in many scenarios.

Depending on the concrete criterion and process element, a weight may belong to an incoming edge, an outgoing edge or to the actual vertex itself. Taking the cellular-based position correction service *CELL* in process S as an example, criteria for accuracy, cost and time are all related to the actual vertex of *CELL*. This is due to the criteria describing characteristics of the correction service. However, the robustness criterion describes stability of communication with the service. Robustness weights belong to the incoming and outgoing edges of *CELL*, reflecting message flows for a request to and a reply from the service.

Before the application of weight annotations, a verification is required to check if the intended graph analysis algorithms support all applied weight types. Since many algorithms like Dijkstra's shortest-path [11] are based on edge weights, it is suggested to translate weights of vertices to edges. This may be done by *i)* splitting a vertex and adding an intermediate edge or by *ii)* applying the weight to incoming/outgoing edges. The latter case results in a more compact graph and is used subsequently.

Following, two different approaches for the application of graph weights are introduced.

Discrete Criteria Graphs. The graph shown in Fig. 3 is duplicated for each criterion of the chosen criteria set. Afterwards, each criterion graph applies weights of the corresponding criterion to the related graph edges. This results in several graphs, where each criterion is allowed to use its own understanding of graph weights (e.g. value interpretation, value range, etc.).

Figure 5 presents the criterion graph for communication robustness of process S. Edge weights represent probabilities $P_w^R \in [0, 1]$ for successful communication on the appropriate process segments. The probabilities of Fig. 5 illustrate that

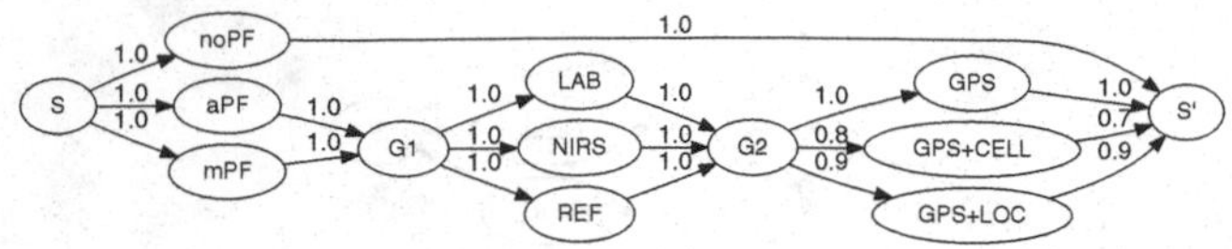

Fig. 5. Robustness graph of S, based on probability edge weights.

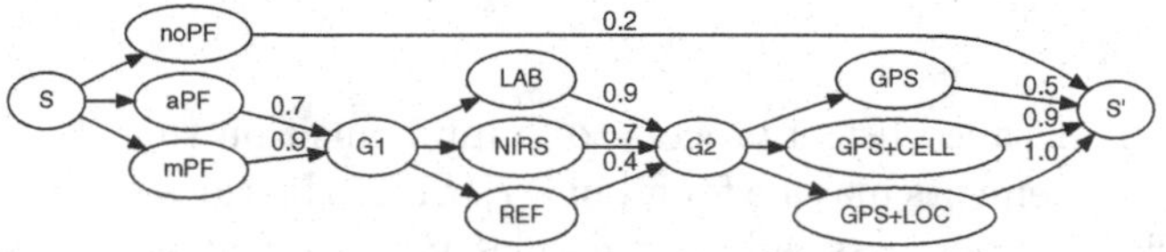

Fig. 6. Accuracy graph of S.

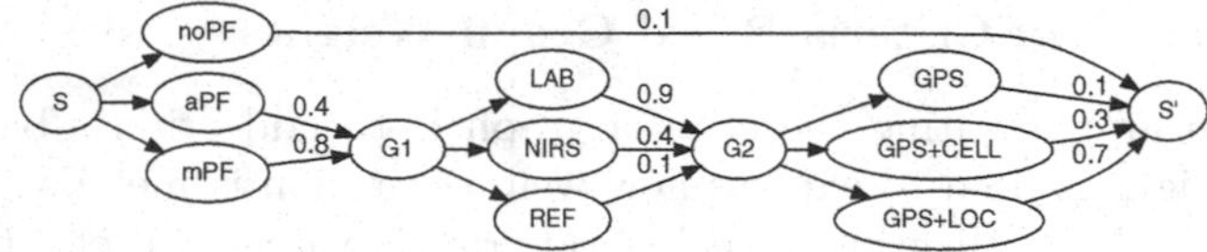

Fig. 7. Cost graph of S.

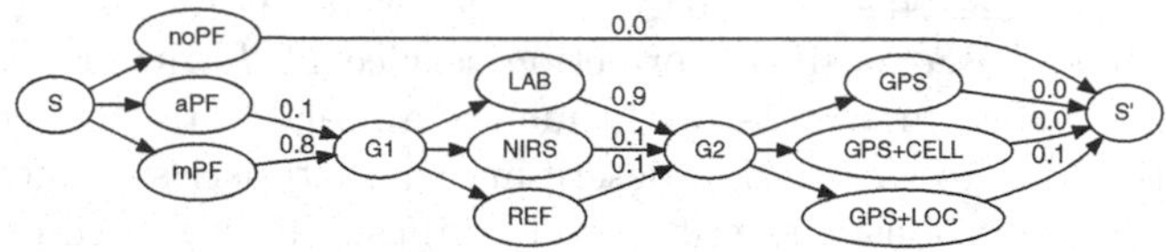

Fig. 8. Time graph of S.

communication issues are only expected for the segments including *CELL* or *LOC*.

Likewise, the criteria graphs for accuracy (Fig. 6), cost (Fig. 7) and time (Fig. 8) apply edge weights $C_w^x \in [0, 1]$. The weights do not reflect probabilities, but give an indication how good or bad a criterion is fulfilled. While accuracy values close to 1 are desired, cost and time aim at low values close to 0. However, different values $C_w^x \in \mathbb{R}$ may be applied by other use cases.

The accuracy graph in Fig. 6 points out the relevance of Precision Farming techniques for highly accurate slurry applications. Certainly, this has an impact on cost in Fig. 7 and time in Fig. 8. Here, the absence of Precision Farming allows low cost and fast operation.

Joint Criteria Graphs. In alternative to separate graphs, a common graph including different criteria may be created by using a weighted decision matrix. This is an appropriate concept for criteria that share a common understanding of edge weights, e.g. aiming at a low weight value. Normalization of criteria values to a consistent scale prior to combination is required. The weights of the decision matrix may be used to prioritize criteria against each other. A subset or the whole set of criteria may be combined using a joint graph.

Table 1 presents a decision matrix comprising the criteria cost and time of operations provided by participants of process S. Both criteria aim at low weight values for optimization. Cost is prioritized with 70% over 30% for time. The summarized criteria values are applied as edge weights in a common graph illustrated in Fig. 9.

Table 1. Weighted decision matrix combining normalized criteria to joint edge weights.

	Weight	*noPF*	*aPF*	*mPF*	*LAB*	*NIRS*	*REF*	*GPS*	*CELL*	*LOC*
Cost	0.7	0.1	0.4	0.8	0.9	0.4	0.1	0.1	0.3	0.7
Time	0.3	0.0	0.1	0.8	0.9	0.1	0.1	0.0	0.0	0.1
Joint	1.0	0.07	0.31	0.80	0.90	0.31	0.10	0.07	0.21	0.52

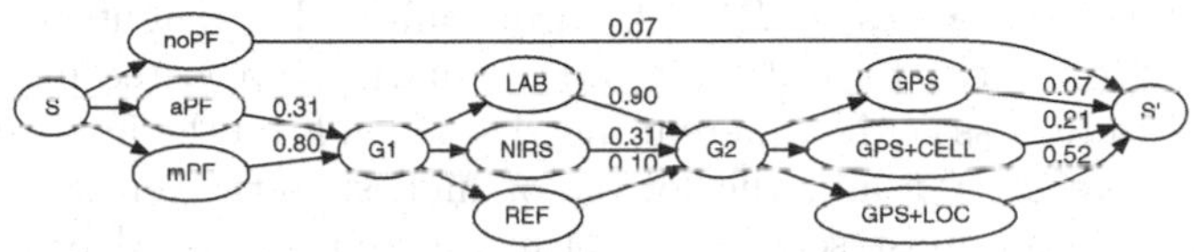

Fig. 9. Joint criteria graph of S for cost and time.

5 Multi-criteria Graph Analysis

After defining the necessary criteria graph(s), an iterative or comparative graph analysis is performed to find the most appropriate process path. The two analysis types are substantial elements to address the varying needs of use cases and criteria sets. The section starts with an introduction of criteria metrics and graph-based search algorithms prior to iterative and comparative graph analysis.

5.1 Criteria Metrics

Criteria metrics are defined in the form of C_y^x, where y represents a certain metric (e.g. t for total path weight) and x stands for a concrete criterion (e.g. R for robustness). For instance, C_t^R describes a total path weight for robustness while C_w^A represents an accuracy weight of an edge. If probabilities are used as edge

Table 2. Criteria metrics.

Semantic	Symbol & Formula	C	P
Criterion placeholder	x (e.g. R → Robustness)	✓	✓
Number of path edges	$n \in \mathbb{N}$	✓	✓
Edge weight	$C_w^x \in \mathbb{R}$	✓	
Total path weight	$C_t^x = \sum_{i=1}^n C_{w_i}^x$	✓	
Lowest path weight	$C_l^x = min(C_{w_1}^x, ..., C_{w_n}^x)$	✓	✓
Highest path weight	$C_h^x = max(C_{w_1}^x, ..., C_{w_n}^x)$	✓	✓
Average path weight	$C_a^x = C_t^x / n$	✓	✓
Median path weight	$C_m^x = median(C_{w_1}, ..., C_{w_n})$	✓	✓
Range of path weights	$C_r^x = C_h^x - C_l^x$	✓	✓
Probability edge weight	$P_w^x \in \mathbb{R} \| 0 \leq P_w^x \leq 1$		✓
Probability of path	$P_p^x = \prod_{i=1}^n P_{w_i}$		✓
Boolean prob. of path	$P_b^x = 0 \quad (\forall\, P_p^x < 1)$ $P_b^x = 1 \quad (\forall\, P_p^x = 1)$		✓

C ⇒ applicable to non-probability-based graphs
P ⇒ applicable to probability-based graphs

weights, the format changes to P_y^x with probability edge weights $P_w^x \in \mathbb{R}|0 \leq P_w^x \leq 1$. Example metrics for criteria graph evaluations are listed in Table 2.

While the usefulness of the different metrics depends on the applied use case, the total path weight C_t^x and the lowest or highest path weight C_l^x and C_h^x are of importance for most scenarios. With probabilities as edge weights P_w^x, the probability of the path P_p^x is a substantial metric. If a criteria requires a probability of 1, the boolean path probability P_b^x is considerable.

5.2 Graph-Based Search Algorithms

The identification of appropriate process paths is provided by graph-based search algorithms. All-path analyses are used to identify every possible process path and to evaluate the different paths with a selection of use-case-driven metrics. An all-path implementation may be based on Breadth-First Search (BFS, [11]) or Depth-First Search (DFS, [22]).

Shortest-path algorithms such as Dijkstra [11] and Bellman-Ford [2] as well as longest-path algorithms (e.g. based on DFS) are especially useful for finding the most appropriate process path in terms of total path weight C_t^x. A shortest-path algorithm is used subsequently to automatically choose a path in the final step of graph analysis.

5.3 Iterative Graph Analysis

The different criteria graphs are analyzed step-by-step in a priority-defined order using the all-path analysis. Every iteration identifies graph paths that fit a defined set of minimum metric values and removes unqualified edges. The following iteration takes over the graph adjustments on its own criterion graph and continues by performing an all-path analysis. This procedure is repeated for each criterion, until a remaining graph fulfilling the defined metric requirements is found.

Depending on the final criterion and the desire for an automated analysis, the last iteration may apply a shortest-path or longest-path analysis to choose the most appropriate path automatically. Alternatively, another all-path analysis is performed on the last criterion. The iterative analysis procedure is summarized in Fig. 10.

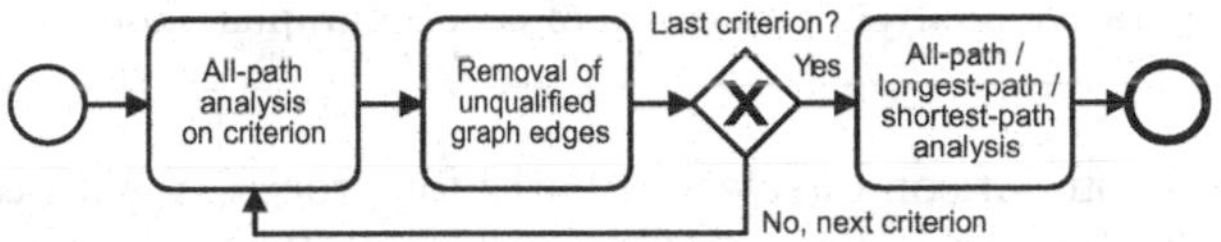

Fig. 10. Iterative analysis procedure of criteria graphs, modeled in BPMN.

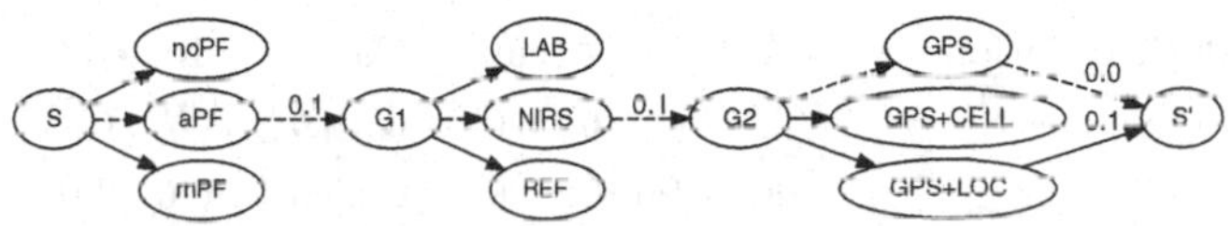

Fig. 11. Final time criterion graph of S with shortest-path after iterative analysis of robustness, accuracy and cost.

In regard to process example S, robustness may be the first priority, followed by accuracy, cost and time. A robustness analysis with a lowest path weight $P_l^R = 0.8$ excludes the correction service *CELL* as possible path by removing the outgoing edge with a weight of $P_w^R = 0.7$. In the accuracy analysis, a lowest path weight $C_l^A = 0.5$ results in removing outgoing edges of *noPF* and *REF*. Following, a highest path weight $C_h^C = 0.7$ for the cost graph eliminates edges of *mPF* and *LAB*. The remaining time criterion graph is illustrated in Fig. 11. A final shortest-path analysis automatically identifies the most appropriate path including *aPF/NIRS/GPS*, depicted by a dashed line.

5.4 Comparative Graph Analysis

Instead of analyzing and modifying graphs in a priority-defined order, all graphs are evaluated using the all-path analysis. Identified paths are compared by a use-case-driven set of criteria metrics to find the most appropriate path available. While this method reflects a broader, more complete type of graph analysis, it may require a higher level of manual interaction in comparing and choosing process paths. A useful approach is to filter process paths by minimum criteria metrics first and to compare the remaining paths afterwards. Figure 12 illustrates the comparative analysis procedure.

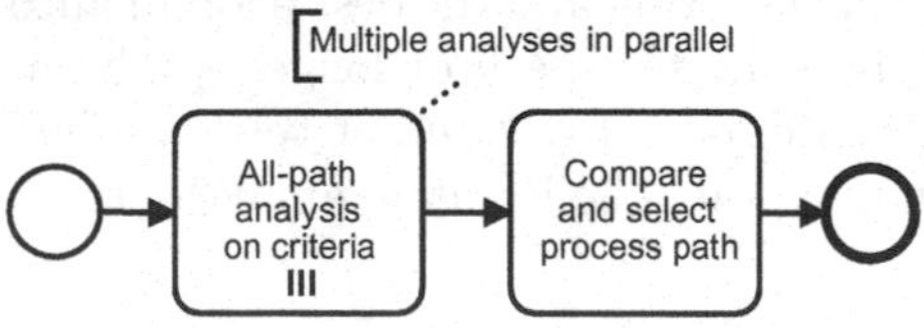

Fig. 12. Comparative analysis procedure of criteria graphs, modeled in BPMN.

Table 3 lists a comparison of selected paths for process S with essential metrics for each criterion, including path probability P_p^x, total path weight C_t^x, lowest and highest path weight C_l^x and C_h^x. In real-world scenarios, the selection of relevant process paths and criteria metrics is done by domain experts.

Table 3. Comparative analysis of criteria graphs for S.

Path variation	Robst.		Accur.		Cost		Time	
$S \rightarrow \ldots \rightarrow S'$	P_p^R	P_l^R	C_t^A	C_l^A	C_t^C	C_h^C	C_t^T	C_h^T
noPF	1.00	1.00	0.2	0.2	0.1	0.1	0.0	0.0
aPF/NIRS/GPS	1.00	1.00	1.9	0.5	0.9	0.4	0.2	0.1
aPF/NIRS/CELL	0.56	0.70	2.3	0.7	1.1	0.4	0.2	0.1
aPF/NIRS/LOC	0.81	0.90	2.4	0.7	1.5	0.7	0.3	0.1
mPF/LAB/LOC	0.81	0.90	2.8	0.9	2.4	0.9	1.8	0.9
mPF/NIRS/LOC	0.81	0.90	2.6	0.7	1.9	0.8	1.0	0.8

For the paths listed in Table 3, a domain expert may conclude the following: The path including *noPF* results in solid robustness, cost and time criteria values, but poor slurry application accuracy. In contrast, high accuracy is guaranteed by paths including *mPF*, but costs and required time are relatively high. A compromise may be found by using a path including *aPF* and *NIRS*. Relatively high accuracy with acceptable robustness, cost and time values may be realized by selecting a path including *GPS* or *LOC* in combination with *aPF* and *NIRS*.

6 Discussion

The exemplary creation and analysis of multi-criteria graphs using an agricultural slurry scenario demonstrated high flexibility of the introduced approach.

While the criteria robustness, accuracy, cost and time have been chosen for this example, others such as error ratio, self-sufficiency level, data volume, performance requirements or failure probability may be used for different scenarios. This also includes scenarios that do not make use of BPMN or *rBPMN*, where the principle of creating separated and extended graph paths remains identical.

An important aspect of the process-to-graph transition is to identify and include all process elements that may be affected by one of the chosen optimization criteria. The examples for the transition of process S and a detailed transition rule list in [17] may help to translate other processes of different domains.

Depending on the criteria set, meanings of criteria edge weights may differentiate significantly from each other. Where possible, weight normalization and a consistent scale (e.g. $C_w^x \in [0, 1]$) increase comparability across different criteria. Discrete and joint criteria graphs allow the definition of edge weights in a flexible way. Joint graphs combine graphs for criteria that share a common understanding of edge weights (e.g. cost and time in process example S). If criteria are diverse in their definition (e.g. value meaning, value range, related edges, and vertices), discrete graphs for each criterion are appropriate.

Various metrics are provided for weight aggregation along a process path. The total path weight C_t^x is a useful parameter for sum-oriented criteria like the reduction of time and cost as well as the increase of accuracy. Lowest path weights C_l^x help to guarantee a minimum weight met by ever edge of a path. Probabilities may be applied as edge weights resulting in product-oriented metrics like the probability of the path P_p^x.

Analysis of criteria graphs is customizable to address the demands of the applied use case and the set of chosen criteria. An iterative analysis is suitable for scenarios with a good understanding of criteria, their priorities and required/expected metric values. Automation of an iterative analysis is straightforward by using clearly defined metrics for the all-path iterations and a shortest-path/longest-path analysis for the final iteration. To avoid the exclusion of too many process paths, it is important to carefully define criteria thresholds when working with an iterative analysis. More comprehensive results may be identified by using a comparative analysis. Comparison is recommended if there are no strict criteria priorities and understanding of metric thresholds/consequences is questionable. While this procedure requires more manual interaction, it helps to find best compromises between criteria.

Since it may be challenging for some use cases to decide on one of the two analysis procedures, a combination of both iterative and comparative may be promising. For instance, a comparative analysis of a process may be applied at design time. After getting familiar with promising criteria metric thresholds, an iterative analysis may be used to automatically optimize process operation at runtime.

While BPMN and *rBPMN* have been used as PMLs in this paper, the optimization approach may be applied to other PMLs by adapting the process-to-graph transition procedure.

7 Conclusion

This paper presents a graph-based multi-criteria optimization approach for business processes. Originally being motivated by finding a decision procedure for different robust process paths, the approach provides high flexibility even for use cases not facing unreliable communication environments. For instance, the approach may identify the process path with the best compromise between operation accuracy, calculation time and energy consumption for its execution on performance-restricted, battery-powered devices.

Discrete and joint criteria graphs may be designed and combined in a use-case-driven way. Joint criteria graphs allow weighted aggregations of criteria and reduce the number of graphs to be analyzed. Depending on the demands of the concrete scenario, the graph analysis may be automatized by applying an iterative procedure in conjunction with the introduced criteria metrics. Alternatively and less priority-oriented, the analysis may be realized in a comparative way by using an all-path analysis on unmodified criteria graphs.

Criteria graphs may help to configure and verify a process at design time. Dynamic optimization of its operation is enabled by applying the approach at process runtime.

References

1. Van der Aalst, W.M.: Business process management: a comprehensive survey. ISRN Softw. Eng. **2013** (2013)
2. Bellman, R.: On a routing problem. Q. Appl. Math. **16**(1), 87–90 (1958)
3. Bocciarelli, P., D'Ambrogio, A.: A BPMN extension for modeling non functional properties of business processes. In: Proceedings of the 2011 Symposium on Theory of Modeling and Simulation, pp. 160–168. Society for Computer Simulation International (2011)
4. Bocciarelli, P., D'Ambrogio, A., Giglio, A., Paglia, E.: Simulation-based performance and reliability analysis of business processes. In: Proceedings of the 2014 Winter Simulation Conference, pp. 3012–3023. IEEE Press (2014)
5. Bocciarelli, P., D'Ambrogio, A., Giglio, A., Paglia, E.: A BPMN extension to enable the explicit modeling of task resources. In: CIISE, pp. 40–47 (2016)
6. Chhun, S., Cherifi, C., Moalla, N., Ouzrout, Y.: A multi-criteria service selection algorithm for business process requirements. arXiv preprint arXiv:1505.03998 (2015)
7. Dijkman, R., Dumas, M., García-Bañuelos, L.: Graph matching algorithms for business process model similarity search. In: Dayal, U., Eder, J., Koehler, J., Reijers, H.A. (eds.) BPM 2009. LNCS, vol. 5701, pp. 48–63. Springer, Heidelberg (2009). https://doi.org/10.1007/978-3-642-03848-8_5
8. Domingos, D., Respício, A., Martinho, R.: Using resource reliability in BPMN processes. Proc. Comput. Sci. **100**, 1280–1288 (2016)
9. Domingos, D., Respício, A., Martinho, R.: Reliability of IoT-aware BPMN healthcare processes. In: Virtual and Mobile Healthcare: Breakthroughs in Research and Practice, pp. 793–821. IGI Global (2020)

10. Dumas, M., La Rosa, M., Mendling, J., Reijers, H.A.: Fundamentals of Business Process Management, 2nd edn. Springer, Heidelberg (2018). https://doi.org/10.1007/978-3-662-56509-4
11. Even, S.: Graph Algorithms. Cambridge University Press, Cambridge (2011)
12. Gounaris, A.: Towards automated performance optimization of BPMN business processes. In: Ivanović, M., et al. (eds.) ADBIS 2016. Communications in Computer and Information Science, vol. 637, pp. 19–28. Springer, Cham (2016). https://doi.org/10.1007/978-3-319-44066-8_2
13. Lohmann, N., Verbeek, E., Dijkman, R.: Petri net transformations for business processes - a survey. In: Jensen, K., van der Aalst, W.M.P. (eds.) Transactions on Petri Nets and Other Models of Concurrency II. LNCS, vol. 5460, pp. 46–63. Springer, Heidelberg (2009). https://doi.org/10.1007/978-3-642-00899-3_3
14. Martinho, R., Domingos, D.: Quality of information and access cost of IoT resources in BPMN processes. Proc. Technol. **16**, 737–744 (2014)
15. Martinho, R., Domingos, D., Respício, A.: Evaluating the reliability of ambient-assisted living business processes. In: ICEIS (2), pp. 528–536 (2016)
16. Mazzola, L., Kapahnke, P., Waibel, P., Hochreiner, C., Klusch, M.: FCE4BPMN: on-demand QoS-based optimised process model execution in the cloud. In: 2017 International Conference on Engineering, Technology and Innovation (ICE/ITMC), pp. 305–314. IEEE (2017)
17. Nordemann, F., Tönjes, R., Pulvermüller, E.: Resilient BPMN: robust process modeling in unreliable communication environments. In: 8th International Conference on Model-Driven Engineering and Software Development (MODELSWARD). Scitepress (2020)
18. Nordemann, F., Tönjes, R., Pulvermüller, E., Tapken, H.: A graph-based approach for process robustness in unreliable communication environments. In: 15th International Conference on Evaluation of Novel Approaches to Software Engineering (ENASE). Scitepress (2020)
19. Object Management Group (OMG): Business Process Model and Notation (BPMN) 2.0 Specification (2011). www.omg.org/spec/BPMN/2.0/About-BPMN. Accessed 05 Mar 2020
20. OMG: Object Management Group: Unified Modeling Language (UML) 2.2 Specification (2017). https://www.omg.org/spec/UML/About-UML. Accessed 09 Dec 2019
21. Respício, A., Domingos, D.: Reliability of BPMN business processes. Proc. Comput. Sci. **64**, 643–650 (2015)
22. Tarjan, R.: Depth-first search and linear graph algorithms. SIAM J. Comput. **1**(2), 146–160 (1972)
23. Van Der Aalst, W.: Process Mining: Discovery, Conformance and Enhancement of Business Processes, vol. 2. Springer, Heidelberg (2011). https://doi.org/10.1007/978-3-642-19345-3
24. Van Der Aalst, W., et al.: Process mining manifesto. In: Daniel, F., Barkaoui, K., Dustdar, S. (eds.) BPM 2011. LNCS, vol. 99, pp. 169–194. Springer, Heidelberg (2011). https://doi.org/10.1007/978-3-642-28108-2_19

Design Optimization of IoT Models: Structured Safety and Security Flaw Identification

Julia Rauscher(✉) and Bernhard Bauer

Software Methodologies of Distributed Systems, University of Augsburg, Augsburg, Germany
{julia.rauscher,bauer}@informatik.uni-augsburg.de

Abstract. More and more devices are being interconnected, thus extending the use of Internet of Things (IoT) systems. However, the larger the networks are the more vulnerable and inscrutable they become. This is a significant challenge especially when IoT is used in safety- and security-critical areas. In these areas, a flawless architecture must be guaranteed already in the design phase. Therefore, a structured possibility is needed to scan models completely for vulnerabilities as early as possible. We developed a pattern recognition framework (PRF) that enables the definition of design patterns and anti-patterns. These patterns are used for a holistic and automated identification of flaws in IoT models during design phase and enable a design optimization.

Keywords: Internet of Things · Design optimization · Pattern recognition · Safety · Security · By design · Wellbeing

1 Introduction

In the age of digitalization there is an increasing number of devices which communicate and interact with each other. This has led to networks including more independent devices that can act and react in a uniquely identifiable and automated manner which are known as Internet of Things (IoT) systems. These systems have two major characteristics respectively challenges. First, they are increasing fast which creates complexity including hidden vulnerabilities. According to [1] by 2025 there will be 75.44 billion connected devices. Second, they aren't self-contained. Hence, they are connected to the internet that leads to possible cyber attacks and other threats. Therefore, IoT has to handle IoT-specific security challenges like data transmission in sensor networks as well as conventional issues like DOS attacks, eavesdropping or virus damages [2]. This set of challenges can arise and occur on plenty times and points. However, studies have shown that 50% of all flaws already emerge during the design phase [3]. Therefore, an approach to recognize vulnerabilities by design is urgently required [4]. Especially in safety- and security-critical areas these challenges are major concerns which require a reliable investigation of possible accidents or threats as early as possible. One example of the plenty application fields of IoT in safety- and security-critical systems is the deployment in the medical field. Not only in hospitals but also in private use as medical smart homes IoT is used in the medical or wellbeing sector. However, this entails danger as shown by examples like

B. Shishkov (Ed.): BMSD 2020, LNBIP 391, pp. 84–102, 2020.
https://doi.org/10.1007/978-3-030-52306-0_6

[5] or [6]. Manipulated baby monitors or captured implantable cardiac devices represent highly critical elements which are difficult to alter afterwards and need observations during design phase.

Since most approaches focus on software level there is a lack of model-based IoT approaches. Additionally, the existing model-based approaches are either generic or cannot be automated. Therefore, to address the above mentioned issues, we have developed a pattern recognition process to present a structured approach to define and examine safety and security architectural patterns and anti-patterns. These are used to identify flaws during the design phase automatically. Thereby, flaws which can be prevented already before the run time are addressed. In addition, this approach enables knowledge conservation of safety and security design challenges and the review of large IoT systems. Since our process includes automated analysis parts, the complexity of IoT systems can be handled.

After introducing the challenges of safety and security in IoT systems, the remaining paper is structured as follows: To differentiate our approach from other concepts Sect. 2 contains related work and background basics of allied fields. Afterwards, we will present the pattern recognition framework and its details in four steps. Section 4 applies an Ambient Assisted Living (AAL) use case to evaluate our diverse approach steps. An outlook on further work and the conclusion completes the paper.

2 Background and Related Work

As described above, most approaches that identify flaws through patterns are conducted after the design phase. Accordingly, these approaches are software-based. Reference [7] offers a review over the attempts to create code patterns to identify bad software decisions. None of these attempts investigates the concept of patterns on architectural level. Another concept of using design patterns in data-intensive systems offers [8]. Though, they aim in detecting design patterns for reverse engineering purposes and not safety or security challenges. Approaches which include IoT and security by design are e.g. [9] and [10]. Reference [9] proposes the application of AADL to be able to model all security related information. Though, their framework doesn't include automated flaw identification possibilities. The work of [10] present the review of the usage of security design patterns in IoT systems. However, like [7] these patterns are made for software architectures. As is often the case, these two approaches do not consider safety.

Analyses on architectural level are often used in other application fields as IoT already. For instance, enterprise architecture management (EAM) applies architecture analyses for diverse goals and even for security analyses. An overview of the available analyses is offered by [11]. E.g. the approaches of [12–14] use defense graphs or extended influence diagrams to assess risks or other security concerns on design level. However, these architecture analysis approaches are only conducted if the vulnerabilities are already known. Therefore, an approach is required to identify these vulnerabilities to enable the application of the assessment.

This literature research has revealed that all concepts are already successfully used, but there is no approach which combines these concepts and applies them in the safety- and security-critical IoT area.

3 Pattern Recognition Framework

Designing an IoT system flawless and without weak points is an almost unmanageable task. We developed an approach to support and simplify this task.

When planning the design or considering design changes two main issues occur. First, designing the details highly depends on expert experience. However, experts are not always available during design phase or afterwards if changes are required in the model. Therefore, a possibility to preserve the knowledge is highly significant. The second issue addresses the complex dependencies, interoperability and requirements of the IoT system components. Hence, a manually verification of all included elements, connections and features is not possible in a reasonable time.

Our approach of a pattern recognition framework (PRF) covers these both challenges. Thus, the PRF has multiple goals. To address the first challenge we created a selection of required information about flaws, risks, avoidable design decisions and possible impacts to offer a structured chance to enable a knowledge conservation. The experience of the experts can be saved for later observations. Therefore, misplaned design mistakes, which already happened before, can be prevented in the design phase during the design check. As the knowledge is conserved in textual readable form, every team member is able to follow it independent of programming language knowledge. To address the second challenge we translate the textual readable form into executable code by using a domain specific language (DSL). Thus, the flaw analysis can be conducted automatically and includes all components of the IoT system.

The knowledge conservation and flaw identification respectively recognition will be conducted through design patterns and anti-patterns. Patterns represent positive and desirable design choices that prevent vulnerabilities, e.g. a highly required authentication mechanism. To recognize possible flawed modelling decisions, model components that do not match these patterns are searched for. During this search, the model components are examined for conditions of the unambiguous pattern definitions. Matches are only displayed if they fulfill all pattern conditions to avoid false positive hits. By contrast, anti-patterns represent negative and avoidable design choices that cause vulnerabilities. The automated flaw identification looks for model components that match the anti-patterns. Our framework enables to define generally applicable patterns which are suitable to all IoT models. Though specifically designed patterns for individual IoT models are also possible and required. When we speak of pattern in the following, this includes anti-pattern as well. In addition, flaw identification and flaw recognition are used interchangeably as our concept is not related to the machine learning research field.

The application of the PRF is described below in four Sects. 3.1–3.4. Sect. 3.1 explains the content of the PRF categories and attribute options, which are used to specify the patterns and anti-patterns textually. Section 3.2 presents the pattern definition language. Finally, Sects. 3.3 and 3.4 show the transformation of the patterns into code and the automated, executable pattern recognition.

To illustrate the context, Fig. 1 provides an overview of the components and usage of our PRF during design time. Independently of the domain, the creation of a model requires a meta model. Therefore, we designed an IoT meta model which can be used to depict IoT networks. This meta model is among others able to depict physical entities, like sensors, actuators or tags, and their virtual counterparts. Additionally, including physical connections with their network specifications, protocol types and encoding mechanism. Furthermore, services with operations, right management and authentication requirements can be presented. In addition, components for business details, stakeholder and their users are contained. As described, the PRF (Sect. 3.1) is applied to define pattern and anti-pattern in textual readable form. The DSL (Sect. 3.2), which is based on the meta model, uses the fulfilled PRF parts, categories and values to configure the pattern language. A pattern database stores the created patterns and anti-patterns. Concurrently, a code generation process (Sect. 3.3) produces executable code for pattern services, i.e. flaw identification services. When a flaw identification is conducted, the database and services are used to examine the IoT model (Sect. 3.4).

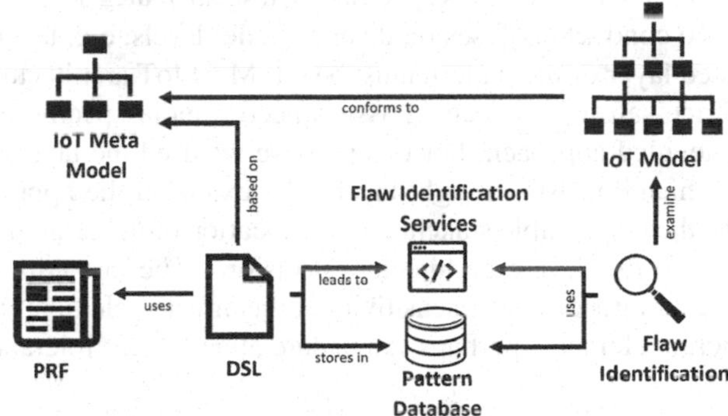

Fig. 1. Structured definition and identification of flaws by using PRF

To realize our approach we need different technologies. Therefore, we use the widely used concepts of EMF to model our IoT meta model. Our IoT models are depicted with the extension Eclipse Sirius [15], whereas the DSL and code generation are conducted with the related concepts Xtext and Xtend. [16, 17].

3.1 Pattern Definition

Following, the components of the PRF are explained in detail with Table 1 to Table 7. As the PRF covers different issues, we need a safety PRF type and a security PRF type. Both types consist of four pattern definition categories. However, the categories vary depending on the PRF type. The structure of the different PRF types consists of:

- a Generic Part (Table 1),
- a Safety OR Security Challenge Part (Table 2 OR Table 3),
- a Safety OR Security Assessment Information Part (Table 4 OR Table 5),
- a Pattern OR Anti-Pattern Implementation Part (Table 6 OR Table 7).

The first three parts are used for knowledge conservation and for later flaw and risk categorization or assessment. The fourth part will be used for the implementation details.

Attributes of the different parts are either of free text style that don't underlay bounds or of enumeration style. Enumerations are predefined sets of possible values.

Every PRF type starts by using a *Generic Part*, which is presented in Table 1 to specify the conditions that are independent of safety or security specific characteristics. To be able to identify the defined patterns in the pattern database an ID and name is required. Apart from this a supercategory for the protected element is included. This supercategory is used for pattern categorization within the pattern database and defines the element type and category, as well as the user group type. The element to protect categories are extracted of the IoT-A project. [18] These categories attempt to cover all aspects of an interactive IoT system and were elaborated of a special IoT security architecture approach. Therefore, users, different kind of devices, software and hardware aspects are covered. Since the kind of hard- and software is decisive of the needed actions, the type of physical connections and services is specified. These attributes are dependent on the used meta model. To conduct analyses on diverse model levels, e.g. layered protection analysis, the affected layer of the pattern must be set. Most IoT architecture approaches use 3–4 layers. Since safety and security issues need a more specific categorization, we chose a more detailed approach. For this purpose we used the layered architecture approach of [19] which consists of eight layers. We extended the approach by a user layer. To determine the responsible stakeholder the location of vulnerability is specified. This attribute helps to divide the architecture decisions. The last attribute views the disruption tolerance to categorize the sensitivity of the affected element. While tolerant and temporary tolerant elements perhaps can endure attacks, zero tolerant elements are highly critical.

Table 1. PRF generic part

Pattern Recognition Framework	
Generic	
ID	*free text*
Name	*free text*
Component	Supercategory: Element to protect
Element Type	*free text*
User Group	*free text*
Element category	Choice: Physical Person, Communication Channel, Leaf of Devices, Intermediate Devices, Backend, Infrastructure, Service, Facilities
HW	*free PhysicalConnection type*
SW	*free Service type*
Architecture layer	Choice: One layer of IoT Layered Architecture
Location	Choice: Local or Cloud
Disruption tolerance	Choice: Tolerant, Temporary tolerant, Zero tolerant

Next definition step is the *Safety* or *Security Challenge Part*. Table 2 defines the specific characteristics security challenges bring along to vulnerabilities. The intent and risk represent the aim and risk of loss of possible attacks. To classify the type of attack the STRIDE categorization is used. [20] The letters represent: Spoofing, tampering, repudiation, information disclosure, denial of service and elevation of privilege. For instance, a distinction is made between spoofing and tampering that are indications how to prevent a weak point. As the goal of attack needs classification as well, an enumeration for attack goals is provided, which is inspired by [21]. It is distinguished whether an attack aims at perhaps less critical information disclosure or in destroying/manipulating a whole network or functions. A capture attack tries to get control or access of an IoT device or critical data. This attack does not necessarily have direct impacts. However, they enable other attacks like DDDD (Disrupt-Degrade-Deny-Destroy). DDDD aims at affecting a system and disabling important functions. These goals bring along manipulation and attacks on diverse points. All these categories are used for assessment and database usage, too.

Table 2. PRF security challenge part

Security Pattern Recognition Framework	
Security Challenge	
Intent	*free text*
Risk	*free text*
Classification	Choice: STRIDE: Spoofing, Tampering, Repudiation, Information disclosure, Denial of service, Elevation of privilege
Attack Goal	Choice: Capture, Disrupt-Degrade-Deny-Destroy, Manipulation, Information Disruption, Host Attack, Network Attack

As described above, every security PRF category has a corresponding safety category which includes safety specific characteristics (Table 3). Within this part the fault and fault class are determined. The fault attribute describes the possible origin of failure. Whereas the fault classes define the possible type of failure. These classes range from hardware causes like attrition to software or logical causes like interface issues or miscalculation. In addition, the hazard describes the consequences of possible faults which can also be classified. For instance, the types distinguish between simple failures, complete outages, single service losses or a system corruption. External problems can be mentioned as well, however these issues are difficult to prevent. Though, countermeasures or security measures can be taken into consideration. These both enumeration categories are extracted of [22].

Table 3. PRF safety challenge part

Safety Pattern Recognition Framework	
Safety Challenge	
Fault	*free text*
Hazard	*free text*
Classification	Choice: Failure, Outage, External Problem, Loss of Service, System Corruption
Fault Class	Choice: Attrition, Energy, Calculation, Change Impact, Configuration Management, Data, Interface, Logic, Omission, Timing, Initialization

After specifying the *Generic* and *Safety/Security Challenge Parts* the details for further assessments of possible risks or hazards can be determined.

The assessment information of security flaws is shown in Table 4. Since assessment information can vary by domain and review reason, the details can be registered free without restrictions. Privacy is often related to security and is taken into consideration during assessment as well. Therefore, personally identifiable information (PII) can be mentioned to ensure attention to this aspect. The *Assessment Information Part* has a supercategory as well, to describe the possible direct impacts and their estimated consequences. These values are based on probability values and are subject to estimations or previous experiences. As direct impacts can vary widely depending on the system an exemplary choice range is given in the framework. The most important aspects are security typical issues like availability, functionality, manipulation of nodes and disclosure of data or structure aspects that allow further attacks. However, the range can be just extended. For every direct impact an estimated probability value can be assigned. E.g. 'Availability 30% down'. These values refer to the defined elements to protect of the *Generic Part* and are used for further impact analyses. Next to direct impacts, also indirect impacts exist. These kinds of impacts are more difficult to estimate and often not obvious. Therefore, the type of indirect impacts can be chosen freely and offer hints for system architects for further design decisions. Related to the impacts is the seriousness of attacks. We extracted our categories from [23] as these are typically used distinctions. An attack can be catastrophic and cause complete system failure, as a critical attack generate issues in important parts, which e.g. are connected with confidential data. Marginal or negligible attacks create threats with moderate or conquerable impact. Attacks with no severity are more or less insignificant as they are not attack critical nodes or data. As last attribute of the *Security Assessment Information Part,* the security requirements are chosen. These requirements include the typical CIA (confidentiality, integrity and availability) security aspects. Since these aspects do not cover all possible IoT issues, the enumeration was extended. For instance, authentication and non-repudiation was added. Authentication is one of the most important and vulnerable aspects of IoT as this process enables the interaction with devices and the access to important data. Whereas non-repudiation is required to ensure the traceability of actions, measurements and node extensions.

Table 4. PRF security assessment information part

Security Pattern Recognition Framework	
Assessment Information	
Assessment Information	*free text*
PII	*free text*
Probable Direct Impacts	Supercategory: Estimated Consequences
Impacts	Choice: Disclosure, Manipulation, Availability, Functionality
Values	*free probability values*
Indirect Impacts	*free text*
Severity	Choice: Catastrophic, Critical, Marginal, Negligible, Non
Security Requirements	Choice: Confidentiality, Integrity, Availability, Manipulation Resistance, Privacy, Authentication, Non-Repudiation

The counterpart of the security assessment displays the *Safety Assessment Information Part*, which is shown in Table 5. Some aspects are equal to the security assessment.

However, these aspects are not included in the *Generic Part* as the values of equal attributes still depend on safety or security specific issues. First attribute of the safety assessment also defines the free information details depending on the domain and assessment reason. Since there are several possible reasons, also multiple information can be set. Likewise, a supercategory for elements to protect is included for estimating the consequences of direct impacts. The enumeration of impacts can be extended as well. These impact categories overlap with security impacts since safety and security are related and cannot be separated completely. Impacts on functionality and availability can cause life-threatening behavior, whereas reliability represent the correct outcome of safety-critical actions. Like the security assessment, safety will be assessed with estimated probability values, too. Since the knowledge on this point also comes largely from experts, knowledge conservation is important. A more critical aspect of safety assessment are indirect impacts as these can cause new safety-critical aspects that can harm human beings. Equally, this challenge is often dependent on experience as well. Safety patterns require other categories for assessment like security since they cover the wellbeing of users. The severity divides between deathly, serious, e.g. internal injuries, and non-serious accidents [24]. Depending on this division, the patterns are ranked in a higher priority within design decisions. An approach to rate the likelihood of occurrence is offered by [23]. Which frequency corresponds to which category depends on the internal guidelines. However, the rough categorization are frequent and probable occurrences for highly possible accidents, whereas less possible accidents are divided in occasionally and improbable. Improbable accidents are defined, because the likelihood of occurrence can change in the future. Since safety brings along its own needs, we specify safety requirements. For instance, typical requirements are the ability of recovery of devices or functions, redundancy of sensitive elements and data/device integrity to ensure right calculations/services.

Table 5. PRF safety assessment information part

Safety Pattern Recognition Framework	
Assessment Information	
Assessment Information	*free text*
Probable Direct Impacts	Supercategory: Estimated Consequences
Impacts	Choice: Functionality, Availability, Reliability
Values	*free probability values*
Indirect Impacts	*free text*
Severity	Choice: Death, Serious Injury, Non serious Injury, No Injury
Likelihood of occurrence	Choice: Frequent, Probable, Occasional, Improbable
Safety Requirements	Choice: Recovery, Redundancy, Failure Resistance, Availability, Data Integrity, Device Integrity

Until this point, the pattern definitions create the basis for the knowledge conservation. Therefore, following parts are responsible for the implementation and automated flaw detection. Additionally, the implementation parts are not safety or security specific. However, they are pattern or anti-pattern intrinsic. Thus, the implementation part of patterns defines positive design decisions that prevent accidents or threats. By contrast, the implementation part of anti-patterns specifies negative design decisions, which cause exploitable or erroneous vulnerabilities. Table 6 presents the *Pattern Implementation Part* that is used to design a desirable architecture. For documentation reasons a textual solution initiates the implementation details. On this occasion a short description of the concrete element, relation and attribute types should be given. This description is displayed after the flaw identification to explain the discovery and to prevent misconceptions. A supercategory includes the specification of required combinations of nodes, attributes and their relations. These combinations represent the elements to protect and their risks. Before specifying the concrete elements, an algorithm is set. How the elements are dealt with and are used for the identification depends on these algorithms. For instance, nodes' attributes can need comparison with other conditions or a simple summation of nodes is required. Section 3.3 is reliant on these algorithm types to conduct the code generation appropriate. Following the concrete node, relation and attribute types are defined. The available types depend on the used IoT meta model. All depictable elements and characteristics must be selectable to check the whole IoT model and to define patterns for all aspects. All nodes connected to the pattern must be selected. Accordingly, the next step is to select the relations that connect these nodes. Finally, the attributes which the nodes must fulfil to be affected by the pattern are selected. To highlight the flaw, the last point of the PRF is a textual documentation of the exact flawed feature.

Table 6. PRF pattern implementation part

Safety/Security Pattern Recognition Framework	
Implementation	
Solution	*free text*
Implementation	Supercategory: Required "Node X Attribute X Relation" Combination
Pattern Algorithm	*free text* (examples: Summation of nodes)
Node2Node	Choice: Available Node types
Node2Relation	Choice: Available Relation types
Node2Attribute	Choice: Available Attribute types
Flaw	*free text*

Our last part of the PRF is shown in Table 7 and is the counterpart of the pattern implementation. The *Anti-Pattern Implementation Part* is similar to the pattern definition. However, as an avoidable design will be described not a solution will be documented. Thus, a security-specific anti-pattern explains a vulnerable design, while a safety-specific anti-pattern documents a hazardous design. Both variants are used for documentation and explanation after the flaw recognition in the IoT model. Furthermore, there is also a supercategory for the required combination of node, attribute and relation types as stated above. The process starts in the same way as mentioned before with a pattern algorithm definition. As before, the algorithm is responsible for further code generation activities and the general handling with the defined elements. Following the contained meta model types are chosen including the related connections and features. Once again, the flaw characteristic description of the element to protect finishes the PRF anti-pattern section.

The presented categories and their enumerations are adaptable and extensible if the used domain requires other topics or values to define or review the model.

Table 7. PRF anti-pattern implementation part

Safety/Security Pattern Recognition Framework	
Implementation	
Vulnerable/ Hazardous Design	*free text*
Implementation	Supercategory: Required "Node X Attribute X Relation" Combination
Pattern Algorithm	*free text* (examples: Summation of nodes)
Node2Node	Choice: Available Node types
Node2Relation	Choice: Available Relation types
Node2Attribute	Choice: Available Attribute types
Flaw	*free text*

3.2 Pattern Specific Language

Through Sect. 3.1 the PRF contained categories and values have been clarified. At this stage, however, the defined patterns and anti-patterns cannot yet be used for automatic flaw detection. Therefore, the patterns must be configured using a DSL. As the domain of our approach is pattern detection, we use Xtext to create a pattern definition language. The patterns are stored in the database in this form. Following, we describe the structure and rules of this DSL.

Our language contains all parts described in Sect. 3.1 and is also structurally oriented towards them. The presented category choices are realized with Xtext respectively Ecore enumerations. These can be extended at this point as well, if the analyzed IoT model requires changes. To enable the full configuration of patterns and complete review of IoT systems, the DSL also contains the IoT meta model elements including all node types, attribute types, relation types and type enumerations. If other safety or security specific features are needed, these can be added on our pattern definition language, too. Since the language cannot be presented fully, by means of code examples an insight should be given.

Figure 2 displays a code extraction of a Xtext pattern definition including the initial feature **patterntype** within the initial start rule ‘PatternDefinitionFramework’ (Line 5–7). The Xtext rule ‘PatternType’ (Line 9–11) delegates either to the rule ‘Security-Pattern’, ‘SafetyPattern’, ‘SecurityAntiPattern’ or ‘SafetyAntiPattern’. We consider the rule ‘SecurityPattern’ exemplarily that starts with a keyword. The rule contains four features each adding one of the PRF parts which are available to choose from. Each of the other rules that are delegated from ‘PatternType’ are structured in this way, however, with its customized choice range.

Afterwards the rules for the generic part, challenge parts, assessment information parts and implementation parts are defined. To offer an insight in one of these parts Fig. 3 views the rule ‘AssessmentInformationSecurityPart’ to configure the assessment details. The rule contains multiple features and keywords (introduced in Table 4). These features are labelled as identifier, String value or a kind of enumeration. The feature **securityRequirements** can add an arbitrary number of values, as several requirements can be needed. The feature **directImpacts** is a special feature as it is a type of the rule ‘ProbableDirectImpacts’ (Line 109–116). This rule configures impacts which can be chosen from security or safety impact enumerations. As impacts don’t necessarily appear

```
//Choice of pattern type
PatternDefinitionFramework:
    patterntype=PatternType;

PatternType:
    SecurityPattern|SafetyPattern|SecurityAntiPattern|SafetyAntiPattern
;

//SecurityPattern definition
SecurityPattern:
    'SecurityPattern' '{'
    generic+=GenericPart
    challenge+=SecurityChallengePart
    assessment+=AssessmentInformationSecurityPart
    implementation+=ImplementationPatternPart
    '}'
;
```

Fig. 2. Xtext code to define the PRF as DSL

```
//Assessment Information Security Part
AssessmentInformationSecurityPart:
    'AssessmentInformationSecurityPart' '{'
    'assessmentFeature' assessment=ID
    'pii' pii=STRING
    directImpacts=ProbableDirectImpacts
    'indirectImpacts' impact=STRING
    'severity' ':'  severity=SecuritySeverity
    'securityRequirements' '{' (requirements+=SecurityRequirements(',')?)* '}'
    '}'
;

ProbableDirectImpacts:
    'ProbableDirectImpacts' '{'
        ('Impacts' ':'  (impactSE+=SecurityImpact)? (',')? (impactSA+=SafetyImpact)?
        'values' ':'
        change+=Change
        value+=INT '%')*
    '}'
;
```

Fig. 3. Xtext code to define the Security Assessment Information Part

```
//Implementation Anti-Pattern Safety Part
ImplementationSafetyAntiPatternPart:
    'ImplementationSafetyAntiPatternPart' '{'
    'hazardousDesign' design=STRING
    implementation=Implementation
    'flaw' (('and')? flaw+=[Node|STRING] ('=' flawValue+=STRING)?)*
    '}'
;

Implementation:
    'PatternRule' rule=ID '{'
    'algorithmType' type=ID
    ('condition' conditionNum+=ID)*
    (('if')? ('and')? ('then')? ('then' 'not')?
        ('equals')? ('or')? node+=Node
    )*
    '}'
;
```

Fig. 4. Xtext code example of the anti-pattern Implementation Part

these values are optional. The concrete values are described with the rule 'Change' and an Integer probability. This rule enables to depict the direction (up or down) of changes.

As last part the implementation parts must be specified with Xtext rules. Figure 4 displays exemplarily a rule for safety anti-patterns. The hazardous design can be described with a String value, whereas the implementation elements themselves depend on the 'Implementation' rule. Every **rule** feature requires an identifier for identification reasons, as well as the **type**. The conditions and correlations of pattern elements are defined with keywords like 'if', 'then' or 'equals'. A **flaw** is determined with specific nodes that were defined with the 'Implementation' rule.

Beside the described or mentioned rules, enumerations, PRF specific rules and meta model rules are components of the pattern definition language.

3.3 Pattern Service Generation

After concluding the first two manually conducted steps the theoretical pattern definition is completed. To enable the automated flaw identification, applicable pattern services are required. To transform the structured, defined patterns and anti-patterns into executable code an automated code generation will be conducted. Part four (Table 6 and Table 7) contains the required implementation details to enable the recognition of patterns or anti-patterns in a model. The transferred details of a DSL (Sect. 3.2) are translated automatically into the needed services through the functions of Xtend. As described before in Sect. 3.1, the code generation acts depending on the chosen pattern algorithm. Once, a pattern or anti-pattern was defined and saved in the pattern database, an automated code generation is conducted and saved as well. Therefore, every specified and saved pattern can be used for design optimization immediately. This code generation process is provided for all kind of pattern.

3.4 Pattern Identification

The last step of our PRF represents the final automated identification of vulnerable or hazardous design flaws in IoT models. The created services (Step C) will be used to analyze and optimize the design automated. The results of the pattern recognition process depend on the kind of defined pattern. In case of identification of an anti-pattern all elements and relations, which match with the definition, are highlighted as they are follow a negative design decision. However, if a pattern identification is conducted to recognize flaws, only the elements that are not matching the definition are highlighted, as the definition represent desirable design. Every IoT Model that complies with the developed IoT meta model can use the content of the pattern database to detect flaws.

4 Evaluation

After explaining the details of the PRF we demonstrate the application to evaluate our approach steps. As described before the usage of IoT in medical cases implicate safety- and security-critical aspects. Therefore, we designed a smart home in manner of an AAL use case for elderly. To create an approved use case for evaluation we take into consideration the approaches of [25–27]. As the devices in our AAL smart home aiming in prevention, it is a wellbeing use case. We define medical devices as wellbeing devices if their main purpose is monitoring, tracking or detecting, i.e. prevention, and do not have direct impact on the body. Figure 5 shows the rough structure and contained devices respectively infrastructure. In our smart home an elderly resident is monitored through multiple devices with different locations and goals throughout the house. For instance, the defibrillator is a fully implanted device to monitor the heart, whereas the insulin pump is a kind of wearable to measure the current insulin level. The other devices are located in diverse places, as the fall detector is positioned in every room and the mobile phone and pillbox vary. To collect and process the data two kind of cloud respectively gateway are included. In addition, the smart home is connected with diverse stakeholder with different goals and rights, like ambulance for critical situations or relatives who may inform about the resident. The network details of our use case were presented in [19].

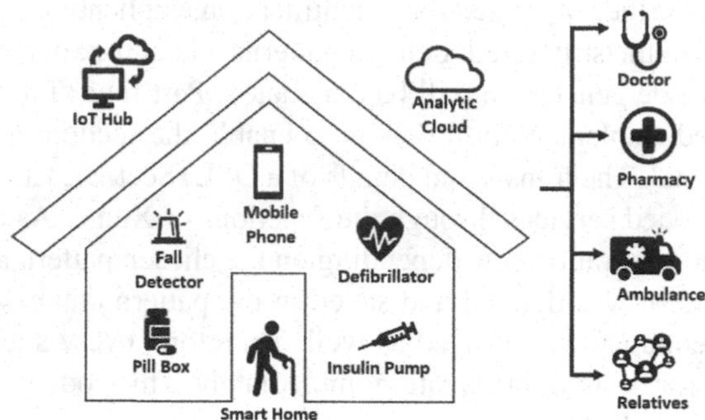

Fig. 5. AAL use case scenario used for evaluation

Our detailed AAL use case architecture and dependencies are modelled based on the developed meta model for IoT systems. Figure 8 shows an excerpt of the IoT system of our AAL use case which conforms to our meta model. In this excerpt some of the included devices with their physical connections, services and users are depicted.

To evaluate the Sect. 3.1–3.4 of Sect. 3, we will present two challenges. For these challenges we will define a pattern respectively an anti-pattern with our PRF to validate the structured way of knowledge conservation. Afterwards, the patterns will be transferred into DSL to enable the code generation for the flaw identification services. To present the added value of our framework, we show the results of the automated flaw identification process applied on our AAL use case model. Following, two safety respectively security challenge examples are considered in detail:

- Example 1 (Security): IoT devices with limited space and energy are easy entry points for cyber attacks as the encryption is missed or neglected
- Example 2 (Safety): Authentication can be a safety issue if life-saving functions are blocked by these methods

For example 1 a pattern will be defined and example 2 is covered through an anti-pattern definition. For both example challenges the PRF is used to define the pattern respectively anti-pattern. Table 8 shows the pattern definition of example 1. The pattern receives an ID and the name *'Lightweight devices without encrypted communication'*. The affected devices in our use case are *defibrillators* which are a kind of *wellbeing IoT devices* and a *leaf of devices*. These are only used for monitoring reasons as they are wellbeing devices and not medical devices in our use case. To communicate with other devices or gateways a *Bluetooth connection* is applied. As described before a *monitoring service* is required which can be affected. Since IoT devices are the basis of every IoT system they are on in the bottom of the layered architecture (*Thing Layer*). However, the location of security attack can be either local or in a cloud. As the defibrillator is only a wellbeing device it is *temporary tolerant* towards attacks. The security challenge aims in *capturing and changing private data on the communication way* that can cause the *theft of PII* and *manipulated analyses results,* as the attack can be classified as *tampering* and the attacker's goals are *capture* and *manipulation.* To assess the impacts of this kind of attack the *integrity* must be taken into consideration to evaluate the correctness of the *measured cardiac conditions.* Since the alteration of data can have impacts on the *functionality* most likely, an estimated change of *70% down* is expected. In addition, *other health recommendations are affected* since the holistic health status is impacted as well. Altered cardiac measurements are of a *critical* nature as these data are used for long-term analytics, e.g. atrial fibrillation monitoring. Security requirements which are affected through a possible attack are *confidentiality, integrity, manipulation resistance* and *privacy.*

Table 8. Pattern definition of security example 1

Pattern Recognition Framework	
Generic	
ID	876543
Name	Lightweight devices without encrypted communication
Component	Supercategory: Element to protect
Element Type	WellbeingIoTDevice (Defibrillators (monitor cardiac conditions))
User Group	Patients
Element category	Choice: Leaf of Devices
HW	Bluetooth Connection
SW	Monitoring Service
Architecture layer	Choice: Thing Layer
Location	Choice: Local, Cloud
Disruption tolerance	Choice: Temporary tolerant
Security Challenge	
Intent	Capture private information, Change of data on comm. way
Risk	Theft of PII, Manipulate data and change analysis results
Classification	Choice: Tampering
Attack Goal	Choice: Capture, Manipulation
Assessment Information	
Assessment Information	Integrity
PII	Cardiac Condition, Measurement values
Probable Direct Impacts	Supercategory: Estimated Consequences
Impacts	Choice: Functionality
Values	70% down
Indirect Impacts	Impact on other health recommendations
Severity	Choice: Critical
Security Requirements	Choice: Confidentiality, Integrity, Manipulation Resistance, Privacy

After we conserved the knowledge of the security attack we define the implementation details to recognize the vulnerability (Table 9). The solution for our example 1 is based on the recommendation of [25]. They suggest prohibiting devices with weak or no encryption algorithms the direct communication to a cloud. These devices should use a field gateway as an intermediary. The field gateway will encrypt the data and deliver them to the analytic cloud. Therefore, the pattern recognition uses an *attribute validation* algorithm to check the types of used gateway. The included nodes are of node types *WellbeingIoTDevice, PhysicalConnection, Encryption* and *Gateway.* Node2Relation specifies the relations between the chosen node types. In addition, the nodes must have corresponding attributes to be included in the pattern. *WellbeingIoTDevices* have to be of the *deviceType: Defibrillator,* whereas their *PhysicalConnections* must use a *Bluetooth protocol.* If the *encryptionType* is *undefined,* the *Gateways* have to be of the type *FieldGateway.* However, if the *gatewayType* is not of type *FieldGateway* a vulnerable design is present.

Table 9. Pattern definition of security example 1

Pattern Recognition Framework	
Implementation	
Solution	Device with weak encryption algorithm has to use a field gateway to connect with a cloud gateway
Implementation	Supercategory: Required "Node X Attribute X Relation" Combination
Pattern Algorithm	Attribute Validation
Node2Node	Choice: WellbeingIoTDevice, PhysicalConnection, Encryption, Gateway
Node2Relation	Choice: physicalconnection, encryption, peereddevice
Node2Attribute	Choice: deviceType: Defibrillator, protocol: Bluetooth, encryptionType: undefined, gatewayType: FieldGateway
Flaw	Flaw: gatewayType= not FieldGateway

After a pattern was defined to prevent security challenges like example 1, the pattern will be transformed into the DSL. Following, we present a Xtext extract of an anti-pattern for example 2 (Fig. 6) and afterwards another snippet of the transformed example 1 (Fig. 7).

As mentioned above we define an anti-pattern for our safety example 2. This negative design decision plans multi-way authentication methods before enabling ambulance calls. Therefore, we use the Xtext rule 'SafetyAntiPattern'. Figure 6 shows the transformed PRF for the *Generic Part, Safety Challenge Part* and *Safety Assessment Information Part.* For the generic information the **ID**, **name**, **component** details and the other categories were transformed. E.g. as an ambulance call corresponds to an acting service of a mobile phone, a 3G connection is required and the affected layer is the *SensingActingLayer.* The DSL also transformed the safety challenge information like possible hazard (*Help cannot be contacted in time*) and classification of this (*Loss of Service).* As last part of the knowledge conservation of our safety anti-pattern the assessment information are transformed. As a service authentication implies *confidentiality* changes this feature will be used for assessment. Depending on the used authentication method indirect impacted misuse of ambulance calls can happen. The implementation part of the anti-pattern specifies the hazardous design of 2-way authentications connected with ambulance calls.

```
SafetyAntiPattern{
    GenericPart{
        id SAAP927392
        name UrgentSituationAuthentication
        Component{
            elementType{ Service }
            userGroup{ undefined }
            elementCategory{ Service,Facilities }
        }
        hardware "3G Connection"
        software "Acting Decision Service"
        layer: SensingActingLayer
        location{ Cloud }
        disruptionTolerance:Temporary tolerant
    }
    SafetyChallengePart{
        fault "Complicated authentication method for ambulance call"
        hazard "Help cannot be contacted fast enough"
        classification{ LossofService }
        faultClass{ ConfigurationManagement,Initialization }
    }
    AssessmentInformationSafetyPart{
        assessmentFeature ConfidentialityAssessment
        ProbableDirectImpacts{ Impacts:Confidentiality values: up 10% }
        indirectImpacts "Misuse of ambulance"
        severity: SeriousInjury
        likelihood: Probable
        safetyRequirements{ Availability }
    }
```

Fig. 6. Defined safety anti-pattern Xtext code example 2

```
47      ImplementationPatternPart{
48          solution "Device with weak encryption algorithm has to use a field gateway
49              to connect with a cloud gateway"
50          PatternRule SEP8765432_1{
51              algorithmType AttributeValidation
52              if
53              WellbeingIoTDevice WellbeingIoTDeviceNameSEP8765432{
54                  deviceType Defibrillator
55                  physicalconnection ( "PhysicalConnectionNameSEP8765432" )
56                  gateway ( "GatewayNameSEP8765432" )}
57              and
58              PhysicalConnection PhysicalConnectionNameSEP8765432{
59                  protocol Bluetooth
60                  encryption{
61                      AsymmetricEncryption AsymmetricEncryptionNameSEP8765432{
62                          type undefined }}}
63              then
64              Gateway GatewayNameSEP8765432{
65                  gatewayType FieldGateway
66                  peereddevice( "WellbeingIoTDeviceNameSEP8765432")}}
67          flaw
68              "GatewayNameSEP8765432" = "not FieldGateway"
69              and
70              "PhysicalConnectionNameSEP8765432.AsymmetricEncryptionNameSEP8765432" = "undefined"}
```

Fig. 7. Defined security pattern Implementation Xtext code example 1

The same transformation has to be conducted for example 1. Figure 7 displays the implementation part of our security pattern, whereas lines 52-66 show the conditional pattern rule. As described above **if** a *WellbeingIoTDevice* with a *Physical Bluetooth Connection* has no defined *Encryption* **then** the *Gateway* has to be a *FieldGateway*, otherwise a flaw exists.

Afterwards, the DSLs of example 1 and 2 are translated into pattern services, i.e. flaw identification services, with Xtend to enable their automated usage. In addition, they are stored in the pattern database.

Since the pattern definition process is finished, we are able to evaluate our last concept step: The flaw identification and model optimization. Figure 8 shows our modelled and analyzed AAL use case with all included physical entities, physical connections, services, clouds, stakeholder, users and their relations among themselves. The elements are colorized depending on their layer type. To optimize this model we apply our automated flaw identification process through the execution of the generated services with Eclipse Sirius Services which highlight the vulnerable elements and their relations in red color: The flaw identification services found the elements and relations 'PhyCo_Hub2Defi', 'SHDefibrillator' and 'SHIoTHub' as this design is not matching our positive design pattern for IoT devices without adequate encryption types and the used gateway type, as 'SHIoTHub' is not a field gateway. As well, identified weaknesses are e.g. 'PhyCo_AmbulanceCall', 'Ambulance Call_Service' and 'SHSmartPhone'. As the service 'Ambulance Call_Service' requires a multi-way authentication and endangers residents, this design matches our negative anti-pattern definition of blocked ambulance calls.

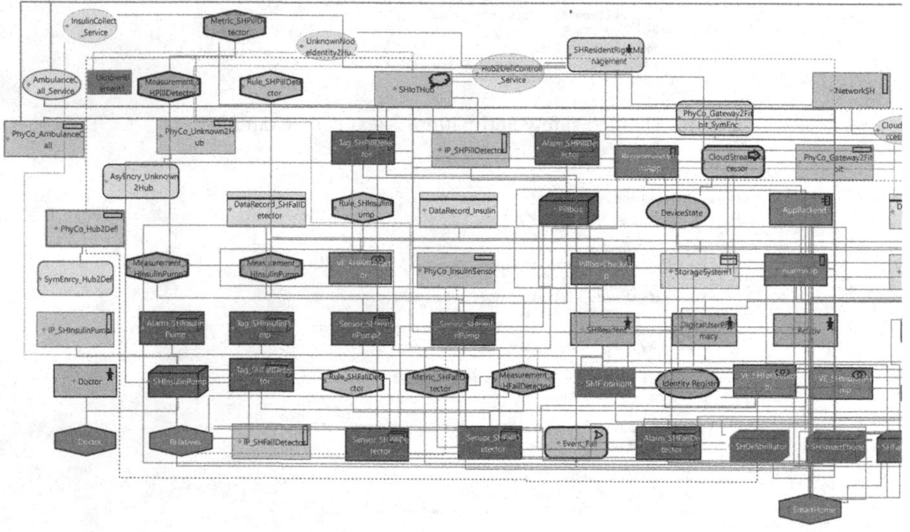

Fig. 8. Flaw identification within the AAL use case model

After applying the pattern recognition the avoidable design decisions can be optimized. The evaluation of our concept was conducted exemplarily on a medical use case. However, the application of the framework is able be deployed in all domains of IoT to optimize the design and identify design smells.

5 Conclusion

In the previous sections, we presented our approach to identify design flaws. While Sect. 3.1, 3.2 and 3.4 are already realized, implemented and applied successfully, Sect. 3.3 is still in progress. Therefore, the next step of future work includes the change of semi-automated code generation to a fully automated code generation process. In addition, to deal with safety and security flaws completely further action is required after the identification. Therefore, future work should include also the assessment of design flaws to evaluate the impacts or severity in detail for diverse quality attributes. Reference [19] already designed a first approach to assess model designs. For this purpose, the approach will be adapted and extended in the future. In addition, to simplify the analysis of already existing IoT systems and the extraction of their models, architecture mining can be considered.

In this paper, we presented an approach to address the issue of safety and security vulnerabilities in IoT systems. As IoT often is applied in safety- and security-critical systems, like medical smart homes, the system must be optimized in the design phase already. Therefore, we introduced our pattern recognition framework which enables the preservation of design knowledge and the structured and automated way to identify flaws in models. The framework consists of four steps. First, the patterns and anti-patterns, which represent desirable or avoidable design, were defined in structured parts. There are parts for generic details, for safety- or security specific information of challenges or assessments and for implementation details to consider the concrete elements and their conditions. Second, a domain specific language was used to realize the defined patterns and anti-patterns. To enable the automated detection of these patterns within the IoT model, a code generation happened in the next step. The last step of our framework represented the identification of vulnerabilities through the defined pattern recognition services. The applicability of our approach was evaluated by an AAL use case. Therefore, we were able to identify two vulnerable design decisions of the IoT system before threats could occur.

Acknowledgment. Electronic Component and Systems for European Leadership (ECSEL) supported the development of this approach within the project CPS4EU (Grant Agreement Number 826276).

References

1. S. R. Department, Internet of Things (IoT) connected devices installed base worldwide from 2015 to 2025 (2020). https://bit.ly/38TUYgO. Accessed 25 Feb 2020
2. Gang, G., Zeyong, L.U.: Internet of Things Security Analysis (2011)
3. Viega, J., McGraw, G.: Building Secure Software: How to Avoid Security Problems the Right Way. Addison-Wesley Professional, Massachusetts (2011)
4. Rauscher, R., Bauer, B.: Safety and security architecture analyses framework for the internet of things of medical devices. In: 2018 IEEE 20th International Conference e-Health Networking, Applications and Services (Healthcom), pp. 3–5 (2018)
5. RAPID7, HACKING IoT: A Case Study on Baby Monitor Exposures and Vulnerabilities (2015). https://bit.ly/1JC9jfS. Accessed 24 Feb 2020
6. FDA: Cybersecurity Vulnerabilities Identified in St. Jude Medical's Implantable Cardiac Devices and Merlin@home Transmitter: FDA Safety Communication (2017). https://bit.ly/2qqkgiA. Accessed 18 Feb 2020
7. Zhang, M., Hall, T., Baddoo, N.: Code bad smells: a review of current knowledge. J. Softw. Maint. Evol. Res. Pract. **23**(3), 179–202 (2011)
8. Zanoni, M., Perin, F., Fontana, F.A., Viscusi, G.: Pattern detection for conceptual schema recovery in data-intensive systems. J. Softw. Evol. Process **26**(12), 1172–1192 (2014)

9. Wortman, P.A., Tehranipoor, F., Karimian, N., Chandy, J.A.: Proposing a modeling framework for minimizing security vulnerabilities in IoT systems in the healthcare domain, pp. 185–188 (2017)
10. Lee, WT., Law, P.J.: A case study in applying security design patterns for IoT software system, p. 978–1 (2017)
11. Rauscher, J., Bauer, B., Langermeier, M.: Characteristics of enterprise architecture analyses. In: Proceedings Sixth International Symposium Business Model. Software Descriptions, pp. 104–113 (2016)
12. Sommestad, T., Ekstedt, M., Johnson, P.: Combining defense graphs and enterprise architecture models for security analysis. In: Conference of EDOC 2008, pp. 349–355 (2008)
13. Ekstedt, M., Sommestad, T.: Enterprise architecture models for cyber security analysis. In: 2009 IEEE/PES Power System Conference Exposition, pp. 1–6 (2009)
14. Johnson, P., Lagerström, R., Närman, P., Simonsson, M.: Extended influence diagrams for enterprise architecture analysis. In: EDOC, pp. 3–12 (2006)
15. EMF, Eclipse EMF (2020). https://bit.ly/3bUNnjU. Accessed 24 Feb 2020
16. Gronback, R.: Eclipse Modeling Project: A Domain-Specific Language (DSL) Toolkit. Pearson Education, London (2009)
17. Xtend/Xtext, Xtend/Xtext (2020). https://bit.ly/2HQcaIc. Accessed 30 Jan 2020
18. Carrez, F.: Internet of Things – Architecture IoT-A Deliverable D1.5-Final architectural reference model for the IoT v3 no. 257521 (2013)
19. Lohmüller, P., Rauscher, J., Bauer, B.: Failure and Change Impact Analysis for Safety-Critical Systems. In: Shishkov, B. (ed.) BMSD 2019. LNBIP, vol. 356, pp. 47–63. Springer, Cham (2019). https://doi.org/10.1007/978-3-030-24854-3_4
20. Microsoft, Microsoft STRIDE (2007). https://bit.ly/37SKuwE. Accessed 17 Feb 2020
21. Covington, M.J., Carskadden, R.: Threat implications of the Internet of Things. In: International Conference Cyber Conflict, CYCON, pp. 1–12 (2013)
22. Wallace, D.R., Kuhn, R.D.: Failure modes in medical device software: an analysis of 15 years of recall data. Int. J. Reliab. Qual. Saf. Eng. **08**(04), 351–371 (2001)
23. Department of Defense USA.: Department of Defense Standard Practice System Safety Amsc. Mctechsystems.Com, pp. 1–98 (2012)
24. IEC.: Standard 62304, Medical device software—Software life cycle processes (2006)
25. Microsoft.: Microsoft Azure IoT Reference Architecture, pp. 1–61 (2018)
26. Dohr, A., et al.: The internet of things for ambient assisted living. In: 2010 Seventh International Conference on Information Technology: New Generations. IEEE (2010)
27. Pires, G., et al.: VITASENIOR-MT: A telehealth solution for the elderly focused on the interaction with TV. In: 2018 IEEE 20th Healthcom. IEEE (2018)

From Business Modeling to Software Design

Bert de Brock(✉)

Faculty of Economics and Business, University of Groningen,
PO Box 800, 9700 AV Groningen, The Netherlands
E.O.de.Brock@rug.nl

Abstract. Graphical system sequence diagrams (SSDs), used in Requirements Engineering and Analysis, are hard to draw for larger use cases. However, we wanted to be able to express SSDs for such use cases as well. While we were designing a grammar for *textual* SSDs, we noted that we needed the same kind of structuring mechanisms as for modeling business processes and programming languages. Only the basic building block differs: e.g., an assignment statement for (imperative) programming languages and a (basic) interaction step for SSDs. Can we generalize this similarity idea, leading to (uniform) grammars for instruction languages in general, and exploit this? This paper presents a grammar for 'structured' Ws (where W stands for 'Whatever'), leading to grammars for (textual) instruction languages. The general grammar contains constructs necessary for specifying all kinds of instructions. We illustrate our theory with examples from several different application areas. A basic building block might even be a picture or an icon, as we will point out. The main contribution of the paper is a powerful and uniform grammar for instruction languages in general, containing generic constructs for specifying various instructions conveniently. Exploiting the similarity between the structuring mechanisms for modeling business processes, (textual) SSDs, and programming languages will ease the translation towards an implementation in a software system. Usually the grammar rules for basic building blocks are *domain specific* and must be specified and added per application.

Keywords: Language design · Grammars · Structuring mechanisms · Instruction languages · Business Modeling · System sequence diagram · Programming language

1 Introduction

While we were designing a 'grammar' for (a 'language' for) textual system sequence diagrams (SSDs), which is in the area of requirements engineering and requirements analysis, it became clear that we needed the same kind of structuring mechanisms as for business process modeling (BPM) and programming languages. Only the basic building block differs: An assignment statement in case of (imperative) programming languages, a basic interaction step in case of SSDs, and a basic action in case of BPM.

B. Shishkov (Ed.): BMSD 2020, LNBIP 391, pp. 103–122, 2020.
https://doi.org/10.1007/978-3-030-52306-0_7

That brought us to the idea to generalize this similarity, leading to uniform grammars for instruction languages in general, and to exploit this opportunity. We could benefit when the languages for these different levels would be aligned. Currently, UML sequence diagrams [1, 2] - which are graphical - are often used in between use cases (text) and programs (also text). So, this is not really aligned. Instead of graphical UML sequence diagrams, we propose our SSDs, which are textual. This alignment will help to bring us *From Business Modeling to Software Design*, as the title of this paper says.

By the way, we are not so much trying to introduce "yet another language" but most of all trying to align several (textual) languages on different levels, in order to ease the translations from the higher (external) level via an intermediate level to the lower (internal) level. We did not find this anywhere else on these requirements levels. We also did not encounter it in the systematic literature review [3], where 119 papers in this area were thoroughly examined. (But one can see such translations from higher levels to lower levels when going from functional languages (4GL) to imperative programming languages (3GL) to - e.g. - ASCII (2GL) and to machine code (1GL) respectively).

A **system sequence diagram** depicts the interaction between the user of a system, the system itself, and other actors (if any), including the messages (with their parameters) between them. Although SSDs are usually drawn as two-dimensional UML-diagrams [1, 2], in [4] we propose *textual* representations, in order to study and analyse them, to reason about them, and to make integration of scenarios easier. An SSD is a kind of stylized use case that makes the prospective inputs, state changes, and outputs regarding the system more explicit. (For the notion of use case, see for instance [3, 5, 6]). Example 3 shows a concrete SSD.

In [4] we propose *textual* representations, mainly emphasizing scenario integration. In [7] we worked out a substantial, industrial strength case study using textual representations in order to show the feasibility. In the current paper we emphasize how to exploit the similarity between the structuring mechanisms for modeling business processes, (textual) SSDs, and programming languages to ease the translation towards an implementation in a software system. In [8] we will add a formal semantics for the constructs.

Generalizing this similarity idea, we design a grammar for 'structured' Ws in this paper (where W stands for 'Whatever'). The general grammar contains constructs necessary for specifying all kinds of instructions: *sequential composition*, *arbitrary order*, *blocks*, *conditionals*, *alternatives*, *case analyses*, *loops* (driven by a condition), *iterations* (for each element in a given set, allowing parallel execution), *options*, *choices*, 'free floating' instructions (such as *interrupts*), (parameterized) *definitions* (including *recursive* definitions), *declarations*, and *calls* (a.k.a. *Includes*). We build up the grammar step by step.

The paper is organized as follows: Sect. 2 starts with a few basic grammar rules. Section 3 contains various examples of Basic Building Blocks, respectively applied to

(1) work instructions, (2) textual SSDs, and (3) computer programs.

We do this by using the same grammar rules in all 3 examples and only changing the basic building blocks (and sometimes the used conditions). Section 4 introduces several additional grammatical constructs, among others the structuring mechanism of (parameterized) 'definitions' (or 'abbreviations'), including *recursive* definitions. This section also treats instructions that are 'free floating' (such as interrupts). They all are illustrated with examples. Section 5 presents the complete version of our grammar fragment for instruction languages (i.e., languages for specifying instructions).

Section 6 illustrates the alignment and shows how the similarity between the structuring mechanisms eases the translation of use cases via textual SSDs towards programs in a software system (Examples 9–11). As a proof of concept, technical report [7] explained and worked out a substantial, industrial strength case study, delivering a textual SSD along the lines presented here. That report can be considered as supplementary to the current paper and gives an impression of the expressiveness, feasibility, and scalability of our proposal in large, complex, real-life situations.

Finally, Sect. 7 mentions another application area as well: These ideas could be applied to the generation of *assembly instructions* too.

2 Some Basic Grammatical Constructs

We start with our grammatical core. As usual, non-terminals will be of the form <…>. Terminals are written in bold. <W> is the start symbol (Fig. 1):

```
<W>::- <BBB>                                   /* Basic Building Block
     | <BBB>; <W>                              /* Sequential composition
     | begin <W> end                           /* Block ('brackets')
     | if <condition> then <W> end             /* Conditional
     | if <condition> then <W> else <W> end    /* Alternative
     | while <condition> do <W> end            /* Loop (driven by a condition)
     | maybe <W> end                           /* Option
     | either <W> or <W> end                   /* Choice
```

Fig. 1. Our core grammar fragment

The difference between a conditional (**if** C **then** W **end**) and an option (**maybe** W **end**): If you can make explicit under which condition W must happen then you can use the conditional; if you only know that W might happen but not under which condition then you can use the option. Hence, a conditional is deterministic whereas an option is non-deterministic. Rephrased informally: An option corresponds to a conditional without a clearly specifiable condition. Conditional and option, together with arbitrary order (see Sect. 4), relate to the OR-gateway (with resp. without explicit condition) in BPM [9].

The difference between an alternative (**if** C **then** W1 **else** W2 **end**) and a choice (**either** W1 **or** W2 **end**) is similar: If you can make explicit under which condition W1 must happen (or else W2) then you can use the alternative; if you only know that either W1 or W2 must happen but not which one under which condition then you can use the choice. Hence, an alternative is deterministic whereas a choice is non-deterministic. Rephrased informally: A choice corresponds to an alternative without a clearly specifiable condition. Alternative and choice relate to the XOR-gateway (with resp. without explicit condition) in Business Process Modeling [9].

Example 1: A generic grammar fragment

As an illustration of our core grammar fragment, we can generate the following structure with this grammar (where we use all grammar rules except the **begin** … **end**):

<BBB>;
while <condition> **do** <BBB>; <BBB> **end;**
maybe <BBB> **end;**
<BBB>;
if <condition> **then** <BBB> **else** <BBB> **end;**
either <BBB> **or** <BBB>; <BBB> **end;**
if <condition> **then** <BBB>; <BBB> **end**

Paper [8] will add a formal semantics for these constructs.

In fact, our core grammar fragment is not yet finished: The grammar rules for the non-terminals <BBB> and <condition> must still be specified. However, they are *domain specific* (see next section).

3 Various Examples of Basic Building Blocks

We will complete Example 1 with additional grammar rules for <BBB> , resulting in a kind of (very) little domain-specific specification language [10] (a.k.a. *little language* or *micro-language*). It concerns a simple 'business process':

Example 2: Work instructions

We want to express work instructions for building a stack of tiles. Available are red, yellow, and blue tiles. Now we give grammar rules for the non-terminal <BBB>:

<BBB> ::= **put** <type> **tile**
<type> ::= **a** <color> | **any**
<color> ::= **red** | **yellow** | **blue**

We give an example of a W, i.e., an instruction that can be generated with this grammar. We use the structure we presented in Example 1. The structuring key words (**while** etc.) are written in bold face. We write the used *conditions* in italics:

> put a yellow tile;
> **while** *the stack is lower than 1 meter* **do** put a red tile; put a blue tile **end;**
> **maybe** put any tile **end;**
> put a yellow tile;
> **if** *it rains* **then** put a blue tile **else** put any tile **end;**
> **either** put a yellow tile **or** put a red tile; put a blue tile **end;**
> **if** *the sun shines* **then** put a red tile; put a blue tile **end**

We have the following so-called postcondition for this work instruction:

> When following the stack upwards, the final stack consists of a yellow tile on the bottom, then zero or more pairs of a red tile with a blue one on top of it (even if we reached the 1 meter already after a red one), then maybe another tile, then a yellow tile, then any tile (or specifically a blue one if it rained at that moment), then either a yellow tile or a red one with a blue one on top of it, and (only if the sun shined at that moment) another red one with a blue one on top of it.

The appendix shows the resulting stack possibilities in a figure.

Next, we want to be able to express system sequence diagrams (SSDs) in a textual form. This application is in the area of Requirements Engineering for a (software) system to be developed. We do this by completing Example 1 with a different set of grammar rules for <BBB>.

Example 3: System Sequence Diagrams

Now we give other grammar rules for the non-terminal <BBB>, where the users of the system can be cashiers and customers:

<BBB> ::= <actor> → <actor>**:** <message> /* Basic step
<actor> ::= **System** /* System under consideration
| <user> /* Actor (≠ **System**) in the SSD
<user> ::= **Cashier** /* 'Domain specific'
| **Customer** /* 'Domain specific' (but more general)

where 'X → Y**:** M' means: Actor X sends message M to actor Y.
If X and Y are equal then it expresses that X itself is executing M.

Again we take the same grammatical structure as before (Example 1), but with different basic building blocks than in Example 2. We take an excerpt from Larman's well-known example *Process Sale* ([1], Section 10.5). We write the structuring key words (**while** etc.) in bold face and the used *conditions* in italics again:

Cashier → System: makeNewSale;
while *more items of customer*
  do Cashier → System: enterItem(itemID; quantity);
    System → Cashier: description; total
end;
maybe Cashier → System: enterCustomerStatus('tax-exempt') **end;**
Cashier → System: endSale;
if *customer has tax-exempt*
  then System → Cashier: total
  else System → Cashier: total with taxes
end;
either Customer → System: makeCreditPayment(credit card; pin code)
  or Cashier → System: makeCashPayment(amount);
    System → Cashier: change due
end;
if *Customer wants receipt*
  then Cashier → System: printReceipt**;** System → Cashier: receipt
end

The last step (**if** *Customer wants receipt* **then** …) might be preceded by the steps

Cashier → Customer: 'Do you want a receipt?';
Customer → Cashier: answer;

This addition shows that interactions between other actors than the system (human actors in this case) could be represented in an SSD as well.

Next, we want to be able to express computer programs. Again we do this by completing Example 1 with a set of grammar rules for <BBB>.

Example 4: Computer programs

To be able to express computer programs we need the following basic building block:

<BBB> ::= <variable> := <expression> /* assignment statement

Below we give an example of a W, i.e., a computer program that can be generated with this grammar. We use the same structure as we used in Example 1. In order to emphasize the structure again, we write the structuring key words (**while** etc.) in bold face and the used *conditions* in italics. With this program we (seem to) compute the height of the stack of tiles (in centimetres) in case the tile height is 2 centimetres.

x := 2;
while *the stack is lower than 1 meter* **do** x := x + 2; x := x + 2 **end;**
maybe x := x + 2 **end;**
x := x + 2;
if *it rains* **then** x := x + 2 **else** x := x + 2 **end;**
either x := x + 2 **or** x := x + 2; x := x + 2 **end;**
if *the sun shines* **then** x := x + 2; x := x + 2 **end**

We can simplify this program considerably:

x := 2;
while *x < 100* **do** x := x + 4 **end;**
maybe x := x + 2 **end;**
x := x + 4; (*)
either x := x + 2 **or** x := x + 4 **end;**
if *the sun shines* **then** x := x + 4 **end**

(*) Because the statement **if** *it rains* ... always results in x := x + 2

This is an example of an imperative program [11]. Section 6 contains an example of an SQL-program, which is a non-imperative program.

In general, the non-deterministic constructs of *option* (**maybe** ... **end**) and *choice* (**either** ... **or** ...**end**) do make sense when it concerns human beings, but less when it concerns machines. In the first case, it means that 'at runtime' the person (user) can choose, in the second case it means that 'at runtime' the system must choose, making the system non-deterministic.

So, normally you will not find an **either-or**-construct or **maybe**-construct in programming languages (i.e., languages to instruct computers).

4 Additional Grammatical Constructs

4.1 Arbitrary Order

We note that 'W1; W2' means: first do W1, then do W2. But sometimes the order is not relevant, i.e., W1 and W2 may be applied in any order. We can denote this 'freedom' as 'W1, W2' meaning: do W1 and do W2, in arbitrary order. (This also allows parallel execution.) Hence, ';' is used when the order is relevant and ',' can be used to indicate that the order is irrelevant. For example, if in the second instruction in Example 2 the semicolon would be replaced by a comma, so

while *the stack is lower than 1 m* **do** put a red tile, put a blue tile **end**

it means that for each pair of a red and a blue tile in the loop the colors can be in any order (i.e., each time again).

Arbitrary order (',') relates to the AND-gateway in Business Process Modeling [9]. [8] will add a formal semantics for the ',' construct.

4.2 Generalized Choice

With the **either**-construction we distinguish (only) two cases. However, sometimes we want to distinguish more cases. Instead of a nested **either**, we might use a repetitive construction, for which the grammar rule is:

either <W> {**or** <W>} **end**

formally indicating that the part between '{' and '}' can be repeated zero or more times (although zero times does not make much sense here, being equivalent to <W> then).

4.3 Case Analysis

With an **if-then-else** construction we also distinguish (only) two cases. However, sometimes we must distinguish (much) more cases. Instead of a nested **if-then-else** we might use a **case**-construction, as a generalization of the **if-then-else**, similar to the **case**-constructions in programming languages. Our **case**-construction has the following form:

case <expression> **is**
<value> **then** <W>, <value> **then** <W>, …, <value> **then** <W>[**else** <W>] **end**

There must be no duplicate values. Depending on the value of the expression, a specific W will apply. The brackets '[' and ']' indicate that the part '**else** <W>' is optional. If no value applies then the **else**-part applies, provided it is there (because the **else**-part is optional); otherwise nothing happens.

For instance, in such a tile example we might sometimes need a **case**-construction of the following form:

case color **is**
red **then** ...,
yellow **then** ...,
blue **then** ...
else .../* for all other colors (if they would be there)

The **case**-construction is a generalization of the **if-then** and the **if-then-else** because

if C **then** W1 [**else** W2] **end** is equivalent to **case** C **is** true **then** W1 [**else** W2] **end**

4.4 Iteration (for Each Element in a Set)

Sometimes we want to express that something similar has to be done for each element in a given set, independently from each other and without the need for a specific order. (This also allows parallel execution.) We could express that with the next grammar rule, which expresses *iteration* over all elements in a given set:

<W> ::= **for each** <set element> **do** <W> **end**

Actually, this construction also can be expressed in terms of a **while**-loop of the form

while more elements in <set> **do** <W> **end**

as we more or less did in Example 3. But then we miss the hint of the parallel execution possibility. Therefore, we do add this grammar rule.

4.5 Definitions and Calls

We will introduce our next wish (i.e., abbreviations) and its solution (definitions and their calls) via an example.

Example 5: Introducing abbreviations

The stacks in Example 2 were such a success that the company wants to build such stacks more often. For instance on both sides of the entrance of a private driveway. It means that one has to build such a stack, move (say) 5 meters, and then build another such stack. Therefore, we would like to 'name' the instruction sequence in Example 2, e.g., as follows:

define makePopularStack **as**
  put a yellow tile;
  while *the stack is lower than 1 meter* **do** put a red tile; put a blue tile **end;**
  maybe put any tile **end;**
  put a yellow tile;
  if *it rains* **then** put a blue tile **else** put any tile **end;**
  either put a yellow tile **or** put a red tile; put a blue tile **end;**
  if *the sun shines* **then** put a red tile; put a blue tile **end**
end

Before we can express our 'driveway-instruction', we need another basic instruction:

<BBB> ::= **move** <number> **meters**

Now we can express the company's 'driveway-instruction' as follows (by simply referring to the old instruction sequence):

  makePopularStack;
  move 5 meters;
  makePopularStack

A side remark: It would be convenient if the name referring to a definition would constitute a hyperlink to the definition itself. We will apply this idea in the sequel.

We can also have parameterized abbreviations:

Example 6: Parameterized abbreviations

Because of its popularity, our 'driveway-instruction' will be used (and referred to) very often. Therefore, we would like to 'name' that instruction sequence as well. But it is not always that 5 meters. So, it should be easily possible to vary that in the instructions. We can do that by letting that distance be a *parameter*:

define makePopularEntrance(x) **as**
  makePopularStack;
  move x meters;
  makePopularStack
end

The instruction to make two such stacks with 6 meters distance in between can now simply be:

makePopularEntrance(6)

We can generalize and formalize the abbreviation idea by introducing the next grammatical constructions, namely defining an abbreviation possibly followed by a parameter list between brackets (where the parameters in the list are separated by semicolons):

define <abbreviation> **as** <W> **end**
define <abbreviation> (<parameter> {; <parameter>}) **as** <W> **end**

For *using* the abbreviation, we can add an extra rule to our grammar fragment for Ws, and take both previous rules into account by indicating that that list is optional:

<W> :::= <abbreviation> [(<expression> {; <expression>})] /* Reference/Call

This is known as a *reference* or a *call* or an *Include*. Note that in a *definition* there should be *parameters* but in a *call/reference/Include* there can be arbitrary *expressions*.

We note that definitions and their calls are related to subroutines/methods and their calls in programming languages and to the Include relationship in UML [1].

4.6 Recursive Definitions

Example 6 shows that the definition of an abbreviation can refer to another abbreviation. And this can be repeated of course. Sometimes it makes even sense that an abbreviation refers to itself, as the next example shows. It is an example of a *recursive definition*.

Example 7: Recursive definitions

The *Towers of Hanoi* is a game/puzzle consisting of three rods and a number of disks of different sizes. Each disk has a hole in the middle, such that the disk fits around each rod. Initially, the disks are placed around the left rod, in such a way that each disk rests on a larger disk; see the picture below.

The goal is to move the stack to the right rod in such a way that each disk always rests on a larger disk. Each time one can move only one of the upper disks.

The puzzle can (recursively) be solved as follows: If n, the number of disks, is 1 then simply move that one disk from the left rod to the right rod. (Hence, we know how to solve it for n = 1.) The idea behind the solution below is that if we know how to move n – 1 disks in a correct way from one rod to another, then we also have a solution for n disks, namely as follows: Move the upper n – 1 disks in a correct way from the left rod to the middle rod. Then move the remaining disk (i.e., the largest one) from the left rod to the right rod. Then move the other n – 1 disks in a correct way from the middle rod to the right rod.

We can formulate this (recursive) solution as follows (where *solveHanoi(n; x; y)* is the instruction *move the upper n disks of rod x in a correct way to rod y*):

```
define solveHanoi(n; x; y) as
   if n = 1
   then move that one disk from rod x to rod y
   else solveHanoi(n – 1; x; z); (*)
        move the remaining disk from rod x to rod y;
        solveHanoi(n – 1; z; y)
   end
end
```

(*) Here z indicates the other of the 3 rods.
(If they are numbered 1, 2, and 3, then z = 6 – x – y.)

So, the instruction to move a stack of 8 disks correctly from rod 1 to rod 3 is:
<u>solveHanoi</u>(8; 1; 3)

4.7 'Free Floating' Instructions

We will introduce our next problem and our grammatical solution again via an example.

Example 8: Instructions that are 'free floating'

Turning back to our stacks of tiles in examples 2, 5, and 6: Sometimes it is necessary to put cement between two tiles. This is up to the judgment of the one who is building the stack at that moment. So, this can happen 0, 1, or more times per stack. Moreover, it is tradition to put one 'lucky dime' in each stack, at an arbitrary place in the stack. These extra actions can (easily) be formulated, but they cannot be put at a specific place in the instruction sequence. So, the instructions for building such a stack of tiles should be something like below.

It starts with the 'old' instruction set for building a stack (see Example 2):

put a yellow tile;
⋮
if *the sun shines* **then** put a red tile; put a blue tile **end;**

extra: put cement between two tiles whenever needed, /* 0, 1, or more times
put lucky dime **once** /* 1 time
end

We can generalize this by introducing the following extra grammar rules:

R1: <W> ::= <W>; **extra:** <W> [<frequency>]{, <W> [<frequency>]} **end**
R2: <frequency> ::= [<qualifier>] <number> **times**|[<qualifier>] **once**
R3: <qualifier> ::= **at most**|**at least**|**less than**|**more than**|**exactly**

Rule R1 in words: a W can be followed by one or more extra Ws (in arbitrary order), where the frequency of occurrence is optional for each extra W. Without a frequency indicated, that extra W can occur any number of times (0, 1, or more times), by default.

The qualifier in R2 is also optional. If there is no qualifier we mean **exactly**, also by default. According to rule R3 there are 5 possible qualifiers. In rule R2 '[<qualifier>] <number> **times**' is only useful when that number is 2 or more, because '[<qualifier>] 0 **times**' is superfluous and '[<qualifier>] 1 **times**' is equivalent to '[<qualifier>] **once**'.

We note that the **extra**-construction is related to interrupts in programming and to the Extend relationship in UML [1].

5 Summary of All Our Grammatical Constructs

We now present the complete version of our grammar fragment so far. The following terminology/explanation applies to the presented grammar rules (Fig. 2):

1. Basic Building Block
2. Sequence
3. Arbitrary order
4. Block
5. Conditional
6. Alternative
7. Case analysis
8. Loop (driven by a condition)
9. Iteration (for each set element)
10. Option
11. General choice
12. Call
13. Free floating Ws
14. Declarations
15. Definition
16. Frequency of occurrence
17. Qualifier

```
<W>          ::= <BBB>                                                         /*  1
               | <BBB>; <W>                                                    /*  2
               | <W>, <W>                                                      /*  3
               | begin <W> end                                                 /*  4
               | if <condition> then <W> end                                   /*  5
               | if <condition> then <W> else <W> end                          /*  6
               | case <expression> is                                          /*  7
                 <value> then <W>{, <value> then <W>} [else <W>] end
               | while <condition> do <W> end                                  /*  8
               | for each <set element> do <W> end                             /*  9
               | maybe <W> end                                                 /* 10
               | either <W> { or <W>} end                                      /* 11
               | <W-name>[(<expression>{; <expression>})]                      /* 12
               | <W>; extra: <W> [<frequency>]{, <W> [<frequency>]} end        /* 13
               | <W> with <definition>{; <definition>}end                      /* 14
<definition> ::= define <W-name>[(<parameter>{; <parameter>})]                 /* 15
                 as <W> end
<frequency>  ::= [<qualifier>] <number> times | [<qualifier>] once             /* 16
<qualifier>  ::= at most | at least | less than | more than | exactly          /* 17
```

Fig. 2. Our complete grammar fragment

All our keywords are taken from colloquial English, making our language a 'pseudo natural language'.

The following binding rule applies: ',' binds stronger than ';'. For instance, we must read '*A*, *B*; *C*' as '(*A*, *B*); *C*', meaning: do *A* and do *B* in arbitrary order, and then do *C*.

As a general guideline for our grammar design, we used ';' when the order is relevant and ',' when the order is irrelevant.

A **maybe** at a particular point in an SSD might trigger the system to explicitly ask for it at that moment ('*Do you maybe want to* …', which is then meant as a reminder).

For practical reasons we consider our keywords (**begin**, **end**, **define**, **while**, etc.) to be case-insensitive. Then we could, for instance, use **begin** … **end** when those two keywords are relatively close to each other, **Begin** … **End** when they further apart, and **BEGIN** … **END** when the distance between the two keywords is very large. (This idea is applied in [7] as well.)

In [1] Larman uses his NextGen point-of-sale system as an illustrative, real-life case study. In particular, he presents *Process Sale* as a running example of a use case. It is a very elaborated, representative real-life use case. However, he did not give an SSD for the complete use case (only for the so called Main Success Scenario). As a proof of concept, technical report [7] explains and works out this non-trivial industrial strength case in detail, delivering a textual SSD along the lines presented here. The example also shows that we do need these language constructs in practice. [7] can be considered as supplementary to the current paper and gives an impression of the form, feasibility, and scalability of our proposal in large, complex, real-life situations.

6 Example of a Conversion of a Use Case via an SSD to a Program

Now we illustrate how the similarity between the structuring mechanisms for *use cases* (elementary business processes), for *textual SSDs*, and for *programming languages* will ease the translation from the requirements analysis results via textual SSDs towards software programs. So, as our title says: From Business Modeling to Software Design.

A use case describes in natural language the sequence of steps to realize a user story, where a user story is a 'wish' of a (future) user which the system should be able to fulfil [12, 13]; e.g., the wish of a university employee to '*Remove a student*'. According to [13] user stories are popular as a method for representing requirements, especially in agile development environments, e.g., using a simple (but popular) template like

'*As a <role>, I want to <wish> [so that <benefit>]*'

Example 9: A user story and an associated use case

As a starting point, we take the user story *As an administrator, I want to remove a student with a given student number*, in the context of a registration system for a university. If in this university a student can only be removed if (s)he paid all her/his debts to the university then the use case for this user story might run as follows:

The user (administrator) asks the system to remove a student with a given number.
The system checks whether the student (number) is known in the system.
If not **then** the system informs the user that the student number is not known;
otherwise

- The system checks whether that student has any debts to the university.
- **If** so **then**
  the system informs the user that the student still has debts and wasn't removed;
  otherwise
  - The system removes the info of that student (including the study results).
  - The system informs the user that it removed the info of that student

We wrote the structuring keywords in bold

This leads to the following textual SSD:

Example 10: A corresponding textual SSD

```
User   → System: RemoveStudent(<number>);
System → System: check whether student <number> is known;
if student <number> is not known
  then System → User: 'Student is not known'
  else System → System: check whether student <number> still has debts;
       if student <number> still has debts
         then System → User: 'No removal because the student still has debts'
         else System → System:  remove the info of student <number>
                                (including all her/his study results);
              System → User:    'Done: The student has been removed'
       end
end
```

Note that the structure in the SSD follows the structure in the natural language!

Suppose we want (or have) to implement it in, say, a relational system. Also suppose that that system has (1) a student table called Stud with (at least) an attribute Snr for the student number and an attribute Debts for the debt size of the student and (2) a table StudRes for the study results, with an attribute Snr referring to the student. We could define a (stored) procedure *RemoveStudent*, with parameter @n for the student number and @output for the output, as follows in (pseudo-)SQL:

Example 11: A corresponding procedure in SQL

```
CREATE PROCEDURE RemoveStudent @n INTEGER,
                               @output VARCHAR OUTPUT  AS

IF @n NOT IN (SELECT Snr FROM Stud)
THEN SELECT @output = 'Student is not known'
ELSE IF (SELECT Debts FROM Stud WHERE Snr = @n) > 0
     THEN SELECT @output =
            'No removal because the student still has debts'
     ELSE DELETE FROM StudRes WHERE Snr = @n;
          DELETE FROM Stud WHERE Snr = @n;
          SELECT @output = 'Done: The student has been removed'
```

We wrote the structuring keywords in bold again.

Note that the structure and language constructs in the procedure follow from those in the SSD! This would also hold when we would have implemented it in an imperative language [11].

This section illustrated the alignment and how the similarity between the structuring mechanisms eases the translation of use cases via textual SSDs towards programs in a software system.

7 Another Application Area

To mention another application area, these ideas could also be applied to the generation of *assembly instructions*. This might be especially useful for companies with many modular products (e.g., furniture) and/or product lines: As shown in Examples 5 and 6, instructions can be grouped together, the instruction sequence can be named, and then that name can be used (repeatedly) elsewhere. When we want to have a detailed and concrete assembly manual for a particular product then instead of referring to the instruction sequence using its name (as we did in Example 6), we could substitute that instruction sequence wherever that name occurs. Per product, the company can then *generate* a detailed and concrete assembly manual, i.e., a manual only containing simple basic instructions for that product, by using their own basic catalogue of core 'sub-manuals' (or 'master-manuals'). A relevant change in a (sub)product then leads to a change in the corresponding 'master-manual' in the catalogue only, i.e., at that moment. But when a concrete assembly manual has to be generated, the change will also appear in the concretely generated product manual.

We note that the basic building block might also be a picture or an icon. For instance, [14] contains a lot of product examples.

8 Summary, Results, and Conclusions

We wanted to design a grammar for expressing system sequence diagrams (SSDs) in a textual way. It turned out that we needed the same kind of structuring mechanisms as for modeling business processes and programming languages, for instance. Only the basic building blocks are different. We took the challenge to generalize this similarity idea and stepwise designed a rich grammar for instruction languages in general.

By using such languages, the interactions between the user and the (IT) system can be expressed in a more precise way, thereby forcing possible interpretation problems (part of users' natural language) to be solved in an early stage of system specification.

In fact, we defined a whole class of *domain-specific* or *little languages* [10] in this way: The grammar rules for the non-terminal <BBB> (basic building block) are domain specific and have to be specified and added per application. Via this concept of Basic Building Block, the basic grammar is decoupled from the domain-specific language elements that are required for writing SSDs in a specific domain.

The (uniform) grammar contains rules for sequential compositions, arbitrary orders, blocks, conditionals, alternatives, case analyses, loops (driven by a condition), iterations (for each element in a given set, allowing parallel execution), options, choices, 'free floating' instructions (such as interrupts), (parameterized) definitions (including *recursive* definitions), declarations, and calls (a.k.a. *Includes*).

We illustrated our theory with various examples, taken from several different application areas. As pointed out, the basic building blocks could even be pictures or icons. Therefore, our approach can also be applied to *assembly instructions* for instance. Our structuring mechanisms might then be useful for companies with product lines and/or modular products, because those companies can *generate* product-specific assembly manuals out of their own basic catalogue of core 'sub-manuals' (or 'master-manuals').

As a special case of our approach, we get a grammar for textual SSDs resp. imperative programming languages when we use basic building blocks of the form

<actor> → <actor> : <message> resp.
<variable> : = <expression>

We showed the advantage of exploiting the similarity between the structuring mechanisms of textual SSDs and programming languages: it eases the translation of SSDs towards an implementation in a software system (Sect. 6).

The approach is based on more than 40 years of experience in the field of the author, both in the position of a scientist and in the position of a practitioner. The approach was also validated with several other experienced experts (each with decades of experience). They were very enthusiastic about the usefulness of the approach. We were even able to find mistakes in their solutions by using our approach.

For further empirical validation of the expressiveness, feasibility, and scalability of our approach, we also applied it to several cases, including a substantial industrial strength example, a non-trivial representative real-life example of a use case, and delivered a textual SSD according to the lines presented here; see [7].

In the last few years we are also teaching this approach to our Computer Science students (in a course called *Problem Analysis and Software Design*), teaching them how they can use the same (sub-)structuring mechanisms and policies as they are used to in programming. On average their reports are clearly improving over the years.

Acknowledgments. We want to thank the reviewers for some useful suggestions.

Appendix

In Fig. 3, we show the resulting stack possibilities for Example 2:

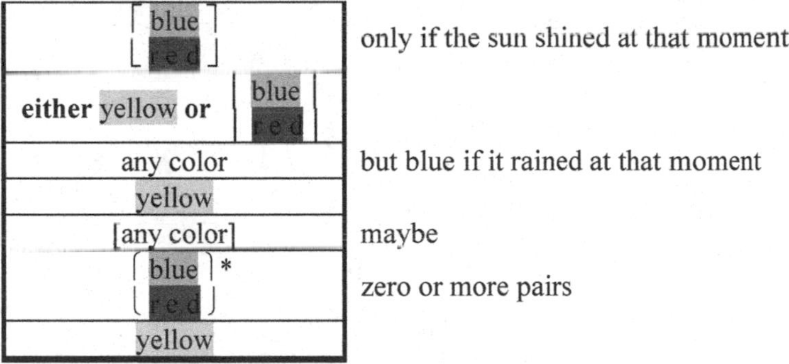

Fig. 3. Stack possibilities for Example 2 (Color figure online)

References

1. Larman, C.: Applying UML and patterns, 3rd edn. Addison Wesley, Boston (2005)
2. https://en.wikipedia.org/wiki/System_sequence_diagram. Accessed on 10 April 2020
3. Tiwari, S., Gupta, A.: A systematic literature review of use case specifications research. Inf. Softw. Technol. **67**, 128–158 (2015)
4. de Brock, E.O.: Scenario integration, under review (2020)
5. Jacobson, I., et al.: Use Case 2.0: The Guide to Succeeding with Use Cases, Ivar Jacobson International (2011)
6. https://en.wikipedia.org/wiki/Use_case. Accessed on 10 April 2020
7. de Brock, E.O.: Converting a non-trivial Use Case into an SSD: An exercise, SOM Research Report 2018011 (2018)
8. de Brock, B.: Declarative semantics of actions and instructions. In: Shishkov, B. (ed.) BMSD 2020. LNBIP, vol. 391, pp. 297–308. Springer, Cham (2020). https://doi.org/10.1007/978-3-030-52306-0_20
9. Dumas, M., La Rosa, M., Mendling, J., Reijers, H.A.: Fundamentals of Business Process Management, 2nd edn. Springer, Heidelberg (2018)
10. van Deursen, A., et al.: Domain-specific languages: an annotated bibliography. ACM SIGPLAN Notices **35**(6), 26–36 (2000)
11. https://en.wikipedia.org/wiki/Imperative_programming. Accessed on 10 April 2020
12. Cohn, M.: User Stories Applied: For Agile Software Development. Addison-Wesley Professional, Boston (2004)
13. Lucassen, G., Dalpiaz, F., van der Werf, J.M.E.M., Brinkkemper, S: The use and effectiveness of user stories in practice. In: Daneva, M., Pastor, O. (eds.) REFSQ 2016. LNCS, vol. 9619, pp. 205–222. Springer, Cham (2016). https://doi.org/10.1007/978-3-319-30282-9_14
14. https://www.ikea.com/us/en/. Accessed on 10 April 2020

Business Process Model Driven Approach for Automatic Use Case Model Generation

Salam Turkman and Adel Taweel(✉)

Computer Science, Birzeit University, Birzeit, Palestine
salma.turk@gmail.com, ataweel@birzeit.edu

Abstract. Requirement elicitation is an essential step for establishing software requirements. They define the outcomes upon which software functionality is produced. However, several studies have shown majority of errors found in software functionality are directly linked to requirement elicitation. To address, this paper proposes a structured approach to derive system requirements automatically using business process models. It employs a systematic mechanism to improve business process models and transformation method to generate requirement models. It employs 26 defined heuristics rules that maps and controls transformation. The proposed approach is evaluated using seven case studies. Results show the viability to generate software requirements from business process models, and the automatic generation of rich UML-based use case diagram. The proposed approach achieves more precise and valid requirement specifications and was able to generate additional valid use case model features compared to other competing approaches.

Keywords: Requirement engineering · Business process modelling · Use case model

1 Introduction

Effective requirement elicitation is an essential process in developing software applications [19]. It necessitates using appropriate requirements elicitation methods for developing successful software projects. They play an important role in determining whether a project delivers the desired business value and meet management constraints, in terms of time and budget [20]. Many large projects fail due to errors in requirement elicitation, with some studies reporting such errors can be very difficult to discover and very expensive to fix [10]. Several alternative promising approaches based on business process models have been proposed to address these issues [21–23]. They identify business processes as essential element to determine software requirements and user needs and demands from the software applications that provide them [22].

Several business process-based approaches have additionally proposed enabling automatic generation of requirement specifications from underlying organization business models, overcoming errors that often result from traditional manual-based requirement elicitation methods. However, these approaches require significant manual intervention. A previous paper proposed a general approach that achieves better transformation of software specifications from business models and reduces manual intervention

B. Shishkov (Ed.): BMSD 2020, LNBIP 391, pp. 123–136, 2020.
https://doi.org/10.1007/978-3-030-52306-0_8

significantly [29]. This paper proposes an approach (named BMSpec) that uses business process models to derive more accurate software requirements, which in majority can be generated automatically. It proposes a new business model-driven approach for the automatic derivation of UML-based requirement specifications from existing business process models. A key advantage of business process modelling that it enables the engagement of end users in requirement elicitation. The proposed approach, equally enables the engagement of end users even longer, additionally in the business process model re-design which helps to produce better engineered business requirements and solution. The proposed approach developed a systematic method that encompasses a set of heuristic rules that transforms an existing business process model into a BMPN-conforming business model inclusive of prospective "To-Be" processes [21]. Introducing a well-defined business process "To-Be" modelling step for generating requirement specifications results into a more successful software product due to the additional engagement of end users in this business re-engineering stage, unlike traditional approaches that usually include only initial engagement of users. The "To-Be" business process model is then automatically transformed to a Use-Case Model, inclusive of both the UML-based Use-Case diagram and the detailed Use Case descriptions.

The proposed approach has been evaluated on seven case studies. Results show accurate transformation compared with other gold-standard based traditional approaches. They also show the dependency, of the transformation, on the input business process model, whereas the more details it includes, the higher the efficiency of the transformation. The generated requirement specifications are represented as Use Case models that include detailed use case descriptions and associations between use cases within minimal manual intervention.

2 Related Work

Derivation of software specification from business process models has been studied by several researchers [1–4, 13, 22]. Some of the approaches proposed an algorithm to automatically transform business model into functional requirements, as a use case diagram [1]. It works by creating meta-models for both the use case diagram and business process model then compares definitions in the two meta-models. It then attempts to map between concepts from across the two models. However, the total error percentage in the generated use case diagram was relatively high at 40%. Another approach used RADs (Role Activity Diagrams) to model business processes to attempt finding associations for use case diagram derivation [2]. However, the notions of a "Role" and an "Actor" in RADs were not clear enough and incompatible with UML, which resulted into a not well-formed use case diagram.

The notion of "automated activity" in an improved RAD model was suggested to map to the notion of "action or function" in the use case diagram to improve the derivation [3]. This approach, however, has shown lack of process visibility with focus on use cases only with no notation of associations between them. A manual transformation to obtain use case model based on business process models was proposed [13]. Although it provided the first approach that attempted to generate use case description from business process models, but it did not focus on generating the use case diagram. A set of rules, predefined from natural language sentences, were used to generate the use case diagram manually from BPMN elements, the resultant use case diagram however did not cover the association between use cases such as extend, include, invoke and precede. A similar manual approach, using business-oriented to requirement elicitation model (BORE), for deriving system requirements from business process models was proposed to integrate requirements engineering and business process engineering [4]. This may be particularly useful when system requirements are in need of early discovery.

The use of DEMO (dynamic essential modeling of organizations) was investigated, as an alternative approach, to find most suitable methods to identify correct use cases [22]. The suggestion is to use a combination of several requirement generation approaches together to enhance use case derivation. Although, the above demonstrate the potential of automatic generation of software specifications from business models, the need is to automate the derivation consistently using standardized notations. Hence the aim of this paper, it proposes a systematic approach based on well-defined heuristic rules on standardized business process BPMN notation.

3 Proposed Approach

The validity of the underlying business process model is the key to represent the process of the organization business processes. A business process model function does not only represent the overall business process, but also can be used for decision-making within an organization. To do so, however, this requires the business model to be sufficiently detailed and consistently represented with valid modeling notations. Therefore, if well defined, such model can be used to generate requirements for the software needed to support business processes.

Thus, the proposed approach developed two new methods to ensure consistent derivation of use cases from business models:

1) TO-BE model preparation: a structured and systematic TO-BE business model preparation method that ensures the production of a valid model. It takes an existing AS-IS model as input and produces a well-defined valid TO-BE model as output. The validity of the TO-BE model is ensured by confirming the consistency of the constraints, the correctness of the representation and modeling notations. The success of the final result depends mainly on this step, because end users as well participate in developing the TO-BE model, and thus the strength of this approach is in enabling the engagement of end users in the design stage and not just in early stage of requirement modelling.
2) USE-CASE transformation: It takes the TO-BE model as input and produces a USE-CASE model as output. This method developed a set of heuristics rules that are employed to derive and transform the TO-BE model into a USE-CASE model.

In the TO-BE model preparation method, to address the input AS-IS model, the proposed approach employed requirement and business model engineering integration from [4]. This step requires manual processing and the required effort depends on the status of the existing AS-IS business process model, in terms of process details, consistency of application of business constraints and of modeling notations. For the USE-CASE transformation, it developed an algorithm that transforms input TO-BE BMPN XML objects into software specifications represented as UML-based USE-CASE XML objects. BMSpec's transformation algorithm employs a developed set of heuristics rules, see Sect. 2.1, that defines relations between TO-BE business process representation (objects) and UML-based USE-CASE representation (objects). These methods are described in further details in the following subsections.

3.1 TO-BE Model Preparation

To achieve consistent transformation of business process models to use-case software specifications, models need to adhere to a consistent and valid representation. However, due to the variation of existing business models in terms of representation, modeling and validity and consistency in the use of modeling (BPMN) notations, a manual transformation is adopted. Manual transformation ensures that AS-IS models are consistently transformed into TO-BE models. Understandably this may introduce additional effort, and requires modeling expertise, but does not require software engineering expertise. The required level of effort heavily depends on the status of the AS-IS model. Where the input is just a manual AS-IS model and does not cover the user interaction with the system, it requires reengineering to build a valid TO-BE model. This may include analysis of the purpose and effect of the software information system on the business processes. At the end of this step is to identify clearly the automated tasks that represent user interactions with the system. Therefore, it is important to follow good modeling practices to result into significant business improvement [6]. In business process reengineering, processes need be reengineered while taking full advantage of automation to improve business outputs, which may require changing how the business function [7, 8]. Both process and information flows need to be considered along with how people interact with systems to achieve integrated business functions [8].

For maximum benefit, process reengineering should focus on both system perspective, i.e. to reach a clearly defined use case, and business process perspective, i.e. to reach clearly defined business needs from the information system [9]. In this step, the proposed approach aims to identify user interaction tasks with the software system. These tasks often represent important functions, or use cases, that the use case model must include. In other words, each identified use case specifies a functionality that the system must provide for an actor to achieve a business function or process. The proposed approach assumes AS-IS model is represented using BPMN notations. To guide process reengineering, it defines a set of rules to achieve the TO-BE business process model:

- **Rule 1:** Define automated tasks that are achieved fully by the system without any action from user as service tasks.
- **Rule 2:** Define tasks that represent an action of the user on the system.
- **Rule 3:** Remove manual tasks (<<task>>) that cannot be achieved by the system.
- **Rule 4:** Ensure gateway (<<gateway>>) are appropriately defined and used.
- **Rule 5:** Specify <<events for task>> not only <<start events>> but also <<intermediate events>> and <<end events>>.
- **Rule 6:** Define all participants as <<Roles>> not as <<pool>> or <<lane>>.

- **Rule 7:** Assign appropriate (performer) for each user <<task>>.
- **Rule 8:** Specify required <<data objects>>.
- **Rule 9:** Specify required <<message flow>>.

On the other hand, in cases where the existing AS-IS models are designed with a clear software system purpose and the role of the software system on the business is clearly defined, the transformation to the TO-BE model is straightforward. However, a manual check is needed to confirm validity and consistency of the use of BPMN modeling and notation. This requires to ensure correct use of BPMN notations, for example, for specifying task types, declaring conditions for gateways, events name and types. To conform to BPMN notations, the proposed approach defines the following set of rules to guide this modification:

- **Rule10:** Set task type as service task, if the task is fully executed by the system.
- **Rule 11:** Set notation description correctly obeying BPMN's notations, i.e.:
- **Rule11.1**: set a name for each <<gateway>>.
- **Rule11.2**: Set a name for each <<condition>>.
- **Rule11.3**: Set a name for each <<data object>>.
- **Rule11.4**: Set a name for each <<data store>>.
- **Rule11.5**: Set a name for each <<start event>>.
- **Rule11.6**: Set a name for each <<intermediate event>>.
- **Rule11.7**: Set a name for each <<end event>>.
- **Rule11.8**: Set a name for each <<message flow>>.

3.2 Use Case Diagram Transformation: Heuristic Rules

Once TO-BE model is re-engineered, it is used as input to for the transformation. The proposed approach depends on the TO-BE model to be consistent and valid. Therefore, it developed a set of heuristic rules that conform to the correct and consistent use of BPMN notations. The heuristic rules are then used to identify and generate actors, use cases, and their associations and transform them into a use case diagram. Therefore, the developed heuristic rules are based on consistency and normalization of the BPMN notations.

To achieve, BPMN have been studied as a language, not just in terms of its notations but also their semantic use and meaning. Although published BPMN resources and guidelines were used as a reference, but in many cases notation and their semantic uses are not précised defined. Therefore, to reach a better-defined semantic use of the notations, 70 real-time business models have been studied and analyzed to arrive at consistent transformation and interruptions of BPMN notations and their combinations. This helped reach a better understanding of applied uses of the notations and to develop heuristic rules that caters variable semantic uses. Generally, heuristic rules define semantic mapping between business model BPMN notation and software requirement UML notation. For example, a task or activity represents user interaction with the system. In a use case diagram, a use case presents functionality a user wants to achieve through the software system [12]. Thus, a heuristic rule takes the assumption that each activity can be mapped into a use case.

To enable automatic transformation, a computational algorithm was developed based on the heuristic rules. The algorithm takes, as input, the TO-BE model represented as BPMN XML objects, saved from a BPMN modeling tool, combines and applies the heuristic rules to generate the USE-CASE model. The generated USE-CASE model, is generated as XML objects, formatted and used as input to UML-based modeling tool, to generate a USE-CASE diagram. The following describes the developed heuristics rules.

HRule1: Map each activity to a use case. The use case name is the activity name (Fig. 1).

Fig. 1. HRule1.

HRule2: Map each performer to an actor. The actor name is the role (Fig. 2).

Fig. 2. HRule2.

HRule3: Map each association between an activity and performer to association between actor and use case in use case diagram (Fig. 3).

Fig. 3. HRule3.

HRule4: Map sequence flow between two activities to "Precede" association between the corresponding use cases (Fig. 4).

Fig. 4. HRule4.

HRule5: Map exclusive decision gateway between two activities to "extend" association between the corresponding use cases (Fig. 5).

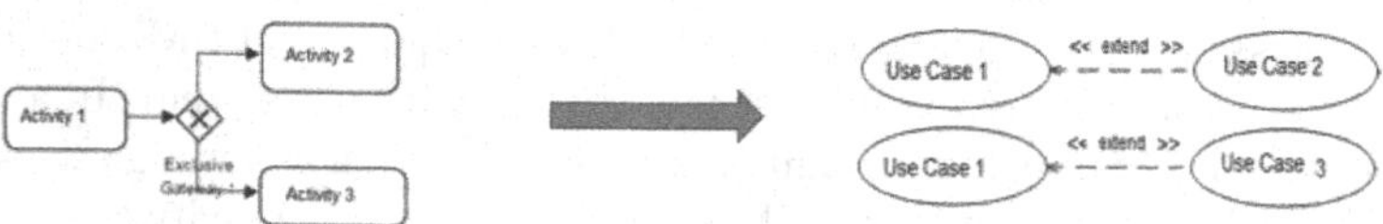

Fig. 5. HRule5.

HRule6: Map data association between activity and input data store to include association between the corresponding use cases (Fig. 6).

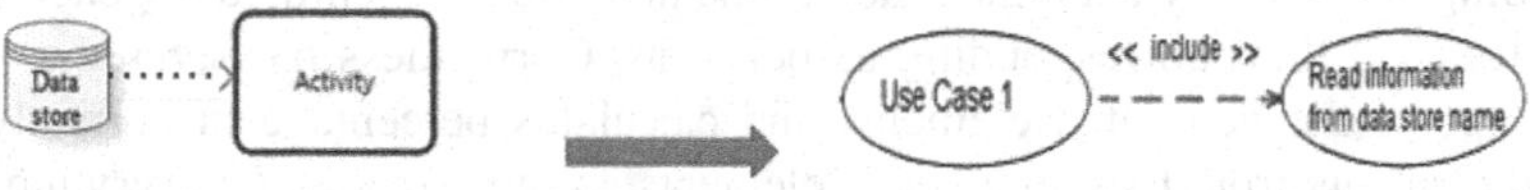

Fig. 6. HRule6.

HRule7: Map data association between activity and output data store to include association between the corresponding use cases as shown in an output data store (Fig. 7).

Fig. 7. HRule7.

HRule8: Map data association between activity and input data object to include association between the corresponding use cases as shown in an output data store (Fig. 8).

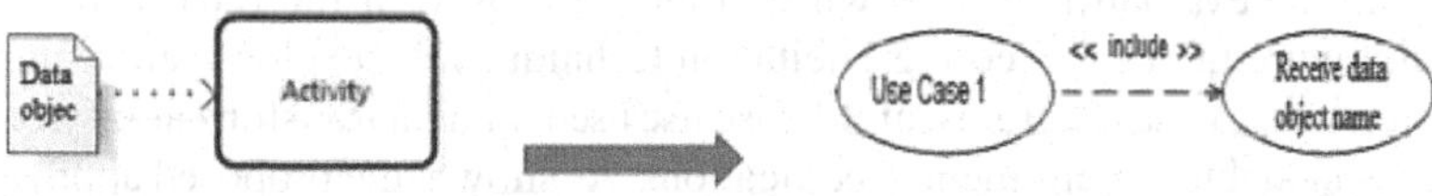

Fig. 8. HRule8.

HRule9: Map data association between activity and output data object to include association between the corresponding use cases as shown in an output data store (Fig. 9).

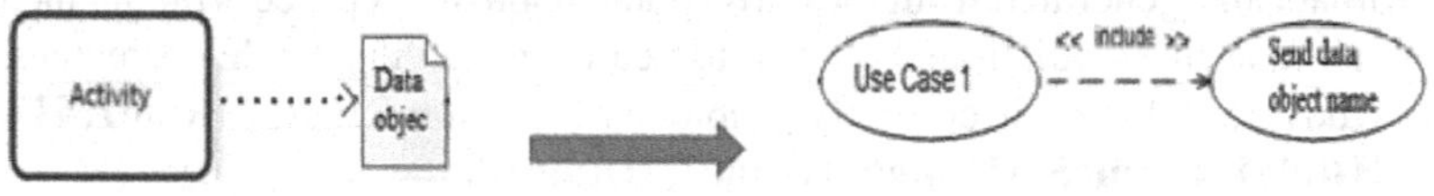

Fig. 9. H Rule9.

HRule10: Map sequence flow between activity and service activity to Invoke association between the corresponding use cases (Fig. 10).

Fig. 10. HRule10.

4 Evaluation and Results

The evaluation methodology aims to evaluate the reproducibility, correctness and validity of the proposed approach's generated use cases, actors and association represented into a use case diagram. Validity examines each of the individually identified or generated use cases, actors and their corresponding associations. Correctness measures the validity of each type of the generated elements and calculates percentage of correctly valid generated elements from total number of elements. In other words, for every input case study and its business process model it should produce or generate a valid use case diagram with correctly identified use cases, actors and associations between them. This is represented in the following equation:

Correctness % = VEt – IEt/ TEt

Where VE: Number of Valid elements of type t; IE: Number of Invalid elements of type t; TE: Total number of generated elements of type t; t: type of generated elements.

The traditional gold standard testing or model evaluation is used [18]. This is conducted by evaluating the output of traditional requirement elicitation techniques, in which software engineers are employed to build use case diagrams manually, against BMSpec generated use case diagrams, for the same scenarios. Although this is an expensive procedure, yet to ensure validity, the evaluation was done on several different case studies.

Table 1 lists the seven evaluated case studies, including a brief description of each. Results from the evaluation are shown in Tables 2 to 8. 6 of these case studies used traditional requirement engineering elicitation techniques to develop their requirement specification as use case diagrams, and 1 case use used manual transformation from business process model to requirement specifications. As shown, the proposed approach was able to identify extra features, which are not supported in other competing approaches [1–4, 14], such as association between use cases (precede, invoke, include, extend).

Table 2 shows outputs from both the traditional manual approach and the BMSpec automated approach for case study 1 (Nobel Prize). In this case study, 10 use cases, 4 actors and 4 associations were manually identified, which the proposed approach has correctly automatically generated from the corresponding business process model including correct generation of associations between use cases, achieving 100% correctness. For this case study, to achieve, it correctly employed Heuristic Rules: **HRule1, HRule2, HRule3, HRule4, HRule5, HRule6, HRule7, HRule10.**

Table 3 shows outputs from both approaches for use case study 2 (Car hire). In this case study, 3 use cases, 2 actors and 4 associations were manually identified, which the proposed approach has correctly automatically generated from the respective business process model including correct generation of associations between use cases, achieving 100% correctness. For this case study, to achieve it correctly employed Heuristic Rules: **HRule1, HRule2, HRule3, HRule4, HRule7, HRule9.**

Similarly, Tables 4, 5, 6, 7, 8 show outputs of both approaches for remaining case studies respectively, generating their respective use case diagram elements correctly in all cases. Figure 11 shows the output use case diagram compared to the manually generated use case diagram for the X-Road Registration case study.

Table 1. Descriptions of evaluated case studies.

Case study name	Case study brief description
Nobel Prize example	A case study in which a paper work [13] used manual transformation from business process model for the Nobel prize case study to generate a use case model. The authors used a set of rules for the manual transformation. We used the same business process model for the Nobel prize case study used in [13], and the validation was conducted against their derived models
Car-Hire case study	A case study in which a team of four expert master degree students developed a software system for car-Hire Company. The team used a traditional requirement elicitation technique to model system requirements. The output system requirement specifications (SRS) document included a UML use case model and a detailed use case description. The final work of the team has been manually checked and validated
Online Bookshop case study	A case study, in which a team of four expert master degree students developed an online bookshop system. The system enables publishers or book suppliers to setup online shops, and customers to browse and search through the shop and purchase books online. The team used a traditional requirement elicitation technique to model system requirements, and generated an SRS document inclusive of UML use case diagram and use case descriptions, which was manually checked and validated
Three X-road services/case studies	Three case studies, obtained from the Ministry of Telecom and Information Technology (Palestine), each representing a service. These processes represent the daily work of three X-Road services: registration on X-Road service, Consume X-Road service and provide X-Road service. A team of two experts from the ministry used a traditional requirement elicitation technique to derive system requirements for the three case studies. The SRS document included detailed description of the X-road services, UML use case diagram and use case descriptions

Table 2. Nobel Prize example case Study.

	Manual		BMSpec		Correctness	Extra elements
	Qty.	valid	Qty.	valid		<<include>> <<extend>> <<precede>> <<invoke>>
Use cases	10	10	10	10	100%	
Actors	4	4	4	4	100%	

Table 3. Car Hire case study (hire car process) case study.

	Manual		BMSpec		Correctness	Extra elements
	Qty.	valid	Qty.	valid		<<precede>> <<include>>
Use cases	3	3	3	3	100%	
Actors	2	2	2	2	100%	

Table 4. Online Bookshop System (make order process).

	Manual		BMSpec		Correctness	Extra elements
	Qty.	valid	Qty.	valid		<<extend>> <<precede>> <<include>>
Use cases	5	5	5	5	100%	
Actors	3	3	3	3	100%	

Table 5. Extra feature calculator.

	Manual		BMSpec		Correctness	Extra elements
	Qty.	valid	Qty.	valid		
Use cases	2	2	2	2	100%	
Actors	1	1	1	1	100%	

Table 6. Registration on X-Road.

	Manual		BMSpec		Correctness	Extra elements
	Qty.	valid	Qty.	valid		
Use cases	4	4	4	4	100%	
Actors	2	2	2	2	100%	

Table 7. Consume X-Road service.

	Manual		BMSpec		Correctness	Extra elements
	Qty.	valid	Qty.	valid		
Use cases	7	7	7	7	100%	
Actors	3	3	3	3	100%	

Table 8. Provide X-Road service.

	Manual		BMSpec		Correctness	Extra elements
	Qty.	valid	Qty.	valid		
Use cases	5	5	5	5	100%	
Actors	2	2	2	2	100%	

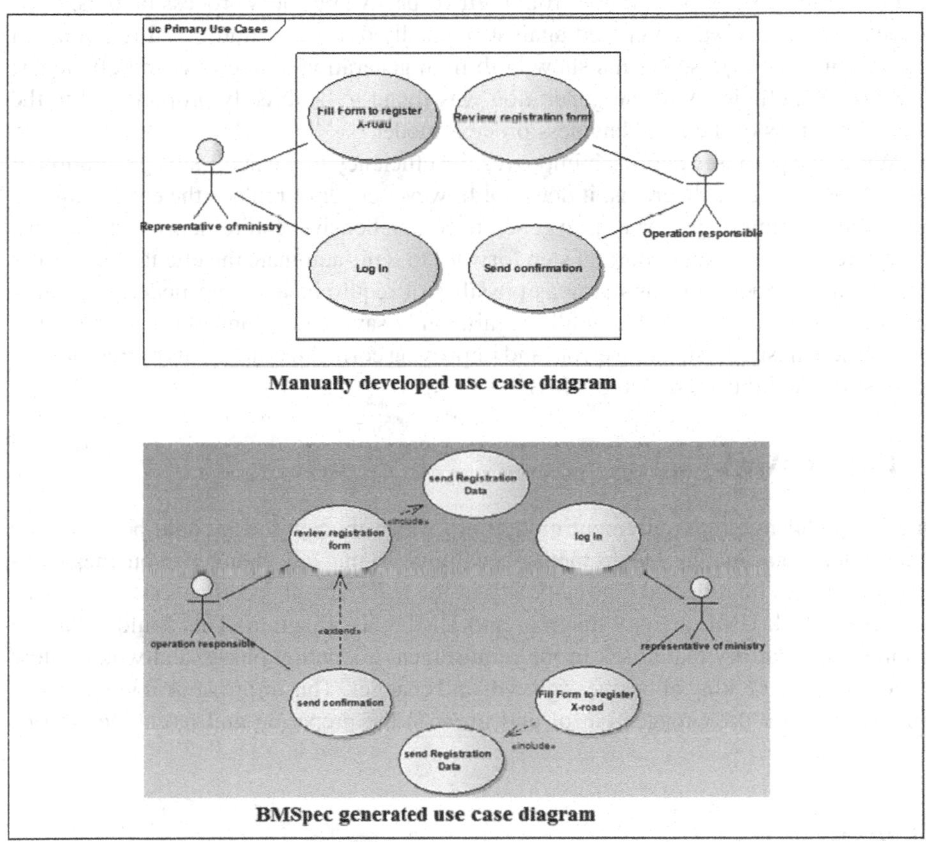

Manually developed use case diagram

BMSpec generated use case diagram

Fig. 11. Use case diagrams for the X-Road Registration service

As shown above, the proposed approach achieved 100% correctness, i.e. identified elements of use case diagrams correctly for all evaluated case studies. Also considering the proposed approach with other competing approaches including [14, 27], it was able to identify and generate additional use case diagram elements and features, including the <<extend>>, <<include>>, <<precede>> and <<invoke >> associations.

5 Conclusion

The paper proposed an approach that shows business models can be used to generate accurate software specifications. The proposed approach employs systematic method that takes a number of systematic steps that processes business process models as input using standardized BPMN notations and produces software specification as UML-based use cases. The approach is evaluated, using gold standard, on seven case studies. Specifications, as UML use case diagrams, of the evaluated case studies were developed using manual traditional requirement engineering techniques and automatically generated using the proposed approach from their respective business process models. Each of the case studies was compared against manually developed traditional requirement engineering techniques. Results show both high generation correctness and efficiency. However, the efficiency of the generation was found to be directly proportional to the level of richness of the input business process model.

While the proposed approach improves the efficiency of the automatic generation of UML-based use case diagrams, it does not however cover or replace the entire requirements engineering stage, nor aims to generate comprehensive requirement specifications. It provides, however, an important step forward to semi-automate the elicitation process through the extraction of as many as possible of requirements from underlying business process models, thus potentially significantly saving development time, reducing requirement misunderstanding errors and improving correct requirements representation using software industry de facto UML.

6 Future Work

One key challenge in requirement modelling, which this approach could be improved to include, is automating requirement traceability, so that any changes in business process model will be reflected automatically in the requirement specifications (e.g. UML use case model, UML activity diagram and UML class diagram).This could solve the problem of volatility that arises in the requirement elicitation phase, and would allow automating the tracking of business growth and changes. This improvement would additionally increase the engagement of end users in the preparing and re-engineering of business models.

References

1. Dijkman, R.M., Joosten, S., Ordina, F.: An algorithm to derive use case diagrams from business process models. In: Proceedings of the 6th International Conference on Software Engineering and Applications, SEA, Anaheim, US (2002)
2. Odeh, M., Richard, K.: Bridging the gap between business models and system models. Inf. Softw. Technol. **45**(15), 1053–1060 (2003)
3. Aburub, F.: Activity-based approach to derive system models from business process models. In: International Conference on Information Society, i-Society. IEEE (2012)
4. Przybylek, A.: A business-oriented approach to requirements elicitation. In: International Conference on Evaluation of Novel Approaches to Software Engineering, ENASE. IEEE (2014)

5. Boehm, B.W.: Software Engineering Economics, vol. 197. Prentice-hall, Englewood Cliffs (1981)
6. Weerakkody, V., Currie, W.: Integrating business process reengineering with information systems development: issues & implications. In: van der Aalst, Wil M.P., Weske, M. (eds.) BPM 2003. LNCS, vol. 2678, pp. 302–320. Springer, Heidelberg (2003). https://doi.org/10.1007/3-540-44895-0_21
7. Hammer, M.: Reengineering work: don't automate, obliterate. Harvard Bus. Rev. **68**(4), 104–112 (1990)
8. Kaplan, R.B., Murdock, L.: Rethinking the corporation: core process redesign. Mckinsey Q. **22**, 27–44 (1991)
9. Eriksson, E., Magnus, P.: Business modeling with UML. Wiley, New York (2000). Business Patterns at Work
10. Dijkman, R., Jorg, H., Jana, K., (eds) Business Process Model and Notation. Springer, Boston (2011). https://doi.org/10.1007/978-0-387-39940-9_1195
11. Pressman, R.S.: Software Engineering: A Practitioner's Approach. Palgrave Macmillan, London (2005)
12. OMG: Unified modeling language (OMG UML), version 2.5, Technical report, Object Management Group (2012)
13. Bloch, M., Sven. B., Jürgen, L.: Delivering large-scale IT projects on time, on budget, and on value, McKinsey Quarterly (2012)
14. Cruz, E.F., Machado, R.J., Santos, M.Y.: From business process models to use case models: a systematic approach. In: Aveiro, D., Tribolet, J., Gouveia, D. (eds.) EEWC 2014. LNBIP, vol. 174, pp. 167–181. Springer, Cham (2014). https://doi.org/10.1007/978-3-319-06505-2_12
15. Indulska, M., Recker, J., Rosemann, M., Green, P.: Business process modeling: current issues and future challenges. In: van Eck, P., Gordijn, J., Wieringa, R. (eds.) CAiSE 2009. LNCS, vol. 5565, pp. 501–514. Springer, Heidelberg (2009). https://doi.org/10.1007/978-3-642-02144-2_39
16. Rajagopal, P., Lee, R., Ahlswede, T., Chiang, C.C., Karolak, D.: A new approach for software requirements elicitation. In: 6th International Conference on Software Engineering, Artificial Intelligence, Networking and Parallel/Distributed Computing and ACIS International Workshop on Self-Assembling Wireless Network, pp. 32–42. IEEE (2005)
17. Brooks, F.P.: No silver bullet: essence and accidents of software engineering. IEEE Comput. **20**, 10–19 (1987)
18. Eriksson, H.-E., Penker, M.: Business Modeling with UML: Business Patterns at Work. Wiley, Hoboken (2000)
19. Kruchten, P.: The Rational Unified Process – An Introduction. Addison-Wesley, Boston (2000)
20. Davis, A., Dieste, O., Hickey, A., Juristo, N., Moreno, A.M.: Effectiveness of requirements elicitation techniques: empirical results derived from a systematic review. In: 14th IEEE International Requirements Engineering Conference, RE 2006, pp. 179–188. IEEE (2006)
21. Neill, C.J., Laplante, P.A.: Requirements engineering: the state of the practice. IEEE Softw. **20**(6), 40–45 (2003)
22. Berry, D.M., Kamsties, E.: Ambiguity in requirements specification. In: do Prado Leite, J.C.S., Doorn, J.H. (eds) Perspectives on Software Requirements. The Springer International Series in Engineering and Computer Science, vol 753. Springer, Boston (2004). https://doi.org/10.1007/978-1-4615-0465-8_2
23. Kitchenham, B.A., Pickard, L., Linkman, S., Jones, P.: A framework for evaluating a software bidding model. Inf. Softw. Technol. **47**(11), 747–760 (2005)
24. Jalote, P.A.: Concise Introduction to Software Engineering. Springer, London (2008). https://doi.org/10.1007/978-1-84800-302-6

25. Mili, H., Tremblay, G., Jaoude, G.B., Lefebvre, É., Elabed, L., Boussaidi, G.E.: Business process modeling languages: sorting through the alphabet soup. ACM Comput. Surv. (CSUR) **43**(1), 4 (2010)
26. Bider, I.: State-oriented business process modeling: principles, theory and practice (Doctoral dissertation, Data-och systemvetenskap) (2002)
27. Hove, S.E., Anda, B.: Experiences from conducting semi-structured interviews in empirical software engineering research. In: 11th IEEE International Software Metrics Symposium, METRICS 2005, pp. 10. IEEE (2005)
28. Shishkov, B., Dietz, J.L.: Deriving use cases from business processes, the advantages of demo. In: ICEIS, no. 3, pp. 138–146 (2003). https://doi.org/10.1007/1-4020-2673-0_29
29. Turkman, S., Taweel, A.: Business process model driven automatic software requirements generation. In: Shishkov, B. (ed.) BMSD 2019. LNBIP, vol. 356, pp. 270–278. Springer, Cham (2019). https://doi.org/10.1007/978-3-030-24854-3_20

Integrated Process Model for Systems Product Line Engineering of Physical Protection Systems

Bedir Tekinerdogan[1(✉)], Sevil Yagiz[2], Kaan Özcan[2], and Iskender Yakin[2]

[1] Research, Information Technology, Wageningen University, Wageningen, The Netherlands
bedir.tekinerdogan@wur.nl
[2] Aselsan A.Ş., Ankara, Turkey
{syagiz,mkozcan,iyakin}@aselsan.com.tr

Abstract. A physical protection system (PPS) integrates people, procedures, and equipment for the protection of assets or facilities against theft, sabotage, or other malevolent intruder attacks. Designing effective PPSs is not trivial and requires the consideration of multiple different concerns. Hence, several PPS methods have been proposed in the literature to design and analyze PPSs to realize the envisioned objectives. These methods have mainly considered the design of a single PPS. Yet, despite the differences, PPSs also share a common design and set of features and likewise can be developed using a systematic large scale reuse approach. Product line engineering (PLE) has been used in various application domains to exploit the potential for large scale reuse, and with this reduce the time-to-market, reduce the cost, and the overall quality of the developed systems. In this paper, we first report on the results of our study to explicitly model the process for developing PPSs. Subsequently, we present the integration of the PPS method with the current PLE method. For modeling the processes, we adopt the Business Process Modeling Notation (BPMN). The resulting method can be applied to the development of various PPSs while considering large-scale reuse.

Keywords: Physical protection systems · Systems engineering · Business process modeling · Product line engineering

1 Introduction

A physical protection system (PPS) integrates people, procedures, and equipment for the protection of assets or facilities against theft, sabotage, or other malevolent intruder attacks [4, 19]. PPSs have targeted the protection of various systems, including airports, rail transport, highways, hospitals, bridges, the electricity grid, dams, power plants, seaports, oil refineries, and water systems. Designing effective PPSs requires careful consideration of the requirements and the resources to provide the protection that is needed. Without a proper assessment and design, valuable resources on unnecessary protection might be wasted or, worse yet, fail to provide adequate protection at critical points of the facility. To avoid both limitations and risks, several PPS design methods have been proposed in the literature to design and analyze PPSs to realize the envisioned objectives.

B. Shishkov (Ed.): BMSD 2020, LNBIP 391, pp. 137–151, 2020.
https://doi.org/10.1007/978-3-030-52306-0_9

In general, a PPS provides *deterrence, detection, delay,* and *response* measures to protect against an adversary's attempt to complete a malicious act. As such, a PPS method considers these concerns explicitly and defines the steps for realizing these in the best possible manner. The existing PPS methods have been successfully applied to design effective PPSs. Yet, it can be observed that despite the differences, PPSs also share a common design and set of features, and likewise can be developed using systematic reuse approach. The current PPS methods, however, have targeted the development of a single system and did not consider the large scale reuse for developing various PPSs.

This paper considers the context of an industrial company that is indeed developing a broad range of PPSs. Each facility that needs to be protected is indeed unique, but on the other hand, also recurring development activities over the entire systems engineering life cycle can be observed. Obviously, there seems to be a large potential for reuse that will support the development process. Reuse has been an important goal in many industrial practices and also broadly addressed in the literature. While reuse was initially focused on a small scale, ad hoc reuse, currently, it is widely recognized that the broadest and the most valuable benefits are derived from a large-scale systematic reuse approach. This idea has culminated in the product line engineering (PLE) approach that indeed focuses on exploiting reuse over the whole lifecycle process [1, 11, 17]. Traditionally, a product line is defined as a set of systems sharing a common, managed set of features that satisfy the specific needs of a particular market segment or mission and that are developed from a common set of core assets in a prescribed way. While PLE has initially focused on software reuse, the development paradigm is now applied in a broader systems engineering context, leading to the notion of systems product line engineering (SPLE). Despite earlier reuse approaches, SPLE aims to provide pro-active, pre-planned reuse at a large granularity (domain and product level) to develop applications from a core, shared asset base.

The benefits of adopting a product line approach have been analyzed and discussed before by several authors [9, 12]. Several studies show remarkable benefits of the organizations that are aligned with commonly held business goals including large-scale productivity gains, decreased time to market, increased product quality, decreased product risk, increased market agility, increased customer satisfaction, more efficient use of human resources, ability to effect mass customization, ability to maintain a market presence, and ability to sustain unprecedented growth.

The PLE process is agnostic to the domain and can be applied to developing a product line for any domain. Yet, for the development of PPSs, we also need to focus on the domain-specific PPS aspects. Hence an integrated PLE process for PPS is needed. To this end, our objective in this paper is to model the PPS method explicitly, and subsequently show the integration with the PLE process. For modeling the methods, we use the Business Process Modeling Notation (BPMN). The provided method is novel and can be applied to the development of various PPSs while considering large scale reuse.

The remainder of the paper is organized as follows. Section 2 presents the product line engineering process. Section 3 elaborates on the goals for process modeling. Section 4 presents the modeling PPS process. Section 5 shows how to integrate the PLE process with the PPS process. Finally, Sect. 6 concludes the paper.

2 Product Line Engineering

Developing PPS can be done using a single systems engineering or product line engineering approach. In the traditional single systems engineering approach in which no PLE is adopted, usually, a product portfolio can exist, but hereby systems are developed separately. This means that no PLE practices such as explicit commonality variability modeling, a product family architecture, and a shared asset base is adopted. The usually adopted process is shown in Fig. 1.

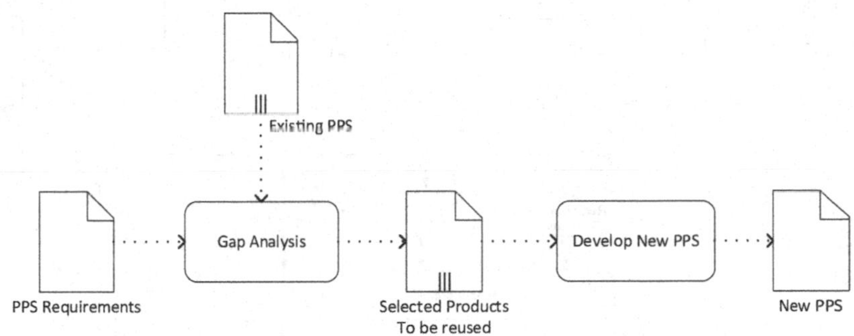

Fig. 1. Ad-hoc, non-PLE reuse strategy for developing PPS

The basic activity in this process is to identify among all the already manufactured or delivered systems, which is the closest one to the requirements and needs expressed formally (through PPS requirements) by a new potential customer. Then the selected engineering artifacts of the previously existing PPS are reused and modified in order to completely fulfill the requirements for the new PPS.

The traditional way of developing PPS fails to see and exploit the potential for reuse. Although PPSs are different, they still share the common structure and features. The larger the commonality is, the more reuse potential we can identify. This means that a company that targets the development of multiple PPS can adopt a smarter, reuse-based approach. Hence, a product line of PPS can be anticipated and developed from a common set of core assets in a prescribed way.

Compared to single system development, applying a product line engineering approach requires additional investments. The initial investment will result in a so-called *return on investment* (ROI). The adoption of product line engineering approach will usually pay off after the development of more than one product. This point is denoted as the *break-even point*. Although different PLE processes have been proposed, they share the same concepts of *domain engineering*, in which a reusable platform and product line architecture is developed, and *application engineering*, in which the results of the domain engineering process are used to develop the products. The overall development process is further controlled by a management process that consists of technical and organizational management. The typical common PLE process is shown in Fig. 2.

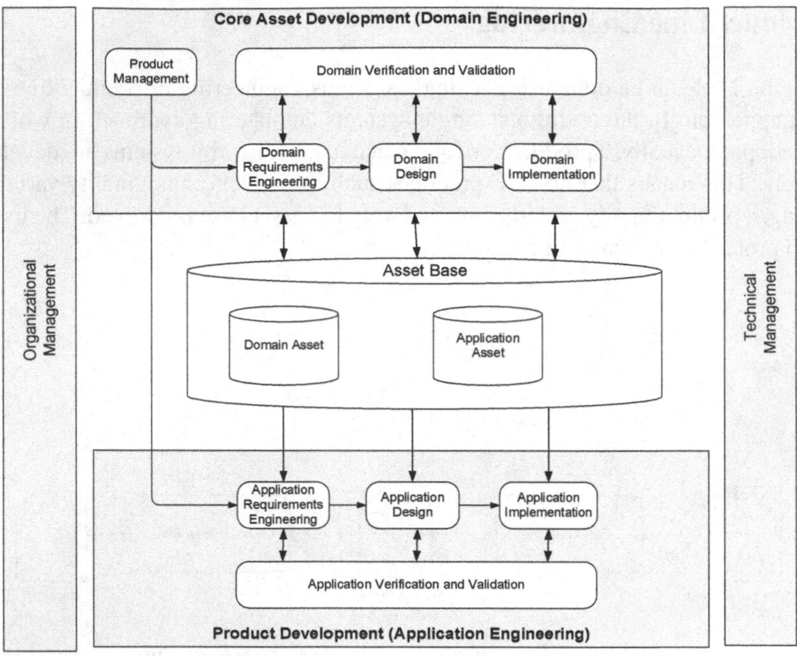

Fig. 2. PLE Process (adapted from: [15])

3 Adopted Design Approach

In this paper, we aim to model the PPS process and integrate this with the PLE process. In general, a process is defined as a collection of related, structured activities or tasks that produce a specific service or product (serve a particular goal) for a particular set of customers. A business process model (BPM) is an abstract representation of a business process. Various objectives can be distinguished for developing explicit process models [15], including (1) Facilitate human understanding and communication (2) Support process improvement (3) Support process management (4) Automate process guidance (5) Automate execution support.

In this paper, the primary goal of process modeling includes communication of the PPS process to different stakeholders, the guidance of the PPS process activities, means to analyze the progress and align the PPS process with the product line engineering process. Our focus is not on automated process guidance and/or automated execution of the process, although this could indeed be considered as a follow-up study.

The adopted design method is shown in Fig. 3. We start with two parallel activities that aim to identify the PLE methods and PPS methods. Both are modeled using BPMN. The final step is the integration of the PPS with the PLE method.

For the PPS methods, we have primarily consulted the methods of the following sources:

- ML. Garcia. Vulnerability Assessment of Physical Protection Systems. Amsterdam: Elsevier Butterworth-Heinemann; 2006 [3].

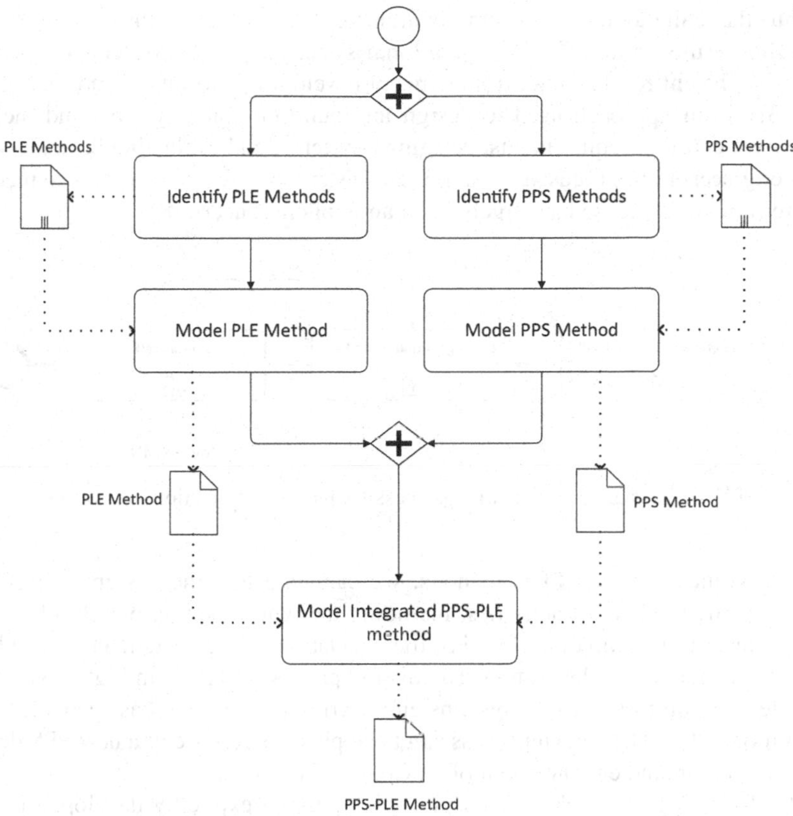

Fig. 3. Adopted design method for deriving integrated PPS-PLE process

- ML. Garcia. The Design and Evaluation of Physical Protection Systems. 2nd ed. Amsterdam: Elsevier Butterworth-Heinemann; 2008 [4].
- L. Fennelly. Effective Physical Security, Fifth Edition (5th. ed.). Butterworth-Heinemann, USA, 2016 [10].
- J.D. Williams, Physical Protection System Design and Evaluation, IAEA-CN-68/29, Vienna, 10–12 November 1997 [19].
- IAEA, Handbook on the Physical Protection of Nuclear Material and Facilities, IAEA-TECDOC-127, March 2000 [6].

For identifying the PLE methods, we have used the traditional methods as published in the PLE community. In this paper, we do not elaborate on the modeling of the PLE method [1, 11] since we have reported on these already in our earlier studies [14–16, 18].

4 PPS Process Model

PPS design is a systematic approach that employs, in particular, a systems engineering approach Systems engineering is an interdisciplinary approach to translating users' needs into the realization of a system, its architecture, and design through an iterative process that results in an effective operational system [5, 7, 9]. Systems engineering applies over the entire life cycle, from concept development to final disposal. Systems engineering is an approach used to design and build complex systems and includes processes for defining requirements, designing systems, and evaluating designs. While systems engineering has focused on defining a systematic life cycle process to meet the quality requirements, reuse has largely been an implicit concern [8].

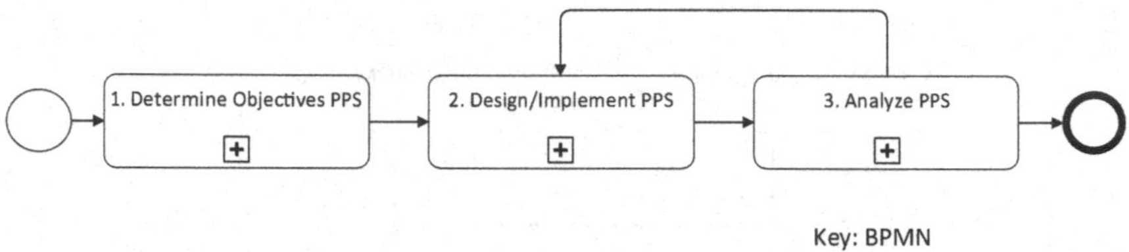

Fig. 4. Design and evaluation process for physical protection systems

Based on the identified PPS methods, we can state that the design of each PPS includes a predefined set of activities, including the determination of PPS objectives, the design and implementation of a PPS, the evaluation of the design, and if needed, a redesign or refinement of the system. The overall process is shown in Fig. 4, which can be considered as an instance of a systems engineering process that has been adapted to the design of a PPS. The shown process can be applied to the case of a new PPS design, or to an adaptation and enhancement of an existing PPS.

In the following, we elaborate on the process using explicitly developed process models.

4.1 Determine PPS Objectives Process

Figure 5 shows the activities for determining the objectives of a PPS. To formulate these objectives, the designer must (1) characterize the facility, (2) identify the targets, and (3) define the potential threats. In parallel, the designer should identify and check the legal and regulatory requirements that are required by the corresponding state laws or standardization organizations. We elaborate on these steps in the following sub-sections.

4.1.1 Facility Characterization Process

The facility characterization process is shown in Fig. 6. The characterization of the facility focuses on the entity that needs protection. Before any design decisions concerning the level of protection needed, in this step, it is aimed to provide an understanding of what is being protected and the surrounding environment.

The results of this step will help identify constraints, document existing protection features, and reveal areas and assets that may be vulnerable. The major areas of investigation for facility characterization that have been defined in the PPS methods include:

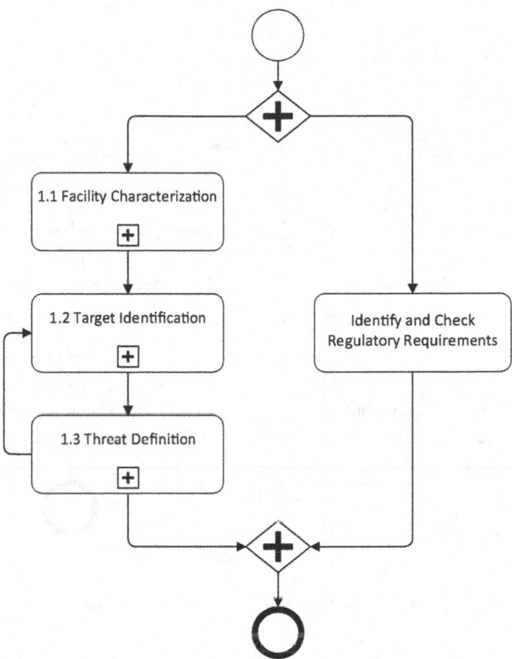

Fig. 5. Process for *determine objectives* physical protection systems

- *physical conditions*
  The physical conditions such as site boundary, location of the facility, access points, existing physical protection features, and other infrastructure details.
- *facility operations*
  The adopted processes in the facility, such as operating conditions (working hours, off-hours, emergency operations), and the types and numbers of employees.
- *facility policies and procedures*
  The written and unwritten policies and procedures used at a facility.
- *regulatory requirements*
  All facilities responsible for some regulatory authority, such as the local fire department, safety, and health regulators, and federal agencies.
- *legal issues*
  cover liability, privacy, access for the disabled, labor relations, employment practices, proper training for guards, the failure to protect, and excessive use of force by guards, to list only a few.
- *safety considerations*
  issues related to safety
- *corporate goals and objectives*
  the goals and objectives of the corporation or facility regarding the protection

Characterization of the facility thus requires both a thorough analysis of the facility and the processes within the facility, together with the identification of any existing physical protection features.

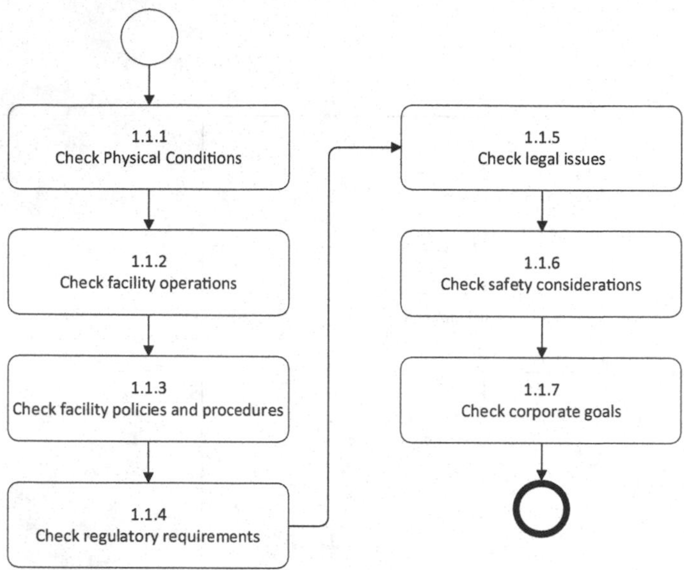

Fig. 6. Facility characterization process

4.1.2 Target Identification Process

The target identification process is shown in Fig. 7. The aim of this process is to identify what to protect without yet considering the potential threats or the means to provide physical protection. This elaborates on the facility characterization process and requires a thorough review of the facility and its assets. Two types of targets can be distinguished, primary targets, and secondary targets. Primary targets may be the physical assets inside the facility and include electronic data, people, or anything that could impact business operations. Secondary targets are the assets that can be attacked to reduce system effectiveness and/or facilitate an attack. The target identification process focuses on the identification of both types. The two techniques for target identification are a manual listing of targets and the use of logic diagrams to identify vital areas [3]. In manual listing, all significant targets to be protected are listed. When the facility is, however, too complex for manual identification of targets, logic diagrams can be used instead of or as a complementary technique. One type of logic diagram called a fault tree graphically represents the combinations of components and events that can result in a specified undesired state [13].

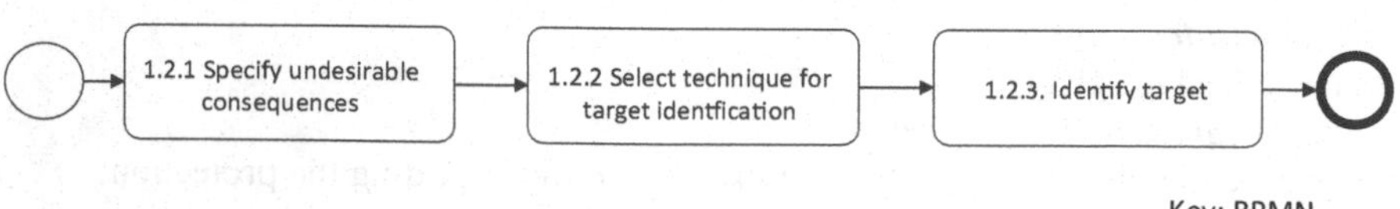

Fig. 7. Target identification process

4.1.3 Threat Definition Process

Facility characterization is followed by the threat definition process that aims to analyze and describe the threats for the corresponding facility and the identified targets.

The threat definition process is shown in Fig. 8. The methodology for *threat definition* consists of three basic parts: (1) List the information needed to define the threat (2) Collect information on the potential threat (3) Organize the information to make it usable. Hereby, the first step aims to identify and describe the information regarding the class of adversary, the range of tactics of the adversary, the range of the adversary's tactics, and the adversary's capabilities [4]. Different classes of adversaries include outsiders, insiders, and outsiders working in collusion with insiders. The range of tactics of adversaries includes deceit, force, stealth, or any combination of these. As defined by Garcia [4], deceit is the attempted defeat of a security system by using false authorization and identification; force is the overt, forcible attempt to overcome a security system; and stealth is any attempt to defeat the detection system and enter the facility covertly.

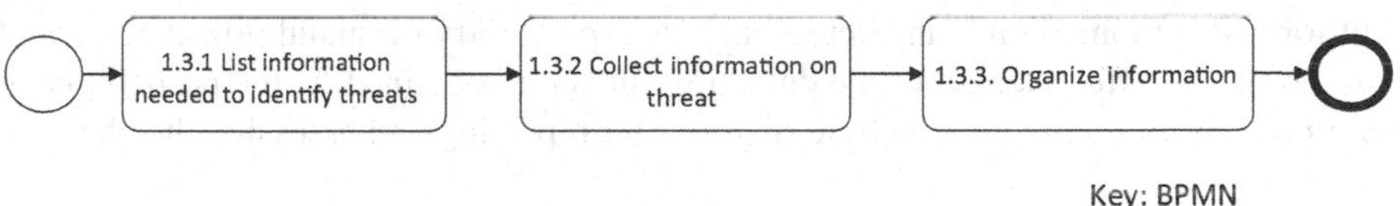

Fig. 8. Threat definition process

4.2 Design PPS Process

Once the PPS Objectives have been defined, the design process can be started. Figure 9 shows the top-level activities for the PPS design process. The outcome of the PPS design process is a PPS design that should meet the defined objectives and operational, safety, legal, and economic constraints of the facility. The design process is structured according to the primary functions of PPS, that is, *detection* of an adversary, *delay* of that adversary, and *response* by security personnel (guard force). All these three functions are essential functions of an effective PPS and must be performed in the order of *detect, delay, response.* Further, the overall period should be within a length of time that is less than the time required for completing the adversary task.

To derive a proper design, several design principles are usually taken into account, such as *defense in depth, graded approach, balanced protection,* and *robustness* [2, 3, 6]. *Defense in depth* implies the usage of a combination of multiple layers of systems and measures that have to be overcome or circumvented before physical protection is compromised. *Graded approach* implies the application of physical protection measures that are proportional to the potential consequences of a malicious act. *Balanced protection*, defines a method to use comparably effective physical protection measures. Finally, *robustness* requires the inclusion of redundancy and diversity in the PPS design to ensure a high probability of effective protection against the range of threats. In the following sub-sections, we elaborate on the steps of the design process.

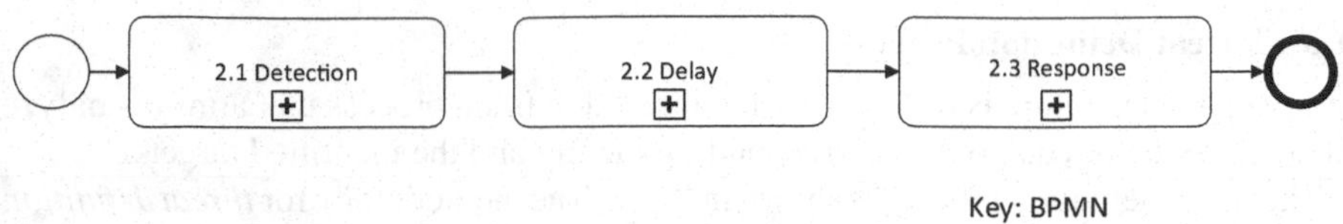

Fig. 9. PPS design process

4.2.1 Detection Process

Detection includes the discovery of an adversary action that is covert or overt. The process for detection is shown in Fig. 10. To detect an adversary action, typically, a sensor reacts to a stimulus, an alarm is initiated, and a report is sent and displayed. The alarm is assessed, and a decision is made, whether it was a false alarm or a real adversary action. Here it is necessary that an alarm is followed by an alarm assessment. Otherwise, this is not considered detection. For realizing the detection, interior and exterior sensors are designed. Detection also includes entry control which allows entry to authorized personnel only and detects the attempted entry of unauthorized personnel or material. The effectiveness of the detection function is defined by the probability of sensing adversary action and the time required for reporting and assessing the alarm.

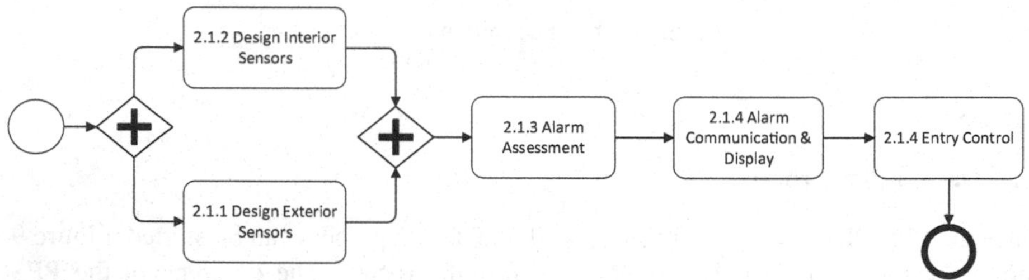

Fig. 10. PPS design process – detection

The measures of the effectiveness of entry control are throughput, false acceptance rate, and false rejection rate. Throughput is defined as the number of authorized personnel allowed access per unit time, assuming that all personnel who attempt entry are authorized for entrance. False acceptance is the rate at which false identities or credentials are allowed entry, while the false rejection rate is the frequency of denying access to authorized personnel.

4.2.2 Delay Process

Delay implies the slowing down of a detected adversary attack. Once the adversary is detected, it is important to delay the adversary so that the response force can interrupt the attack before the goal is achieved. Delay can be realized by human personnel, barriers, locks, and activated delays. Since it is not feasible to provide a response force at every attack point, some type of adversary delay is needed. The process for the delay in PPS is shown in Fig. 11. In essence, it includes two parallel steps *provide active barriers* and *provide passive barriers.* Active barriers can, on command, stop or delay an adversary from accomplishing the objective. For example, a door or security barrier is active because it can be moved to allow access but keeps adversary agents outside. Passive barriers are relatively immovable, and no manual or electronic action is required for the barrier to perform its function.

After an adversary has been detected, delay elements will prevent completion of the adversary act, provide delay until an adequate response force can arrive. The adversary may be, of course, delayed prior to detection, but this has no value to the effectiveness of the PPS since it does not provide additional time to respond to the adversary. Delay before detection is primarily a deterrent [4].

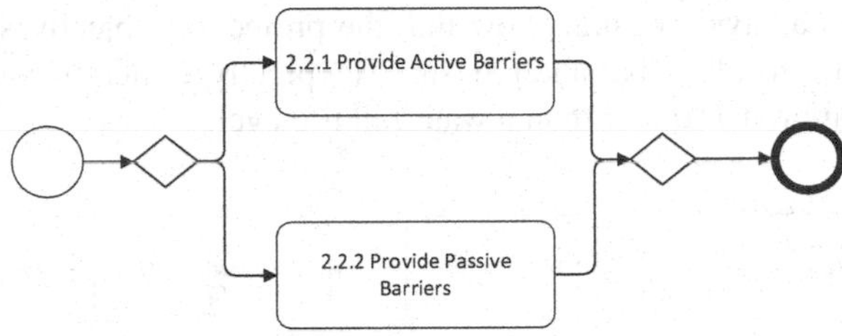

Fig. 11. PPS design process – delay

4.2.3 Response Process

The response function consists of the actions taken by the response force to prevent adversary success and can include both *interruption* and *neutralization*. Interruption is the activity of a sufficient number of response force personnel at the appropriate location to stop the adversary's progress. For this, it is needed to communicate the accurate information about adversary actions to the response force and select and deploy the response force. Neutralization includes the actions and effectiveness of the responders after interruption. Two major categories of response forces can be distinguished, immediate on-site response (timely response) and after-the-fact recovery. The use and combination of these forces will depend on the needs and objectives of a facility and the potential targets. An important metric is the response time that defines the time between receipt of a communication of adversary action and the interruption of the adversary action. Figure 12 shows the design process for the PPS response activity. It includes two steps, the design of the response force and the corresponding communication.

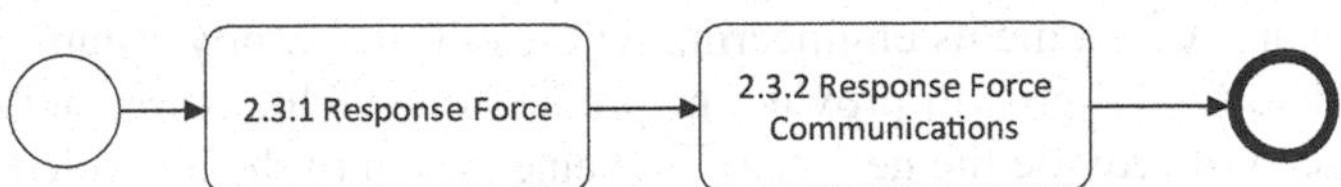

Fig. 12. PPS design process – response

4.3 Evaluate PPS Process

The final step in the design process is the evaluation of the design PPS. The process for this is shown in Fig. 13. Several techniques can be distinguished here, including Path Analysis, Scenario Analysis, and System Effectiveness Analysis. For more details about these approaches, we refer to [3, 4, 10].

The outcome of this process a system vulnerability assessment. The analysis of the PPS design can lead to either to the conclusion that the design is feasible and effectively achieves the protection objectives, or it will still identify unnoticed weaknesses. In the first case, the design and analysis process is completed. However, if the PPS does not fulfill the objectives for effective protection, then a redesign will be considered. This might also need to reconsideration or adaptation of the initial PPS objectives. This cycle continues until the analysis results show that the protection objectives are met. Note that the overall process of design and redesign is typically an iterative and incremental lifecycle process approach rather than a waterfall life cycle.

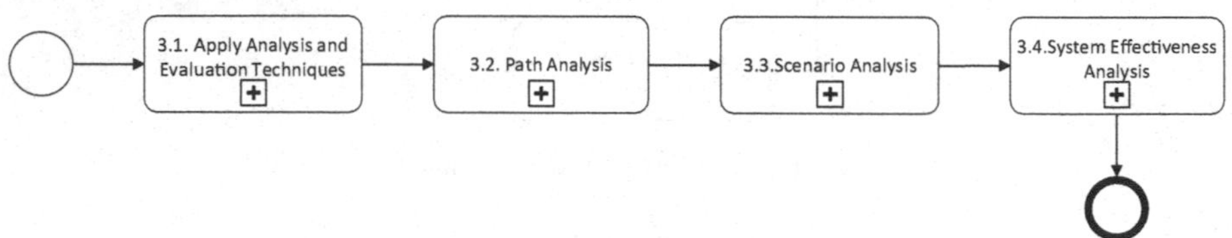

Fig. 13. PPS evaluation process

5 Integration of PLE and PPS Processes

In Sect. 2, we have provided the SPLE process, which we have also modeled in our earlier work [14–16, 18]. The previous section has provided an explicit process model for PPS. The SPLE process is, in general, domain agnostic, and can thus be applied to multiple application domains, and as such, fails to address domain-specific process concerns. On the other hand, the PPS process focuses on the development of a single PPS and does not explicitly consider reuse. To provide a systematic product line engineering for PPS, we have integrated both processes, which is shown in Fig. 14.

In essence, the dominant process model is the two-life cycle process of the PLE process consisting of a domain engineering process and an engineering process. In the domain engineering process, the core assets for the PPSs that are envisioned can be developed. In a sense, this does not change the conventional domain engineering process steps. The domain requirements engineering will result in a family requirements specification, the domain design will provide the product line architecture, and the domain implementation will provide the necessary implementation of the identified core assets for the PPSs.

The PPS method, shown on the right part of the figure, is integrated with the application engineering process, which starts by identifying the objectives and requirements of a particular PPS. These objectives and requirements, however, are not developed from

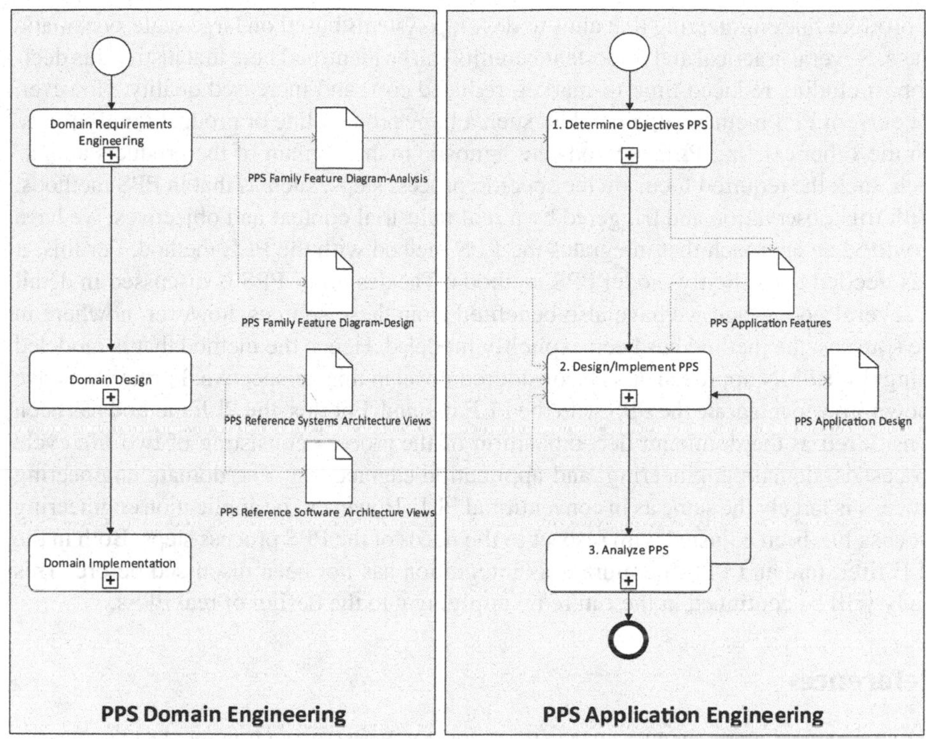

Fig. 14. PPS design process integrated within the PLE process

scratch but reused from the reusable asset base that is the result of the domain engineering process. Similarly, the design process follows the exact same process steps that we have described in the previous section but will primarily reuse the assets and the design that is needed for developing the PPS. Finally, the analysis of the PPS is based on the evaluation of the designed PPS.

Before, we stated that we wish to provide large scale systematic reuse for developing PPS. This is, in particular, necessary if a company is developing multiple different PPSs, which are based on a common product line architecture and a substantially large part of commonality. One could state that this could be just developed using conventional PLE methods. However, in particular, PPS design requires very domain-specific specific steps regarding the design of deterrence, detection, delay, and response actions. As such, it is needed to represent not only the artifacts but also the PPS process steps in the PPS product line engineering. The method shown in Fig. 14 accomplishes both goals. On the one hand, it ensures that the key concern of PPS that is protection is properly addressed. On the other hand, it helps to develop PPSs faster, with lower cost, and higher quality.

6 Conclusion

In this paper, we have focused on the design of PPS systems. In contrast to the single system perspective that is adopted in current PPS methods, we have discussed the adoption of product line engineering that aims to develop systems based on large scale systematic reuse. Several practical and important benefits can be identified here that justify this decision, including reduced time-to-market, reduced cost, and increased quality. However, the current PPS methods do not adopt such a large product line or product family focus. On the other existing PLE methods are agnostic to the domain of the products and, as such, lack the required focus on the specific process steps, such as that in PPS methods. With this observation and triggered by a real industrial context and objectives, we have provided an approach that integrates the PPS method with the PLE method. For this, it was needed to explicitly model PPS methods. The design of PPS is discussed in detail in several books, and we have also benefited from these sources, however, nowhere in the sources, the method has been explicitly modeled. Hence the method that is modeled using the BPMN approach can be considered novel in this perspective. Further, we have shown how to integrate the PPS with the PLE method. For this, the PLE method has been considered as the dominant decomposition of the process consisting of two life cycle processes, domain engineering, and application engineering. The domain engineering process is largely the same as in conventional PLE. However, the application engineering process has been adjusted with respect to the needs of the PPS process steps. Both in the PLE literature and PPS literature, this integration has not been discussed before. This study will be continued in the future by applying it to the design of real PPSs.

References

1. Clements, P., Northrop, L.: Software Product Lines: Practices and Patterns. Addison-Wesley, Boston (2002)
2. Drago, A.: Methods and techniques for enhancing physical security of critical infrastructures, Ph.D. thesis, University of Naples, March 2015
3. Garcia, M.L.: Vulnerability Assessment of Physical Protection Systems. Elsevier Butterworth-Heinemann, Amsterdam (2006)
4. Garcia, M.L.: The Design and Evaluation of Physical Protection Systems, 2nd edn. Elsevier Butterworth-Heinemann, Amsterdam (2008)
5. Guide to the Systems Engineering Body of Knowledge (SEBoK), October 2016
6. IAEA: Handbook on the Physical Protection of Nuclear Material and Facilities, IAEA-TECDOC-127, March 2000
7. Walden, D.D., Roedler, G.J., Forsberg, K.J., Hamelin, R.D., Shortell, T.M. (eds.): INCOSE Systems Engineering Handbook: A Guide for System Life Cycle Processes and Activities, 4th edn. Wiley, New York (2015)
8. INCOSE Product Line Engineering International Working Group. http://www.incose.org/ChaptersGroups/WorkingGroups/analytic/product-lines. Accessed October 2017
9. International Council on Systems Engineering (INCOSE), INCOSE Systems Engineering Handbook, Ver. 3.2, INCOSE-TP-2003-002-03.2, January 2010
10. Fennelly, L.: Effective Physical Security, 5th edn. Butterworth-Heinemann, Oxford (2016)
11. Pohl, K., Böckle, G., van der Linden, F.: Software Product Line Engineering – Foundations, Principles, and Techniques. Springer, Heidelberg (2005). https://doi.org/10.1007/3-540-28901-1
12. Schmid, K., Verlage, M.: The economic impact of product line adoption and evolution. IEEE Softw. **19**(4), 50–57 (2002)
13. Tekinerdogan, B., Sozer, H., Aksit, M.: Software architecture reliability analysis using failure scenarios. Elsevier J. Syst. Softw. **81**(4), 558–575 (2008)

14. Tekinerdogan, B., Ozkose Erdogan, O., Aktug, O.: Supporting incremental product development using multiple product line architecture. Int. J. Knowl. Syst. Sci. (IJKSS) **5**(4), 1–16 (2014)
15. Tekinerdogan, B., Duman, S., Gümüşay, Ö., Durak, B.: Devising integrated process models for systems product line engineering. In: 2019 International Symposium on Systems Engineering (ISSE), Edinburgh, United Kingdom (2019)
16. Tekinerdogan, B., Duman, S., Caner, H., Durak, B.: Customizing a feature ontology for product line engineering within a system-of-systems context. In: 2019 International Symposium on Systems Engineering (ISSE), Edinburgh, United Kingdom (2019)
17. Tüzün, E., Tekinerdogan, B., Kalender, M.E., Bilgen, S.: Empirical evaluation of a decision support model for adopting software product line engineering. Inf. Softw. Technol. **60**, 77–101 (2015)
18. Tüzün, E., Giray, G., Tekinerdogan, B., Macit, Y.: Modeling software product line engineering with essence framework. Int. J. Inf. Technol. **11**(1), 99–109 (2018)
19. Williams, J.D.: Physical Protection System Design and Evaluation, IAEA-CN-68/29, Vienna, 10–12 November 1997

From Adaptive Business Processes to Orchestrated Microflows

Andreas Daniel Sinnhofer[1,2](✉), Roy Oberhauser[3], and Christian Steger[1]

[1] Institute of Technical Informatics, Graz University of Technology, Graz, Austria
a.sinnhofer@alumni.tugraz.at, steger@tugraz.at
[2] NXP Semiconductors, Gratkorn, Austria
[3] Computer Science Department, Aalen University, Aalen, Germany
roy.oberhauser@hs-aalen.de

Abstract. Nowadays, businesses with focus on consumer-products are challenged by short production cycles, high pricing pressure, and the need to deliver new features and services in a regular interval. Currently, businesses are tackling these challenges by automating their business processes, while yet trying to be flexible by introducing methods for process variability modeling. However, for larger processes and variability models, it becomes difficult to consider, maintain, and optimize all process variations in the various execution contexts. In software development, highly agile requirements are usually tackled with a flexible microservice architecture. Nonetheless, the fast-changing service landscape is often not fully reflected in the underlying business processes, leading to inefficiency and loss of profit. With this work, we extend our framework for process variability modeling with concepts of Microflows, allowing agile business process modeling and orchestration while utilizing the full flexibility of underlying microservices. In addition, we present a case study, showing how this approach is used in the context of an IoT application.

Keywords: Business processes · Workflow management systems · Microservices · Software Product Lines

1 Introduction

Today's society is heavily driven by an ever-changing and interconnected world. Heavily shaped through the digital transformation, new technologies like Internet of Things (IoT) are pushed as a solution for our daily problems. Generally speaking, IoT refers to the connection of our everyday objects with a network like the Internet [1]. Each of these devices is equipped with different kinds of sensors to observe its environment, making the device a smart object. In combination with embedded systems, IoT promises to increase the quality of our daily lives by taking over simple tasks like controlling the room temperature or cooking coffee. For businesses, this means that feature-rich systems are demanded by the customers, with the ability to unlock new services and features on a regular

B. Shishkov (Ed.): BMSD 2020, LNBIP 391, pp. 152–168, 2020.
https://doi.org/10.1007/978-3-030-52306-0_10

basis. Consequently, new methods are investigated on how to efficiently model process and product variability [2].

Business Process (BP)-oriented organizations are known to perform better regarding highly flexible demands of the market [2]. A workflow describes the automation of a BP by applying a set of procedural rules [3]. By using a workflow management system (WfMS), workflows are defined, created, and managed. However, while adaptive WfMS can handle a certain degree of flexibility, they usually require manual intervention and rework. As such, context-aware BP modeling techniques were introduced to cope with fast changing requirements [4]: by analyzing the context states of the environment and by mapping the suitable BPs to their related software systems, flexibility is gained that can then be used to automatically select, adapt and execute a process variant. Problems of this approach are that such systems are often developed independently from each other [2]. Consequently, operating and maintaining these variants can lead to unnecessary overhead.

Since recent years, software services or microservices are often utilized in software development to support a digital automation [5]. As described by Fowler and Lewis [6], microservices provide an agile and loosely-coupled partitioning of business capabilities into service implementations. Each service is individually evolved, deployed, and executed. However, due to the rising number of services and automation expectations, approaches for a dynamic webservice orchestration are needed. Service orchestration can be split into: (1) centralized approaches, e.g., using flow descriptions – and (2) decentralized approaches, e.g., using collaborative interaction of services [7]. However, an integration of these approaches to dynamically plan and invoke processes remains a challenge.

The reuse of software components is an important step for an industrial company to survive in a flexible and competitive market [8]. By applying a microservice architecture, the focus on reuse is often lost: teams focus on delivering work quickly and independently, often avoiding dependencies to other teams or to shared code that is not maintained by them. However, we think that software reuse is essential also in the context of webservice development to raise software quality and to minimize time-to-market. Software Product Lines (SPLs) have proven to be highly effective in reusing software artifacts [9]. The most critical phase during the design of an SPL is the identification of the variable parts and the common parts of a product family [8]. In the context of webservice architectures, SPL can be beneficial for the implementation of common libraries that are shared across different teams, and to define common solution architectures. However, an integrated view on BPs is often missing, leading to inefficient development overhead [10].

With this work, we focus on extending our framework [2,8,11] with capabilities of Microflows [12] to allow an automatic orchestration of microservices based on annotated processes. In a nutshell, the annotated process model describes the pre-conditions and constraints that must be met to execute the process and the post-conditions that are a consequence of executing the process. Pre-conditions can be as simple as a specific input parameter, or constraints about the execution sequence (e.g., before execution of process X or after Y). By applying our framework for combined variability management, we enforce a strong link between the developed software artifacts and the business processes in which they participate, take full advantage of SPL Engineering techniques for reusing software artifacts, and enable high variability within workflows.

This work is structured in the following way: we present related work in Sect. 2. Section 3 summarizes the basic concepts of SPL Engineering (SPLE), Business Process Modeling (BPM), as well as Microflows that we have applied in this paper. Section 4 summarizes our approach for combined variability modeling of business processes and software architectures, and how automated process orchestration can be applied. In Sect. 5, we describe how the proposed framework was applied in the context of an IoT case-study. And finally, Sect. 6 concludes this work.

2 Related Work

IBM defines a Microflow as short-lived BPEL processes [13]. However, in this work, we use the definition found in [12], defining it independent of any specific Business Process Management System (BPMS).

Web-Service composition [14], provides a survey of prototypes and standards for composition of webservices. Rajasekar et al. [15] presents a technique to orchestrate microservices based on a distributed event-condition-action rule engine. Rao and Su [16] present a framework for webservice orchestration by using an explicit composite service.

Traditionally, BP modeling languages do not explicitly support the representation of families of process variants [17]. As a consequence, a lot of work can be found which tries to extend traditional process modeling languages with notations to build adaptable process models. Having such a variability modeling for BP models builds the foundation of this work. Thus, related work which utilizes similar modeling concepts is presented in the following:

Derguech [18] presents a framework for the systematic reuse of process models. In contrast to this work, it captures the variability of the process model at the business goal level and describes how to integrate new goals/sub-goals into the existing data structure. The variability of the process is not addressed in this work.

Gimenes et al. [19] presents a feature-based approach to support e-contract negotiation based on webservices (WS). A meta-model for WS-contract representation is given and a way is shown how to integrate the variability of these contracts into the BPs to enable process automation. It does not address the variability of the BP itself but enables the ability to reuse BPs for different e-contract negotiations.

While our framework to model process variability reduces the overall process complexity by splitting up the process into layers with increasing detail, the PROVOP project [20–22] focuses on the concept that variants are derived from a basic process definition through well-defined change operations (deletion, addition, moving of model elements, or the adaptation of an element attribute). In fact, the basic process expresses all possible variants at once.

The work of Gottschalk et al. [23] presents an approach for the automated configuration of workflow models within a workflow modeling language. The term workflow model is used for the specification of a BP, which enables the execution in an enterprise and WfMS. The approach focuses on the activation or deactivation of actions and thus is comparable to the PROVOP project for the workflow model domain.

La Rosa et al. [24] extends the configurable process modeling notation developed from [23] with notions of roles and objects, providing a way to address not only the variability of the control-flow of a workflow model but also of the related resources and responsibilities.

The Common Variability Language (CVL) [25] is a language for specifying and resolving variability independent from the domain of the application. It facilitates the specification and resolution of variability over any instance of any language defined using a MOF-based meta-model. CVL-based variability modeling in combination with a BP model with an appropriate model transformation could lead to similar results as presented in this paper.

The work of Zhao and Zou [26] shows a framework for the generation of software modules based on BPs. They use clustering algorithms to analyze dependencies among data and tasks captured in BPs.

3 Background

This section summarizes the basic concepts of SPLE, BP Modeling, and Microflows that are applied in this work. This section is based on our previous publications that form the foundation of this work [2,5,11,12,27].

3.1 Software Product Line Engineering (SPLE)

SPLE applies the concept of product lines to software products. Thus, SPLE delivers diverse, high-quality software products of a product family in a short time and at low price [9]. Instead of writing software for every individual system, SPLE makes use of software components (domain artifacts) which are diversified and combined in order to generate the final software product. As described in [9,28], the SPLE can be split into two main phases, the *Domain Engineering* and the *Application Engineering*:

During the domain engineering, the domain is modeled and the variabilities and the commonalities of the according domain are identified and reflected in the implemented domain artifacts. Domain artifacts are reusable development artifacts like the software architecture, or software components and their corresponding unit-tests [9].

In the application engineering phase, the final software products are created by combining and diversifying the domain artifacts which were implemented in domain engineering. The main goal of application engineering is to maximize reuse of domain artifacts. Additionally, implemented logic usually just consists of glue-logic between the different domain artifacts, which is often fully generated. Consequently, the rapid creation of high-quality products can be achieved. The degree of domain artifact reuse depends to a large extent on the application requirements. Hence, a major concern of the application engineering is the detection of deltas between the application requirements and the available capabilities of the SPL. During the lifetime of a product line, these deltas often result in additional domain artifacts which can be reused in future products.

In the context of webservices, SPLE provides capabilities for reusing common implementations (like user-interfaces, library implementations, and others), leading to a more robust and mature software base for each service.

3.2 Business Process Modeling

Business Processes (BPs) are a specific sequence of activities or (sub-) processes which are executed in a dedicated sequence to produce output with value to the customer [8,29]. In this work, we use the modeling paradigm defined by Oesterle [30]: The BPs are split-up into different layers until the microscopic level is reached. This is achieved when all tasks are detailed enough so that they can be used as work instructions. The top level (macroscopic level) is a highly abstract description of the overall process, while each subprocess is further described in lower levels. Consequently, higher levels of the process are usually independent of the production facility, the infrastructure, and environmental specifics. Thus, the higher level is more stable with respect to changes and can be reused in different contexts and production environments. The microscopic levels, however, require adaptation to be reused in different contexts.

Variability of such process structures can be modeled through a variable process structure (i.e. by adding/removing activities in a process) or by replacing sub-processes with different ones. In the scope of this work, we use BPMN (Business Process Model and Notation) [31] as a modeling notation for BPs, but the general framework is not limited to BPMN as long as the modeling notation supports concepts like events, activities, responsibilities, data objects (used to describe inputs and outputs), and control flow elements (to model, e.g., choices and parallel executions).

3.3 Microflows

A Microflow can be seen as a short-lived process execution, which is defined by an execution of webservices. The following enumeration lists the important principles used for modeling and orchestrating Microflows in the context of this work (for a full list of principals, see [5]):

Microservice Semantic Self-description Principle: A microservice provides sufficient metadata to support autonomous client invocation.

Client Agent Principle: We chose Belief-Desire-Intention (BDI) agents for the client realization, were belief is provided via knowledge, desire via goals, and intention are represented in the resulting workflow.

Graph of Microservices Principle: microservices / workflow activities are represented as nodes in a graph. Each node is annotated with properties. Edges depict the directed connections between the nodes.

Microflow as Graph Path Principle: A directed graph of nodes corresponds to a workflow, and is determined by an algorithm applied to the graph. During the workflow execution, each node and respectively the underlying microservice is executed, with inputs and outputs as specified in the annotated microprocess.

Declarative Principle: Any workflow requirement specification take the form of goal and constraint modeling statements. It contains the starting microservice, the end microservice, and additional constraints that must be met during the workflow execution.

Path Weighting Principle: Any edge of the microservice graph can be weighted with a potentially dynamic cost which helps in quantifying and comparing path alternatives. As such, the navigation from one node to another node can be dynamically adjusted based on collected process execution data (like response time).

4 From Adaptive Processes to Orchestrated Microflows

In this section, we give details on how we model variability of BPs, how to generate BP variants, and how to orchestrate BPs using BDI agents.

4.1 Managing Variability in Business Processes

A detailed description of our framework for modeling variability of BPs and software architectures can be found in [2]. In the scope of this work, we will briefly summarize the concept and present the extensions to the original framework. The extensions allow a combined variability modeling not only for higher-order processes, but also for processes which make use of webservices to trigger actual actions on the systems. Figure 1 shows the overall extended framework. The original framework consists of two essential parts: The *Process Variability Framework* and the *Product Software Product Line*, while the extended framework introduced the *Microflow Orchestrator*.

Process Variability Framework (c.f. [11,27,32]) is a framework used to manage variability of BPs by applying concepts of SPLE. As such, maintaining and evolving process variants of a family is done by automatically applying changes to the model. These changes are automatically propagated to all process variants. By using rich constraint checking engines and code generation methods, it is ensured that the generated process variants are consistent. The starting point for the variability modeling is the process of domain modeling and process-template creation: during this process, the requirements of the domain are analyzed and appropriate process templates are created. In addition, variation points (VPs) are identified and reflected in the variability model. The framework supports variability management of a whole process hierarchy, starting at the top

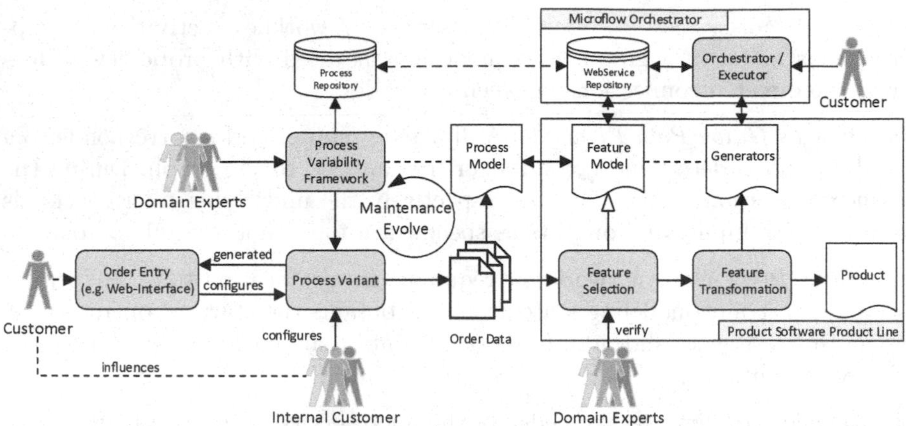

Fig. 1. Overall framework for combining process variability and product variability based on [32], extended with runtime service aspects using Microflows.

level (macroscopic processes) to the lowest level (microprocesses). On each level, certain transformations can be applied which are: replacing non-atomic activities/subprocesses with different ones, adding and removing activities and resequencing process steps.

Product Software Product Line is a SPL which allows configuration and generation of software products during product order: the variable parts of the process variants are mapped to the variability model of the product line using identifiers, ensuring a traceable link between both models. To support the process of modeling, we have defined mapping rules whereby standard BPMN processes can be translated into a basic feature model skeleton of the product: activities are reflected by features, and process inputs are reflected as configuration options [2]. By analyzing the structure of the process model, the system can also identify which features are mandatory, which ones are optional, and what basic constraints are defined between them. In this manner, we have shown in [8] that product configurations can be automatically generated based on, e.g., an order defined by the customer.

To summarize, the original framework provides a configurable solution, which allows the configuration of adaptive BPs, for instance during product order, based on customer/stakeholder inputs. In addition, a SPL is automatically configured using the input configuration of the (order) process, and the final software products are automatically generated. One limitation of this system is that some of the actions still required manual interaction, like triggering the source-code generator, uploading files to a server, etc.

With this work, we want to extend the scope of the framework, in order to support a WS-oriented business to automatically create and execute Microflows without the need for manual interaction during the execution. To allow this, we assume the following:

- An atomic activity can be modeled as a WS (microservice) call.
- A *microprocess* consists of a sequence of atomic activities.
- A *microprocess* defines meta-information on how and when it can be triggered (see Sect. 4.2 for details).
- A Microflow can be modeled as a sequence of *microprocess* executions.

The concept of *microprocesses* consisting of multiple microservice executions is purely used for grouping and modeling purposes (i.e., allowing a single model to generate multiple WS variants) and could be seen as a smaller Microflow. If the provided desire and conditions are met, a Microflow can be created dynamically on the fly by defining a start condition, an end condition, and additional constraints that must be met. In order to support a flexible design of *microprocesses*, we apply our Process Variability Framework to model process variants and to publish them in a repository. By applying the concept of combined variability modeling, we can generate microservice descriptions which must be implemented by the developers, while still providing a concept for reusing shared functionality.

4.2 Orchestration of Microprocesses Based on Annotated Process Models

By using the concept described in Sect. 4.1, a repository of business microprocesses is generated and available. To support their automated orchestration, each microprocess is annotated with additional meta-information, allowing an algorithm to calculate possible paths through the set of available microprocesses in order to achieve a defined goal. In this work, we specifically make use of a shortest path algorithm, but the overall framework is not limited to this algorithm. The set of annotations required to calculate possible paths can be summarized as:

- *Path weight*: The path weight gives an indication on how "expensive" it is to execute a specific microprocess. By allowing dynamic path weights (e.g., updated due to process execution logs, or different weights based on different execution environments), it is possible to gain flexibility and increase the quality of service.
- *Constraints*: A list of constraints that must be met. Our framework makes use of the following classes of constraints:

  - *Input Parameter*: Input parameters that are necessary in order to execute a process. These parameters can either be provided by a client, or can be the outcome of another microprocess execution.
  - *Output*: The outcome(s) of a process execution. To allow flexible modeling of process executions, it is also possible to define meta-data output that is only used for planning purposes.
  - *Before Node*: Constraint used to model that specific microprocesses must be executed before the execution of this microprocess. This can also be modeled using specific types of input parameter and output values, but by using the concept of a *Before Node*, more flexibility is gained.

- *After Node*: Constraint used to model that specific microprocesses must be executed after the execution of this microprocess. Identical to a before node constraint if defined in reversed order.
- *Exclude Node*: Constraint to indicate that a specific microprocess must not be executed at all (neither before, nor after).

In our approach, we do not fully dynamically re-calculate the next node during process execution. For a simpler and more lightweight framework: we make use of a planning phase where a BDI agent takes a goal and additional constraints to find an appropriate schedule of microprocess executions. Mandatory constraints for the agent are the selection of the start node, the end node, and may optionally contain additional microprocesses that must be invoked during the execution. Only in case where the execution of a microprocess fails, we recalculate an alternative path by invoking the planning phase again. By doing this, we can ensure that at least one valid alternative Microflow path exists which fulfills the requirements, prior to invoking an error recovery.

In a nutshell, the currently implemented path finding algorithm performs the following steps: First, it identifies the start node and determines which nodes can be directly reached while meeting the defined constraints. Secondly, for each direct connection, the algorithm basically calls itself recursively with the new node being the start node, and it updates its constraints. The updated constraints basically contain the output(s) from the former start node as additional available input parameter, and a call history containing the start node. This is necessary to prevent visiting the same node twice. The algorithm continues by recursively calling itself until a list of possible execution paths are collected. These paths are then evaluated using the defined path weights and the shortest one is taken. In case multiple paths converge to the same weight, implementations can implement various strategies like round-robin, or choosing a random one.

5 Case Study

For illustration purposes, we look at an exemplary IoT use-case which we are currently working on with our research partners: In a home automation scenario, various IoT devices and actuators are installed. The overall concept is illustrated in Fig. 2. Some IoT devices may be installed in a fixed location, with a power supply, while others may be battery powered and mobile (like a smartphone). Additionally, devices may be produced by different vendors. From a technical perspective, each IoT device implements some functionality like reading sensor values, returning the health status (battery level), and enabling/disabling output ports. Each device is connected either directly, or via a gateway to an IP network having access to a so-called *Service Platform*. For this example, we assume that this *Service Platform* is a local reachable Server in the LAN network. Specific services can be installed to the *Service Platform* that can be utilized by the customer. Each service accesses functionality of the IoT devices and/or the actuators. For development purposes, the *Service Platform* provider (i.e., a company

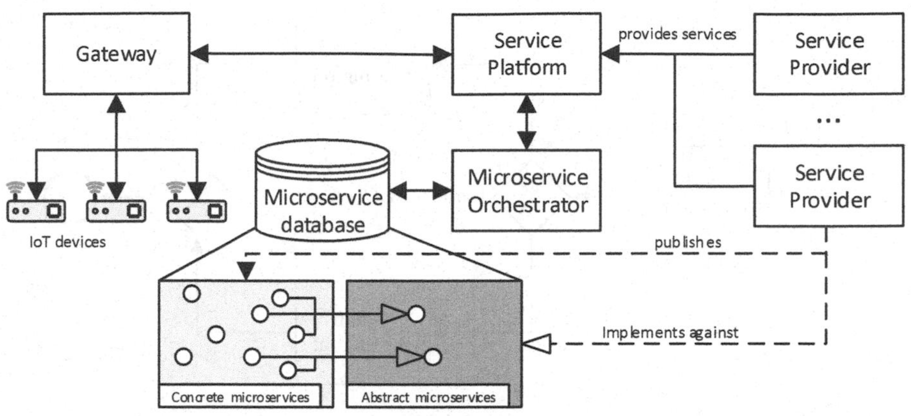

Fig. 2. System overview of the case study.

offering a platform for IoT Services) makes use of our introduced framework for modeling and implementing small microservices for accessing functionality of the IoT network. Consequently, a *Service Provider* does not need to implement code to access functionality of the linked devices. However, a provided service uses abstract webservice invocations to get and set information in the IoT network. Consequently, the *Service Platform* is responsible for WS orchestration and execution based on the desire and constraints defined by the service.

The *Service Platform* may provide abstract microservices like readSensorValue and setOutputValue, which internally are represented by a sequence of microservice calls like connect, authenticate, readSensorValue, and setOutputValue. Each of these microservices can be implemented in several different ways depending on the used hardware and supported protocols. For example, if a *Service Provider* implements a service for regulating the room temperature (i.e., switching a heating element on or off, depending on the current room temperature), the service formulates the desire to set the output voltage of an outlet (setOutputValue), with the constraint of first sensing the room temperature and afterwards doing some calculation (a micro-service provided by the service provider).

5.1 Example Microflow: Measuring the Room Temperature

In the following, we will take a closer look at an example. First, we start with a simple case: The network consists of identical IoT nodes, having the same capabilities (i.e., each node is equipped with a temperature sensor). All of them are permanently powered. From a high level perspective, the *Service Provider* models his business process as depicted in Fig. 3: In a regular interval, he requests the current room temperature from the IoT network, decides with a very basic decision if the temperature is above or below a certain threshold (23 °C), and

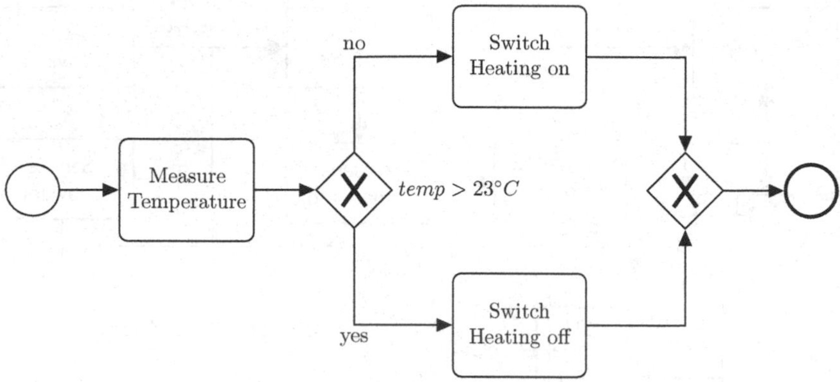

Fig. 3. Business Process for regulating the room temperature (Macroscopic level).

switches the heating system on or off. To keep this example simple, we consider the room temperature regulation process on the Macroscopic level as a "normal" BP, while each sub-process of the BP is modeled as a Microflow. In the following, we will take a look at the details of the *Measure Temperature* microflow. The microservice database consists of the following microservices which are of interest:

- **Connect**: Is an abstract microservice which takes care of connecting to an IoT device using a protocol that is supported by the device. The actual implementation of this microservice takes care of handling device and protocol specific aspects.
- **Authenticate**: Is an abstract microservice which takes care of authenticating the *Service Provider* to the device. The actual implementation of this microservice depends on the communication protocol and device capabilities. In the following we group authentication protocols based on symmetric and asymmetric cryptography.
- **Read Temperature**: Is an abstract microservice which takes care of reading the current temperature from a device. The actual implementation of this microservice depends on the communication protocol and the authentication method (e.g., command sent via a secure communication channel).
- **Close Connection**: Is an abstract microservice which takes care of closing the communication to an IoT device. The actual implementation of this microservice depends on the communication protocol and the authentication method.

The particular implementations of the above mentioned microservices are provided by the IoT device/system manufacturer. This allows *Service Providers* to define services independent of the used hardware. For this example, we consider that a connection to the IoT devices can be established via Bluetooth,

Table 1. Overview of the constraints for each microservice

	Input parameter	Output	Before node	After node
Connect*	deviceAddress	connection	–	–
Authenticate*	connection	channel	–	–
Read Temperature	channel	temperature	Close Connection	–
Close Connection	–	–	–	–

*Each implementation defines its own input and output types to allow an automatic orchestration. For illustration, only the abstract input/output types are shown in this table.

WiFi, or via Zigbee. For each of these communication protocols, we consider two possible authentication methods/protocols: one based on asymmetric cryptography (like Transport Layer Security (TLS)), and one based on symmetric cryptography (like Secure Channel Protocol (SCP)). We will not look into the details of the *Read Temperature* or *Close Connection* webservices. The constraints of the individual microservices are illustrated in Table 1. Note that each concrete implementation of the abstract microservice can define different input and output parameter. For example, a webservice connecting to the device via WiFi may require an IP address and a port number as input, while a connection via Bluetooth may only need the Bluetooth device address as input. In addition, by using different output types, the orchestrator can take care of selecting the correct subsequent microservice in case there are execution dependencies. For example, if a specific authentication method requires a dedicated connection interface, the connection interface could produce an output that can only be consumed by this special authentication method. Other possibilities would be to define a more fine grained constraint model in which each concrete service implementation defines specific *Before Node* and *After Node* constraints.

The desire of this Microflow is measuring the *temperature* which is the output data of the *Read Temperature* microservice. Thus, the path finding algorithm is able to calculate a Microflow fulfilling the desire: *Read Temperature* requires a channel as input parameter. Consequently, *Authenticate** must be executed prior to reading the temperature, which requires *Connect** to be executed before to establish a connection. And finally, after reading the temperature value – and returning it to the *Service Provider* – the *Close Connection* webservice has to be called. Noteworthy is the input parameter of the *Connect** webservice: The deviceAddress must be provided by the *Service Platform* which keeps track of all the registered devices in the network, as well as their capabilities. The generated Microflow is illustrated in Fig. 4. For Microflow execution, the Microflow Orchestrator receives a list of devices, calculates the path for each device to produce the desire (the temperature value), rates the generated variants according to the path weight, and selects the path with the lowest path weight. Various strategies can be used in case multiple paths lead to the same path weight, like round-robin or randomly choosing a device.

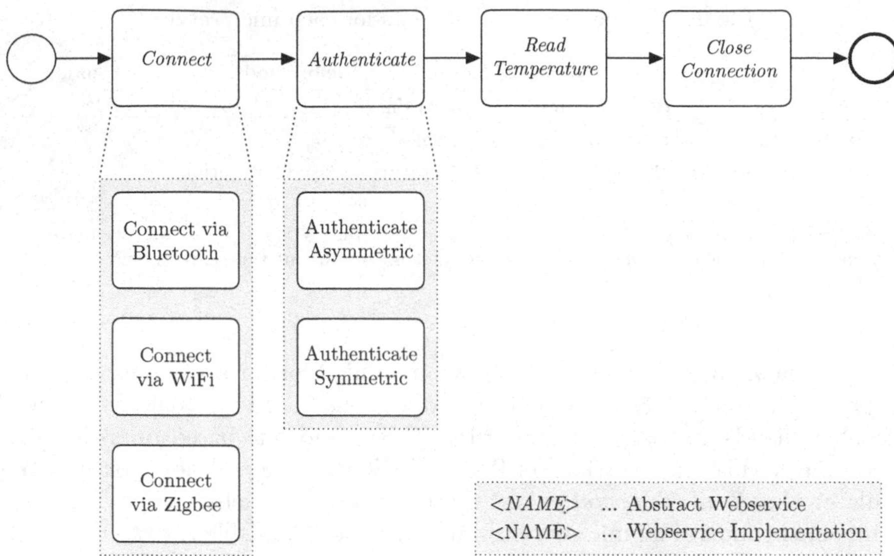

Fig. 4. Schematic overview of the generated Microflow, indicating the pool of concrete service implementations used during execution of the flow.

In case a failure happened during the execution of the Microflow, error recovery strategies need to be implemented. In case of IoT use-case, devices tend to terminate connection unexpectedly due to bad signal strength, power failures, or similar issues. Error recovery strategies can be quite complex, especially if some of the previous execution steps need to be reverted in order to not leave the network in an unstable state. In the context of this example, the strategies can be as simple as a retry mechanism. This means that the current webservice is executed a second time, or the whole Microflow is restarted at the start node. In case a retry also did not result in a successful process execution, the Microflow Orchestrator chooses an alternative route (e.g. measuring the temperature via a different device). If all strategies have failed, the *Service Provider* (i.e., the actual service implementation) is notified via an exception. As such, alternative error-recovery strategies can be implemented on this level as well.

Last but not least, we will shortly discuss the impact of using different IoT devices in a more complex setup and how this impacts the service orchestration: The IoT network consists of various different devices. A number of devices is battery powered, each device can only support one communication protocol, and the equipped temperature sensors are of varying quality. To model these additional constraints, each webservice is annotated with additional meta-data used for path calculation, like: energy consumption, execution time, sensor accuracy, and others. Each of these categories can be individually weighted: If the service requires a highly accurate temperature value, accuracy can be weighted more heavily then others, or if the field of application requires highly energy efficient implementations, energy consumption can be rated more heavily. In the current state of the implemented framework, these path weights are not updated automatically, but only manually by a user, or system administrator. In future work, we want to investigate possible solutions on how to update these weights automatically by making use of e.g., observed system properties like the received signal strength (to enable or disable communication protocols), the battery state, and others.

To summarize the examples above, the Microservice Orchestrator takes care of identifying the registered IoT devices. During Microflow execution, the Measure Temperature Microflow is expanded with context specific executions. In case a node is not reachable during webservice execution, error-recovery strategies are used which may trigger the path finding algorithm a second time, finding an alternative node to get the room temperature. The presented examples highlight, that the approach helps to create an abstraction for service developers to access functionality of IoT devices without the need of developing vendor specific code. By using complex mechanics for adapting path weights, the system can be optimize according to different strategies, like power consumption or quality of service.

While we heavily discussed microservice orchestration and Microflow execution, we only gave little information on how to create constraint models and how to benefit from variability modeling. In most of the cases, a *Service Provider* is not interested to create such constraint models, nor cope with execution sequences on the microscopic level. The *Service Provider* is usually only interested in reading or setting values of the IoT network. Thus, orchestration of webservices is mostly relevant on a higher abstraction level. For the microscopic process level, the *Service Platform* usually provides convenience models which can also be used as templates for custom services. In this case study, we applied our framework for modeling business process variability [2], but instead of limiting the usage to order processes, we extended it with runtime aspects and custom model transformation engines: The above example was derived from a variability model which is partially illustrated in Fig. 5: The feature model shows a generic model of Microflows which are capable of measuring either the temperature or the luminous intensity. Features on higher levels represent abstract webservices (i.e. abstract microprocesses), while child features (i.e., the leafs in the tree) represent the actual implementations.

The *Measure Temperature* Microflow – which was used as example in this case study – was created by selecting the *Temperature* feature and transforming the model. Other selections – like the connection method or the particular authentication method – are not chosen during model transformation, but are selected during Microflow invocation. To allow a transformation of the feature model into the constraint model defined in Table 1, additional information has to be annotated to the feature model: For each feature, we define input parameter and output values. *Before Node*, *After Node* and *Exclude Node* constraints can be partially derived by the dependencies between the specific features: A *requires* dependency indicates a dependency on the sequence of execution. However, a pure feature model does not clearly define which feature has to be

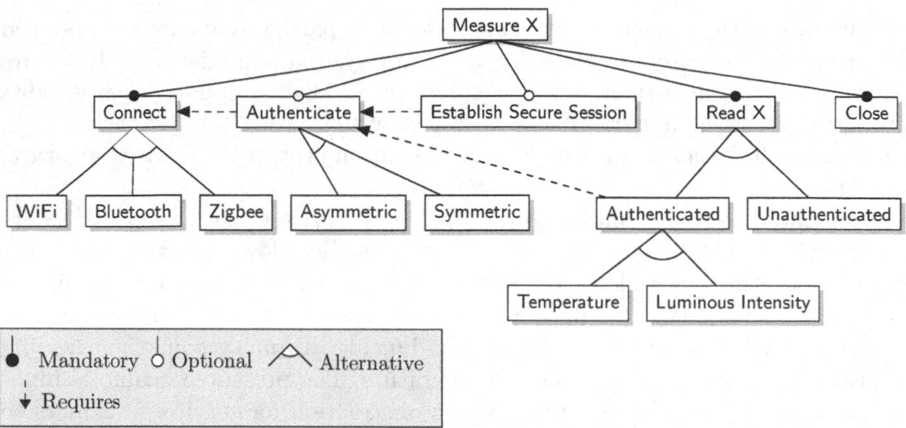

Fig. 5. Extract of the feature model that was used to derive the Microflow constraints of the Measure Temperature Microflow.

executed prior to other ones. As such, we additionally annotate *Before Node* and *After Node* constraints if they cannot be derived based on input/output value dependencies. Consequently, the Microflow constraint model can be derived by applying simple model transformation rules. Thus, changes to the feature model are automatically propagated to the microservices and respectively to the micro-processes. This has the positive side effect that also development teams get a view on where and how their actual implementations are used within a business process. In addition, a strong connection is built between the process modeling team and the implementation team [2].

6 Conclusion

Today's industry is heavily driven by the digital transformation, short development cycles and highly flexible requirements from the market. We proposed a framework to use SPLE techniques for a combined variability modeling of BP models and software architectures. This leads to an integrated view of product variability from a business perspective as well as from a technical perspective.

In addition, we have shown how concepts of dynamic Microflow planning and execution allows workflow-based variability and WS orchestration during runtime. As illustrated in the case study, this is especially useful for industries providing service platforms such as IoT, where a number of service providers are publishing new WS. These WS can also make use of abstract microservices provided by the service platform to support access to the functionality of IoT devices in an abstract way, allowing third parties to develop microservices independent of the used infrastructure.

Future work will focus on extending the support for microservice orchestration, introducing advanced verification and validation techniques and a more fine-grained model to dynamically calculate path weights.

Acknowledgements. The project is funded by the Austrian Research Promotion Agency (FFG).

References

1. Xia, F., Yang, L.T., Wang, L., Vinel, A.: Internet of things. Int. J. Commun. Syst. **25**(9), 1101–1102 (2012)
2. Sinnhofer, A.D., et al.: Combining business process variability and software variability using traceable links. In: Shishkov, B. (ed.) Bus. Model. Softw. Des., pp. 67–86. Springer, Cham (2018). https://doi.org/10.1007/978-3-319-78428-1_4
3. WFMC: Workflow Management Coalition Terminology and Glossary (WFMC-TC-1011). Technical report, Workflow Management Coalition, Brussels (1999)
4. Saidani, O., Nurcan, S.: Towards context aware business process modelling. In: 8th Workshop on Business Process Modeling, Development, and Support, BPMDS 2007, CAiSE, vol. 7, p. 1 (2007)
5. Oberhauser, R., Stigler, S.: Microflows: leveraging process mining and an automated constraint recommender for microflow modeling. In: Shishkov, B. (ed.) Bus. Model. Softw. Des., pp. 25–48. Springer, Cham (2018). https://doi.org/10.1007/978-3-319-78428-1_2
6. Lewis, J., Fowler, M.: Microservices. IEEE Softw. **32**(1), 116 (2014)
7. Bouguettaya, A., Sheng, Q.Z., Daniel, F. (eds.): Web Services Foundations. Springer, Cham (2014). https://doi.org/10.1007/978-1-4614-7518-7
8. Sinnhofer, A.D., Pühringer, P., Potzmader, K., Orthacker, C., Steger, C., Kreiner, C.: Software configuration based on order processes. In: Shishkov, B. (ed.) BMSD 2016. LNBIP, vol. 275, pp. 200–220. Springer, Cham (2017). https://doi.org/10.1007/978-3-319-57222-2_10
9. Pohl, K., Böckle, G., van der Linden, F.J.: Software Product Line Engineering: Foundations Principles and Techniques. Springer, New York (2005). https://doi.org/10.1007/3-540-28901-1
10. Sinnhofer, A.D., Oppermann, F.J., Potzmader, K., Orthacker, C., Steger, C., Kreiner, C.: Increasing the visibility of requirements based on combined variability management. In: Shishkov, B. (ed.) Bus. Model. Softw. Des., pp. 203–220. Springer, Cham (2018). https://doi.org/10.1007/978-3-319-94214-8_13
11. Sinnhofer, A.D., Pühringer, P., Kreiner, C.: Varbpm – a product line for creating business process model variants. In: Proceedings of the Fifth International Symposium on Business Modeling and Software Design - Volume 1: BMSD 2015, pp. 184–191 (2015)
12. Oberhauser, R.: Microflows: automated planning and enactment of dynamic workflows comprising semantically-annotated microservices. In: Shishkov, B. (ed.) Bus. Model. Softw. Des., pp. 183–199. Springer, Cham (2017). https://doi.org/10.1007/978-3-319-57222-2_9
13. IBM: IBM business process manager 8.6.0 (2020)
14. Sheng, Q., Qiao, X., Vasilakos, A., Szabo, C., Bourne, S., Xu, X.: Web services composition: a decade's overview. Inf. Sci. **280**, 218–238 (2014)
15. Rajasekar, A., Wan, M., Moore, R., Schroeder, W.: Micro-services: a service-oriented paradigm for scalable, distributed data management. In: Kosar, T. (ed.) Data Intensive Distributed Computing: Challenges and Solutions for Large-scale Information Management. IGI Global, Hershey (2012)

16. Rao, J., Su, X.: A survey of automated web service composition methods. In: Cardoso, J., Sheth, A. (eds.) SWSWPC 2004. LNCS, vol. 3387, pp. 43–54. Springer, Heidelberg (2005). https://doi.org/10.1007/978-3-540-30581-1_5
17. Rosa, M.L., Aalst, W.M.P.V.D., Dumas, M., Milani, F.P.: Business process variability modeling: a survey. ACM Comput. Surv. **50**(1), 2:1–2:45 (2017)
18. Derguech, W.: Towards a framework for business process models reuse. In: The CAiSE Doctoral Consortium (2010)
19. Gimenes, I., Fantinato, M., Toledo, M.: A product line for business process management. In: International Software Product Line Conference, pp. 265–274 (2008)
20. Hallerbach, A., Bauer, T., Reichert, M.: Guaranteeing soundness of configurable process variants in provop. In: IEEE Conference on Commerce and Enterprise Computing, CEC 2009, pp. 98–105. IEEE (2009)
21. Hallerbach, A., Bauer, T., Reichert, M.: Issues in modeling process variants with Provop. In: Ardagna, D., Mecella, M., Yang, J. (eds.) BPM 2008. LNBIP, vol. 17, pp. 56–67. Springer, Heidelberg (2009). https://doi.org/10.1007/978-3-642-00328-8_6
22. Reichert, M., Hallerbach, A., Bauer, T.: Lifecycle support for business process variants. In: vom Brocke, J., Rosemann, M. (eds.) Handbook on Business Process Management 1. Introduction, Methods and Information Systems. Springer, Cham (2014). https://doi.org/10.1007/978-3-642-45100-3
23. Gottschalk, F., van der Aalst, W.M.P., Jansen-Vullers, M.H., La Rosa, M.: Configurable workflow models. Int. J. Cooper. Inf. Syst. **17**, 177–221 (2007)
24. La Rosa, M., Dumas, M., ter Hofstede, A.H.M., Mendling, J., Gottschalk, F.: Beyond control-flow: extending business process configuration to roles and objects. In: Li, Q., Spaccapietra, S., Yu, E., Olivé, A. (eds.) ER 2008. LNCS, vol. 5231, pp. 199–215. Springer, Heidelberg (2008). https://doi.org/10.1007/978-3-540-87877-3_16
25. Haugen, O., Wasowski, A., Czarnecki, K.: Cvl: common variability language. In: Proceedings of the 17th International Software Product Line Conference, SPLC 2013 (2013)
26. Zhao, X., Zou, Y.: A business process-driven approach for generating software modules. Softw. Pract. Exp. **41**(10), 1049–1071 (2011)
27. Sinnhofer, A.D., Pühringer, P., Potzmader, K., Orthacker, C., Steger, C., Kreiner, C.: A framework for process driven software configuration. In: Proceedings of the Sixth International Symposium on Business Modeling and Software Design - Volume 1: BMSD 2016, pp. 196–203 (2016)
28. Weiss, D.M., Lai, C.T.R.: Software Product-line Engineering: A Family-based Software Development Process. Addison-Wesley Longman Publishing Co. Inc, Boston (1999)
29. Hammer, M., Champy, J.: Reengineering the Corporation - A Manifesto For Business Revolution. Harper Business, New York (1993)
30. Österle, H.: Business Engineering - Prozess- und Systementwicklung. Springer, Heidelberg (1995). https://doi.org/10.1007/978-3-642-61437-8
31. OMG: Business process model and notation (BPMN) version 2.0 (2011)
32. Sinnhofer, A.D., Höller, A., Pühringer, P., Potzmader, K., Orthacker, C., Steger, C., Kreiner, C.: Combined variability management of business processes and software architectures. In: Proceedings of the Seventh International Symposium on Business Modeling and Software Design - Volume 1: BMSD, INSTICC, pp. 36–45. SciTePress (2017)

Model-Driven ML-Ops for Intelligent Enterprise Applications: Vision, Approaches and Challenges

Willem-Jan van den Heuvel[1] and Damian A. Tamburri[2](✉)

[1] Jheronimus Academy of Data Science (JADS), Tilburg University, Tilburg, The Netherlands
w.j.a.m.vdnheuvel@jads.nl

[2] Jheronimus Academy of Data Science (JADS), Eindhoven University of Technology, Eindhoven, The Netherlands
d.a.tamburri@tue.nl

Abstract. This paper explores a novel vision for the disciplined, repeatable, and transparent model-driven development and Machine-Learning operations (ML-Ops) of intelligent enterprise applications.

The proposed framework treats *model abstractions of AI/ML models* (named AI/ML Blueprints) as first-class citizens and promotes end-to-end transparency and portability from raw data detection- to model verification, and, policy-driven model management.

This framework is grounded on the intelligent Application Architecture (iA^2) and entails a first attempt to incorporate requirements stemming from (more) intelligent enterprise applications into a logically-structured architecture. The logical separation is grounded on the need to enact MLOps and logically separate basic data manipulation requirements (data-processing layer), from more advanced functionality needed to instrument applications with intelligence (data intelligence layer), and continuous deployment, testing and monitoring of intelligent application (knowledge-driven application layer).

Finally, the paper sets out exploring a foundational metamodel underpinning blueprint-model-driven MLOps for iA^2 applications, and presents its main findings and open research agenda.

Keywords: ML-Ops · ML Blueprints · Methodological support to AI · AI software engineering · TOSCA

1 Introduction

Over the past few years, Artificial Intelligence (AI) has swiftly evolved in the main tech driver that is currently reshaping the way in which we conduct business and live our daily lives [1], witnessing a plethora of tantalizing AI-driven innovations in industry and

This work is sponsored by the EU ISFP ProTECT grant on Public Resilience using TEchnology to Counter Terrorism.

B. Shishkov (Ed.): BMSD 2020, LNBIP 391, pp. 169–181, 2020.
https://doi.org/10.1007/978-3-030-52306-0_11

society at large. They range from better ways to detect and treat melanoma relying on convolutional neural networks, to harnessing interactive entertainment bots with speech recognition, leveraging improvements in cyber security with Machine-Learning (ML), and, fostering computer vision for safety and security scenarios relying on a mix of deep- and transfer learning approaches.

Indeed, AI is now quickly maturing and finally delivering industry-strength applications—often referred to as *AI-software*—breaking away from experimental, non-scalable 'toy' prototypes devoid of practical enterprise value. This has paved the way for Machine-Learning applications with full-fledged DevOps pipelines to maintain them: a piece of software engineering fabric often termed as MLOps (see Fig. 1).

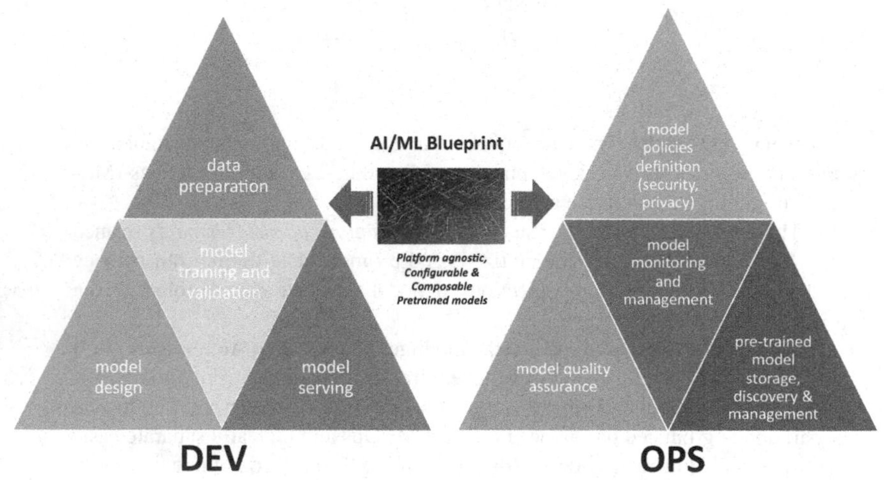

Fig. 1. ML-Ops, activities overview.

This latest AI-trend has led to the software engineering to seriously turn their attention to infuse AI-techniques, technologies and platforms (such as Google AI platform, TensorFlow, IBM's Watson Studio and Microsoft's Azure) in their software development practices. Notably, AI-techniques are increasingly deployed to foster automatic code-generation, continuous testing and integration, and software design. Thus, exiting new research and development opportunities are to be found at their cross-roads.

On the one hand, AI has delivered significant techniques and tools in (biology-inspired) computational heuristics for exploring optimum solutions in highly unstructured, complex, fuzzy, unpredictable and/or incomplete discourses. Software engineering, on the other hand, has proven its value in factoring well-understood, relatively stable, and clearly demarcated solution spaces into code [2, 3]. Model-driven development has proven additional value to exploit models—other than ML models—as representational often box-and-line, discrete artefacts summarizing a specific software code concept or construct (e.g., an *if* statement in procedural programming, or the concept of a *statement* in any programming language). In this way, the solution space can be typically decomposed into smaller and simpler problems—each of which can be addressed discretely—and then composed into large-scale systems.

Unfortunately, however, current ML/AI approaches, platforms and tools do not harness any such model-based or model-driven software engineering approaches, with the word *model* itself comprising an entirely different meaning altogether. Many challenges are associated to this disconnect.

Firstly, they typically lack model transparency during the entire end-to-end workflow to ascertain explainability, interpretability, and accountability. Second, ML-models tend to operate as a "black box" making it very hard to impossible, to effectively understand, assess and control their operations.

At the same time, completely open transparency would enlarge vulnerability to attacks. This dichotomy is referred to as the "transparency paradox" [4]. Thirdly, integrated methodological support for the AI/ML model governance is very sparse, overlooking critical "deployment and operation time" aspects such as model versioning, security, privacy and compliance monitoring.

And finally, AI/ML platforms tend to (implicitly) embrace a coding-oriented, "modeling-validation-training-(hyper parameter) optimization" workflow, that is hard to transpose from one platform to another, promoting vendor lock-in and resisting change. This makes management of AI/ML models, e.g., in terms of portability and maintainability, an extremely difficult endeavor that relies on craftmanship (learned through many failures), rather than a predictable engineering approach.

In this paper, we introduce, and explore a novel vision for the disciplined, repeatable, and transparent model-driven development and Machine-Learning operations (ML-Ops) of intelligent enterprise applications. The proposed framework treats *model abstractions of AI/ML models* as first-class citizens and promotes end-to-end transparency and portability.

Figure 1 graphically depicts our ML-Ops vision, synthesizing the diptych of development and operation activities. The development tenet encompasses the following four key activities (see left-side from top to bottom in this Figure): data preparation (including data detection, data transportation and transformation, data reconciliation, and data integration), model design, model training and validation, and model serving. The operations tenet complements the development view with: model quality assurance; model monitoring (including quality monitoring) and maintenance/management; storage, discovery, and management of pre-trained models; and, model policy definition to specify security, safety and other non-functional requirements and soft/hard constraints.

In this vision, a single artefact, namely an *AI/ML blueprint*, is bound to contain all necessary knowledge representation and reasoning constructs to allow for the aforementioned software governance, maintenance, and evolution activities.

The remainder of this article is as follows. In the following section we will further explore and assess the cutting edge in AI engineering: the convergence software engineering and artificial intelligence. In Sect. 3, we will then introduce a stratified architecture for developing intelligent enterprise applications, and outline a meta-model that forms the foundation on which the methodological framework has been devised (Sect. 4). Section 5 concludes the article summarizing the key findings, and plotting a roadmap for further research.

2 Related Work

The model-driven MLOps framework that is induced in this paper draws upon industrial and scientific concepts, methods and techniques from the domain of artificial intelligence and software engineering. In the following we will summarize the most relevant ones.

2.1 Automated Machine Learning (AutoML) and MLOps

Since the 1990s automated approaches have been studied and offered commercially to improve the way in which machine learning applications are constructed with very limited to no human intervention ([5, 6]). This strain of automation of machine learning is shortly referred to as AutoML.

Basically, such approaches apply ML themselves to generate more optimized ML solutions. Undeniably, without AutoML, developing effective ML pipelines is a complex, time-consuming, iterative "trial-and-error" task involving multiple actors such as data modelers and domain experts.

AutoML approaches investigate novel ways to calibrate hyperparameters to optimize performance by better fitting them to the problem at hand, selecting the optimal mix of choices about the systems architecture, cost functions and regularization. This is shortly referred to as Hyper Parameter Optimization (HPO). For example, as early as 1994 HPO via grid search was studied, e.g., [7].

From 2018 onwards, the field of AutoML gained renewed attention with the advent of new commercial offerings, configurable data-pipelines and significant improvements to their performance from several hours to several minutes [8].

Another important development in turning Machine-Learning into an engineering discipline constitutes improved collaboration and coordination activities between all stakeholders involved in the ML lifecycle, ranging from data analysts, data/AI engineers to domain experts [9]. As alluded to in the introduction, this is briefly referred to as MLOps.

MLOps has emerged from the DevOps philosophy and associated practices [10] that streamline the software development workflow and delivery processes. Like DevOps, MLOps adopts the continuous integration and continuous testing cycle to produce and deploy production-ready new micro-releases and versions of intelligent enterprise applications.

This implies a culture shift between data analysts, data engineers, deployment and system engineers, and domain experts, with improved dependency management (and thus transparency) between model development, training, validation and deployment. As such MLOps clearly requires sophisticated policies based on metrics and telemetry such as performance indicators like F^1, and accuracy scores, as well as software quality [11].

Whilst the exact boundary between MLOps and DevOps is blurry, a prominent example of MLOps can be found in Amazon WebServces that offers an integrated ML workflow—albeit vendor-locked—from build, testing and integration, supporting continuous delivery with source control and monitoring services.

Unfortunately, however, current methods and approaches to AutoML and ML-Ops provide little to no support for portability as well as transparency (and therefore explainability). Similarly, little or no support is provided to typical design-phase operational considerations including latency, performance, reliability, deployability, or other essential dependability [22] system properties.

2.2 Data Governance for AI

To minimize the risks and their potential impact associated to the (mis)use of ML/AI in practice, a set of guidelines and monitoring and control mechanisms is of paramount importance. AI-centric Data Governance [12] is set to ensure transparency, accountability and explainability of AI in enterprise applications, some of which can be autonomous; we referred to this class as intelligent enterprise applications.

In light of establishing data governance along the AI lifecycle many organizations have begun to define and minor their own normative, and measurable standards and guidelines; see f.e. Google [13]. In addition, governmental entities such as the EU have recognized the importance to regulate data governance for AI, witnessing laws like the GDPR. In addition, standardization organizations and professional associations have defined codes of conduct, such as the IEEE and ACM, e.g., the US Policy Council principles for algorithmic transparency and accountability [14].

Regrettably, existing ML & AI approaches and technologies, such as AutoML, largely fail to effectively and explicitly consider the key principles of data governance, notably transparency, accountability and explainability [15].

2.3 Complex AI Models: Transfer-Leaning

Transfer learning -often referred to as inductive transfer- loosens the implicit assumption underpinning many machine learning approaches that training and testing data are taken from the same feature space and data distribution. By doing so, transfer learning allows ML/AI models to be reused across different domains, tasks and data distributions [16]. This in order of previous investments in collecting and curating preparing datasets, pre-training and pre-testing the ML-models (often relatively expensive in terms of GPU-time), and expert knowledge, to be reused [17].

A well-known example is the reuse of a previously trained localization model that was trained to sniff and localize smart phones during a particular event (let's say the 2019 Glastonbury festival) for another time zone (two years later), or for another event with different perimetry, that same year.

With the rise of interest in transfer, a number of proprietary and open digital repositories of (well-organized) datasets and models with pre-trained weights have arisen. Current popular examples of open repositories include, OpenML[1], ModelDepot[2], and ModelZoo[3], whilst TensorFlow Hub, IBM's Watson ML Repository are examples of proprietary ones. Typically, these repositories like ModelZoo comprise pretrained models implemented in multiple AI-frameworks like Caffe/2, PyTorch, Chainer, and, Keras.

[1] https://www.openml.org/.

[2] https://modeldepot.io/.

[3] https://modelzoo.co/.

Clearly, transfer learning techniques in conjunction with these repositories hold the promise to boost the efficiency and effective of ML/DL to resolve actual business problems by non-experts, and minimal investments. Nevertheless, there is to the best of our knowledge no way to better render these model artifacts abstractly in a more user-friendly, and implementation-agnostic manner. Also, the policies under which such models can be re-trained and re-deployed typically remain hidden and/or unspecified.

2.4 Model-Driven Development

Model-driven development has emerged from the UML modeling language and the Meta Object Facility initiatives sprung off by the Object Management Group in the late 90 s. From its beginning, the MDD's fabric is woven with three key constituent threads [18]: domain-specific languages, model transformation and management facilities, and, supporting infrastructure to facilitate automation from higher-application and platform-abstractions down to physical source code and engines. In this way wicked problems can be caught and resolved pro-actively, while iteratively and fluidly 'yoyoing' back-and-forth between abstract model representations of the problem domain and the physical infrastructure [19].

To date, MMD has mainly focused on the disciplined forward- and reverse-engineering of enterprise applications, transforming computational independent models, to platform-specific model and physical code. The domain of ML/DL is largely terra incognita. It is the purpose of this article to commence explorations on how to reap the benefits of MMD for developing intelligent enterprise applications that leverage ML/DL.

In the next section, we will now first further define the notion of intelligence enterprise applications, and dissect their key internal organization.

3 A Novel Solution: Intelligent Enterprise Applications Architectures (iA^2) Blueprinting for MLOps

Novel enterprise applications are increasingly exploiting ML/DL code in order to make their systems more "intelligent". This imposes additional requirements on traditional service-oriented application architectures [20], including derivates such as micro-service and serverless-computing architectures, which have been cultivated into an international de-facto reference.

The intelligent application architecture - iA^2 - entails a first attempt to incorporate requirements stemming from (more) intelligent enterprise applications into a logically-structured architecture.

iA^2 constitutes a stratified architecture encompassing three layers (see Fig. 2) promoting logical separation of concerns, loose-coupling and reuse. The logical separation is grounded on the need to logically separate basic data manipulation requirements ("data processing services"), from more advanced functionality needed to: (a) instrument applications with intelligence that facilitate reasoning including root-cause analysis and predictive/prescriptive analytics, and (b) continuous deployment, testing and monitoring of intelligent applications.

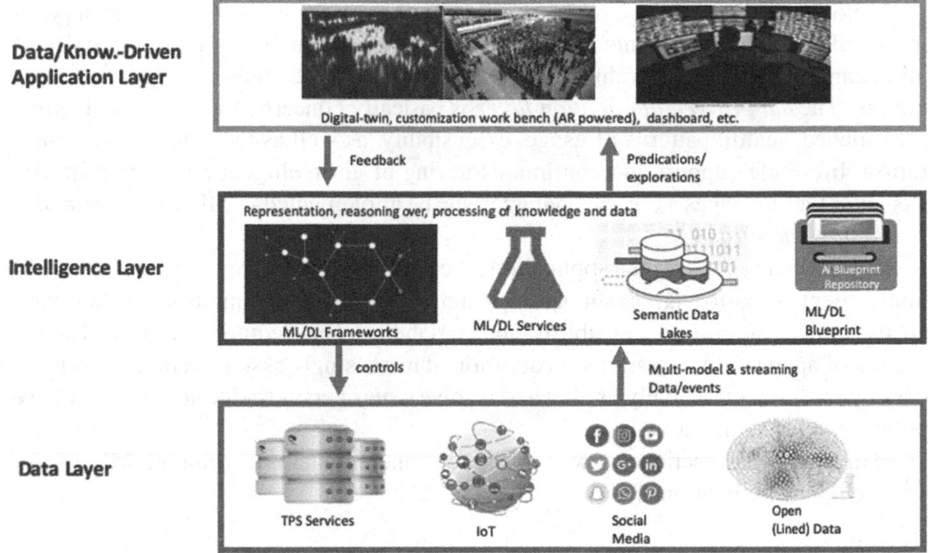

Fig. 2. Intelligent Enterprise Application's Architecture

The bottom layer of the iA^2 is akin of *traditional data processing services*, facilitating multi-model data storage capturing data from various heterogenous (static and streaming) data sources such as: IoT (sensor) devices, open and linked data, social media data, and, traditional transaction-oriented crunching systems. It is important to note that data may include data training, validation and tests sets, aside of operational data that is produced in the execution environment.

In a normal scenario employing this basic data layer in iA^2, a data engineer designs, develops and deploys a *data-pipeline* including data preparation, feature engineering, data transformation, data management and governance functionality.

The Intelligence layer of the iA^2 encompasses necessary roles and functionality for *developing, training and finetuning ML/DL models* that collectively embody the key "intelligence" exploiting data from the layer below. Typically, data scientists/data analysts, and/or AI experts will exploit existing DL/ML frameworks such as Google's AI,Microsoft's Azure, and IBM's Watson—and increasingly AutoML platforms—that provision (semi-)automated AI/DL services such as sentiment analysis, recommendation systems, purchase predication, spam detection, and others.

Resulting model artifacts can be stored and published as parameterized, discoverable and re-instantiable AI/DL models with pretrained weights, which may be re-utilized by data scientists/data analysts/AI experts for future projects. Such blueprints do not simply package pre-trained AL/DL models, but also attach associated policies that future clients need to understand. For example, security policies may express location-constraints, encryption protocols, and pre-configured access/control stipulations. We refer to such pre-trained, policy-enabled AI/DL models as blueprints in Figure-2.

The intelligence layer makes use of *semantic data lake* that comprises meta-data descriptors, which may range from simple label identifiers to full-fledged semantic ontologies. The purpose of the semantic data lake is to capture and convey the meaning in context of the AL/DL models and their associated datasets.

Deploying and managing intelligence enterprise applications in the iA^2 even imposes more challenging requirements. Failures, performance anomalies or unexpected degradation can propagate in the architecture, and impact the health of other application components. The *data-driven application layer* is basically concerned with the availability, performance, health, patterns of usage, extensibility, as well as the control and configuration, life-cycle support and continuous testing of an intelligent application in iA^2. This layer thus manages a critical characteristic be implemented in ML-Ops: *continuous application operations.*

Essentially, the data-driven application layer provides service-level agreement (SLA) management, monitoring, dashboarding and auditing (including trouble-shooting), and dynamic scalability, extensibility and portability. This requires end-to-end transparency of application operations. In addition, it increasingly assumes application managers/operators to proactively predict and resolve issues versus traditional, more reactive application management.

In the following section we will introduce a metamodel underpinning MLOps for iA^2 intelligent applications [21].

4 Blueprinting Intelligent Enterprise Applications Architecture: A Metamodel Sample

The proposed metamodel (see Fig. 3) provides a first attempt to define the core artifacts for blueprinting enterprise intelligent applications in a semi-formal manner.

The metamodel is defined into three essential meta-areas:

(1) in the top, the blueprint shall provide an operational `context` for the *`model`* that stipulates under which conditions it can be transferred, e.g., a task x can be reused in another context (aka can be transferred) if the tasks to be executed are equivalent, yet the domains have different feature spaces. This implies the basic mechanisms of transfer learning can be applied to the ML/AI blueprints, supporting both `heterogenous` and `homogeneous transfer` [16]. In addition, the blueprint shall provide detail over the *`model`*(s) involved in its operation, models themselves shall in turn be defined by means of their `cost function` optimization (e.g., hyperparameter tuning routines).

(2) in the middle, `operational policies` that may be applied to the model are defined (mid right-hand side in Fig. 3). In particular, this compartment of the metamodel defines the policies that may be applied to the model, including, `security policies` (e.g., RBAC-policies), `privacy policies` (e.g., differential privacy), `QoS policies` (such as the required F^2, precision and recall), `compliance policies` (e.g., constraints with respect to profiling, and `monitoring policies` (e.g., thresholds for average CPU/GPU consumption rates or available memory space).

(3) in the bottom, the blueprint shall outline every architecture element [22] composing the AI/ML model parameters. A variety of AI/ML models may be supported such as `Support Vectors Machines`, `Bayesian Models`, and `Neural Networks`.

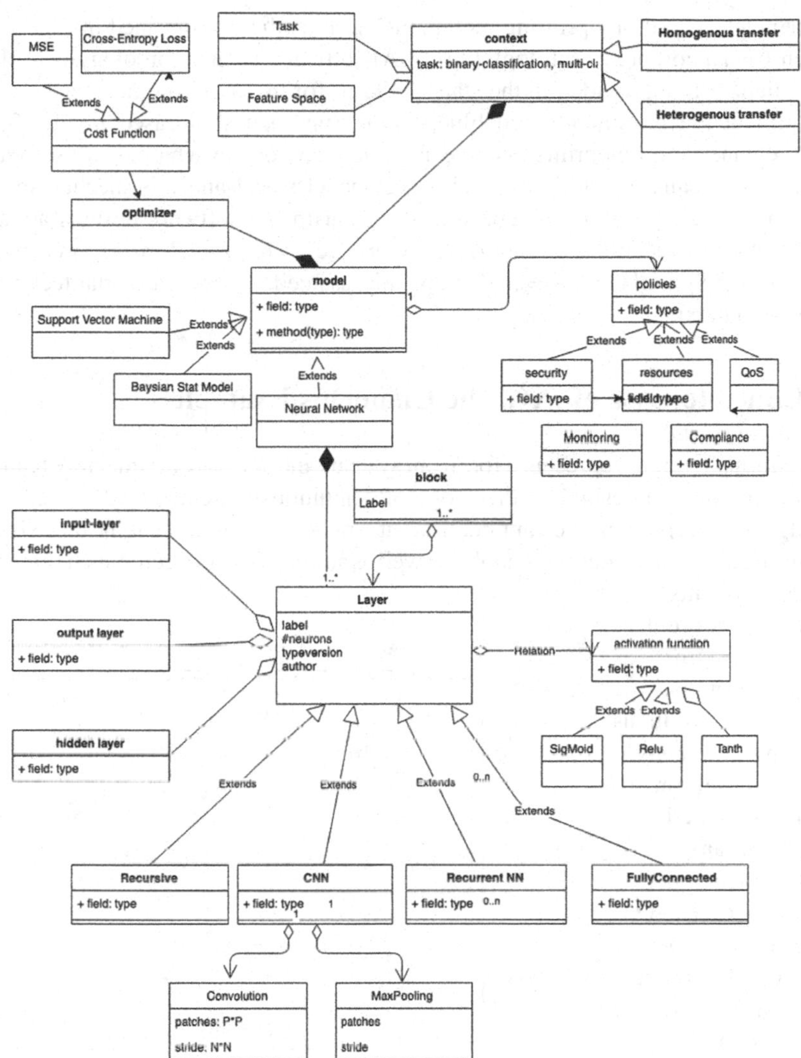

Fig. 3. Intelligent Application Blueprints, a Metamodel.

As part of the architecture specification (meta-area (3) of the blueprinting metamodel in Fig. 3, as outlined above) the iA^2 blueprints shall specify the instances of all types of ML technological components in the application, detailing the internals of such components at a fine-grained level of abstraction.

For example, in the sample provided in Fig. 3, `Neural-Networks` are used as a basis for the AI-software being developed while the metamodel constrains, in the scope of a Convolutional Neural Networks (CNN) [23], the input of parameters such as `convolution` *layering details*, `maxPooling`which need to be specified.

In principle, a full blueprinting metamodel such as the one outlined in Fig. 3 shall be drawn from a complete Ontology [24] of AI-software; such an ontology is itself yet to be formalized and provided in the state of the art for use in this context.

As part of the aforementioned blueprinting approach showcased in Fig. 3, AI-software engineering blueprints become first-class citizens in which, analyses can be performed by means of whatever established model-based analysis mechanism may be available. In the proposed blueprinting mechanism, AI software designs are separated from specific technologies and AI techniques (e.g., Keras or TensorFlow), and can therefore be configured to fit—even dynamically, as needed—to a particular technology application context.

5 A Concrete Case of iA^2: The ChainOps Example

Blockchain applications represent a forefront systems and software architecture featuring a blockchain-oriented design. In the scope of continuously architecting as well as re-designing and re-deploying such applications, it is rather obvious to imagine the existence of ML applications that cater for, enable, as well as automatically execute such re-designs and re-deployments.

We call the aforementioned paradigm as *ChainOps*, that is, the usage of continuous architecting, integration, and evolution of blockchain-oriented designs by means of AI-enabled systems across an automated DevOps pipeline. In the scope of such a complex orchestration and software lifecycle scenario, the existence and operation of MLOps blueprints is almost obligatory since, without a blueprinting artefact to handle the complexity of overall (re-)designing as well as (re-)deploying such ChainOps examples, their feasibility in action would be impossible. Figure 4 provides an example of the intended

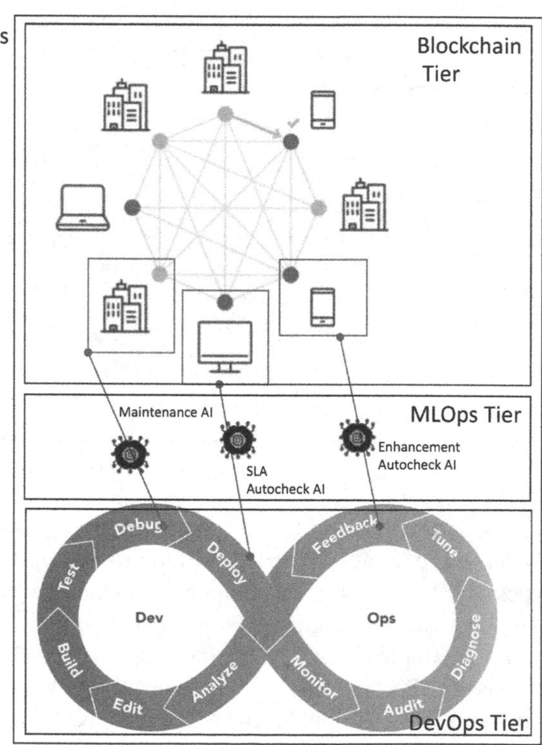

Fig. 4. MLOps enabled ChainOps

ChainOps instance entailed in the aforementioned definition. The figure shows a complex orchestration scenario in which different blockchain nodes part of a blockchain-oriented design where each node may be in a different DevOps lifecycle phase (lifecycle in the bottom part of the Figure) but the complex orchestration of the DevOps phases is choreographed by individual MLOps activities (red boxes and red links from the Figure).

In the complex orchestration scenario depicted in the figure the MLOps layer acts as a glue between the blockchain operations and the actionable insights stemming from the blockchain-oriented operation itself.

At the same time, a single blueprinting artifact (left-hand middle side of the Figure) is capable of synthesizing the orchestration components for operations engineers as well as business-tier stakeholders to predicate upon.

6 Conclusions and Roadmap

The visionary promise of AI-driven enterprise applications – often referred to as AI-software—is that they will go well beyond simple data-processing and cater for sophisticated near- to real-time data analytics, and improved decision making.

This article proposes and explores a novel approach in which software based on artificial intelligence (AI) components can be offered in the form of a *blueprint,* namely, a versionable, analyzable and coherent model-driven artefact akin to the model-driven engineering tenets and concepts.

In such a way, AI-software blueprints can be versioned, verified for properties - including policies, contextualized, explained, used for portable AI-tech transfer (e.g., model-driven transfer learning) and similar state-of-the-art model-driven engineering activities and tool-supported software actions.

To substantiate the aforementioned proposal, a sample blueprinting metamodel was provided which illustrates the basic tenets—and research challenges—behind the proposition. In terms of tenets, the proposed approach would, in principle, inherit most if not all of the established concepts and benefits typical in model-driven software engineering solutions.

The research reported in this article constitutes core research results in nature. Indeed, many critical research challenges remain unanswered. From our side, we intent to utilize, extend and improve the metamodel presented herein to make ML model transformations a reality, defining AI/ML blueprint operators and their operational semantics. Secondly, the development of a full-blown, semantic, and rigorous ML-ontology that builds on top of the metamodel and her operators is envisioned. In addition, a prototypical and experimental prototype is foreseen that revolves around the ML/AI blueprint repository, and allows to exploit "recipes" for continuous integration and testing. Lastly, and probably most importantly, real-world experiments are planned in the context of the EU ISFP ProTECT project to feed the envisioned approach with empirical and experimental data of the model-driven ML approach "in action", and iteratively drive the approach, AI/ML blueprints and supporting ID to a higher level of maturity.

References

1. Soni, Neha, et al.: Artificial intelligence in business: from research and innovation to market deployment. Proc. Comput. Sci. **167**, 2200–2210 (2020)
2. Ford, L.: Artificial intelligence and software engineering: a tutorial introduction to their relationship. Artif. Intell. Rev. **1**, 255–273 (1987). https://doi.org/10.1007/BF00142926
3. White Paper on Artificial Intelligence: a European approach to excellence and trust, February 2020. https://ec.europa.eu/info/sites/info/files/commission-white-paper-artificial-intelligence-feb2020_en.pdf
4. Burt, A.: The AI transparency paradox, Harvard Business Review, web article, December 2019. https://hbr.org/2019/12/the-ai-transparency-paradox
5. Zöller, M.A., Huber, M.: Benchmark and survey of automated machine learning frameworks, January 2020. arXiv:1904.12054
6. Tuggener, L., et al.: Automated machine learning in practice: state of the art and recent results. In: 6th Swiss Conference on Data Science, SDS, Bern, Switzerland, pp. 31–36 (2019)
7. Ripley, B.D.: Statistical aspects of neural networks. In: Barndorff-Niels, O.E., et al. (eds.) Networks and Chaos—Statistical and Probabilistic Aspects, pp. 40–123. Chapman & Hall, London (1993)
8. Feurer, M., Hutter, F.: Hyper parameter optimization. In: Hutter, F., et al. (eds.) Automated Machine Learning: Methods, Systems. Challenges. Springer, Heidelberg (2019). https://doi.org/10.1007/978-3-030-05318-5
9. Masood A., Hashmi A.: AIOps: predictive analytics & machine learning in operations. In: Cognitive Computing Recipes. Apress, Berkeley, CA (2019)
10. Ebert, C., et al.: DevOps. IEEE Softw. **33**(3), 94–100 (2016)
11. Nogueira, A.F.: et al.: Improving La Redoute's CI/CD pipeline and DevOps Processes by applying machine learning techniques. In: The Proceedings of the 11th International Conference on the Quality of Information and Communications Technology, QUATIC, Coimbra, pp. 282–286. IEEE (2018)
12. Gasser, U., Almeida, V.: A layered model for AI governance. IEEE Internet Comput. **21**(6), 58–62 (2017)
13. Perspectives on Issues in AI Governance, Google. https://ai.google/static/documents/perspectives-on-issues-in-ai-governance.pdf. Visited 7 April 2020
14. ACM U.S. Public Policy Council. Statement on algorithmic transparency and accountability. https://www.acm.org/binaries/content/assets/public-policy/2017_usacm_statement_algorithms.pdf.2017
15. Kroll, J.: Data science data governance. IEEE Secur. Priv. **16**(6), 61–70 (2018)
16. Pan, S.J., Yang, Q.: A survey on transfer learning. IEEE Trans. Knowl. Data Eng. **22**(10), 1345–1359 (2010)
17. Day, O., Khoshgoftaar, T.M.: A survey on heterogeneous transfer learning. J. Big Data **4**, 29 (2017). https://doi.org/10.1186/s40537-017-0089-0
18. Schmidt, D.C.: Model-driven engineering. Comput. IEEE Comput. Soc. **39**(2), 25 (2006)
19. Bucchiarone, A., et al.: Grand challenges in model-driven engineering: an analysis of the state of the research. Softw. Syst. Model. **19**, 5–13 (2020)
20. Papazoglou, M.P. van den Heuvel, W.J.: Service oriented architectures: approaches, technologies and research issues. VLDB J. **16**(3), 389–415 (2007). https://doi.org/10.1007/s00778-007-0044-3
21. Virmani, M.: Understanding DevOps & bridging the gap from continuous integration to continuous delivery. In: Fifth International Conference on the Innovative Computing Technology, INTECH 2015, Pontevedra, pp. 78–82 (2015)

22. Bass, L., Clements, P., Kazman, R.: Software Architecture in Practice. Addison-Wesley, Boston (2003). ISBN: 9780321154958
23. Wendler, C., Püschel, M., Alistarh, D.: Powerset convolutional neural networks, pp. 927–938 (2019)
24. Gaševic, D., et al.: Software engineering approaches to ontology development. In: Model Driven Engineering and Ontology Development, pp. 177–205. Springer, Heidelberg. (2009). https://doi.org/10.1007/3-540-32182-9_6. ISBN: 978-3-642-00281-6

Managing Human and Artificial Knowledge Bearers

The Creation of a Symbiotic Knowledge Management Approach

Marcus Grum(✉)

University of Potsdam, 14482 Potsdam, Germany
mgrum@lswi.de

Abstract. As part of the digitization, the role of artificial systems as new actors in knowledge-intensive processes requires to recognize them as a new form of knowledge bearers side by side with traditional knowledge bearers, such as individuals, groups, organizations. By now, artificial intelligence (AI) methods were used in knowledge management (KM) for knowledge discovery, for the reinterpreting of information, and recent works focus on the studying of different AI technologies implementation for knowledge management, like big data, ontology-based methods and intelligent agents [1]. However, a lack of holistic management approach is present, that considers artificial systems as knowledge bearers. The paper therefore designs a new kind of KM approach, that integrates the technical level of knowledge and manifests as Neuronal KM (NKM). Superimposing traditional KM approaches with the NKM, the Symbiotic Knowledge Management (SKM) is conceptualized furthermore, so that human as well as artificial kinds of knowledge bearers can be managed as symbiosis. First use cases demonstrate the new KM, NKM and SKM approaches in a proof-of-concept and exemplify their differences.

Keywords: Knowledge management · Artificial Intelligence · Neuronal systems · Design of knowledge-driven systems · Symbiotic system design

1 Introduction

Being faced with the role of new technical and digital actors and knowledge bearers, such as Artificial Intelligence (AI)-based systems, the danger is present, that artificial systems are evolving and generate knowledge, that is undesired from the viewpoint of an organization. An example refers to the generation of selling recommendations: Although these might perform well on training and test data sets, they disregard the human's knowledge need in its business process context. Further, humans might reject AI-based insights, because they cannot reason for the system's plausibility and its conformance with organizational objectives.

Inadvertence towards the management of knowledge of all kinds of knowledge bearers can hold enormous risks. For instance, one cannot identify if the system focuses on wrong influence factors and one blindly must follow its recommendations. However, the compelling necessity for an instrument becomes transparent that enables the prevention of undesired knowledge bases of an organization. This includes human-based knowledge bases as well as technical knowledge bases of individual machines.

B. Shishkov (Ed.): BMSD 2020, LNBIP 391, pp. 182–201, 2020.
https://doi.org/10.1007/978-3-030-52306-0_12

Although being faced with numerous AI method uses in KM, such as for knowledge discovery, the reinterpreting of information, and the implementation for KM, like big data, ontology-based methods and intelligent agents [1], the joint management of human and technical knowledge bearers has not been issued so far. This is supplemented by contemporary attempts to develop AI-based systems. Since these focus on the learning task specified, neither the manageable development of AI-based systems, which is with regard to objectives of an organization, nor the management of knowledge generated by AI-based systems have been issued, yet.

If it was possible to systematically and efficiently guide the evolution of an organization's joint knowledge bases, so namely human knowledge bases as well as artificial knowledge bases, the trustworthy and ethical justifiable use of AI-based systems is supported. So, the following research will focus on the optimization of knowledge bases with the intention to answer the following research question: "How can machine-based knowledge and human-based knowledge be managed efficiently in an integrated way?" Sub-research questions addressed are:

1. "How can AI-based systems be considered as knowledge bearers, so that traditional KM is enhanced?"
2. "How can human knowledge be considered at knowledge-driven enterprise information systems, so that dealing with AI-based systems is enhanced?"

This paper contributes with a new kind of KM approach, that enables the symbiotic management of technical and human knowledge bases. Since the approach proposed intends to enable the traditional KM by knowledge from artificial knowledge bearers, throughout the paper, the linking with traditional KM will be regarded. The focus is set on how human-based knowledge can be managed more efficiently (first sub-research question). For instance, the approach will enable the question how the knowledge need of a professional buyer having a need for market analyses and the knowledge supply of an ANN system about the prediction of market prices can be allocated efficiently.

Further, the symbiotic management approach proposed intends to enable the dealing with AI-based systems, by knowledge from human knowledge bearers. Since this must be compatible with traditional KM activities, throughout the paper, the reinterpretation of KM activities in ANN context is regarded. So, the manageable development of AI-based systems will be enabled. Further, new kinds of KM roles and management levels have been derived and the focus is set on how machine-based knowledge can be managed efficiently (second sub-research question).

The research approach is intended to be design-oriented as Peffers proposes [2] and the structuring of this paper is derived from the Design-Science-Research Methodology (DSRM) as follows: The second section provides a theoretical foundation and underlying concepts. The third section presents a methodological required specification for the management of knowledge bearers: requirements are derived, which are separated from the design of required artifacts. So, they can function as quality gates for artifacts in the fourth section. Here, the Symbiotic Knowledge Management (SKM approach) is set up that considers a KM and the novel Neuronal Knowledge Management (NKM). The fifth section demonstrates the application in case studies, so that the requirement fulfillment can be evaluated (sixth section). The final section concludes the paper and presents implications for a contemporary management of knowledge and enhanced ANN system development.

2 Background of Managing Knowledge

Underlying concepts for the research presented here refer to the definition of knowledge (first sub-section) and the domain of KM (second sub-section). As ANN systems are considered as technological knowledge bearer manifestation, relevant concepts of the domain of ANN are presented in a third sub-section. As both kinds of knowledge bearers are evolving over time, contemporary insights of a knowledge development are considered in the fourth sub-section. The literature review is issued finally.

2.1 Theoretical Foundation

Knowledge. Attempts to define the term knowledge can be traced back to ancient times. Inter alia, attempts for definitions can be found in the following.

- *Everyday understandings* recognize knowledge as an awareness of something [3,4], which results because of family resemblances among items to be aware of [5,6].
- *Philosophical definitions* focus on the nature of knowledge as an insight from an epistemological perspective. It therefore has to stand different levels of justification [7,8].
- *Educational contexts* consider knowledge to be a concept of competences enabling individuals to act in specific situations [9,10].
- *Pedagogical and cognitive-psychological definitions* consider knowledge to be a fluent information schemata being perceived by a person and integrated in the person's long-term memory [11,12]
- *KM- and Knowledge-Logistic-oriented approaches* recognize knowledge as the unity of skills, cognition and capabilities, which are used for the solution of problems [13,14]. So, knowledge has a contextual meaning, dynamic nature, tacit dimension, is socially constructed [15], and it can be used in order to realize a competitive advantage [16].
- *Information-System-oriented and AI-based definitions* recognize knowledge to be information, which is valuable in specific situations and supports the identification of decisions [17]. Issuing the distinction of data, information and knowledge, definitions focus on the interlinking and organization of information.
- *Neuro-Scientific and Cognitive-Scientific attempts* recognize knowledge as information stored, integrated and organized inside the brain [18]. So, by the act of selecting, comparing, evaluating and drawing consequences, knowledge is made from the resource of information [19].

As the SKM approach intends to integrate the traditional KM and AI system development, and the identification of knowledge within neuronal structures is intended, an adequate definition of knowledge must bring together aspects form a non-machine side inspired by the KM domain (everyday, philosophical, pedagogical and knowledge management contexts, etc.) as well as aspects from a machine side inspired by the AI domain (information system, machine learning contexts), so that a knowledge definition supports the everyday understanding about knowledge-related concepts and can stand as a foundation for knowledge objects to be managed.

Knowledge Management. The knowledge management (KM) deals with the creating, sharing, using and managing of knowledge and information of an organization [20]. Principally, there are two kinds of KM [15,21–27]:

- *Resource-oriented KM*, which focus on the management of knowledge as resource, so that knowledge is recognized to be administrated.
- *Process-oriented KM*, which focus on the utilization of knowledge. It appreciates knowledge to have a value and to be part of the entire value chain of a company.

Concrete KM models and concepts e.g. refer to [15,28–31]. Although not any KM model addresses a machine-based knowledge, the Potsdam KM model [15] is attractive to stand as a foundation for the conceptualization of SKM approach in particular, as it provides an ordering system, which is based on the dimensions of the following three: (1) the organizational range providing a foundation of traditional knowledge bearers, (2) the procedural range providing a foundation of by knowledge traditionally affected areas, and (3) the personnel range providing a foundation of traditional KM stakeholders. Further, the Business-Process-Oriented KM model (BPO-KM, [15,30,31]) is attractive to stand as a foundation since it provides valuable framework conditions.

Artificial Knowledge Bearers. Having a long history, the origin of Artificial Intelligence (AI) is typically dated back to the 1950 [32]. Often, it is differentiated by the degree of intelligence [33,34]:

- *Narrow AI* focuses on the automation of a precisely defined task. Here, knowledge refers to a limited set of capabilities.
- *General AI* addresses systems having the physical and intellectual capabilities of a human person. Here, knowledge refers to a circumstantial and complex set of capabilities.
- *Super AI* issues systems that are much more intelligent than humans. Here, knowledge refers to the most complex and ambitious set of capabilities.

Further, the AI is differentiated by its interpretability, which centers symbols [34, 35]:

- *Symbolic AI* tries to capture a certain knowledge domain by explicit symbols. As these traditionally are coming from the human model creator, the intelligent performance of a system is realized on behalf of a top-down approach and with the aid of symbols of a conceptual level. Hence, its interpretability is not an issue. Often it is referenced orthodox AI or as GOFAI (Good-Old-Fashioned AI). Here, one can argue to deal with explicit knowledge.
- *Neuronal AI* tries to capture a certain domain of knowledge with the aid of data. Hence, it rather refers to a bottom-up approach, which is enabled by an as precisely rebuilding of the human brain as possible. Here, the system behavior is difficult to interpret since knowledge is not explicitly constituted by symbols and one can argue to deal with tacit knowledge.
- *Symbolic Distributed AI* tries to combine the first two kinds of AI, as it recognizes the symbolic nature of knowledge and considers a distributed processing. Here, one can argue to deal with both explicit and tacit knowledge.

So far, the issue with AI-based systems, such as ANN, refers to the fact that no explicit, human understandable model is created [36, p. 136]. Its learning and so the structure building of a knowledge generation entirely builds on the optimization of thousands weights and floating point parameters. Implicitly, they function as tacit knowledge. Principally, this limits the capability of the SKM approach by now, as only knowledge from a symbolic AI can be issued. However, the interpretability of neuronal AI systems, such as ANN, is improving and these may not be excluded from an organization-wide management of knowledge.

Since AI-based systems operate on base of the generation of floating point parameters, the very atomic neuronal activity is considered to be a foundation for the SKM approach. Building on neuronal activations, that hold floating point parameters, knowledge can be considered as a neuronal pattern. This refers to a current, evolves over a certain period of time and causes a specific behavior of consecutive neurons [37]. As the smallest denominator of a knowledge definition, the SKM approach will be based on this knowledge understanding. Following a constructivist approach, here, the assumption is implemented, that each neuronal knowledge object is considered as an activation-based, codified form of knowledge that is considered with sooner or later complexity levels as clearly recognizable knowledge from the perspective of KM and everyday understandings.

Knowledge Development. As contemporary pedagogical and cognitive-psychological approaches assume knowledge to be combined successively to more complex schemata and by this, a knowledge structure evolves over time [12], the learning and the development of knowledge is realized phase-wise and needs to be supported (e.g by pedagogical valuable designs):

- In the first phase, knowledge is prepared to be crystallized by *fluid systems*, such as the phonological loop, episodic buffer, visuo-spatial sketch pad and the central executive [38–40]. As these deal with schemata individually, different kinds of individual capacities and learning barriers need to be addressed, so that they do not overload the working memory in the sense of the cognitive-load theory [41,42]. This goes along with the respecting of individual emotional factors of human learners [43].
- In the second phase, knowledge is anchored within the crystallized knowledge base, e.g. by repetition. So, the volatile knowledge constructed by fluid systems is stored sustainably in the long-term memory, which therefore is called *crystallized system* [44].

Regarding to the current focus of a learning phase, each schemata demands for an individual support of pedagogic designs. These are valuable for the symbiotic KM because of the appropriate addressing of learning characteristics. By the realization of activities with the aid of pedagogic designs, the efficient guiding of a human or machine-based learner is enabled. Therefore, an adequate management of knowledge, which intends to systematically evolve an organizational knowledge base, needs to address the knowledge development with regard to the following three: first, the individual knowledge bearer, second, the schemata and third, the learning phase.

2.2 Literature Review

Alavi and Leidner have reviewed KM literature. They identified detailed processes and the role of information systems [45]. Weinreich and Groher reviewed contemporary KM activities and they identified architectures for the efficient capturing of KM activities [46]. On base of a great collection of KM activities, well documented KM processes and information systems, one can recognize the KM as foundation for the efficient management of human knowledge bearers.

Tsui et al. reviewed the roles of AI in KM. They argue if AI systems are ready to converse with humans [47] - from this perspective, they won't demand for management. Liao reviewed KM technologies and AI applications and identified an integration of qualitative and quantitative methods at that time [48]. Having reviewed recent attempts of AI methods and KM systems, Begler and Gavrilova identified AI methods as tools simplifying isolated KM activities [1]. A management approach recognizing AI-based systems as knowledge bearers, which need to be managed, has not been issued, yet. Also, a holistic approach for the common management of human and artificial knowledge bearers is not present.

Although Tsui et al. have reviewed KM approaches, they argue if KM is a brand name of knowledge engineering. Being dominated by computer scientists and AI researchers in particular, the construction of intelligent agents and ontologies is issued [47]. Neither an integration of AI-based knowledge with the organizational knowledge base nor the controlled or educative knowledge building is present. The AI system development rather focuses on the performance-oriented training and generalization [49]. So, the organization's holistic objectives - these go beyond the limited context of a specific learning task - are disregarded. Further, contemporary approaches lack at the identification of a common understanding of knowledge, that is in the sense of traditional KM and corresponds to AI-based systems.

In contrast to the above work, this contribution specifically focuses on the joint management of human and artificial knowledge bearers. Synthesizing existing models, in the sense of a holistic framework, an approach is presented, that identifies a joint understanding of knowledge as well as its management with regard to organizational objectives.

3 Requirements for the Management of Knowledge Bearers

In accordance with Design-Science oriented research [2], requirements are defined before the artifacts are conceptualized. Since these will serve as design maxims for the SKM approach set up, they issue the following: First, the SKM approach will be based on contemporary research presented in Sect. 2.1. Second, the SKM approach will progress the state-of-the-art presented in Sect. 2.2. Third, they support the comparability of subsequent research. Having set up these requirements in a workshop session, these were confirmed by three experts from the field of KM, business process management and ANN construction each. Table 1 presents an overview.

Table 1. Requirements for the management of knowledge bearers.

Req.	Description
1.	The SKM approach needs to stand as management approach for the following three kinds of combinations: first, organizational knowledge only (cf. knowledge at Sect. 2.1), second, neuronal knowledge only (cf. artificial knowledge bearers at Sect. 2.1), and third, both kinds of knowledge jointly
2.	The SKM approach needs to reflect contemporary ontological dimensions. This requirement recognizes knowledge to be constructed on traditional ontological levels (cf. KM at Sect. 2.1) and includes AI-based knowledge bearers (cf. artificial knowledge bearers at Sect. 2.1)
3.	The SKM approach needs to reflect the educative dimension of knowledge bearers (cf. knowledge development at Sect. 2.1). Here, human as well as machine-based knowledge bearers are faced with limited capacities, learning burdens, emotional factors, and different kinds of memories. This requirement issues the efficient knowledge development
4.	The SKM approach needs to reflect different kinds of stakeholders because the dealing with human and technical knowledge bearers demands for different competences. While some experts are coming from the process domain and deal with KM issues (cf. KM at Sect. 2.1), others are coming form the ANN domain and deal with the construction of AI-based systems (cf. artificial knowledge bearers at Sect. 2.1)
5.	The SKM approach needs to reflect the contemporary procedural range. This recognizes knowledge to be constructed on different procedural levels (cf. process-oriented KM at Sect. 2.1). For instance, this refers to the biological plausible knowledge processing of ANN and its anchoring in business processes
6.	The SKM approach needs to reflect KM activities (cf. KM at Sect. 2.1), which are able to function as interventions and modify current environmental conditions [50]
7.	The SKM approach needs to reflect framework conditions of a KM (cf. KM at Sect. 2.1). This requirement recognizes each activity to be realized within a certain environment and having influencing factors

4 Design of a Symbiotic Knowledge Management Approach

Since not any contemporary KM considers educational perspectives and framework conditions, the following sets up a KM approach. Since the Potsdam KM Model has been identified as a powerful representative to carry out KM [15], it has served as starting point for an extension with BPO-KM framework conditions [31,51,52]. The approach designed is denominated as *KM approach* from hereon and its components have been indicated by highlighting the bottom left (blue) corner in Fig. 1.

Since not any contemporary KM further considers neuronal perspectives and not any approach to deal with ANN considers traditional KM activities, the following establishes a Neuronal Knowledge Management (short: NKM). Based on the requirements (cf. Sect. 3), the *KM approach* mentioned before has been transferred to the neuronal context, so that a *NKM approach* has been constructed in a second step. Its components have been indicated by highlighting the top right (green) corner in Fig. 1.

In a third step, an approach has been designed, which issues the *ANN Process Domain*, and therefore integrates the KM approach from the *Process Domain* and the NKM approach from the *ANN Domain* [37]. In the following, this integrating approach is called Symbiotic Knowledge Management approach (short: *SKM approach*). With regard to Req. 1, it has been composed and therefore addresses activities from the one domain in the other domain and vice versa. The joint KM and NKM components of the SKM approach have been indicated by a gray shading in Fig. 1. Hence, by their joint visualization, the integration of three individual approach becomes transparent. Each of their components are issued in detail by the following sub-sections.

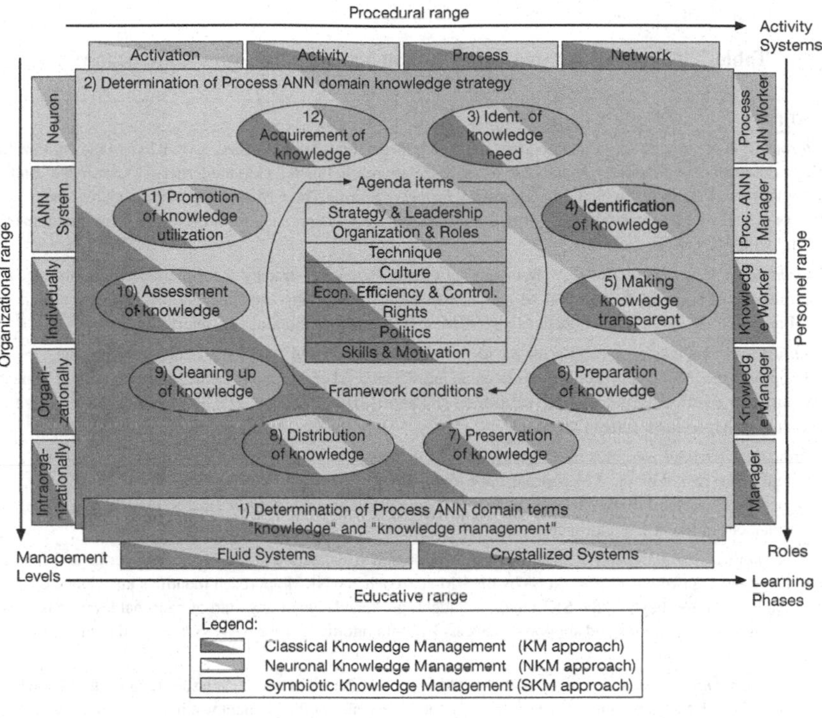

Fig. 1. Design of the symbiotic knowledge management approach. (Color figure online)

Activity Collection. Beside the classical KM activities, that have been described by the Potsdam KM Model (cf. [15, p. 49]), the SKM approach and the NKM approach consider the same activities within the ANN domain. Although having the same naming, they follow an interpretation within the neuronal context. Jointly, they are referred to as *ordering amounts*. Hence, the Table 2 provides a new structuring of activities for the dealing with ANN systems by a reinterpretation of KM activities. The numbers visualized in Fig. 1 refer to the following explanations but they do not represent a sequential order.

Educative Range Specification. The educative range of Fig. 1 focuses on the question, in which phase the learning system currently is, so that KM and NKM measures support the target-oriented knowledge development. This considers the type of the system, its individual capacities and learning burdens as well as its current knowledge state (cf. knowledge development at Sect. 2.1). The educative range is supported by pedagogical valuable interventions. Its manifestations are ordered by the learning progress of management levels. Since an educative proceeding has not been considered by any KM approach, yet, and all activities of Sect. 4 are affected by the educative range, Table 3 deals with differences between the KM approach, NKM approach and SKM approach.

Table 2. Activities for managing human and artificial knowledge bearers.

ID	Description
1.	*Determination of terms:* A common understanding of relevant terms is established, so that the whole organization is able to communicate efficiently. In the case of the SKM approach, this refers to the terms of "knowledge" and "knowledge management", which reflect the *ANN Process Domain*. The KM approach would address the process-oriented KM context only (*Process Domain*) and the NKM approach would focus on terms about the dealing with ANN (*ANN Domain*)
2.	*Determination of knowledge strategy:* Being part of the organizational strategy, the importance of knowledge is determined from both, the KM and NKM perspective. While the KM approach disregards NKM objectives and the NKM approach disregards KM objectives, the SKM approach regards all kinds of objectives
3.	*Identification of knowledge need:* Beside the identification of KM-based knowledge needs issued by the KM approach, the NKM approach examines on an individual level of a group of neurons, which kind of knowledge is required for an effective process step realization and knowledge generation. The SKM approach identifies the need on all kinds of management levels
4.	*Identification of knowledge:* Beside the recognition of the personal, organizational and inter-organizational knowledge base issued by the KM approach, the joint knowledge base of ANN systems is examined by the SKM approach in regard to the currently available knowledge. This includes ANN-based knowledge representations of the NKM approach
5.	*Making knowledge transparent:* Beside the identification and visualization of knowledge of internal and external knowledge carriers (knowledge workers) by the KM approach, the NKM approach identifies knowledge on a neuronal level. Going beyond, the SKM approach identifies knowledge of any kind of neuronal level, makes it transparent by visualizations and supports its access by meta information for ANN systems and human knowledge carriers
6.	*Preparation of knowledge:* In harmony with the KM approach, the SKM approach issues the idea that knowledge is transformed to a KM-friendly and a NKM-friendly form. This allows the efficient use in current and future task realizations. In distinction of the SKM approach, the NKM approach transforms knowledge to a NKM-friendly form only, which disregards the KM-friendly form
7.	*Preservation of knowledge:* Beside the structuring, decontextualization and backing up knowledge from the KM perspective, the SKM approach and the NKM approach consider the structuring and backing up of ANN-based knowledge. Just the SKM approach harmonizes the structuring and backing up of knowledge, so that an effective exchange of ANN-based and human knowledge is supported
8.	*Distribution of knowledge:* A knowledge distribution within the organization must not be limited with respect to by management or by culture induced knowledge distributions, as the KM approach issues. The NKM approach issues the distribution of knowledge within ANN systems. The SKM approach further supports the distribution of ANN systems and knowledge generated by them within the organization. It further supports the distribution of knowledge of the organization within ANN systems
9.	*Cleaning up of knowledge:* Beyond the correction, renewing and deletion of knowledge by the KM approach, the NKM approach cares about the correction, renewing and deletion of ANN-based knowledge. So, negative effects of knowledge not supporting the organization's objectives can be avoided
10.	*Assessment of knowledge:* The assessment of the current knowledge base of an organization in regard to its value within the entire value chain is issued by the KM approach. The SKM approach additionally includes the assessment of the knowledge base generated by ANN systems. The NKM approach limits the knowledge assessment on neuronal systems only
11.	*Promotion of knowledge utilization:* In addition to the creation and modification of new organizational structures, processes and systems that support the knowledge use (KM approach), the SKM approach includes the creation and modification of new ANN structures, systems, subsystems and neurons. The NKM approach only focuses on the transmission of neuronal signals and is with regard to the ANN performance
12.	*Acquirement of knowledge:* In distinction from the elimination of a knowledge deficit by external acquisition or education, which is issued by the KM approach, the ANN knowledge deficit is treated by the NKM approach. Since the SKM approach includes the KM and NKM, the knowledge acquisition by education or external parties is considered for ANN system deficits, as well as ANN systems are considered for the elimination of a knowledge deficit within an organization

Table 3. Learning phase-specific systems of human and artificial knowledge bearers.

ID	Description
1.	*Fluid Systems:* During the first learning phase, capacities are addressed by measures and activities, that reduce learning barriers and enable the schemata building in fluid systems. While KM measures and activities address capacities of traditional knowledge workers and human process participants, NKM measures and activities address capacities of ANN systems and machine-based process participants. The SKM approach considers KM measures and NKM measures jointly, so that interdependencies can be treated
2.	*Crystallized Systems:* During the second learning phase, free capacities for the storing of fluid schemata are addressed, so that knowledge crystallizes and is integrated with and anchored in the crystallized knowledge base sustainably. Primary, KM measures and activities address the crystallization of schemata of traditional knowledge workers and human process participants, that have been built during the first learning phase. Corresponding NKM measures and activities address the crystallization of schemata of ANN systems and machine-based process participants. The SKM approach jointly considers the sustainable knowledge anchoring of schemata coming from any kind of fluid system

Although various phases are adequate for an educative development of learning systems, as a rough first level, pedagogical and cognitive-psychological types of systems and corresponding learning phases, capacities and burdens have been considered. Further possibilities refer to e.g. the refinement of phases for different kinds of systems, such as phonological loop, episodic buffer, visuo-spatial sketch pad, central executive, or the six competence levels of Bloom, such as *Knowing*, *Comprehending*, *Applying*, *Synthesizing*, *Analyzing* and *Evaluating* [53]. The essential point of this range rather refers to the systematic education of learning systems than the concrete design. A comparable training and testing procedure for ANN systems has not been issued in literature, yet.

Organizational Range Specification. The organizational range of Fig. 1 focuses on the question, which areas of an organizational structure are affected by a KM measure and its concrete KM activities [15, p. 49]. Its manifestations are ordered by the amount and size of organizational structures participating in a certain KM measure. While the NKM approach only considers the level of *Neurons* to be affected by NKM measures and NKM activities, for the SKM approach, the KM approach has been extended by the elements of *ANN Systems* and *Neurons*, so that a NKM is enabled. Table 4 presents an overview.

Since dealing with knowledge is recognized throughout all management levels presented and the interplay of these levels is enabled because of a joint knowledge definition (cf. knowledge at Sect. 2.1), the social construction of knowledge is reflected in the management approaches designed.

Table 4. Management levels for managing human and artificial knowledge bearers.

ID	Description
1.	*Neuronal:* The neuronal manifestation issues the very atomic knowledge carriers as management level. It refers to compartments that jointly construct individual ANN systems
2.	*ANN System:* The ANN system manifestation substantiates higher management levels, such as the *individual* in whatever detail by ANN mechanisms and algorithmic representations, the manifestation of ANN systems issues KM and NKM measures or rather activities that affect neuronal representations
3.	*Individual:* Beside the idea, that KM measures and activities affect persons like Max Mustermann, issued by the KM model, the SKM approach includes the idea that these affect ANN systems as well. Since NKM measures and activities also affect individuals, the SKM approach integrates the *Process Domain* and the *ANN Domain*
4.	*Organizational:* The SKM approach introduces the idea that NKM measures and activities can affect organizational entities, such as groups, teams, departments and sections. These in turn affect ANN systems by KM measures
5.	*Intraorganizational:* Going beyond the traditional addressing of the collaboration between enterprises as well as the relation to suppliers and external service providers e.g., the SKM approach reflects NKM measures and activities for the affecting of intraorganizational entities

Procedural Range Specification. The procedural range of Fig. 1 focuses on the question, which areas of a process organization are affected by a KM measure and its concrete KM activities [15, p. 49]. Its manifestations are ordered by a kind of complexity and complicatedness of manifestations participating in a certain KM measure. The KM approach has been extended by the element of addressing neuronal activities, the so called *Activation*. So, a NKM is enabled by neuronal activities, which are relevant for a certain behavior of an ANN system. Table 5 presents an overview.

Personnel Range Specification. The personnel range of Fig. 1 focuses on the question, which persons are part of the realization of a KM measure and carry out concrete KM activities [15, p. 49]. Its manifestations are ordered by a kind of professional hierarchy. The KM approach has been extended by the element of *Process ANN Manager* and *Scientific Expert*, so that a NKM is enabled. So, Table 6 issues implications from the KM approach, NKM approach and SKM approach.

Framework Conditions. The framework conditions of Fig. 1 focus on the question, which environmental agenda items need to be addressed by a KM measure and its concrete KM activities. Its manifestations jointly refer to [52, p. 109, 108, 107, 113] and [15] and do not have an ordering. As these are considered in the neuronal context, Table 7 issues implications from the KM approach, NKM approach and SKM approach.

Table 5. Activity systems considering human and artificial knowledge.

ID	Description
1.	*Activation:* As the key activity on the neuronal level (cf. artificial knowledge bearers at Sect. 2.1), the neuronal activity brings together ANN mechanisms from the *ANN Domain* and a process understanding of the process domain. It refers to the most atomic activity system available at all and translates measures of a KM as well as a NKM to the neuronal context
2.	*Activity:* The activity manifestation of the KM approach addresses the idea, that a measure or activity of KM can affect an individual activity. By the SKM approach, additionally, NKM-based measures and activities are also assumed to affect individual activities. So, the SKM approach addresses an integrative activity understanding in the sense of the *ANN Process Domain*: first, measures or activities of KM can affect corresponding ANN representations, second, measures or activities of NKM can affect activities of process participants and knowledge carriers. The NKM approach is designed to not consider this kind of activity system, since NKM measures and activities focus on the efficient Machine Learning task realization
3.	*Process:* Since measures or activities of NKM are also considered to affect entire processes, and measures or activities of KM can affect corresponding ANN representations, the SKM approach addresses an integrative process understanding in the sense of the *ANN Process Domain.* The NKM approach is designed to disregard this kind of activity system, since NKM measures and activities focus on the efficient Machine Learning task realization
4.	*Network:* The network manifestation of the KM approach issues the most complex and complicated activity system level of non-sequential processes, that must be considered as a mesh of processes. In addition, the SKM approach considers also measures or activities of NKM to affect entire networks, and measures or activities of KM to affect corresponding ANN representations. Having a clear focus of NKM measures and activities, the NKM approach disregards this kind of activity system

5 Demonstration of New Knowledge Management Approaches

As demanded by the design-oriented research [2], the demonstration applies designed artifacts and demonstrates their use. Being faced with numerous management activities at the SKM approach and NKM approach the following exemplifies the use of each new approach by one scenario. Since the KM approach corresponds to an extension of traditional KM attempts and the KM approach is part of the SKM approach, it will be demonstrated with the latter approach jointly.

Table 6. Roles for managing human and artificial knowledge bearers.

ID	Description
1.	*Manager:* Beside the persons caring about the efficient realization of a model, which is issued by the KM approach, because of the SKM approach, the manager will be faced with the efficient and economic realization of a model of the *ANN Process Domain*. Focusing on the NKM approach only, this does not consider the management role directly, because the effect of a manager is decoupled from the technical Machine Learning task realization
2.	*Knowledge Manager:* The knowledge manager cares about the efficient dealing with the resource of knowledge within the company [54]. As the SKM approach establishes a NKM in addition, the knowledge manager includes knowledge generated by ANN systems, subsystems and neurons, so that the organizational knowledge base is supplemented. Since knowledge managers are not considered for the technical Machine Learning task realization, these rather serve as domain-specific experts for the design, the NKM approach does not consider this kind of role directly
3.	*Knowledge Worker:* According to the KM approach, the process participant is referred to as knowledge worker, that carries out knowledge-intensive processes. In the context of the SKM approach, the knowledge worker will also operate with the ANN constructed. It further enables the ANN construction by its process experience. Additionally, autonomous systems are considered as knowledge worker on an equal footing with human workers
4.	*Process ANN Manager:* This role must be seen as counterpart of the knowledge manager. The process ANN manager cares about the efficient dealing with the resource of knowledge within a company on behalf of contemporary *ANN Process Domain* approaches. Since neither the NKM approach nor the KM approach consider systems from the other domain, this role functions as a bridge between different kinds of systems
5.	*Process ANN Worker:* As a kind of complement for the process ANN manager, the process ANN worker issues the very specific competence of an scientific expert. It provides expertise from at least one domain that enables the *ANN Process Domain*. Here, one can find the wide range of biologists, neuro-scientists, and doctors, who care about state-of-the-art biologic mechanisms, as well as computer scientists and simulation experts caring about the algorithmic processing of simulations. Further, one can find ANN experts caring about the ANN system building, as well as experts from the specific field of application (e.g. chemist, physicians, astronomers, engineers). While the NKM approach considers this role only for the application of NKM measures, a classical KM approach so far has not accessed this kind of role because of the focus on KM measures and activities

5.1 Interventions by the NKM Approach

Focusing on the artificial knowledge base of an ANN system design only, the use of the NKM approach can be demonstrated as follows: Imagine in this scenario to realize interventions addressing the different activities and learning phases. These are realized by the *Process ANN worker*, who is operating on an *Activation* level by the dealing with

Neurons. Please trace this by the green components presented at Fig. 1 (highlighted top right corner).

For the initialization of an ANN system, the architectural structures are set up and weights are initialized randomly [55]. This refers to the NKM activity *Acquirement of knowledge* on the *Fluid System* level. The specification of training material can be associated with the activity called *Preparation of knowledge*. Of course, this material needs to be prepared by data experts before (fourth NKM activity, cf. Fig. 1). Here, an intervention could improve the expert's skills for this kind of knowledge identification.

As one e.g. recognizes compartments of an ANN to generalize efficiently, the knowledge utilization can be promoted by the reuse of these structures for the design of

Table 7. Framework conditions for managing human and artificial knowledge bearers.

ID	Description
1.	*Strategy & Leadership:* The KM approach focuses on traditional measures for an active management, that supports an autonomous, self-determined acting of process participants. In particular, this refers to the acting as coach and to the acknowledging of employees and external knowledge carriers [52, p. 109]. On the other side, the NKM approach issues measures for an active management supporting the self-determined acting of ANN systems as well as the acting as coach for ANN-based knowledge carriers. Considering all of them, the SKM approach provides measures for an active management by and of ANN systems as well as human process participants, which includes the educative knowledge development
2.	*Organization & Roles:* In addition to measures providing appropriate processes, roles and an internal organization of communities to embed KM services in a company's structure, the NKM approach addresses measures for the provision of appropriate processes, roles and communities for the embedding of NKM services. Jointly, the SKM approach addresses corresponding measures for the embedding of KM services and NKM services
3.	*Technique:* The KM approach focuses on measures for the establishment of an appropriate infrastructure, software and hardware, that allows the provision and utilization of KM services. As a supplement, the SKM approach cares about the provision of an appropriate infrastructure, software and hardware, which allows the provision and utilization of NKM services as well
4.	*Culture:* Measures need to address attitudes, qualifications, role understanding and missions of actors of the social system, which all support the utilization of KM services and reduce barriers. In the sense of the SKM approach, all of them also need to support the utilization of NKM services. In this way, knowledge will be recognized as procedural phenomenon being able to be managed by an adequate environment
5.	*Economic Efficiency & Controlling:* The KM approach demands for measures about the assurance of the beneficial, cost- and time-effective KM service use for the social system actors. It further addresses the examination of the successful realization of predefined KM targets. The SKM approach additionally includes the audit of the beneficial, cost- and time-effective NKM service utilization and the fulfillment of predefined NKM targets by hard and soft indicators. It so builds on the NKM approach
6.	*Rights:* The KM approach demands for measures about the assurance of legal issues, such as property rights of third parties and conditions for governmental approvals about the provision of KM services, as well as for the explanation of rights and duties for knowledge workers, that are relevant for the dealing with KM services. In distinction from this approach, the NKM approach issues the compliance of legal issues of NKM services and the explanation of rights and duties for the dealing with NKM services. Going beyond, the SKM approach draws attention to all
7.	*Politics:* In addition to KM approach measures providing organizational resources in regard with legal circumstances, that allow the use of KM services, the NKM approach builds on governmental regulations affecting the provision of organizational resources, that allow the use of NKM services, and tries to adjust legal circumstances. The SKM approach jointly draws attention to all
8.	*Skills & Motivation:* Going beyond measures of the KM approach, that demand for an enhancement of individual skills that are relevant for business process realizations, and the motivation of employees to conduct effective KM activities [52, p. 108], the SKM approach demands for the enhancement of individual skills relevant for neuronal process realizations, and the motivation of employees to conduct effective NKM activities. It so builds on the NKM approach

further ANN systems (eleventh NKM activity). For instance, it has been identified that a certain target system needs to establish a behavior, which is comparable to the behavior of the reference system (third NKM activity - *Identification of knowledge need*). Then, attractive structures of the reference system can be recreated at the target system (eighth NKM activity). In the case one aims to transfer ANN compartments from one customer to another, the framework conditions of *Rights* must allow this.

In the case, a system generates unpleasant recommendations, which have been identified because the corresponding knowledge has been assessed (tenth NKM activity), these ANN compartments simply can be deleted, which are responsible for this recommendation (ninth NKM activity - *Cleaning up of knowledge*). This might be related to political regulations (framework condition of *Politics*), as for example laws demand for the transparent backing up of data and information systems.

When learning has finalized successfully, and one intends to continue training processes, it might be useful to preserve the current ANN structures as crystallized memories (second learning phase). By the provision of new capacities, such as additional neurons at the ANN trained, these can focus on fluid knowledge while crystallized structures care about learned memories (seventh NKM activity - *Preservation of knowledge*).

5.2 Interventions by the SKM Approach

Focusing on the organization-wide knowledge base, the use of the SKM approach can be demonstrated as follows. Imagine in this scenario to realize interventions addressing the different activities and learning phases. These are addressed by all kinds of roles, that are operating on all kind of activity systems (procedural range). Further, they are dealing with all kinds of management levels (organizational range). Please trace this by the gray components presented at Fig. 1 (shaded components).

Let's assume to initialize ANN systems again (*Fluid System* level). The *Knowledge Worker* can guide the knowledge identification best because of its experiences from the daily routines in the knowledge-intensive process that is issued (fourth SKM activity). For this, the *Knowledge Manager* guides the selection of knowledge workers across the processes. Here, the knowledge manager reflects the *Activity* level since knowledge is identified at the realization of an operational task. Further, the knowledge manager reflects the *Process* level because knowledge from the one task will be distributed among other tasks. The *Manager* cares about the consideration of economic dimensions and the organization's vision. E.g. the manager intends do "reduce process durations" by the reuse of knowledge across the processes (eighth SKM activity). Here, he focuses on the *Network* level. The *Process ANN Worker* finally trains the ANN systems. The *Process ANN Manager* regards the training progress and cares e.g. about the efficient implementation of the knowledge acquisition. This includes the backing up of knowledge and ANN systems by the marking as *crystallized system*.

An example for the interplay of all kinds of management levels refers to the following: Let's assume to have established a crystallized organizational knowledge base, which e.g. can be seen at the availability of standards, routines and a team-wide behavioral pattern (*Organizational* management level). Then, a new colleague (*Individual* level) or intelligent machine (*ANN System* level) might cause a change of this long-term memory because of the integration of new knowledge objects and the current knowledge base. Here, it is essential that the organization's culture (fourth framework condition) supports the inclusion of external expertise.

6 Evaluation

In order to satisfy design-science-oriented research approaches [2], the following evaluates how far requirements of Sect. 3 have been fulfilled.

- Req. 1 has been fulfilled, as three kinds of KM approaches have been superpositioned. By this, the three kinds of approaches (KM/NKM/SKM) can stand individually within its own domain, or they can integrate the *Process Domain*, the *ANN Domain* and the *ANN Process Domain*.
- Req. 2 has been fulfilled, as contemporary knowledge bearers (or management levels) have been considered by the SKM approach on an equal footing. Here, the traditional ontological levels, such as *Individuals*, *Organizations* (groups, teams, departments) and *Intraorganizations*, have been positioned next to AI-based systems, such as *ANN Systems* and its compartments (*Neurons*).
- Req. 3 has been fulfilled, as contemporary pedagogical concepts have been considered by the SKM approach. Here, learning phases have been put side-by-side, so that a focus is set on the dealing with fluid and crystallized systems.
- Req. 4 has been fulfilled, as contemporary roles have been considered by the SKM approach on an equal footing. Here, traditional ontological levels, such as the *Manager*, the *Knowledge Manager* and *Knowledge Worker* have been positioned next to the novel roles of *Process ANN Managers* and *Process ANN Workers*.
- Req. 5 has been fulfilled, as contemporary activity systems have been considered by the SKM approach. Here, traditional systems, such as *Activities*, *Processes* and *Networks*, have been positioned next to AI-based systems (*Activations*).
- Req. 6 has been fulfilled, as different kinds of KM activities have been considered by the SKM approach. With this, a systematic ANN system realization is enabled by the NKM.
- Req. 7 has been fulfilled, as environmental factors have been considered by the SKM approach by categories or rather agenda items.

7 Conclusion

Having updated traditional KM by one further approach (KM approach), and having formulated a neuronal knowledge management and its approach (NKM approach), further, a joint approach has been created (SKM approach). This considers human as well as artificial knowledge bearers to be in a symbiosis, and with whom they jointly can be managed. The approach components have been demonstrated individually, so that the approach interplay and the accessing of its individual domains has been clarified.

Critical Appraisal: The first research question (*"How can AI-based systems be considered as knowledge bearers, so that traditional KM is enhanced?"*) can be answered with the design of the SKM approach. The traditional KM can be enhanced as ANN systems are considered as a new kind of knowledge bearers, which are treated on an equal footing with traditional knowledge bearers. By this, a more powerful organization-wide knowledge base can be accessed, that includes decentralized individual knowledge bases of autonomous machines.

The second research question (*"How can human knowledge be considered at knowledge-driven enterprise information systems, so that dealing with AI-based systems is enhanced?"*) can be answered by the design of the NKM approach, which transfers traditional KM activities and framework conditions to the context of ANN system designs. For the first time, the dealing with ANN-based knowledge can be systematized, which results in new activities in the training and testing of ANN systems. Oriented to contemporary psychological concepts, this further considers different learning phases and introduces a pedagogical valuable, incremental knowledge building in the dealing with ANN systems.

So, the main research question (*"How can machine-based knowledge and human-based knowledge be managed efficiently in an integrated way?"*) can be answered by the joint consideration of machine-based and human knowledge by one management approach. This is based on the superposition of a traditional KM and the new form of neuronal KM, so that the joint SKM is set up in the *ANN Process Domain*. This claims to be efficient, as ANN-based knowledge becomes manageable for the first time and further considers interdependencies among the different kinds of KM approaches. Further, because of the pedagogical valuable addressing of capacities, learning burdens and emotional factors, the efficient and learner-specific management is supported. As a wide research field of the operationalization of this new kind of management, the concrete addressing of them by valuable pedagogic designs and Machine Learning algorithms need to be examined.

Limitations: Although first use cases demonstrate the use of NKM approach and SKM approach, only a sparse collection of theoretical use cases has been presented. However, these focused on the exemplary clarification of measures or interventions of the one domain affecting the other and the complete demonstration of the ordering system has not been presented, yet. Further, the validity level is low as demonstrations presented refer to abstract descriptions only.

Outlook: Faced with given limitations, the collection of use cases is to be extended. This must include the circumstantial description of technical effects by an activity. With this, the initial assumption of having a potential for organizations, because of the joint management of human kinds as well as technical kinds of knowledge bearers, needs to be verified empirically. Further, it will be examined, how far the trustworthy and ethical justifiable use of AI-based systems is supported with the aid of the SKM approach and NKM approach.

References

1. Begler, A., Gavrilova, T.: Artificial intelligence methods for knowledge management systems. Working Papers 15106, Graduate School of Management, St. Petersburg State University (2018)

2. Peffers, K., et al.: The design science research process: a model for producing and presenting information systems research. In: 1st International Conference on Design Science in Information Systems and Technology (DESRIST), vol. 24, pp. 83–106 (2006)
3. Eberhard, J.: Johann August Eberhards synonymisches Handwörterbuch der deutschen Sprache, p. 1802. Schimmelpfennig
4. Schlabach, P.: Sitte, Ethik und Moral: eine Begründung. Tredition (2018)
5. Wittgenstein, L.: Philosophische Untersuchungen. Suhrkamp Verlag, Frankfurt am Main (1953)
6. Prechtl, P., Burkard, F.: Metzler Lexikon Philosophie: Begriffe und Definitionen. J.B. Metzler, Stuttgart (2015)
7. Brendel, E.: Wissen. In: Jordan, S., Nimtz, C. (eds.) Lexikon Philosophy - Hundert Grundbegriffe, pp. 308–311. Reclam (2013)
8. Gettier, E.L.: Is justified true belief knowledge? Analysis **23**(6), 121–123 (1963)
9. Weinert, F.E.: Vergleichende Leistungsmessung in Schulen - eine umstrittene Selbstverständlichkeit. In: Weinert, F.E. (ed.) Leistungsmessungen in Schulen, pp. 17–32. Beltz, Weinheim (2001)
10. Heyse, V., Erpenbeck, J.: Kompetenztraining: 64 modulare Informations- und Trainingsprogramme für die betriebliche, pädagogische und psychologische Praxis. Schäffer-Poeschel (2009)
11. Schmidt, C.: Arbeitsgedächtnis und fremdsprachliches leseverstehen. Zeitschrift für Fremdsprachenforschung **1**(11), 83–101 (2000)
12. Wellenreuther, M.: Forschungsbasierte Schulpdagogik. Schneider Verlag, Hohengehren (2012)
13. Davenport, T.H., Prusak, L.: Working knowledge: how organizations manage what they know. Ubiquity, vol. 2000, August 2000
14. Polanyi, M., Sen, A.: The tacit dimension. University of Chicago Press, reissue edn. (2009)
15. Gronau, N.: Wissen prozessorientiert managen: Methode und Werkzeuge für die Nutzung des Wettbewerbsfaktors Wissen in Unternehmen. Oldenbourg Wissenschaftsverlag (2009)
16. North, K., Brandner, A., Steininger, T.: Die Wissenstreppe: Information – Wissen – Kompetenz, pp. 5–8. Springer, Wiesbaden (2016)
17. Lämmel, U., Cleve, J.: Künstliche Intelligenz. Carl-Hanser Verlag, München (2012)
18. Solso, R.L.: Kognitive Psychologie. Springer-Lehrbuch. Springer, Heidelberg (2005)
19. Reinmann-Rothmeier, G., Mandl, H.: Wissen. In: Lexikon der Neurowissenschaft. Spektrum Akademischer Verlag, Heidelberg (2000)
20. Girard, J., Girard, J.: Defining knowledge management: toward an applied compendium. Online J. Appl. Knowl. Manag. **3**(1), 1–20 (2015)
21. Scheer, A.: ARIS - Modellierungsmethoden, Metamodelle, Anwendungen, 3rd edn. Springer, Heidelberg (1998). https://doi.org/10.1007/978-3-642-97731-2
22. Becker, J., Schütte, R., Geib, T., Ibershoff, H.: Grundsätze ordnungsmäßiger modellierung (gom)/westfälische wilhelms–universität münster-institut für wirtschaftsinformatik, ids scheer ag, josef friedr. Bremke & Hoerster GmbH & Co (2000)
23. Remus, U.: Prozessorientiertes wissensmanagement. konzepte und modellierung, Juni 2002
24. Fettke, P., Loos, P.: Referenzmodellierungsforschung. Wirtschaftsinformatik **46**, 331–340 (2004)
25. Gronau, N., Müller, C.: Wissensarbeit prozessorientiert modellieren und verbessern (2005)
26. Gronau, N., Müller, C., Korf, R.: KMDL - capturing, analysing and improving knowledge-intensive business processes. J. Univers. Comput. Sci. **11**, 452–472 (2005)
27. Hinkelmann, K., Thönssen, B., Probst, F.: Referenzmodellierung für e-government-services. Wirtschaftsinformatik **47**(5), 356–366 (2005)
28. Davenport, T., Jarvenpaa, S., Beers, W.: Improving knowledge work processes. Sloan Manag. Rev. **37**(4), 53–65 (1996)

29. Allweyer, T.: Modellbasiertes wissensmanagement. Inf. Manag. **13**(1), 37–45 (1998)
30. Hinkelmann, K., Karagiannis, D., Telesko, R.: PROMOTE—Methodologie und Werkzeug für geschäftsprozessorientiertes Wissensmanagement, pp. 65–90. Springer, Heidelberg (2002)
31. Heisig, P.: Geschäftsprozessorientiertes Wissensmanagement: effektive Wissensnutzung bei der Planung und Umsetzung von Geschäftsprozessen, ch. GPO-WM: Methode und Werkzeug zum geschäftsprozessorientierten Wissensmanagement, pp. 47–64. Xpert.press. Springer, Heidelberg (2002)
32. Russell, S., Norvig, P.: Artificial Intelligence: A Modern Approach, 3rd edn. Prentice Hall Press, Upper Saddle River (2009)
33. Bostrom, N.: Superintelligence: Paths, Dangers Strategies, 1st edn. Oxford University Press Inc., Oxford (2014)
34. Fettke, P.: Conceptual modelling and artificial intelligence: overview and research challenges from the perspective of predictive business process management. In: Companion Proceedings of Modellierung 2020 Short, Workshop and Tools & Demo Papers co-located with Modellierung 2020, Vienna, Austria, 19–21 February 2020, pp. 157–164 (2020)
35. Peschl, M.: Cognitive Modelling: Ein Beitrag zur Cognitive Science aus der Perspektive des Konstruktivismus und des Konnektionismus. DUV, Datenverarbeitung, Deutscher Universitätsverlag (1990)
36. Evermann, J., Rehse, J.-R., Fettke, P.: Predicting process behaviour using deep learning. Decis. Support. Syst. **100**, 129–140 (2017). Smart Business Process Management
37. Grum, M., Gronau, N.: A visionary way to novel process optimizations – the marriage of the process domain and deep neuronal networks. In: Shishkov, B. (ed.) BMSD 2017. LNBIP, vol. 309, pp. 1–24. Springer, Cham (2018). https://doi.org/10.1007/978-3-319-78428-1_1
38. Baddeley, A.: Oxford Psychology Series, no. 11. Working Memory, New York, NY, US (1986)
39. Baddeley, A.J.: The episodic buffer: a new component of working memory? Trends Cogn. Sci. **4**, 417–423 (2000)
40. Baddeley, A.: Working memory: theories, models, and controversies. Annu. Rev. Psychol. **63**(1), 1–29 (2012). PMID: 21961947
41. Sweller, J., van Merrienboer, J.J.G., Paas, F.G.W.C.: Cognitive architecture and instructional design. Educ. Psychol. Rev. **10**, 251–296 (1998)
42. Clark, R.C., Nguyen, F., Sweller, J., Baddeley, M.: Efficiency in learning: evidence-based guidelines to manage cognitive load. Perform. Improv. **45**(9), 46–47 (2006)
43. Lufi, D., Okasha, S., Cohen, A.: Test anxiety and its effect on the personality of students with learning disabilities. Learn. Disabil. Q. **27**(3), 176–184 (2004)
44. Heymann, H.: Üben und wiederholen - neu betrachtet. Pädagogik **10**, 7–11 (1998)
45. Alavi, M., Leidner, D.E.: Review: knowledge management and knowledge management systems: conceptual foundations and research issues. MIS Q. **25**(1), 107–136 (2001)
46. Weinreich, R., Groher, I.: Software architecture knowledge management approaches and their support for knowledge management activities: a systematic literature review. Inf. Softw. Technol. **80**, 265–286 (2016)
47. Tsui, E., Garner, B.J., Staab, S.: The role of artificial intelligence in knowledge management. Knowl. Based Syst. **13**(5), 235–239 (2000)
48. Liao, S.: Knowledge management technologies and applications—literature review from 1995 to 2002. Expert Syst. Appl. **25**(2), 155–164 (2003)
49. Schmidhuber, J.: Deep learning in neural networks: an overview. Neural Netw. **61**, 85–117 (2015)
50. Grum, M., Rapp, S., Gronau, N., Albers, A.: Accelerating knowledge – the speed optimization of knowledge transfers. In: Shishkov, B. (ed.) BMSD 2019. LNBIP, vol. 356, pp. 95–113. Springer, Cham (2019). https://doi.org/10.1007/978-3-030-24854-3_7

51. Heisig, P.: Integration von Wissensmanagement in Geschäftsprozessen. Dissertation, Technische Universität, Berlin (2005)
52. Mertens, K.: Knowledge Management: Best Practices in Europe. Springer, Heidelberg (2001). https://doi.org/10.1007/978-3-662-04466-7. http://publica.fraunhofer.de/documents/n-4420.html
53. Bloom, B.S., Engelhart, M.B., Furst, E.J., Hill, W.H., Krathwohl, D.R.: Taxonomy of Educational Objectives. The Classification of Educational Goals. Handbook 1: Cognitive Domain. Longmans Green, New York (1956)
54. Probst, G., Raub, S., Romhardt, K.: Wissen managen - Wie Unternehmen ihre wertvollste Ressource optimal nutzen, 5th edn. Gabler Verlag, Wiesbaden (2006)
55. Hochreiter, S., Schmidhuber, J.: Long short-term memory. Neural Comput. **9**, 1735–1780 (1997)

Adaptable Knowledge-Driven Information Systems Improving Knowledge Transfers

Design of Context-Sensitive, AR-Enabled Furniture Assemblies

Marcus Grum(✉) and Norbert Gronau

University of Potsdam, 14482 Potsdam, Germany
mgrum@lswi.de

Abstract. A growing number of business processes can be characterized as knowledge-intensive. The ability to speed up the transfer of knowledge between any kind of knowledge carriers in business processes with AR techniques can lead to a huge competitive advantage, for instance in manufacturing. This includes the transfer of person-bound knowledge as well as externalized knowledge of physical and virtual objects. The contribution builds on a time-dependent knowledge transfer model and conceptualizes an adaptable, AR-based application. Having the intention to accelerate the speed of knowledge transfers between a manufacturer and an information system, empirical results of an experimentation show the validity of this approach. For the first time, it will be possible to discover how to improve the transfer among knowledge carriers of an organization with knowledge-driven information systems (KDIS). Within an experiment setting, the paper shows how to improve the quantitative effects regarding the quality and amount of time needed for an example manufacturing process realization by an adaptable KDIS.

Keywords: Augmented reality · Knowledge transfers · Empirical studies · Context-aware computing · Adaptable software systems · Business process improvement

1 Introduction

Many aspects of knowledge-intensive processes have been examined in-depth, e.g. modeling methods, the use of information systems in business processes and the potential of knowledge management systems (KMS) for knowledge transfers [1]. Findings on the speed of knowledge transfers are quite rare and just have been quantified by empirical findings once [2]. Since knowledge-intensive business processes are characterized by the exchange of knowledge and information among process participants [3–7] as well as the knowledge application within concrete situations [1], the amount of knowledge required for the knowledge application and time required for the correct knowledge application are suited for empirical examinations. Grounding on statistically proven models, which quantify the influence of the velocity and quality of knowledge transfers, the knowledge transfer itself as well as its situation can be controlled. Applying these controlling mechanisms in knowledge-driven enterprise information systems (KDIS), the effective knowledge transfer among organizational units can be assumed to be supported.

B. Shishkov (Ed.): BMSD 2020, LNBIP 391, pp. 202–220, 2020.
https://doi.org/10.1007/978-3-030-52306-0_13

Following the motivation to improve knowledge transfer velocity by concrete adjustments of the manifestation of knowledge transfers in their concrete situation and application context, here called intervention, the modification of statistically proven influence factors affecting the speed of knowledge transfers can directly be connected to the adaptability of KDIS: If it was possible to adapt information systems to their situational and knowledge context, the design of information systems, their integration within business processes as well as their combination with knowledge management systems will be enabled.

Hence, the following research will focus on the improvement of knowledge transfers with the intention to answer the following research question: "How can the speed of knowledge transfers in knowledge-intensive processes be improved?" As the assembly of components can be interpreted to be always based on individual experiences and assembly instructions, knowledge is transferred among product development situations and assembly situations via persons and/or media. Hence, the product assembly context is very suited for the observation of knowledge transfers. Further, research methods of Albers et al. [8] become attractive, since the transfer of knowledge in the context of product assembly is based on the transfer of knowledge between situations, which is similar to knowledge transfers between product generation situations already examined.

This paper intends not to draw an all-embracing description of concrete, technical realizations of those novel process improvement techniques. It intends to set a first step to a speed-improved business process design with the help of AR techniques. Before the implementation of concrete AR interventions in context-sensitive, adaptable KDIS, their functioning was proven in laboratory studies described in the following. Hence, sub research questions addressed are:

1. "How can time-dependent knowledge-transfer models be used in order to derive AR interventions, which improve speed of knowledge-intensive business processes?"
2. "How can AR interventions be considered in knowledge-driven enterprise information systems?"

Based on the assumption that AR-based process interventions do not improve the entire set of situations available in reality, but at least they follow the empirically proven knowledge transfer models of [2] and they therefore improve the reference process, their consideration by KDIS needs to be context-sensitive and adaptive. Only then, the optimal setting for the process realization can be supported by the KDIS.

The research approach is intended to be design-oriented as Peffers proposes [9]. The structuring of this paper is derived from this as follows: The second section provides a theoretical foundation and underlying concepts. The third section presents a methodology for the improvement of knowledge transfer speed improvement in knowledge-intensive processes with AR techniques. Objectives are derived, which are separated from the design of required artefacts, so that they can function as quality gates for artefacts in the fourth section. The fifth section demonstrates their application in laboratory studies. These are evaluated in the sixth section, so that the optimal intervention can be identified by KDIS. The final section concludes the paper and presents implications for the AR-enabled, adaptable and context-sensitive KDIS implementation.

2 Theoretical Foundation

Underlying concepts for the research presented here refer to the domain of process improvement (first sub section). As AR technologies are considered in order to increase the knowledge transfer velocity, relevant concepts of the domain of knowledge management are presented in a second sub section.

2.1 Process Improvement

Following the intention to improve a process in regard to a certain objective, any adjustment of them is called process improvement. In general, all activities and decisions that lead to a desired improvement of business processes, are designated as *business process improvement* [10]. With the focus on the improvement of knowledge-intensive business processes, all activities and decisions that lead to the improvement of a certain knowledge transfer in its concrete situation and application context, are designated as *knowledge transfer intervention* [8]. The success of an improvement or intervention is measured by key performance indicators (KPIs), such as assembly times, failure and success rates, the number of assembled components, etc. Principally, one can find two basic approaches for business process improvements that are reflected in various methods and variations:

(1) A management concept called *Kaizen*, that has originally be inspired by a Japanese living and working philosophy, realizes an iterative never ending improvement of processes and products in small steps, which are referred to as *Continuous Improvement Process* (CIP) cycles. In accordance to Imai, the key principles include a *feedback* mentality, which demands for an everlasting search for *efficiency*. Since processes or products are reflected continuously, suboptimal processes are identified and improved in an evolutionary manner, so that rather small than giant adjustments are carried out [11]. Management concepts following cyclic procedures can be found in numerous variations: Shewhart Cycle [12], Deming Wheel [13], a second Shewhart Cycle [14], PDSA Cycle [15]), PDCA Cycle [16] and a second PDCA Cycle [17]. Commonly, those concepts start with planning activities (*plan*). Then, the process adjustment is implemented and carried out (*do*). Feedback is collected in order to be compared with the planned output (*check*). If the comparison gives evidence for inefficient implementations, adequate objectives are derived (*act*), before this cyclic procedure is started again.

(2) The fundamental over-thinking of as-is processes refers to an improvement concept called *Business Process Reengineering* (BPR) [18]. Mostly, this is connected with far reaching changes or a completely redesign of products and processes. Since adjustments of processes are designed as if the organization was built a new, improvements are carried out top-down and are initiated by the management. Hence, in accordance to Hammer and Champy, BPR can be characterized by the following: Decisions are *decentralized*, process step sequences are *reorganized* and different *process variations* can be considered. Further, the *localization* of working content is organized meaningfully, the need for *control* and required *coordination efforts* are reduced and centralized contact points (e.g. for customer requests) are established.

In conclusion, as both kinds of improvements realize adjustments of a process, AR interventions can be considered in both, either in cyclic adjustments of small steps or in fundamental process redesigns. Since CIPs consider adjustments in small steps, and an available process can stand as reference, a cyclic process improvement seems attractive for a first experimentation with AR interventions. Here, knowledge transfer situations can be improved systematically without running in danger to loose knowledge transfer situations because of process redesigns.

2.2 Knowledge Transfers

Based on a consensus of the domain of knowledge management, *knowledge* is defined to be the unity of skills, cognition and capabilities which are used by individuals for the solution of given problems [19–21]. An example can be found in knowledge, which is used for the assembly of a cupboard.

As the assembly is carried out with the help of instructions, knowledge is to be transferred from the instruction to the individual. Hence, a definition of knowledge transfer has to consider the transfer process itself as well as its content to be transferred. This refers for example to the fact, that a certain screw is to be fixed at a certain hole of an assembly component. Since the solution of a given problem is part of the knowledge definition presented, the successful application of knowledge by individuals must be considered. Therefore, building on the conceptual model of Minbaeva et al. [22], this research defines a *knowledge transfer* as the identification of knowledge, its transfer from knowledge carrier to knowledge receiver, and its application by the knowledge receiver. Considering forms of knowledge to refer either to person-bound knowledge (tacit knowledge) or to externalized knowledge of physical and virtual objects (explicit knowledge) [23], for the example process issued, the knowledge transfer at an assembly process considers the instruction as knowledge carrier providing explicit knowledge, the assembler as knowledge receiver having tacit knowledge and the application of knowledge at the final assembly object in form of explicit knowledge. Hence, a successful knowledge transfer can be measured by the correct assembly.

Measuring the time for the successful transfer of knowledge, the *knowledge transfer velocity* can be established, which Gronau and Grum define as the relation of a clearly distinguishable amount of knowledge, which is required for the successful solution of a certain task and transferred from a knowledge carrier to a knowledge receiver within a certain amount of time [2]. Aiming to compare processes of paper-based instructed assemblies with processes of AR-based instructed assemblies, the definition of knowledge transfer velocity implies the following for an experimentation:

- The same amount of knowledge is to be transferred, either coming from the paper-based assembly instruction or from the AR-based assembly instruction.
- The same amount of knowledge is to be applied measured at the finalization of the assembly.
- The clearly distinguishable amount of knowledge refers to atomic assembly operations.
- The time for a correct assembly must be measured.

The only available empirical model about a knowledge transfer velocity is given by Gronau and Grum [2, 24] and sets focus on the following variables: As the *competence* of process participants is raised, the knowledge transfer velocity can be increased. As the *stickiness* of knowledge to be transferred is raised, the knowledge transfer velocity can be increased. This had been declared to be the attribute of knowledge tending to remain at the outgoing perception border of a knowledge carrier or to remain at the incoming perception border of a knowledge receiver and thus retard the transfer of knowledge is defined as stickiness of knowledge [24]. As the *complexity* of the knowledge transfers required for the task to be solved is lowered, the knowledge transfer velocity can be increased. For the application of an AR knowledge transfer intervention focused here, this means a consideration of the only available empirical model inclusive its influence variables. Following the research overview, the application of an empirical knowledge transfer velocity model in form of interventions has not be realized yet. Hence, the application of an AR knowledge transfer intervention focused here is missing, too. A research gap becomes visible.

3 Methodology and Objectives

Following the Design-Science-Research-Methodology (DSRM) of Peffers [9], requirements are defined before the design of artefacts is carried out, so that the latter serve as the design maxims for the experiment design, paper instruction design and AR application design. Since artefacts can only be finalized when all requirements are fulfilled, they work as quality gates for artefacts presented here. Further, they can stand as quality gates for subsequent research and guarantee a comparability.

3.1 Proceeding

With the intention to create the first AR-based knowledge transfer intervention, which will be applied in KDIS, the DSRM approach of Peffers will be embedded in the proceeding oriented to Albers et al. [8], who examined the intervention-based improvement of knowledge transfers in the domain of product development. As a mixed method design, this allows the design-science oriented examination suggested by Peffers and the systematically correct implementation of knowledge transfer interventions of Albers et al. Hence, advantages of both methodologies can be accessed in order to realize a sufficient explanatory power isolated method cannot generate [25]. Figure 1 illustrates the procedure model for accelerating inefficient knowledge transfers within organizations. The procedure model has been extended for desired application design. One can observe seven sequential phases and three possibilities for an iterative proceeding that enable the consideration of insights made in consecutive phases. Those only demand for adjustments of the previous phase, so that later insights are connected with any previous phase. Each phase of the procedure model is described in the following.

The first phase deals with the acquisition of knowledge transfer improvement projects, and includes sale activities, contractual issues, marketing, etc. The second phase defines the focus on knowledge transfer improvement and so makes the use of methods presented here plausible. Based on company strategic objectives and

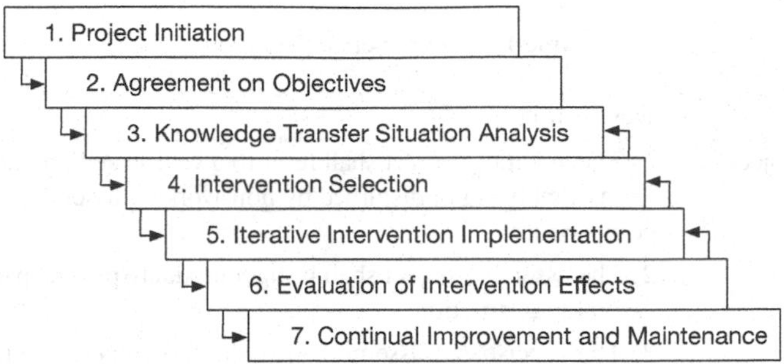

Fig. 1. Procedure model.

constraints, knowledge-intensive processes are identified. Key performance indicators (KPIs) are selected to be improved, such as the quality of knowledge transfers (e.g. measured by failure rates of knowledge applications) or velocity of knowledge transfers (e.g. measured by the time required for the correct knowledge application). Within the third phase, knowledge transfers of selected processes are analyzed. KPIs identified in the second phase are used to quantify as-is situations. Empirically proven factors are considered for the characterization of the situation, which have an influence on selected KPIs as dependent variables. So, an improvement potential can be identified precisely. Then, in the fourth phase, interventions are identified, which are attractive for an improvement of selected knowledge transfer situations and realize the improvement potential identified in the third phase. Since interventions are characterized by the same influence factors that are used for the situation analysis, a match of the most attractive interventions can be detected easily. The fifth phase designs and carries out interventions. Since we are working on a research level, we recommend to do this iteratively following Peffer's design-science-oriented methodology and start with small contexts like pretests, laboratory studies, etc. Later iterations will focus on prototype departments, regional companies and consider greater contexts. The sixth phase considers KPIs identified in the second phase and evaluates, if the implementation of interventions lead to an improvement. Only then, interventions are attractive for a permanent use and an implementation in greater contexts. As an intervention, a combination or parts of interventions are kept, they need to be provided by the corresponding KDIS. They are defined to stand as new process reference and the application developed and applied in the seventh phase is considered in continual improvement process (CIP) cycles and demands for maintenance.

3.2 Requirements

Aiming to prepare an experimentation of the acceleration of knowledge transfers in assembly contexts with AR technologies, this section presents a set of requirements that has to be taken into account in the realization of artefacts. Requirements are presented category-wise in Table 1. The first category of requirements deals with the selection of an assembly object. Since we assume AR-based instructions to effect the time

Table 1. Requirement collection.

Focus	Description
Assembly object	1) The assembly object shall refer to a well-tested product, so that the assembly is not disturbed by non-working assembly components
	2) The assembly object shall bring a product-specific, paper-based assembly instruction
	3) The paper-based assembly instruction shall be well-practiced, so that the assembly is not disturbed by badly described assembly steps
Assembly instruction	4) The paper-based assembly instruction shall consider a selection of assembly steps, that realizes a product as a whole. So, expectations of test persons to realize a final product are met
	5) The preparation of the AR-based and paper-based assembly instruction shall both bring the same knowledge content. Only as the same amount of knowledge is transferred, results can be compared
	6) Both kinds of assembly instructions shall enable an assembly on base of picture elements. Any kind of variations of visualizations because of technique inherent advantages must not change the amount of knowledge transferred
	7) Both kinds of instructions shall enable the visualization of the *previous* and the *next* assembly step. In the case former steps have been forgotten or need to be revised, the application needs to provide forward and backward functions. These simulate the page turning of a paper-based instruction
Experiment	8) Each experiment is to be observed by an observant, who guarantees a correct time measurement. Further, the observant identifies and documents failures, even those that might not have been reflected in the experiment design
	9) The failure surveying is to be carried out by a tool, so that common failures can be documented efficiently
	10) The time measurement is to be carried out by a tool, so that measurements are objective
	11) For the experimentation, competencies of test persons are to be surveyed after the assembly, so that test persons are not biased. For the live system implementation, these might be integrated with KMS providing the test person's competence profile, so that the application is able to adapt to the test person automatically
	12) The stickiness of knowledge to be transferred must not be disturbed by a repetitive experiment realization. Its focus shall lie on repetitive kinds of assembly steps. For the test person selection, this means to guarantee that test persons do not realize the experiment more than one time

required for knowledge transfers and failures being made, the second category focuses on requirements for the design of assembly instructions. The third category presents the experimental conditions.

While the AR-based instruction simplifies the knowledge transfer by the positioning of operations within the real world, the paper-based instruction simplifies knowledge transfers by the presentation of a best angle on the assembly object. Since both kinds of simplifications refer to technique inherent advantages, the focus was set on the original technique use. As a consequence, visualization differences were compensated as follows: The paper-based instruction provides a zoomed version of relevant components, which draws the assembler's attention to a selection of components relevant at that assembly step. Since this kind of visualization does not correspond to the original AR technique use of realistic positioning, this has been compensated at the AR-based instruction by additional text instructions drawing attention to the best viewing angle and colors highlighting relevant components.

4 Design

Beside the application design of an AR-based instruction, its interpretation as knowledge transfer intervention will be designed here. All will be connected in one experimentation design, that intends to empirically validate the functioning of an acceleration of knowledge transfers with AR technologies.

4.1 Assembly Object Selection

The assembly object was chosen from a well-known furniture company called IKEA. Here, the wall cupboard called METOD was selected [26] because of the following:

- The product has been sold for a long period, so that its assembly components have been proven in practice.
- The paper-based instructions have been used by hundreds of customers, which is an indicator for a well-tested instruction.
- The company sells products worldwide, which simplifies the reproduction of experiments presented here.

Components of METOD to be assembled or required for the assembly are visualized in Fig. 2. Here, Fig. 2a presents seven small components. Those have been collected in Fig. 2b in a small paper box in the center. Further, the picture on the right presents bigger components like the two cupboard sidewalls, its back, ceiling panel and floor panel. The three tools called gavel, flat-tip screwdriver and cross-tip screwdriver can be found in both sub figures. Please note the different color of the two screwdriver types, which only will be used in the AR-based instruction.

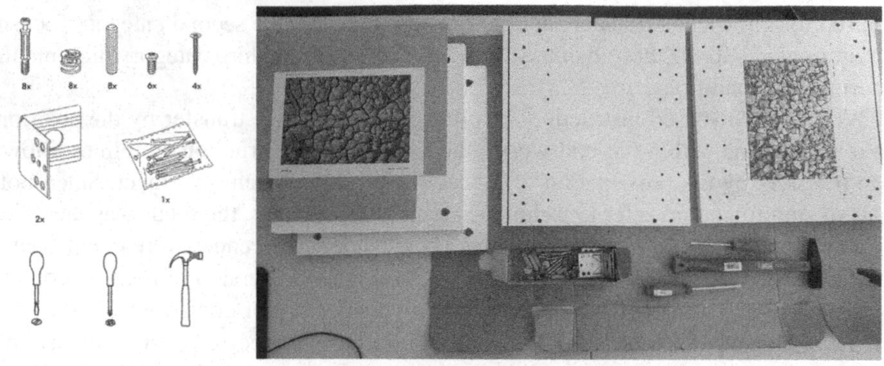

(a) Small assembly parts. (b) Large assembly components and initial experiment setting.

Fig. 2. Assembly components.

4.2 Instruction Design

The instruction design refers to two kinds of instructions. Since the AR-based instruction brings an augmentation of the paper-based instruction, the latter was designed first. Both designs can be found in the following.

Paper-Based Instruction: Since the instruction of IKEA was very well prepared, only the following was done in order to design the paper-based instruction of the experiment:

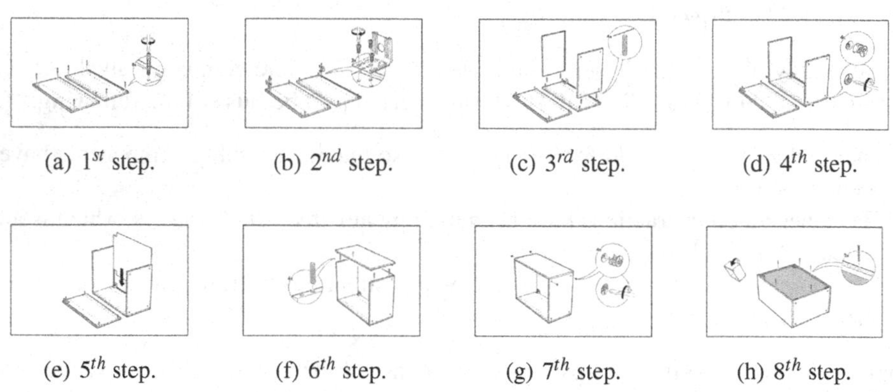

(a) 1st step. (b) 2nd step. (c) 3rd step. (d) 4th step.

(e) 5th step. (f) 6th step. (g) 7th step. (h) 8th step.

Fig. 3. Paper-based assembly instruction.

The eight most important assembly steps were selected, which are required for the construction of a cupboard. Here, minor steps such as the assembly of cupboard door parts, detailed instructions for the back fixation and the installation on a wall were dismissed. Cryptic item numbers were erased from schematics. Further, security tips in a collection of 35 languages and schematics were dismissed. The installation of further products, such as UTRUSTA inlays were dismissed. The final paper-based design can be found in Fig. 3.

AR-Based Instruction: Although various ways to carry out AR-based applications exist and were discussed by [24], the application design for the AR-based instruction was carried out as follows:

The AR components were connected to real proportions, visualizations were coupled to their physical position and target images were sticking on its corresponding physical object. Although the identification could have been realized because of the recognition of the physical object itself (without target images), the poor-featured, white surface of the assembly components did not enable a robust recognition at all. Therefore, the recognition on behalf of target images was chosen for realization.

In accordance to assembly steps presented in the paper-based instruction, augmentations were prepared, which are visualized as an image target was detected by the AR device camera. As can be seen in Fig. 2b, two well working image-targets from VUFORIA were used. One printed version was sticked at the floor panel and one was sticked at the cupboard's back. The precise size adjustment of 3D models was a very arduous path and essential for the interplay of physical objects and augmentations.

Two digital buttons realized the switching between assembly steps. The *next* button was placed at the lower right corner, the *previous* button was placed at the upper left corner and augmentations were visualized in between. Hence, the tablet was intended to be hold with two hands and the two thumbs were able to switch between assembly steps easily. A step-specific instruction text was displayed at the top center. The final AR-based instruction design can be found in Fig. 4.

Pretests: Although test persons being instructed by the AR-application were allowed to simultaneously built and augment, pretests have shown that test persons preferred first studying augmentations and then laying the tabled aside in order to use both hands for assembly operations. Further details can be found at [24].

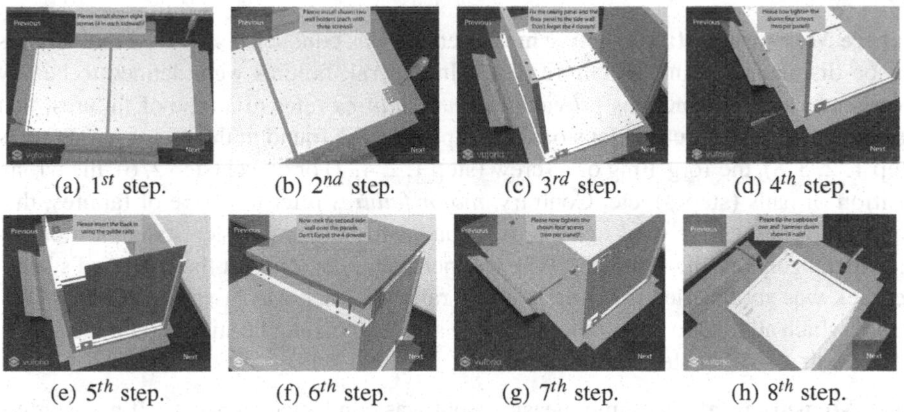

(a) 1st step. (b) 2nd step. (c) 3rd step. (d) 4th step.

(e) 5th step. (f) 6th step. (g) 7th step. (h) 8th step.

Fig. 4. AR-based assembly instruction.

4.3 Experiment Design

The design of experiments (DoE) was carried out by the specification of an *experiment process*, an operationalization of the *failure measurement* and a *time measurement* operationalization.

Experiment Process: At the beginning of the experiment, test persons were asked not to be cleverer than the instructions in order to avoid the following:

- anticipate and realize several assembly steps once,
- use the flat-tip screwdriver for cross-tip screws,
- use anything else than the gavel to fix nails.

Figure 2b shows the initial experiment setting, which was prepared before any experimentation. Each test person encountered assembly components as they can be seen here. The observation is designed to be carried out by an individual observant, who accompanied the test person and guaranteed the disturbance-free experiment realization. Besides the focus on the correct time measurement, the observant documented failures made by the test person. Here, the online tool called LIMESURVEY was used, so that the observant was able to document failures with the help of a tablet and the test person was not disturbed by the documentation process. The documentation of the most common failures was realized by a simple activation of checkboxes. Text boxes per assembly step allowed the documentation of unexpected failures. Faced with the great responsibility of the observants for the successful experimentation, observants were educated in the experimentation objectives, the efficient conductance of failures, thoughts about the design of artefacts presented here, a common and warmly welcome and farewell of test persons and operational issues during the experimentation. At the end of the experiment, as the assembly was finalized, the competence of test persons was conducted.

Failure Measurement: The failure measurement was conducted step-wise and failures can be distinguished in two failure types. In general, failures were defined to be any divergence from instructions provided. *Minor failures* refer to a type of failures, that would not rule consecutive steps out. Examples can be found in the use of wrong tools (step 1, 2, 3, 8), the forgetting of a screw (step 1, 2, 4, 7) or dowel (step 2, 6), the wrong position of nails (step 8), etc. Contrary, *major failures* refer to a type of failures, that would rule consecutive steps out. Focusing on the fifth assembly step, examples for this failure category are the following: The test person forgot to insert the cupboard's back, the back was not inserted using the guiding rails, the back was inserted the wrong way round, which all lead to the problem that the side wall cannot be sticked onto the panels in the sixth assembly step.

Time Measurement: The time measurement was conducted step-wise. It was started, as the test person indicated its willingness to start an assembly step. As the test person indicated the willingness to end the current assembly step, the time measurement was stopped. It only has been prolongated, if major failures were made. If major failures have been avoided successfully at the end of an assembly step, test persons were allowed to start the next assembly step.

5 Demonstration

As demanded by the methodological approach of Sect. 3.1, the demonstration applies designed artefacts and is structured by its phases. The following describes results and definitions of each phase.

1. **Project initiation:** The demonstration example can be categorized as an experimental example that was created with the intention of developing a small, easily understandable process improvement setting.
2. **Objectives:** The general objective was to compare the current assembly procedure of do-it-yourself assemblies (paper-based instruction) with AR-based instructions. Furthermore, since paper-based assemblies stand as a reference point, the use of AR techniques instead can be seen as intervention being evaluated by the improvement of required time and failures that have been made.
3. **Knowledge transfer situation analysis:** Within the process of instructed assemblies, each assembly step can be identified as an individual knowledge transfer situation. Any situation is characterized by a certain complexity, stickiness and competence level.
4. **Intervention selection:** Aiming to establish an AR-based knowledge transfer improvement, the use of AR techniques was selected as intervention. As it was explained in Sect. 4, the complexity was designed to be reduced by the positioning of augmented assembly components beside physical objects. The stickiness was designed to be reduced by repetitive and realistic augmentations. The competence was designed to be reduced by the increased experience about the assembly of a certain product.
5. **Iterative intervention implementation:** A first implementation of designed process variants focused on three pretests and a greater experimental study. The experimental study was conducted with students of the Blinded University. Each participant was allowed to assemble the given object once in order to not distort effects of stickiness and competence faced with the here presented kind of operationalization. Test persons were assigned randomly either to experiments using paper-based instructions or AR-based instructions. Finally, 24 AR-based experiment runs and 20 paper-based experiments have been realized.

Table 2 summarizes time and failure measurement in accordance to the eight assembly steps provided and the two groups *amateurs* and *experts*. Test persons have been categorized in accordance to questions regarding their knowledge about the specific product (assembly object). Experts already had assembled the assembly object presented and therefore have more competences. As results separated assemblies of paper-based instructions from assemblies of AR-based instructions, the number of participants n is provided column-wise.

On the left of the table, one can see the average time in seconds. Although the time measurement had the precision of a thousandth of a second, values have been rounded. On the right of the table, one can see the average numbers of failures made at the assembly. Here, values have been rounded to a thousandth.

Table 2. Time and failure measurement per assembly step.

	Average time in s				Average failures in pieces			
	Amateurs		Experts		Amateurs		Experts	
assembly steps	Paper	AR	Paper	AR	Paper	AR	Paper	AR
	n=12	n=18	n=8	n=6	n=12	n=18	n=8	n=6
Step 1	124	112	111	97	0.08	0.00	0.00	0.17
Step 2	151	125	130	101	0.17	0.00	0.13	0.00
Step 3	104	102	73	62	0.08	0.28	0.38	0.00
Step 4	72	69	60	54	0.42	0.50	0.38	0.50
Step 5	43	54	28	45	0.33	0.39	0.13	0.17
Step 6	58	58	48	48	0.08	0.06	0.00	0.00
Step 7	50	57	52	50	0.25	0.33	0.38	0.33
Step 8	197	162	55	217	0.08	0.22	0.50	0.33
All	**798**	**739**	**558**	**673**	**1.50**	**1.78**	**1.88**	**1.50**

Table 3. Time and failure improvement because of stickiness.

	Average time in s				Average failures in pieces			
	Amateurs		Experts		Amateurs		Experts	
assembly steps	Paper	AR	Paper	AR	Paper	AR	Paper	AR
	n=12	n=18	n=8	n=6	n=12	n=18	n=8	n=6
Step 3	104	102	73	62	0.08	0.28	0.38	0.00
Step 6	58	58	48	48	0.08	0.06	0.00	0.00
Optim	✓	✓	✓	✓	-	✓	✓	-
Step 4	72	69	60	54	0.42	0.50	0.38	0.50
Step 7	50	57	52	50	0.25	0.33	0.38	0.33
Optim	✓	✓	✓	✓	✓	✓	-	✓

6. **Evaluation of intervention effects:** Based on a comparison of results of the as-is process (paper-based instruction) and the to-be process realized by the AR knowledge transfer intervention (AR-based instruction), a change to the to-be process is attractive in various points. This regards both, time that is required for knowledge transfers and failures that have been made at the assembly. A detailed explanation can be found in the following section.
7. **Continual improvement and maintenance:** Consecutive phases have not been taken into account because of the experimental nature of the demonstration example presented here. Considering the experimentation insights presented, the corresponding KDIS is ready to be implemented.

6 Evaluation

The evaluation of the laboratory study reflects three perspectives. First, the *competence perspective* evaluates, if a higher competence results in faster knowledge transfers and lower failure rates. With this, AR-based interventions can be assesses to behave similar to common process-support techniques. Second, the *stickiness perspective* evaluates, if a reduced stickiness results in faster knowledge transfers and lower failure rates. With this, AR techniques can be confirmed to fit empirical models. Third, the *complexity perspective* evaluates, if a reduced complexity results in faster knowledge transfers and lower failure rates. Here, augmentations can be evaluated in regard to their reference complexity level, which is here the paper-based instruction.

Competence: Faced with absolute, average time measurements of Table 2, amateurs required more time for the assembly then experts. This applies for both, paper-based and AR-based experiments.

The time difference of assembly steps realized by amateurs and assembly steps realized by experts is visualized in Fig. 5a. As the average time of expert assembly steps is subtracted from the average time of amateur assembly steps, assembly steps for paper-based and AR-based instructions that improved because of a higher competence of test persons can be found above the x-axis. Hence, we denoted them as *expert advantage*. Steps having values below zero, indicate assembly steps having an *amateur advantage*.

With exception of a single assembly step, any step can be accelerated by higher competencies for both, paper-based and AR-based instructions. A reason for the exceptional assembly step (8th AR-based step) can lie in the higher complexity of the AR-based instruction, which will be explained in the paragraph of the complexity perspective.

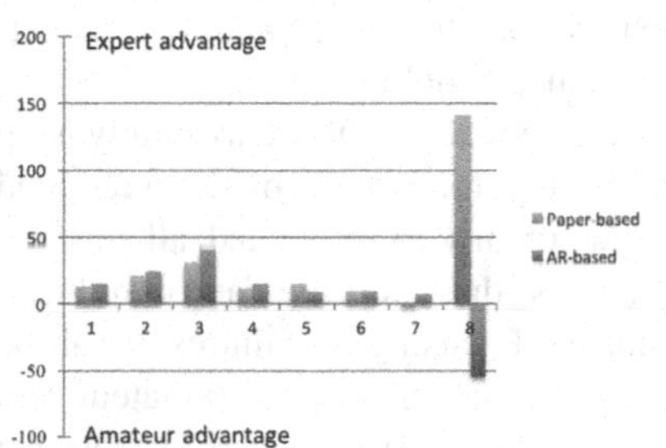

(a) Expert time advantage (average time of assembly steps realized by experts subtracted from average time of assembly steps realized by amateurs).

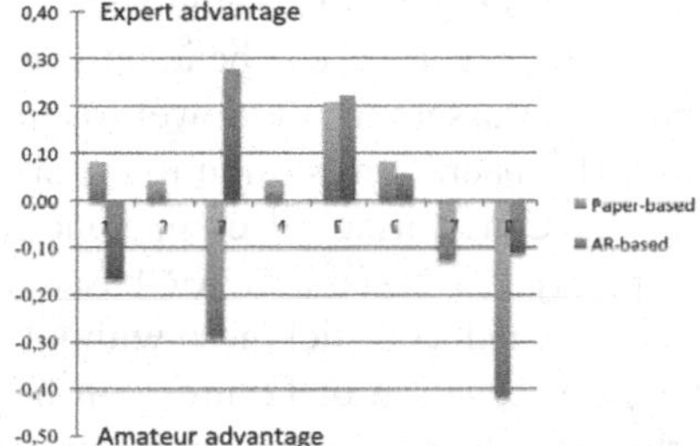

(b) Expert failure advantage (average failure of assembly steps realized by experts subtracted from average failure of assembly steps realized by amateurs).

Fig. 5. Expert advantage.

Faced with absolute, average failure measurements of Table 2, amateurs following paper-based instructions made less failures than experts. This surprises and can come from the expert opinion to be cleverer than the instruction. Maybe, they are more careless than amateurs because their belief to know and anticipate correctly. In contrary, test persons with higher competence following AR-based instructions showed a reduced number of failures. Maybe, the newness of AR-based solutions keeps the attraction of expert test persons high.

The failure difference of assembly steps realized by amateurs and assembly steps realized by experts is visualized in Fig. 5b. As the average number of expert failures per assembly step is subtracted from the average number of amateur failures per assembly step, assembly steps for paper-based and AR-based instructions that improved because of the competence of test persons can be found above the x-axis. Again, we denoted them as *expert advantage*. Steps having values below zero, indicate assembly steps being better realized by amateurs.

Focusing on AR-based assemblies, only the first and eighth assembly steps resulted in more failures as the competence raises. Any other assembly step either leads to an improved average failure rate or at least remains unaffected. An explanation for the two exceptions might be the unbiased instruction realization of amateurs.

The improvement of paper-based assemblies in regard to the competence mainly result in less failures. Exceptions can be found at the third, seventh and eighth assembly step since amateurs produced less failures. This might be because of the unbiased instruction realization of amateurs, which is faster than the instruction realization biased with the competence of experts.

Faced with evaluations about the competence, AR-based instructions can be identified to behave similar to paper-based instructions for all competence types (amateur and experts) in regard to time: The higher competences are, the faster knowledge transfers are carried out. In regard to failures, AR leads to a failure reduction with higher competences while paper-based instructed, more competent test persons made more failures.

Stickiness: The effect of the stickiness on paper-based and AR-based instructions can be observed at repetitive assembly steps. In the experimentation presented, two knowledge transfer situations can be identified to have a reduced stickiness.

First, the assembly of dowels is realized twice: Since the third assembly step demands for operations similar to the sixth assembly step, the latter provides a reduced stickiness. Considering all competence types (amateur and experts) and all instruction types (paper-based and AR-based), Table 3 shows, that the time can be reduced because of a reduced stickiness without any exception. Focusing on failures, it can be seen that a reduction of failures can be found at all competence types (amateur and experts) and all instruction types (paper-based and AR-based) with two exceptions: paper-based instructed amateurs and AR-based instructed experts don not show any failure reduction. The latter can be explained easily because AR-based instructed experts were failure-free. In analogy, paper-based instructed amateurs show a very low failure rate.

Second, the assembly of screws is realized twice: Since the fourth assembly step demands for operations similar to the seventh assembly step, the latter must be characterized with a smaller stickiness than the fourth step. Table 3 again shows, that any knowledge transfer situation can be improved by a reduced stickiness. Considering the time, there is no exception. Having a focus on failures made, the only exception refers to paper-based instructed experts. Here, none effect can be observed. It seems that failures made here are not dependent on the stickiness.

Faced with evaluations about the stickiness, AR-based instructions can be identified to behave similar to paper-based instructions for all competence types (amateur and experts).

Complexity: Faced with absolute, average time measurements of Table 2, AR-based instructed test persons required less time for the assembly then paper-based instructed test persons as they are amateurs. Experts were faster if they were paper-based instructed.

The time difference of paper-based assembly runs and AR-based assembly runs is visualized in Fig. 6a. As the average time of AR instructed assembly steps is subtracted from the average time of paper instructed assembly steps, assembly steps that improved because of the use of AR-techniques can be found above the x-axis. Hence, we denoted them as *AR instruction advantage*. Steps having values below zero, indicate assembly steps being better realized by paper-based instructions.

Considering amateur runs, with exception of the fifth and seventh assembly step, all assembly steps can be accelerated with AR techniques. An explanation for this might be the introduction of the second target image, which was sticked on the cupboard's back and raised complexity because of the difficulty to focus on both, the image target recognition and augmented object recognition.

The sixth step does not show any preference for AR-based and paper-based instructions. This might be because of the reduced stickiness effects explained previously.

Focusing on expert runs, all assembly steps can be accelerated with AR techniques, but the fifth and eighth steps. Those are slowed down so that paper-based instruction are more attractive here. A reason for the slower fifth step might be the use of the second image target. The slower eight step realization might be because of an increased complexity as follows: AR-based instructions are considered as realistic instructions and enable the perfect positioning of nails on a continuous spectrum. In contradiction, test persons following paper-based instructions do not consider the perfect positioning at all since they interpret instructions as schematics. Hence, the complexity of the paper-based instruction is smaller here.

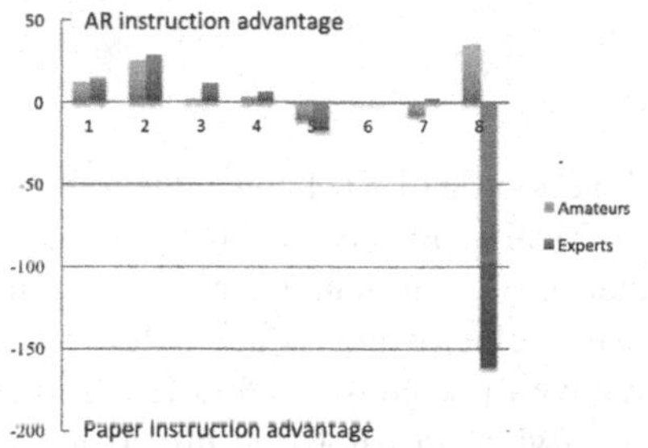

(a) AR time advantage (average time of AR instructed assembly steps subtracted from average time of paper instructed assembly steps).

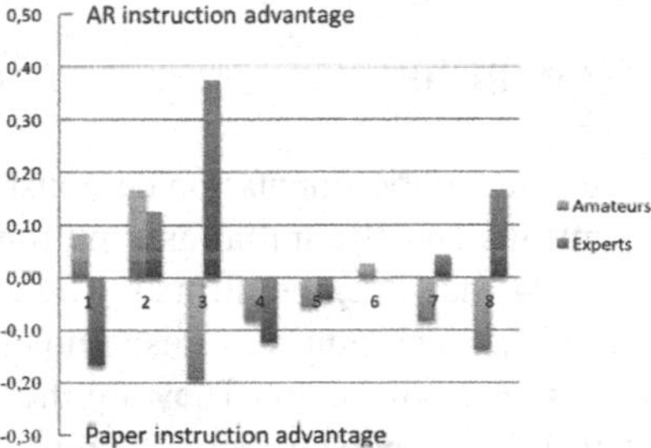

(b) AR failure advantage (average failure of AR instructed assembly steps subtracted from average failure of paper instructed assembly steps).

Fig. 6. AR advantage.

Faced with absolute, average failure measurements of Table 2, AR-based instructed test persons made more failures at the assembly then paper-based instructed test persons as they are amateurs. Experts made less failures if they were AR-based instructed.

The failure difference of paper-based assembly runs and AR-based assembly runs is visualized in Fig. 6b. As the average number of failures of AR-instructed assembly steps is subtracted from the average number of failures of paper-instructed assembly steps, assembly steps that improved because of the use of AR-techniques can be found above the x-axis. Again, we denoted them as *AR instruction advantage*. Steps having values below zero, indicate assembly steps being better realized by paper-based instructions.

Focusing on amateur runs, only the first, second and sixth assembly steps can be improved with AR techniques, since less failures were made. This might be because AR-instructions enable a more precise and clear positioning of assembly components than the paper-based instruction does, which was especially in the first dealing with screws relevant. Other assembly steps show more failures when AR-based instructions are used. This might be because schematics of the paper instruction supports the understanding of the basic idea.

Considering expert runs, with exception of the first, fourth and fifth assembly steps, all assembly steps can be improved with AR techniques. This can be an indicator for experts being best supported by realistic visualizations because the are able to identify the correct focus efficiently. A reason for the exceptional assembly steps might be found in the following: operations required here, are not only needed for the METOD cupboard and well known from paper-instructions of other products. The sixth assembly step does not show any improvement at all. A reason for this can be effects of the stickiness mentioned at the paragraph of the stickiness perspective.

Faced with evaluations about the complexity, AR-based instructions show time advantage and failure disadvantages for amateurs. Experts are faced with AR-based time disadvantages and failure advantages. Hence, recommendations have to trade-off here.

7 Conclusion

The presented experimentation demonstrates the functioning of AR knowledge transfer interventions and the initial assumption to fit empirically proven knowledge transfer models [24] has been confirmed. The experimentation further demonstrates the dominance of AR techniques to raise knowledge transfer velocity and reduce failure rates in certain assembly steps. They are therefore attractive to be considered in KDIS, that adapt to the test person and situation occurring. A switch to AR-based instruction is recommended, here. The effect of AR interventions even can be improved as its situational conditions are improved. Examples refer to a raised initial competence, a reduced stickiness or reduced knowledge transfer complexity. Corresponding interventions can be recommended by the KDIS before the process realization. Since other assembly steps demonstrate a dominance of paper-based instructions, a closer look on the specific knowledge transfer situation by the KDIS is required.

Critical Appraisal: The first research question which improve speed of knowledge-intensive business processes?) can be answered with the design of an AR intervention presented. Empirically proven influence factors are used for the design and characterization of concrete AR knowledge transfer interventions. Their selection in the fourth phase of the procedure model of Fig. 1 on base of the fit to the need of an individual knowledge transfer situation, will improve the speed of knowledge-intensive business processes efficiently.

The second research question can be answered by an application that builds on the procedure model designed (Fig. 1). It therefore analyzes the situation on base of the factors of the time-dependent knowledge-transfer model. As context-aware, adaptable software system, it then suggests the optimal process design, which is derived from the empirical findings of an experimentation. As the process improvement refers to different process designs depending on the situation analysis (Table 2), the KDIS selects best process designs and visualizes either paper-based instructed assembly steps (Fig. 3) or AR-based instructed assembly steps (Fig. 4).

With regard to the main research question one can identify a potential in KDIS by the adaption to the current knowledge transfer situation and the improvement of knowledge transfers. By the KDIS conceptualized, this counts for the time and quality dimensions of knowledge transfer outcomes.

Limitations: The results and insights presented are somewhat limited in regard to the following points. Although the results demonstrate clear dominance of AR techniques to raise knowledge transfer velocity and reduce failure rates in certain assembly steps, this yet cannot stand as a generalization since the applied contexts incorporates only a small scenario. The scenario was not verified in company-specific production settings, yet. Further, results only focus on the assembly of one specific product. Hence, results cannot stand for generalizations but show clear evidence for promising further research.

Outlook: Over the course of this research, many points for future research were identified. Among them, the most urgent are addressed below:

First, future research should incorporate limitations of the current work. This means, it should try to broaden the study context systematically. The identification of further, successful AR knowledge transfer interventions and their application in greater settings having more complex tasks is essential to generalize obtained results correctly.

Second, the final KDIS conceptualized by this contribution, which is able to identify best interventions in dependence of the current situation and test person, as well as to present either paper-based or AR-based instructions when attractive, needs to be implemented and examined in a greater experimentation. Here, test persons are either equipped by the adaptable KDIS flexibly providing best instructions or by the ordinary installation routine.

Third, alternatives for the experiment process, time and failure operationalizations can lead to interesting insights. So, the time measurement can differentiate between the knowledge application and knowledge transfer. Conditions for the experimentation can be relaxed. E.g. test persons are allowed to anticipate, so that the effect of AR techniques on creativity can be observed. Repetitive assemblies and assembly variations can help to detect, if AR techniques have effects on the remembering and forgetting.

References

1. Alavi, M., Leidner, D.E.: Review: knowledge management and knowledge management systems: conceptual foundations and research issues. MIS Q. **25**(1), 107–136 (2001)
2. Gronau, N., Grum, M.: The creation of a time-dependent knowledge transfer model. Work Report WI-2018-01, University of Potsdam, February 2018
3. Gronau, N., Weber, E.: Management of knowledge intensive business processes. In: Desel, J., Pernici, B., Weske, M. (eds.) BPM 2004. LNCS, vol. 3080, pp. 163–178. Springer, Heidelberg (2004). https://doi.org/10.1007/978-3-540-25970-1_11
4. Gronau, N.: Modeling and Analyzing Knowledge Intensive Business Processes with KMDL: Comprehensive Insights Into Theory and Practice. Series on Business Information Systems. Gito, Berlin (2012)
5. Strambach, S.: Knowledge-intensive business services (KIBS) as drivers of multilevel knowledge dynamics. Int. J. Serv. Technol. Manage. **10**(2–4), 152–174 (2008)

6. Sigmanek, C., Lantow, B.: A survey on modelling knowledge-intensive business processes from the perspective of knowledge management. In: KMIS 2015 - Proceedings of the International Conference on Knowledge Management and Information Sharing, Part of the 7th International Joint Conference on Knowledge Discovery, Knowledge Engineering and Knowledge Management (IC3K 2015), Lisbon, Portugal, 12–14 November 2015, vol. 3, pp. 325–332, 2015
7. Marjanovic, O., Freeze, R.: Knowledge intensive business processes: theoretical foundations and research challenges. In: 2011 44th Hawaii International Conference on System Sciences, pp. 1–10, January 2011
8. Albers, A., et al.: Influencing factors and methods for knowledge transfer situations in product generation engineering based on the SECI model. In: NordDesign, Linköping, Sweden, 14–17 August 2018 (2018, in Press)
9. Peffers, K., et al.: The design science research process: A model for producing and presenting information systems research. In: 1st International Conference on Design Science in Information Systems and Technology (DESRIST), vol. 24, pp. 83–106, August 2006
10. Grum, M., Gronau, N.: A visionary way to novel process optimizations. In: Shishkov, B. (ed.) BMSD 2017. LNBIP, vol. 309, pp. 1–24. Springer, Cham (2018). https://doi.org/10.1007/978-3-319-78428-1_1
11. Kaizen, M.I.: The Key to Japan's Competitive Success. McGraw-Hill Education Ltd., New York (1986)
12. Shewhart, W.A., Deming, W.E.: Statistical method from the view-point of quality control. IX + 155 p. The Graduate School, Department of Agriculture, Washington, D.C., (1939)
13. Deming, W.E.: Elementary principles of the statistical control of quality: a series of lectures. Nippon Kagaku Gijutsu Remmei (1950)
14. Deming, W.E.: Out of the Crisis. MIT Press, Cambridge (1986)
15. Deming, W.E.: The New Economics, pp. 51–56. MIT Center for Advanced Engineering Study, Cambridge (1993)
16. Moen, R., Norman, C.: Evolution of the PDCA cycle (2006)
17. Ishikawa, D.K.: What Is Total Quality Control?: The Japanese Way (Business Management). Prentice Hall Trade, Upper Saddle River (1985)
18. Hammer, M., Champy, J.: Reengineering the Corporation: A Manifesto for Business Revolution. Harper Business (1993)
19. Davenport, T.H., Prusak, L.: Working knowledge: How organizations manage what they know. Ubiquity, vol. 2000, August 2000
20. von Krogh, G., Ichijo, K., Nonaka, I.: Enabling Knowledge Creation: How to Unlock the Mystery of Tacit Knowledge and Release the Power of Innovation. Oxford University Press, New York (2000)
21. Polanyi, M., Sen, A.: The tacit dimension. University of Chicago Press, May 2009
22. Minbaeva, D., Pedersen, T., Björkman, I., Fey, C.F., Park, H.J.: MNC knowledge transfer, subsidiary absorptive capacity, and HRM. J. Int. Bus. Stud. **34**(6), 586–599 (2003)
23. Nonaka, I., Takeuchi, H.: The Knowledge-creating Company: How Japanese Companies Create the Dynamics of Innovation. Oxford University Press, New York (1995)
24. Gronau, N., Grum, M., Zaiser, A., Rapp, S., Weber, E., Albers, A.: Knowledge Transfer Speed Optimizations in Product Development Contexts. GITO mbH Verlag, Berlin (2019)
25. Johnson, R.B., Onwuegbuzie, A.J., Turner, L.A.: Toward a definition of mixed methods research. J. Mixed Methods Res. **1**(2), 112–133 (2007)
26. IKEA. "Metod," Assembly Instruction AA-675849-3, Inter IKEA Systems B.V. 1999–2018 (2012). https://www.ikea.com/de/de/catalog/products/S09926341/

VR-EAT: Visualization of Enterprise Architecture Tool Diagrams in Virtual Reality

Roy Oberhauser[1(✉)], Pedro Sousa[2,3], and Florian Michel[1]

[1] Computer Science Department, Aalen University, Aalen, Germany
roy.oberhauser@hs-aalen.de, florian.michel@studmail.hs-aalen.de

[2] Instituto Superior Técnico, University of Lisbon, Lisbon, Portugal
pedro.manuel.sousa@tecnico.ulisboa.pt

[3] Link Consulting, Lisbon, Portugal

Abstract. The digital transformation occurring in enterprises results in an increasingly dynamic and complex IT landscape that in turn impacts enterprise architecture (EA) and its artefacts. New approaches for dealing with more complex and dynamic models and conveying EA structural and relational insights are needed. As EA tools attempt to address these challenges, virtual reality (VR) can potentially enhance EA tool capabilities and user insight but further investigation is needed in how this can be achieved. This paper contributes a VR solution concept for visualizing, navigating, and interacting with EA tool dynamically-generated diagrams and models using the EA tool Atlas. An implementation shows its feasibility and a case study using EA scenarios is used to demonstrate its potential.

Keywords: Virtual reality · Enterprise architecture · Enterprise modeling · Enterprise architecture tools · Visualization

1 Introduction

A major *digital transformation* of industries is underway (Muro et al. 2017). While the digitalization rate (digital score) may vary across industries and economies, it is nevertheless impacting business strategies and necessarily the enterprise architecture (EA) that supports the business. Increased digital automation in turn affects business functions and processes, and thus affects and changes the actual EA. The IT infrastructure expands and becomes more dynamic and complex to support these both rapidly changing and highly-integrated business processes, resulting in a complex EA.

Enterprise architecture (EA) comprises the structural and behavioral aspects needed for an enterprise to function and adapt in alignment with some vision. To this end, it involves comprehensive and cohesive modeling and documentation. Considering the trends and challenges mentioned, the reality that EA is attempting to comprehensively model, document, and change has become much more complex than in previous decades. EA seeks to provide a comprehensive set of cohesive models to describe the enterprise structure and functions, while individual models are logically arranged to provide further detail about an enterprise (Jarvis 2003). Healthy enterprises necessarily evolve,

B. Shishkov (Ed.): BMSD 2020, LNBIP 391, pp. 221–239, 2020.
https://doi.org/10.1007/978-3-030-52306-0_14

and they thus the need to maintain explicit knowledge of their EA, be it for enterprise governance, engineering, compliance, maintenance, etc. Architectural representations are an enterprise asset that must be governed (Hoogervorst 2009). However, the effort required to keep architectural views updated is known to be very high in current organizations (Sousa 2018), mainly because the organization's structure is the result of an asynchronous, distributed, and heterogeneous process, producing representations in different languages/notations, with different levels of detail, in different tools at different times. But timepoints are actually a more complex issue, because enterprise models are also a moving target, as enterprises need architectural views that refer to different points in time, namely past, present and future. So, one aspect of our research has been in finding a low effort method that supports updated architectural views regardless of the point in time (past, present or future).

The Atlas tool (Sousa 2018) was developed under the Enterprise Cartography paradigm (Sousa 2009; Tribolet 2014) to minimize the effort required to keep architectural views up-to-date in fast changing organizations. In Atlas, all architecture views are generated on-the-fly and include a time bar where one can navigate in time and see the architecture evolution from any point in the past to any point in the future. The view´s contents regarding the future are computed, processing the plans of transformation initiatives pipeline (both ongoing and planned) to produce a consolidated state in any point in time. Therefore, one can foresee the contents of an architecture view in some desired future date by consolidating the current view´s content with the expected changes of ongoing and planned transformation initiatives whose completion date precedes the desired date (Sousa 2009, 2018a). Atlas is also able to generate and support time navigation in BPMN models (Sousa 2019; Colaço 2017; Cardoso 2020).

In general, modeling provides an abstracted or simplified representation of a system that can assist with understanding relationships between elements or concepts of interest. Typically, views are used to address stakeholder concerns and portray relevant aspects of a model. However, with typical 2D view depictions, one can lose insight into the interrelationships across views and relevant model elements. For certain EA-related tasks, as EA complexity increases, the need to visualize and inspect multiple related model views is limited by the current 2D capabilities.

Virtual Reality (VR) could potentially assist with visualizing this growing and complex set of models and their interrelationships simultaneously in a spatial structure. VR is defined as a "real or simulated environment in which the perceiver experiences telepresence" (Steuer 1992), a mediated visual environment which is created and then experienced. VR has made inroads in various domains and become readily accessible as hardware prices have dropped and capabilities improved. As EA models grow in complexity and reflect the deeper integration of both the business and IT reality, an immersive EA environment could provide an additional visualization capability to comprehend the "big picture" for structurally and hierarchically complex and interconnected diagrams, while providing an immersive experience for EA models in a 3D space viewable from different perspectives.

In prior work, VR-EA (Oberhauser and Pogolski 2019) presented a VR solution concept for visualizing, navigating, annotating, and interacting with ArchiMate (Open Group 2017) EA models and our generalized VR modeling framework (VR-MF), while

VR-BPMN (Oberhauser et al. 2018) described a solution concept for visualizing Business Process Model and Notation (BPMN) (OMG 2011) models in VR. The Atlas EA tool and meta-model (Sousa 2018) consolidates various EA model and data sources into a single repository and provides coherent visualization and view capabilities. This paper presents our solution concept VR-EAT (EA Tool) for integrating EA tool visualizations into VR, in particular making any number of dynamically generated EA diagrams from the EA tool Atlas available and enhancing these with 3D depth, inter-diagram element connections. By leveraging the unlimited space in VR, overall interrelationships of the models and views can be indicated and considered adjacent to one another, while sensory immersion can support task focus while limiting visual distractions that typical 2D display surroundings incur.

The remainder of this paper is structured as follows: Sect. 2 discusses related work while Sect. 3 provides background detail on the EA tool Atlas. In Sect. 4 our solution concept VR-EAT is described. Section 5 then provides details on our prototype implementation. The evaluation is described in Sect. 6, and a conclusion follows in Sect. 7.

2 Related Work

Work related to EA visualization includes (Rehring et al. 2019), who applied 3D visualization in augmented reality in support of EA decision making. (Naranjo et al. 2014) describe PRIMate based on PRIMROSe, a visual graph-based enterprise analysis framework, and show a graph, treemap, and 3D visualization of an the ArchiSurance ArchiMate model. As to harmonizing ArchiMate, BPMN, and UML, (van den Berg 2012) analyzes the various metamodels and shows how one could practically combine the notations across views and diagrams. We are unaware of research applying VR to the EA area with EA tool (meta-)model and non-standard multidiagram integration into VR, including support for model visualization of ArchiMate and BPMN to VR.

Our VR-EAT solution concept enables VR-centric visualization with integration with the EA tool Atlas. It is implemented with standard game engine technology (Unity) using common VR hardware. It supports hypermodeling, e.g., combining ArchiMate, BPMN, and EA tool models in the same space, provides automatic layout of views as stacked 3D hyperplanes, visualizes the reality of inter-view relations of elements, and integrates non-standard EA diagrams for an immersive experience to support deeper EA analysis across multiple diagrams and stakeholder concerns.

3 Background on the EA Tool Atlas

Atlas is an EA tool with a repository holding a fully configurable metamodel that generates views (also fully configurable), including all the information required to represent the views at any point in time as well as representing each artifact in its lifecycle state (Sousa 2018). Thus, architectural views are movies, not pictures. This is a unique feature of Atlas and, in our experience, a fundamental one to reduce the effort of maintaining architectural views in large organizations.

Atlas is far from providing all the architectural view types one may find in well-known tools (Roth 2014), but it supports the time-travel mechanism in all the views types it supports. It supports the configuration of the view types according to the metamodel defined by the user. Figure 1 shows some view types supported by Atlas.

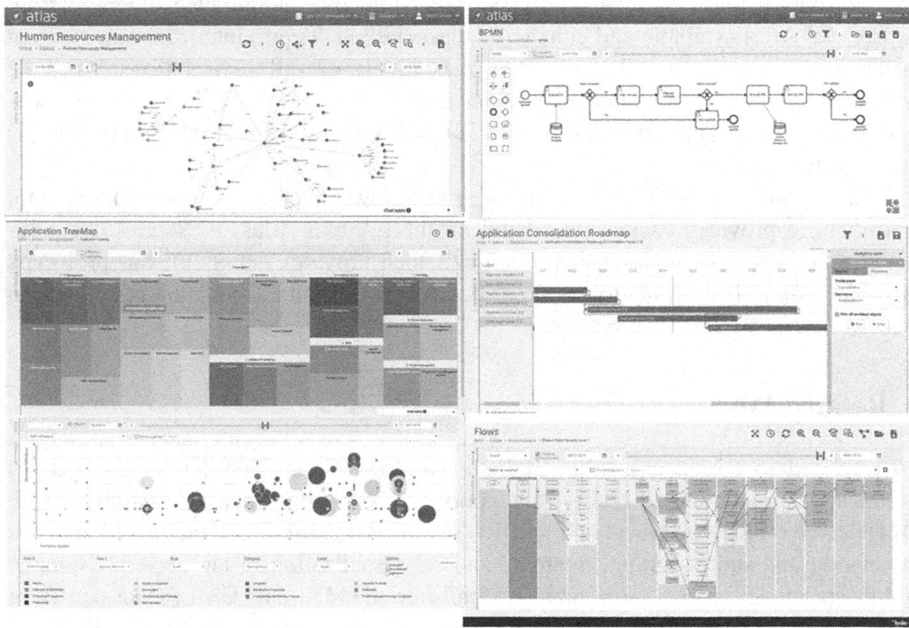

Fig. 1. Various view types supported by Atlas.

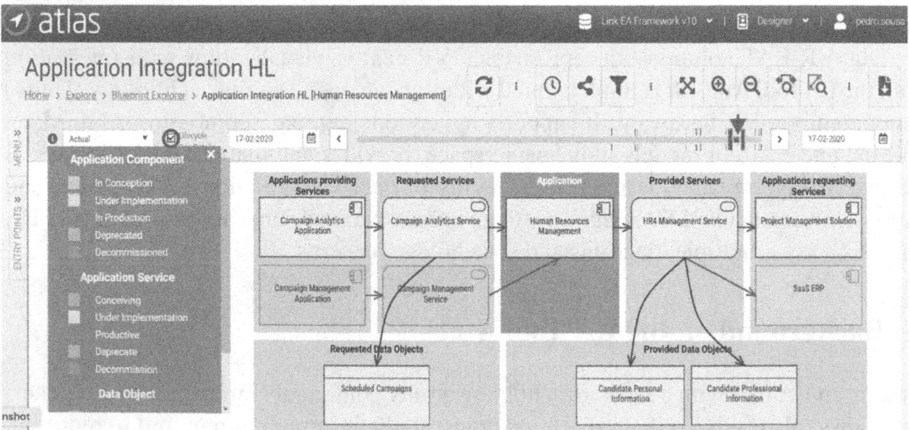

Fig. 2. High-level Application Integration Blueprint for HR Management application.

A key aspect Atlas addresses is the generation of up-to-date architectural views with near zero effort as has been done for some cases (Sousa 2011, 2014), even with the previous generation of the tool named EAMS. Users define templates of architectural views that are instantiated on request to particular objects. Figure 2 illustrates the generated view for the Human Resources (HR) Management application, presented in the middle container. Moving leftwards, one can see the Services requested by the HR Management application and the applications providing such services. Moving rightwards, one can see the service realized by the HR Management application and the applications that request it. Below it data objects used in the services.

Since the Lifecycle option is selected (red circle), artefacts symbols are shaded according with their lifetime state on the date defined by the time handler position in the time bar (top red arrow). The legend on the left presents the lifecycle states defined for Application Components and Application Services. In this case, on the selected date (17/02/2020) the Campaign Management application and service are Deprecated (light blue on the left), and the SaaS ERP application is In Conception (grey, on the right). To feed Atlas with the information required to produce such architectural views, one uses the information made available by project plans, be it simple lists of created and decommissioned artefacts or models in some notation such as ArchiMate. In this last case, since ArchiMate does not provide a way to state that some work package creates/deletes/or changes any artefact, one uses association relationships named as "created by", "decommissioned by" or "changed by". Atlas also provides a transformation engine that allows end users to configure how each concept in an imported model (such as in ArchiMate) maps into the concepts defined in its metamodel.

Atlas also allows end users to define the propagation rules between a project milestone dates and the lifecycles of the artefacts created/decommissioned and changed by the project. A default rule for artefact creation is that objects created by a project become productive upon project completion. So, whenever a project is delayed, Atlas can update the lifecycle of dependent artefacts. Finally, end users can also define the rules the establish dependency between projects. A default rule is that a project A is dependent of a Project B if it uses some artefact created, changed or decommissioned by project B. So, whenever a project termination date is delayed, Atlas can alert (e.g., email) the actor responsible for the impacted ongoing or planned projects.

4 Solution Concept

As shown in Fig. 3, our generalized VR Modeling Framework (VR-MF) (Oberhauser and Pogolski 2019) provides a VR-based domain-independent hypermodeling framework that addresses three primary aspects of modeling in VR: visualization, navigation, and interaction. Rather than requiring unique and specific 3D shapes to represent various model elements, since most models already have 2D graphical element notations, we chose the more pragmatic principle of utilizing cubes to represent elements, since its sides can be viewed from all perspectives an optional 2D type icon can easily be portrayed as a material on the cube's sides. Furthermore, relationships between elements can be shown in 3D space, and related elements can be grouped in 3D layers or views as appropriate. VR-EA provides specialized direct support and mapping for EA models in

VR (Oberhauser and Pogolski 2019), including both ArchiMate as well as BPMN (VR-BPMN) models (Oberhauser et al. 2018). VR-EAT (EA Tool) is our solution concept for integrating EA tool data and visualizations in VR. The VR-EAT solution concept is generic and its feasibility is demonstrated with the EA tool Atlas.

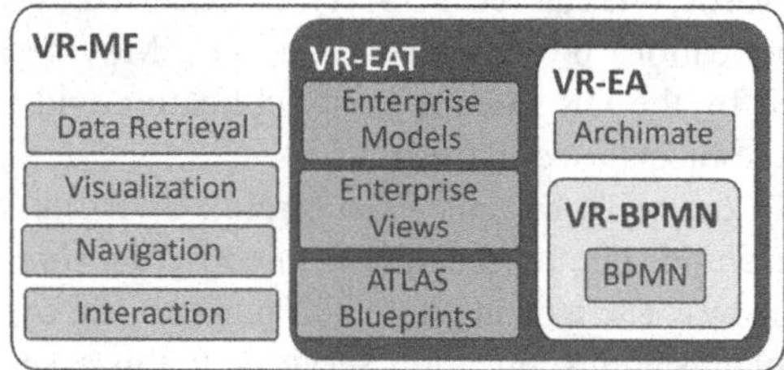

Fig. 3. The VR-MF (general) and VR-EAT (EA Tool) solution concept

ArchiMate models use a graphical notation consisting of a collection of concepts to portray a wide scope of EA elements and relationships. Elements can be behavioral, structural, motivational, or some composite. These concepts can participate in various layers: strategy, business, application, technology, physical, and implementation & migration, the layers having colors associated with them. Cross-cutting aspects involved include: passive structure, active structure, behavior, and motivation. Views are used to convey information addressing concerns of specific stakeholders. On the other hand, BPMN models focus on business processes and consist of Business Process Diagrams (BPDs) composed of graphical elements consisting of flow objects, connecting objects, swim lanes, and artifacts (OMG 2011). On the other hand, Atlas, as a representative EA tool, provides access to diverse EA-related data in a coherent repository and meta-model and is not restricted to certain standards or notations.

Visualization. While many visual options and metaphors are possible, diverging too far from the 2D diagrams and notations familiar to EA tool users would reduce comprehension. Yet to place 2D images like flat screens in front of users would provide little added value. As a transitional hybrid before we have full VR EA tooling, to differentiate elements by type 3D boxes provide depth in the diagrams and project the relevant 2D object type notation from the EA tool onto all sides as a texture, which can thus be perceived from all angles. In contrast to 2D space, one challenge in 3D space element placement is that one can never be sure if an element is not hidden behind another element at any particular vantage point if the element is opaque. However, if one makes the element partially transparent, then it can become confusing as to which element one is actually focusing on. We thus chose to make the elements opaque in order to avoid this visual confusion, and by briefly adjusting one's perspective one can visually check that nothing is hidden behind an element. Moreover, visualizing text is an issue in VR due to the relatively low resolutions currently available and the distance from the virtual camera position to the text. Also, labels for elements can differ widely in length, yet should not interfere with understanding the underlying diagram structure. We thus place element labels on the top of the sides. For dealing with longer element labels, on selection (when element is of interest) the full label is displayed. For visualizing and differentiating the various diagrams, hyperplanes are used to take advantage of the 3D space, with each plane representing one diagram.

Navigation. The immersion afforded by VR requires addressing how to intuitively navigate the space while reducing the likelihood of potential VR sickness symptoms. Two navigation modes are included in the solution concept: the default uses gliding controls, enabling users to *fly through* the VR space and get an overview of the entire model from any angle they wish. Alternatively, teleporting permits a user to select a destination and be instantly placed there (i.e., by moving the camera to that position); this can be disconcerting but may reduce the likelihood of VR sickness that can occur when moving through a virtual space for those prone to it.

Interaction. VR interaction with VR elements has not yet become standardized. In our VR concept, user-element interaction is done primarily via the VR controllers. Views are stacked hyperplanes and can be made visible or invisible by selecting the plane or equivalent icon. Inter-view connections can be enabled or disabled. A specific connection can be selected by selecting an element to emphasize it. To reduce visual clutter, one mode permits visualizing only the inter-view connections for the element of interest, hiding all others.

5 Realization

Figure 4 shows our solution concept realization for VR-EAT. The Unity block denotes our VR-MF realization, and besides Atlas Blueprint views includes direct support for ArchiMate and BPMN models (VR-EA). A Data Hub is shown in the center while below it, MongoDB is used for local data storage and to update data within Unity. The top left shows the integration with the EA tool Atlas, including repository data and service access via REST/JSON. A command line extension shown on the left provides helper functions for configuration, mapping, and data loading for the Data Hub. Initially, due to time and resource constraints, our realization primarily addresses visualization and navigation of existing views and models in Atlas. Future work will include support for creating and improving views and models from within VR.

The integration with Atlas was done in a VirtualBox VM with Win10Pro 1903 with 8 GB RAM, 4-core CPU @4.6 GHz, 50 GB. The VR-EAT implementation used Unity 2019.1.14f1 with IL2CPP, Blender 2.8, SteamVR 1.9.16, MongoDB 4.2.2. The Data Hub uses NuGet packages CommandLineParser 2.7.82, MongoDB.Driver 2.10.0, Newtonsoft.Json 12.0.3, and .NET system packages. The Data Hub, Command Line Extension, and Unity run on the .NET Framework 4.6.

Our sample Atlas repository contained about 66 core blueprints without parameter choices, and resulting in 7900 different blueprints considering all selection combinations. We load these in the Data Hub and save them to MongoDB in our schema, to permit us to transform and annotate the data as needed for VR.

Initially an empty blueprint placeholder (Fig. 5 top) is shown with menu options as a local menu attached to the plane. After menu option parameters have been specified,

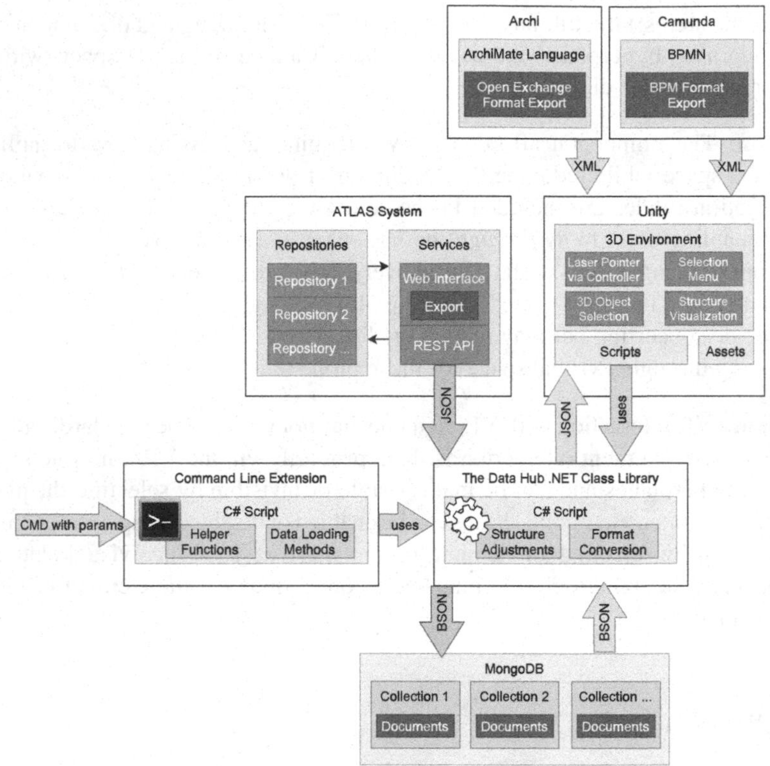

Fig. 4. VR-EAT solution concept realization.

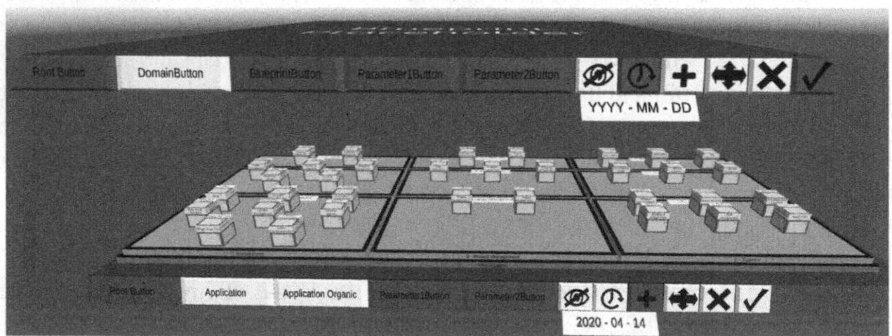

Fig. 5. Application/Application Organic blueprint in VR.

the generate button (checkmark) causes the VR blueprint to be displayed (Fig. 5 bottom) equivalent to that of Atlas (Fig. 6). In VR, the elements in red are elements that do not exist at that timepoint, having been decommissioned (past) or to exist (future). The top diagram also shows an empty placeholder after adding a view (+).

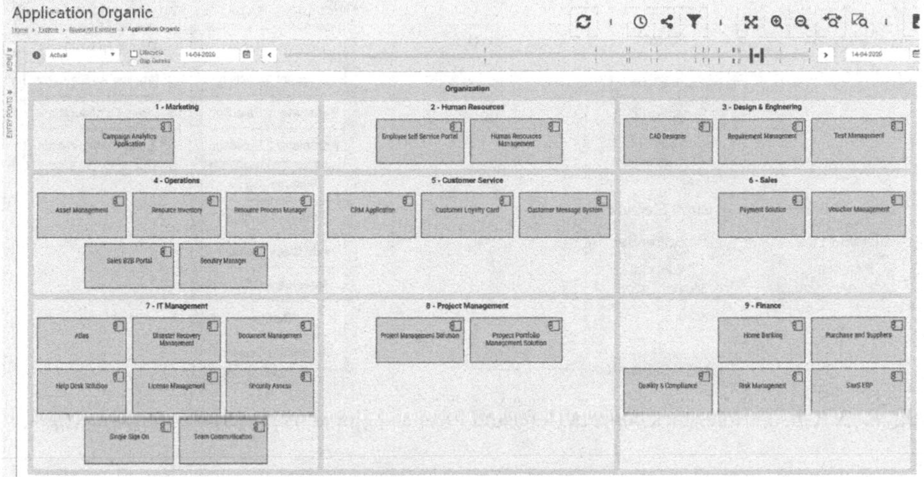

Fig. 6. Application/Application Organic blueprint in Atlas.

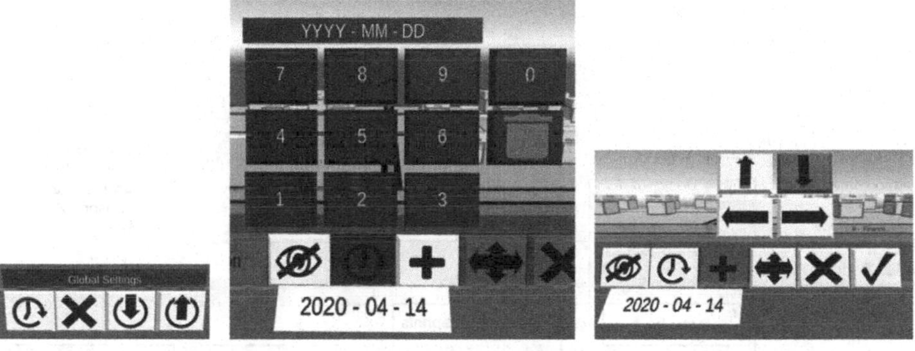

Fig. 7. VR-EAT menus: floating global (left), timepoint (center), and local (right).

Our menu options concept (Fig. 8 right) includes a floating Global Options Menu (realized as Fig. 7 left) and a local Options Menu (realized as Fig. 7 right). As to our solution concept for organizing spatial placement of Atlas blueprints, a stack-based scheme (Fig. 8 left) with a maximum of three parallel stacks is used (arbitrary to consolidate diagrams in relative proximity), with no limit on the views in any stack. The floating Global Options Menu supports deleting all views, setting a timepoint for all views, and saving/loading the configuration, while the local blueprint Options Menu supports Domain/Blueprint/Parameter, hide (eye symbol), timepoint (Fig. 7 center), add stack element above (+ symbol), move element within/between stacks (arrows in Fig. 7 right), delete element (x symbol), generate blueprint based on parameter selection (checkmark), and domain selection (leftmost Root button) to switch between root repositories.

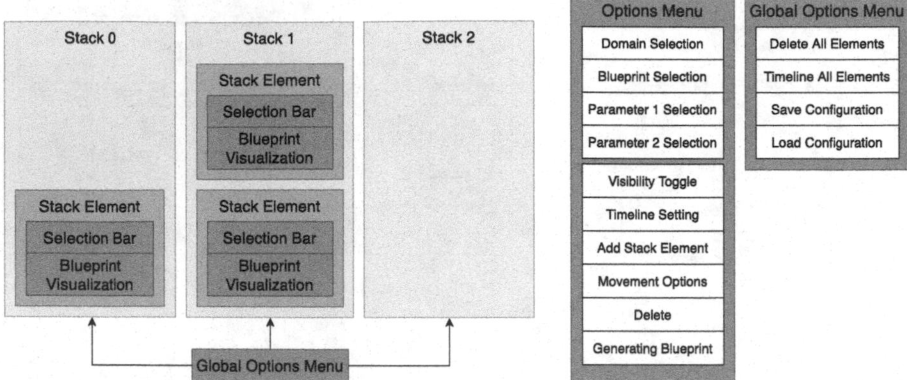

Fig. 8. VR-EAT triple stack concept (left) and local and global menu selection options (right).

Since hundreds of parameters are possible, selection of the domain/blueprint/parameter1/parameter2 button dynamically shows the available choices as buttons upon selection (see Fig. 9 concept and Fig. 10 VR implementation).

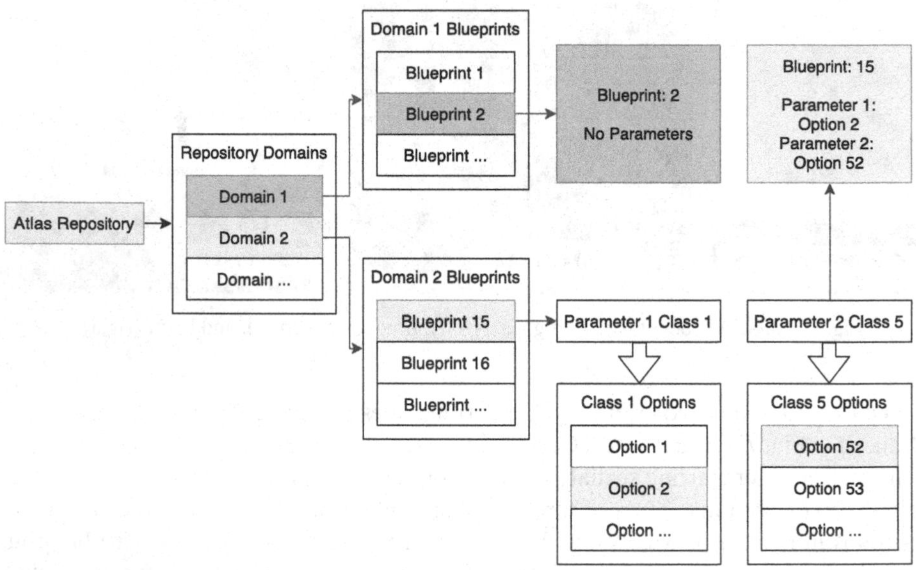

Fig. 9. VR-EAT local blueprint selection.

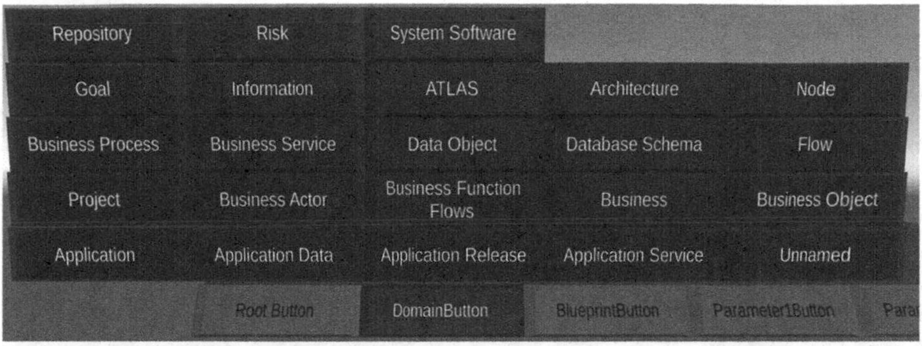

Fig. 10. VR-EAT local blueprint selection.

Figure 11 shows elements with icons and labels placed on the sides, containment is indicated with raised, colored, and named plates, dependencies are shown with black connectors, and a selected element is indicated with a pink glow and an indicator of that same element in other views.

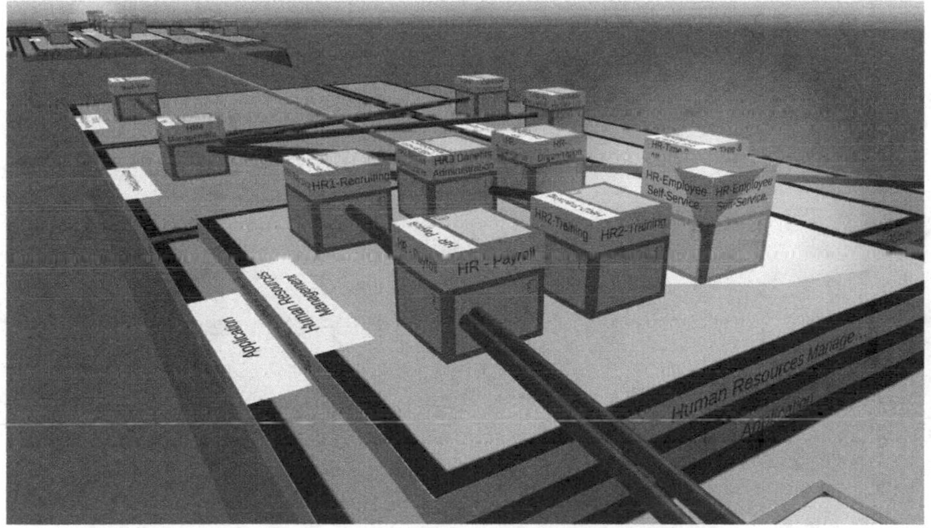

Fig. 11. VR-EAT container and element selection (glow) visualization.

In Fig. 12, a side-by-side comparison of timepoints 1-1-2010 on left and 16-03-2020 on right is shown, whereby in Atlas two browser windows are shown (top) and in VR-EAT (bottom) a side-by-side depiction is supported. Figure 13 shows support for multiple EA models side-by-side in VR to support analysis, with VR-EAT Atlas blueprints (left) and (on the right) VR-EA with the ArchiSurance Archimate model.

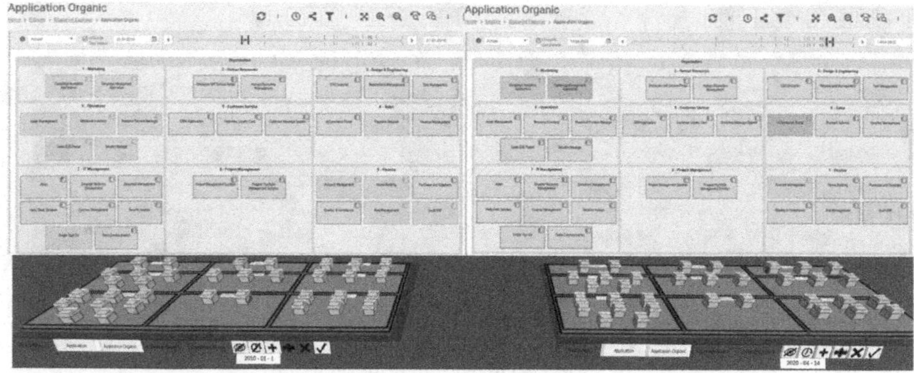

Fig. 12. Time delta in Atlas (top) in 2 browser windows with 1-1-2010 left and 14-04-2020 right, and equivalent VR-EAT with via visual marking in red of non-current elements (bottom).

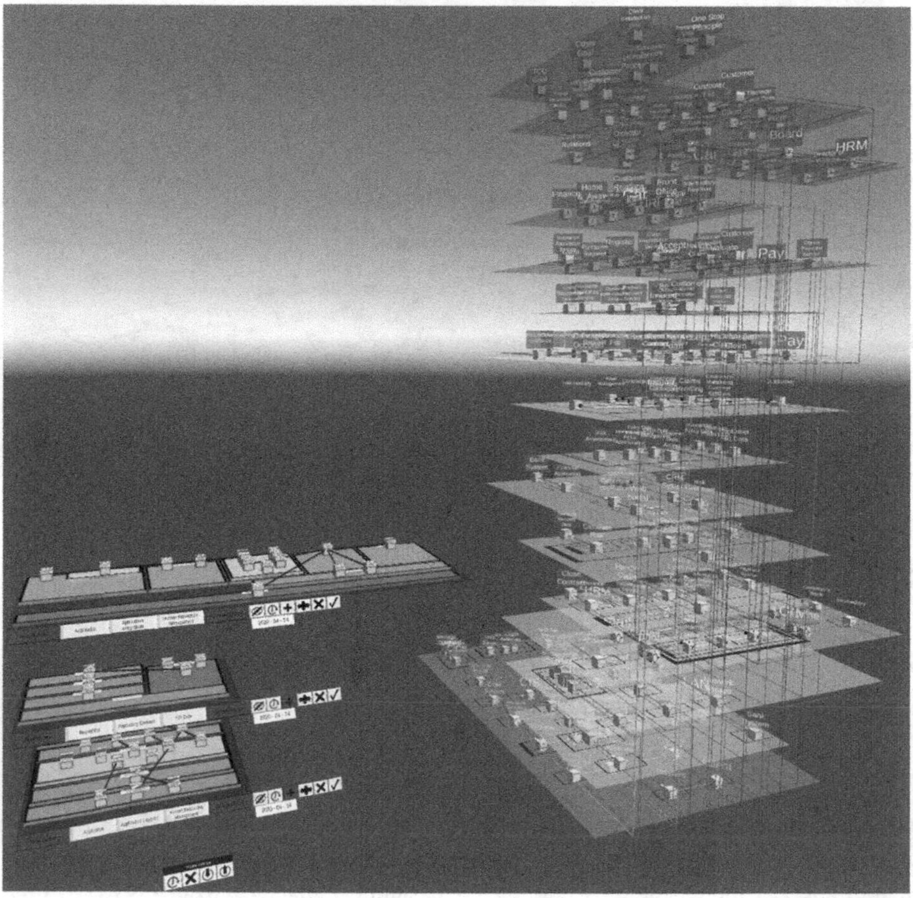

Fig. 13. VR-EAT showing Atlas blueprints (left) and VR-EA with the ArchiSurance Archimate model (right) side-by-side in VR to support analysis.

6 Evaluation

A case study is used to evaluate the practicality of the VR-EAT concept and implementation. Two scenarios that require multiple views (blueprints) to assess the situation will be used to exemplify usage of VR-EAT: (1) EA system replacement and (2) data storage consolidation.

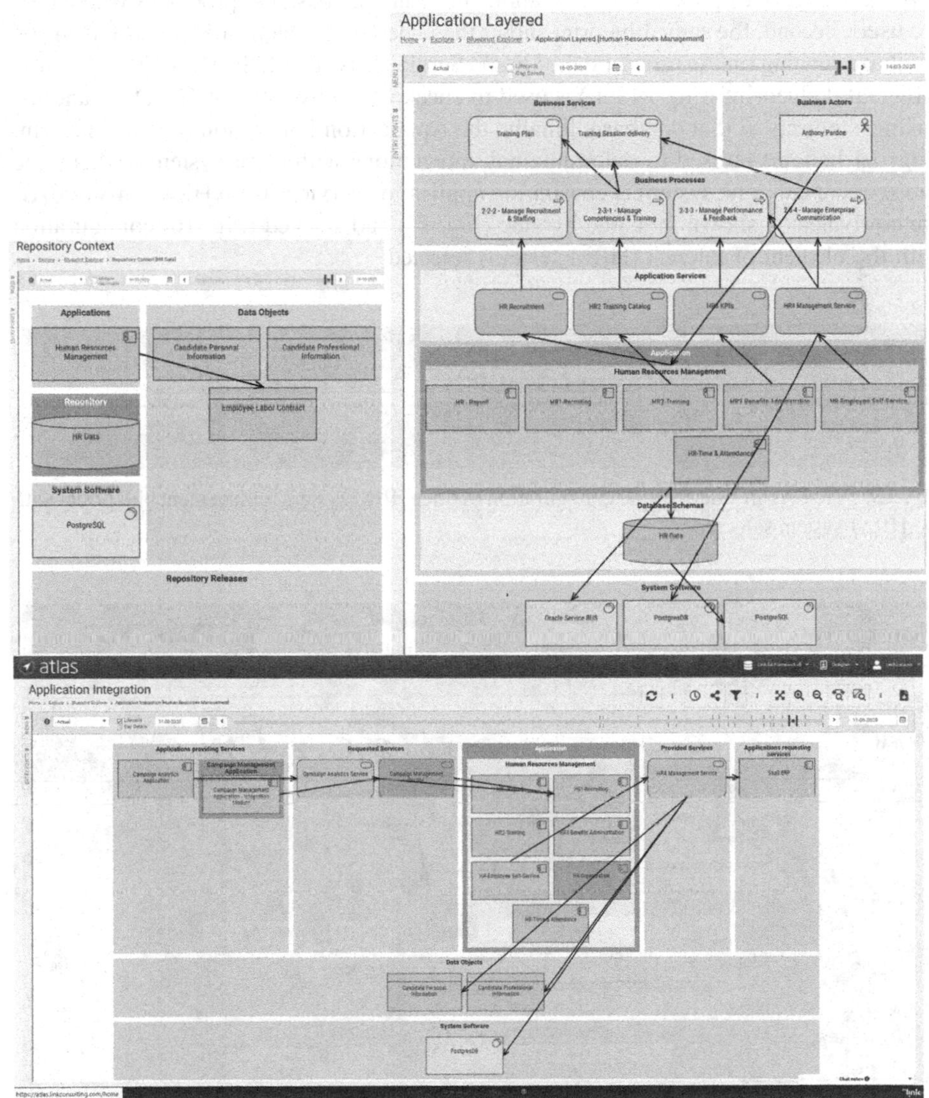

Fig. 14. Repository Context [HR Data] (top left), Application Layered [HRM] (top right), and Application Integration [HRM] (bottom) blueprints in Atlas.

6.1 System Replacement Scenario

When considering system replacement (perhaps due to increased licensing costs), various blueprints must be consulted to identify dependencies of the system, both current and planned at the time of system replacement. First, the application landscape blueprint is used to drill down into the Application Layered [Human Resource Management] (HRM) blueprint (Fig. 14 right) and determine any impacted business processes: one sees four application services provided by this application and the business processes where they are used. Second, the same blueprint shows the underlying system software used: an HR database running on Postgres and the Oracle Service Bus. Third, the Repository Context [HR Data] blueprint (Fig. 14 left) is used to check what else uses the HR Data, and the business objects in that database. Finally, the Application Integration [HRM] blueprint (Fig. 14 bottom) is used to determine any integrations with other systems, where one can see that only one system is consuming application services from HRM. In VR-EAT, the equivalent is shown in a side-by-side (Fig. 15) and stacked (Fig. 16) configuration with the element of interest (HRM system) selected.

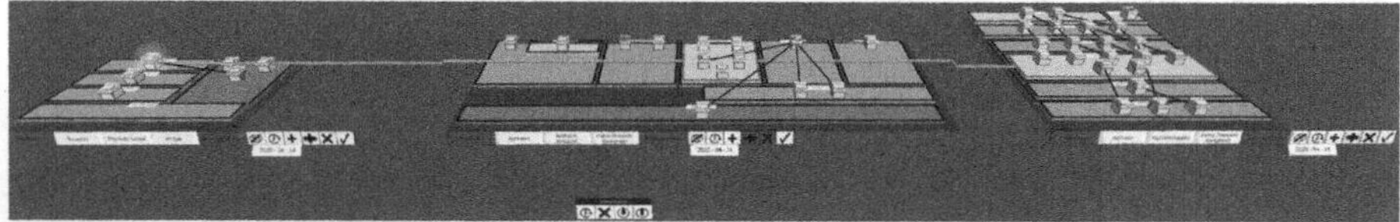

Fig. 15. VR-EAT in side-by-side configuration of three HRM system replacement blueprints with the HRM system selected.

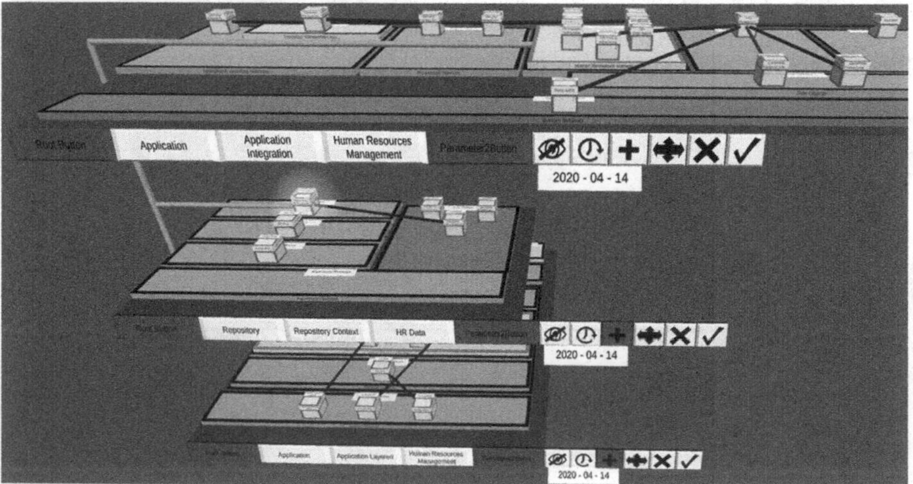

Fig. 16. The three HRM Application system replacement blueprints stacked in VR-EAT.

6.2 Data Storage Consolidation Scenario

Views are specific to a stakeholder and their interest. In larger enterprises with many possible blueprints (our sample database alone offers 7900), the question that can linger in the mind of an EA analyst is: Did I miss something? Have I looked at all the relevant diagrams? Have I considered all possible impacts?

For this case study, let us consider the question if consolidation of databases onto one product/vendor is realistic? How many different ones are even used, and by which applications for what scenarios? How critical are these to the business?

For that, multiple blueprints might be used. We suggest that a hybrid approach of non-VR and VR be used. Direct use of Atlas (non-VR) would be more efficient for quickly ascertaining the various relevant blueprints, for example the four blueprints as shown in Fig. 17 where Application Layered [Financial] (left) and Repository Context [HR Data] (right) both involve PostgreSQL and Fig. 18 where System Software Layered [PostgreSQL] (left) shows applications using PostgreSQL and Application Context [Financial] (right) involves use of the Oracle Service Bus and may affect vendor lock-in. Once these are identified, in VR-EAT these could be stacked or laid side-by-side for deeper analysis and element of interest selection in VR as shown in Fig. 19.

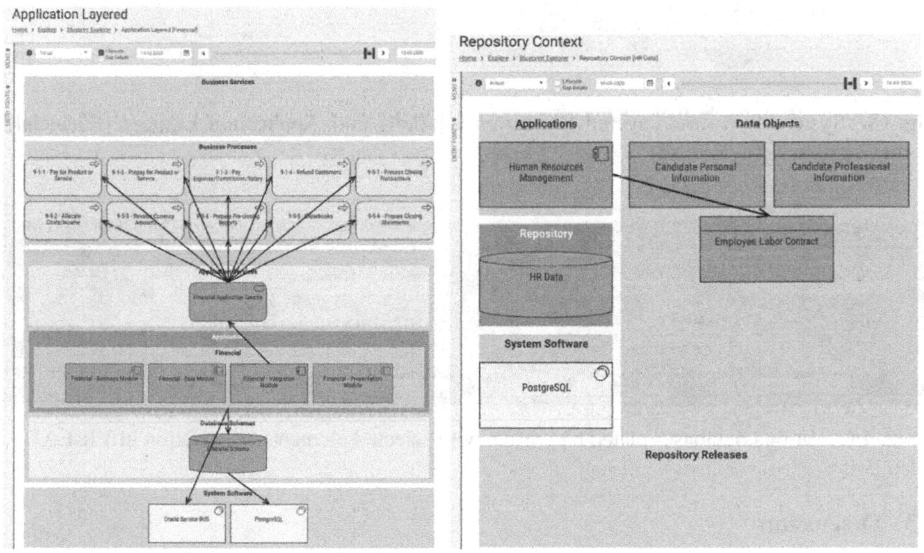

Fig. 17. Application Layered [Financial] (left) and Repository Context [HR Data] (right).

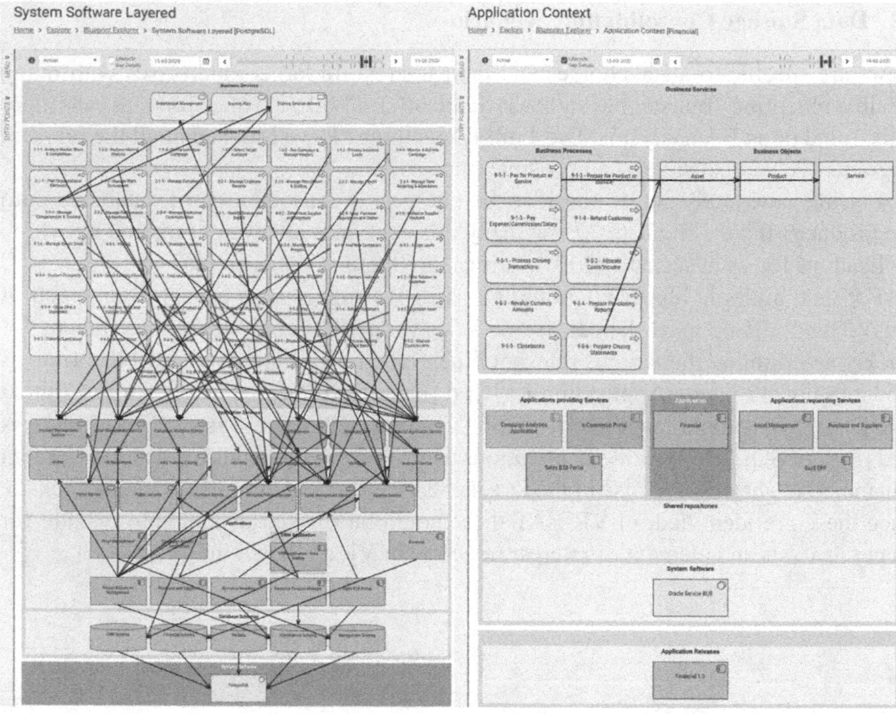

Fig. 18. System Software Layered [PostgreSQL] (left) and Application Context [Financial] (right).

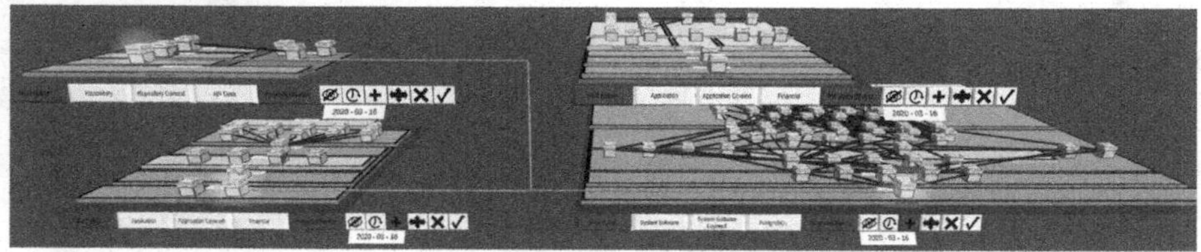

Fig. 19. Various database-related blueprints with selected element visualization in VR-EAT.

6.3 Discussion

As to the benefits of an immersive VR experience vs. 2D, (Müller et al. 2014) investigated a software analysis task used a Famix metamodel of Apache Tomcat source code dependencies in a force-directed graph. They found that VR does not significantly decrease comprehension and analysis time nor significantly improve correctness (although fewer mistakes were made). While interaction time was less efficient, VR improved the user experience (more motivating, less demanding, more inventive/innovative, and more clearly structured). Analogously, we believe VR-EAT shows that EA tool dynamically-generated diagrams can be brought into VR to support EA stakeholders as EA complexity grows. VR-EAT benefits include: unlimited simultaneous diagrams without screen space limitations, structured placement of diagrams, inter-diagram dependencies. By providing an immersive VR experience to fly-in, navigate and get a feel for the context and surrounding elements involved, it removes other visual distractions in our surroundings that 2D displays inherently involve. It is analogous to being outside an aquarium versus swimming with the fish.

Thus, VR-EAT can support EA decision-making by making multiple EA views and models and their interdependencies simultaneously available, and in combination with VR-EA, these can be visualized and tied to other available EA models such as Archimate. VR-EAT can be positioned as providing a (transitional/hybrid) way to access and utilize the 2D diagrams and models that are common to EA users and available in EA tools today, and enable VR-based EA modeling to utilize these. VR does involve challenges, including limiting cognitive overload and visual clutter and ascertaining the intentions of the user, and as VR is still relatively new and not commonplace for IT work environments, interaction models with elements have not yet been standardized, incurring additional interaction and training overhead.

7 Conclusion

As enterprises evolve and EA models increase in complexity, new and practical approaches for integrating available EA tool diagram and model information sources and dynamically-generated diagram visualizations are needed. With VR-EAT we demonstrated the specific capability to integrate advanced EA tools such as Atlas and convey their available EA-related dynamic diagrams into VR for an immersive VR experience. VR-EAT is founded on the general VR modeling framework VR-MF and enhances VR-EA with direct EA tool support. A prototype implementation of VR-EAT demonstrated its feasibility with Atlas. Our evaluation case study showed its potential to support various EA scenarios that require analysis of multiple diagrams in conjunction with one another.

As EA complexity increases, we see a great potential in VR to visualize objects (that have symbolic meaning to the users) in a spatial format and allow them to navigate and interact with them in this immersive space. While views have their place for simplifying the enterprise reality for specific stakeholder interests, for more complex analytical tasks involving multiple stakeholders, 2D graphical visualizations are limited in the ability and area on which multiple diagrams and inter-model aspects are analyzed. Future work will enhance the interactive and informational capabilities of VR-EAT, provide a more integrated synchronization and immersive experience between the Atlas diagrams and other EA models, and investigate VR-EAT usage in an empirical study.

Acknowledgements. The authors would like to thank Ricardo Santos Leal for his technical assistance with Atlas.

References

Cardoso, D., Sousa, P.: Generation of stakeholder-specific BPMN models. In: Aveiro, D., Guizzardi, G., Borbinha, J. (eds.) EEWC 2019. LNBIP, vol. 374, pp. 15–32. Springer, Cham (2020). https://doi.org/10.1007/978-3-030-37933-9_2

Colaço, J., Sousa, P.: View integration of business process models. In: Themistocleous, M., Morabito, V. (eds.) EMCIS 2017. LNBIP, vol. 299, pp. 619–632. Springer, Cham (2017). https://doi.org/10.1007/978-3-319-65930-5_48

Hoogervorst, J.: Enterprise governance and enterprise engineering. Springer, Heidelberg (2009). https://doi.org/10.1007/978-3-540-92671-9

Jarvis, B.: Enterprise Architecture: Understanding the Bigger Picture - A Best Practice Guide for Decision Makers in IT. The UK National Computing Centre (2003)

Müller, R., Kovacs, P., Schilbach, J., Zeckzer, D.: How to master challenges in experimental evaluation of 2D versus 3D software visualizations. In: 2014 IEEE VIS International Workshop on 3DVis (3DVis), pp. 33–36. IEEE (2014)

Muro, M., Liu, S., Whiton, J., Kulkarni, S.: Digitalization and the American Workforce. Brookings Institution Metropolitan Policy Program (2017). https://www.brookings.edu/wp-content/uploads/2017/11/mpp_2017nov15_digitalization_full_report.pdf

Naranjo, D., Sánchez, M., Villalobos, J.: Towards a unified and modular approach for visual analysis of enterprise models. In: 2014 IEEE 18th International Enterprise Distributed Object Computing Conference Workshops and Demonstrations, pp. 77–86. IEEE (2014)

Oberhauser, R., Pogolski, C.: VR-EA: virtual reality visualization of enterprise architecture models with ArchiMate and BPMN. In: Shishkov, B. (ed.) BMSD 2019. LNBIP, vol. 356, pp. 170–187. Springer, Cham (2019). https://doi.org/10.1007/978-3-030-24854-3_11

Oberhauser, R., Pogolski, C., Matic, A.: VR-BPMN: visualizing bpmn models in virtual reality. In: Shishkov, B. (ed.) BMSD 2018. LNBIP, vol. 319, pp. 83–97. Springer, Cham (2018). https://doi.org/10.1007/978-3-319-94214-8_6

OMG: Business Process Model and Notation (BPMN) Version 2.0. OMG (2011)

Open Group: ArchiMate 3.0.1 Specification. The Open Group (2017)

Rehring, K., Greulich, M., Bredenfeld, L., Ahlemann, F.: Let's get in touch - decision making about enterprise architecture using 3D visualization in augmented reality. In: Proceedings of 52nd Hawaii International Conference on System Sciences (HICSS), pp. 1769–1778. IEEE (2019)

Roth, S., Zec, M., Matthes, F.: Enterprise architecture visualization tool survey. Technical Report, Sebis, Technical University Munich (2014)

Sousa, P., Gabriel, R., Tadao, G., Carvalho, R., Sousa, P., Sampaio, A.: Enterprise transformation: the Serasa Experian case. In: Harmsen, F., Grahlmann, K., Proper, E. (eds.) PRET 2011. LNBIP, vol. 89, pp. 134–145. Springer, Heidelberg (2011). https://doi.org/10.1007/978-3-642-23388-3_7

Sousa, P., Cardoso, D., Colaço, J.: Managing multi-view business processes models in the Atlas tool. In: Proceedings of the 19th Enterprise Engineering Working Conference Forum, vol. 2408. CEUR-WS.org (2019)

Sousa, P., Lima, J., Sampaio, A., Pereira, C.: An approach for creating and managing enterprise blueprints: a case for IT blueprints. In: Albani, A., Barjis, J., Dietz, Jan L.G. (eds.) CIAO!/EOMAS -2009. LNBIP, vol. 34, pp. 70–84. Springer, Heidelberg (2009). https://doi.org/10.1007/978-3-642-01915-9_6

Sousa, P., Sampaio, A. Leal, R.: A case for a living enterprise architecture in a private bank. In: 8th Workshop on Transformation & Engineering of Enterprises (TEE 2014), vol 1182. CEUR-WS.org (2014)

Sousa, P., Carvalho, M.: Dynamic organization's representation. Linking project management with enterprise architecture. In: IEEE 20th Conference on Business Informatics (CBI), vol 2, pp. 170–174. IEEE (2018)

Sousa, P.; Leal, R.; Sampaio, A.: Atlas: the enterprise cartography tool. In: 18th Enterprise Engineering Working Conference Forum, vol. 2229. CEUR-WS.org (2018)

Steuer, J.: Defining virtual reality: Dimensions determining telepresence. J. Commun. **42**(4), 73–93 (1992)

Tribolet, J., Sousa, P., Caetano, A.: The role of enterprise governance and cartography in enterprise engineering. Enterpr. Modell. Inf. Syst. Architect. **9**(1), 38–49 (2014)
van den Berg, M.: ArchiMate, BPMN and UML: an approach to harmonizing the notations. Orbus Software white paper (2012)

Understanding the Augmented and Virtual Reality Business Ecosystem: An e^3-value Approach

Julian Schuir[1(✉)], Jannis Vogel[2], Frank Teuteberg[1], and Oliver Thomas[2,3]

[1] Accounting and Information Systems, Osnabrück University, Osnabrück, Germany
{julian.schuir,frank.teuteberg}@uni-osnabrueck.de
[2] Information Management and Information Systems, Osnabrück University, Osnabrück, Germany
jannis.vogel@uni-osnabrueck.de, oliver.thomas@dfki.de
[3] Smart Enterprise Engineering, German Research Center for Artificial Intelligence, Osnabrück, Germany

Abstract. In recent years, augmented and virtual reality have increasingly gained attention. To date, a multitude of solutions has been developed and implemented both in research and in practice. As a result, these technologies create new business opportunities. Particularly in Germany, a variety of startups tried to enter the market. By analyzing 141 tech startups, this paper visualizes the 25 generic roles and value streams within the augmented and virtual reality business ecosystem using the e^3-value method. Furthermore, we evaluate the model with semi-structured interviews to verify validity. Practitioners can use the model to identify competitors or collaboration opportunities. Theoretically, our research contributes to the body of knowledge by systematically depicting the services related to augmented and virtual reality. Finally, we provide directions for future research.

Keywords: Generic value network · e^3-value method · Augmented reality · Virtual reality · Business ecosystem

1 Introduction and Motivation

Innovative technologies by themselves may have great potentials but no single objective values. Consequently, the economic value of a technology remains undeveloped until it is transformed into a product or service that generates a value [1]. Two emerging technologies that have the potential to create economic values in such a way are augmented reality (AR) and virtual reality (VR) [2]. According to a recent forecast, the global market size of both technologies will be around 160 billion US dollars by 2023, as their use could revolutionize some industries such as education or manufacturing [3].

As stated by Milgram et al. (1994), augmented and virtual reality are parts of the reality-virtuality-continuum. Augmented reality refers to the display of additional information into the user's field of vision. Specific devices incorporating see-through displays such as smart glasses (e.g. Google Glass) and AR glasses (e.g. Microsoft HoloLens) are

B. Shishkov (Ed.): BMSD 2020, LNBIP 391, pp. 240–256, 2020.
https://doi.org/10.1007/978-3-030-52306-0_15

used for this purpose. Virtual reality, on the contrary, completely immerses the user in a simulated environment using devices like virtual reality headsets (e.g. Oculus Rift) [4]. Both technologies have increasingly attracted the attention of researchers and practitioners in recent years due to their great potential for economic applications, especially for improving information provision [5, 6]. For instance, smart glasses can improve repairing processes efficiency by allowing workers to access remote support and work hands-free at the same time [7]. Virtual reality, on the other hand, is regarded as a promising tool for the acquisition of procedural skills, since various scenarios can be simulated realistically and without danger in the virtual environment [8].

As a result, the amount of startups providing AR and VR solutions has continuously increased during the last years. Hence, the technologies established their own business ecosystem [2]. In general, the term business ecosystem describes the network of companies with "co-evolv[ing] capabilities around a new innovation" [9], with both competitive and collaborative activities [10]. According to Bezegová et al. (2018), AR and VR are overlapping industries heavily depending on their innovative strength and research activities. In particular, Germany is seen as a central player in the global AR and VR scene, as it has a long tradition of VR research and applications in the manufacturing industry, which are steadily increasing due to the High-Tech Strategy of the German Federal Government [2, 11]. Consequently, the number of employees in Berlin in this sector grew from 300 to 1200 between 2016 and 2018 [12]. Against this background, startups need to increase networking and partnering with experienced organizations to profit from synergies between companies [13], especially for identifying common value delivery channels such as platforms [14], to co-create new products and to further improve the maturity of these technologies [2].

In this regard, it is problematic that only a few studies are available dealing with the downstream value network of these technologies [14–16]. So far, business-oriented research on these technologies has been limited to examining the market potential of individual services [17] or business models [18]. Particularly the AR and VR industry itself has not yet been depicted scholarly, although it is repeatedly associated with disruptive products and services as well as high market volumes [18, 19]. Furthermore, a holistic understanding of the ecosystem is advantageous in order to identify necessary interfaces of software design at an early stage and to promote diffusion. To close this research gap, the following research question (RQ) can be derived:

RQ: *What are the actors and value streams in the ecosystem of augmented and virtual reality and how can they be represented abstractly in a generic model?*

Thus, the goal of this paper is to create a generic value model of the AR and VR business ecosystem depicting the actors and value streams. Therefore, we follow the research approach of Riasanow et al. (2017) by analyzing 141 companies using the e^3-value approach [20]. Basing on value modelling patterns, this methodology allows economic evaluations by visualizing the exchange of values between various actors in a network [21]. Due to its design-oriented character, this research project can be assigned to the Design Science Research (DSR) approach aiming to develop a model [22], which is besides constructs, methods, and instantiations the main type of DSR projects [23].

To answer the RQ, we structured our study as follows: First, we present related work and our methodological approach. Then we present the identified roles and actors as parts of their business models. Next, we illustrate the generic value model using the e^3-value approach, followed by an evaluation of the model. Finally, we discuss the implications, limitations, and future research opportunities.

2 Related Work

2.1 Businesses Based on Augmented and Virtual Reality

To build this paper on a solid base, we applied the method of a systematic literature review according to vom Brocke et al. (2009). As a first step, we defined the review scope and focused on research on business models related to AR and VR [24]. In general, the term business model describes "the heuristic logic that connects technical potential with the realization of economic value" [25] and covers the core activities of a company. Since business models are closely related to value network research, this perspective offers an initial starting point for the design of our model [26]. We therefore applied the search string *("augmented reality" OR "virtual reality") AND ("business model" OR ecosystem OR startup)* to databases like EBSCO, Science Direct, Scopus and SpringerLink to receive scientific, peer-reviewed papers. To enlarge to the number of papers we used forward and backward search.

In general, technological innovations such as virtual reality as well as the increasing digitalization of business processes are seen as the main drivers of business growth and transformation. For instance, the industry 4.0 concept will change business models by connecting the factory to various virtual reality applications according to Ignat [27]. In the literature, AR and VR are referred to be important tools to improve value delivery for customers by improving customer experiences [28]. The explicit impacts of the technologies on value creation have been hardly investigated yet.

Cranmer & Jung (2014) examine the opportunities of using augmented reality for touristic purposes. According to their study, the commercial use of AR for tourism requires a carefully considered business model. Therefore, the authors propose to investigate how to build up business models using augmented reality [19]. Jimenez et al. (2016), who previously designed a location-based AR system for utility management, examine the market potential for such a system. In order to prepare the commercialization of the product, the authors analyze its competitive advantages, identify potential markets and describe the services to be commercialized [17]. Mütterlein & Hess (2017) investigate the impacts of VR on business models in the media industry using the business model concept in combination with qualitative case studies and semi-structured interviews. The findings indicate that especially companies creating and selling VR content for value creation are transformed by the technology itself. Compared to this, VR's effect on companies that only use the technology for internal purposes is relatively weak [18].

Overall, the results of the systematic literature review indicate that the value creation with AR and VR has so far been investigated primarily at the individual meso-level. Several authors show that AR and VR can have a strong economic impact by enabling new business opportunities such as 3D content creation [18, 19]. However, a comprehensive analysis of this network in research is still lacking, although the number and diversity of the companies operating within it have increased steadily in recent years [2]. This research gap motivates us to perform a coherent analysis of the ecosystem using the e^3-value method as it enables the abstraction of similar organizations to an abstract level [21] and is explicitly suitable for large ecosystems with a diversity of actors and economic value streams [10].

2.2 e^3-Value Methodology

The e^3-value method was introduced and developed by Gordijn and Akkermans at the Free University of Amsterdam in 2001 [29, 30]. The approach allows to analyze and to represent how actors create, distribute, and consume values in a network. In this context, the term *value* refers to economic values such as money, products, and services that are exchanged between the stakeholders of a business ecosystem [29]. In contrast, ethical values such as sustainability, privacy, and accountability as known from Value-Sensitive Design are not part of the e^3-value methodology, as it was originally developed for economic evaluations [31]. An e^3-value model consists of different concepts with specific notation elements such as *actors*, *market segments*, *value interfaces with value ports*, and *value exchanges with value objects* (see Fig. 1).

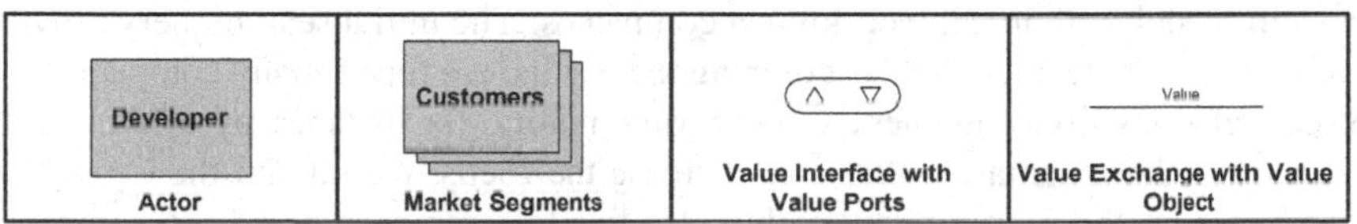

Fig. 1. e^3-value Notation Elements in accordance to Gordijn and Akkermans (2001)

An *actor* is an entity that generates profit for itself by carrying out activities and therefore refers to product and services offered. *Market segments* represent similar actors that share the same value interfaces and objects. Thereby, one or more *value interfaces* can be attached to an actor. They visualize that an actor undertakes ingoing and outgoing value offerings via *value ports* that present the provision or request of *value objects*. These can be products, services, money, or consumer experiences. The value objects being exchanged on a connection between two value ports are designated as value exchanges [21, 29].

This methodological approach has already been used in order to analyze the business landscape in different innovative areas of interest that were significantly influenced by the digital transformation, such as the cloud computing market [32], the automotive industry [33], the e-commerce business landscape [21], the insurance industry [34] and digital platform ecosystems [10].

3 Research Approach

To identify the actors in the business ecosystem of augmented and virtual reality with their value streams and develop the model in a rigorous manner, we applied the Design Science

Research Methodology in accordance to Peffers et al. [39]. After having *identified the problem* and the *objectives of our solution* in the previous sections, we briefly outline the steps of our research process including the *design and development, demonstration,* and *evaluation* (cf. Fig. 2).

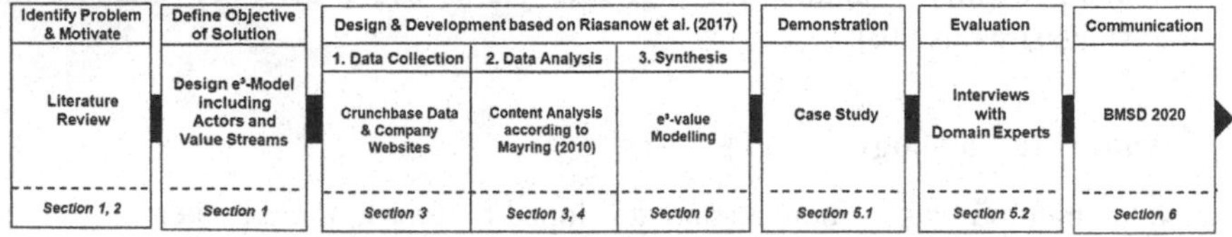

Fig. 2. Research approach based on Peffers et al. [39]

First, we adopted the approach of Riasanow et al. (2017) to identify actors and develop our model [20]. For data collection, we selected Crunchbase database[1]. Crunchbase contains datasets about companies and startups in the high-tech sector [35, 36]. We used the Crunchbase category system and limited the results to actively operating, German companies in the pre-defined categories of *virtual reality, 3D technology, augmented reality, wearables,* and *Google Glass*. A restriction to Germany took place because in Germany, many new AR and VR solutions based on Industry 4.0 initiated by the German Federal Government were developed [11, 37]. Further, it allows verifying the ecosystem model with local, well-known companies. The initial search query provided approximately 325 results. While screening the results, we found many companies with no direct relationship to augmented and virtual reality, for instance by offering smart watches or trackable smart wallets. To increase the focus, we filtered the Crunchbase search engine by the search term "reality" leading to a sample size of 176 companies. The results containing company name, company description, founding year, company size, company website URL and sector were exported to an excel file in December 2019. Then 35 other companies not related to AR and VR were excluded, resulting in a final sample size of 141. To complete the data collection, we supplemented the database with information from the company's websites, which include the products and services offered.

Afterwards, we conducted a qualitative content analysis according to the renowned German sociologist Phillipp Mayring (2010) by scanning the textual descriptions of the companies' profiles [38]. This step aimed to get an overview of the different market actors. To this end, we chose the inductive approach and first extracted the roles [38]. For example, the role *3D Modeler* was originated by the appearance of words like *3D Models, Autodesk, Texturing*. We applied the same approach to the analysis of the value streams by examining product offerings and reports. Two independent raters coded the companies in order to ensure inter-coder-reliability. To conclude the design phase, we adopted the e^3-value methodology according to Gordijn (2002) in order to model the generic value network for the AR and VR business ecosystem using Microsoft Visio [29].

To ensure the applicability of the model, we subsequently performed a demonstration by conducting case study research as proposed by Peffers et al. [39]. The literature recommends concentrating on an extreme and critical case when conducting a single case study. Resulting from this, a highly diversified company was selected from the

[1] Crunchbase is accessible via http://www.crunchbase.com.

sample and classified into the model of the ecosystem. Various data sources consisting of the company's website and whitepapers were used for data collection in accordance to Benbasat et al. [40].

Finally, we evaluated the model by conducting semi-structured interviews according to Gläser and Laudel [41]. To choose the evaluation method, we followed the Design Science Evaluation Framework by Venable et al. [42]. The primary objective of the evaluation was to verify the validity of the model and to identify areas of improvement as suggested by Hevner et al. [22]. We interviewed two entrepreneurs with a professional background in the AR/VR startup community, two AR/VR developers and two management consultants with an academic background in business modelling. Before the interview, each participant was given an introduction to the e^3-value-methodology and the business ecosystem itself. The interviews lasted an average of 37 min. The transcripts of the interviews served as the basis for the qualitative content analysis [38].

4 The Value Network of the AR and VR Business Ecosystem

Based on the research approach described above, we identified a total of 25 roles. In general, a role refers to a range of similar services offered by the market participants to similar customer segments. Since some companies offer services and request services at the same time, they can be found in different types of roles [34]. In the following, we will introduce the actors according to the underlying technologies in terms of AR, VR as well as AR and VR. Table 1 gives an overview of the actors and roles related to both AR and VR.

Table 1. Generic roles related to augmented and virtual reality

Role	Description	Example(s)
Developer for Augmented and Virtual Reality Applications	An AR and VR developer needs to be able to realize projects using Unity, Unreal, and C#. Typical platforms include Microsoft HoloLens and HTC Vive	Viality, SpotAR, Ad4VR, SALT AND PEPPER
Hardware Engineer	Hardware engineers design and develop AR/VR technologies like HMD-devices, tracking systems, and controllers	Nxtbase, Holo-Light
Technology and Process Consulting	Consultants help with the integration of AR/VR technologies into business processes. Essential activities include the elicitation of the actual processes, requirements analysis, and the target design of the technology-induced processes, i.e. to design use cases	Ubimax, Digital Devotion Group, SALT AND PEPPER
Low-code Platform	A low-code platform enables the design of AR and VR applications. The main advantage is that people without IT knowledge can create and adapt applications with the help of a graphical editor [43]	Frontline Creator, REFLEKT, simplifier

(*continued*)

Table 1. (*continued*)

Role	Description	Example(s)
3D Data Visualization	3D data visualization enables real-time data representation of 3D objects. Simple 2D data graphics can be interpreted more easily using a 3D object	Holo-light, Viaity, begehungen.de, Graphtwerk
Hardware Provider	Hardware providers offer AR/VR devices such as smart glasses, head-mounted displays, and sensors to customers	Gestigon, vality, nxtbase, Ubimax
3D Product Presentation Platform	3D product presentation enables three-dimensional visualization of products for business purposes such as online-shops	Vuframe, Visard, room
3D Modeler	3D artists texture and illuminate 3D models of objects (i.e. products). They prepare the resources needed for AR and VR applications using software like Maya, Autodesk, and Blender	Viality, begehungen.de, Metaphysics, Graphtwerk
Rental Service	A rental service provider lends hardware such as head-mounted displays, 360° cameras, and beacons to other companies for a fee. These companies make use of this service especially for trade fairs and events	INVR.Space, Ijsfontein, Design4Real
Community	A community serves the networking of users, developers, and entrepreneurs who deal with AR and VR. Typically, they are networked via an online platform and can exchange information about applications, hardware and trends	Erster Deutscher Fachverband für Virtual Reality, Catchar
3D Scanning	3D scanning companies offer a service to create digital images of real objects. The resulting 3D models can be used, for example, for virtual product presentations or as building blocks for virtual worlds	VIRAO, Pointreef
Consumer	Among other things, the consumer asks for software solutions for business or private use. The consumer is sometimes at the same time a prosumer, because he uses and creates a service	Design4real, INVR.Space
Software Development Kit (SDK)	A software development kit (SDK) is a collection of programming tools and program libraries that are used to develop software. It supports software developers in creating applications	Vision Lib, Photon

(*continued*)

Table 1. (*continued*)

Role	Description	Example(s)
Science and Research	Scientific projects and research companies collaborate with developers and companies in order to derive research findings which help to improve business functions	Erster Deutscher Fachverband für Virtual Reality, VIRAO
3D Marketplace	A marketplace to buy 3D assets. A known marketplace is, for example, the unity asset store	Unity

The results illustrate how closely the AR and VR industries are connected and thus form a single business ecosystem. For example, a variety of services are offered relating to three-dimensional content required for AR and VR applications. These include *3D Modelers, 3D Scanning,* and *3D Marketplaces.* In addition, there are a number of *Communities* that are explicitly dedicated to both technologies in order to promote networking between the individual stakeholders of this business ecosystem. Nevertheless, we identified some actors that can be exclusively assigned to the field of augmented reality, as Table 2 shows.

Table 2. Generic roles and market actors due to augmented reality

Role	Description	Example(s)
AR Application	Augmented reality applications allow additional information to be displayed in the user's field of vision [16]. Typically, wearable devices such as smart glasses and head-mounted displays with semitransparent displays are used in this context [4]	*XPICK by Ubimax, Pulsio FLEX AR by REFLEKT One*
AR Cloud Services	Augmented Reality Cloud Services enable the cloud-based superimposition of additional information into the user's field of vision based on sensor and camera data transmitted in real-time	*Watchar, Visualix*
Remote Customer Support System	A remote customer support system supports the employee by sending his live stream to the back office. The expert in the back office can then provide help and instructions to the working person in the field of vision, for example using markers or textual hints	*Ubimax, REFLEKT, simplifier, nxtbase*

Apart from individual, specific applications, which we have grouped together under the term *AR Application*, the sample particularly includes *Remote Customer Support Systems* from different providers such as *Ubimax* or *Reflekt*. Moreover, some *AR cloud services* such as *Watchar* have already established themselves, which enable cloud-based superimposition of additional information into the user's field of vision. In addition to this, we identified seven roles with a focus on virtual reality. Table 3 gives an overview of the roles, descriptions, and examples.

Table 3. Generic roles and market actors due to virtual reality

Role	Description	Example(s)
VR Collaboration Platform	A VR collaboration platform enables shared viewing, interaction, and communication in a virtual space. 3D prototype evaluations, building planning, training, or market research can be carried out in the virtual world	Stage (vr-on), we are, VIREED, room, VIRAO
VR Gaming	VR gaming services deals with the conception and development of virtual reality games. In addition, some of these companies distribute the games themselves	Playsnak, Ijsfontein, Massive Miniteams
Co-Location VR System	A co-location VR system allows users in the same physical room to visit a virtual room together. In contrast to shared online experiences, all users see a superimposition of the virtual world that is aligned with the physical reality	HoloDeckVR
VR Application	Virtual reality applications make it possible to work in three-dimensional, virtual spaces [8]. The user interacts with the virtual world. Typically, virtual reality headsets are used for such applications, which allow the user to immerse themselves into the virtual world	Boxplan by SALT AND PEPPER, VIREED MED
VR Streaming Platform	VR streaming platforms enable VR and 360° streaming experiences. Use is subject to payment of a fee	VR Delight

(continued)

Table 3. (*continued*)

Role	Description	Example(s)
VR Event Agency	VR Event Agencies are specialized in the planning, coordination, and execution of events using Virtual Reality. Well-known application examples include exhibitions, trade fairs, and corporate events	A4VR
VR Photo and Video Production	VR photo and video production service companies are specialized in the capture and processing of photo and video materials in VR. Many companies focus on 360° recording, i.e. in the housing sector	Design4real, INVRSpace

The findings reveal the emergence of a number of services in the field of virtual reality that serve entertainment purposes (e.g. *VR Gaming*, *VR Streaming Platform*). It is also noticeable that some *VR Event Agencies* have already specialized providing VR hardware and the corresponding infrastructure for companies at mass events.

5 Generic Value Model of the AR and VR Business Ecosystem

Based on the analysis, we present a coherent generic model for the AR and VR business ecosystem. Using the e^3-value approach, our model visualizes the identified roles and the value exchanges that occur between them as displayed in Fig. 3 [29].

To improve clarity and to underline the contribution of the roles to the value network, we make a fundamental distinction between the clusters *enabling service providers*, *software solution providers*, *hardware-related service providers*, *support service providers*, and *special service providers*.

Hence, the roles shown in the previous section have been assigned to these clusters. Enabling service providers is a cluster of actors that provide value objects e.g. a Software Development Kit (SDK) or 3D models that software solution providers need to implement their software. Developers or 3D modelers use these enabling services to create added value with their skills, which is then sold to the customer as an app or software. Therefore, software solution providers is a cluster that includes actors or entities that are elemental in the AR and VR industry. The hardware-related service providers cluster consists of actors whose main initial value is generated by the rental and sale of hardware. Besides, it refers to the design of new hardware. Since AR and VR technologies are elusive and have to be explained to the mass market, support service providers such as science and research or community assemblies improve the perception and understanding of the technology in society. In particular, advantages and use cases must be communicated at corporates [2].

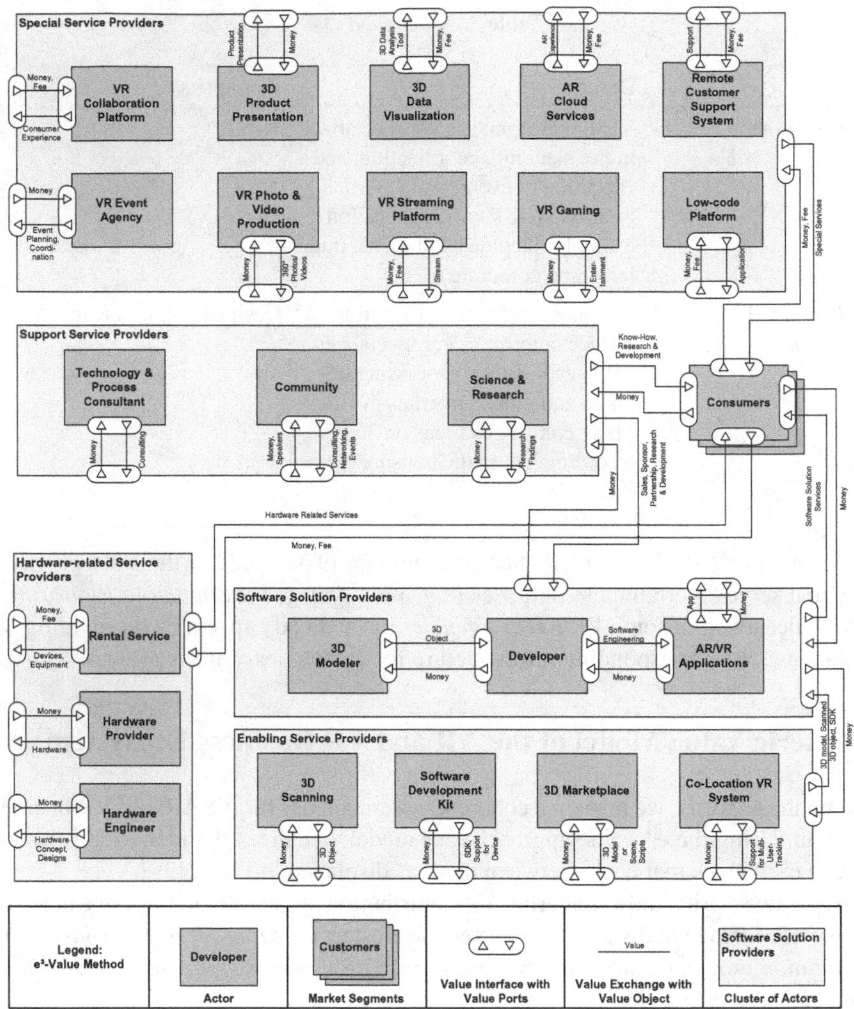

Fig. 3. Generic e^3-value model of the AR and VR business ecosystem

5.1 Demonstration

In order to illustrate the applicability of the model, we first present an example company that specializes in the development and distribution of wearable AR solutions. The developed ecosystem model is then used to name the actors and roles of the company and the associated value streams.

Ubimax GmbH is a German IT company headquartered in Bremen, Germany [44]. The company was founded in 2011 following an expired research project. According to the company, Ubimax is the European market leader in wearable computing for industrial companies in 2019. The main business areas of Ubimax GmbH include the development and sale of software and hardware for smart glasses in industrial companies. The company also offers consulting services and remote service support systems. Additionally, it cooperates with the scientific community in terms of university collaborations. Given this background, the visualization of the company's assignment in the model is shown in Fig. 4.

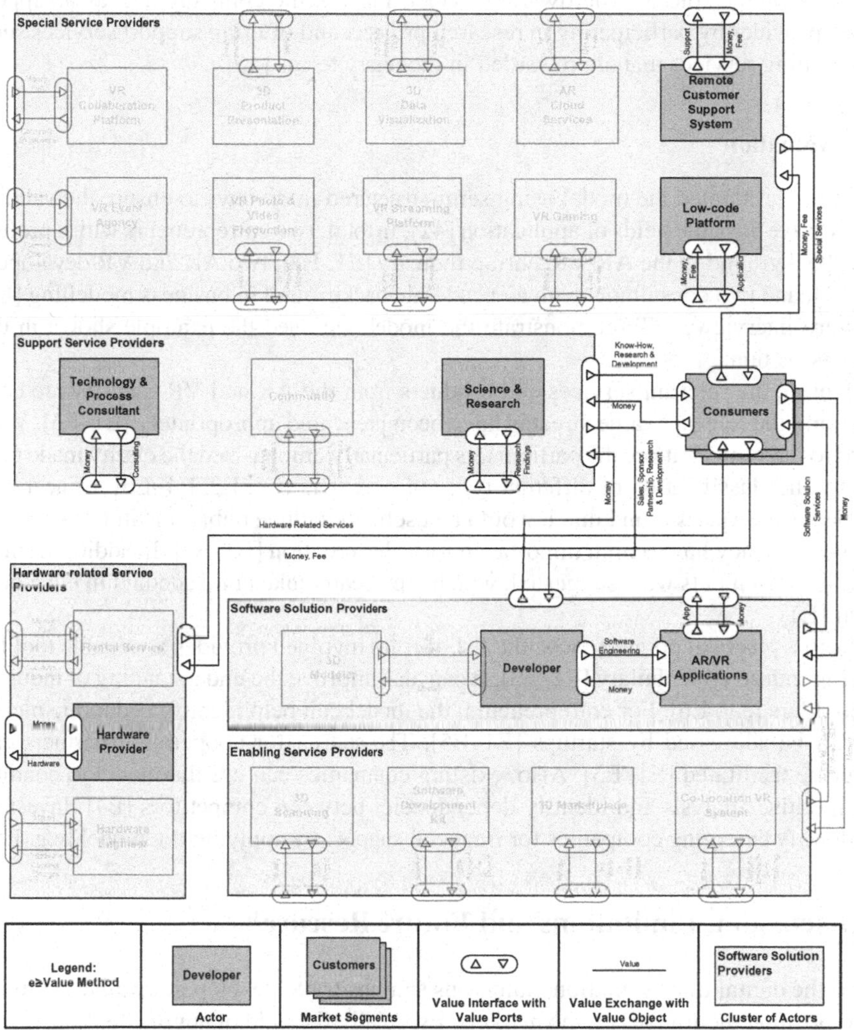

Fig. 4. Application example

Since Ubimax develops and sells its own AR applications for smart glasses and AR Glasses (i.e. XPICK), it is part of the group of software solution providers. Revenues in the form of money are generated by the customers using these software services. The company employs its own developers, who participate in the software engineering processes and are compensated with part of the revenue generated. Ubimax also belongs to the special service providers, as the company offers low-code platforms and remote customer support systems. The latter can be utilized by the customers against payment of a fee. Similarly, Ubimax customers can use the low-code platform to create their AR applications. The payment of a fee is also a requirement for this. As Ubimax also offers hardware such as AR glasses and smart glasses and charges a price for it, the company also takes on the role of a hardware provider. Finally, the company acts as a support service provider by participating in research projects and offering support services such as consulting services that are rewarded in monetary terms [45].

5.2 Evaluation

Finally, we evaluated the model using semi-structured interviews to ensure the validity and to derive possible fields of application [42]. In total, two entrepreneurs with a professional background in the AR/VR startup industry [E1, E2], two AR and VR developers [E3, E4], and two consultants with an academic background in business modelling [E5, E6] were interviewed. To demonstrate the model, we used the example shown in the previous section.

Overall, the relevant services and products from the AR and VR industry are contained and the relevant value streams have been presented appropriately [E1–E5]. With regard to the visualization, the participants particularly emphasized the clarity made possible by the classification of different types of providers [E1, E2, E4–E6]. Concerning the roles, two experts found that it would be useful to include public institutions such as museums, as they have a high importance for value creation [E2, E5]. In addition, small visual improvements were suggested, which are already taken into account in the model shown [E1].

From a practical point of view, the list of roles involved provides a valuable tool for unifying industry vocabulary [E2, E3]. It can also improve the understanding of industry stakeholders [e.g. E6]. For entrepreneurs, the model can help identify economic niches that can be addressed by startups [E1–E5]. The search for cooperation partners can further be facilitated [E1, E3]. Also, existing companies can use the model to conduct a competitive analysis and identify dependencies between competitors [E4]. Investors can identify emerging companies for financial support by applying the model [e.g. E5].

6 Discussion, Limitations and Future Research

Due to the digital transformation, numerous startups try to develop innovative solutions and to position themselves on the markets. Especially the field of augmented and virtual reality has been described as a fast-growing industry. Drawing on the e^3-value approach, this article illustrates the business ecosystem for the AR and VR industry based on 25 generic roles, of which seven are related to virtual reality, three to augmented reality, and 15 to both technologies.

Even though the use of AR and VR in business practice is still at an early stage [2], a technology-specific ecosystem of its own has already been established. The results show that it is not only software developers, vendors, and customers who operate in the market. In the meantime, a number of enabling services have been established that deal, for example, with the provision of technology-specific support tools (e.g. SDKs).

In addition, there are individual, specialized services that are accessible to the mass market. These include, for example, VR gaming applications or 3D product presentations. The quantitative assessment of the individual actors indicates that so far more services involving a link to virtual reality have been offered than those involving augmented reality. This is probably a result of the higher level of technological maturity [2]. As shown by the evaluation, the value model evolved is valid, comprehensive and useful. The presented results have both practical and academic implications.

From a practical point of view, already established startups can profit from our work by partnering with experienced organizations to minimize the complexity of this business ecosystem and to profit from synergies between companies. New startups planning to provide solutions for the AR/VR industry can benefit from our work by identifying potential economic niches. Moreover, potential investors may use our model in order to find startups that they can support by evaluating the allocation of costs, benefits, and risks across the actors in the ecosystem [20]. In view of the increasing importance of digital platforms [21], this article also provides a first insight into which services from the field of AR and VR may be provided on these platforms in the future.

Theoretically, this contribution is a first step towards closing the research gap of organizational effects of augmented and virtual reality, since previous studies in this area have been mainly of a technical nature. Through the systematic identification of the relevant actors, their relationship, and visualization using the e^3-value method, a holistic, theoretical model of this business ecosystem, driven in particular by the hardware innovations brought to the market since 2013, was presented. Future investigations can use our model to classify services and DSR artefacts terminologically. Besides, we aim to deliver a common understanding of the industry itself across different disciplines.

As every qualitative approach, our work has several limitations that need to be mentioned and offer starting points for future research. First, we had to rely on publicly accessible data by using Crunchbase. Thus, not all existing companies were included in the sample. Besides, Crunchbase does not include important value streams like patents or non-disclosure agreements. Future research might focus on the analysis of patents to uncover further value streams. Second, when coding the actors and roles, sometimes different types of AR and VR applications were grouped into generic terms. Further investigations could address this lack of granularity by developing taxonomies to classify different AR and VR applications. Moreover, since AR and VR often integrate other technologies such as artificial intelligence in their applications [2], an investigation of the impact on other technology-specific ecosystems as well as their relations should be considered for future research. Third, we limited our analysis solely to German companies. It should be noted that country-specific ecosystems can be very diverse. By comparing different country-specific ecosystems (e.g. Germany and China), important insights can be gained into how technology adoption differs and how markets are influenced by politically motivated economic strategies (e.g. High-Tech Strategy and Made in China 2025). Therefore, we would like to encourage other researchers to examine startups in their country. Fourth, the evaluation results may have been influenced by subjective impressions due to the small sample size and the coding process. Hence, we therefore propose to evaluate our model with a larger sample in order to perform a more detailed evaluation with several different perspectives. Finally, it should be noted that the

AR/VR market is characterized by dynamic developments, which may require a further adjustment of our model in the medium term.

Acknowledgement. The authors would like to thank the reviewers for their constructive feedback. This research is funded by the "Graduiertenkolleg va-eva: Vertrauen und Akzeptanz in erweiterten und virtuellen Arbeitswelten" at the University of Osnabrück (https://www.vaeva.uni-osnabrueck.de).

References

1. Chesbrough, H.: Business model innovation: opportunities and barriers. Long Range Plann. **43**, 354–363 (2010)
2. Bezegová, E., Ledgard, A., Molemaker, R.-J., Oberč, B.P., Vigkos, A.: Virtual Reality and its Potential for Europe. Ecorys, London (2018)
3. Liu, S.: Forecast augmented (AR) and virtual reality (VR) market size worldwide from 2016 to 2023 (in billion U.S. dollars). https://www.statista.com/statistics/591181/global-augmented-virtual-reality-market-size/. Accessed 20 Feb 2020
4. Milgram, P., Takemura, H., Utsumi, A., Kishino, F.: Mixed Reality (MR) Reality-Virtuality (RV) Continuum. In: SPIE, vol. 2351, pp. 282–292 (1994). Telemanipulator Telepresence Technol.
5. Martín-Gutiérrez, J., Mora, C.E., Añorbe-Díaz, B., González-Marrero, A.: Virtual technologies trends in education. EURASIA J. Math. Sci. Technol. Educ. **13**, 469–486 (2017)
6. Rauschnabel, P.A., Ro, Y.K.: Augmented reality smart glasses: an investigation of technology acceptance drivers. Int. J. Technol. Mark. **11**, 123–148 (2016)
7. Niemöller, C., Metzger, D., Thomas, O.: Design and evaluation of a smart-glasses-based service support system. In: Proceedings of the 13th Internationale Tagung Wirtschaftsinformatik, pp. 106–120 (2017)
8. Metzger, D., Niemöller, C., Wingert, B., Schultze, T., Bues, M., Thomas, O.: How machines are serviced – design of a virtual reality-based training system for technical customer services. In: Proceedings of the 13th Internationale Tagung Wirtschaftsinformatik, pp. 604–618 (2017)
9. Moore, J.F.: Predators and prey: a new ecology of competition. Harv. Bus. Rev. **71**, 75–86 (1993)
10. Riasanow, T., Jäntgen, L., Hermes, S., Böhm, M., Krcmar, H.: Core, intertwined, and ecosystem-specific clusters in platform ecosystems: analyzing similarities in the digital transformation of the automotive, blockchain, financial, insurance and IIoT industry. Electron. Mark. (2020). https://doi.org/10.1007/s12525-020-00407-6
11. Bundesregierung, D.: Hightech-Strategie 2025. https://www.hightech-strategie.de/de/hightech-strategie-2025-1726.html. Accessed 20 Feb 2020
12. Mühlhans, T.: Virtual Reality/Augmented Reality - Bestandsaufnahme und Best Practices (2018)
13. Capgemini Research Institute: Augmented and Virtual Reality in Operations (2018)
14. European Comission: Augmented and Virtual Reality. https://ec.europa.eu/growth/tools-databases/dem/monitor/sites/default/files/DTM_AR_VR-vf.pdf. Accessed 20 Feb 2020
15. Walsh, K.R., Pawlowski, S.D.: Virtual reality: a technology in need of is research. Commun. Assoc. Inf. Syst. **8**, 297–313 (2002)
16. Harborth, D.: Augmented reality in information systems research: a systematic literature review. In: Twenty-Third Americas Conference on Information Systems, Boston, pp. 1–10 (2017)

17. Jimenez, R.J.P., Becerril, E.M., Nor, R.M., Smagas, K., Valari, E., Stylianidis, E.: Market potential for a location based and augmented reality system for utilities management. In: 2016 22nd International Conference on Virtual System & Multimedia (VSMM), pp. 1–4 (2016)
18. Mütterlein, J., Hess, T.: Exploring the impacts of virtual reality on business models: the case of the media industry. In: ECIS Proceedings 2017, pp. 3213–3222 (2017)
19. Cranmer, E., Jung, T.: Augmented reality (AR): business models in urban cultural heritage tourist destinations. In: 12th APacCHRIE Conference (2014)
20. Riasanow, T., Galic, G., Böhm, M.: Digital transformation in the automotive industry: towards a generic value network. In: 2017 Proceedings of 25th European Conference on Information and Systems, ECIS 2017, pp. 3191–3201 (2017)
21. Gordijn, J., Akkermans, J.M.: Value-based requirements engineering: exploring innovative e-commerce ideas. Requir. Eng. **8**, 114–134 (2003). https://doi.org/10.1007/s00766-003-0169-x
22. Hevner, A.R., March, S.T., Park, J., Ram, S.: Design science in information systems research. MIS Q. **28**, 75–105 (2004)
23. March, S.T., Smith, G.F.: Design and natural science research on information technology. Decis. Support Syst. **15**, 251–266 (1995)
24. vom Brocke, J., Simons, A., Niehaves, B., Riemer, K., Plattfaut, R., Cleven, A.: Reconstructing the giant: on the importance of rigour in documenting the literature search process. In: 17th European Conference on Information and Systems, ECIS 2009 (2009)
25. Chesbrough, H., Rosenbloom, R.S.: The role of the business model in capturing value from innovation: evidence from Xerox Corporation's technology spin-off companies. Ind. Corp. Chang. **11**, 529–555 (2002)
26. Tian, C.H., Ray, B.K., Lee, J., Cao, R., Ding, W.: BEAM: a framework for business ecosystem analysis and modeling. IBM Syst. J. **47**, 101–114 (2008)
27. Ignat, V.: Digitalization and the global technology trends. In: IOP Conference Series: Materials Science and Engineering, vol. 227 (2017)
28. Ibarra, D., Ganzarain, J., Igartua, J.I.: Business model innovation through Industry 4.0: a review. Procedia Manuf. **22**, 4–10 (2018)
29. Gordijn, J., Akkermans, H.: Designing and evaluating e-business models. IEEE Intell. Syst. **16**, 11–17 (2001)
30. Veit, D., Clemons, E., Benlian, A., Buxmann, P., Hess, T., Kundisch, D., Leimeister, J.M., Loos, P., Spann, M.: Business models: an information systems research agenda. Bus. Inf. Syst. Eng. **6**, 45–53 (2014)
31. van den Hoven, J.: ICT and value sensitive design. In: Goujon, P., Lavelle, S., Duquenoy, P., Kimppa, K., Laurent, V. (eds.) The Information Society: Innovation, Legitimacy, Ethics and Democracy In honor of Professor Jacques Berleur s.j. IIFIP, vol. 233, pp. 67–72. Springer, Boston (2007). https://doi.org/10.1007/978-0-387-72381-5_8
32. Böhm, M., Koleva, G., Leimeister, S., Riedl, C., Krcmar, H.: Towards a generic value network for cloud computing. In: Altmann, J., Rana, Omer F. (eds.) GECON 2010. LNCS, vol. 6296, pp. 129–140. Springer, Heidelberg (2010). https://doi.org/10.1007/978-3-642-15681-6_10
33. Riasanow, T., Flötgen, R.J., Setzke, D.S., Böhm, M., Krcmar, H.: The generic ecosystem and innovation patterns of the digital transformation in the financial industry. In: PACIS (2018)
34. Greineder, M., Riasanow, T., Böhm, M., Krcmar, H.: The generic InsurTech ecosystem and its strategic implications for the digital transformation of insurance industry. In: 40th GI EMISA (2019)
35. Perotti, V., Yu, Y.: Startup Tribes: Social Network Ties that Support Success in New Firms (2015)
36. Marra, A., Antonelli, P., Dell'Anna, L., Pozzi, C.: A network analysis using metadata to investigate innovation in clean-tech - implications for energy policy. Energy Policy **86**, 17–26 (2015)

37. KPMG: Neue Dimensionen der Realität - The New Media Consortium (2016)
38. Mayring, P.: Qualitative Inhaltsanalyse. In: Handbuch qualitative Forschung in der Psychologie, pp. 601–613. Springer (2010)
39. Peffers, K., Tuunanen, T., Rothenberger, M.A., Chatterjee, S.: A design science research methodology for information systems research. J. Manag. Inf. Syst. **24**, 45–77 (2007)
40. Benbasat, I., Goldstein, D.K., Mead, M.: The case research strategy in studies of information systems. MIS Q. Manag. Inf. Syst. **11**, 369–386 (1987)
41. Gläser, J., Laudel, G.: Experteninterviews und qualitative Inhaltsanalyse. Verlag für Sozialwissenschaften, Wiesbaden (2010)
42. Venable, J., Pries-Heje, J., Baskerville, R.: A comprehensive framework for evaluation in design science research. In: Peffers, K., Rothenberger, M., Kuechler, B. (eds.) DESRIST 2012. LNCS, vol. 7286, pp. 423–438. Springer, Heidelberg (2012). https://doi.org/10.1007/978-3-642-29863-9_31
43. Richardson, C., Rymer, J.R.: New Development Platforms Emerge For Customer-Facing Applications (2014)
44. Crunchbase: Ubimax on Crunchbase https://www.crunchbase.com/organization/ubimax-gmbh#section-overview. Accessed 08 May 2020
45. Ubimax: Ubimax. https://www.ubimax.com/de/unternehmen/#about. Accessed 08 May 2020

Short Papers

Business Model Dependencies: Towards Conceptualizing Dependencies for Extending Modeling Languages for Business Models

Christian Vorbohle(✉), Daniel Szopinski, and Dennis Kundisch

Paderborn University, Paderborn, Germany
{christian.vorbohle,daniel.szopinski, dennis.kundisch}@wiwi.uni-paderborn.de

Abstract. Digital innovation continues to give technical and economic dependencies within and between business models an increasingly important role. Despite the steadily growing interest in business models in various disciplines such as software design, amongst others, there is no common understanding about the constituent parts of business model dependencies that define the relationships within and between business models of different market participants. On the basis of a literature analysis across more than 250 articles from business model research, we comprehensively review the understanding of business model dependencies. Thereby, we identify dependencies that are specific to business models. In doing so, this study pursues two objects: First, to explicate tacit knowledge about dependencies in business model research. Second, to review this knowledge to conceptualize business model dependencies. This study proposes five distinct types of business model dependencies and thereby lays the ground for conceptualizing business model dependencies. In this way, this study contributes to information systems research and software design by providing the basis for extending modeling languages for business models by introducing business model dependencies.

Keywords: Business models · Business model innovation · Business model dependencies · Business modeling languages

1 Introduction

Business models describe the mechanisms of how organizations create, deliver and capture value for their customers [1] and innovating business models is of paramount importance for the competitiveness of organizations of all sizes and industries [2]. The interplay of business models and technology is crucial as "a mediocre technology pursued within a great business model may be more valuable than a great technology exploited via a mediocre business model" [3, p. 354]. Put differently, in the words of Teece, "technological innovation does not guarantee business success [and] should be coupled with a business model" [4, p. 83]. The nexus between technology and business models is an illustrative example of dependencies within and between business models. A frequently tried and tested way to explicate dependencies are modeling languages.

B. Shishkov (Ed.): BMSD 2020, LNBIP 391, pp. 259–265, 2020.
https://doi.org/10.1007/978-3-030-52306-0_16

There are many different modeling languages for making business models concrete and tangible [5]. To the best of our knowledge, dependencies are not explicitly provided in these modeling languages for business models. Consequently, before extending business model modeling languages, it is essential to understand BMDs.

Considering such dependencies is new in the context of business models. The importance of dependencies has already been demonstrated in other contexts such as business process models (e.g., [6, 7]), IT project portfolio management (e.g., [8]) and enterprise architecture management (e.g., [9]). Other than in these contexts, there is no common understanding of the constituent parts of business model dependencies (BMDs). Conceptualizing BMDs is vital because technology-driven innovation possesses some highly distinctive characteristics that have important practical and theoretical implications [10]. We illustrate three characteristics and their consequences for BMDs:

1. Digitalization extensively changes existing BMDs and creates new ones because physical or analog business model elements are transformed into digital ones.
2. Moore's law rapidly increases the speed in which BMDs change because the range of what is technically and economically feasible advances business model elements.
3. Network effects alter the significance of BMDs because some business model elements become more valuable to adopters as the size of the adopter network grows whereby such platform-based business models require aligning platform owners, content producers and content consumers.

2 Method

To provide an overview of how business model research considers dependencies, we comprehensively reviewed this stream of literature. Therefore, we employed a three-step keyword search to identify relevant articles: (1) We developed the following search string: *"business model*" AND (relation* OR link* OR connection* OR *dependence*)*, (2) we selected relevant journals (see Appendix), (3) we searched in titles, abstracts and keywords.

As a result, we obtained an initial result set of 252 articles. We required articles to fulfil two criteria: The article deals with (A) the concept of business models and (B) the concept of dependencies. Therefore, the first and second authors independently read the title, abstract, and figures of each article as well as searched for keywords (e.g., business model, relation, link, connection, dependency). Based on this reading, each of the first and second authors identified relevant articles that deal with business models and dependencies. We validated the coding of the articles by calculating the interrater reliability (88%). In the few cases of disagreement, the co-authors discussed their opinions to come to a joint verdict about inclusion or exclusion of an article. As a result, we identified 219 articles that do no deal with business models and/or dependencies and deem 33 articles as being relevant to conceptualize BMDs.

3 Findings

We found that there is research on BMDs, but this research refrains from considering dependencies as a distinct sub-concept within the concept of business models (i.e., it conceptualizes BMDs). Towards conceptualizing BMDs, our literature review reveals that business model research considers dependencies from two different angles: The level of integration of BMDs and the location of the causation of BMDs. The level of integration revolves around three major types of BMDs, namely Intra- (6 articles), Inter- (13 articles) and Extra-BMDs (14 articles). Inter- and Extra-BMDs can be further differentiated with regard to the location of causation, namely endogenously-induced and exogenously-induced dependencies. On the basis of the level of integration and the location of causation, we propose five distinct types of BMDs. We consider these types to be atomic (i.e., they cannot be further divided). These atomic BMDs can be combined with each other to form complex BMDs that are made up of several atomic BMDs (Fig. 1).

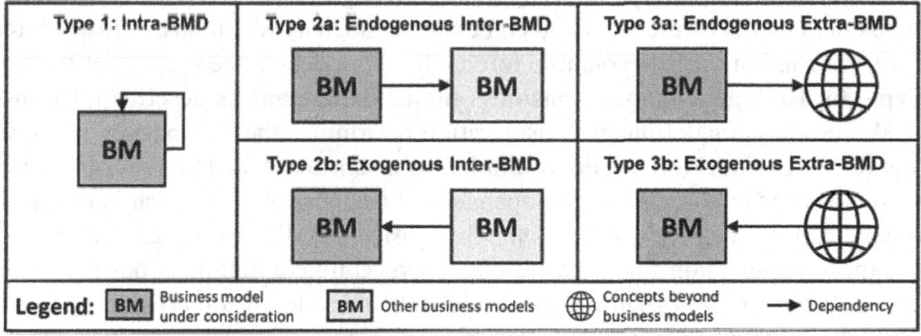

Fig. 1. Five distinct types of business model dependencies (BMDs)

In the following, we describe the five atomic types of BMDs and illustrate each of them by an example taken from the literature analysis.

Type 1: Intra-business model dependencies describe relations within a business model. This means that a business model element depends on another business model element within the same business model. For example, Cosenz and Noto [11] describe Intra-BMDs in the context of business venture strategies. A firm's business model considers BMDs with regard to a business model's profitability that depends on key partners. The difference between revenue and costs affects the ability of a firm to acquire new key partners for implementing its business model (e.g., investors to increase equity funding or suppliers to improve purchasing conditions).

Type 2: Inter-business model dependencies describe relations between two or more business models. This means that a business model element depends on an element from another business model.

Type 2a: Endogenous inter-business model dependencies describe relations in which the business model under consideration determines the dependency on another business model. For example, Leiponen and Delcamp [12] describe endogenous inter-BMDs in the context of patent licensing in business models. A license firm's business model considers BMDs with regard to the business model of other license firms. Unlike an independently licensing firm, the business model of an affiliation-based licensing firm affects the business model of other licensing firms, depending on how much value the firm creates solely on its business model and how much value the firm creates jointly with affiliated licensing firms.

Type 2b: Exogenous inter-business model dependencies describe relations in which another business model determines the dependency of the business model under consideration. For instance, Dawar and Stornelli [13] describe exogenous inter-BMDs focusing on the relationship between manufacturers and retailers. A manufacturer's business model considers BMDs with regard to a retailer who distributes a manufacturer's products or services. The business model of the manufacturer, therefore, depends on the business model of the retailer. This is because the way the retailer creates value for its customers affects the manufacturer's business model as the manufacturer provides products and services required for the retailers' business model.

Type 3: Extra-business model dependencies describe relations between a business model and other concepts beyond business models (e.g., trends and forces). This means that a business model element depends on elements such as key trends, industry forces, market forces and/or macro-economic forces (for more details see [1, p. 200f.]).

Type 3a: Endogenous extra-business model dependencies describe relations in which the business model under consideration determines the dependency to another concept (e.g., trends and forces). For example, Kortmann and Piller [14] describe endogenous extra-BMDs with regard to the openness of business models towards integrating customers. A manufacturer's business model considers BMDs with regard to the openness of the value creation for and with customers. Unlike a non-open business model of a manufacturer (who produces goods and sells them to customers), an open business model of a manufacturer (who collaborates with customers when producing goods) affects elements such as industry forces (e.g., when customers produce the goods and the manufacturer becomes the platform operator) and societal and cultural trends (e.g., when customers identify with a firm and its business model).

Type 3b: Exogenous extra-business model dependencies describe relations in which another concept (e.g., trends and forces) determines the dependency on the business model under consideration. For example, Hannon et al. [15] describe exogenous extra-BMDs reflecting the technological progress. A manufacturer's business model considers BMDs with regard to new or advanced technologies available to develop products or services. The business model of the manufacturer is therefore exogenously dependent on technology trends.

4 Outlook

This study is part of a larger research program that aims to conceptualize BMDs. For explicating tacit knowledge about BMDs, we first comprehensively reviewed how business model research currently understands BMDs. Based on this literature analysis, we contribute to business modeling and software design in two respects: First, we lay the ground for extending and refining business model modeling languages to include dependencies within and between business models for reflecting the dynamic and interactive nature of business model innovation in these modeling languages [16]. Second, we provide an initial set of semantic components to visualize BMDs and thereby advance existing visual approaches to business IT alignment which integrate business models into enterprise architectures [17, 18].

In further studies, we will leverage the valuable body of knowledge on dependencies in modeling languages in other contexts (e.g., dependencies in process modeling languages such as BPMN or software modeling languages such as UML). First and foremost, we will triangulate our initial findings by integrating them into a taxonomy design project to foster conceptualizing BMDs both, conceptually and empirically. In this way, we seek to broaden and deepen the scope of this ongoing research. By consolidating the findings on dependencies that are specific to business models, this study lays the ground for purposefully extending business model modeling languages such as the Business Model Canvas [1]. The five distinct types of BMDs have the potential to inform the semantic, syntax and pragmatics of future extensions of the modeling languages for business models [5].

Acknowledgments. This work was partially supported by the German Research Foundation (DFG) within the Collaborative Research Center "On-The-Fly Computing" (CRC 901, project number 160364472SFB901).

Appendix

To conceptualize business model dependencies based on business model research, we searched in the same journals that have already been used in the well-received article by Massa et al. (2017) to conceptualize the business model concept. In addition, we also searched in two further relevant journals (see Table 1).

Table 1. Article selection criteria applied to the initial search output.

Journal	Rationale for selecting journal
Academy of Management Journal	Massa et al. (2017)
Academy of Management Review	Massa et al. (2017)
Administrative Science Quarterly	Massa et al. (2017)
Journal of Management	Massa et al. (2017)
Journal of Management Studies	Massa et al. (2017)
Management Science	Massa et al. (2017)
MIS Quarterly	Massa et al. (2017)
Organization Science	Massa et al. (2017)
Strategic Entrepreneurship Journal	Massa et al. (2017)
Strategic Management Journal	Massa et al. (2017)
Industrial and Corporate Change	Massa et al. (2017)

(continued)

Table 1. *(continued)*

Journal	Rationale for selecting journal
Research Policy	Massa et al. (2017)
Long Range Planning	Massa et al. (2017)
Technovation	Massa et al. (2017)
Journal of Business Ethics	Massa et al. (2017)
Journal of Cleaner Production	Massa et al. (2017)
Business and Society	Massa et al. (2017)
Energy Policy	Massa et al. (2017)
California Management Review	Massa et al. (2017)
Harvard Business Review	Massa et al. (2017)
MIT Sloan Management Review	Massa et al. (2017)
Academy of Management Annals	Massa et al. (2017) was published in this journal
Journal of Business Models	This journal is devoted to establishing the discipline of business models as a separately recognized core discipline in academia

References

1. Osterwalder, A., Pigneur, Y.: Business Model Generation. A Handbook for Visionaries, Game Changers, and Challengers. Wiley, Hoboken (2010)
2. Massa, L., Tucci, C.L., Afuah, A.: A critical assessment of business model research. Acad. Manage. Ann. **11**, 73–104 (2017)
3. Chesbrough, H.: Business model innovation: Opportunities and barriers. Long Range Plann. **43**, 354–363 (2010)
4. Teece, D.J.: Business models, business strategy and innovation. Long Range Plann. **43**, 172–194 (2010)
5. John, T., Kundisch, D., Szopinski, D.: Visual languages for modeling business models: a critical review and future re-search directions. In: Proceedings of the 38th International Conference on Information Systems (ICIS), Seoul, Korea (2017)
6. Meyer, A., Pufahl, L., Fahland, D., Weske, M.: Modeling and enacting complex data dependencies in business processes. In: Daniel, F., Wang, J., Weber, B. (eds.) BPM 2013. LNCS, vol. 8094, pp. 171–186. Springer, Heidelberg (2013). https://doi.org/10.1007/978-3-642-40176-3_14
7. Wetzstein, B., Leitner, P., Rosenberg, F., Dustdar, S., Leymann, F.: Identifying influential factors of business process performance using dependency analysis. Enterp. Inf. Syst. **5**, 79–98 (2011)
8. Meier, C., Kundisch, D., Willeke, J.: Is it worth the effort? Bus. Inf. Syst. Eng. **59**, 81–95 (2017)
9. Winter, R., Fischer, R.: Essential layers, artifacts, and dependencies of enterprise architecture. In: 10th IEEE International Enterprise Distributed Object Computing Conference Workshops (EDOCW), Hong Kong, China (2006)
10. Fichman, R.G., Dos Santos, B.L., Zheng, Z.: Digital innovation as a fundamental and powerful concept in the information systems curriculum. MIS Q. **38**, 329–343 (2014)

11. Cosenz, F., Noto, G.: A dynamic business modelling approach to design and experiment new business venture strategies. Long Range Plann. **51**, 127–140 (2018)
12. Leiponen, A., Delcamp, H.: The anatomy of a troll? patent licensing business models in the light of patent reassignment data. Res. Policy **48**, 298–311 (2019)
13. Dawar, N., Stornelli, J.: Rebuilding the relationship between manufacturers and retailers. MIT Sloan Manage. Rev. **54**(2), 83–90 (2013)
14. Kortmann, S., Piller, F.: Open business models and closed-loop value chains: redefining the firm-consumer relationship. Calif. Manage. Rev. **58**, 88–108 (2016)
15. Hannon, M.J., Foxon, T.J., Gale, W.F.: The co-evolutionary relationship between Energy Service Companies and the UK energy system: implications for a low-carbon transition. Energy Policy **61**, 1031–1045 (2013)
16. Pigneur, Y., Fritscher, B.: Extending the business model canvas a dynamic perspective. In: Proceedings of the Fifth International Symposium on Business Modeling and Software Design, pp. 86–95. SCITEPRESS - Science and Technology Publications (2015)
17. Fritscher, B., Pigneur, Y.: A visual approach to business it alignment between business model and enterprise architecture. Int. J. Inf. Syst. Model. Des. **6**, 1–23 (2015)
18. Fritscher, B., Pigneur, Y.: Business IT alignment from business model to enterprise architecture. In: Salinesi, C., Pastor, O. (eds.) CAiSE 2011. LNBIP, vol. 83, pp. 4–15. Springer, Heidelberg (2011). https://doi.org/10.1007/978-3-642-22056-2_2

Concepts for Comparison in Models to Support Decision Making

Ella Roubtsova(✉) and Rachelle Bosua

Open University, Valkenburgerweg 177, 6419 AT Heerlen, The Netherlands
{ella.roubtsova,rachelle.bosua}@ou.nl

Abstract. The cognitive basis of any decision making process is a comparison. This paper presents evidence from two distinct cases showing that decision making is facilitated by selecting specific sets of business concepts for comparison. The first case illustrates modelling of a new business process that does not exist yet. In this case, the concept for comparison is found outside the modelled business system. The second case presents an improvement of an existing business process, where the concepts for comparison are found inside the model of the existing system and compared with the concepts used in the model of the modified system. These cases identify two ways of selecting concepts for comparison that help to make the key decision to implement or not implement a proposed system model.

Keywords: Purpose of modelling · Conceptual model · Enterprise model · Concepts for comparison · Decisions on models

1 Introduction

Businesses need to constantly propose changes to their business processes or system structures to gain competitive advantage in a rapidly changing business market. Business management roles often have to make key decisions related to whether a proposed change is worthwhile to implement. The cognitive basis of any decision is a comparison, providing there is adequate information to make an informed decision. However, the cognitive restriction of the human decision making process is that a human being "can differentiate among only a small number of objects" and has "difficulty dealing with more than three or four relationships concurrently" [9].

We observe that modelling techniques are beginning to consider the comparison of concepts as an important cognitive basis for decision making. For example, building the as-is and to-be models is normally carried out using Enterprise modelling [12]. There is always a goal of changes to direct what concepts to include into the to-be model. Some authors [5] propose to see any model change as a trigger for model evaluation and simulation. Another suggestion is to extract a gap-of-changes view from the as-is and to-be Enterprise architectures [2,4] and present this to decision makers for comparison with respect to the goal of

B. Shishkov (Ed.): BMSD 2020, LNBIP 391, pp. 266–275, 2020.
https://doi.org/10.1007/978-3-030-52306-0_17

changes. However, there is no support for decision making through comparison in the case where a completely new business process or system structure is proposed. As the decision about implementation of changes is based on model analysis and evaluation with respect to the goal of changes, the research question of this paper is the following:

What is an indication that a model of changes is complete to decide that it enables the achievement of a given goal of changes?

In this paper we present two cases that cover two variants of answers to our research question observed by the authors in practice. The structure of the paper is the following. Section 2 positions our research within existing modeling and decision-making research domains. Section 3 presents a change associated with the design of a new business process and the corresponding conceptual model. Section 4 presents a change of an existing business process. Section 5 discusses the answers to the research question. Section 6 concludes the paper and presents some ideas for future work.

2 Positioning Within Related Work

The usefulness of concepts in a model for decision making can be positioned in the context of model quality. The quality of models is a constant topic of discourse in a number of different modelling communities as outlined in the next subsections.

In the data modelling community, there are clear arguments [11] for separating the mechanical view on model quality from the fitness of a model for a purpose: "Assessing the quality of anything, models included, has two parts. One comes from measuring the right things, in the right way, with the right yardsticks. But the heart of quality comes from the second aspect; judging something based on its intended function and purpose."

The search for quality starts by asking what the purpose of a data model is. The characteristics related to the fitness of the model for a purpose are proposed in [8]. These characteristics are correctness, completeness, simplicity, flexibility, and understandability, and they are in line with the cognitive restrictions of decision making. For example, cognitive decision making may be ineffective if a model lacks correctness, and(or) completeness, and(or) simplicity.

In the business process modelling community the quality of models is either seen mechanically [14] based on five system design principles: coupling, cohesion, complexity, modularity and size, or is assessed as "good enough or bad", based on the so-called "Process Excellence Principles" [6]. The Process Excellence Principles are predefined purposes of a business process, such as "Customer Value and Economic profit", "Employee well-being", "Focus on standard processes". It is assumed that any business process model always has many purposes. The business process modelling community uses the term "fairness" to express the fitness of the model for several purposes. Fairness [13] is defined in the context of a decision tree whereby: "All choices are made (implicitly or explicitly) by applications, humans or external actors. Clearly, they should not introduce an infinite loop". "Strong fairness means in every infinite firing sequence, each transition fires infinitely often. The weaker forms of fairness with just local conditions, e.g., if a transition is enabled infinitely often, will fire eventually" [1]. In the practice of business process modelling, some of the purposes (goals) are transformed to modelling constraints, and the small number of purposes remain and the chosen amount of transitions should fire fairly.

In the enterprise architecture modelling community, fitness for a purpose is considered as a basic quality characteristic of any enterprise model. The characteristics proposed for data models [8] have been adapted by [7] and [10] and reduced to two characteristics: correctness and completeness. Correctness is seen as a syntactic quality characteristic: "Correctness refers to how well the enterprise model conforms to the rules of the modelling technique" [7]. Completeness reflects fitness of the model for purpose: "Completeness is the degree to which all relevant facts of the problem domain are included in the enterprise model" [7].

In terms of [7,10], our paper is about "completeness" of the model for the purpose of decision making about the worthwhileness of the implementation of the proposed changes. We assume that a goal of business changes is given. We assume also that each model is created to make a decision on whether or not the proposed model or model change sufficiently contributes to the goal. The proposed model or model changes should be "complete", i.e. contain the concepts and the relations of the concepts needed for this decision. However, the concepts representing the objects for comparison, needed for decision making, are not always included in models and not always clearly selected. Therefore, the completeness of the model for decision making needs special attention in modelling.

3 Concepts from Different Domains Enabling Decisions

Our first case study shows that the concepts of objects needed for decision making may demand model extension with concepts from a different domain.

3.1 Model for the Case of Marketing of a Children's Savings Account

Let us consider a model of a marketing campaign in a bank. A bank tries to win new customers by advertising savings accounts for children, in the hope that the child will continue to do business with the bank as an adult. *The bank should design a new process, assess this process and make a decision if it is worthwhile to implement this process gauging whether it sufficiently contributes to the goal of winning new customers.*

First, the bank designs a new business process. The *strategic goal* of the bank is to *increase the number of customers by inviting minor customers (to join).* The *strategic goal* is refined by the business process goal, which is to *Register New Minor Customers*, and the goal to *Measure Effectiveness of Marketing.* These goals separate the domains of the underlying business process and measurement.

The business process goal *Register New Minor Customers* is refined by the milestones of the marketing process:

- A marketing employee mails an invitation to all its adult customers to open a children's savings account.
- An adult customer may ignore the invitation, or submit an application for a children's savings account.
- Upon receipt of an application for a children's savings account, if the child is under the age of 11 years, and does not yet have such an account, a back-office employee registers the child as a minor customer, who will retain that status until reaching the age of 18.

The goal *Measure Effectiveness of Marketing* is refined to:

- Conversion rate of Invitations to Applications;
- Conversion rate of Applications to Minor Customers;
- Conversion rate of Invitations to Minor Customers.

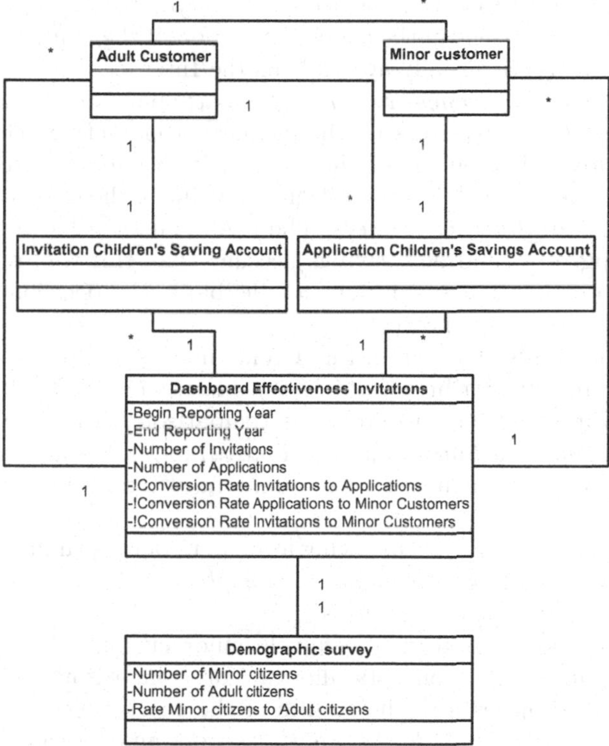

Fig. 1. Conceptual model of the case study of marketing of a children's savings account with external concept *Demographic survey*.

The concepts derived from the refined goals, are shown in Fig. 1. The reader can see *Adult Customer*, *Minor Customer*, *Invitation Children's Saving Account*, *Application Children's Saving Account* and *Dashboard Effectiveness Invitations*. The attributes of the Dashboard are the parameters of measurement (*Begin Reporting Year*, *End Reporting Year*) and the indicators (*Number of Invitations, Conversion Rate Invitations to Applications*, *Conversion Rate Applications to Minor Customers*, *Conversion Rate Invitations to Minor Customers*). The character "!" means that there is a formula associated with the indicator.[1]

Even if the bank measures the number of new bank customers transformed from the minor customers, it is difficult to estimate if this number is sufficient to implement the new marketing process. There are no concepts for comparison possibilities in winning new customers with the results of marketing.

3.2 Concepts for Comparison

The decision making about worthwhileness of implementing the new process is a goal by itself: *Make a decision if the marketing is worthwhile to implement.* In order to make a decision one needs an estimation. This estimation can be taken outside the marketing process model, from a *Demographic survey* presenting the population of minor citizens in the country or region of the bank's location. Such a *Demographic survey* is usually available on the Internet.

The *Dashboard Effectiveness Invitations* has attribute *Conversion Rate Invitations to Minor Customers* to keep the measure of marketing achievements. A *Demographic survey* is used to get the value of its attribute *Rate Minors citizens to Adult citizens*, which is a top estimation value of the measure *Conversion Rate Invitations to Minor Customers*. The bank cannot achieve better results in the marketing of a children's savings account than this top estimation. If a part of this top estimation is sufficient for the bank, the decision can be made to implement the proposed process.

The conceptual model shown in Fig. 1 contains this external concept *Demographic survey* and its attribute *Rate Minor citizens to Adult citizens* used for the decision support. If implemented, the comparison of the *Conversion Rate Invitations to Minor Customers* and the *Rate Minors citizens to Adult citizens* in the country (or region) can be used to assess the effectiveness of the marketing process.

This case study provides the following answers to our research question: *What is an indication that a model of changes is complete to decide that it enables the achievement of a given goal of changes?*

The goal of changes is to win as much minor customers as possible. The model should contain the concepts allowing for comparison between the top estimation of possibilities and the results of the marketing. In this case, the concept *Rate Minors citizens to Adult citizens* from an extension of the system model by the concept *Demographic survey* is compared with the *Conversion*

[1] The formulas are not relevant to this paper. For the interested readers, the formulas and executable model can be found in Burg-Lehmkuhl, K. (2018). *Specifying measures that suit the need.* Master thesis, available on request.

Rate Invitations to Minor Customers from the system model. The indication of the model completeness is the presence of concepts to decide that the proposed changes enable achievement of the goal of changes.

4 Concepts from Different Time Points Enabling Decisions

Our second case study shows that the concepts of objects for decision making may be found inside the same domain and demand model versions at different time points.

4.1 Planning and Scheduling at a High School

We illustrate the comparison of concepts and relations in a pair of as-is and to-be models of a case of changing the planning and scheduling applications at a High School, inspired by [3].

The goal of changes in this case is to *Achieve consistency of plans and schedules at a High School*. The goal is refined to the business rules: *(1) Any data item (any business object) is created once and used in the Planning and Scheduling application. (2) The Planning and Scheduling application should avoid manual coordination of activity codes.*

Among business objects used by a High School are the designed *Many years plan*, *Year plan*, *Lesson (group) year plan* and *Period plan*. A *Many years plan* is designed from exams that have to be taken by students during a *Many years period*. Each *Exam* has its unique *Exam Code*. A *Many years plan* is composed from instances of the business object *Year plan*. An *Year plan* contains the exams in a year within the corresponding *Exams plan* and extends exams with instances of *Lesson activity* and *Learning activity* that should be taken to pass the exams.

An *Year plan* is used to make a *Lesson (group) year plan* for each study year by adding the teachers delivering the lessons, and other employees supporting the courses, and the students following the courses. From a *Lesson (group) year plan*, the *Period plans* are derived and extended with the information about the time and location of the lessons.

The as-is enterprise model (Fig. 2) of planning and scheduling at a High School reflects the situation when a *Spreadsheet application* is used to create an *Exam plan* and a *School year plan*.

An *Exam plan* is created using the concepts *Exam*, *Exam Name* and *Exam Code*. Instances of the concept *Activity* corresponding to the *Exam plan* are searched manually using the *Exam Code*. Manual assigning of codes for a search of activities is error prone. As this search should be done both for an *Exams plan* and for an *Year plan*, it can be a source of inconsistency of plans.

Further, a *School year plan* is manually inserted into a scheduling package to create a *Lesson (group) year plan*. The groups of students are created for each school year. The *Faculty* and the *Employee* are assigned to support the educational process. The scheduling package is further used to create instances of the concept *Period Plan* by assigning times and locations to a *Lesson (Group) Year Plan*.

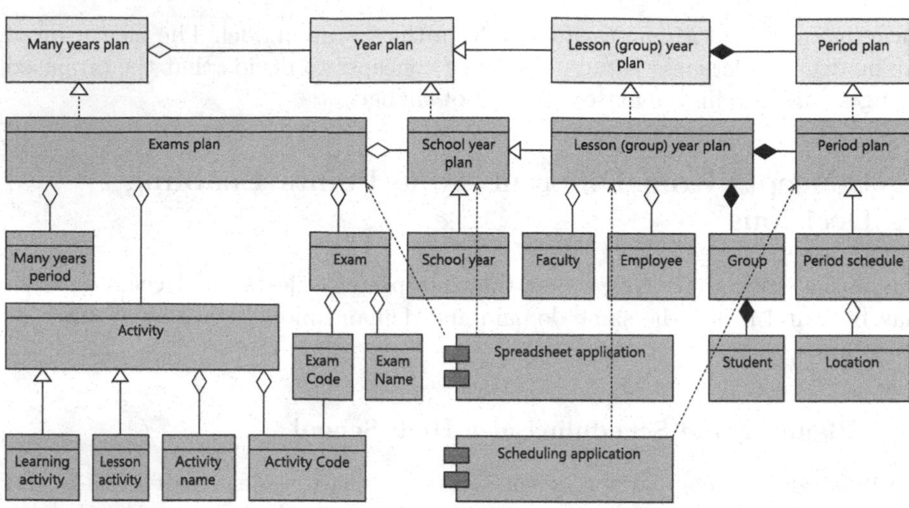

Fig. 2. As-is Enterprise model of planning and scheduling at a High School

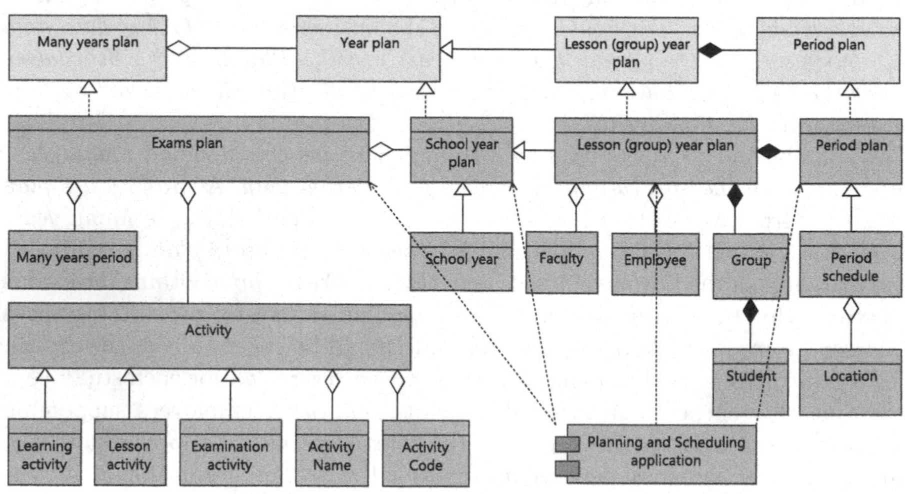

Fig. 3. To-be Enterprise model of planning and scheduling at a High School

The to-be Enterprise model is shown in Fig. 3. All plans and schedules are supported with one *Planning and Scheduling application.* The data structure does not contain an independent concept *Exam.* The concept *Activity* is extended with a new specialisation concept *Examination activity.* The other specializations are *Lesson activity* and *Learning activity.* Each instance of *Activity* has an *Activity Name* and an *Activity code.* Each of these items is created once when an activity is defined. A business procedure for course designers can be used for creating instances of *Examination activity* in combination with the corresponding instances of *Lesson activity* and *Learning activity.*

This case study provides the following answer to our research question: *What is an indication that a model of changes is complete to decide that it enables the achievement of a given goal of changes?* The goal of changes has been refined to two rules to avoid manual coordination of plans and schedules and their items. The indication of completeness of the model is the ability to identify the subsets of concepts in the as-is model that enable scenarios that demonstrate confrontation to the rules and the subsets of concepts in the to-be model that enable scenarios that are compliant with both rules.

First, a pair of concepts *Spreadsheet application* and *Scheduling application* in the as-is model is compared with the concept *Planning and Scheduling application* in the to-be model. This means that the manual uploading of plans from one application to another is avoided.

However, the key support for comparison in this case is the relation between concepts *Exam* and *Activity*. In the as-is model, *Exam* and *Activity* are independent concepts. They can be made related indirectly, using their codes *(Exam–Exam Code–Activity Code–Activity)*. In the to-be model, the *Examination activity* concept is one of specializations of the *Activity* concept among other specializations. The specialization enables interfaces and automatic controls of codes for course designers and automatic selection of activities for *Many years plan* and *Year plans*.

The to-be model can be used to mentally play the scenarios of planning. The instances of activities are created by course designers, the codes of activities are generated. A plan designer selects examination activities for an *Exams plan* from the available examination activities. From an *Exam plan* the instances of *School year plan* are generated for each *School year* with activities associated with each examination by design. The manual code coordination of activity codes is avoided. From a *School year plan* a form for a *Lesson (group) year plan* is generated to be filled in with faculties, employees and groups of students. The completed *Lesson (group) year plan* is used to make a *Period plan* to be filled in with a given period and locations. These scenarios show that manual coordination of plans is avoided as each next plan extends the previous plan with new data items.

5 Comparison of the Answers to the Research Questions in Two Case Studies

In both modelling case studies the indication of completeness of the model is the presence of concepts that enable scenarios that need to be analysed to make a decision. The presence of concepts enables mental enacting of scenarios needed to decide that the proposed changes enable achievement of the goal of changes.

In the first case study, the conceptual model of a marketing process in a bank has been deliberately extended with an external concept from a different domain allowing for the comparison of marketing results with the available population of minor citizens and making a decision about the implementation of the proposed marketing process. The conversion rate of new minor customers following the invitation sent to adult customers is compared with the rate of minor citizens to adult citizens. By mentally enacting different scenarios using this model, a decision maker can make a top estimation of the number of potential clients that can be achieved by this marketing process and decide about the worthwhileness of implementing this marketing process.

In the second case study, two versions of the conceptual model of the planning and scheduling process in a High school has been made: as-is and to-be, and the subsets of concepts used in the scenarios needed to make a decision have been identified. By mentally enacting different scenarios using the as-is model, the manual association of *Exam code* and *Activity code* and the manual uploading of an *Year plan* to the *Scheduling application* have been identified as sources of inconsistency of plans. The to-be model contains one *Planning and Scheduling application* that excludes manual uploading of instances of the *Year plan*. The uniform data structure for all activities including the *Examination activity* eliminates the errors of code coordination. By mentally enacting scenarios of constructing plans using the to-be model, a decision maker can see that the data instances are created ones and then used for constructing all plans and schedules, and can decide that the to-be model is worthwhile to implement.

6 Conclusion and Future Work

This paper has presented two deliberately chosen case studies that identify two different ways (or dimensions) to find the supported concepts for a decision. One way is to compare concepts from the system model with the concepts found outside the system model. This can be seen as an extension of a system model for decision making. Another way is to compare the existing concepts in one version of the system model (as-is) and the concepts in another version of the system model (to-be). These two different ways can be used by researches looking for relating concepts with goals and decisions made on the basis of models.

In future work, the attention to concepts used for comparison may result in patterns of finding concepts related to specific classes of decisions with respect to specific goal classes. Moreover, the attention to compared concepts (and their relations) also contributes to the choice of the right level of model abstractions as only a selection of a small set of concepts for comparison supports a decision with respect to a given goal.

Acknowledgement. The authors thank Kirsten Burg-Lehmkuhl and Martijn Bos for their graduation project work on the modelling of cases.

References

1. van der Aalst, W.M.: Challenges in business process management: verification of business processes using Petri nets. Bull. EATCS **80**(174–199), 32 (2003)
2. Bakelaar, R., Roubtsova, E., Joosten, S.: A framework for visualization of changes of enterprise architecture. In: Shishkov, B. (ed.) BMSD 2016. LNBIP, vol. 275, pp. 140–160. Springer, Cham (2017). https://doi.org/10.1007/978-3-319-57222-2_7
3. Bos, M.: Evaluation of two ArchiMate based visualization techniques. How to keep track of changes when replacing a spreadsheet application with an information system? Technical report (2018). https://research.ou.nl/en/studentTheses/evaluatie-van-twee-oparchimate-gebaseerde-visualisatietechnieken
4. Dijkstra, R., Roubtsova, E.: Analytic pattern and tool for analysis of a gap of changes in enterprise architectures. In: Proceedings of the 14th International Conference on Evaluation of Novel Approaches to Software Engineering. SCITEPRESS-Science and Technology Publications (2019)
5. Gaaloul, K., Guerreiro, S.: A decision-oriented approach supporting enterprise architecture evolution. In: 2015 IEEE 24th International Conference on Enabling Technologies: Infrastructure for Collaborative Enterprises, pp. 116–121. IEEE (2015)
6. Krogstie, J.: Quality of business process models. Quality in Business Process Modeling, pp. 53–102. Springer, Cham (2016). https://doi.org/10.1007/978-3-319-42512-2_2
7. Larsson, L., Segerberg, R.: An approach for quality assurance in enterprise modelling. Ph.D. thesis, MSc thesis, Department of Computer and Systems Sciences, Stockholm University (2004)
8. Moody, D.L., Shanks, G.G.: Improving the quality of data models: empirical validation of a quality management framework. Inf. Syst. **28**(6), 619–650 (2003)
9. Pohl, J.: Cognitive elements of human decision making. In: Phillips-Wren, G., Ichalkaranje, N., Jain, L.C. (eds.) Intelligent Decision Making: An AI-Based Approach. Studies in Computational Intelligence, vol. 97, pp. 41–76. Springer, Heidelberg (2008). https://doi.org/10.1007/978-3-540-76829-6_2
10. Sandkuhl, K., Stirna, J., Persson, A., Wißotzki, M.: Quality of enterprise models. Enterprise Modeling. TEES, pp. 203–216. Springer, Heidelberg (2014). https://doi.org/10.1007/978-3-662-43725-4_12
11. TDAN: Measuring the Quality of Models (2000). http://tdan.com/measuring-the-quality-of-models/4877
12. The Open Group: ArchiMate 3.1 Specification (2012–2019). https://pubs.opengroup.org/-architecture/archimate3-doc/
13. Trautmann, S.T., Wakker, P.P.: Process fairness and dynamic consistency. Econ. Lett. **109**(3), 187–189 (2010)
14. Vanderfeesten, I., Cardoso, J., Mendling, J., Reijers, H.A., van der Aalst, W.M.: Quality metrics for business process models. In: BPM and Workflow Handbook, vol. 144, pp. 179–190 (2007)

Model-Based Hypothesis Engineering for Supporting Adaptation to Uncertain Customer Needs

Sebastian Gottschalk(✉), Enes Yigitbas, and Gregor Engels

Software Innovation Lab, Paderborn University, Paderborn, Germany
{sebastian.gottschalk,enes.yigitbas,gregor.engels}@uni-paderborn.de

Abstract. To build successful products, the developers have to adapt their product features and business models to uncertain customer needs. This adaptation is part of the research discipline of Hypotheses Engineering (HE) where customer needs can be seen as hypotheses that need to be tested iteratively by conducting experiments together with the customer. So far, modeling support and associated traceability of this iterative process are missing. Both, in turn, are important to document the adaptation to the customer needs and identify experiments that provide most evidence to the customer needs. To target this issue, we introduce a model-based HE approach with a twofold contribution: First, we develop a modeling language that models hypotheses and experiments as interrelated hierarchies together with a mapping between them. While the hypotheses are labeled with a score level of their current evidence, the experiments are labeled with a score level of maximum evidence that can be achieved during conduction. Second, we provide an iterative process to determine experiments that offer the most evidence improvement to the modeled hypotheses. We illustrate the usefulness of the approach with an example of testing the business model of a mobile application.

Keywords: Hypothesis Engineering · Model-based · Customer need adaptation · Business model · Product features

1 Introduction

To build successful products, the developers have to continuously adapt their product features [7,11] and the underlying business model [2,3] to the actual customer needs. Due to the uncertainty in the actual customer needs, the usage of experimentation to validate and disapprove hypotheses with potential customers has been carried out as a promising approach. This experimentation is implemented by different similar concepts like rapid experimentation [2], discovery-driven planning [8], experiment-driven development [7], or data-driven software

This work was partially supported by the German Research Foundation (DFG) within the Collaborative Research Center "On-The-Fly Computing" (CRC 901, Project Number: 160364472SFB901).

B. Shishkov (Ed.): BMSD 2020, LNBIP 391, pp. 276–286, 2020.
https://doi.org/10.1007/978-3-030-52306-0_18

development [11] in the literature. These concepts are covered by the emerging research field of Hypothesis Engineering (HE) [10] as a subfield of Requirement Engineering (RE), in which different hypotheses have to be tested with evidence. Evidence refers to the certainty with which a hypothesis is either validated or disapproved. Both help developers to adapt their products to actual customer needs. For this, the usage of models can support the visualization and traceability of the HE process. Traceability, in turn, is important to document the adaptation to the customer needs and identify experiments, whose conduction increases evidence. To support this, introduce the hypotheses modeling and mapping support HypoMoMap (see Fig. 1) which can be used by a business developer to iterative test hypotheses about the product features and business models of the product. For this, we need to define a structure and a process.

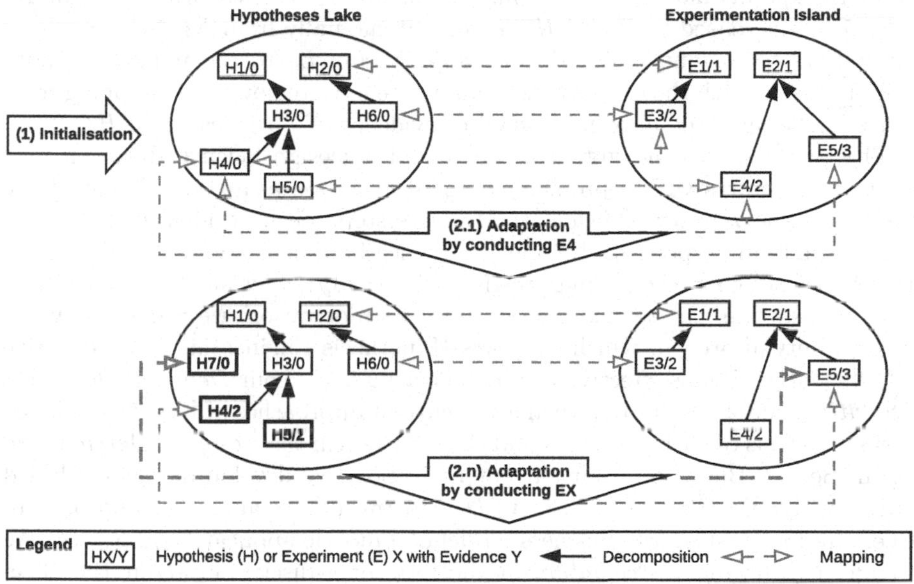

Fig. 1. Overview of the modeling and mapping approach

The structure (i.e. nodes in *Hypotheses Lake* and *Experimentation Island*) consists of hierarchies of hypotheses and experiments. While the hypotheses consist of a state (validated, disapproved, untested) together with a score level of the current evidence and priority, the experiments consist of a score level of maximum evidence that can be achieved during conduction and costs that are generated during conduction. Figure 1 provides a simplification by assuming that all hypotheses and experiments have the same priority, state, and cost.

The engineering process consists of a single phase for (1) Initialisation and repetitive phases for (2) Adaptation. In the **(1) Initialisation**, the business developer models the first set of hypotheses and corresponding experiments in a structure with hierarchical interrelationships. Moreover, the developer creates a mapping of the hypotheses to all experiments, which conduction can validate or disapprove the hypotheses. As an example in Fig. 1, we have modeled six hypotheses (i.e. *H1* to *H6*) and five experiments (i.e. *E1* to *E5*) together with mappings between them (e.g. *H2* and *E1*). In the repetitive **(2) Adaptation**, our approach selects the experiment that provides the best ratio of increased evidence scores among all hypotheses and generated costs. The developer conducts the experiment and uses the result to update the hypotheses by changing the evidence score of each tested hypothesis. Moreover, the developer adds new hypotheses that can occur by the conduction and remove mappings to experiments, which can not improve the scores of the hypotheses. This adaption phase is repeated until there exists no mapping between hypotheses and experiments, which means that it is not possible to improve the evidence of the hypotheses with the experiments. By conducting *E4* in Fig. 1, the evidence scores of *H4* and *H5* are increased to 2, and *H7* is derived manually from *E4*. Next, we have mapped *H7* to *E3* and removed the mapping from *E4* to *H4* and *H5*, because both are tested with the experiment. Finally, we have removed the mapping from *E3* to *H4* because the maximum score of evidence of *E3* is less than *H4*.

The paper shows the first design cycle of a Design Science Research process [13] and starts with a problem-centered initiation as an entry point of the process. In the *Identify Problem & Motivate* step, we have identified the lack of traceability in Hypothesis Engineering which has the advantage to document the adaptation to the customer needs and identify experiments that conduction increases the gained evidence at most. As motivation, we want to develop a traceability approach, which supports Hypothesis Engineering in an effective and efficient way. This effectivity and efficiency are also our *Define[d] Objectives of Solution*. For this solution, we analyze current approaches of Hypothesis Engineering in terms of their structure and their process in the *Design & Development* step in Sect. 2. Based on their current limitation, we develop our model-based approach HypoMoMap in Sect. 3. As *Demonstration*, we apply our approach to the example of testing the business model of a mobile application in Sect. 4. We provide a preliminary *Evaluation* in the form of a discussion about the effectiveness and efficiency of our approach together with limitations we found by developing business models for the app. Finally, our *Communication* step will be done with a conclusion in Sect. 5 and the publication of the paper.

2 Background and Challenges

Hypothesis Engineering [10] is used to validate and disapprove hypotheses by running experiments and gather qualitative and quantitative results from metrics. In their paper [10], the authors found Hypothesis Experiment Data-Driven Development (HYPEX) [11] and Rapid Iterative value creation Gained through High-frequency Testing (RIGHT) [4] as two models for evaluating product features with quantitative metrics. Based on our review of literature, we add Qualitative/quantitative Customer-driven Development (QCD) [12] for qualitative

Table 1. Challenges for modeling from the Hypothesis Engineering approaches

	HYPEX	RIGHT	QCD	DDP	TBI
Hypotheses	✓	✓	✓	✓	✓
With State	✗	✗	✗	✓	✓
With Priorities	✓	✓	✓	✓	✓
With Evidence Scores	✗	✗	✗	✗	✓
With Refinement	✗	✗	✗	✗	✗
Experiments	Feature Test	Feature Test	✓	✓	✓
With Evidence Scores	✗	✗	✗	✗	✓
With Costs	✗	✗	✗	✓	✓
With Refinement	✗	✗	✗	✗	✗
Artifacts	Product Feature	Product Feature	✓	✓	✓
Mapping	Single Experiment	Single Experiment	Single Experiment	✓	Single Experiment
With Metrics	Actual Behavior	Resulting Data	✓	✓	✓

metrics of product features together with Discovery-Driven Planning (DDP) [8] and Testing Business Ideas (TBI) [2] to consider also the business model. We analyze these five approaches to derive the challenges, we need to consider in our mapping and modeling approach. *HYPEX* [11] is a conceptual model for analyzing product goals to develop a prioritized feature backlog. For this, they assume an expected behavior, implement the feature, and calculate the possible gap between expected and actual behavior based on quantitative observations. If there is a gap, they develop new hypotheses about the feature, otherwise, they continue with the next feature in the feature backlog. *RIGHT* [4] is similar to HYPEX by deriving hypotheses from the business model, test them in a product feature, and use the result to update the business model and product features. *QCD* [12] improves the concept of HYPEX and RIGHT, which use only quantitative measurements, by adding qualitative customer feedback to the continuous experimentation. *DDP* [8] has its foundation in the adaptation of business models. For this, they put the experiments in relation to hypotheses that can be tested together and focus on the created costs. *TBI* [2] is an approach that provides an iterative process from a good idea to a validated business. For this, the authors provide a catalog of 44 experimentation types and focus on the different levels of costs and evidence these experiments provide.

All approaches consist of a process where an initial set of hypotheses is defined, which is further tested by selecting hypotheses and conducting an experiment. This iterative testing is similar to the cycles in LEAN-Development [14], experiments in Experimental Software Engineering, or sprints in SCRUM. All processes except TBI focus on the test of hypotheses with high priority but neglect the overall evidence gain by testing multiple hypotheses through a single experiment. In our approach, we adopt the concept of the LEAN-Development cycle to build an iterative process together with the usage of evidence score as mentioned in TBI. Moreover, the process of incremental refinement can be supported by our previous work in [5], where we intertwine the development of a business model and product functions based on feature models.

None of the existing approaches provides an explicitly modeled structure representing the hypotheses and the experiment. Therefore, we analyze the existing approaches to derive the modeling challenges for our approaches (see Table 1) from their implicit requirements. In this analysis, we can see that HYPEX and RIGHT are quite similar in their modeling structure. Both consist of a hypotheses backlog, where hypotheses together with a priority are stored. To test the hypotheses they can run a single experiment of a feature test, where the usage of the feature is measured. QCD improves this by running different experiments and gather the corresponding feedback. DPP works on the limitation of a single mapping from a hypothesis to an experiment by testing multiple hypotheses with a single experiment. TBI covers the different evidence scores of the hypotheses and experiments but only covers a single hypothesis per experiment. Nevertheless, none of the approaches covers the refinement of hypotheses which can be used to decompose the hypotheses into smaller, easier validatable assumptions. Refinement is one advantage of a model-based approach, which is also used for product features [1], non-functional properties of products [17], and business models [15]. In our approach, we adapt the structure of Goal Oriented Requirements Engineering (GORE) [17]. The adaption of GORE will allow us to easily adapt the formal verification of models with techniques like deductive reasoning, which are not the focus of our first design cycle. We refine this structure with states of hypotheses (untested, validated, disapproved), score levels (priorities, evidence scores, costs), and a mapping between hypotheses and experiments.

3 Modeling and Mapping Approach

In this section, we present our hypotheses modeling and mapping approach HypoMoMap by introducing a structure and an engineering process.

3.1 Structure of the Approach

The structure of the approach can be seen in Fig. 2. It consists of the two components of a *Hypotheses Lake* and an *Evaluation Island*. In the **Hypotheses Lake**, different elements of hypotheses (*Validated Hypotheses*, *Disapproved Hypotheses*, *Untested Hypotheses*) can be modeled with corresponding evidence score (e.g. *Kids* with a score of 2) and a priority (e.g. *Kids* with a priority of 2). The scores and priorities can have a value from 1 (lowest) to 5 (highest). The hypotheses interrelate to each other in a hierarchical order (e.g. *Customer* is decomposed into *Kids*). The hierarchy consists of *AND/OR-Relationships*. While with an *OR-Relationship* each hypothesis in a higher hierarchy level can be validated with a single lower interrelated hypothesis (e.g. *Customer* or *Kids*), the *AND-Relationship* provides only validation to a higher hypothesis by validating all lower interrelated hypotheses (e.g. *Kids* into *Age* and *Gender*). Moreover, each hypothesis is mapped to the experiments which can be used to validate or disprove the hypothesis (e.g. validate *Gender* with *Data Analysis*). For the mapping, we explicitly model the metric, which is used to validate the hypothesis.

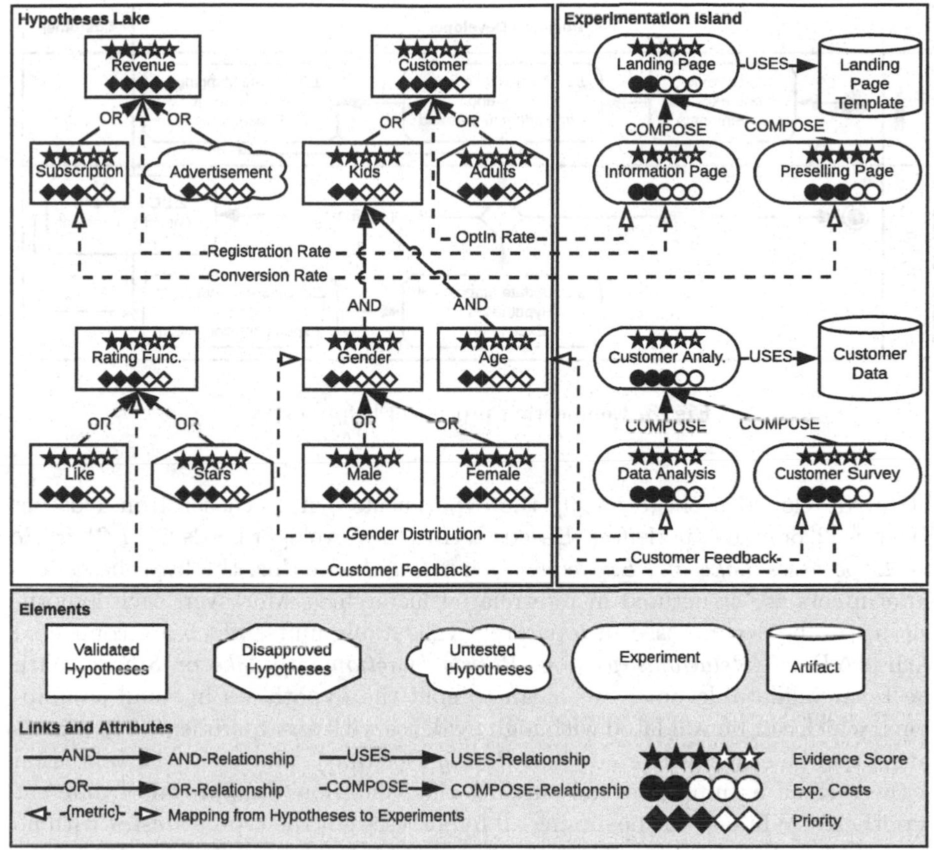

Fig. 2. Visual notation of HypoMoMap

On the **Experimentation Island**, different elements of *Experiments* (e.g. *Data Analysis*) and corresponding *Artifacts* (e.g. *Customer Data*) are modeled. Each experiment has a maximum score of evidence that can be achieved by conducting the experiment and costs that are generated by the conduction (e.g. *Data Analysis* with a score of 3 and costs of 3). Moreover, each experiment can use different provided artifacts (e.g. *Customer Analysis* uses *Customer Data*). Moreover, the experiments are decomposed to more accurately experiments.

3.2 Engineering Process of the Approach

The engineering process of the approach is depicted in Fig. 3. It consists of the two phases of the Initialisation and the Adaptation. In the **(1) Initialisation** phase, the business developer has to *(1.1) define hypotheses and experiments* at the beginning. While the hypotheses of the business model and the product features can be derived from the business strategy and its product goals

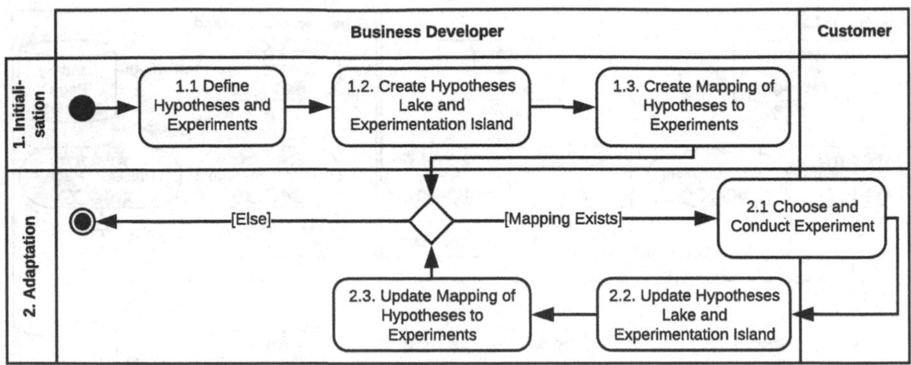

Fig. 3. Engineering process of HypoMoMap

[11] or developed user stories [9], the experiments can be chosen from existing libraries [2] or own experiences. Based on this, the developer needs to *(1.2) create the Hypotheses Lake and Experimentation Island.* For this, the hypotheses and experiments are structured in interrelated hierarchies. Moreover, each hypothesis has to be decomposed in separately validatable units, which are connected with *AND/OR-Relationships* (e.g. *Rating Function* into *Like* or *Stars*). With the term validatable units, we mean to split the hypotheses in small assumptions, which can be validated with high evidence with an experiment (e.g. a *Stars* rating can be easier validated than *Rating Function*). Moreover, the validation of these small assumptions can support the validation/disapproval of different hypotheses. While at the beginning all hypotheses got the type *Untested* with no estimated evidence, the developer has to estimate the maximum score of evidence and generated costs of the experiments (e.g. *Landing Page* with a score of 2 and costs of 3). To support this process, the developer can use the experimentation catalog, which has proposed in [2]. Moreover, the developer has to prioritize the hypothesis to consider the most important hypotheses at the beginning. After that, the developer needs to *(1.3) create the mapping of hypotheses to experiments* where the hypotheses are mapped to experiments that can be used for testing the hypotheses. Here it is important to choose multiple experiments for the hypotheses to test these different hypotheses with the same experiment.

In the **(2) Adaptation** phase, the developer has to *(2.1) choose and conduct an experiment.* Because this choice is a critical part, we provide different techniques, which can be used for different situations because of their outcomes: With *Highest Priority*, a hypothesis with the highest priority is chosen. This setting is also used by other models [4,11] and ensures that the most important assumptions are validated first. Nevertheless, it has the disadvantage that more iteration cycles are needed for the validation of the model. For *Best Estimated Ratio*, the developer looks at each experiment and chooses the maximum of hypotheses evidence gain which can be validated in a single execution of the experiment in comparison to the costs of the experiment. The hypotheses evidence gain is defined by cumulated evidence scores between the current evidence score and the estimated evidence score with the experiment of all selected hypotheses. This setting is used to maximize validated learning by considering the costs but has the disadvantage to not consider the most critical hypotheses at the beginning. With *Best Discounted Ratio*, we discount the hypotheses evidence gain of single hypotheses in the Best Estimated Ratio with their priority to focus the validated learning on the most important assumptions. Nevertheless, it has the disadvantage that the calculation is quite complex without tool support.

After that, the developer needs to *(2.2) update Hypotheses Lake and Experimentation Island*. For this, each tested hypothesis is typed as *Validated* or *Disapproved* with the evidence score of the experiment. Here it is also possible to use a lower evidence score if the experiment turned out as less effective as expected. Additionally, the evidence scores are propagated to the higher levels of the hierarchy. While with an *OR-Relationship* the higher hypothesis is set to the highest evidence score of the lower hypothesis, the *AND-Relationship* assumes the lowest evidence score of all lower hypotheses. Moreover, new hypotheses that are derived by the experiment can be added to the model. In the end, the developer needs to *(2.3) update the mapping of hypotheses to experiments*. For this, the developer removes all mappings between hypotheses and experiments which do not provide further evidence gain adds new mappings which are derived from the experiment. At every adaptation of the model, it is important to save the existing model together with the results of the experiments to provide traceability. The adaptation phase is repeated until no experiment that can improve the evidence in the hypotheses.

4 Instantiation

We illustrate the usefulness of our approach by testing the business model of a mobile to-do app. The main functionality of the app is to provide customers an organization of their daily tasks. For this, we structure the hypotheses according to the customer-side (Customer Segments, Value Propositions, Customer Relationships, Channels, Revenue Streams) of the Business Model Canvas and model the product features as different value propositions. Because of the multitude of hypotheses, we develop a preliminary version of a tool-support based on [6].

In the **(1) Initialisation**, we need to define the hypotheses we want to validate together with corresponding experiments. For developing a new business model, Teece [16] argues that a deep analysis of the market, the existing competitors and potential customers are needed. We apply this by analyzing the market of mobile applications, the existing competitors (e.g. Microsoft ToDo, Any.do, Todoist), and three selected customer segments (Business Improver, Fitness Improver, Life Improver). The full analysis is shown in [6]. Out of the analysis, we generate 96 hypotheses. We structure them into the five main hypotheses of the customer-side on the canvas (e.g. Customer Segments → Target Group → Business Improver; Value Propositions → Automatic Task Scheduling,

Workflow Tracking) so that the overall goal is to create a canvas where all building blocks are validated. While the features for the competitive advantage get a high priority to test them at the beginning, the existing features of competitors are already validated by them and therefore receive less priority. Moreover, we use the test catalog of Bland et al. [2] to create five experiments (Landing Page, Clickable Prototype, Single-Feature Minimum Viable Product, Split-Test, Customer Survey) with three artifacts (Facebook-Page, Landing Page, Mockup) to derive a mapping from the hypotheses (e.g. Customer Segment $\rightarrow$ Landing Page, Workflow Tracking $\rightarrow$ Clickable Prototype). In the **(2) Adaptation**, we need to test the hypotheses by conducting experiments. We use the strategy of *Best Discounted Ratio*, to maximize the validated learning by considering also the experimentation costs. Here, we saw that many hypotheses can be combined and test together in single experiments. An example of this is the Split-Test with a Facebook-Page to test hypotheses about the Customer Segments and Facebook as a potential channel. Moreover, a Landing Page with the corresponding artifact can be used to test hypotheses about the Revenue Streams and the Channels. By choosing the experiments identified with our modeling and mapping approach, we could efficiently reduce the number of adaptation loops to validate the model.

We conduct a preliminary evaluation by analyzing the effectiveness and efficiency of our approach. The effectiveness is supported by the explicit modeling of hypotheses and experiments. With this modeling, it is possible to gather an overview of the currently tested hypotheses and whether important assumptions not tested. Moreover, by refining these hypotheses into small validatable units, the validation of fuzzy hypotheses can be replaced. The efficiency is supported by the explicit mapping of hypotheses to experiments. With this mapping, it is possible to validate different hypotheses at the same time by conducting a single experiment. Moreover, by analyzing old hypotheses and experiments, the selection of matching experiments for new hypotheses is supported. A potential limitation is the manual modeling complexity, which is time-consuming due to the multitude of hypotheses and corresponding experiments the developer can choose. To solve this limitation, we want to classify different hypotheses types with a literature review and map these types to suitable experiments. With this, it is possible to provide tool-support, which supports the modeling of hypotheses and experiments together with an automated mapping between them.

5 Conclusion

Hypothesis Engineering (HE) is used to build successful products by conducting experiments to test hypotheses about uncertain customer needs. We introduce a modeling and mapping support for HE, which provides traceability in terms of documentation of the adaptation of customer needs and identification of experiments which provides the most evidence gain in the customer needs. For this, we model the hypotheses with evidence scores in interrelated hierarchies and map them to corresponding experiments with maximum evidence and costs. By conducting the identified experiments based on the best ratio of increased evidence and estimated costs, we support the process of improving the evidence in the customer needs. In the future, we plan to classify different hypotheses types with a mapping to experiments to support a questionnaire-based engineering process for automated experiment derivation. Moreover, we want to evaluate the applicability of our approach with a student seminar on lean development.

References

1. Apel, S., Batory, D., Kästner, C., Saake, G.: Feature-Oriented Software Product Lines. Springer, Heidelberg (2013). https://doi.org/10.1007/978-3-642-37521-7
2. Bland, D.J., Osterwalder, A.: Testing Business Ideas. Wiley, Hoboken (2020)
3. Chesbrough, H.: Business model innovation: opportunities and barriers. Long Range Plan. **43**(2–3), 354–363 (2010). https://doi.org/10.1016/j.lrp.2009.07.010
4. Fagerholm, F., Sanchez Guinea, A., Mäenpää, H., Münch, J.: The RIGHT model for Continuous Experimentation. J. Syst. Softw. **123**, 292–305 (2017). https://doi.org/10.1016/j.jss.2016.03.034
5. Gottschalk, S., Rittmeier, F., Engels, G.: Intertwined development of business model and product functions for mobile applications: a twin peak feature modeling approach. In: Hyrynsalmi, S., Suoranta, M., Nguyen-Duc, A., Tyrväinen, P., Abrahamsson, P. (eds.) ICSOB 2019. LNBIP, vol. 370, pp. 192–207. Springer, Cham (2019). https://doi.org/10.1007/978-3-030-33742-1_16
6. Gottschalk, S., Rittmeier, F., Engels, G.: Hypothesis-driven adaptation of business models based on product line engineering. In: International Conference on Business Informatics (CBI). IEEE (2020). https://doi.org/10.1109/CBI49978.2020.00022
7. Lindgren, E., Münch, J.: Raising the odds of success: the current state of experimentation in product development. Inf. Softw. Technol. **77**, 80–91 (2016). https://doi.org/10.1016/j.infsof.2016.04.008
8. McGrath, R.G.: Business models: a discovery driven approach. Long Range Plan. **43**, 247–261 (2010). https://doi.org/10.1016/j.lrp.2009.07.005
9. Melegati, J., Wang, X.: QUESt: new practices to represent hypotheses in experiment-driven software development. In: International Workshop on Software-intensive Business (IWSiB), pp. 13–18. ACM (2019). https://doi.org/10.1145/3340481.3342732
10. Melegati, J., Wang, X., Abrahamsson, P.: Hypotheses engineering: first essential steps of experiment-driven software development. In: RCoSE/DDrEE, pp. 16–19. IEEE (2019). https://doi.org/10.1109/RCoSE/DDrEE.2019.00011
11. Olsson, H.H., Bosch, J.: The HYPEX model: from opinions to data-driven software development. In: Bosch, J. (ed.) Continuous Software Engineering, pp. 155–164. Springer, Cham (2014). https://doi.org/10.1007/978-3-319-11283-1_13
12. Olsson, H.H., Bosch, J.: Towards continuous customer validation: a conceptual model for combining qualitative customer feedback with quantitative customer observation. In: Fernandes, J.M., Machado, R.J., Wnuk, K. (eds.) ICSOB 2015. LNBIP, vol. 210, pp. 154–166. Springer, Cham (2015). https://doi.org/10.1007/978-3-319-19593-3_13
13. Peffers, K., Tuunanen, T., Rothenberger, M.A., Chatterjee, S.: A design science research methodology for information systems research. J. Manag. Inf. Syst. **24**(3), 45–77 (2007). https://doi.org/10.2753/MIS0742-1222240302
14. Ries, E.: The Lean Startup: How Today's Entrepreneurs Use Continuous Innovation to Create Radically Successful Businesses. Crown Business, New York (2014)

15. Samavi, R., Yu, E., Topaloglou, T.: Strategic reasoning about business models: a conceptual modeling approach. Inf. Syst. E-Bus. Manag. **7**(2), 171–198 (2009). https://doi.org/10.1007/s10257-008-0079-z
16. Teece, D.J.: Business models, business strategy and innovation. Long Range Plan. **43**(2–3), 172–194 (2010). https://doi.org/10.1016/j.lrp.2009.07.003
17. van Lamsweerde, A.: Goal-oriented requirements engineering: a guided tour. In: International Symposium on Requirements Engineering, pp. 249–262. IEEE (2001). https://doi.org/10.1109/ISRE.2001.948567

An Agent-Oriented Methodology for Business Process Management

Sara Zouad[1,2(✉)] and Mahmoud Boufaida[1]

[1] LIRE Laboratory Abdelhamid Mehri, Constantine 2 University, Constantine, Algeria
Sarazed03@gmail.com, boufaida@hotmail.com

[2] Computer Sciences Department, Larbi Ben Mhidi University, Oum-El-Bouaghi, Algeria

Abstract. In recent years, agent-oriented methodologies have emerged in the academic domain, each one having its specificities: agent model, formalism, programming, and application domain. However, no methodology has ever been extended to the domain of business processes. The goal of this paper is to use the agent paradigm, i.e. the general logic and the conceptual aspects of its technologies, in the development of a methodology dedicated to the business process management. The proposed approach is inspired by existing agent-based methodologies and from the study of business processes and their modeling. It follows the waterfall model, in which the traditional development phases are easily performed with a return to the previous ones. This approach permits an easy and simple transition from the analysis phase to the implementation one through a general and architectural design. Also, it aims to improve and to optimize the management, interoperability, and reusability of the different business processes that compose the organization and to harmonize the collaborative work of their components. Our methodology consists of four main phases: Analysis, architectural design, general design, and implementation.

Keywords: Agent methodology · Business process · Waterfall model · Interoperability · Reusability

1 Introduction

Agent-oriented methodologies [1] are useful for modeling real-life systems since the agent concept can be a useful reflection of stakeholders' features. Nevertheless, none of the widely popular agent-oriented methodologies has been adequately and exhaustively used in the field of business processes [2].

This is a challenge because current software development essentially counts on the underlying enterprise that modeling that is in turn featuring business processes. However, we cannot ignore business processes because we are currently facing evolution complexity featuring sophisticated market environments that concern massive developments related to information and communication technologies. It appears to be crosscutting about all aspects of life, organizational activities, and business.

Nonetheless, the importance of business processes and the need to optimize their management in companies are not receiving enough attention in the multi-agent-systems

B. Shishkov (Ed.): BMSD 2020, LNBIP 391, pp. 287–296, 2020.
https://doi.org/10.1007/978-3-030-52306-0_19

Community, with some exceptions, such as the works of Konstantin Aksyonov [3] and Yushuai Lin [4] that are nevertheless with limited impact.

Inspired by this challenge, we propose in the current paper a methodology that is dedicated to business process management [5] while being rooted in the agent paradigm, i.e. the general logic and the conceptual aspects of multi-agent systems.

The remainder of the paper is organized as follows: In Sect. 2, we present a state-of-the-art analysis featuring six recognizable agent-oriented methodologies, namely: Adelfe, Gaia, Ingenias, MaSE, Prometheus, and Tropos. On that basis, we present in Sect. 3 our proposed methodology leaning towards business process management. In Sect. 4, we analyze the usefulness and applicability of our proposed methodology (compared to some of the six methodologies, analyzed in Sect. 2). Finally, we conclude with current and future directions for this research in Sect. 5.

2 State of the Art

In this section, we give an overview of some main methodologies of SMA conception, and we make a comparison between them based on the used development process and the limits that they present (See Table 1).

We can observe that each methodology proposes a complete and clear development cycle, and overall, that is no "perfect" methodology. Each methodology has its specificities in terms of architecture, formalism, or models. However, none of this popular agent-based methodology has been adopted for the business process domain.

The study of the six methodologies mentioned above had led us to establish a comparison between them after having defined some criteria based on the using of AMAS (Adaptative Multi-Agent System) [12], the taking into account le BDI (Belief Desir Intention agents) [13] agents, the representation based on conceptual tools, the facility degree, the reusability, and the business process management. In Table 2, we show the principal characteristics that we have analyzed.

Table 1. Comparative table of methodologies

Methodology	Methodology development process	Limits
Adelfe [6]	Preliminary requirements, Final requirements, Analysis, Conception, Implementation, Test	No coherence management or error checking is possible; The notations lack precision in modeling and expressiveness in the representation of logical reasoning; Considering complexity only through structuring into packages, models, and subsystems Adelfe only integrates the notion of an agent in analysis and design Management of quality is identical to that proposed by the RUP and does not cover the problems of the agent

(*continued*)

Table 1. (*continued*)

Methodology	Methodology development process	Limits
Gaia [7]	Analysis, Architectural design, Detailed design	The resources available are quite limited It requires solid expertise in temporal logic It is difficult for developers to adopt it It is limited to applications with highly granular agents, few in number, and with a static organization, which makes it difficult to scale It has no particular notations or modeling techniques Despite some work on a specification of directives for a transition to the JADE platform, Gaia does not propose any implementation guidelines
INGENIAS [8]	Analysis, Design, Implémentation	INGENIAS only modifies the analysis and design activities. It take into account the agent problem, without worrying about technological solutions during implementation
MaSE [9]	Analysis: Identify the roles, Identify the use cases and create sequence diagrams, Transform goals into sets of roles, Conception: Assign roles to specific classes of agents, and identify conversations, Build conversations, Define the internal classes of agents, Define the overall architecture of the system	- MaSE does not consider dynamic systems where the agents can be created, destroyed, or moved during the execution - Communication between agents is point-to-point
Prometheus [10]	Specification of the system, Architectural design, Detailed design	In Prometheus, the requirements are not much discussed. The test, validation, deployment, and maintenance phases are absent, as well as quality management and project management It is suitable for user-oriented applications, not for problem-solving or simulation Prometheus is associated with two tools: JDE (JACK development environment) and PDT. JDE (Prometheus Development Tool) permits editing the proposed models to export them to the JACK platform but some consistency checks have to be done on some models

(*continued*)

Table 1. (*continued*)

Methodology	Methodology development process	Limits
Tropos [11]	Analysis of initial requirements, Analysis of final requirements, Architectural design, Detailed design, Implementation	Tropos lacks the tools to allow the transition from one step to the next It does not provide compliance with all types of systems It does not consider the environment It does not exploit use cases

Table 2. Characteristics of the studied methodologies

Criterium	Methodology					
	Adelfe [6]	Gaia [7]	Ignesias [8]	MaSE [9]	Prometheus [10]	Tropos [11]
Using Adaptative Multi-Agent System AMAS [12]	Yes	No	No	No	No	No
Considering Belief Desir Intention agents BDI [13]					Yes	Yes
Used Conceptual Tools: UP [14], RUP (Rational Unified Process) [14] or UML [15]	Yes	No	Yes	Yes	No	No
Facility Degree	Difficult			Easy	Easy	Not very difficult
Reusability				Little		
Business Process Management [5]	No	No	No	No	No	No

3 Description of the Proposed Methodology

Our proposed methodology has been inspired by some of the agent-based methodologies considered in the previous section and also by our previous studies concerning business process modeling. Moreover, we stick to the Waterfall model [16] whose traditional development phases are performed one after another, with a return on the previous ones.

The proposed methodology also covers the "micro-level" (e.g., the structure of a single agent) as well as the "macro-level" (e.g., the structure of the entire organization), to permit an easy and straightforward transition from analysis to implementation through general and architectural design.

Overall, the methodology focuses on optimizing the management, interoperability, and reusability between different business processes that make up the company and on harmonizing the collaborative work of their components.

3.1 General Features

As it concerns the proposed methodology, the starting point is ANALYSIS (coming through requirements analysis (identifying functional and non-functional requirements), identification of business processes, identification of roles and responsibilities, and in the end - the task of determining the agent-to-agent interactions). As it concerns the design, it is two-fold:

- The global conception where each agent and its internal functioning must be represented;
- The architectural conception where the modeling of interactions and the general structure of the system is done.

3.2 Different Phases

Our proposed methodology consists of four main phases: Analysis, Architectural conception, General conception, and Implementation. Each major phase is divided into several sub-phases (see Fig. 1).

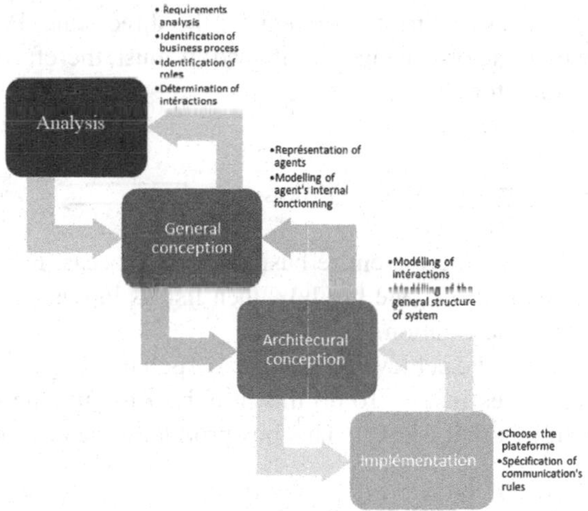

Fig. 1. Phases of the methodology

Analysis. The first phase of a methodology must always be the analysis. It is divided into five (5) sub-phases:

Requirements Analysis. During this step, the analyst must determine the functional and non-functional requirements of the system to satisfy the client. During this step the questions are answered:

- What or which is the system to be developed?
- Why or what are the problems to be solved?
- How or what is the best way to solve these problems?

Alternatively, an iterative process such as in prototyping design could be used to refine the requirements as much as possible.

In this step, business rules are also defined, i.e. the rules that determine the course of a business process, i.e. they influence and control it. These rules must be clear, unambiguous, and comprehensible to everyone.

Identification of Business Processes. It consists of the identification of the company's objectives. During this phase, we were inspired by TIBCO Software's idea [17] of business process management by aligning business processes with the company's goals. This approach facilitates the development and simplifies the identification of business processes because the flow of a business process is the sequencing of its activities to achieve the goal.

By identifying the company's objectives with the help of its direction, it will be easier for us to identify the basic business processes.

Identification of the Company's Processes. The work of identifying processes, particularly the elementary processes, must be done with the directorate. Process mapping is the foundation on which the organization is aligned. It must, therefore, be fully verified and validated by the directorate.

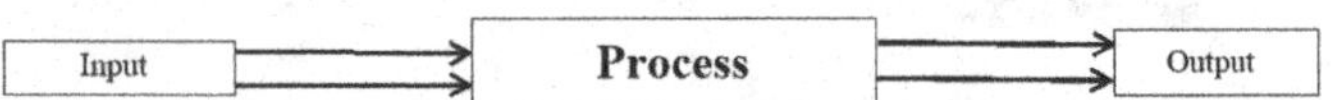

The first step is to describe the entire business as a process. For example, we can represent the entire company as one big box, then list its inputs and outputs and sort them by provenance and destination.

Once this first step will be achieved, it is time to open this large box and to discover the network of small boxes inside. To do this, it is best to take the first of its entries and identify the small box that takes it. This box produces one or more outputs, which should be listed.

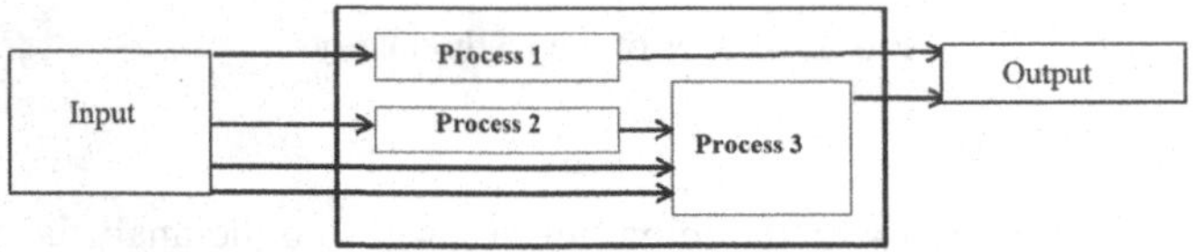

Finally, following what was done for the biggest box, we must describe with a simple sentence the scenario that must happen in the small one.

Thus the first process has just been identified and described. It is more simple, to treat all the inputs in the same manner. Of course, many inputs may be placed in the same small box. It is also possible, that one of their outputs corresponds to one of the big boxes.

Therefore, the identification of all the business processes of the organization will be done.

Identification of Business Objects. To identify the business processes, it is possible to start by identifying the business objects, which are the elements manipulated by the actors of the organization every day. It is relatively easy to list the main business objects. They are often the same from one organization to another: products, commands, contracts, materials, they are contained in the business process.

Identification of Roles and Responsibilities of Agents. After having determined the final requirements and the business processes of the organization, we move on to the third step of the analysis which focuses on the roles of the agents that will be used to realize the system, this sub-phase is divided into two steps:

- The decomposition of functions: Once the necessary functions have been determined, they will be broken down into sub-functions. These sub-functions will represent the tasks that an agent must perform to achieve his role in his organization.
- The identification of agent roles: This step consists of identifying the role(s) of each agent or group of agents and determining their responsibilities by specifying what an agent must do when an agent has to do something and how has to interact with other agents.

Determination of Interactions Between Agents. From the perspective of information flow in multi-agent systems and business processes, it becomes evident that there is a need to determine the interactions between agents in the same multi-agent system, that are all working to make the business process management system work efficiently. These interactions are between agents within the same organization or between agents belonging to different organizations, which may be part of a single business process, multiple business processes, or the business process management system.

It is possible to determine for each agent his connections. An agent's connections are the agents perceiving and therefore interacting with it. One way to formalize them is to give them to the agents at the outset. We can also want the connections to be built through proximity in the environment, depending on the model and its hypotheses. It is important to be aware that the choices made in building connections can lead a model in one direction or another.

General Conception. The general design is as follows:

Representation of Agents. This step consists of mapping the roles and types of agents and creating the right number of instances of agents of each type. It is necessary to represent the static aspect of the agent graphically, i.e. to represent the agent as a class with a name, one or many roles, belonging to one or many organizations, and having one or many capabilities. A type of agent can be an aggregation of one or more agent roles. The best way to represent an agent would be a class diagram, for example, the class diagram of AUML (Agent Unified Modeling Language) [18].

Modeling the Internal Functioning of Agents. This step consists in modeling agents according to their role(s) in the business process(es), because according to the role of an agent, we define the functionalities through which it performs specific tasks to achieve the goal.

For example, we could use the UML activity diagram to model the activities that follow each other within an agent to achieve its goal.

Architectural Conception. This phase is divided into two sub-phases:

Modeling of Interactions Between Agents. One of the characteristics of the agent is his sociability, that's why, in a society of agents, the agents must communicate. In their communication, agents alternate between active and passive roles and vice versa. In other words, they switch from agents who ask questions to agents who answer them by exchanging series of messages while respecting communication protocols for example:

- Negotiation protocols
- Coordination protocols
- Cooperation protocols
- Interoperability protocols

It is useful to model the interactions of the agents in the system during the design phase to facilitate the implementation, there are different formalisms of representation of the interactions we can mention:

- Sequence diagrams in AUML.
- Transition state diagrams in AUML.
- Petri nets
- Reasoning graphs
- Protocol description languages, and;
- Formal languages.

Modeling the General Structure of the System. During this phase, the architectural design of the system must be realized by modeling its general structure through the definition of the agents in their organization(s) and their interactions. This model does not define the messages exchanged but rather the communication paths between the different agents in the different organizations through the business process management system. For example, the UML deployment diagram could be used in this step.

Implementation. The last phase of our methodology is divided into two sub-phases:

Choice and Configuration of the Software Development Platform. There are many platforms for agent development. At this step, we have to choose the one that is the most appropriate for the technological requirements and the application field.

Specification of Agent Communication Rules. In this step, the communication protocols are specified in detail as well as the agent communication language.

4 Discussion

Due to the importance of business process modeling and the observation of that none of the popular agent-based methodologies was oriented for this, we proposed a methodology that will serve as a basis for further research in guiding the construction of a framework in the domain of business process management. To validate, the ideas that we proposed in the specification of our approach, we have chosen an example related to a travel agency for its application in this methodology. The role of this agency is to organize travel for its clients, providing them with travel, accommodation, transport if needed, and day trips. Therefore, we can deduce that the travel agency works with Airline companies and then to make reservations for its clients. The agency must know the destinations proposed by the airline companies and the availability of the flights. Also, it must have a wide range of hotels to be able to accommodate the customer according to his wishes. For this, we specified three hypotheses:

- We assume that a business process is a web service,
- We assume that in our system there is a fixed number of business processes,
- We assume that our system is a closed environment.

5 Conclusion and Futures Works

In the current paper, we have proposed an agent-oriented methodology, inspired by the observation that agent-oriented. Further, we have directed our proposed methodology towards business process management, observing that none of the popular agent-oriented methodologies has this strength and acknowledging the increasing importance of business process modeling for all technological developments.

In support of our work, we have performed a state-of-the-art analysis featuring six of the most popular agent-oriented methodologies. On that basis, we have presented our proposed methodology, consisting of four main phases, namely: Analysis, Architectural conception, General conception, and Implementation. It supports two levels, namely: the "agent level" (featuring the structure of a single agent) and the "organization level" (featuring the structure of the global organization). This permits an easy and simple transition from the analysis phase to the implementation one through a general and architectural design. Also, this aims at improving and optimizing the management, interoperability, and reusability of the different business processes that compose the organization and also harmonizing the collaborative work of their components.

The proposed approach was only tested on a theoretical level, without direct verification on concrete organizations, which limits the ability to provide an evaluation of its usefulness in real situations.

As futures work, we are planning to improve the methodology, by adding a test phase, as well as creating a CASE tool [19] for the methodology's development and taking account of mechanisms allowing the dynamic composition of semantic Web services during the Business Process Management.

References

1. Iglesias, C.A., Garijo, M., González, J.C.: A survey of agent-oriented methodologies. In: Müller, J.P., Rao, A.S., Singh, M.P. (eds.) ATAL 1998. LNCS, vol. 1555, pp. 317–330. Springer, Heidelberg (1999). https://doi.org/10.1007/3-540-49057-4_21
2. Aguilar-Savén, R.S.: Business process modelling: review and framework. Int. J. Prod. Econ. **90**, 129–149 (2004)
3. Aksyonov, K., et al.: Tools and methodologies for business processes formalization: application to multi-agent systems. In: Proceedings - UKSim 5th European Modelling Symposium on Computer Modelling and Simulation, EMS 2011 (2011)
4. Lin, Y., Zhu, J., Li, Q.: A BPK-CRIO methodology for the design and implementation of a multi-agent based business process monitoring system. In: Proceedings - 11th International Conference on Signal-Image Technology and Internet-Based Systems, SITIS 2015 (2016)
5. Van der Aalst, W.M.P.: Business process management: a comprehensive survey. ISRN Softw. Eng. **2013**, 37 (2013)
6. Capera, D., Picard, G., Gleizes, M.-P., Glize, P.: A sample application of ADELFE focusing on analysis and design the mechanical synthesis problem. In: Gleizes, M.-P., Omicini, A., Zambonelli, F. (eds.) ESAW 2004. LNCS (LNAI), vol. 3451, pp. 231–244. Springer, Heidelberg (2005). https://doi.org/10.1007/11423355_17
7. Wooldridge, M., Jennings, N.R., Kinny, D.: The Gaia methodology for agent-oriented analysis and design. Auton. Agent. Multi. Agent. Syst. **3**, 285–312 (2000). https://doi.org/10.1023/A:1010071910869
8. Pavón, J., Gómez-Sanz, J.J., Fuentes, R.: The INGENIAS methodology and tools. In: Agent-Oriented Methodologies (2005)
9. DeLoach, S.A.: The MaSE methodology. In: Bergenti, F., Gleizes, M.P., Zambonelli, F. (eds.) Methodologies and Software Engineering for Agent Systems. Multiagent Systems, Artificial Societies, and Simulated Organizations (International Book Series), vol. 11, pp. 107–125. Springer, Boston (2004). https://doi.org/10.1007/1-4020-8058-1_8
10. Winikoff, M., Padgham, L.: The Prometheus methodology. In: Bergenti, F., Gleizes, M.P., Zambonelli, F. (eds.) Methodologies and Software Engineering for Agent Systems. Multiagent Systems, Artificial Societies, and Simulated Organizations (International Book Series), vol. 11, pp. 217–234. Springer, Boston (2004). https://doi.org/10.1007/1-4020-8058-1_14
11. Bresciani, P., Perini, A., Giorgini, P., Giunchiglia, F., Mylopoulos, J.: Tropos: An agent-oriented software development methodology. Auton. Agent. Multi. Agent. Syst. **8**, 203–236 (2004). https://doi.org/10.1023/B:AGNT.0000018806.20944.ef
12. Georgé, J.P., Gleizes, M.P., Glize, P.: Conception de systèmes adaptatifs à fonctionnalité émergente: La théorie Amas. Rev. d Intelligence Artif. **17**, 591–626 (2003)
13. Rao, A., Georgeff, M.: BDI agents: from theory to practice. In: Proceedings of the First International Conference on Multi-Agent Systems (ICMAS-95) (1995)
14. Jacobson, I., Booch, G., Rumbaugh, J.: Unified process. IEEE Softw. (1999)
15. Booch, G.: The unified modeling language. Perform. Comput. Rev. (1996)
16. Royce, W.W.: Managing the development of large software systems: concepts and techniques. In: ICSE 1987 Proceedings of 9th International Conference on Software Engineering (1987)
17. Margulius, D.L.: Tibco: Promoting flexibility through BPM and analytics. InfoWorld (2003)
18. Odell, J., Parunak, H.V., Bauer, B., Arbor, A.: Extending UML for Agents. Group (2000)
19. Cossentino, M., Potts, C.: A CASE tool supported methodology for the design of multi-agent systems. In: 2002 International Conference on Software Engineering Research and Practice (2002)

Declarative Semantics of Actions and Instructions

Bert de Brock(✉)

Faculty of Economics and Business, University of Groningen, PO Box 800, 9700 AV Groningen, The Netherlands
E.O.de.Brock@rug.nl

Abstract. A complete information modeling method must address both the process- and data-perspectives, preferably in an integrated manner (i.e., also specifying which state change each process should achieve exactly). However, most approaches either emphasize only data or only processes. And when an approach handles both data and processes, there is usually no integration of processes and data. A language must have a precise semantics if tools are to perform intelligent operations on models expressed in the language. Moreover, formal semantics helps in detecting errors in and reasoning about specifications.

We give a precise, declarative, model-theoretic semantics for a large class of instruction languages that treats processes and data in an integrated manner. The instruction expressions are interpreted against a 'state space' (i.e., a set of 'states') and we consider the semantics of an instruction as the set of possible state transitions it can achieve. As a result, we can provide the integration of the different scenarios of a use case into one (textual) system sequence diagram with a well-defined semantics. We can also formally prove the semantic equivalence of several instructions, even for non-deterministic instructions.

The class of instruction languages provides a fruitful similarity between the structuring mechanisms for modeling business processes, textual system sequence diagrams, and programming languages, among others. This will ease the translation towards an implementation in a software system.

Keywords: Action · Instruction · State transition · Transaction · Syntax · Meaning/interpretation · Declarative semantics · (Non-)deterministic · Compositionality · State space · Semantically equivalent

1 Introduction

Any complete information modeling method must address the data-, process-, and behavioral perspectives [1]. And it should do so in an integrated manner.

The problem is that most approaches either emphasize data (e.g. ORM) or they emphasize processes (e.g. BPM). And when an approach handles both data and processes, like UML, there is usually no integration of processes and data. What we mean by that, is that it should also be specified which state change each process should achieve exactly (expressed in terms of the input and the state at hand).

B. Shishkov (Ed.): BMSD 2020, LNBIP 391, pp. 297–308, 2020.
https://doi.org/10.1007/978-3-030-52306-0_20

The semantics, being an essential part of a language, must be precise if tools are to perform intelligent operations on models expressed in the language, like consistency checks and transformations from one model to another [2]. Moreover, formal semantics helps in detecting errors in specifications and to reason about specifications.

We tackle the problem by giving a precise, declarative, model-theoretic semantics for a large class of instruction languages that treats processes and data in an integrated manner. Those instruction languages were introduced in [3] and generalized in [4]. Those papers explained the meaning of the constructs informally, but no formal semantics was given. [3] proposed *System Sequence Descriptions* (i.e., textual System Sequence Diagrams) as a semi-formal modelling notation suitable for scenario integration within use cases. A System Sequence Description (SSD) emphasizes the interactions between the primary actor (user), the system, and other actors (if any). SSDs can form the bridge between the users' world and the developers' world. [3] introduced a suitable (context-free) grammar for SSDs, actually designing a (stylized) language for instructions, which include non-deterministic instructions (e.g., providing the user the choice 'Either do A or do B'). [4] generalized the grammar such that it is suitable for arbitrary instruction languages. As pointed out there, this leads to uniform grammars for general instruction languages. In this way one can obtain a fruitful similarity between the structuring mechanisms for modeling business processes, (textual) SSDs, and programming languages, for instance. This will ease the translation towards an implementation in a software system [3].

The rest of the paper is organized as follows. Section 2 sketches an overall picture of our approach. Section 3 discusses some other approaches. Section 4 explains our syntax for instructions informally, followed by the formal grammar in Sect. 5. It is a slightly different version of the grammar in [4]. Section 6 informally introduces and explains the ideas behind our declarative semantics for instructions. Section 7 contains the necessary auxiliary mathematical definitions and terminology before Sect. 8 defines the semantics of instructions formally. Section 9 contains the main conclusions.

We use a running example (*Process Sale*) for illustration purposes, with the final example illustrating the integration of processes and data.

2 Overall Picture

Any complete information modeling method must address the data-, process-, and behavioral perspectives [1]. And it should do so in an integrated manner.

In this paper we present a formal, declarative model-theoretic semantics (Sect. 8) for our grammar for instruction languages (Sect. 5), in order to be able to uniformly treat and integrate processes and data. This also enables us to formally prove several properties, e.g., the correctness of meaning-preserving transformations.

3 Other Approaches

From the perspective of uniformly treating and integrating processes and data, we look at some other approaches:

Business Process Model and Notation (BPMN) will provide businesses with the capability of understanding their internal business procedures in a graphical notation [5]. BPMN is intended for modeling behaviour/processes, but not for modeling data.
Object Role Modeling (ORM) is a method for designing and querying database models at the conceptual level [6]. ORM is intended for modeling data and retrieval, but not for modeling behaviour/processes.
Unified Modeling Language (UML) emphasizes object-oriented application coding. Although UML has structure diagrams as well as behavior diagrams, they are not integrated. UML will not be useful to software developers, mainly because software developers work with code, not with pictures or diagrams [7, 8].

It is commonly accepted that a language needs a formal specification to be unambiguous. According to [9], the semantics of UML defines how the UML concepts are to be realized by computers. The sections on semantics in [9] are in fact explanations only. Anyway, at best UML has some kind of operational semantics, see [2] for instance, but no declarative, model-theoretic semantics.

4 The Syntax for Instructions Informally Explained

We have the following instruction compositions, with the following informal meaning:

'e1; e2'	means 'first do e1, then do e2',
'e1, e2'	means 'do e1 and e2, in any order',
'**while** c **do** e **end**'	means 'do e as long as c holds',
'**begin** e **end**'	just means 'do e',
'**skip**'	means 'do nothing',
'**either** e1 **or** e2 **end**'	means 'choose between doing e1 or doing e2',
'**maybe** e **end**'	abbreviates '**either** e **or skip end**',
'**repeat** e **until** c'	abbreviates 'e **; while not** c **do** e **end**', and

'**do** n' means 'do the instruction n stands for' (a.k.a. an *Include* or a *Procedure Call*).

We also have '**if** C **then** S {**else if** C **then** S} [**else** S] **end**', which essentially is a nested **if-then-else**: The meta-symbols '{' and '}' indicate that the part '**else if** C **then** S' can be repeated 0 or more times. The meta-symbols '[' and ']' indicate that the part '**else** S' is optional. So, in fact we have a sequence of 1 or more occurrences of '**if** C **then** S', optionally followed by '**else** S'.

Informal (operational) semantics: Only the instruction after the first *true* condition must be executed. If no condition is true then the **else**-part applies, if it is there; otherwise nothing happens. Hence, a lacking **else**-part is equivalent to **else skip**. Therefore, we can always consider the **else**-part to be present.

Example 1: A nested *if-then-else*

To illustrate the use of our nested **if-then-else**, and inspired by Larman's well-known example *Process Sale* plus its extensions [10], the instruction for a cashier to process the items of a customer could have the form:

```
if item has a machine-readable ID then e1                 /* First consider this
 else if item has a human-readable ID then e2             /* else consider this
 else if item has a tag with a price on it then e3        /* else consider this
 else either e4 or e5 end                                 /* else either do e4 or do e5
end                                                       /*
```

So, if an item has (1) no machine-readable ID, (2) no human-readable ID, and (3) no tag with a price on it, then the cashier must choose between doing e4 or doing e5.

When the part '**else if** C **then** S' does not occur, we get the classical rules for **if-then** and **if-then-else** as special cases (both regarding the syntax and the meaning):

S ::= **if** C **then** S [**else** S] **end**

In theory, the abbreviations **repeat-until** and **maybe** are redundant, but they are convenient in practice!

5 A Grammar for Instructions

Now we specify our grammar for instruction languages formally.

A grammar for instruction languages

Using standard BNF-notation, our grammar rules for instruction languages are:

S ::= A | **skip** | S ; S | **begin** S **end** | **while** C **do** S **end** | **either** S **or** S **end** | **do** N
S ::= S , S | **maybe** S **end** | **repeat** S **until** C
S ::= **if** C **then** S {**else if** C **then** S } [**else** S] **end**
C ::= B | **true** | **false** | **not** C | (C **and** C) | (C **or** C)
D ::= **define** N **as** S **end**

where the non-terminal S stands for 'instruction', A for 'atomic instruction', C for 'condition', N for 'instruction name', B for 'basic condition', and D for 'definition'.

In order to avoid ambiguity, we use the binding rule that ',' binds stronger than ';'. We can break through this standard reading by using the 'brackets' **begin** … **end**.

The non-terminals A (for 'atomic instruction'), B (for 'basic condition'), and N (for 'instruction name') have to be worked out per application (they are 'domain-specific').

The atomic instructions in an imperative programming language are the *assignment statements*, which typically are of the form v := e, where v is a variable and e is an expression. Normally you will not find the non-deterministic instructions **maybe** or **either-or** in an imperative programming language. The choice **either-or** relates to the XOR-gateway (without explicit condition) in Business Process Modeling [5].

Instead of the usual *graphical* (system) sequence diagrams [9, 10], *textual* system sequence descriptions (SSDs) are proposed in [3]. The atomic instructions in case of such textual SSDs are of the form

Actor ➡ Actor: Message

expressing that the 1st Actor sends *Message* to the 2nd Actor. If the 2nd actor is **System** (the system under consideration) then *Message* is an instruction for **System** (often implying a state change). If the 1st actor is **System** (and unequal to the 2nd actor) then *Message* is an output of **System** sent to that 2nd actor (with no state change).

The following example illustrates most of our grammar constructs. It is an SSD for a variant of Larman's *Process Sale* [10]. It also shows how we can integrate a Main Success Scenario and its alternative scenarios (in this case, the priced item alternative and the choice between cash payment and credit payment).

An underlined instruction name constitutes a hyperlink to the definition itself.

Example 2: A (textual) system sequence description

```
DEFINE processSale AS
  Cashier ➡ System : makeNewSale ;
  while customer has more items do
      do handleItem ;
      System ➡ Cashier : description, running total
  end ;
  Cashier ➡ System : endSale ;
  System ➡ Cashier : total ;
  do handlePayment(total) ,
  System ➡ InvSys  : sale information ;            /* external Inventory System
  System ➡ Cashier : receipt ;
  maybe Cashier ➡ System : printReceipt end
END /* processSale

DEFINE handleItem AS
  if item is normal
    then Cashier ➡ System : enterItem(itemID, quantity)
    else Cashier ➡ System : enterPricedItem(category, price)
  end
END /* handleItem

DEFINE handlePayment(amount) AS
  either Cashier  ➡ System : makeCashPayment(amount)
      or Customer ➡ System : makeCreditPayment(credit card nr., pin code, amount)
  end
END /* handlePayment
```

6 Towards a Declarative Semantics for Instructions

We consider the semantics/essence/effect of an *action* to be the state transition it achieved, i.e., from an 'old' state to a 'new' state. Therefore we model the *semantics* of an individual action as a *state transition*, i.e., a pair of states (s; s′), where we call s the 'old' state and s′ the 'new' state (in that action context).

A *transaction*, on the other hand, is a function that assigns to any ('old') state a ('new') state, informally speaking. So, a *transaction* is more generic than a *transition*.

Example 3: Transitions versus transactions

In a program *run* (or *execution*), v := e achieves a transition, namely the one where the value of the variable v in the 'new' state will be the value of the expression e in the 'old' state, while everything else stays the same.

In contrast, in a program the instruction v := e expresses a transaction, i.e., a function that assigns to *each* ('old') state a ('new') state, viz. the one in which the value of the variable v will be the value of the expression e in the 'old' state, while everything else stays the same.

In principle, different actions can have the same semantics, just as different mathematical expressions can have the same semantics (e.g., the two mathematical expressions $1 + 2$ and $2 + 1$ have the same semantics).

Example 4: Different actions with the same result

If a golf player hits the ball, say starting from the tee (the 'old' state), and the ball ends at some point (the 'new' state) and later another golf player hits the ball also starting from the tee, and the ball ends at the same point, then the effect is the same, even if the balls came there via completely different routes (e.g., one ball rolled back from a hill).

We also need a semantics for *instructions* (or shortly called *tasks*). Where we model the *semantics* of an action as a *transition*, we might model the *semantics* of an instruction as a *transaction*, i.e., a function that assigns to any relevant 'old' state a 'new' state. We note that 'executing an instruction' corresponds to an action, which formally corresponds to applying the function to the current state, thus arriving at the next state.

We note that an instruction can be non-deterministic (e.g., 'Either do A or do B'). Therefore - being more general - we will model the *semantics* of an instruction as a relation, namely *the set of possible transitions* the instruction can achieve. We note that 'executing a non-deterministic instruction' corresponds to choosing one of the possible 'new' states as the next state.

7 Auxiliary Definitions and Terminology

Before we can define the semantics of instructions formally, we need some auxiliary definitions and terminology. We use the symbols '$\Leftrightarrow$' and "$\stackrel{\text{def}}{=}$" to mean 'is defined as'.

- R is a **relation** ⇔ R is a set of ordered pairs
- If R is a relation then:

  <u>dom(R)</u> $\stackrel{def}{=}$ { x | (x;y) ∈ R }, called the **domain** of R. /* so, all 1st coordinates

  <u>rng(R)</u> $\stackrel{def}{=}$ { y | (x;y) ∈ R }, called the **range** of R. /* so, all 2nd coordinates
- If U is a set then: <u>id(U)</u> $\stackrel{def}{=}$ { (s;s) | s ∈ U }, called the **identity** on U
- If R1 and R2 are relations then we define the **composition** of R1 with R2 as:

  <u>R1 □ R2</u> $\stackrel{def}{=}$ {(x;z) | ∃y∈ dom(R2): (x;y) ∈ R1 and (y;z) ∈ R2}
- If R is a relation then:

  R^0 $\stackrel{def}{=}$ id(dom(R)) /* the set of all '0-step' transitions in R

  R^{n+1} $\stackrel{def}{=}$ R^n □ R /* set of transitions possible in R in n+1 steps (n ≥ 0)

  R* $\stackrel{def}{=}$ ⋃ { R^n | n ∈ N} /* set of transitions possible in R in 0 or more steps
- If U is a set, R ⊆ U × U (i.e., **R being a relation on U) and f : U ⟶ {0,1}** (i.e., f being a function from U into {0,1}), then:

  <u>R ⧖ f</u> $\stackrel{def}{=}$ { (x;y) ∈ R | f(x) = 1 }, called the **positive limitation** of R by f

  <u>R ⧗ f</u> $\stackrel{def}{=}$ { (x;y) ∈ R | f(x) = 0 }, called the **negative limitation** of R by f

We note that R1 □ R2 consists of all the 'combinations' of transitions in R1 'interlinked with' transitions in R2.

If R1 and R2 happen to be functions then R1 □ R2 = R2 ○ R1, i.e., the well-known <u>function composition</u>, defined by R2 ○ R1 (x) = R2(R1(x)) for all x ∈ dom(R1) for which R1(x) ∈ dom(R2). This follows easily by looking at the definition of R1 □ R2: if R1 and R2 are functions then y = R1(x) and z = R2(y), so z = R2(R1(x)).

Regarding the 2 limitations of R by f, we note that **R ⧖ f** and **R ⧗ f** partition R, i.e.:

(1) R ⧖ f ⊆ R (2) R ⧗ f ⊆ R (3) R ⧖ f ∪ R ⧗ f = R (4) R ⧖ f ∩ R ⧗ f = ∅

8 A General Declarative Semantics for Instructions

Section 4 explained the meaning of the syntactic constructs informally. Section 5 presented the grammar itself. Section 6 introduced and explained the ideas behind our declarative semantics for instructions. In this section, we define the semantics formally.

A language (i.e. a set L of 'expressions') is typically generated by a set of (context-free) grammar rules. To link expressions to semantics, usually an 'interpretation function' m over L is introduced [11]. If e ∈ L then m(e) can be read as the <u>meaning/interpretation</u> of expression e. We call expressions e and e′ **semantically equivalent** iff m(e) = m(e′), i.e. iff they have the same meaning.

The expressions are usually interpreted against a set U (of 'possible worlds' or 'states'), where U is called a 'universe of discourse' or 'state space' [12].

Within a program, a <u>state</u> is typically a function that assigns to each variable in the program a value and the <u>state space</u> is a set of such functions.

The state space in case of SSDs might become some (usually large) mathematical structure. This mathematical structure plus the SSDs can form the basis for an implementation, e.g., an OO-implementation (with a class diagram and methods) or a relational implementation (with a database schema and stored procedures).

Example 5: A state space

In Fig. 1 we sketch the minimally needed state space we envisage to support the *Process Sale* SSD in Example 2, presented here in the form of a data model.
Some additional explanation:

- In each concept the value (or combination of values) of the attribute(s) preceded by 'o' is unique; in other words, that attribute (combination) forms a key
- Attributes between the brackets '[' and ']' do not need to have a value (i.e., they are optional); for all other attributes, values are required

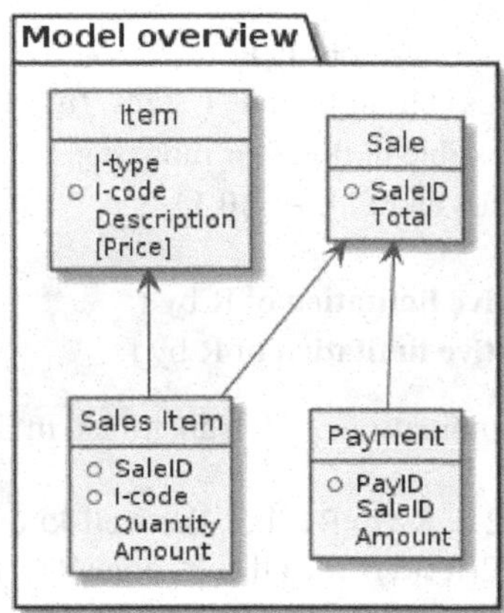

- For the attribute *I-type* of concept *Item*, the set of possible values is {normal, priced}
- The attribute *I-code* of the concept *Item* represents the itemID for normal items and the category for priced items
- The attribute *Price* of the concept *Item* is optional (only relevant for normal items) and represents the price per unit
- The attribute *Total* of the concept *Sale* represents the total amount of the Sale
- The attribute *I-code* of the concept *Sales Item* refers to *Item*
- The attributes *SaleID* of the concepts *Sales Item* and *Payment* refer to *Sale*

Before we give the general semantics, we note that without the meta-symbols '[', ']', '{', and '}', our grammar rules are (with the non-terminal X standing for 'auxiliary'):

S ::= **if** C **then** S X **end**
X ::= **else if** C **then** S X | **else** S

Semantics

We consider a set U (of 'possible worlds' or 'states').

(a) If c is a condition (so generated from the non-terminal C) then m(c) : U → {0,1}, where m(c)(s) indicates for a state s whether c is true in s, i.e. m(c)(s) = 1, or c is false in s, i.e. m(c)(s) = 0.

(b) If e is an (atomic) instruction or instruction name (so generated from A, S, or N) then m(e) ⊆ U × U, representing the set of transitions possible with e. (We recall that we considered the semantics of an instruction as the set of possible transitions it can achieve.)

We could call a transition (s;s') *c-positive* iff m(c)(s) = 1 and *c-negative* iff m(c)(s) = 0.
We could call an element of m(e) an *e-transition*.

For instructions e generated from the non-terminal S we define m(e) inductively in terms of its constituents (Compositionality principle [11]), following the grammar rules in Section 5:

m(**skip**) ≝ id(U)
m(e1; e2) ≝ m(e1) □ m(e2)
m(**begin** e **end**) ≝ m(e)
m(**while** c **do** e **end**) ≝ (m(c) ⧖ m(c))* □ { (s;s) | s ∈ U and m(c)(s) = 0 }
m(**either** e1 **or** e2 **end**) ≝ m(e1) ∪ m(e2)
m(**do** n) ≝ m(e) *if we have introduced n by:* **define** n **as** e **end**

m(e1, e2) ≝ (m(e1) □ m(e2)) ∪ (m(e2) □ m(e1))
m(**maybe** e **end**) ≝ m(**either** e **or skip end**)
m(**repeat** e **until** c) ≝ m(e ; **while not** c **do** e **end**)

m(**if** c **then** e x **end**) ≝ (m(e) ⧖ m(c)) ∪ (m(x) ⧗ m(c)) /* cf. S::= **if** C **then** S X **end**
m(**else if** c **then** e x) ≝ (m(e) ⧖ m(c)) ∪ (m(x) ⧗ m(c)) /* cf. X::= **else if** C **then** S X
m(**else** e) ≝ m(e) /* cf. X::= **else** S

We note that m(**while** c **do** e **end**) and hence m(**repeat** e **until** c) only contain the results of the *terminating* executions.

For conditions c generated from non-terminal C (given in Section 5), we define m(c) inductively for each s ∈ U as follows:

m(**not** c)(s) ≝ 1 − m(c)(s)
m(**true**)(s) ≝ 1
m(**false**)(s) ≝ 0
m((c1 **and** c2))(s) ≝ min[m(c1)(s), m(c2)(s)] /* their minimum
m((c1 **or** c2))(s) ≝ max[m(c1)(s), m(c2)(s)] /* their maximum

Given the formal semantics, we could now formally prove several properties, e.g., whether certain transformations are meaning-preserving. (For instance, we can see that the expression 'e1, e2' is semantically equivalent to '**either** e1;e2 **or** e2;e1 **end**'.)

Our 'universal instruction grammar' and its semantics (including non-determinism) is strongly based on ideas and principles from mathematical logic (see [13]), modal logic (see, e.g., [12]), logics of computation (see, e.g., [12]), in particular dynamic logic [14], and design of languages and their semantics (see, e.g., [11]). We could not find anything like this in [10, 15–17], which together cover more than 120 papers in this area. Our semantics is much simpler and straightforward than the one in [18], for instance.

As an illustration of the semantics of atomic instructions in case of SSDs, we treat the ones in the *Process Sale* example of Sect. 5 and sketch their state transitions. It also illustrates the integration of processes and data, integrating the process described in Example 2 and the data described in Example 5.

We start bottom-up with the subtasks (handleItem and handlePayment) and then we treat the 'main task' processSale. The concepts that get a change are in italics and are also underlined.

Example 6: Illustrating semantics of SSD-instructions / Integrating processes and data

(1) We start with the subtask handleItem.

The step Cashier ➡ **System:** enterItem(x, q) adds a *Sales Item* entry, where the SaleID is the one of the 'running' Sale, the I-code is x, the quantity is q, and the amount is q × the price of the item with I-code x. It also adds that amount to the total of the 'running' *Sale*.

The step Cashier ➡ **System:** enterPricedItem(c, p) adds a *Sales Item* entry, of which the SaleID is the one of the 'running' Sale, the I-code is c, the quantity is 1, and the amount is p. It also adds that amount to the total of the 'running' *Sale*.

In summary: handleItem adds a *Sales Item* entry based on the entered parameter values, where the SaleID is the one of the 'running' Sale. It also adds the amount of the Sales Item entry to the total of the 'running' *Sale*.

(2) We continue with the subtask handlePayment(a).

The step Cashier ➡ **System:** makeCashPayment(a) adds a *Payment* entry, with a system-generated PayID, the SaleID of the 'running' Sale, and the amount a.

The step Customer ➡ **System:** makeCreditPayment(ccn, pc, a) adds a *Payment* entry, with a system-generated PayID, the SaleID of the 'running' Sale, and the amount a. We note that the credit card nr. ccn and the pin code pc are needed for doing the credit payment but are not stored in the state space.

In summary: handlePayment(a) adds a *Payment* entry with a system-generated PayID, the SaleID of the 'running' Sale, and the amount a.

(3) Now we are ready for the 'main task' processSale. Many steps are 'informing steps', i.e., they inform the user or some external system but do not lead to a state change.

The step Cashier ➡ **System:** makeNewSale adds a *Sale* entry, with a system-generated SaleID and the total 0.

The step **do** handleItem adds a *Sales Item* entry based on the entered parameter values (with the SaleID of the 'running' Sale) and it also adds the amount of the Sales Item entry to the total of the 'running' *Sale*, as we concluded under (1).

The step **System** ➡ Cashier: description, running total shows the description of the item at hand and the current total of the sale at hand (but does not change the state).

The step Cashier ➡ **System:** endSale only triggers the next step (but no state change).

The step **System** ➡ Cashier: total shows the final total of the sale at hand (but does not change the state).

The step **do** handlePayment(total) adds a *Payment* entry with a system-generated PayID, the SaleID of the 'running' Sale, and the parameter value total as the amount, as we can conclude from (2).

The step **System** ➡ InvSys: sale information sends all Sales Item entries of the sale at hand to the external Inventory System (but does not change the state of **System**). For the system InvSys - in its turn - this input can be considered as an instruction.

The step **System** ➡ Cashier: receipt shows the relevant information of all Sales Item entries (i.e., the description of the item, the quantity, and the amount) as well as the Payment entry of the sale at hand (but does not change the state).

The step Cashier ➡ **System:** printReceipt delivers a print of the above information (but does not change the state).

In summary: processSale adds the *Sale* entry, all *Sales Item* entries, and the *Payment* entry of the sale at hand, informs the system InvSys about it, shows the relevant information of the sale (also in between), and maybe delivers a print of that sale information.

In a translation towards an OO-implementation, the 'shows' above use a `GET` and the 'adds' a `SET`. Translating towards an SQL-implementation, the 'shows' use a `SELECT` and the 'adds' an `INSERT` (but the 'adds amount' in handleItem an `UPDATE`).

9 Main Conclusions

A complete information modeling method must address both the process- and data-aspects, preferably in an integrated manner. Also, a language must have a precise semantics if tools are to perform intelligent operations on models expressed in the language. In this paper we gave a precise, declarative, model-theoretic semantics for a large class of instruction languages that treats processes and data in an integrated manner. The general grammar for the instruction languages contain rules for sequential compositions, arbitrary orders, blocks, (nested) conditionals, loops, options, choices, definitions, and calls (a.k.a. *Includes*). All keywords in our grammar are taken from colloquial English, making the languages 'pseudo natural languages'.

The class of instruction languages provides a fruitful similarity between the structuring mechanisms for modeling business processes, textual system sequence diagrams, and programming languages, among others. This will ease the translation towards an implementation in a software system. We are now also able to prove formally the semantic equivalence of several instructions (i.e., that they have the same meaning), even for non-deterministic instructions. As another result, we can provide the integration of the different scenarios of a use case into one SSD with a well-defined semantics. All in all, the paper contributes to the foundations of business modelling, among others for information systems analysis and design.

A limitation is the lack of exception handling. We want to work on it in near future.

References

1. Olle, T.W., et al.: Information Systems Methodologies: A Framework for Understanding. Addison-Wesley, Boston (1991)
2. Övergaard, G., Palmkvist, K.: A formal approach to use cases and their relationships. In: Bézivin, J., Muller, P.-A. (eds.) UML 1998. LNCS, vol. 1618, pp. 406–418. Springer, Heidelberg (1999). https://doi.org/10.1007/978-3-540-48480-6_31
3. de Brock, E.O.: On system sequence descriptions. In: Proceedings NLP4RE (2020)
4. de Brock, E.O.: From business modelling to software design. In: Proceedings BMSD (2020)
5. http://www.bpmn.org/. Accessed 16 May 2020
6. http://www.orm.net/. Accessed 16 May 2020
7. https://archive.eiffel.com/doc/manuals/technology/bmarticles/uml/page.html. Accessed 16 May 2020
8. https://www.techwalla.com/articles/the-disadvantages-of-uml. Accessed 16 May 2020
9. https://www.omg.org/spec/UML/. Accessed 16 May 2020
10. Larman, C.: Applying UML and Patterns. Addison Wesley Professional, Boston (2005)
11. Stanford Encyclopedia of Philosophy, Stanford (in particular Compositionality and its Formal Statement). Accessed 16 May 2020
12. Goldblatt, R.I.: Logics of time and computation. CSLI Lecture Notes 7, Stanford (1992)
13. Montague, R.: Universal grammar. Theoria **36**(3), 373–398 (1970)

14. Harel, D., Kozen, D., Tiuryn, J.: Dynamic Logic. MIT Press, Cambridge (2000)
15. Jacobson, I., et al.: Use Case 2.0: The Guide to Succeeding with Use Cases. Ivar Jacobson International (2011)
16. Cockburn, A.: Writing Effective Use Cases. Addison Wesley, Boston (2001)
17. Tiwari, S., Gupta, A.: A systematic literature review of use case specifications research. Inf. Softw. Technol. **67**, 128–158 (2015)
18. Sinnig, D., et al.: LTS semantics for use case models. In: Proceedings of SAC, pp. 365–370 (2009)

Bridging the Gap Between Business and Technical Infrastructures of Enterprise Information Systems: Addressing the "Vertical Fit" Problems

Sahbi Zahaf[1,2(✉)], Khaoula Fatnassi[1], and Faiez Gargouri[1]

[1] HICM, MIRACL Laboratory, University of Sfax, 242-3021 Sfax, Tunisia
sahbi.zahaf@isi.utm.tn, khaoula_fatnassi@yahoo.com, faiez.gargouri@isims.usf.tn

[2] Higher Institute of Computer Sciences, University of Tunis El-Manar, Tunis, Tunisia

Abstract. Enterprise Information Systems supporting business processes are to be characterized by integrity, flexibility, and interoperability. Nevertheless, the "three fit" problems (considered in the current paper) obstruct the achievement of those desired features both at the business-infrastructure and technical-infrastructure EIS levels: "vertical fit" problems – concerning the business infrastructure; "horizontal fit" problems and "transversal fit" problems – concerning the technical infrastructure. We argue that for overcoming those problems, it is necessary to: (a) narrow the gap between the business infrastructure and the technical infrastructure; (b) facilitate the integration, communication and coordination between components in each of the infrastructures. Featuring our approach directed towards dealing with the "three fit" problems, we present in this paper our contribution related to the "vertical fit" problems. This concerns in particular our proposal featuring the challenge of addressing integrity, flexibility, and interoperability with regard to EIS business infrastructures. Moreover, we define solutions for guaranteeing interoperability between EIS business infrastructures and EIS technical infrastructures. We apply this to organize the BPIS (Bid Process Information System).

Keywords: EIS · Integrity · Interoperability · Flexibility · Bid Process · BPIS · BPMN · BPEL · WS · SOA · Big Data

1 Introduction

Enterprises often operate in unstable environments. They have to adequately address saturated markets, increasing competition, customers' requirements, and so on [12]. In this, the enterprise competitiveness depends on the following as according to [13]: The enterprise's degree of integrity with respect to the Business Processes covered by the enterprise; Its degree of interoperability with regard to the customers, partners, and suppliers, it has to coordinate; Its flexibility as it concerns the enterprise's power to adapt

B. Shishkov (Ed.): BMSD 2020, LNBIP 391, pp. 309–319, 2020.
https://doi.org/10.1007/978-3-030-52306-0_21

skills and resources for supporting the market requirements. Often the successful development of an enterprise depends on the Enterprise Information Systems (EIS) it uses and manipulates. Nevertheless, the use of EIS reaches a limit in collaborative environments because enterprises management methods diverge and EISs are mainly inflexible resource packages that are not built with an interoperability objective. Consequently, we need to make EISs integrated, flexible and interoperable in order to achieve the needed gains competitiveness and performance [11]. In fact, an EIS implementation is a delicate issue that is hard to achieve – since the conception until the exploitation and evolution [13]. The urbanization approach allows for implementing an EIS, featuring two infrastructures [4]: The Business Infrastructure that concerns the EIS design – it is about identifying and modeling processes operated by the enterprise; The Technical Infrastructure that concerns the EIS implementation – it is about specifying applications that cover the defined processes. We count on this approach as it concerns the specification of EIS featuring corresponding enterprises. In this we nevertheless are faced by the so called "three fit" problems [12]: (a) "vertical fit" – lack of integrity and lack of extensibility; (b) "horizontal fit" – lack of flexibility and lack of internal interoperability; (c) "transversal fit" – lack of openness and lack of external interoperability.

Featuring our approach directed towards dealing with the "three fit" problems, we present in this paper our contribution related to the "vertical fit" problems. This concerns in particular our proposal featuring the challenge of addressing integrity, flexibility, and interoperability with regard to EIS business infrastructures. Moreover, we define solutions for guaranteeing interoperability between EIS business infrastructures and EIS technical infrastructures. This all is based on BPMN modeling [8] and corresponding executions using the BPEL-WS language [7]. As it concerns the data transmission between Web Services (WS) [2] it is realized via JSON messages [6]. We apply this to organize the so-called "BPIS" (Bid Process Information System) [12] and we present an example: it is about exploiting interoperability criteria between a BPIS business infrastructure and a BPIS technical infrastructure. Actually, we use Big Data techniques (such as "MongoBD") [1] as it concerns the "application view", we demonstrate that our communication interface allows for ensuring the availability of bid data for large volumes and varieties of data (structured and unstructured). We prove that our approach allows for resolving the problems of integrity, flexibility, and interoperability (between business infrastructures and technical infrastructures). We apply our contributions to organize the BPIS [12].

The remaining of the current paper is structured as follows. Section 2 presents relevant background information and points to related work. Section 3 introduces the abovementioned approach. In Sect. 4, we present the application of the approach, while providing also further elaborations with regard to the approach itself. We conclude the paper in Sect. 5.

2 Background

As mentioned already, we base our work on the "Urbanization Approach" [4] as it concerns the implementation of EIS. This approach concerns four levels: BUSINESS VIEW – representing the modeling of the business processes used by the enterprise; FUNCTIONAL VIEW – representing the functions and information flows towards the business processes, regardless of the technologies used; APPLICATION VIEW – representing the applications used to support functions and flows, and to facilitate the processes; PHYSICAL VIEW – representing the "material" infrastructure. Further, the EIS is to be integrated, flexible, and interoperable.

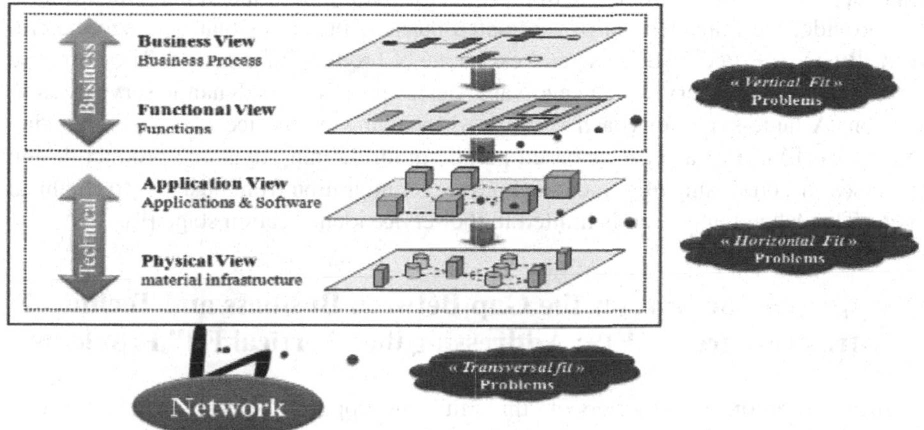

Fig. 1. EIS Urbanization model [4]: Addressing the "three fit" Problems [12].

Nevertheless, the abovementioned approach has to deal with the "three fit" problems [12], as mentioned already – see Fig. 1. The VERTICAL FIT concerns the gap between the EIS business infrastructure (that is abstract) and the EIS technical infrastructure (that represents real implementations) – this is hence about the lack of integrity and of extensibility. Moreover, this is the lack of interoperability between EIS business infrastructures and EIS technical infrastructures. The HORIZONTAL FIT reflects software deficiencies to the business level (induced by the "vertical fit" problems) and this is also about the detection of intra-applicative communication problems. It is thus difficult to ensure interactions among software instances within the same EIS technical infrastructure. This is hence about the lack of flexibility and of internal interoperability. The TRANSVERSAL FIT concerns the inter-applicative communication problems carried out dynamically through a network – this is hence about the lack of openness and of external interoperability. As studied in [12], such problems handicap the achievement of integrity, interoperability, and flexibility as it concerns the development of EIS.

In the following, we focus to the "vertical fit" problems. Several works have proposed solutions for bridging the gap between business and technical infrastructures.

The approach outlined by [10] enables synchronization between analysis model and implementation model respectively from the business and technical domains. Consistency and interaction synchronization are the necessary and sufficient conditions for an operational alignment between these domains. The authors focus their research on the "discontinuity" between the business and IT perspectives, the "business-IT gap". The defined approach ensures consistency between heterogeneous models. However, it is limited for guaranteeing interoperability between EIS business infrastructures and EIS technical infrastructures. Moreover, the consistency of an EIS depends utterly on its degree of integrity, flexibility and its internal interoperability. While its agility always depends on its flexible capacities and external interoperability [12].

The works of [5] outline a Service Oriented Approach (SOA) [2] that facilitates design process flexibility in Product Lifecycle Management (PLM) systems. PLM systems support data in the life cycle of a product including design and manufacturing. It also provides the management of associated business processes that organize the creation, Business Process (BP) use and exchange of product information. They propose reusable activities as services and evolvable design processes as dynamic services composition. A three-stage approach is outlined including (i) service identification using catalogues (ii) use of a services based paradigm for defining dynamic product design processes (iii) proposing alignment techniques for migration from business to technical levels. The defined approach is limited to the service identification stage [9].

3 Approach for Narrow the Gap Between Business and Technical Infrastructures of EIS: Addressing the "Vertical Fit" Problems

In order to overcome the barriers of "three fit", our proposal featuring the challenge of addressing integrity, flexibility, and interoperability with regard to EIS at its both business and technical infrastructures. Integration at the EIS business level covers the coordination of functions that manage, control and monitor business processes. Integration at the EIS technical level deals with interoperability of software applications and database systems in heterogeneous computing environments. This integrity assumption is valid only if internal interoperability inside the EIS is carried out without ambiguity. Henceforth, interoperability is a necessary condition for EIS to describe it as integrated.

The flexibility assumption is valid only if integrity inside the EIS is guarantee. However, this last feature is ensured if we solve the interoperability requirements inside the EIS (internal interoperability) and between different EIS (external or dynamic interoperability). However, the non-satisfaction of the interoperability requirement incurs significant costs associated primarily to time and resources which are presented to develop exchange information interfaces and knowledge sharing (technical interoperability), following a common semantics (semantic interoperability) and which are supposed to train actors and adapt organizational procedures (organizational interoperability). Such assumptions influence negatively the overall performance of enterprises [12].

Based on the related work in the previous section, we present, in the following, our solutions for guaranteeing interoperability between EIS business infrastructures and EIS technical infrastructures. Through a business process-lifecycle, consistency is difficult to be maintained between models from different environments. The successive developments and changes made by different stakeholders lead to the development of inconsistencies between models. In fact, each enterprise has its own strategy to define its processes flows. Integration can be achieved by unification [9]: standards methods, architectures, and reusable models help to guarantee interoperability of the EIS at the business level. We propose a method allowing the control of business processes, from their modelling to their implementation within an application view. This all is based on BPMN modeling [8] and corresponding executions using the BPEL-WS language [7]. Table 1 shows our choices for these languages featuring the integrity, flexibility, and interoperability.

Table 1. BP languages evaluation according: integrity, flexibility and interoperability.

		Business Process Definition Languages			Business Process Execution Languages	
		UML 2.0	BPMN 2.0	YAWL	XPDL	BPEL
Integrity	Functional	+	++	+	+	++
	Behavioral	+	++	++	-	++
	Informational	++	-	-	+	+
	Organizational	+	+	-	+	++
	Operational	+	+	+	+	++
Flexibility	Design	+	+	+	+	++
	Change	-	-	-	-	-
Interoperability	Intra-process	+	++	-	-	++
	Inter-process	-	+	-	-	+

The BPEL supports business transactions by standardizing the format definition of business processes flows. The interoperability is guarantee by using Web Services (BPEL-WS). In fact, BPEL can orchestrate business processes interactions between Web Services in a standardized way by using XML documents. These processes can be executed on any platform. However, BPEL was criticizing by the difficulty to implement in the "application view" functions defined at the business infrastructure, thus a discontinuity between business and technical infrastructures appears

For bridging the gap of this "vertical fit" barrier, we rely to the SOA [2] approach for defining functions as services at the "functional view". This solution facilitates the alignment and coherence between business and technical infrastructures of an EIS. In this, SOAP [6] permits to implement WS [2] and allows the transmission of data between remote applications located on different machines while ensuring their security. However, this transmission was characterizing by the heaviness of the XML documents exchanged by the SOAP services. To overcome this limitation, we propose to integrate REST-WS [6] technology with the JSON format; it ensures transmission more faster than XML. Note that REST uses HTTP protocol for data transmission and JSON format for data reception [6]. We use SOAP/XML as a "repository" and we convert XML to JSON format in the Controller.

4 Application for Resolve the Barrier of the BPIS "Vertical Fit"

The owner calls for a bid in manufacturing domain to benefit from a product. After a certain delay, he receives proposals from different participating competitors, which submit their contributions to this call for tenders (bid process). A bid process embodies a techno-economic proposal (a technical expertise backed by a financial offer). Such a contribution translates the product design activity by optimizing factors of production (cost, quality of services, risks), and it must be respect the deadlines and the constraints formalized in the specifications. The owner focuses on the best offer, which meets its requirements and which covers the eminent interests [12]. It is clear that the differentiation with competitors in manufacturing product is based on additional services. These services are created by gathering and assembling information coming from value chain partners.

The executing support of the bid process so-called “BPIS” or Bid Process Information System can increase the product value thanks to additional services (built on data associated to the product) in order to meet and fit better owner’s needs. However, this system influences the internal and external environmental requirements of partners. The problem is that partners exploit different processes and applications; which leads to vertical, horizontal and transversal barriers of BPIS interoperability.

We address integrity, interoperability and flexibility by defining four dimensions to describe the BPIS [13]: OPERATIONAL DIMENSION – serves to exploit business processes used by the enterprise in its different bid projects; ORGANIZATIONAL DIMENSION – organizes the expertise that the enterprise acquired during its previous bid projects. Such assumption permits an eventual adaptation and reutilization of these skills in future bid projects; DECISION-MAKING DIMENSION – aims to make the right decisions that concern the enterprise participation in different bid projects. COOPERATIVE DIMENSION – covers the intra-enterprise communications and the inter-enterprise communications in order to contribute on the techno-economic bid proposition. We define these dimensions while creating techno-economic bids propositions. Thus, Table 2 illustrates the different approaches used to describe these four dimensions of the BPIS.

Table 2. BPIS 4-dimensions featuring the integrity, flexibility, and interoperability [13].

		Flexibility		
		Integrity		External Interoperability
		Internal Interoperability		
		“Vertical fit”	*“Horizontal fit”*	*“Transversal fit”*
Operational Dimension	Organizational Dimension	PRIMA / Engineering Systems / Lean Manufacturing / SOA / BPM	Knowledge Management	Knowledge Management
	Decision Dimension		Business Intelligence	
	Cooperative Dimension		SOA / Web Service	SOA / Web Service / Cloud Computing

In the following, we present an application of our contributions (see Sect. 3), for addressing integrity, flexibility, and interoperability with regard to BPIS business infrastructure. Figure 2 materializes our bid process modelling by using BPMN 2.0. It distinguishes three main processes: “assessment for the eligibility of the bid”, “elaboration of the bid proposition”, and “closure of the bid process” [13].

We focus on the “elaboration of the bid proposition” sub-process that corresponds to the planning of the design activity of the product [13]. During this phase, the expert must

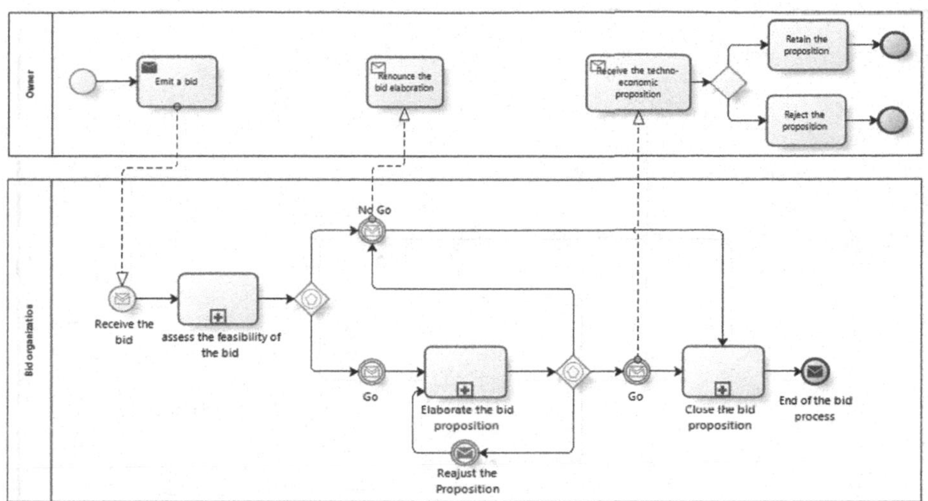

Fig. 2. BPMN modelling: Addressing the phases for the achievement of the Bid Process [13].

identify the manufacturing tree whose root is the final product, and whose leaves contain the purchased components and raw materials. Based on this work, the expert can specify the products to manufacture and others to purchase from suppliers. For each product to manufacture, the expert relies on a specific process, which describes the construction of this product in relation with its direct components. Note that each process contains a set of phases, and each phase consumes resources. The expert can also detect the risks related to the exploitation of resources. Figure 3 presents an extract of our BPEL implementation of the product design activity [3].

In the following, we present the list of services that covers the techno-economic bid proposition: (a) services for build technical solution required for product design activity; (b) services for cost-management to assess the cost of the technical solution and for the price-management to check the future price on the market of the designed-product; (c) services for risk-management to specify risks relying the techno-economic proposition.

Figure 4 describes an extract of the fragment of code in BPEL that represents the selection type of product required to build the technical solution [3].

In order to resolve interoperability problems between business and technical infrastructures of the BPIS, we propose to support BPEL by SOAP-WS. As it concerns the data transmission between WS it is realized via JSON messages. Figure 5 shows an extract of the conversion from BPEL to SOAP/XML [3].

We present an example: it is about exploiting interoperability criteria between a BPIS business infrastructure and a BPIS technical infrastructure. In fact, we propose to evaluate the response time of request that permits to insert documents describing the characteristics of manufactured products (code, cost, price, risks, label, quantity, etc.). We use Big Data techniques (such as "MongoBD") [1] as it concerns the "application view". Our communication interface allows for ensuring on real time the availability of bid data for large volumes and varieties of data (structured and unstructured).

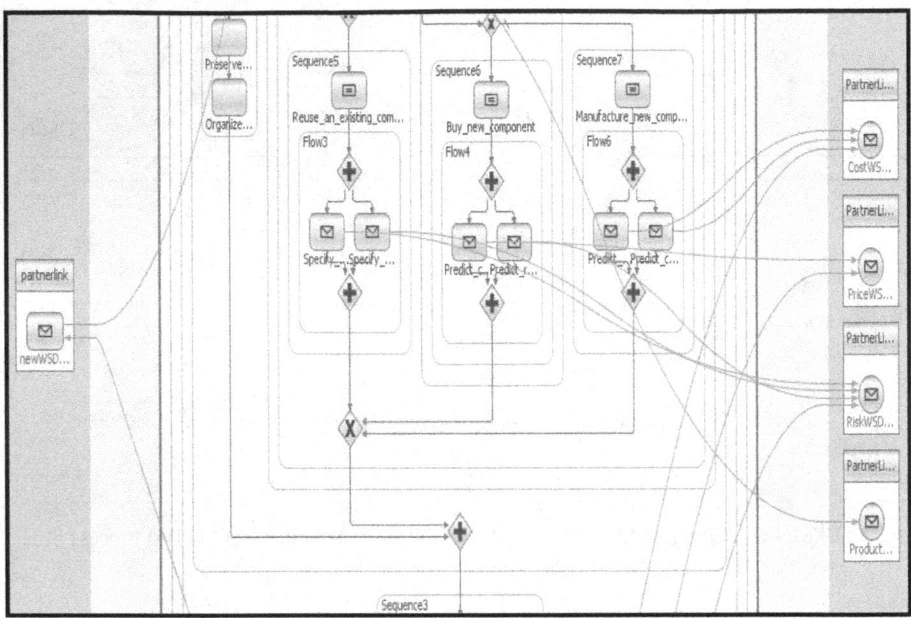

Fig. 3. BPEL Implementation extract: Addressing the product design activity for the techno-economic Bid proposition.

```
<invoke name="Select_technical_component" partnerLink="PartnerLink3" operation="ProductWSDL1Operation" xmlns:tns="http://j2ee.netbeans.org/wsdl/BpelModule1/ProductWSDL1" portType="tns: ProductWSDL1PortType" inputVariable="ProductWSDL1OperationIn" outputVariable="ProductWSDL1OperationOut"/>
        <if>
          <condition> ns1:doXslTransform(stub(), stub(), stub(), stub(), $ProductWSDL1OperationOut.part3) </condition>
          <sequence name="Sequence5" xmlns:tns="http://j2ee.netbeans.org/wsdl/BpelModule1/RiskWSDL1">
            <assign name="Reuse_an_existing_component">
              <copy>
                <from> concat('hello', $ProductWSDL1OperationIn.part3) </from>
                <to variable="ProductWSDL1OperationOut"/>
              </copy>
            </assign>
              <flow name="Flow3">
                <invoke name="Specify_risks_related_use_component" partnerLink="PartnerLink5" operation="RiskWSDL1Operation" xmlns:tns="http://j2ee.netbeans.org/wsdl/BpelModule1/RiskWSDL1" portType="tns:RiskWSDL1PortType" inputVariable="RiskWSDL1OperationIn" outputVariable="RiskWSDL1OperationOut"/>
                  <invoke name="Specify_component_risk" partnerLink="PartnerLink5" operation="RiskWSDL1Operation" xmlns:tns="http://j2ee.netbeans.org/wsdl/BpelModule1/RiskWSDL1" portType="tns:RiskWSDL1PortType" inputVariable="RiskWSDL1OperationIn1" outputVariable="RiskWSDL1OperationOut1"/>
              </flow></sequence>
          <elseif>
  <sequence name="Sequence6">
              <assign name="Buy_new_component">
                  <copy>
                    <from variable="ProductWSDL1OperationIn" part="part3"/>
                    <to variable="ProductWSDL1OperationOut" part="part3"/>
                  </copy>
                  </assign>
                  <flow name="Flow5">
            <invoke name="Predict_component_price" partnerLink="PartnerLink6" operation="PriceWSDL1Operation" xmlns:tns="http://j2ee.netbeans.org/wsdl/BpelModule1/PriceWSDL1" portType="tns:PriceWSDL1PortType" inputVariable="PriceWSDL1OperationIn" outputVariable="PriceWSDL1OperationOut"/>
```

Fig. 4. BPEL fragment: Addressing the selection type of product.

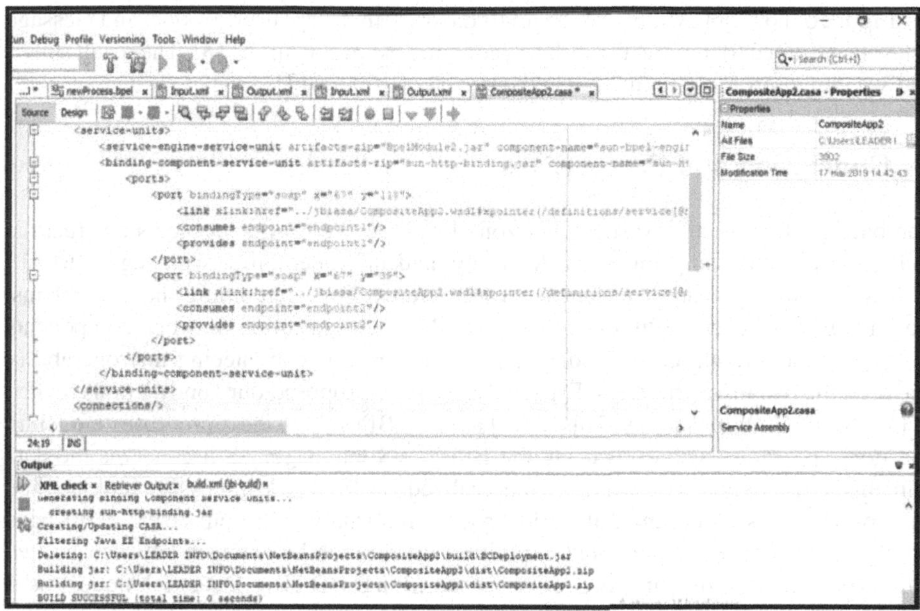

Fig. 5. Extract of the conversion from the BPEL techno-economic Bid proposition to SOAP/XML Web Services.

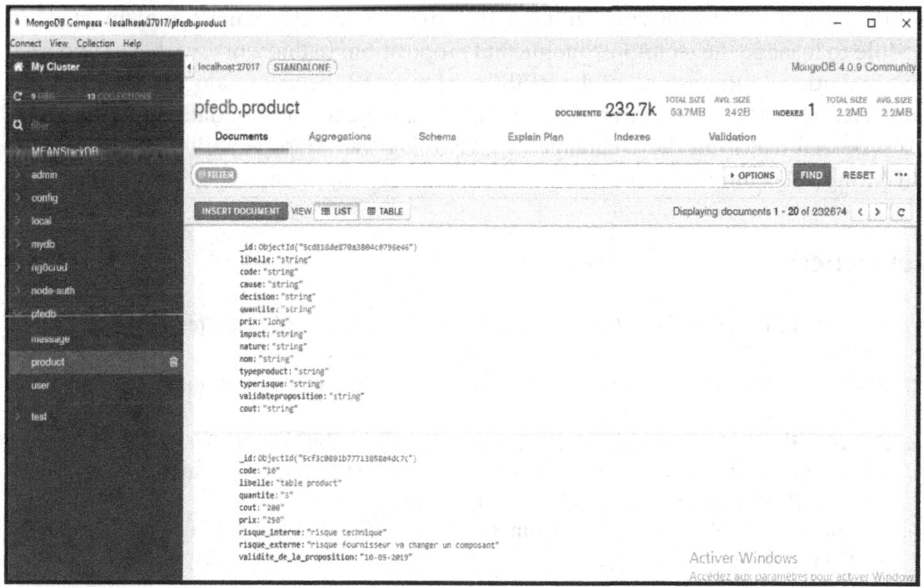

Fig. 6. A set of data addressing the product design activity stored with MongoDB.

Figure 6 shows an extract of MongoDB database that store user, product and message datasets, required to definite the techno-economic bid proposition [13]. The result shows that we can insert more than 2.6 k in the period of 100 ms [3].

5 Conclusion and Perspectives

The barrier of "three fit": vertical, horizontal and transversal fits problems obstruct the challenge of addressing integrity, flexibility, and interoperability with regard to EIS both at its business and at technical infrastructures. For overcoming those problems, we have presented our solutions to facilitate the communication between components in each of the infrastructures and to narrow the gap for guaranteeing interoperability between the two infrastructures. Especially, we have proposed our contributions related to the "vertical fit" problems. This all is based on BPMN business processes modeling and corresponding executions using the BPEL-WS language. As it concerns the data transmission between Web Services, it is realized via JSON messages. We have applied our contributions to organize the Bid Process Information System (BPIS). We have even presented an example about exploiting interoperability criteria between its two infrastructures. In this context, we have used MongoBD (Big Data techniques) as it concerns the "application view"; we have demonstrated that our communication interface allows for ensuring the availability of bid data for large volumes and varieties of data (structured and unstructured). Note that we have proposed in our previous researches [13] to rely on Enterprise Resource Planning "Odoo" for defining the "operation dimension" and thus, the "application view" of the BPIS. In this context, we have implemented our module to manage the techno-economic bid proposition. In this work, we have supported the "operational dimension" of the BPIS by MongoDB, because Odoo uses a relational database, which is not able to store and analyse a large amount of data. In future work, our proposal featuring the challenge of addressing the interoperability between Odoo and MongoBD, and thus to deal with "horizontal fit" and "transversal fit" problems.

References

1. Berman, J.: Principles and Practice of Big Data 2nd edn. Academic Press, London (2018). eBook ISBN: 9780128156100
2. Bean, J.: SOA and Web Services Interface Design, Principles, Techniques and Standards. Elsevier, Burlington (2010)
3. Fatnassi, K., Zahaf, S., Gargouri, F.: Resolving interoperability problems of the Bid Process Information System (BPIS). In: 11th Conference on ENTERprise Information Systems, 16–18 October 2019, Sousse, Tunisia. Elsevier Ltd (2019)
4. Fournier-Morel, X., Grojean, P., Plouin, G., Rognon, C.: SOA le Guide de l'Architecture du SI. Dunod, Paris (2008)
5. Hachani, S., Gzara, L., Verjus, H.: A service-oriented approach for flexible process support within enterprises: application on PLM systems. Enterp. Inf. Syst. **7**(1), 79–99 (2013)
6. Juris, T., Grabis, J.: Comparison of SOAP and REST based web services using software evaluation metrics. Inf. Technol. Manage. Sci. **19**(1), 92–97 (2016)
7. OASIS. Web Services Business Process Execution Language Version 2.0. Technical report, OASIS, (2007). http://docs.oasis-open.org/wsbpel/2.0/OS/wsbpel-v2.0-OS.html

8. OMG. Business process model and notation (BPMN) version 2.0. Technical report, Object Management Group (OMG), (2011). http://taval.de/publications/BPMN2.0
9. Panetto, H., Cecil, J.: Information systems for enterprise integration, interoperability and networking: theory and applications. Enterp. Inf. Syst. **7**(1), 1–6 (2013). https://doi.org/10.1080/17517575.2012.684802.hal-00686500
10. Ulmer, J.-S., Belaud, J.-P., Le Lann, J.-M.: A pivotal-based approach for enterprise business process and IS integration. Enterp. Inf. Syst. **7**(1), 61–78 (2013)
11. Zacharewicz, G., Diallo, S., Ducq, Y., et al.: Model-based approaches for interoperability of next generation enterprise information systems: state of the art and future challenges. Inf. Syst. e-Bus. Manage. **15**, 229–256 (2017)
12. Zahaf, S., Gargouri, F.: ERP Inter-enterprises for the operational dimension of the urbanized bid process information system. In: 6th Conference on ENTERprise Information Systems, Troia, Portugal, Journal of Procedia Technology, vol. 16, pp. 813–823. Elsevier Ltd (2014)
13. Zahaf, S., Gargouri, F.: The urbanized bid process information system. In: 21th International Conference in Knowledge Based and Intelligent Information and Engineering Systems, 06–08, Marseille, France, Journal of Procedia Computer Science, vol. 112, pp. 874–885. Elsevier Ltd (2017)

IoT System Design of a V2X Application

Evangelos D. Spyrou(✉), Konstantinos Skoufas, and Dimitris Mitrakos

School of Electrical and Computer Engineering,
Aristotle University of Thessaloniki, Egnatia Street,
Panepistimioupoli, Thessaloniki, Greece
{evang_spyrou,mitrakos}@eng.auth.gr, skoukons@ece.auth.gr

Abstract. We live in the Internet of Things era. Daily activities are being handled via the Web. One of the major sectors that has been impacted is intelligent transportation. As such Vehicle to Everything (V2X) has emerged whereby Road Side Units (RSU)s assist vehicle drivers to make decisions such as routing. The successful implementation and deployment of such a system requires a thorough design. To this end there exist certain methodologies that can be used to construct a detailed design of the system. In this paper, we utilise the Unified Modeling Language (UML) to capture the requirements of an intelligent IoT V2X system and design it. We provide a detailed design, where use cases, sequence diagrams and a statechart make the demands of such a system clear, in order to provide a fully designed IoT V2X application. We argue that such a design can provide significant assistance to the developers and engineers and become the beginning of a newly formed visual modeling language.

Keywords: IoT · V2X · UML · Use cases · Sequence diagrams · Statechart

1 Introduction

Noways, the vastly expanding Internet of Things has reached a point which requires thorough preparation and planning in order for a technological idea to become feasible. To this end, business modeling can play a decisive role and is considered by many one of the best approaches [1,2], always having its own challenges [3]. Furthermore, the usage of the Unified Modeling Language is of great importance [4] and can be used to achieve the modeling of the desirable system.

It comes as no surprise, that UML and business modeling can also be used in describing the structural and functional processes of intelligent transportation systems [5]. By doing so, the main idea, the structure and the function of such systems - even if it is a complex one - breaks down to simpler parts that can be visually monitored. Thus, it is easier for the team that develops the system to examine them for possible flaws and if flaws exists, to make the proper designing adjustments. In addition, with the project split into multiple parts, each one can

B. Shishkov (Ed.): BMSD 2020, LNBIP 391, pp. 320–330, 2020.
https://doi.org/10.1007/978-3-030-52306-0_22

be given to specific sub-team and the collaboration between the teams becomes more smooth. The problem of system design is of particular significance, since it can result in a proper implementation of a system. Especially in IoT systems there have been approaches that the UML paradigm was used to model dependencies and relationships in IoT components, as we can see in [6] and references therein. Furthermore, using the UML language we aim to bridge the gap between technical and non technical people of a project. A UML design can be an initial point of a new IoT based language extension that will assist in all stages of a project, similar to other works that have been proposed in [7,8], albeit in this work we are focusing on the IoT application.

Towards this direction, in this paper, we take on board a complete IoT V2X system, which we model and design its architecture in full, using UML. The main goal of this system is to achieve optimal vehicle routing and give the fastest route to the infotainment system of the vehicle that made the request. More specifically, we capture the requirements of this system and describe them as use cases. Thereafter, we proceed with the design of the sequence diagrams of each identified actor, for simplicity, and we finish with the detailed statechart. The statechart shows the possible states of the system, together with possible problems that may arise during the system implementation. Note that ongoing work is done for the representation of the system in a class diagram, specific for an IoT application using our case study. That way, the whole process of the actual creation of the V2X system breaks down to less complex parts, the goal becomes more clear and the complexity drops by a big factor. The main objective of this work is to attempt a new visual language based on UML to describe different aspects of the system. As such, this is an initial work on an attempt of an abstracted notation specific for the Internet of things for transportation.

The remainder of this paper includes the following; Sect. 2 provides the specifications of the system, Sect. 3 presents the system breakdown to UML diagrams and finally, Sect. 4 provides the conclusions of the work done in this paper.

2 Specifications

IoT systems belong is an immediate step from wireless sensor networks. Usually they consist of devices that perform some kind of sensing and they transmit their data over the Internet. These devices are equipped with wireless transceivers, which operate in order to lead data into a server. Furthermore, sensing units perform every day activities, which correspond to the application of an IoT system, such as traffic monitoring in our case. A complete IoT system performs specific services that can be modeled before the implementation stage. In our particular case, we have three subsystems, which comprise the traffic light subsystem, the vehicle subsystem and a server, which they are represented by their functionalities in terms of software.

For the better understanding of the functionality of the system we first provide its hardware structure. The systems consists of two subsystems, one that is meant to be implemented on traffic lights and one for the vehicles. In addition, it utilises a central server. Both of the devices and the server cooperate to create an Internet of Vehicles (IoV) network which gathers data according to the real time traffic conditions. With the data gathered by the system, the optimal routing is achieved by implementing a backpressure algorithm.

The traffic lights subsystem consists of an Arduino Uno Rev3[1] and a Raspberry Pi 3 model B+[2] with the former being a non-expensive microcontroller and the latter a non-expensive microcomputer and the central processing unit of the traffic lights subsystem. We suggest Wi-Fi communication to send/receive data from/to the traffic lights subsystem and from/to the server, using the Raspberry's build in Wi-Fi while also implementing GSM communication medium via the Arduino, in order to have more options in case the Wi-Fi communication fails. Thus, we selected the Adafruit FONA 808 Shield – Mini Cellular GSM + GPS[3] for the Arduino Uno, in order to utilize its GPRS-GSM capability. The main responsibility of the traffics lights subsystem is to count the passing vehicles in front of the traffic light; thus, we needed to select a camera for the Raspberry Pi. Depending of the method, vehicle detection and counting can be a heavy in processing power task. In addition, cameras can be very expensive, hence, in order to achieve a tradeoff between cost and processing power, we select and the Pi v2 Camera Module[4] vehicle detection and counting. The usage of the Arduino seems secondary but is of great importance, due to its flexibility in its usage with various sensors. The Raspberry Pi handles the heavy in processing power vehicle counting and that makes the Arduino a great hardware that provides the traffic lights subsystem with great flexibility. The components and the connections of the traffic lights subsystem can be seen in Fig. 1.

For the vehicles subsystem we once again selected the Arduino Uno for the microcontroller. Our goal is to take data from the On Board Diagnostics (OBD-II) system of the vehicle and transmit it together with data that is useful to the traffic lights subsystem, in order to initiate the routing process. Vehicles will be able to communicate between them for other purposes as well, which would provide flexibility in our further applications. Thereafter, we needed a communication device compatible with the Arduino Uno. We once again selected the Adafruit FONA 808 Shield – Mini Cellular GSM + GPS. To connect with the OBD-II of any vehicle, we use a simple ELM327 USB cable (a cable with an ELM327 microcontroller[5]). The Arduino is not a USB host; thus, we use a USB Host Shield[6] for the Arduino to be able to connect to the vehicle of interest. The components and connections of the vehicle subsystem can be seen in Fig. 2.

[1] Arduino Uno Rev3, www.arduino.cc.

[2] Raspberry Pi 3 Model B, www.raspberrypi.org.

[3] Adafruit FONA 808 Shield – Mini Cellular GSM + GPS, https://www.adafruit.com/product/2636.

[4] Pi v2 Camera Module, https://www.raspberrypi.org/products/camera-module-v2/.

[5] ELM 327 USB Cable, https://www.totalcardiagnostics.com/elm327/.

[6] USB Host Shield, https://store.arduino.cc/arduino-usb-host-shield.

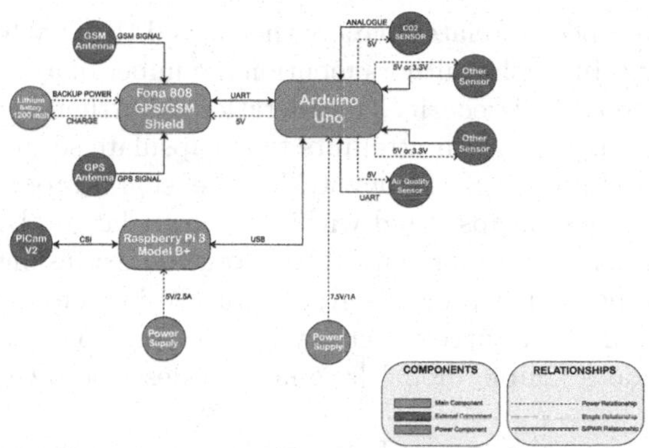

Fig. 1. Block diagram of traffic lights device [9]

The main purpose of the two subsystems is to communicate with each other and with the central server, calculate the fastest route and give it to the infotainment system of the driver that made the request. The complexity of the system leads to the usage of UML diagrams to better explain how the communication will be achieved and what course will the gathered data follow in order for the fastest route to be calculated.

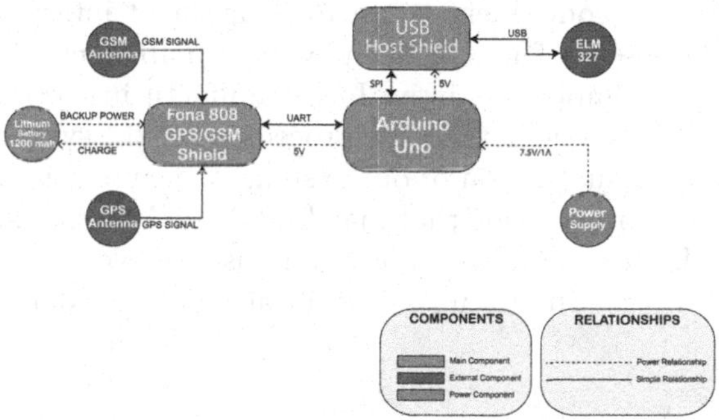

Fig. 2. Block diagram of vehicles device [9].

3 Diagrammatic Design of the IoT V2X System

Initially we present specific related papers that paved the way towards the completion of this work. In [7] the authors mention a number of approaches that aim to model IoT systems and security considerations. Furthermore, they propose a UML/SysML extension, which attempts to encapsulate security knowledge to model IoT systems. In particular, a new UML extension is proposed, which characterises security issues encapsulated within a nomenclature, UML stereotypes, in order to model common actors and UML notation extensions. The aim is to move IoT development at a previous step from the implementation stage; the designing phase. This work targets security concerns in IoT development; hence, the authors provide a simple model language to describe security actions and entities.

In [6], the authors propose an IoT visual domain language designed with UML, having considered different types of users that may be of a technical background or not. They showed different representations of IoT entities with respect to UML notation. The authors, however, do not show the full extent of the language in its different steps; they focus on attempting to visually characterise IoT entities.

In [8], the authors describe the UML4IoT approach, whereby a developer can design a component of a cyber-physical system using known system design standards, such as UML and SysML. This design can assist towards the transformation of each component to an Industrial automation thing, using a UML profile. The purpose is the generation of the IoT-compliance interface of the components, in order to automate the development process of the corresponding wrapper. Furthermore, this approach can be used even in the absence of a specification by applying it at the source code level, in order to properly annotate the properties of the cyber-physical component. Thus, a layer is automatically built, which wraps the component to an IoT-compliant interface. These mechanisms address the issues of new cyber-physical components development and integration of legacy components in an IoT manufacturing setup.

In order to be able to understand the procedures of the system, we proceeded in the diagrammatic visualisation of our system. We emphasise to the fact that this work describes an application that may lead to a UML extension for IoT. The correct design of the subsystems of our system as a whole, initially requires the requirements capture coming from the specification of the complete application.

3.1 Use Cases

The use cases of a system are of great importance in the cycle of the software design [10]. We can see the use cases of our system in Fig. 3. In particular, our system comprises 4 actors with their respective use cases. The actors are a) the traffic light system, b) the vehicle system, c) the server and d) the driver. For the sake of clarity we list the use cases of each actor in Table 1. These use cases will be useful at the design stage, in order to distinguish the different functionalities of our complete system. Note that the abbreviation BW is the backpressure weight.

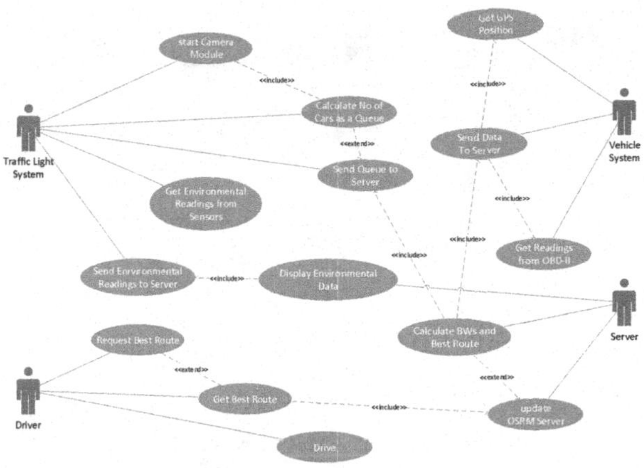

Fig. 3. Use cases diagram

Furthermore, we can see that there are certain connections between the use cases. Specifically, we utilise the <<include>> and <<extend>> connections. The <<include>> connection dictates that our use case, which is the origin includes the terminal one to finish its functionality. The <<extend>> connection shows that the uses case which is the origin extends its functionality to the terminal use case.

3.2 Sequence Diagrams

Thereafter, we proceed with the design of our IoT V2X system, beginning with the sequence diagrams of our use cases. In order to keep the simplicity of our design, in this paper we provide the core sequence diagrams, instead of a sequence diagram for each use case. We present the sequence diagrams for the Traffic Light Subsystem, the Vehicle Subsystem, the Driver and the Server in the Figs. 4, 5, 6 and 7.

The sequence diagram for the traffic light subsystem initiates with the Raspberry Pi giving the command to its connected camera to start obtaining the video. Upon arrival of the video from the camera, the Raspberry Pi, calculates the number of cars as a queue; hence the self ending message. The queue is then sent to the server for the calculation of the BW. Furthermore, the Raspberry Pi requests the environmental readings from the Arduino. The Arduino samples the sensors and obtains the readings. The environmental readings are returned to the Raspberry Pi and sent to the server.

In the sequence diagram of the vehicle, the system starts with the Arduino activating the on board data acquisition from the vehicle using the OBD-II reader. Then the data is requested from the vehicle brain whereby important information about the vehicle's status are obtained, such as the speed of the vehicle. The data is forwarded internally to the Arduino microprocessor. Then, the Arduino requests the Global Positioning System (GPS) position by the respective module, in order

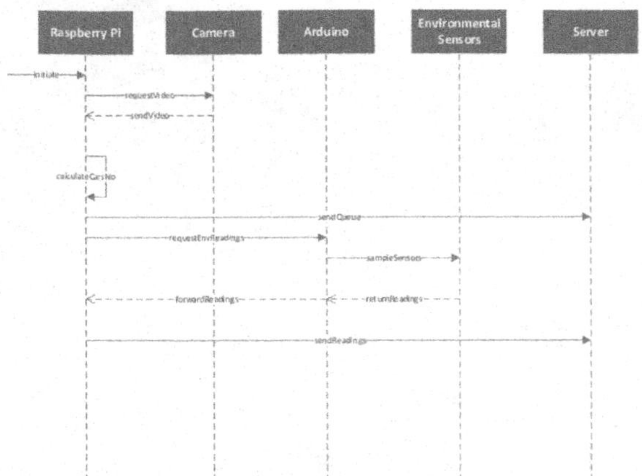

Fig. 4. Traffic light subsystem sequence diagram.

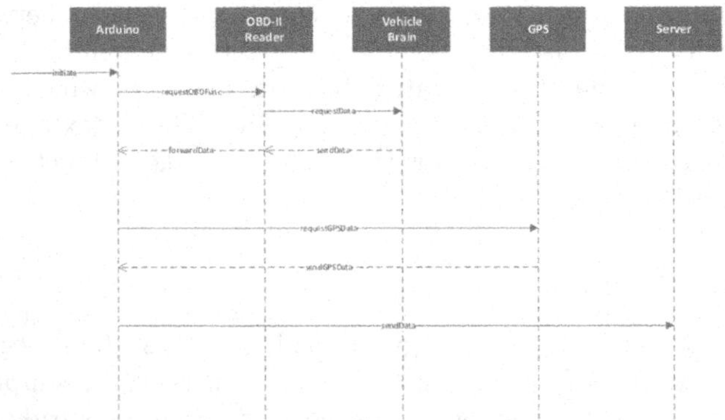

Fig. 5. Vehicle subsystem sequence diagram

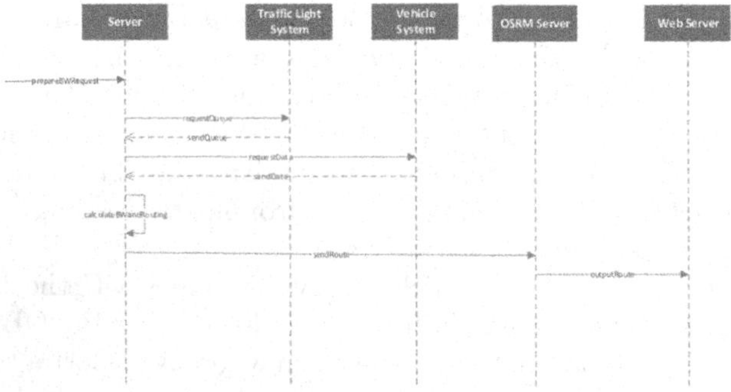

Fig. 6. Server sequence diagram

Table 1. Use cases list

Actors	Traffic Light System	Vehicle System	Driver	Server
Use cases	Start Camera Module	Get GPS Position	Request Best Route	Calculate BWs and Best Route
	Calculate No of Cars as a Queue	Send Data to Server	Get Best Route	Update OSRM Server
	Send Queue to Server	Get Readings from OBD-II	Drive	Display Environmental Data
	Get Environmental Readings from Sensors			
	Send Environmental Readings to Server			

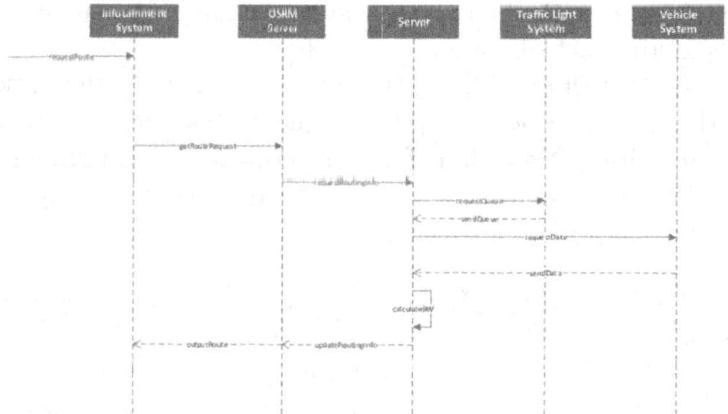

Fig. 7. Driver sequence diagram

to obtain its position in the road network. The GPS module return the data to the Arduino. The data obtained by both the OBD-II reader and the GPS are then sent to the server for the calculation of the Backpressure weight.

Examining the driver's sequence of events, we can see that the routing is requested from the infotainment system. Thereafter, the request is forwarded to the Open Source Routing Machine (OSRM) server. The OSRM essentially calculates the distance between the points and outputs the best route, based on vehicles' speed. In order to be able to obtain the route the request is forwarded to the server, where the necessary traffic lights are identified, which will obtain the necessary information to calculate the BW. Note that we can cross reference the vehicle speeds and the BWs; however this is beyond the scope of this paper. After the identification of the traffic lights, the server communicates with them and gets the queues. Also, the server gets the necessary data from the respective vehicles as well. The server obtains the traffic light queue and the data from the vehicle to calculate the BW. Finally, the data is sequentially transferred down to the Infotainment System, where the route is displayed.

The server sequence diagram starts with the BW request reaching the server. Thereafter, the server communicates with the traffic light system requesting its queue of vehicles. The traffic light subsystem sends its queue to the server. Then, the server requests the data from the respective vehicles. The vehicles return their data to the server, which then calculates the BW. Finally, the server is updating the route on the OSRM server and the route is displayed to the web server, being accessible to the vehicles.

3.3 Statechart

A necessary activity for the full design of the IoT V2X system and its routing decisions, is the derivation of the states that the system enters. We utilise the statechart, in order to determine possible deadlocks and other situations that are essential to be covered during the implementation of the subsystems. We can see the detailed statechart of the system in Fig. 8.

Essentially, the statechart follows the activities taken from the sequence diagrams. In the diagram the boxes represent the states and the arrows represent the connecting activities. Note that if a connecting arrow originates from a solid coloured circle then it is the former and if it terminates in a solid coloured circle

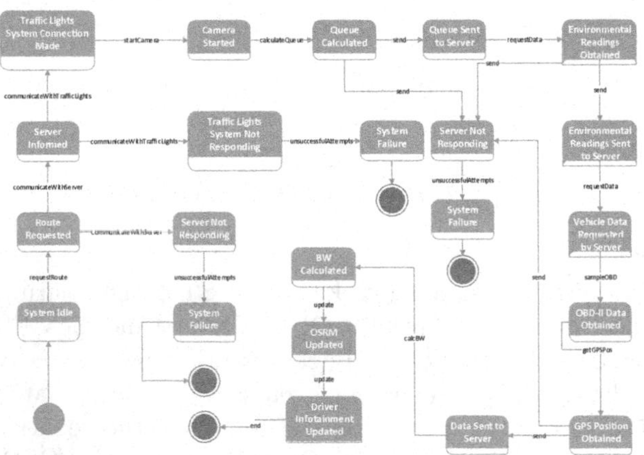

Fig. 8. Statechart

within a circle it s a termination of the system. The four subsystems of our complete application are fully explained in terms of system states. We constructed the statechart with respect to the system as a whole, meaning that our purpose is to show the cooperation between the subsystems into forming a full application. Additionally, the statechart includes some system failure terminal states. The authors could have expanded to more potential faults and failure; however, this would have made the statechart much more complex.

The full system starts with an idle state. Thereafter, the route is requested, which means that the server is informed. The server might be in a faulty state; hence we have a state where it is not responding and a system failure is reported. The server then communicates with the respective traffic lights and a connection is made. Here we have our second potential faulty process, whereby the traffic light system is not responding and our system concludes with a final state of system failure. After the traffic light system connection is made the camera is started and the queue is calculated. The queue is sent to the server. Another system failure is reported as well. The system then resumes with the server requesting the environmental data, which is sent to the server. Thereafter, the vehicle data is requested and the OBD-II data is obtained. The GPS data is also obtained and the date is sent to the server. Then the BW is calculated, the OSRM is updated and the driver infotainment system is updated as well before the full system termination.

4 Conclusions

In this paper we exhibited the full system design of a complete IoT V2X system. We started by identifying the use cases of our system and we showed that we have 4 actors. Moreover, we proceeded with the main sequence diagrams in order to show the upcoming functionality of our system, which we broke down to 4 subsystems. Lastly, we provided the system statechart, whereby the states of the system have been identified in conjunction with potential faults and lack of communications. We consider our work as the initial step into designing a new visual modeling extension for IoT systems.

Our future work includes the formal verification of our system using appropriate tools, as well as the its implementation to constitute a practical IoT V2X system. The formal verification tools will verify that there are no deadlocks in our design and that specific properties are satisfied, such as the communication between the subsystems. The implementation of such a system will follow the UML design and will be carried out separately as subsystems, and then integrated into a full application. Initial experiments will take place in a laboratory setting.

Acknowledgment. Co-financed by the European Union and Greek national funds through the Operational Program Competitiveness, Entrepreneurship and Innovation, under the call RESEARCH – CREATE - INNOVATE (project code: T1EDK-04012)

References

1. Chan, H.C.: Internet of Things business models. J. Serv. Sci. Manag. **8**(04), 552 (2015)
2. Fleisch, E., Weinberger, M., Wortmann, F.: Business Models and the Internet of Things. Bosch IoT Lab White Paper (2014)
3. Westerlund, M., Leminen, S., Rajahonka, M.: Designing business models for the Internet of Things. Technol. Innov. Manag. Rev. **4**(7), 5–14 (2014)
4. Fowler, M.: UML Distilled: A Brief Guide to the Standard Object Modeling Language. Addison-Wesley Professional, Boston (2004)
5. Arrayangkool, A., Unakul, A.: A flexible Intelligent Transportation System architecture model with object oriented methodology and UML. In 2009 9th International Symposium on Communications and Information Technology, pp. 741–746. IEEE (2009)
6. Eterovic, T., Kaljic, E., Donko, D., Salihbegovic, A., Ribic, S.: An Internet of Things visual domain specific modeling language based on UML. In 2015 XXV International Conference on Information, Communication and Automation Technologies (ICAT), pp. 1–5. IEEE (2015)
7. Robles-Ramirez, D.A., Escamilla-Ambrosio, P.J., Tryfonas, T.: IoTsec: UML extension for Internet of Things systems security modelling. In: 2017 International Conference on Mechatronics, Electronics and Automotive Engineering (ICMEAE), pp. 151–156. IEEE (2017)
8. Thramboulidis, K., Christoulakis, F.: UML4IoT–a UML-based approach to exploit IoT in cyber-physical manufacturing systems. Comput. Ind. **82**, 259–272 (2016)
9. Skoufas, K., Spyrou E.D., Mitrakos D.: Low cost V2X traffic lights and vehicles communication solution for dynamic routing. In: Proceedings of the Eighth International Conference on Telecommunications and Remote Sensing (2019)
10. Shishkov, B., Dietz, J.L.: Deriving use cases from business processes: the advantages of DEMO. In: Camp, O., Filipe, J.B.L., Hammoudi, S., Piattini, M. (eds.) Enterprise Information Systems V. Springer, Dordrecht (2004). https://doi.org/10.1007/1-4020-2673-0_29

Stakeholder Tensions in Decision-Making for Opening Government Data

Ahmad Luthfi[1,2(✉)], Marijn Janssen[1], and Joep Crompvoets[3]

[1] Faculty of Technology, Policy and Management, Delft University of Technology, Jaffalaan 5, 2628 BX Delft, The Netherlands
{a.luthfi,m.f.w.h.a.janssen}@tudelft.nl

[2] Universitas Islam Indonesia, Yogyakarta, Indonesia
ahmad.luthfi@uii.ac.id

[3] Katholieke Universiteit Leuven, Leuven, Belgium
joep.crompvoets@kuleuven.be

Abstract. Various types of stakeholders are often involved in the process of deciding to open data. However, the influence of multiple–actors on the decision-making process is ill-understood. Stakeholders play different roles and have different interests in opening and analyzing datasets. The objective of this paper is to understand the influence of the stakeholder's roles and their interests in the decision-making process to open data. The roles-interest grid method is used to determine the stakeholder's concerns and how they influence the decision-making process to open data. In addition to stakeholder theory, we employ muddling through and bounded rationality theories to create a comprehensive analysis of the decision-making process. Stakeholders are found to be diverse, where some are proponents of opening data, and others are risk-averse and do not favor disclosing data. Stakeholder's responsible for the actual opening of data are often focused on the risks resulting in a tension between the ambitions of politicians to open data, and the practices of administrators and decision-makers. Understanding the stakeholder's roles and their tensions can help to ensure better decisions are made. We recommend creating incentives for generating shared objectives.

Keywords: Stakeholder · Open government data · Decision-making · Roles · Interest · Muddling through · Bounded rationality

1 Introduction

Making decision process to either open or closed the dataset by the government institutions is not trivial and faces many complexities. The main challenge encountered is the involvement of stakeholders having various interests and concerns in the decision-making process, like politicians, executive boards, decision-makers, civil servants, and administrative officers, all with their distinct perspectives and agendas [1]. These stakeholders play all different roles in the decision-making process of opening data ranging from setting the objectives and ambitions to the actual opening of data.

B. Shishkov (Ed.): BMSD 2020, LNBIP 391, pp. 331–340, 2020.
https://doi.org/10.1007/978-3-030-52306-0_23

The diversity of actors and their interests, various interpretations of strict regulations, limited knowledge and expertise, lack of personal skills, and barriers of technology acceptance at the management level are all influencing the decision-making process of opening data [2, 3]. As a result, the decision-making process becomes fuzzy, and the objectives of opening data are not realized. Besides, the different roles and interests of the heterogonous actors in the internal government organization might create an erratic and slow decision-making process.

For example, some decision-makers might have high authority to publish or keep closed the dataset. Furthermore, some public servants might be risks-adverse, whereas others might just open datasets without thinking about the possible negative consequences. In general, perceptions on the pros and cons of open data can be different among stakeholders. The dominating view on deciding to open data is that of being a systematic and structured process in which a careful trade-off is taken between the pros and cons of opening data, and then the best decision is made. However, reality might be more cumbersome due to the complex relationships and different roles and interests of stakeholders.

The objective of this paper is to analyze the stakeholder's roles and their interests in the decision-making process to open data. This should result in the identification of tensions between stakeholder's roles and their interest. The role versus interest grid method is to analyze stakeholder positions and can help to effectively engage and support all the stakeholders in the decision-making process [4, 5]. This method can determine the concern stakeholders have and how they influence the decision-making process in opening data.

In order to make a comprehensive analysis, we employed two theories, namely muddling through and bounded rationality. The first theory is used to analyze complex problems in the decision-making process to open data by considering the obstacles that stand between the initial problem state and the goal state. Bounded rationality is used to analyze decisions when rationality is limited. When the executives make decisions, they will trace the decision problems by taking account of their cognitive limitations, available resources, and time restriction.

2 Related Work

There are different types of stakeholders. Some of them have a higher degree in the organizational hierarchy and can decide the course of action [6]. Some decision-makers can approve or veto decisions on a decision-making process [7]. Another set of stakeholders can aid with their expert opinion and knowledge [8]. Moreover, several stakeholders help oversee the project from the beginning, during implementing and making the decisions [6]. Hence, stakeholders should understand how the project scope, goals, and performance indicators.

In the domain of Open Government Data (OGD), the backgrounds of multiple actors in the decision-making process are often heterogeneous. Some stakeholders set the policy, others might want to know the progress of the current decision-making process, the time to make a decision, and the outcome of the decisions. However, not all stakeholders are equally involved in the decision-making process from the beginning. Some are positioned to take responsibility to direct or provide input for others to make a decision. Therefore, in this study, stakeholder analysis contributes to analyze the stakeholder positions and how to engage these different types of stakeholders.

2.1 The Science of Muddling Through

In the science of muddling through, the decision-making process is looked at as a complex process with many vague small steps [9]. Decision-makers have to cross through the mud (muddling through) and big steps are not possible [9, 10]. As a result, changing policy is in most cases an evolutionary process instead of a revolutionary process [9]. For example, Lindblom, who was the originator of the theory of muddling through, wondered why the government used rational methods with their absolute belief when people are rationally limited [11].

Lindblom introduced two ideal types of policy-making method, namely the root and branch method. First, the "root" method or rational comprehension method refers to the view in which decisions are made at the bottom level of the root [11]. The problem is decomposed down completely rationally [9]. However, this method did not suitable in some cases, because people are limited rational to solve decision-making problems or these are usually too complicated [9, 11]. Second, "branch" method or also known as successful limited comparison method where this always small steps in decisions [11]. Afterward, narrow down the steps to find at what happens and make decisions iteration [9, 12].

Furthermore, the root method believes that it is possible to reach an agreement on organizational goals [10]. These goals can then be used to allocate resources, including human, technology and systems, and procedures [9, 11]. The "branch" method, on the other hand, assumes that it is almost impossible to set clear goals due to the overly interests of stakeholder's involvement [11]. The resources used are usually also only available at that time and not necessarily require the best ones [11, 12]. The environment analysis of the root method is therefore much broader than that of the branch method [9]. The first method depends heavily on theory, but the second one does not need this because there is the frequent use of comparisons and the adjustment of goals [9, 10].

To sum up, with the root method, good policy is to achieve the objectives with the available resources. According to Lindblom, decision-makers and other policy-making stakeholders should implement the root method, but take into consideration the practice cases using the branch method [9, 10]. Therefore, in this study, the muddling through theory contributes to a better understanding of the decision-making process to open data. This suggests that the opening of data is a less relational process and might be dependent on the persons who are involved. A study [13] found that the different organization makes different decisions about a similar type of data. This results in some datasets being opened by certain agencies, whereas other agencies do not open these types of datasets. This arbitrariness originates from differences in the decision-making process.

2.2 Bounded Rationality

The bounded rationality theory was introduced by Simon in 1957. Simon described that decision alternative is not given per situation, but it should be found, one after the other alternatives [14]. The bounded rationality is an approach to process decision-making when decision-makers have limited rationality [15]. Simon proposed the theory of bounded rationality as an alternative to substitute the fact that rationality decisions are often difficult to adapt in practice due to the intractability of natural decision-making problems [14].

Full rationality by stakeholders in the decision-making process may require unlimited cognitive capabilities [14]. In an organization, having a person who has capabilities in many fields like mathematics, computations, statistics, and decision-making expertise can be an ideal situation. However, in reality, human beings' cognitive competences are limited. For this reason, the decision-making behavior of stakeholders cannot accommodate the optimal decisions [14, 15].

To summarize, the theory of bounded rationality proposes that decision-makers have bounded rationality when faced with organizational decision-making problems. In this study, there are three main reasons the use of bounded rationality theory in the stakeholder's analysis domain. First, cognitive limitations can lead to different perception gaps among stakeholders in open data. Second, incomplete information and a lack of resources the stakeholders can create a wrong interpretation of the decision alternatives. Third, a lack of time to process decisions can affect decision-making delays. Besides, recognizing the diversity of stakeholders and their perspectives and interests is essential to understand the decision-making process to open data. Therefore, the bounded rationality contributes to a strategy when the rationality thinking of the stakeholders to process the decision-making is limited.

3 Analyzing Stakeholders Using a Role-Interest Grid

In this paper, we use electronic procurement (e-procurement) case study in Indonesia to capture the context of the decision-making process to OGD. We employ experimental case study to the stakeholders, which consist of 43 participants in total derived from several different organizations like governments, universities or academia, and professionals, or communities. The objective of this experimental case study is to identify the roles and interests of the stakeholders in the decision-making process to open or to analyze the government's datasets. There are two main steps to develop a role-interest grid of the decision-making process in the open data domain. First, we identify and construct a role-interest of different stakeholders to show the position and level of each stakeholder in terms of four quadrants. Second, we analyze the decision-making process.

3.1 Identify and Construct a Role-Interest of the Different Stakeholders

In this research, we define several main stakeholders who are involved as primary and secondary stakeholders. The primary stakeholders are derived from internal government entities, including the politicians, executive boards, policy-makers, decision-makers, civil servants, and administrative officers [16]. The secondary stakeholders are acquired from non-governmental ecosystems, including data enthusiasts, researchers, journalists, business enablers, and civil societies [2, 16, 17].

Moreover, the primary stakeholders refer to the actor of data publishers who have formal, official, hierarchical, and contractual relationships. These actors have a direct and degree of roles in the decision-making process. In addition, the secondary stakeholders represent the multiple actors of open data users. They are influenced by the open government datasets but less formal and do not directly contribute to the decision-making process of opening data.

The objective of the construction step is to show the group and prioritize these stakeholders. Here, we categorize the stakeholders in terms of their roles or influence, interests or impact, and levels of participation in the decision-making process to open data. The roles and interests of stakeholders' analysis presented in Fig. 1 reveal the following tensions:

1. The policy-makers and decision-makers have a strong influence and high interest in the decision-making process. The policy-makers set the policy-making agendas and translate the ideas into the execution of the policies. Decision-makers are responsible for providing decision alternatives and high interest to reuse the datasets to make better decisions at the same time. The decision-makers should follow the policies set by the government. Nevertheless, the policies are often not clear for a given dataset. Policy-makers and decision-makers may have a sufficiency of knowledge and resources to make decision alternatives.
2. The politicians and executive boards have a high role and less interest. The politicians can control both content and presence the open data legislation in the legislative level. Yet, most of the politicians are not interested in using the datasets for their individual benefits because of the cognitive limitation in analyzing the datasets. Executive boards, they can contribute to the decision-making process to open data. However, executive boards have a very limited time to re-analysis the datasets because of the organizational agendas.
3. The civil servants and administrative officers have a moderate role and moderate interest level in the decision-making process. The civil servants can play a role regularly to manage the coordination between internal stakeholders. Concurrently, the civil servants are moderately interested in re-analyze the impact of released datasets. Administrative officers maintain the open data portal and provide visual information to the public. At the same time, the administrative officers are moderately fascinated to re-analyze the dataset to know the impacts of opening datasets. Resources are scarce and the opening of data often comes as an afterthought. Data enthusiasts and business enablers have a moderate role and high interest in the decision-making process. These stakeholders require analyzing the datasets to an individual or organizational benefits. The business enablers can use the datasets for in-depth analysis to generate the customers' demand for a product. Their ambitions are often in tension with the civil servants that are more conservatives and risk-averse.
4. The researchers, journalists, and civil societies can all high interest in using datasets, but they are hardly engaged in the decision-making process. Being the external entities of government institutions, it makes these stakeholders difficult to involve in the decision-making process to open data. Even though researchers have sufficient knowledge and decision rationalities, the role gap between the internal and external stakeholders may become challenging. They might not be even aware of certain datasets, as these are not published.

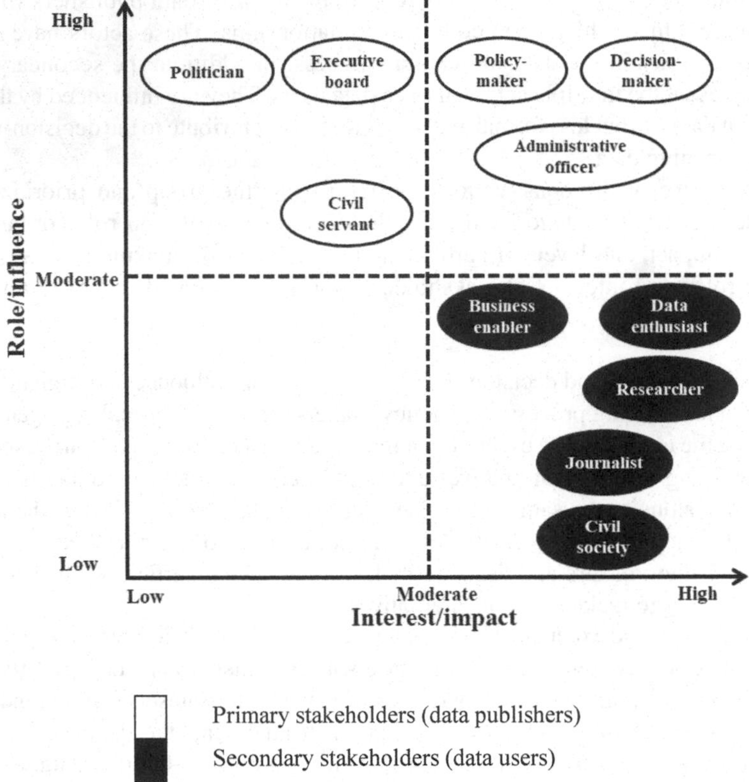

Fig. 1. Role and interest grid of stakeholders (Based on the framework from [4])

3.2 Analyzing the Decision-Making Process

In the domain of OGD, not all data publishers like executive boards, decision-makers, and administrative officers behave rationally. The difference between high-level and low-level capabilities in decision-making can create a perception-cognition gap [18]. For some decision-makers, using a formal method in the decision-making process is possible to implement, while others are not able to use such a method. Besides, the decision-makers cannot have access to all the required information and relevant resources to make the best decisions [15, 19]. Apart from incomplete information, their perspectives are bounded by cognitive limits and thus making it difficult to process appropriately [14].

From the two theories of the muddling through, we classify stakeholders operate in the root or branch domain. Data publishers are classified in the root domain. The stakeholders who are part of the regulators and decision-makers, they are dominantly following rational thinking and rigor to achieve the predetermined organization's objectives. While data users and other potential data enablers are classified in the branch domain, they might use small and irregular steps and iterate unsatisfactory results to find the best decision alternatives. They may feel reluctant to use rational thinking because of the limited resources they have. Therefore, the stakeholders in this group do not require such a theoretical approach. They tend to employ comparison techniques and their expertise to adjust personal and organizational objectives. Moreover, there is a standard decision-making process that criteria are not well-defined. Also, the importance of decision-making is different per organization. In contrast, some have procedures and processes in place and have even tool support; most of them leave it up to the civil servants involved in the process to open the data. These civil servants might even not be aware of the need for opening data, have limited knowledge about opening data, and did not receive any training.

There are two main points to represent the result analysis of role-interest levels. First, the primary stakeholders include politicians, decision-makers, executive board, civil servants, and administration officers; they all have their role in influencing the decision-making process. Besides, the use of the root method with procedural steps in these types of stakeholders is still dominant. Some of them are aware of the decision impacts that can cause disadvantages. While others may use their authority to refuse the decisions because of too fanatic with rationality thinking and conventional method. From the bounded rationality theory, the limitation of the cognitive competencies of stakeholders can affect the optimal decisions they made. Therefore, the decision-makers cannot access all the required information and relevant resources to which dataset should be opened.

Second, the secondary stakeholders include the data enthusiast, business enabler, researcher, journalist, and civil society the all have high interest to analyze and reuse the datasets. However, they cannot actively engage in the decision-making process. Although some of them have sufficient knowledge and rational sense in the decision-making complexities, these theories cannot be ultimately implemented.

4 Findings and Recommendations

4.1 Why Decision-Making Processes Are Not Trivial?

This study finds many stakeholder tensions in the decision-making process to open data. We define eight important factors to capture the challenges of data publishers to make the decision to open data. First, stakeholders have different interests and opinions about opening data. Some stakeholders are risk-averse to avoid making mistakes, whereas others promote transparency and accountability. Second, different stakeholders represent different concerns. Each stakeholder has its own goals and objectives to use and re-analyze datasets. This results in tensions between ambitions and the actual opening of data. Third, in the internal organization level, there is a tension between the value of open data and the avoiding of risks. Some stakeholders are consistent to provide new knowledge to the public, while others tend to be risk-averse. Fourth, there are no clear priorities and objectives to guide decision-making. Authorities play a huge role in determining which objectives dominate and how many resources are allocated for this and if the staff gets the necessary training and tools to open data.

Fifth, the high political ambitions are in stark contrast to the limited resources, a lack of good infrastructure and supporting methods for making decisions. Sixth, stakeholders are already overloaded and have limited time resulting in the quick release of datasets which often have limited value. The focus is on reaching the target of opening a number of the dataset (quantity) instead of looking at the value (quality). Seventh, for some data, there is a clear 'yes' or 'no' for opening data, but many datasets are in a grey area. The stakeholders have a lack of cognitive and limited time to an in-depth analysis of the datasets. It definitely requires training and high-skills in mathematics and computing, whereas the level of education is often low. Finally, there is a potential of conflicting interests between the data publishers about the extent to which data should be opened, and it will affect the decision-making delays.

The challenges result in tensions in the level of ambitions, the allocation of resources, acquiring technical infrastructure, and training. As a consequence, data is all too often not disclosed.

4.2 Recommendation for Data Publishers

Based on the several challenges found in this study, we also provide some recommendations to the government institutions to make better engagement in the decision-making process in opening data. First, establish a committee to make clear authorization to open data. The committee can provide the detailed roles of the stakeholders and prioritize the allocation of scarce resources. Second, establish a decision-making committee composition including ethics, politician, and external organizations to gain positive feedback about their concern, interest, and possible risk-averse of opening data. Third, create a knowledge-based repository that can be shared among stakeholders to make evidence-based decisions. This repository can avoid duplication of the making of mistakes and foster learning from each other best practices. Fourth, analyze the stakeholder decision-making process and address the stakeholder tensions. Finally, create an incentive or reward to make more motivation for the data publisher to open their data. This intensive should guide all stakeholders towards pursuing the same direction.

5 Conclusion

In the case, we found many tensions between stakeholders, which result in opening fewer data. The ambitious objectives of transparency, accountability, and participation were in sharp contrast to the resources allocated to open data and the providing of training and infrastructure for supporting deciding to open data. This cause of the different stakeholders has other concerns, e.g., avoiding any risks of opening data and allocate scarce resources to issues that have priority.

The decision process was still dominated by the risk-averse culture, in doubt the process was halted, and not data was opened. Some policy guidelines were used for opening data, but no rational trade-off was often made, relevant expertise was lacking, and stakeholders took hardly time for making informed decisions. The science of muddling through used in this paper helped to determine which stakeholders dominantly following rational thinking and which types of stakeholder favorably using irregular decision steps.

From the case study, we found that the data publishers, like politicians, decision-makers, executive board, civil servants, and administration officers; they all have dominantly influenced the decision-making process. The use of root method with decomposed sequential steps can make several of these data publisher stakeholders aware of the potential disadvantages of decision impacts. While others might use their veto power or intervention to refuse the decisions because of overly dogmatist with rationality methods. Besides, we classified the data users in the branch method, whereby they might use irregular steps and iterate unsatisfactory decisions to find the best results. Therefore, they do not need such theoretical strategies, and tend to employ comparison techniques based on their expertise to calibrate personal and organizational expectations.

From the bounded rationality theory, the limitation of the cognitive competencies of the open data stakeholders can influence the optimal decisions they made. Decision-makers cannot access all the required information and relevant resources to which dataset should be opened. In order to tackle the cognitive gaps between the stakeholders, in this study, we recommend the data publishers to establish a knowledge-based repository that can help to make evidence-based decisions, and to encourage learning from other stakeholder's best practices. Also, we recommend to align the stakeholder interests by providing the right incentives and avoiding to be overly ambitious and stay focus on opening as many datasets as possible. Besides, we suggest to ensure the datasets offering value are disclosed to the public.

References

1. Jetzek, T.: Managing complexity across multiple dimensions of liquid open data. Gov. Inf. Q. **33**(1), 89–104 (2016)
2. Luthfi, A., Janssen, M., Crompvoets, J.: Framework for analyzing how governments open their data: institution, technology, and process aspects influencing decision-making. In: EGOV-CeDEM-ePart 2018. Donau-Universität Krems, Edition Donau-Universität Krems, Austria (2018)
3. Luthfi, A., Janssen, M., Crompvoets, J.: A causal explanatory model of Bayesian-belief networks for analysing the risks of opening data. In: Shishkov, B. (ed.) BMSD 2018. LNBIP, vol. 319, pp. 289–297. Springer, Cham (2018). https://doi.org/10.1007/978-3-319-94214-8_20
4. Bryson, J.M.: What to do when stakeholders matter. Public Manag. Rev. **6**(1), 21–53 (2004)
5. Ackermann, F., Eden, C.: Strategic management of stakeholders: theory and practices. Long Range Plan. **44**, 179–196 (2011)
6. Gonzales-Zapata, F., Heeks, R.: The multiple meanings of open government data: understanding different stakeholders and their perspective. Gov. Inf. Q. **32**, 441–452 (2015)
7. Mitchell, R.K., Agle, B.R., Wood, D.J.: Toward a theory of stakeholder identification and salience: defining the principle of who and what really counts. Acad. Manag. Rev. **22**(4), 853–886 (2012)
8. Savage, G.T., et al.: Strategies for assessing and managing organizational stakeholders. Acad. Manag. Perspect. **5**(2), 61–75 (1991)
9. Lindblom, C.E.: The science of "muddling through". Public Adm. Rev. **19**(2), 79–88 (1959)
10. Kopecka, J., Santema, S., Buijs, J.: Designerly ways of muddling through. J. Bus. Res. **65**(6), 729–739 (2012)
11. Johnston, W., Low, B., Wilson, T.: Scientific muddling: decision making through a Lindblomian lens. J. Bus. Res. **65**(6), 717–719 (2012)
12. Scherizer, R.: The internationalization process of SMEs: a muddling-through process. J. Bus. Res. **65**(6), 745–751 (2012)
13. Kuk, G., et al.: Exploring the implementation blind spots: selective decoupling of freedom of information. In: Thirty Eight International Conference on Information Systems. Association for Information Systems, Seoul (2017)

14. Gigerenzer, G., Selten, R.: Bounded Rationality - The Adaptive Toolbox. MIT Press, Cambridge (2002)
15. Simon, H.A.: Theories of bounded rationality. Decis. Organ. **1**(1), 161–176 (1972)
16. Zuiderwijk, A., Janssen, M., David, C.: Innovation with open data: essential elements of open data ecosystems. Inf. Polity **19**(2–3), 17–33 (2014)
17. Janssen, M., Charalabidis, Y., Zuiderwijk, A.: Benefits, adoption barriers and myths of open data and open government. Inf. Syst. Manag. **29**(4), 258–268 (2012)
18. Hoffmann, S.: Bridging the gap between perception and cognition: an overview. In: Performance Psychology, pp. 135–149 (2016)
19. Wang, L., Jiang, Y.: Escape dynamics based on bounded rationality. Phys. A: Stat. Mechan. Appl. **531**, 121777 (2019)

Automated System for Monitoring of Educational Processes: Collection, Management, and Modeling of Data

Lyazzat Atymtayeva(✉), Kanat Kozhakhmet, and Alexander Savchenko

Suleyman Demirel University, Kaskelen, Kazakhstan
lyazzat.atymtayeva@sdu.edu.kz

Abstract. Currently, the most of the processes at the educational analytical centers entirely depend on the human factor. Automation of the real-time monitoring system for the educational processes can be possible through the development and improvement of the information technologies, algorithms and computational methods, such as machine learning methods, analysis and visualization of big data processes. This paper covers the issues of the development of automated system for monitoring of educational processes from the point of view of data collection, data management, and data modeling. It includes the stages of data collection with the description of data engineering methods, data management procedures, algorithms of data cleaning and filtering, data modeling and visualization processes as well as the description of intelligent algorithms for scoring analysis of results. The principal feature that characterizes the development of the mentioned automated system is the using of availability of user experience data from existing educational sites and other open data sources that allow us to create a complete vision of the educational processes' state at various levels.

Keywords: Education · Data collection · Data modeling · Machine learning

1 Introduction

Nowadays, the most of the processes at the educational analytical centers entirely depend on the human factor. Frequently, the calculations and visualization of analysis the results occur in the manual mode that casts doubt on the accuracy of the performed calculations. Such a manual analysis also significantly slows down the receipt of the relevant information in real time. The automation of analysis of educational processes and its automated monitoring significantly reduces the time for processing of results; releases the human resources involved to the processes; and gives the accurate real-time analysis for actuality of information. Automation of the real-time monitoring system for the educational processes can be possible through the development and improvement of the information technologies, algorithms and computational methods, such as machine learning methods, analysis and visualization of big data processes.

The practice of creating such automated systems points out to the existence of recommendation systems, including content filtering systems, collaborative filtering, and

B. Shishkov (Ed.): BMSD 2020, LNBIP 391, pp. 341–351, 2020.
https://doi.org/10.1007/978-3-030-52306-0_24

hybrid systems [1, 2]. In the world practice, the similar systems were successfully implemented in the different fields and allowed to save big amounts of money, as well as they improved the quality of information and data received.

By having certain previously collected and processed information the development of recommendation systems [1–3] helps to predict which objects will be in the focused interest of the user. Using of the basic methods for recognizing and classifying big data, among which the artificial intelligence, machine learning, multimodal recognition of the architecture of algorithms with recommendations for adapting more relevant content, analyzing aggregated data and visualizing results [4–8] aims to develop the effective recommendation systems.

By using main principles of the recommendation systems development we can create the automated system for monitoring of the educational processes that allows informing the relevant state bodies in a timely manner about the emerging trends in the declining of education level in a particular region. It will help to make decisions to prevent problems and improve the situation in the educational processes. Among others, the adaptive learning is also a part of the given automated system. This direction contains the tasks for the development of a personalized training program that will contribute to effective learning, depending on mental abilities and interests of the users. An opportunity to have access to a quality personalized training program, which will no longer depend on the location of the user, is a one of the advantages of automated system. It is equally effective in both urban and rural environments. An automated monitoring system for vulnerable representatives of the educational environment helps to determine and build a special education strategy to improve the adequacy and adaptability of certain segments of the population.

The principal feature that characterizes the automated system for monitoring of educational processes (ASMEP) is the availability of user experience data from existing educational sites and other open data sources that allow us to create a complete vision of the educational processes' state at various levels.

This paper is devoted to the description of the processes for the development of the mentioned automated system from the point of view of data collection, management, and modeling. It includes the stages of data collection with the description of data engineering methods, data management procedures, algorithms of data cleaning and filtering, data modeling and visualization processes as well as the description of intelligent algorithms for scoring analysis of results.

2 Data Collection

The increasing use of digital technologies in educational systems has been led to the storage of large amounts of data about the students. At present, various database management systems (DBMS) are applied in the field of education and science directly. However, the issue of extracting useful knowledge from the raw data remains open. The so-called extracted useful knowledge is valuable. They have a significant impact on the decision making processes in the management of educational activities. Therefore, the development of methods for extracting such data is important for the effective use of the DBMS.

The ASMEP is designed to implement the methods of useful knowledge extraction, or methods of data engineering, that is also needed to improve teaching and learning processes. As experience shows, the similar automated systems can be used in many tasks, including identifying the risks for learners' groups, identifying the priority of learning needs for different groups, increasing the number of graduation classes, effectively assessing school performance, increasing productivity, maximizing the use of the digital transformation resources, and optimizing subject matters for updating of the curriculum.

In the Fig. 1 we can see the structure of data engineering of ASMEP in accordance with the stages of Knowledge Discovery in Databases (KDD) as a process of finding useful knowledge in raw data.

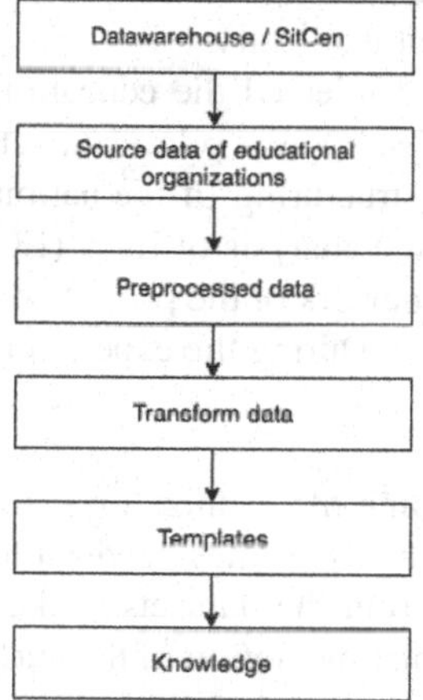

Fig. 1. Structure of data engineering for the automated system

The Knowledge Discovery in Databases process consists of the following steps:

1. Preparation of the original data set. This step consists of creating the data set from the various sources, selecting a training sample, etc. For this purpose, we used the model of statistical processing.
2. Preprocessing of data. For preprocessing of data and applying Data mining effectively we use the data processing in terms of elimination of omissions, noise, abnormal values as well as removing of data redundancy or insufficiency.
3. Transformation, data normalization. At this stage we transform data to calibrated view with a range of values of independent variables or data attributes. This method has been applied to the tasks for determining the level of education digitalization by regions and tasks for the forecasting of the level of training equipment indicators and the level of academic performance. For these tasks we also applied the clustering methods that include the special python libraries such as pandas, numpy, matplotlib.
4. Data Mining. During this stage we use Data mining techniques for our tasks.
5. Post-processing of data with the interpretation of the results and using of the obtained knowledge in applications.

After applying procedures of KDD we can talk that the automated system meets all the requirements for successful interaction with an expert (analyst):

- A single platform where expert can go through all the steps of Knowledge Discovery in Databases;
- All operations are performed with the help of machine learning methods, which reduce the requirements for the expert's mathematical knowledge;
- Possibility of arbitrary combination of any processing methods;
- A wide range of methods for visualizing the obtained results;
- Batch execution of all data processing activities.

To get the result, the expert just needs to select the necessary report. The information by request will be represented automatically.

In developing of ASMEP we selected the educational organizations of Turkestan region (South Region of Kazakhstan) as a pilot data set. We developed the system of data collection, processing and structuring of the national educational database using the API as well as we provided the analysis of Egov (EGovernment) Open Data on the possibility of their use in the framework of the projects on automation of public services including the educational services. During the experimental works we implemented the following tasks:

- Carrying out the partial mapping of organizations from database of our system and the national educational database by names of educational organizations and regions;
- Data checking and cleaning from the datasets of the national educational database that were necessary for the implementation of the current projects on the automation of public services;
- Data obtaining on unified national testing in the context of schools throughout the Turkestan Region;
- Development of the system of data collection from the national educational database that includes API for data collection, processing, validation, and structuring with subsequent transfer for processing and analysis in the relational DBMS.

In the Fig. 2 you can see the simplified scheme of DBMS used in the system.

During the development of the system we used various programming tools such as Python programming language, MongoDB DBMS, etc. Figure 3 shows a simplified scheme of data collection and processing with applying of mentioned programming tools.

As we mentioned above, for system data management we implemented the partial mapping of organizations from the national educational database and the internal database of the system for automation of public services. We used the special toolkits for the mapping procedures by help of the ElasticSearch search engine and add-on for PostgreSQL and ZomboDB databases. Figure 4 demonstrates a simplified scheme of the search and mapping of organizations by name and location. To develop a toolkit for automatic updating of data from the national educational database, we used the mapping by tables of entity relationships and relationship diagrams.

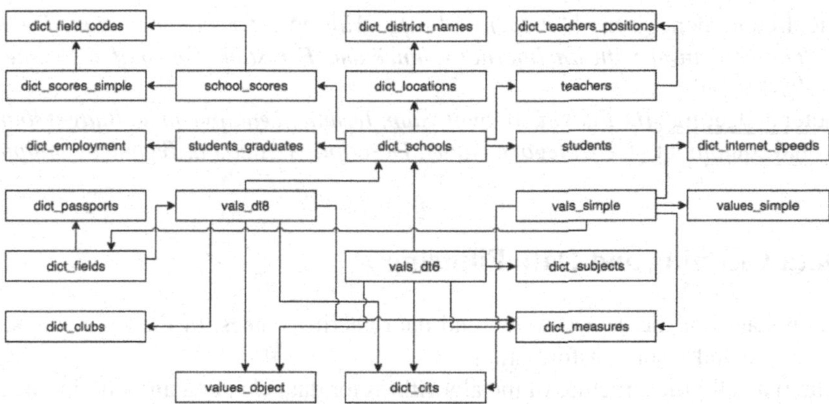

Fig. 2. Simplified DBMS scheme for automated system

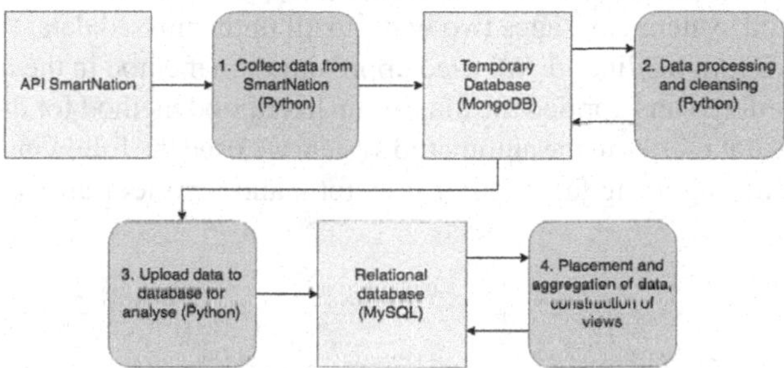

Fig. 3. Simplified scheme of the data collection and processing for automated system

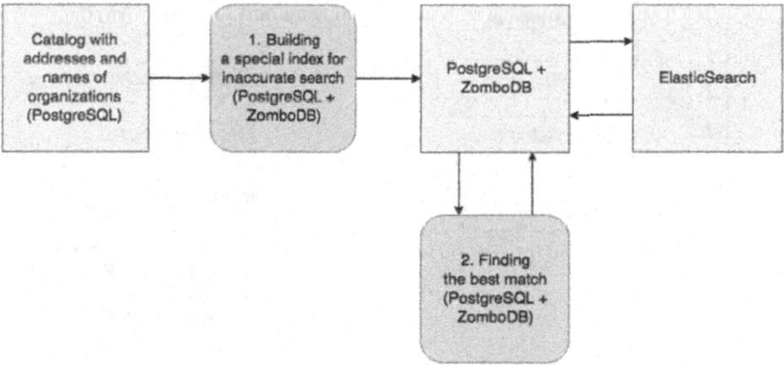

Fig. 4. Simplified scheme of the search and mapping of organizations by name and location

As an example we can show the mapping of entities by the following characteristics:

Summary table with information on technical equipment of the school (indexes) {*ID, Educational organization ID, projector(unit), Interactive display(unit), Antivirus (unit), 3D-printers, Robotics equipment, Local network, Personal computer, Local network type, Internet connection, Interactive display, Internet connection speed, Access point of internet connection, Devices for students*}

Technical equipment (json) {*ID, General info, With an Internet connection, For education, For education with an Internet connection, For stuff, For stuff with internet connection*}
Computer budgeting {*ID, Budget, Amount, Sum, Technical equipment Id, Budget source*}
Additional equipment {*ID, Category, Name, Description, Amount, Technical equipment ID*}

3 Data Cleaning and Data Filtering

The main stages of the data cleaning and data filtering consist of the following steps: Data cleaning and Data transformation.

Schematically the structure of the algorithms for data cleaning and filtering that we used in ASMEP is represented in the Fig. 5.

Data cleaning consists of partial preprocessing, including anomaly editing, filling empty data, smoothing, as well as the detection of duplicates and inconsistencies.

The automated system envisages two ways to fill in the missed data: the approximation and the maximum likelihood. We used approximation method in the rows where the data have been ordered and applied the maximum likelihood method for disordered data. For smoothing of data series in the automated system we used the following two methods: low-frequency filtering using fast Fourier transform and wavelet transformation.

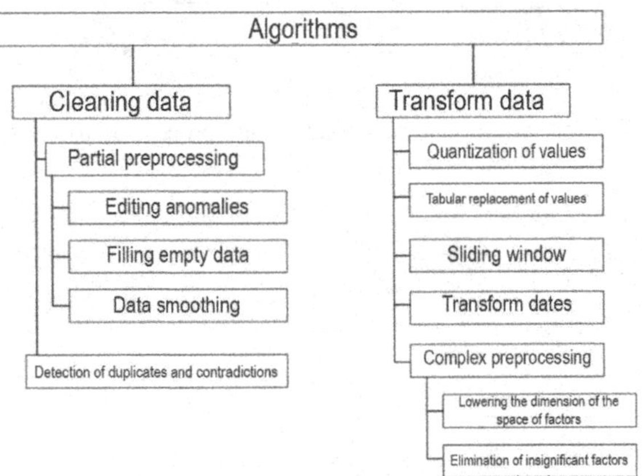

Fig. 5. Algorithms for data cleaning and filtering

Data transformation consists of three steps in a strict sequence (each of which, however, can be omitted): quantization of values, tabular replacement of values, "Sliding window" and transformation of dates as well as complex preprocessing.

Quantization is performed by the both interval and quantile method. At the result of the process of substitution in the table of values (so-called substitution table) we could replace the pairs of the input and output values by the tabular values. At the process of the development of automated system we used the method of data selection called as "sliding window" that can be applied to the solving the tasks of the forecasting time series with the help of a neural networks. Also we used date transformation for the analysis of various indicators for a certain period (day, week, month, quarter, year). During the complex preprocessing stage the pre-express data analysis has been used in order to assess whether the factor is significant or not, or whether all factors are taken into account to explain the behavior of the resulting value.

4 Set of Algorithms for Data Scoring

From the point of view of data structure we can distinguish important categories of algorithms for system development such as Search, Sorting, Insertion, Update, Delete.

The data structure of the system consists of the following components:

1. Additional education;
2. Results of the Unified National Testing;
3. Material-technical base;
4. Building/Hostel/Boarding school;
5. Teaching staff;
6. Level of digitalization and provision.

The overall rating according to these 6 criteria was calculated on the basis of the average value.

Each of the items consists of a subset of criteria with an individual weighting system, affecting the rating category.

Each data structure has an interaction interface and a set of supporting operations. The interface only provides a list of supported operations, the type of parameters they can accept, and returns the type of these operations. For our automated system the interface was developed on the basis of Microsoft's Business Intelligent Solutions (MS Power BI) technology.

Determination of data is provided by a set of algorithms and operations, such as operations with arrays, search, update, etc. The internal representation of the data structure is supplied by implementation of algorithms used in the data structure of accepted educational processes of Kazakhstan.

During the work with data structures we used the adaptive and non-adaptive sorting algorithms as well as scoring algorithms of the educational system of the Republic of Kazakhstan.

Within the framework of the creation of automated system the thorough "scoring" of quantitative and qualitative indicators of school institutions of the Turkestan region has been developed. It can be available by the link [9].

Algorithms of building key "scoring" models in the educational sphere are based on the classical methods of statistical analysis. However, due to the growing level of digitalization, the additional data sources are using to assess the educational institutions activities. New approaches to information processing, such as a set of big data technologies, are applied in scoring models. In addition, the specialized analytical software has been improved to allow using improved data analysis and modeling tools for faster and more efficient processing of large volumes of data. Currently, many institutions are increasingly applying sophisticated derivative forecast models based on big data and machine learning analysis.

The set of evaluation parameters for scoring systems is quite standardized and remains almost unchanged for a long time. Scoring models are characterized by separating (differentiating) ability, stability of results of model application over time and interpretability of its components. At the same time, they have good predictive capability, because they use the quantitative data. The models use the maximal content of internal information available to the educational institution.

Categories of assessment indicators are based on 6 selected structures of the educational system mentioned above.

The overall rating for these 6 criteria was calculated based on the average of all categories of indicators.

Each of the items consisted of multiple criteria with an individual weighting system and impact on the rating category.

In the Table 1 you can see the part of the set of multiple criteria with individual weights (only for 1 criteria) created during the development of ASMEP.

The final rating dashboard for automated system can be found by link [9]. We can notice that all blocks are linked to each other and after the selection of criteria they can be filtered. For example, we can view the data only for one school from the list of "Top 10 Schools" or "Worst 10 Schools" or filter the list by districts.

Within the framework of the development of ASMEP we have created the analytical systems of assessment of quantitative and qualitative indicators of educational institutions, in particular, the set of analytical data on the region of South Kazakhstan. Given analytical systems that are called Basqarma SmartNation and SitCen reflect the full range of data on 6 main criteria that adequately assess the current state of educational institutions and identify the rating of "the best" and "the worst" educational institutions.

Further, we have developed the simulation model that can predict one or another trend of development in educational institutions. For these purposes we used the expert simulation model on the base of fuzzy logic interface in Matlab software platform that is the conceptual model for decision making systems [10].

Below you can find the description of the linguistic input variables for simulation model.

Additional education: ZERO{No}, PS{availability of less than 2 electives}, PM{availability of more than 5 electives}, PB{complete additional training (extension)}
UNT results: BAD{Below the average}, NORM{average figures}, GOOD{good and excellent performance}
Material and technical base: WEAK{poor equipment, lack of media boards, computers, etc.}, NORM{average equipment}, EXCELLENT{complete equipment}
Teaching levels: WEAK{teachers without any category}, NORM{teachers with and without mixed categories}, EXCELLENT{top categories},
Level of digitalization: POOR{low level of digitalization}, SATISFY{the level of digitalization is satisfactory}, GOOD{high level of digitalization, availability of media systems in all classes, etc.}

Table 1. Set of criteria with individual weights (only 1 criteria)

Criteria	Component	Weight
Additional education	Camp availability	15%
	Museum availability	2.5%
	Number of UMLs for children with special educational development needs	2.5%
	Playroom for 5–6 year olds	2.5%
	Number of circles and sports sections by type	50%
	Presence of yard clubs in this organization	10%
	Availability of ensemble (orchestra, choir)	2.5%
	Number of special classes/groups	15%
	The presence of a logo point	5%
	Programmes for the prevention of drug addiction and behavioural diseases are being implemented	2.5%

In the MatLab environment we elaborated the interfaces for implementation the input variables and output evaluation factors, descriptions of the accessory function for each input variable, descriptions of the accessory function for each output variable, and developed the knowledge base.

The developed algorithms allow applying the corrections of the simulation model for other regions. In general, it allows using the adequate solutions to each region separately (see Fig. 6).

Fig. 6. Results of modeling the scoring data in Arys city (South Kazakhstan) and simulation results for the predictive model

5 Conclusion

The development and implementation of ASMEP for different regions of Kazakhstan has shown the significant advantages of automation in general, even at the stages of collecting, modeling and analyzing data. It helped reducing the processing time and assisting experts in making decisions. At the same time, the using available data on user experience by applying the machine learning methods made it possible to predict emerging trends in the educational process in situational analytical centers. For example, the relevance of the taken decisions helped to predict the budget for the construction of the schools accurately, taking into account the required number of seats, material and technical base, and the teaching staff.

The authors of this paper carry out various studies in the direction of creating intelligent expert systems and their heterogeneous focus using data mining and machine learning methods. In particular, these are researches in the field of security auditing [11], the development of intelligent security tools [12], methods for developing smart interfaces for web applications [13], expert systems in healthcare [14, 15], data mining of insurance systems [16], fuzzy logic in determining market metrics [17], fuzzy logic in project management [18], etc. There are a number of works in the direction of modeling business processes using intelligent security tools [19, 20]. This work is a continuation of these studies in the field of the intelligent systems development.

Acknowledgement. This research was supported by grant of the program of Ministry of Education of the Republic of Kazakhstan BR05236699 Development of a digital adaptive educational environment using Big Data analytics. We thank our colleagues from Suleyman Demirel University (Kazakhstan) who provided insight and expertise that greatly assisted the research. We express our hopes that they will agree with the conclusions and findings of this paper.

References

1. Tariq, A., Rafi, K.: Intelligent decision support systems - a framework. J. Inf. Knowl. Manag. **2**(6), 2514–2523 (2012)
2. Ltifi, H., Trabelsi, G., Ayed, M.B., Alimi, A.: Dynamic decision support system based on Bayesian networks. Int. J. Adv. Res. Artif. Intell. (IJARAI) **1**(1), 22–29 (2012)
3. Merkert, M., Mueller, H., Hubl, B.: A survey of the application of machine learning in decision support systems. In: Proceedings ECIS 2015, Paper 133, pp. 1–16 (2015)
4. Zadeh, L.A.: Fuzzy sets and their application to pattern classification and clustering analysis. In: Proceedings of Advanced Seminar by the Mathematical Research Center, The University of Wisconsin-Madison, 3–5 May 1976, pp. 251–299 (1977)
5. Celebi, M.E.: Partitional Clustering Algorithms. Springer, Heidelberg (2015). https://doi.org/10.1007/978-3-319-09259-1. eBook, ISBN 978-3-319-09259-1
6. Graves, D., Pedrycz, W.: Kernel-based fuzzy clustering and fuzzy clustering: a comparative experimental study. J. Fuzzy Sets Syst. **161**(4), 522–543 (2010)
7. Acuña, E., Rodriguez, C.: The treatment of missing values and its effect on classifier accuracy. In: Banks, D., McMorris, F.R., Arabie, P., Gaul, W. (eds.) Classification, Clustering, and Data Mining Applications. Studies in Classification, Data Analysis, and Knowledge Organisation, pp. 639–647. Springer, Heidelberg (2004). https://doi.org/10.1007/978-3-642-17103-1_60

8. Melnykov, V., Michael, S., Melnykov, I.: Recent developments in model-based clustering with applications. In: Celebi, M. (ed.) Partitional Clustering Algorithms, pp. 1–39. Springer, Cham (2015). https://doi.org/10.1007/978-3-319-09259-1_1
9. Link to the website of the system. http://bit.ly/2pdO04a
10. Cordón, O.: A historical review of evolutionary learning methods for Mamdani-type fuzzy rule-based systems: designing interpretable genetic fuzzy systems. Int. J. Approx. Reason **52**(6), 894–913 (2011)
11. Atymtayeva, L., Kozhakhmet, K., Bortsova, G.: Some issues of development of intelligent system for information security auditing. In: Proceedings of the CCIIS 2012, London, UK, vol. 2, pp. 725–731 (2012)
12. Nurmyshev, S., Kozhakhmet, K., Atymtayeva, L.: Architecture of web based intellectual vulnerability scanners for OWASP web application auditing process. Int. J. AETA Nat. Sci. Publ. **5**(3), 51–55 (2016)
13. Sheriyev, M.N., Atymtayeva, L.B., Beissembetov, I.K., Kenzhaliyev, B.K.: Intelligence system for supporting human-computer interaction engineering processes. Int. J. Appl. Math. Inf. Sci. (AMIS) Nat. Sci. Publ. **10**(3), 917–925 (2016)
14. Duisenbayeva, A., Beisembetov, I., Atymtayeva, L.: Using fuzzy logic concepts in creating the decision making expert system for cardio-vascular diseases (CVD). In: Proceedings of the 10th IEEE AICT 2016, pp. 807–812 (2016)
15. Sagdoldanova, A., Atymtayeva, L.: Expert system for pharmacy. In: Proceedings of 10th IEEE AICT 2016, pp. 827–832 (2016)
16. Ata, F., Atymtayeva, L.: Overview of data mining techniques for CRM management at insurance broker. Int. J. AETA Nat. Sci. Publ. **7**(1), 9–13 (2018)
17. Mirseidova, S., Inoue, A., Atymtayeva, L.: Applying soft computing to estimation of resources' price in oil and gas industry. In: Proceedings of the 23rd MAICS 2012, USA, pp. 6–10 (2012)
18. Artykov, D., Atymtayeva, L.: A fuzzy linear programming approach for resource-constrained project scheduling. Int. J. AETA Nat. Sci. Publ. **4**(3), 47–52 (2015)
19. Atymtayeva, L., Tulemissova, G., Nurmyshev, S., Kungaliyev, A.: Some issues in the re-engineering of business processes and models by using intelligent security tools. In: Proceedings of the 7th BMSD 2017, Spain, pp. 199–205 (2017)
20. Atymtayeva, L., Abdel-Aty, M.: Improvement of security patterns strategy for information security audit applications. In: Proceedings of the 5th BMSD 2015, Italy, pp. 199–205 (2015)

Exploration of Data Analytics for Ground Segment in Space Systems

Bedir Tekinerdogan[1(✉)], Bedia Acar[2], Çağrı Cabıoğlu[2], Damla Savaş[2], Nebi Vuran[2], Şenol Tekdal[2], and Ümit Gürsoy[2]

[1] Information Technology, Wageningen University & Research, Wageningen, The Netherlands
bedir.tekinerdogan@wur.nl

[2] TUBITAK Space Technologies Research Institute, Ankara, Turkey
{bedia.acar,cagri.cabioglu,damla.savas,nebi.vuran,senol.tekdal, umit.gursoy}@tubitak.gov.tr

Abstract. Space systems have to deal with massive spatio-temporal Earth and Space observation data collected by space-borne and ground-based sensors. Despite the data latency in communications, data is collected at enormous rates, and a sophisticated network of ground stations is set up to collect and archive telemetry data. The data that is received at the ground segment can be made available to the end-users. Beyond archiving data, the available data provides opportunities for data analytics that can support the decision-making process or provide new insight for the target requirements. Unfortunately, for practitioners, it is not easy to identify the potential and challenges for data analytics in the space domain. In this paper, we reflect on and synthesize the findings of existing literature and provide an integrated overview for setting up and applying data analytics in the space systems context. To this end, we first present the process as adopted in space systems, and describe the data science and machine learning processes. Finally, we identify the key questions that can be mapped to data analytics problems.

Keywords: Space systems · Ground segment · Data analytics

1 Introduction

In the context of spaceflight, a satellite is an artificial object which has been intentionally placed into orbit. Such objects are sometimes called artificial satellites to distinguish them from natural satellites such as the Moon. A space system consists basically of three segments, including Ground Segment, Launch Segment, and Space Segment [5–7, 9]. Each segment by itself is a complex system integrating hardware and software. Space systems have to deal with massive spatio-temporal Earth and Space observation data collected by space-borne and ground-based sensors. Despite the data latency in communications, data is collected at enormous rates, and a sophisticated network of ground stations is set up to collect and archive telemetry data [13]. The data that is received at the ground node can be made available to the end-users. Beyond archiving data, the available data provides opportunities for data analytics that can support the decision-making process or provide new insight for the target requirements.

B. Shishkov (Ed.): BMSD 2020, LNBIP 391, pp. 352–361, 2020.
https://doi.org/10.1007/978-3-030-52306-0_25

In this context, the term Big Data usually refers to data sets with sizes beyond the ability of commonly used software tools to capture, curate, manage, and process data within a tolerable elapsed time [1, 2, 12, 14, 16]. The extraction of useful information out of the big data is done using data analytics. Data analytics includes inspection, pre-processing, and modeling of data to discover useful information. The data analytics processes have been typically automated using machine learning and/or deep learning algorithms. In principle, four different types of data analytics can be distinguished. *Descriptive analytics* describes what has happened over a given period. *Diagnostic analytics* focuses on why something has happened. *Predictive analytics* aims to find out what is likely going to happen in the near term. Finally, *prescriptive analytics* suggests a course of action.

Like in many industrial domains, we can observe that data science in general and (big) data analytics, in particular, has triggered opportunities for creating smart space systems based on information derived from raw data. Unfortunately, for practitioners, it is not easy to identify the potential and challenges for data analytics in the space domain. Several studies discuss the application of data analytics to specific space domain problems but a general overview is largely missing. As such, we reflect on and synthesize the findings of existing literature and provide an integrated overview for setting up and applying data analytics for the ground segment in the space systems context. In particular, we aim to answer the following research questions:

RQ1. What are the important questions for the ground segment of space systems?
RQ2. Which type of data analytics will be required to answer these questions?
RQ3. What are the required machine learning approaches for these data analytics problems?

Our aim is not to provide a detailed analysis to derive the analysis for these questions, but rather to provide an overview of the current literature that will help practitioners identify the key solution directions. This objective was directly derived from our own industrial context of space domain projects. To this end, we first present the background and the process as adopted in space systems, together with an overview of data science and machine learning processes.

The remainder of the paper is organized as follows. In Sect. 2, we shortly describe the overview of space systems, thereby focusing on the ground segment. In Sect. 3, we discuss the problem statement. Section 4 presents the approach, and finally, we conclude the paper in Sect. 5.

2 Space System

Figure 1 shows a conceptual model of a typical space system consisting of the ground segment and space segment. The space segment has onboard computers, data-handling systems, attitude and orbit control systems, all of which contain software. The ground segment has command and control systems, simulators, flight-dynamics systems, mission-analysis tools, communications networks, and ground-station data systems such as telemetry and telecommand processors, as well as 'downstream processing' systems for payload data. These all contain software, often of considerable complexity. The results of the ground segment are typically used by external systems, which include application-specific software.

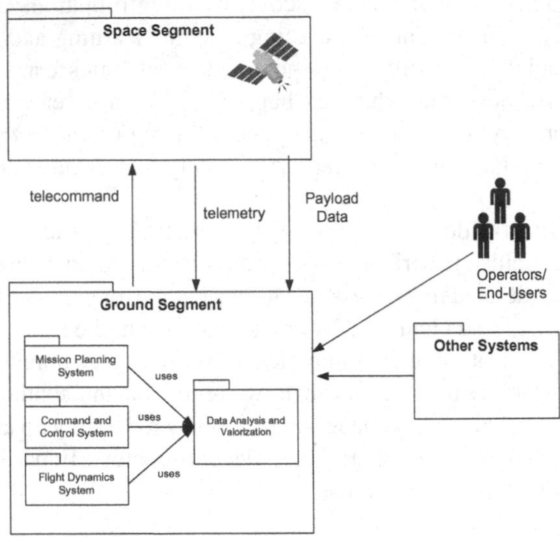

Fig. 1. Conceptual architecture of space system

The ground segment can send so-called *telecommands* to the satellite (through radiofrequency links), to initiate behaviour of the satellite, and sometimes to override internal decisions taken by the onboard software [10]. Telecommands are normally sent as asynchronous data packets, and are always received by the satellite central computer (the OBDH computer). Depending on the type of mission, the link with the ground station can be continuous or extend only over a section of the orbit.

The satellite on its turn can send *data* to the ground, which can be divided into two broad categories [10]:

- *The payload data* (mission data) represents the data collected by the satellite. In the case of an astronomical telescope, for instance, the telemetry contains the pictures taken by the telescope.
- *Housekeeping data* (telemetry) gives information about the general status of the satellite. Telemetry data are sent in packets.

Data analytics is typically part of the ground segment, which is the system set up on Earth to manage and control a space mission, and to receive and process the data produced by a spacecraft's instruments, and if necessary, to send out and archive any generated products. A principal telecommunications device of the ground station is the parabolic antenna. When a satellite is within a ground station's line of sight, the station is said to have a view of the satellite. It is possible for a satellite to communicate with more than one ground station at a time. The ground segment consists of the following systems:

Mission Planning System
Mission planning is defined as the task of preparing, organizing, and planning all relevant activities that happen during the mission, onboard as well as on-ground. It is important that the plan is correct and conflict-free and, as such, needs to be thoroughly verified.

Command and Control System
Command and control system manages satellites orbit, usually from the point of lift-off up to the orbit, and the end of the mission. From the ground system, a staff of flight controllers monitor all aspects of the mission using telemetry, and send commands to the satellite.

Flight Dynamics System
Spacecraft flight dynamics includes functionality for the management of the performance, stability, and control of satellites. In general, spacecraft flight dynamics involve three forces: propulsive force, gravitational force exerted by the Earth or other celestial bodies; and aerodynamic lift and drag.

Data Analytics and Valorization
As shown in Fig. 1 the above three modules use the Data Analytics and Valorization module that focuses on the clearing and pre-preprocessing of the received raw data to derive information and likewise to support the decision making. The decision making process on its turn can support the other three functionalities of mission planning, command and control and flight dynamics.

3 Data Science and Machine Learning

To identify the needs for data science for the ground segment modules we will first focus on the conventional data science process. Data science includes a process for obtaining raw data and converting it into information useful for decision-making by users. Data science consists of the following steps [9, 15, 18, 19]:

Data collection is a systematic approach for gathering and measuring information from a variety of sources. *Data pre-processing* defines the step in which the data is transformed and prepared to bring it to such a state that it can be further processed by an algorithm. This is often an essential and time-consuming step since data is often taken from different sources using different formats. Data pre-processing includes substeps such as data cleaning (e.g. missing, duplicate, noisy data), data transformation (e.g. normalization), and data reduction (e.g. dimensionality reduction). *Data processing* includes the analysis and analytics of the data to derive useful information from the preprocessed data in order to support further understanding and/or decision-making process. *Data visualization* is the graphic representation of the acquired information in order to communicate the relationships among the represented data.

For processing the data and as such realizing data analytics machine learning (ML) can be applied. ML enables computer programs to perform complex tasks such as prediction, diagnosis, planning, and recognition by learning from historical data. Figure 2 shows the traditional process for machine learning. The process consists of two steps, training and prediction. In the training process a ML model is developed that can be used to predict the outcome for new data. For training the model, the initial raw data must be first pre-processed after which the necessary features are extracted for which we wish to analyze the correlations. In training activity the data is split up in a training set and validation set (for tuning so-called hyperparameters). In the evaluation step the model is tested using a test data set and a final ML model is provided. In the prediction activity, the new data can be prepared, and the features extracted, and an outcome can be predicted using the provided ML model. As stated above we distinguish between payload data and housekeeping data. The payload data depends on the mission of the satellite and as such a broad set of ML applications can be identified here. The housekeeping data is often based on structured data that needs to conform to the standards as defined in the space domain.

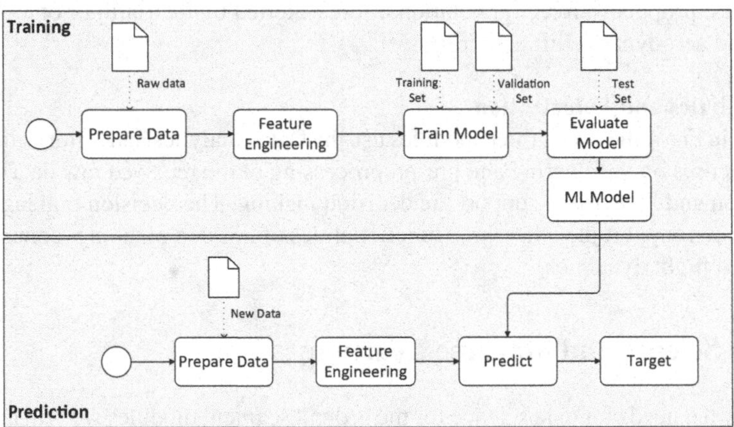

Fig. 2. Machine learning process

In the literature, different ML types can be distinguished [19]: In *supervised learning* a function or predictor is derived from a set of labeled training data. *Unsupervised learning* looks for previously undetected patterns in a data set with no pre-existing labels and with a minimum of human supervision. Unsupervised learning is usually used when relationships among input variables are not known. In several cases, only a small portion of the data is labeled while the majority of the data points are unlabeled. In that case, *semi-supervised learning* algorithms can be used to train a model with both labeled and unlabeled data, which can provide better accuracy compared to the supervised model that uses very limited labeled data. Finally, *reinforcement learning* adopts agents that observe the environment, perform some actions, and get some rewards (negative/positive) based on the selected action, upon which the model is updated accordingly. These machine learning types are agnostic to the application domain data, and as such, can be applied to support the questions of the mission planning, command and control and flight dynamics of the groud segment in space systems.

Besides of ML types, a number of ML task are distinguished in the literature. *Classification* maps input features to one of the discrete output variables. The output variable represents a class for the underlying problem. For binary classification, the output variable can only be one or zero. For *multi-class classification*, the output variable can consist of several classes. *Regression* maps the input features to a numerical continuous variable. The output variable can be either an integer or a floating-point number. *Clustering* divides data points into relevant groups. This grouping is based on the similarity pattern between data points. Similar points are grouped together and provide valuable information to data scientists. *Data reduction* tasks can reduce the number of features for building models faster. This task is mainly used as an auxiliary method for other machine learning tasks

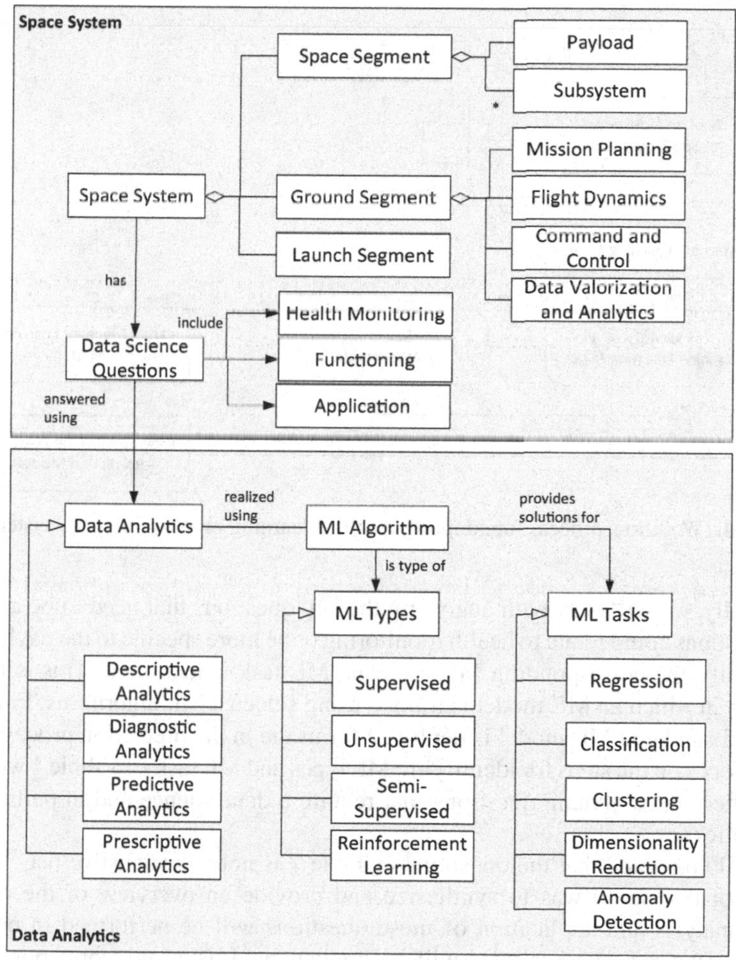

Fig. 3. Metamodel for big data analytics for space systems

such as regression and classification. *Anomaly detection* is usually handled with unsupervised learning methods. Similar to clustering, anomaly detection algorithms group the samples and aims to determine the outliers. In Fig. 3, we summarize the concepts in a metamodel that we can use for our further analysis of data science for the space domain.

4 Data Analytics for Space Domain

As stated before, space systems concern the collection of a large amount of data and as such we can identify an important opportunity to process this raw data using data analytics. In Fig. 4, we show the process of guiding this activity.

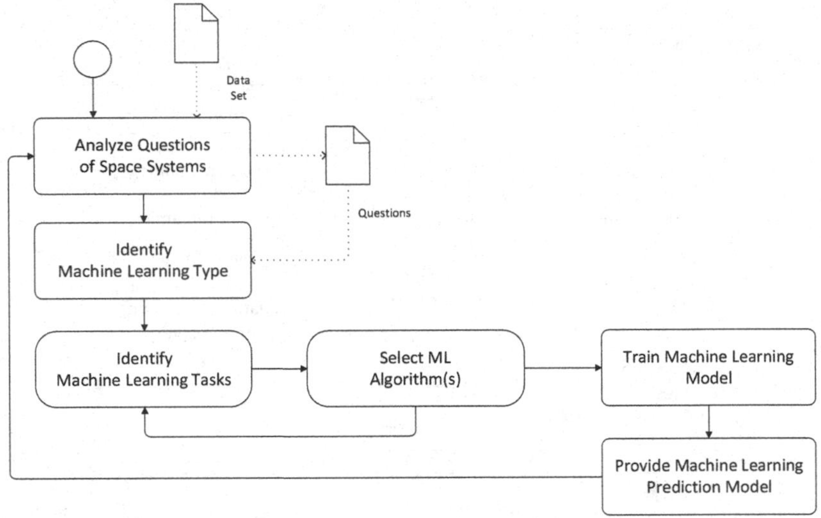

Fig. 4. Workflow process for adopting machine learning process for space systems

Typically, we will start with analysing the key questions that need to be answered. These questions could relate to health monitoring or be more specific to the payload data. Subsequently, the corresponding ML type and ML task is identified. This is followed by the step in which an ML model is trained using selected ML algorithms. Finally, the trained and validated ML model is deployed for usage in the prediction process. In this paper we focus on the steps for identifying ML types and ML tasks. In Table 1 we present the identified space domain questions that require a data science and in particular big data analytics approach.

It should be noted that the questions in Table 1 is not an exhaustive list. The main objective of this study was to synthesize and provide an overview of the concepts. Detailed analysis and application of these questions will be performed in our future work. The required data analytics will be implemented using the corresponding ML tasks. Table 2 shows the identified ML tasks that were derived from the literature [3, 5, 8, 11, 13, 15, 17, 21, 22].

Table 1. The identified space domain questions and the relation to data analytics type

Data analytics	Identified space domain questions
Descriptive analytics	Satellite orbit monitoring; Satellite maneuver monitoring; Orbit determination; Non-reliable data source identification
Diagnostics analytics	Health monitoring (Failure Diagnosis)
Predictive analytics	Health monitoring; Fuel consumption prediction; Lifetime-prediction of satellite subsystem; Maneuver prediction; Conjunction analysis; Orbit determination; Orbit propagation; Initial orbit determination; Orbit drift prediction; Satellite simulator of ground segment
Prescriptive analytics	Health monitoring; Radio resource allocation; Maneuver mission planning; Mission planning scheduling Payload re-configuration

Table 2. The identified ML tasks

ML task	Identified space domain problems/tasks
Regression	Health monitoring; Telemetry prediction Fault diagnosis; Orbit determination Precise orbit prediction; Initial orbit determination Orbit propagation; Lifetime-prediction of satellite subsystem; Conjunction analysis
Classification	Satellite stability prediction; Maneuver classification; Non-reliable data source identification (Security); Maneuver prediction
Clustering	Health monitoring; Telemetry prediction; Anomalous orbital behavior prediction
Dimensionality reduction	Pre-processing step for telemetry mining applications to reduce high-dimensional telemetry data
Anomaly detection	Anomaly detection of power unit; Anomaly detection of the subsystems; Satellite telemetry data anomaly detection

5 Related Work

In this paper we have provided a general and conceptual overview of the space domain and the potential for exploiting the available data analytics techniques in the literature. This idea is not new and a number of studies have been reported about the application of specific techniques to the identified questions in this paper.

Hassanien et al. [13] explore in their edited book the concepts, algorithms, and techniques of data mining in analyzing telemetry data of satellites for health monitoring. Three key domains are distinguished including health monitoring, telemetry data analytics and applications, and security issues in telemetry data.

We have provided a general reference model for the data analytics. Complementary to this is the need to develop a proper architecture for data-intensive space systems. In this context, the Consultative Committee for Space Data Systems (CCSDS) [4] has proposed the Reference Architecture for Space Data Systems (RASDS) [14]. This reference architecture can be used to design concrete space data systems, support reuse, and likewise reduce the cost and time of development of space data systems.

In our earlier work, we have focused on model management and analytics [19] which can be considered as a special case of data analytics. Model Management and Analytics for Large Scale Systems covers the use of models and related artefacts (such as metamodels and model transformations) as central elements for tackling the complexity of building systems and managing data. Also in the space domain a large number of various models are generated which are amenable for further processing to derive useful insight. The integration of model analytics and the selection and development of the corresponding model platform [20] is part of future research.

6 Conclusion

A massive amount of data is collected at the ground segment of space systems, which can be made available to the end-users for further processing. In this position paper we have indicated the potential for data analytics that can support the decision-making process or provide new insight for the target requirements. We have reflected on the current space system domain from a data science perspective and developed the metamodel that integrates the important concepts. Three key modules of the ground segment have been identified, including mission planning, command and control, and flight dynamics. We have stated that each of these modules can benefit from data analytics. Further, we have identified the key data analytics approaches, the machine learning techniques and machine learning tasks. We can conclude that there is indeed huge potential for applying data science techniques in the space domain, which have not yet been fully explored. This paper complements on the initiated studies in this domain and aims to further pave the way for future work. In our own future work, we aim to address the key research questions using various machine learning and deep learning approaches.

References

1. Avci Salma, C., Tekinerdogan, B., Athanasiadis, I.: Feature driven survey of big data systems. In: Proceedings of the International Conference on Internet of Things and Big Data, Rome, pp. 348–355 (2016)
2. Avci Salma, C., Tekinerdogan, B., Athanasiadis, I.: Domain-driven design of big data systems based on a reference architecture. In: Mistrik, I., Bahsoon, R., Ali, N., Heisel, M., Maxim, B. (eds.) Software Architecture for Big Data and the Cloud, pp. 49–68 (2017)

3. Bradley Knox, W., Mengshoel, O.: Diagnosis and reconfiguration using Bayesian networks: an electrical power system case study. In: Twenty-First International Joint Conference on Artificial Intelligence (2009)
4. Consultative Committee for Space Data Systems (CCSDS). http://www.ccsds.org. Accessed May 2020
5. Dibona, P., Foster, J., Falcone, A., Czajkowski, M.: Machine learning for RSO maneuver classification and orbital pattern prediction (2019
6. Eickhof, J.: On-Board Computer, On-Board Software, and Satellite Operations. Springer, Heidelberg (2012). https://doi.org/10.1007/978-3-642-25170-2
7. European Cooperation for Space Standardization (ECSS): Space Engineering – Ground systems and operations - Telemetry and telecommand packet utilization (2003). (ECSS-E-70-41A)
8. Ibrahim, S.K., Ahmed, A., Eldin Zeidan, M.A., Ziedan, I.: Machine learning methods for spacecraft telemetry mining. IEEE Trans. Aerospace Electron. Syst. **55**, 1816–1827 (2018)
9. Fortescue, P., Swinerd, G., Stark, J.: Spacecraft Systems Engineering (2011)
10. Garcia, P.A.: Satellite Ground System Architecture (2006)
11. Gremyachikh, L., et al.: Space Navigator: A Tool for the Optimization of Collision Avoidance Maneuvers (2019)
12. Han, J., Kamber, M., Pei, J.: Data Mining: Concepts and Techniques, 3rd edn. Morgan Kaufmann Publ. Inc., San Francisco (2011)
13. Hassanien, A.E., Darwish, A., El-Askary, H. (eds.): Machine Learning and Data Mining in Aerospace Technology. Studies in Computational Intelligence. Springer, Heidelberg (2019). https://doi.org/10.1007/978-3-030-20212-5
14. ISO 13537:2010: Space data and information transfer systems—reference architecture for space data systems (2015)
15. Lee, B.S., Hwang, Y., Kim, D.W., Kim, W.G., Lee, J.: Machine learning approach to initial orbit determination of unknown LEO satellites. In: 15th International Conference on Space Operations (2018)
16. Marz, N., Warren, J.: Big Data: Principles and Best Practices of Scalable Realtime Data Systems. Manning Publications Co. (2015)
17. Mital, R., Cates, K., Coughlin, J., Ganji, G.: A machine learning approach to modeling satellite behavior. In: Proceedings - 2019 IEEE International Conference on Space Mission Challenges for Information Technology (SMC-IT 2019) (2019)
18. Pääkkönen, P., Pakkala, D.: Reference architecture and classification of technologies, products and services for big data systems. Big Data Res. **2**(4), 166–186 (2015)
19. Tekinerdogan, B., Babur, Ö., Cleophas, L., van den Brand, M., Akşit, M.: Model Management and Analytics for Large Scale Systems. Elsevier, Amsterdam (2020). https://doi.org/10.1016/C2018-0-00106-1
20. Tekinerdoğan, B., Bilir, S., Abatlevi, C.: Integrating platform selection rules in the model driven architecture approach. In: Aßmann, U., Aksit, M., Rensink, A. (eds.) MDAFA 2003-2004. LNCS, vol. 3599, pp. 159–173. Springer, Heidelberg (2005). https://doi.org/10.1007/11538097_11
21. Yairi, T., Kawahara, Y., Fujimaki, R., Sato, Y., Machida, K.: Telemetry-mining: a machine learning approach to anomaly detection and fault diagnosis for space systems (2006)
22. Wang, Y., Ma, Z., Yang, Y., Wang, Z., Tang, L.: A new spacecraft attitude stabilization mechanism using deep reinforcement learning method. In: 8th European Conference for Aeronautics and Space Sciences (EUCASS) (2019)

Understanding Human Generated Decision Data

Johan Silvander(✉)

Software Engineering Research Lab Sweden, Blekinge Institute of Technology, Karlskrona, Sweden
Johan.Silvander@bth.se

Abstract. In order to design intent-driven systems, the understanding of how the data is generated is essential. Without the understanding of the data generation process, it is not possible to use interventions, and counterfactuals. Interventions, and counterfactuals, are useful tools in order to achieve an artificial intelligence which can improve the system itself. We will create an understanding, and a model, of how data about decisions are generated, as well as used, by human decision makers. The research data were collected with the help of focus group interviews, and questionnaires. The models were built and evaluated with the help of, bayesian statistics, probability programming, and discussions with the practitioners. When we are combining, probabilistic programming models, extended machine learning algorithms, and data science processes, into a directed acyclic graph, we can mimic the process of human generated decision data. We believe the usage of a directed acyclic graph, to combine the functions and models, is a good base for mimic human generated decision data. Our next step is to evaluate if flow-based programming can be used as a framework for realization of components, useful in intent-driven systems.

Keywords: Human decisions · Bayesian statistics · Probabilistic programming

1 Introduction

In areas where human experts are involved in critical decision making, the datasets might be "not-quite-big-enough". The datasets might be "not-quite-big-enough" because the same type of decision is not taken very often, the problem at hand is complex and it is not easy to compare the decisions between different problems, all decision points are not possible to record, some available information are not recorded, etc.

When faced with human generated decision data, which is in the form of "not-quite-big-enough" datasets, bayesian statistics [7], and probabilistic programming [3], are tools which can support the data analysis.

Independent of the size of the dataset, it is important to understand, and model, how the data was generated [10]. If the data generation process is known,

B. Shishkov (Ed.): BMSD 2020, LNBIP 391, pp. 362–374, 2020.
https://doi.org/10.1007/978-3-030-52306-0_26

it might be possible to build a mimic of such a process, with the help of reusable components. This type of cause and effect models are not common in today's decision support systems.

In order to mimic how humans generates decision data, algorithms from the fields of fuzzy logic [13], deep learning [4], and probabilistic programming [11] are used or extended. We are inspired by Bayesian networks [15], which split a problem into sub-problems in the form of a directed acyclic graph.

Together with Ericsson AB we are investigating, and elaborating, the requirements needed to design an intent-driven system. In order to design an intent-driven system, the knowledge of how humans generate decision data is crucial to be able to, evaluate, learn, and improve, the functionality of the system itself.

In Sect. 2 we present the background, the methodology is described in Sect. 3, and the results are presented in Sect. 4. The analysis of the results, and a discussion are presented in Sect. 5, and finally, in Sect. 6, the conclusion and future research are presented.

2 Background

During our work with intent-driven systems, we were presented with a dataset based on human decisions. The dataset contains information about patients with stomach cancer, and a decision if an operation should be performed or not. The dataset was generated over several years. The analysis of the dataset became a challenging tasks. It is a small data set with only 55 records. Out of this 55 records, 16 has missing data.

We investigated how two different types of machine learning algorithms could explain the decisions taken by the practitioners. The two different types of machine learning algorithms are a binary decision tree, and logistic regression, [1].

When we removed all records which contain missing data, the dataset became a "not-quite-big-enough" dataset. It was not possible to use this dataset, since the chosen algorithms could not produce a result. Instead, we explored different methods of counter measures to the missing data. The combination of a binary decision tree, and a counter measure based on using the mean values with dependencies on the output values, produced the best model but did not have a high accuracy.

When we presented our findings to practitioners, they questioned the resulting decision rules. During our meeting with the practitioners, we decided to investigate why there were many records with missing data, and how the decisions about operations are taken. However, this study will concentrate on how the decisions about operations are taken.

3 Methodology

3.1 Study Design

In order to understand how the decision data is generated, we used evaluation research [12]. The research data was collected in two different ways, during focus group [19] interviews, and with the help of questionnaires.

The focus group interviews were approximately two hours in length and were based on semi-structured focus group interviews [12] with the interview questions adapted to the findings during the previous focus group interviews or questionnaire analysis. The validation and correction of the captured material was conducted with the members of the focus group on the same day as the interview was held.

The questionnaires consist of several features, and their measurement values, for fictive patients. The practitioners decide the impact of each value, and if a treatment should be considered or not. The use of fictive patients tries to make sure that only the measurement data will be used to decide if a treatment should be considered or not. The use of impact values will create an understanding of how the different features, and their values, impacts a decision about a treatment. After the questionnaires were answered, samples from the questionnaire were discussed among the practitioners.

The questionnaire data were analyzed with the help of R-Studio [14] for Mac (x86 64-bits) including the Rethinking package [8] which supports Bayesian statistics. The questionnaire instruments are described in Sect. 3.2.

3.2 The Questionnaire Data

Together with the practitioners we decided to use different cases in the questionnaire. These cases are described in Table 1. The idea is to test the model portability between different cases, and to find indication factors of the different cases. In this study we do not develop the indication factors, but studies from Hansen et al. [5], and Harambam et al. [6] might be useful when we continue our work.

Table 1. The different cases

Case	Name	Description
1	Stomach cancer	The patient is scheduled for an operation, regarding stomach cancer, within 48 h. Does the information about age, CRP, current BMI, and difference between BMI values, indicate a recommendation of an operation?
2	Appendix inflammation	The information from the patient indicates a possible inflammation in the appendix. Does the information about age, CRP, current BMI, and difference between BMI values, indicate a recommendation of an operation?

It was decided that each participant should get a dataset containing data from 12 different fictive patients. The data from the 12 fictive patients were the same for the different cases. Each of the practitioners got different datasets. The idea behind this was two fold: We will get an understanding of the different effects a value has on the decision for different cases, and, by using fictive patients the unknown factors should not influence the decision, i.e. the decision should be based on the data itself. The instructions for grading the impact of a feature value are shown in Table 2.

Table 2. Impact gradings

Grade	Description
2	Major increased risk for the patient, if a treatment is not given
1	Minor increased risk for the patient, if a treatment is not given
0	Neutral risk for the patient
−1	Minor increased risk for the patient, if a treatment is given
−2	Major increased risk for the patient, if a treatment is given

The questionnaires captures five independent features, and two dependent features. These features are described in Table 3.

Table 3. Questionnaire features

Name	Description
CRP	C-reactive protein [16] is a measurement of the infection rate
Age	The age of the patient
BMInow	The Body Mass Index [17] (BMI) value measured when the decision shall be taken
BMIbefore	The previous measured BMI value. This measurement should not be more than 12 months old
BMIdiff	The difference between BMInow and BMIbefore, in percentage
BMIeff	Used by the practitioners to show if the BMI information favors a treatment or not
Treatment	Used by the practitioners to indicate if the patient should have a treatment or not

Three of the features have predefined ordinal scales. The predefined ordinal scale for $BMInow$, $BMIbefore$, and CRP are described in Table 4. Each feature can have three different types of values, as described in Table 5.

Table 4. The feature grading

Feature	Value range	Grade	Description
BMI	0–18.5	−1	Underweight
	18.5–25.0	0	Normal
	25.0–30.0	1	Overweight
	30.0 -	2	Obese
CRP	0–10	0	Normal
	10–50	1	Infection
	50 -	2	High infection

Table 5. The different values types a feature can have

Notation	Description	Comments
$feature_m^n$	Measured value	-
$feature_g^n$	Existing ordinal scale	BMI, and CRP (Table 4)
$feature_i^n$	Practitioner decided impact	The impact a value of a feature is considered to have on the treatment decision, Table 2

3.3 The Model Equations

We are using logistic regression [1] to create models which describes how the practitioners take decisions. There are two different dependent variables, $Treatment$ and $BMIeff$. The $Treatment$ variable indicates if a treatment should be considered or nor. The $BMIeff$ variable indicates if the BMI information favors a treatment or not.

The logistic regression model can be divided into two different parts. One part is the use of a binomial distribution [8], described by Eq. 1, where p is the probability. The second part is described by Eq. 2, where the probability is calculated via a logit function [8] which can be seen as a linear equation with an intercept α, plus one coefficient ($\beta_{feature^n}$) for each feature, $feature^n$, which is part of the model. If nothing else is stated, the priors of the intercept and the priors of the coefficients are initialized according to Eqs. 3 and 4. We consider the priors to be weakly informed.

$$dependent\_variable \sim Binomial(1, p) \tag{1}$$

$$logit(p) = \alpha + \beta_{feature^i} * feature^i_{value} + ... + \beta_{feature^j} * feature^j_{value} \tag{2}$$

$$\alpha \sim Normal(0, 10) \tag{3}$$

$$\beta_{feature^n} \sim Normal(0, 1) \tag{4}$$

4 Result

We focus on Case 1, described in Table 1, during our analysis of the questionnaire data. The reason is that we will compare the Case1 questionnaire data with the real world Case 1 data, discussed in Sect. 2. By using the Case 1 questionnaire data as a base, we can investigate if our findings can be generalized between different cases, e.g. Case 2 which is described in Table 1.

4.1 Information from the Practitioners

We started with a questionnaire which only contained measured values for the following features; *CRP*, *Age*, *BMInow*, *BMIbefore*, and the dependent variable *Treatment*. During the first data gathering, updates to the questionnaire were discussed with the practitioners.

The following updates to the questionnaire were performed; One feature with derived measured value was added, *BMIdiff*. *BMIdiff* is the difference between *BMInow*, and *BMIbefore*, in percentage. One supporting dependent variable was added, *BMIeff*. *BMIeff* is used to build a model of how the BMI information will effect the decision of *Treatment*.

Three of the measured values were translated into the predefined ordinal scales, described in Table 4, and provided in the questionnaire, as a support to the practitioners.

During one of the focus group meetings with the practitioners, we discussed the problem with missing data in the real world datasets. The conclusion was, the problem can get some remedy if it will be possible for the practitioners to fill in the BMI grades from Table 4, instead of the actual BMI value, if the actual BMI value is not capture.

Several of the practitioners expressed frustration when confronted with the questionnaire data. The practitioners are used to have an interaction with the patients, which will help them to take their decisions. Another vital remark was that the data alone might not be enough, but need to be combined with visual information, an example is the BMI information. The shape of the body can indicate if obese shall be considered as a risk or not.

The practitioners mentioned something called "the eight seconds rule". The "the eight seconds rule" can be explained as the impressions a practitioner get during the first eight seconds of a meeting with a patient, e.g. how a person walk, talk, shake ones hand, if someone is assisting the patient, etc.

This first impression influence the decisions, made by the practitioners, by adding vital information into the decision process.

4.2 Supporting the Data Analysis

During the study we introduced three new value types in addition to those described in Table 5. The added value types are described in Table 6.

Table 6. The additional values types a feature can have

Notation	Description	Comments
$feature_o^n$	Practitioner ordinal scale	Table 7 shows the ordinal scales for certain features
$feature_r^n$	Practitioner eReLU scale	Calculated with the help of Eq. 5
$feature_{lr}^n$	Rearranged grades	Make sure that the output value of the gradings is monotonically decreasing, or increasing

Table 7 shows how the impact values of a certain feature are mapped to the values of that feature. This mapping is done by the practitioners. The values a, b, a_g, and b_g, are used to create an ordinal scale for a specific feature, $feature^n$.

Table 7. Impact values for the different values of the features

$feature^n$	$feature_i^n = 0$	$\|feature_i^n\| = 2$	a	b	ag	bg
CRP	<25	≥75	25	75	1	3
Age	<75	≥90	75	90	1	3

The $v_g(v)$ is the eReLU value of a feature, $feature^n$, with the measured value of v. The data used in Eq. 5 is shown in Table 7. Equation 5 can be regarded as an extended version of the Rectified Linear Unit (ReLU) algorithm [4], which we name eReLU.

$$v_g(v) = \begin{cases} a_g & \text{if } v < a \\ \frac{v-a}{b-a} * (b_g - a_g) + a_g & \text{if } a \leq v \leq b \\ b_g & \text{if } v > b \end{cases} \tag{5}$$

4.3 Simplified Models of Human Decision Making

The aim is to find a simplified model which represents how the practitioners are using the data to make a decision. With the help of the Eqs. 6–13, we are trying to find the model which best fits the data. Table 8 shows the results of the different models.

$$Treatment \sim Binomial(1, p) \tag{6}$$

$$logit(p) = \alpha + \beta_{CRP} * CRP_m + \beta_{Age} * Age_m + \beta_{BMInow} * BMInow_m + \beta_{BMIdiff} * BMIdiff_m \tag{7}$$

$$logit(p) = \alpha + \beta_{CRP} * CRP_m + \beta_{Age} * Age_m \tag{8}$$

$$logit(p) = \alpha + \beta_{CRP} * CRP_m + \beta_{Age} * Age_o \tag{9}$$

$$logit(p) = \alpha + \beta_{CRP} * CRP_o + \beta_{Age} * Age_m \tag{10}$$

$$logit(p) = \alpha + \beta_{CRP} * CRP_m + \beta_{Age} * Age_r \tag{11}$$

$$logit(p) = \alpha + \beta_{CRP} * CRP_m + \beta_{Age} * Age_o + \beta_{BMIeff} * BMIeff \tag{12}$$

$$logit(p) = \alpha + \beta_{CRP} * CRP_m + \beta_{Age} * Age_r + \beta_{BMIeff} * BMIeff \tag{13}$$

$$logit(p) = \alpha + \beta_{CRP} * CRP_m + \beta_{Age} * Age_r + \beta_{BMInow} * BMInow_{lr} + \beta_{BMIdiff} * BMIdiff_m \tag{14}$$

$$logit(p) = \alpha + \alpha_{Prac[i]} + \beta_{CRP} * CRP_m + \beta_{Age} * Age_o + \beta_{BMIeff} * BMIeff \tag{15}$$

$$logit(p) = \alpha + \alpha_{Prac[i]} + \beta_{CRP} * CRP_m + \beta_{Age} * Age_r + \beta_{BMIeff} * BMIeff \tag{16}$$

$$\alpha_{Prac[i]} \sim Normal(0, \sigma), \sigma \sim HalfCauchy(0, 1) \tag{17}$$

$$BMIeff \sim Binomial(1, p) \tag{18}$$

$$logit(p) = \alpha + \beta_{BMInow} * BMInow_m + \beta_{BMIdiff} * BMIdiff_m \tag{19}$$

$$logit(p) = \alpha + \beta_{BMInow} * BMInow_g + \beta_{BMIdiff} * BMIdiff_m \tag{20}$$

$$logit(p) = \alpha + \beta_{BMInow} * BMInow_{lr} + \beta_{BMIdiff} * BMIdiff_m \tag{21}$$

Table 8. The results of how the different models fit to the data

logit(p) equation	Accuracy (%)	Comments
7	81	Using the measurement values of CRP, Age, BMInow, and BMIdiff
8	83	Using the measurement values of CRP and Age
9	86	Using the measurement values of CRP and the practitioner ordinal scale of Age
10	81	Using the practitioner ordinal scale of CRP and the measurement values of Age
11	94	Using the measurement values of CRP and the eReLU of Age
12	89	Using the measurement values of CRP and the practitioner ordinal scale of Age, together with the BMIeff
13	94	Using the measurement values of CRP and the eReLU of Age, together with the BMIeff

4.4 Clustering of Decision Data

The $BMIeff$ value is an artificial feature, used to indicate if the BMI information favors a treatment. In order to create a model which estimates the $BMIeff$, based on $BMInow$ and $BMIdiff$, we use the Eqs. 18–21. In Eq. 19 we use the measured value of both the $BMInow$ and the $BMIdiff$. In Eq. 20 we are using the gradings in Table 4 for the $BMInow$ feature.

When inspecting the data we observe the impact indicated by the practitioners regarding $BMInow$ forms a valley. The absolute value of the impact is high on grade -1, and grade 2, but lower in between. Since we are using logistic regression a valley might cause problems for the algorithm. In order to remedy this problem we change the grade of the values in grade -1 into grade 3. The new grading is used in Eq. 21. Table 9 indicates an improvement of the model when the grading value was rearranged.

Table 9. Results of the models regarding the BMI effect

logit(p) equation	Accuracy (%)	Comments
19	94	Using the measured values
20	94	Using the BMI grades from Table 4 for $BMInow$
21	100	Rearrange the grading in order to improve the model

4.5 Multilevel Models

Since we would like our models to capture the different practitioners knowledge, and beliefs, we are investigating the use of a multilevel model. In a multilevel model, each practitioner contributes with its own intercept parameter $\alpha_{Prac[i]}$, which contributes to the total model.

Equation 6 and Eqs. 15–17 are used to create two different multilevel models. The contribution from each practitioner is model with Eq. 17. We model the intercept priors as a normal distribution with a mean of zero and a none negative, weakly informed, σ. Table 10 shows that the use of multilevel models can improve the models accuracy.

Table 10. Multilevel models

logit(p) equation	Accuracy (%)	Comments
12	89	CRP_m, Age_o and BMIeff
15	92	Model 12 as a multilevel model
13	94	CRP_m, Age_r and BMIeff
16	94	Model 13 as a multilevel model

4.6 Decisions Taken in Different Steps

During one of the focus group meetings with the practitioners, we discussed the problem with external factors which affects the decision about if the BMI information. It was concluded, using a binary value indicating if external factors have changed the value of $BMIeff$, will be useful for the understanding of the decision making.

Since $BMIeff$ is affected by external factors, the direct effect of the BMI features, $BMInow$ and $BMIbefore$, on the $Treatment$ is removed. By creating the model in two steps, we introduce the effect of the $BMIeff$ on the $Treatment$. Table 11 shows the difference between models when we only are using the measured values, compared to when we use our gained insight about how the practitioners are reasoning when taking decisions.

Table 11. Comparing measured data models with insight models

logit(p) equation	Accuracy (%)	Comments
7	81	Using the measured values for all the features
14	92	Creates the model in one step, using eReLU and rearranged grading
16	94	Creates the model in two steps, using eReLU and rearranged grading

4.7 Using the Gained Knowledge

We apply our gained knowledge on the Case 2 dataset, Table 1. We cannot reuse the treatment model since CRP_m influence the decision about a treatment in an opposite way, compared to Case 1. However, the eReLU, the logic regression compensation of $BMInow_g$, and the $BMIeff$, are vital components in order to improve the accuracy of Case 2 from 86% to 92%.

We use our gained insight on the real world data, discussed in Sect. 2. In order to simulate the impact of external factors, we use out-layer detection to filter out decisions which are plausible to be judge as impacted by external factors. The results in Table 12 show improvements when compensating for external factors.

Table 12. Real world data without, and with, compensation for external factors

logit(p) equation	Accuracy (%)	Comments
8	84	Using the measurement values of the different features
15	86	CRP_m, Age_o and BMIeff as multilevel
16	86	CRP_m, Age_r and BMIeff as multilevel
15	90	Compensation for external factors
16	94	Compensation for external factors

During one of the focus group meetings with the practitioners, we discussed the problem with external factors which affects the decision about if the $Treatment$. It was concluded, using a binary value indicating if external factors have changed the value of $Treatment$, will be useful for the understanding of the decision making.

5 Analysis and Discussion

Table 8 shows the results of the different models. We started to create a model which only uses measured values of the features, Eq. 7. Since the accuracy is only 81%, we looked for other models to explain the data. We started with models which could fit the data without taking the BMI into consideration. We focus on how Age and CRP can be represented to fit the data in the best possible way.

When we used the measurement values of the *Age* feature, and altered the way how the *CRP* is represented, as described in Eqs. 8 and 10, we found the measurement value to be the best way to fit the data (83%) compared to practitioner ordinal scale (81%).

When we altered the way how the *Age* is represented, and used the measurement values of the *CRP* feature, as described in Eqs. 8, 12, and 13, we found eReLU to be the best way to fit the data (94%) compared to practitioner ordinal scale (89%), and the measurement value (83%).

CRP and *Age* seems to be handle in different ways by the practitioners, when used in the decision process. The *CRP* measurement value has a distinct meaning as a factor in the decision process. On the contrary, *Age* itself is not a factor, instead *Age* embracing several different generalized factors, e.g. higher risks when doing operation, slow recovering pace, etc. Since the emphasis is put on a certain part of the value range, the eReLU is a good candidate to fit the model to the data.

There are many different type of functions available in the literature. We are inspired by fuzzy logic [13] and deep learning [4] functions. Since we intend to model how humans use data to take decisions, we are looking for a function which can put the emphaci on a specific part of the value range. We considered the Sigmoid function [13] but we chose a linear function since a linear function is easy for humans to relate to. By combining the ideas from the Sigmoid function and the ReLU function [4] we constructed the eReLU function, Eq. 5.

The value of $BMIeff$ reflects the combined effect of the BMI values, on the $Treatment$, better than the BMI values them selfs. The creation of $BMIeff$ improves the overall accuracy since a step-wise approach can be used during the decision making, as shown in Table 11.

A visualization of the results is shown in Fig. 1. Figure 1 shows the functions used to transform the feature information, the models used to fit the dataset to the results, and the external factors impacting the decisions.

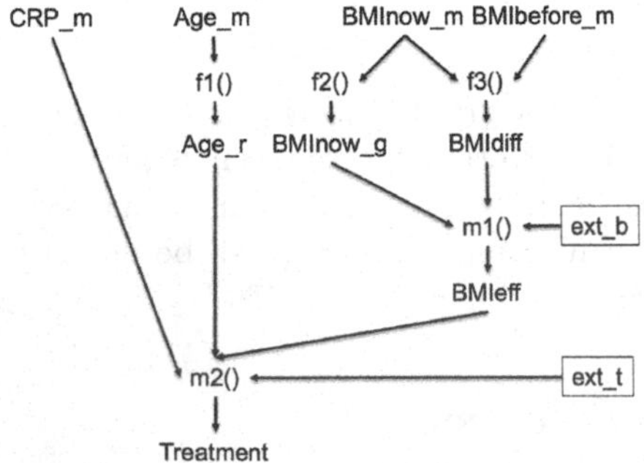

Fig. 1. A visualization of the results

Function $f1()$ is the eReLU algorithm, Eq. 5, while $f2()$ is the function implementing what is shown in Table 4, and Function $f3()$ generates the difference between $BMInow$, and $BMIbefore$, in percentage. The models used to fit the data is named $m1()$ and $m2()$. Model $m1()$ is used to fit the data to $BMIeff$. We use Eq. 21 to implement $m1()$. We use Eq. 16 to implement $m2()$, which is used to fit the data to the treatment. Unknown factors or not recorded factors, will influence the decision. These type of factors are named ext_b, and ext_t. One example of the external factor ext_b, which influence the decision about $BMIeff$, is the shape of the body of a patient. The "the eight seconds rule" is an example of external factors influencing the Treatment decision, as described in Sect. 4.1. These external factors are named ext_t in Fig. 1.

It is possible to use the structure of Fig. 1 to improve the accuracy of other cases, compared to applying machine learning algorithms directly on the measured data. We used our model on the Case 2 datasets and increased the accuracy from from 86% to 92%. In this case we do not have to consider the external factors.

When we use Fig. 1 on the real world dataset for Case 1, we need to consider the external factors. We use out-layer detection to identify decisions which are plausible to judge as impacted by external factors, which increased the accuracy from 84% to 94%. The detected data points were discussed with practitioners and regarded as plausible.

6 Conclusion and Future Work

In this study, we have investigated, and suggested, a way to mimic a processes of how humans generate decision data. We have used the structure of a directed acyclic graph to orchestrate components which make it possible to mimic the process of human generated decision data. These components are probabilistic programming models, extended machine learning algorithms, and data science processes.

During the study we constructed the eReLU function, Eq. 5. When confronted with a feature which values is not a factor but rather embracing several different generalized factors, e.g. higher risks when doing operation, slow recovering pace, etc., the eReLU function is a good estimate of how the feature affects a decision. The eReLU function is a combination of the ideas from the Sigmoid function [13], and the ReLU function [4].

In order to be able to apply the results in an intent-driven system, we need to find a framework which can be used to realize the processes. Since an intent-driven system needs interventions, and counterfactuals, in order to achieve an artificial intelligence which can improve the system itself, we will investigate how we can combine flow-based programming [2,18] with causality, as described by Pearl [9]. The investigation has to include the possibilities to handle external factors, and embrace them as a vital part of the model.

References

1. Burkov, A.: The Hundred-Page Machine Learning Book. Andriy Burkov, Quebec (2019)
2. Crakci, M.: Dataflow and Reactive Programming Systems. CreateSpace Independent Publishing Platform, North Charleston (2014)
3. Davidson-Pilon, C.: Bayesian Methods for Hackers, 1st edn. Addison Wesley Data & Analytics Series, Boston (2016)
4. Goodfellow, I., Bengio, Y., Courville, A.: Deep Learning. MIT Press, Cambridge (2016)
5. Hansen, J., Meservy, R., Wood, L.: Indexing tree and pruning concepts to support case-based reasoning. Omega **22**(4), 361–369 (1994)
6. Harambam, J., Makhortykh, M., Bountouridis, D., Van Hoboken, J.: Designing for the better by taking users into account: a qualitative evaluation of user control mechanisms in (NEWS) recommender systems. In: RecSys 2019–13th ACM Conference on Recommender Systems, pp. 69–77 (2019)
7. McElreath, R.: Statistical Rethinking. CRC Press, New York (2016)
8. McElreath, R.: Rethinking package (2017). https://github.com/rmcelreath/rethinking. Accessed 09 Dec 2019
9. Pearl, J.: Causality, 2nd edn. Cambridge University Press, Cambridge (2009)
10. Pearl, J., Glymour, M., Jewell, N.P.: Causal Inference in Statistics. Wiley, Chichester (2016)
11. Pfeffer, A.: Practical Probabilistic Programming. Manning Publications, Greenwich (2016)
12. Robson, C.: Real World Research: A Resource for Users of Social Research Methods in Applied Settings, 3rd edn. Wiley, Chichester (2011)
13. Ross, T.: Fuzzy Logic with Engineering Applications, 4th edn. Wiley, Chichester (2017)
14. RStudio: RStudio (2019). https://rstudio.com/. Accessed 09 Dec 2019
15. Scutari, M., Denis, J.B.: Bayesian Networks. CRC Press, New York (2015)
16. Wikipedia: C-reactive protein (2018). https://en.wikipedia.org/wiki/C-reactive_protein. Accessed 19 Feb 2018
17. Wikipedia: Body mass index (2019). https://en.wikipedia.org/wiki/Body_mass_index. Accessed 12 Dec 2019
18. Zarrin, B., Baumeister, H., Sarjoughian, H.: Towards domain-specific flow-based languages. In: MODELSWARD 2018 - Proceedings of the 6th International Conference on Model-Driven Engineering and Software Development, January 2018, pp. 319–325 (2018)
19. Zrake, J., MacFadyen, A., McEnery, J.E., Racusin, J.L., Gehrels, N.: Numerical simulations of driven supersonic relativistic MHD turbulence. Ann. Rev. Sociol. **22**, 102–105 (2011)

Enabling Collaborative Business Process Elicitation in Virtual Environments

Ludger Pöhler(✉), Julian Schuir, Simon Lübbers, and Frank Teuteberg

Accounting and Information Systems, Osnabrück University, Osnabrück, Germany
{ludger.poehler,julian.schuir,sluebbers,
frank.teuteberg}@uni-osnabrueck.de

Abstract. With increasingly globalized markets and the growing digitization, business process redesign has steadily become more important in recent years. Despite its increasing relevance, the actual process elicitation still poses a major challenge as global distribution of company locations makes the carrying out of process modelling workshops difficult, and especially novices have problems with the modeling itself. To meet these challenges, virtual reality based systems were estimated to be an efficient and promising way. Consequently, this paper deals with the development of a virtual reality application for participatory process modelling. Using the Design Science paradigm, the work identifies issues occurring in business process elicitation from the literature and translates them into meta-requirements. With the help of these meta-requirements, design principles were derived that were considered in the development. Using these design guidelines, a prototype to enable collaborative process elicitation in VR was developed and subsequently evaluated by a focus group.

Keywords: Virtual reality · Collaborative process elicitation and modelling

1 Introduction

In order to compete in increasingly globalized and intensified markets, it is essential for companies to collectively reengineer their business processes [1]. Despite its growing importance, the actual process elicitation is still a major challenge for many companies due to the lack of experience in process modeling [2], the poor knowledge of process modeling notations [3] and the geographical distribution of the stakeholders involved [4]. To meet these challenges, recent research suggests a diversity of digital support tools such as process mining techniques [5], smart glasses and tablet applications [6]. Beyond that, virtual reality (VR) based process elicitation tools have been valued as a promising approach by enabling the employees involved in a business process to move from the passive role of information sources to the active role of process modelers [7, 8]. At the same time, the technology allows real working environments to be experienced virtually, thus enabling the spatial modeling of business processes in simulations of real environments [8].

In general, virtual reality refers to "the use of computer graphics systems in combinations with various display and interface devices to provide the effect of immersion

B. Shishkov (Ed.): BMSD 2020, LNBIP 391, pp. 375–385, 2020.
https://doi.org/10.1007/978-3-030-52306-0_27

in the interactive 3D computer-generated environment" [9]. For instance, Brown et al. [10] implemented a 3D world for collaborative process modelling in Second Life. The results reveal that process documentation can be improved by increasing user involvement and making the mutual development of process models easier, even when the relevant stakeholders are geographically distributed [10].

With the advances in VR technology in recent years, research especially considers the use of head-mounted displays (HMD) to be beneficial by strongly engaging employees and improving the cognitive availability of information significantly compared to PC-based approaches [11]. An evaluation by Oberhauser et al. demonstrated that users can solve modeling tasks in immersive virtual reality more efficiently compared to common software tools [7]. In addition, VR environments offer unlimited modeling space and enable the representation of complex and extensive processes at different aggregation levels resulting from changes in perspective [8, 10].

Previous work especially focused on the representation of business processes in virtual worlds using 3D monitor-based approaches [7, 8, 10] as well as their added value [12, 13], and developed suitable modelling languages based on BPMN [7, 14]. Nevertheless, modern VR hardware in terms of HMD systems has not yet used for the collaborative process elicitation. Precisely the latter is considered to be advantageous due to its highly immersive character and the intuitive user interface [15]. To our knowledge, there is only one technical concept by Vogel and Thomas, which has yet to be implemented [16]. In view of this gap, the following research question (RQ) can be derived:

RQ: *How can a virtual reality based system be designed in order to enable collaborative and intuitive process elicitation?*

Consequently, this contribution pursues the goal of creating a collaborative VR-based process elicitation application (VR-ModTool). In the sense of the participatory modeling approach, companies should be enabled to model and evaluate business processes in VR by including employees participating in the process with the help of this application. In view of the corona pandemic, where face-to-face meetings cannot take place, such tools can offer a promising alternative for workshops by bridging geographical distances and by simultaneously engaging its users.

The remaining part of this publication is structured as follows: Sect. 2 presents the research approach of this contribution. Section 3 gives an overview of the identified issues, meta-requirements and design principles. The implementation of these design principles and the evaluation of the application of the prototype form Sects. 4 and 5. Section 6 finally summarizes the main findings and provides future research directions.

2 Research Approach

The artifact development follows the Design Science Research (DSR) Methodology in accordance to Peffers et al. [17]. Figure 1 illustrates the research approach including six main stages.

First, the current state of research was examined with a literature research and issues occurring in participatory process elicitation were identified. Therefore, we combined

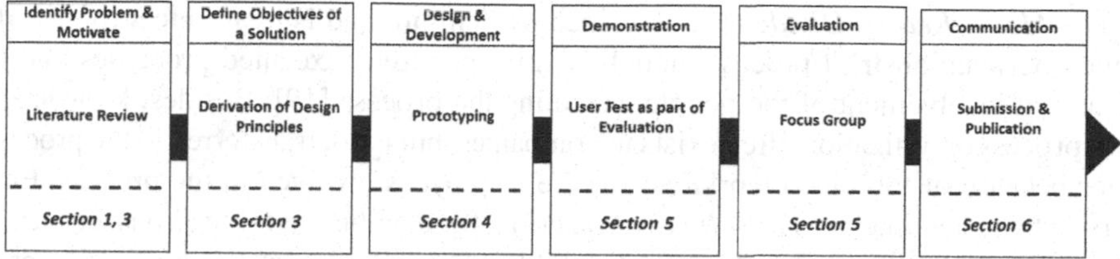

Fig. 1. Design science research approach based on [17]

the term *business process modeling* with the terms *collaborative, participative, social* and queried the scientific databases Scopus, IEEE, EBSCO and Google Scholar. Second, we defined the goals of our solution by deriving meta-requirements (MR) based in the issues (I) identified in the literature [17]. The MRs were consolidated into three design principles (DP), which served as guidelines for the subsequent development process [17]. Third, a concept for the application as well as an associated architecture was developed and implemented. Fourth, the developed prototype was tested with regard to its functionality by eight employees of a VR software company in groups of two prior to the subsequent evaluation within a focus group discussion. The evaluation consisted of the following elements: introduction (5 min), presentation of the prototype (5 min), testing (40 min) and discussion (40 min). Finally, the evaluation enabled us to assess the design principles and to derive needs for further development cycles.

3 Issues, Meta-Requirements and Design Principles

Based on our literature review, we identified nine Is, which in turn led to eight MRs, from which three DPs were finally generated. Figure 2 illustrates the issues identified from literature and their relation to the meta-requirements and design principles.

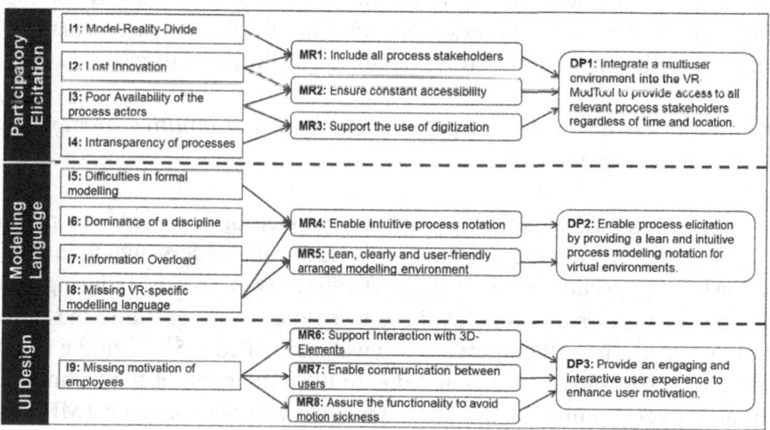

Fig. 2. Derivation of the design principles (following [18], p. 6)

The *Model-Reality-Divide* (I1) described by Schmidt and Nurcan refers to the difference between abstract process models and the concrete, executed processes due to the lack of involvement of the people executing the process [19]. Besides, knowledge about process optimization often exists in companies, but is not transferred to the process owner because of too much workload for the employees involved in the process. Erol refers to this phenomena as *Lost Innovation* (I2) [20]. Combining these two issues leads to the conclusion, that the VR-ModTool should include all relevant employees like process actors or process owners (MR1). Lost Innovation combined with barriers like *poor availability of the process actors* (I3), for example caused by geographic distribution of companies, leads to the need for constant accessibility (MR2), independent of time and location. In addition, *intransparency* (I4), especially on the technical level, makes it more difficult to document and track processes. By targeting the use of digitization (MR3), IT-enabled support for users modelling can be ensured. At the same time, the use of digital tools can promote the IT skills and understanding among employees [21]. Based on these MRs the following DP can be derived:

DP1: *Integrate a multiuser environment into the VR-ModTool to provide access to all relevant process stakeholders regardless of time and location.*

In addition to these social and organizational issues, there are often problems associated with the existing modeling languages: For instance, inexperienced modelers have difficulties in *transferring information into a formal process model* (I5) [3]. Furthermore, in interdisciplinary settings, conflicts between individual disciplines can occur. This is especially the case when the dominance of *one discipline prevails within a department* (I6). This in turn can lead to an increased use of discipline-specific notation elements and thus process participants from outside the field are overstrained [22]. Given this background, an intuitive language is necessary (MR4). Another issue relating to complex process models is the *information overload* (I7). According to Miller [23], a novice can recall an average of seven elements in short term memory. This leads us to the conclusion on the need for a lean and user-friendly modelling notation and corresponding tools (MR5). Given the *lack of process modeling kits for immersive worlds* (I8) which support interaction using modern VR hardware, the following DP results:

DP2: *Enable process elicitation by providing a lean and intuitive process modeling notation for virtual environments.*

Apart from the modeling-specific issues mentioned above, there are problems in practice concerning the motivation of the individual stakeholders, which in turn hinder collaboration [24]. Especially the *lack of motivation of employees* (I9) during interviews and workshops is a major obstacle, as these techniques still constitute the most effective elicitation approach if all employees are well motivated [25]. With the help of VR, employees can be specifically motivated due to the immersion of the technology [15]. An important aspect of immersion is the interaction with the elements (MR6), such as operating a menu or gripping objects. To intensify the motivation of the users, communication tools can additionally be deployed in the virtual world. This can be achieved, for example, by integrating avatars representing the users in virtual environment or by enabling the writing of text and audio messages [10]. In view of this, the application needs to support the communication between the users (MR7). Another technology-specific problem in virtual reality is the so-called motion sickness, which results from high latency times and low frame rates [26]. Thus, to avoid this side effect, the technical functionality of the prototype must be ensured (MR8). To conclude, the following DP can be derived:

DP3: *Provide an engaging and interactive user experience to enhance user motivation.*

Overall, we derived three key design principles. Each of them refers to at least one meta-requirement and was taken into account during the development phase.

4 Concept and Implementation

We propose a solution consisting of the three basic components *Immersive 3D Environment* (referring to DP3), *Multiuser Access* (referring to DP1) and *Process Modelling Kit* (referring to DP2). The concept implemented in Unity Engine version 2019.2.0f1 is shown in Fig. 3.

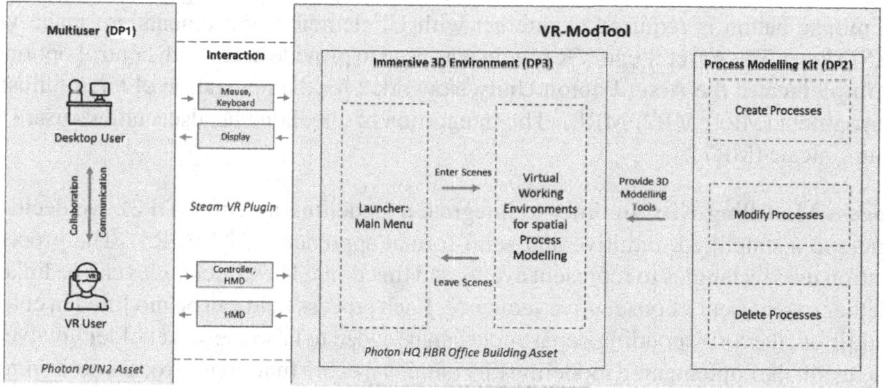

Fig. 3. Solution concept

Immersive 3D Environment: Considering the high potential for user engagement, we decided to deploy in an immersive environment based on virtual reality (MR3) for process modeling (DP3). With regard to the spatial design of this environment, we decided to create a realistic, job-related environment in the form of a virtual building with several rooms using the Photon HQ HBR asset. After the initial login, the user first enters a virtual launcher scene, from where he can enter different virtual office rooms that are used for modelling (see Fig. 4). The intention of providing virtual offices was to allow the components available in the room, such as PCs, to be included in the process modelling (MR6). Thus, for example, it would be imaginable to integrate CAD data from real working environments into the tool in the future. To avoid complications such as motion sickness, we aimed to ensure a high resolution by implementing the asset TextMeshPro.

Fig. 4. Main menu and starting scene

Multiuser Access: To provide access to all relevant process stakeholders regardless of time and location, we implemented two different roles in the form of a desktop user and a VR user. The VR user is able to interact with the virtual objects, to move and to teleport within the virtual space. During implementation, the application was adapted to HTC Vive and the associated controllers. The desktop user controls the avatar with his mouse and keyboard. The mouse is used to change the viewing direction and the left mouse button is required to interact with UI elements. Movements are made via WASD keys. The Asset SteamVR plugin was used to provide users with control options. We implemented the Asset Photon Unity Network 2 for the realization of the multiuser environment (MR1, MR2, MR8). The integration of telephone headsets allows users to communicate (MR7).

Process Modelling Kit: In order to integrate a modelling notation (DP2), we decided to pursue a simplified, intuitive and semi-formal approach (MR4, MR5). The process notation uses rectangles to represent events and functions. These rectangles can be linked together to represent a consecutive sequence. Each process field can be modified in color. In addition, the corresponding department can be added to label the stakeholder involved. As a result, the implemented modeling kit contains six core functions: Process description (InputField Description), the organizational unit (Dropdown Department), selecting the color (Button Change Color), delete the process function (Button Delete Process), create edge (Button Add Edge) and accept edge (Button Receive Edge). Figure 5 shows these elements.

Fig. 5. Process Modelling Kit

Once a user enters the virtual office, these functions can be accessed. We defined the roles as follows: The desktop user only is authorized to enter the process description text. The remaining elements can be manipulated by the VR user. When targeting the *Department* button, a drop-down menu opens from which the appropriate department can be selected. To delete a process function for all users, the UI element Button *Delete Process* is used, which is displayed as a trash can in the lower right-hand corner of the panel. An edge is created on the right side of a process function and it is connected to the left side of another process function. The corresponding UI buttons are visualized by the arrow symbol. Once a process is documented, users can save the scene and quit. The process models stored in the individual scenes can be re-entered and modified by the users.

5 Evaluation

The subsequent focus group discussion as part of the evaluation focused in particular the functionality and the usability of the prototype. According to Morgan, between three and twelve reviewers are suitable for a focus group discussion [27]. Therefore, we invited eight employees of a VR software development company to participate in the evaluation. Before the discussion, the participants had to go through a functional test in groups of two with one acting as the VR user and the other one as the desktop user. Each group had to model a short, predefined process in the virtual world by controlling the avatar, instantiating and, if necessary deleting process functions. Furthermore, the users had to label the department involved. To provide a connection between tasks and environment, the participants were asked to model common tasks that need to be carried out an office environment with the principle of dual control. For example, the case *Leaving the office* includes the steps *Close the entrance door, Leave the office clean and tidy* and *Check the status of internal company servers* (see Fig. 6). An introduction to the handling was not given since we aimed to assess the usability.

Fig. 6. Insights from the experimental results

Overall, all tasks were solved quickly and without complications by the evaluators. The motion control was adapted in a short time for both the desktop and VR avatar. Likewise, all participants applied the instantiation and linking of process functions intuitively. In doing so, they used the objects available in virtual space to create logical links between the spatial environment and the processes. For example, the *close door* function was placed at the door. During the focus group discussion, the collaboration in the virtual environment was positively emphasized as task sharing allowed the users to concentrate on their role in the process. It was mentioned, that *"a clear distribution of roles between the desktop and the VR user should be communicated in the future"*, since in individual cases complications arose when two users simultaneously worked on the same process model. Moreover, the idea of providing a 2D view for the desktop user was introduced. With a top-down view, the user could get a better overview of more complex processes. The process modeling language and its notation were described as *"easy to understand, as the limited number of elements supports the intuitive handling"*, especially for VR users. However, four participants mentioned the need to integrate functionality to model several alternative paths by providing connectors as known from BPMN. In addition, the integration of fold-out processes should be enabled in the future. Concerning the pursued approach of spatial modelling in virtual working environments, the participants emphasized that it can be helpful depending on the application area. As stated by the participants, virtual reality process modelling *"is an advantage where a spatial component is relevant"*, i.e. if a process is shaped by different locations as it is the case for logistic processes. At the same time, the participants emphasized that where spatial components are not relevant, e.g. in software development or sales, *"the added value of VR process modeling is very limited"*.

6 Discussion, Limitations and Future Work

According to our evaluation, participatory modelling can be promoted by a VR-based multi-user environment, as it allows different users to access the system independent of time and location, as long as the required infrastructure is available (DP1). It is important, especially for novices, that the process notation is easy to use by consisting of a concise number of elements (DP2). However, the evaluation outcomes suggest that a VR-based modelling language needs to integrate important connectors (like AND or XOR) from existing languages as well as a function for folding and unfolding processes in order to model complex business processes. Basically, collaborative and interactive VR applications offer the advantage that their immersive character encourages their users to participate (DP3), so VR systems provide an entertaining user experience compared to conventional, rather homogeneous user interfaces. Nevertheless, the evaluation results show that the three-dimensional representation of process models in virtual working environments only offers advantages for specific application areas in which spatial components are involved. We believe that the tool is especially useful for collaborative and security-critical processes that require the principle of dual control (e.g. logistics processes like cash transport or production processes). In the case of processes where spatial conditions are not relevant (e.g. software development), the tool is less suitable. With this knowledge our work has both academic and practical implications.

From an academic point of view, the derived and recently refined design principles offer starting points for the development of further VR systems, can be critically examined by researchers and tested in more realistic application scenarios. Furthermore, they can be extended to contribute to the scientifically based development of VR applications for process modelling. In addition, this paper contributes to growing body of DSR literature by presenting our application. Practitioners can use our results to find new solutions for participatory business process engineering. Our results suggest that virtual reality is a valuable tool for collaborative activities such as process elicitation.

This work is subject to limitations that provide approaches for future research. First, literature research in this paper has only been addressed peripherally. Second, the focus in the development was especially on realization of the intuitive multiuser environment, therefore the modeling kit needs to be extended and improved in the future. Specifically, the integration of operators to connect the processes is essential. We further intend to enable the import of digital twins of real working environments in order to link the virtual space more closely with the process models. Likewise, the integration of a transformation system, which enables the export into standardized process modelling languages (i.e. BPMN), remains the focus of future work. From our point of view, this enables to combine the advantages of intuitive elicitation and standardized visualization. Finally, the findings of the evaluation are very limited because the participants only modelled light and predefined processes. Besides, the results are based on a homogeneous and small sample since all participants were already familiar with VR systems before the evaluation. Therefore, more in-depth evaluations with a heterogeneous and larger sample are necessary to evaluate the system in a rigorous manner.

Acknowledgement. The authors would like to thank the reviewers for their feedback. This contribution was prepared within the research project *SoDigital* (German Federal Ministry for Education and Research, funding code 02L18B570–02L18B575).

References

1. Börger, E.: Approaches to modeling business processes: a critical analysis of BPMN, workflow patterns and YAWL. Softw. Syst. Model. **11**, 305–318 (2012). https://doi.org/10.1007/s10270-011-0214-z
2. Brown, R., Rinderle-Ma, S., Kriglstein, S., Kabicher-Fuchs, S.: Augmenting and assisting model elicitation tasks with 3D virtual world context metadata. In: Meersman, R., et al. (eds.) OTM 2014. LNCS, vol. 8841, pp. 39–56. Springer, Heidelberg (2014). https://doi.org/10.1007/978-3-662-45563-0_3
3. Nolte, A., Brown, R., Anslow, C., Wiechers, M., Polyvyanyy, A., Herrmann, T.: Collaborative business process modeling in multi-surface environments. In: Anslow, C., Campos, P., Jorge, J. (eds.) Collaboration Meets Interactive Spaces, pp. 259–286. Springer, Cham (2016). https://doi.org/10.1007/978-3-319-45853-3_12
4. Attaran, M.: Exploring the relationship between information technology and business process reengineering. Inf. Manag. **41**, 585–596 (2004)
5. Leyh, C., Bley, K., Seek, S.: Elicitation of processes in business process management in the era of digitization – the same techniques as decades ago? In: Piazolo, F., Geist, V., Brehm, L., Schmidt, R. (eds.) ERP Future 2016. LNBIP, vol. 285, pp. 42–56. Springer, Cham (2017). https://doi.org/10.1007/978-3-319-58801-8_4
6. Vogel, J., Zobel, B., Jannaber, S., Thomas, O.: BPMN4SGA: a BPMN extension for smart glasses applications to enable process visualisations. In: Czarnecki, C., Brockmann, C., Sultanow, E., Koschmider, A., Selzer, A. (eds.) Workshops der INFORMATIK 2018 - Architekturen, Prozesse, Sicherheit und Nachhaltigkeit, Bonn, pp. 259–273 (2018)
7. Oberhauser, R., Pogolski, C., Matic, A.: VR-BPMN: visualizing BPMN models in virtual reality. In: Shishkov, B. (ed.) BMSD 2018. LNBIP, vol. 319, pp. 83–97. Springer, Cham (2018). https://doi.org/10.1007/978-3-319-94214-8_6

8. Leinenbach, S.: Interaktive Geschäftsprozessmodellierung: Dokumentation von Prozesswissen in einer Virtual Reality-gestützten Unternehmungsvisualisierung. Springer, Heidelberg (2013). https://doi.org/10.1007/978-3-322-90707-3
9. Pan, Z., Cheok, A.D., Yang, H., Zhu, J., Shi, J.: Virtual reality and mixed reality for virtual learning environments. Comput. Graph. **30**, 20–28 (2006)
10. Brown, R., Recker, J., West, S.: Using virtual worlds for collaborative business process modeling. Bus. Process Manag. J. **17**, 546–564 (2011)
11. Weitlaner, D., Guettinger, A., Kohlbacher, M.: Intuitive comprehensibility of process models. In: Fischer, H., Schneeberger, J. (eds.) S-BPM ONE 2013. CCIS, vol. 360, pp. 52–71. Springer, Heidelberg (2013). https://doi.org/10.1007/978-3-642-36754-0_4
12. Leyer, M., Brown, R., Aysolmaz, B., Vanderfeesten, I., Turetken, O.: 3D virtual world BPM training systems: process gateway experimental results. In: Giorgini, P., Weber, B. (eds.) CAiSE 2019. LNCS, vol. 11483, pp. 415–429. Springer, Cham (2019). https://doi.org/10.1007/978-3-030-21290-2_26
13. West, S., Brown, R.A., Recker, J.C.: Collaborative business process modeling using 3D virtual environments. In: Proceedings of the 16th Americas Conference on Information Systems: Sustainable IT Collaboration around the Globe. AIS (2010)
14. Abdul, B.M., Corradini, F., Re, B., Rossi, L., Tiezzi, F.: UBBA: unity based BPMN animator. In: Cappiello, C., Ruiz, M. (eds.) CAiSE 2019. LNBIP, vol. 350, pp. 1–9. Springer, Cham (2019). https://doi.org/10.1007/978-3-030-21297-1_1
15. Vogel, J., Schuir, J., Thomas, O., Teuteberg, F.: Gestaltung und Erprobung einer virtual-reality-Anwendung zur Unterstützung des Prototypings in design-thinking-Prozessen. HMD Praxis der Wirtschaftsinformatik **57**, 1–19 (2020). https://doi.org/10.1365/s40702-020-00608-9
16. Vogel, J., Thomas, O.: Towards a virtual reality-based process elicitation system. In: EMISA 2018, pp. 15–28 (2018)
17. Peffers, K., Tuunanen, T., Rothenberger, M.A., Chatterjee, S.: A design science research methodology for information systems research. J. Manag. Inf. Syst. **24**, 45–77 (2007)
18. Meier, P., Beinke, J.H., Fitte, C., Behne, A., Teuteberg, F.: FeelFit – design and evaluation of a conversational agent to enhance health awareness. In: Proceedings of International Conference on Information System, pp. 1–17 (2019)
19. Schmidt, R., Nurcan, S.: BPM and social software. In: Ardagna, D., Mecella, M., Yang, J. (eds.) BPM 2008. LNBIP, vol. 17, pp. 649–658. Springer, Heidelberg (2009). https://doi.org/10.1007/978-3-642-00328-8_65
20. Erol, S., Granitzer, M., Happ, S., Jantunen, S., Jennings, B., Johannesson, P.: Pattern detection for conceptual schema recovery in data-intensive systems. J. Softw. Evol. Process. **26**, 1172–1192 (2014)
21. Baumgärtner, K., et al.: Arbeit als subjektivierendes Handeln. Handlungsfähigkeit bei Unwägbarkeiten und Ungewissheit. Springer, Wiesbaden (2017). https://doi.org/10.1007/978-3-658-14983-3
22. Herrmann, T.: Kreatives Prozessdesign: Konzepte und Methoden zur Integration von Prozessorganisation, Technik und Arbeitsgestaltung. Springer, Heidelberg (2012). https://doi.org/10.1007/978-3-642-24370-7
23. Miller, G.A.: The magical number seven, plus or minus two: some limits on our capacity for processing information. Psychol. Rev. **63**, 81 (1956)
24. Majchrzak, A., Wagner, C., Yates, D.: Corporate Wiki users: results of a survey. In: Proceedings - 2006 International Symposium on Wikis (WikiSym 2006), pp. 99–104 (2006)
25. Davis, A., Dieste, O., Hickey, A., Juristo, N., Moreno, A.M.: Effectiveness of requirements elicitation techniques: empirical results derived from a systematic review. In: 14th IEEE International Requirements Engineering Conference (RE 2006), pp. 179–188. IEEE (2006)

26. Tcha-Tokey, K., Loup-Escande, E., Christmann, O., Richir, S.: Effects of interaction level, framerate, field of view, 3D content feedback, previous experience on subjective user eXperience and objective usability in immersive virtual environment. Int. J. Virtual Real. **17**, 27–51 (2017)
27. Morgan, D.L.: The Focus Group Guidebook. Sage Publications (1997)

Business Processes and the Safety of Stakeholders: Considering the Electromagnetic Pollution

Magdalena Garvanova(✉), Ivan Garvanov, and Ivan Kashukeev

Faculty of Information Sciences, University of Library Studies and Information Technologies, Sofia, Bulgaria
{m.garvanova,i.garvanov}@unibit.bg, ikashukeev@gmail.com

Abstract. Enterprise models are featuring business processes and corresponding stakeholders. In this paper, we are interested in those stakeholders who are humans. They are reflected in enterprise models with mainly considering regulations (what laws and business rules they should stick to) and public values (to what public values, such as safety privacy, and so on their behavior should conform). Nevertheless, we have seen no enterprise models that reflect the effect on human health, for example concerning the electromagnetic "pollution" each human is exposed to. We argue that avoiding electro-magnetic pollution as much as possible is a sensible goal as it concerns the behavior of any human stakeholder. Hence, this can be considered as another desired behavioral restriction, next to regulations and public values. In this paper, we discuss in detail the electro-magnetic pollution and its effect on human health, and we propose ways to reducing it. Finally, we give recommendations on how to reflect those issues in enterprise models, such that the safety of stakeholders is taken into account.

Keywords: Business process · Stakeholder · Electro-magnetic pollution

1 Introduction

Enterprise modeling is about modeling business processes and corresponding stakeholders, capturing all relevant rules and restrictions [33]. Stakeholders in turn can be humans, artificial entities, and so on. In this paper, we are particularly interested in those stakeholders who are humans – in the remaining of the paper, by "stakeholder" we mean a stakeholder who is a human. Hence, it is a challenge specifying rules and modeling restrictions that concern stakeholders. Our focus is on the RESTRICTIONS: What restricts the behavior of stakeholders involved in business processes? Shishkov & Mendling claim that regulations and public values are to be taken into account when studying business processes and corresponding stakeholders [34]. Indeed, any stakeholder involved in a business process is restricted: (i) By the laws in the particular country, by the contracts that are underlying with regard to the business processes, and so on; (ii) By the public expectations for meeting particular public values – not to expose at risk the safety of others, not to disclose their personal data, and so on. We argue that

B. Shishkov (Ed.): BMSD 2020, LNBIP 391, pp. 386–393, 2020.
https://doi.org/10.1007/978-3-030-52306-0_28

both regulations and public values are well covered in recent literature as concerning business processes (and corresponding involved stakeholders). What remains insufficiently covered, in our view, is the EFFECT ON HUMAN HEALTH – we have not seen papers proposing enterprise modeling methodologies that take into account the health of the relevant human stakeholders. Indeed, regulations and public values are important for the "organizational health", for the "societal health" but where is the personal health of a stakeholder?

Fig. 1. The exposure to EMF - possible biological and physical effects

Stakeholders act, surrounded by power transmission lines, various electrical appliances, such as TV and radio, wireless sensors, smart phones, and so on – this is all about electromagnetic waves; actually, life on Earth has always depended on the presence of an electromagnetic field [1]. The effect such waves have on the human body, is related to the maintenance of the biological clock and hormonal balance, the regulation of the body immune defenses, and so on. Further, the communication among wireless communication devices is carried out using signals transmitted by electromagnetic waves (we observe that more and more wireless devices and sensors are being used in our daily life, this leading to the exposure to Electro-Magnetic Field (EMF) of all living organisms on Earth – this assumes high levels of EMF irradiation) – this all is illustrated in Fig. 1, and we refer to this exposure as to an "invisible pollution", as considered also by the World Health Organization; it is alarming that this pollution is dramatically increasing with the increased use of mobile phones [2]. The effect of Radio-Frequency EMF (RM-EMF) on humans is studied with regard to cancer [3], genetic damage [4], neurological diseases [5, 6], reproductive disorders [7, 8], immune dysfunction [9, 10], kidney diseases [11, 12], as well as electromagnetic hypersensitivity [13], and cognitive effects [14]. Recent studies have shown that RF-EMFs are transmitted from cell phones and absorbed in the brain to a degree that can interfere with the human neuronal activity [15]. Some technology developers claim that most currently used communication devices use a low-energy EMF that is non-ionizing and that its frequency and power are insufficient to affect human health (a non-ionizing EMF is completely different from ionizing radiation that is associated with X-rays and gamma rays). At the same time, they do not dispute the fact that the body temperature increases when using mobile phones – the so-called "thermal effect", which can be detected by a simple thermal camera [16, 17]. We assume that wireless technologies will be increasingly used; this in turn will lead to increasing the number of EMF transmitters – this points to a secondary application of some of the existing EMFs.

Hence, we are facing two challenges, as follows:

- We need to reduce electromagnetic pollution, creating in this way a better environment for stakeholders;
- We need to adequately model this pollution and its effect on stakeholders, such that they are "forced" to restrict their actions accordingly, for the benefit of their health.

With regard to the first challenge, we propose (in this paper) a model for secondary application of wireless technologies as an option to reduce electromagnetic pollution and improve people's lifestyles. SAWT is a technology that uses existing Electro-Magnetic Waves (EMWs) in the space not for their intended purpose, but for solving new problems [18, 19]. For example, the existing TV signal should not be used for television viewing; with appropriate signal processing, it can be used to create a radio barrier that can be applied for the benefit of border security, for detecting vehicles, for controlling traffic lights, for measuring the time difference of arrival (TDOA), for the benefit of navigation processes, and so on.

With regard to the second challenge, and based on our proposal (mentioned above), we give some recommendations about reflecting those issues in enterprise models.

The remaining of the current paper is organized as follows: The abovementioned model for secondary application of wireless technologies is presented in Sect. 4 while our recommendations are presented in Sect. 5 (the Conclusions). Before this, we are providing further elaboration as it concerns electromagnetic fields (Sect. 2) and the effect on humans, particularly in a physiological perspective (Sect. 3).

2 Sources of Artificial Electromagnetic Fields

Electromagnetic waves can be classified according to the wavelength range, which is a function of the wave frequency - EMF (Fig. 2). Extremely low ELFs, ultra-low SLFs, and infrared ILFs are characterized by frequencies in the 3–3000 Hz range and are generated by electronics and electrical conductors, used in our homes and offices. ELF-EMF is also emitted by power lines that transmit electricity from the power stations to our homes.

Radio waves are in the range of 3 kHz to 300 GHz and are distributed in space, when the radio signal is transmitted by an antenna with suitable sizes. RF-EMF are emitted by devices such as mobile phones, Wi-Fi systems, satellite communication systems, radio, TV stations, and interactive radio stations. The sensors, used in the Internet-of-Things [35], are also in this radio range, as their increasing number and the need to increase the data transfer between them leads to a continuous growth of the frequency of the used radio signal. These devices operate on the principle of electromagnetic waves. These waves are absorbed by human and animal bodies, with a specific absorption rate (SAR). SAR refers to the amount of radio wave energy absorbed per unit mass per human body (1 kg or 1 g); units are W/kg or mW/g. The electromagnetic waves, emitted by mobile phones, are of high frequency and cause a rise in body temperature. This thermal response is quantified by SAR. The principle of warming when using RF-EMF can be explained by the principle of operation of the microwave oven, i.e. EMF causes vibrations of charged or polar molecules in the body, which is crucial for human health and safety. IEEE sets a standard for SAR, which for a mobile phone averages 2.0 W/kg, per 10 g of tissue.

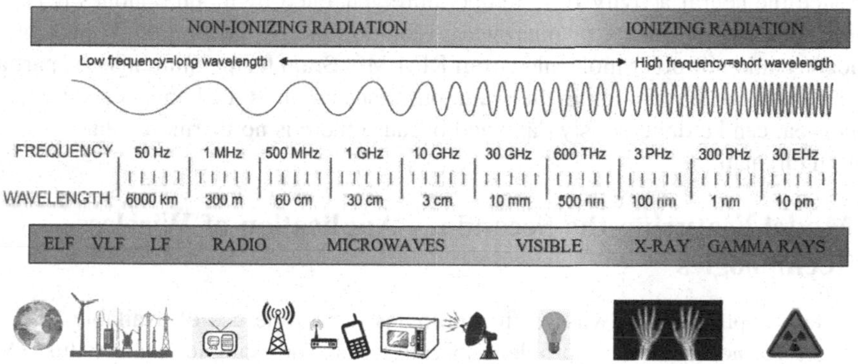

Fig. 2. Electromagnetic spectrum

Microwaves include decimeter, centimeter, and millimeter wavelength range of approximately 1 m to 1 mm and a frequency of 300 MHz to 300 GHz, respectively. They are absorbed by molecules in liquids (which have a dipole moment). In the microwave oven, this effect is used to heat food. Low-intensity microwave radiation is also used in wireless telecommunications. It is noteworthy that there are no definite boundaries between the types of electromagnetic radiation. Light, X-ray and gamma rays are characterized even with higher frequencies. Typical of these rays is that they consist of high-energy photons. These waves are of no interest in this article.

3 Effects of EMF on Human Physiology

In [20], the RF-EMF as possibly carcinogenic to humans with prolonged exposure to EMF is defined. With the development of IoT people are supposed to live in the so-called "smart homes" and "smart cities" and work in "smart factories", where most of objects, including cars and machines, will communicate wirelessly with each other via electromagnetic signals. This means that people will be surrounded by radio pollution throughout the entire frequency range. The results of the impact of these technologies on human health will emerge over time, but they can be considered with the results of the impact of mobile technologies on humans.

There is much research on the impact of GSM technology on humans, some of which claim that different neurological effects may occur due to the proximity of the mobile phone to the head and the cranial nervous system. These neurological dysfunctions include headache [21], changes in sleep habits [22], and changes in EEG [23]. In addition, significant statistical results have been reported through various epidemiological studies on neurological cognitive disturbances such as headache, tremor, dizziness, memory loss, loss of concentration, and sleep disorders due to excessive exposure to RF-EMF [24]. Electromagnetic waves, in particular RF-EMFs emitted from mobile phones, are absorbed into the brain to such extent that they can interfere with neuronal activity [25].

The studies have shown that RF-EMFs, emitted from mobile phones, activate metabolic processes in the human brain [26]. The thermal effects of RF-EMF can influence the neural activity from temperature generated by mobile phones [27]. The established thermal effects of microwave radiation are the generation of heat by the induced rotation of polar molecules from RF-EMF. Brain temperature may be partially lowered by blood circulation in the brain, but tissues such as the human eye, especially the cornea, can be dangerously damaged because there is no thermoregulatory system through circulation.

4 Model Featuring the Secondary Application of Wireless Technologies

Secondary application of wireless technologies means the use of available EMFs in the space for non-traditional problem-solving tasks. For example, using radio, TV or GSM signals to create radio barriers to detect moving objects, evaluate their parameters, classify objects, and more. This information can be used to manage road traffic in smart cities over time, without having to create new radio barriers by installing additional radio transmitters. Similarly, it is possible to create different security systems, both in rooms with available WiFi and outdoors using available radio, TV, GSM or GPS signals (Fig. 3). The use of GPS as a secondary application system for wireless technologies is very convenient for implementation both inside and outside settlements, including all over the globe [28–30]. Knowing the location of the transmitters (base stations, TV- and radio transmitters, different sensors used by IoT) and measuring the TDOA, it is possible to create different navigation systems. In recent years, alternative solutions have been offered for navigation systems using natural sources of radio signals, coming from space, namely the use of pulsar signals. The creation of such technology will make it impossible to maintain artificial navigation systems such as GPS, GLONASS, BeiDou, Galileo and others.

The use of signals from pulsars and other natural space sources of EMFs can be directed to detecting meteorites and other cosmic bodies on the principle of radio barriers [31]. The development of passive communication systems and the secondary application of available communication signals can significantly reduce the number of EMF transmitters. In recent years, various technologies that use the information from the radio shadow, obtained from an object, have been offered. The shadow has been used for millennia before us as a source of information for orienting in space or determining time. With the currently available equipment, it is possible to detect the radio shadow from different objects, evaluate the parameters and solve various useful tasks in practice such as improving navigation, detecting and classifying objects, etc. [32].

Establishing systems for secondary application of wireless technologies will reduce the radiofrequency pollution, as it will be useful for practice. To obtain these applications, it is necessary to apply specific knowledge from various professional fields, as well as to offer specialized software solutions.

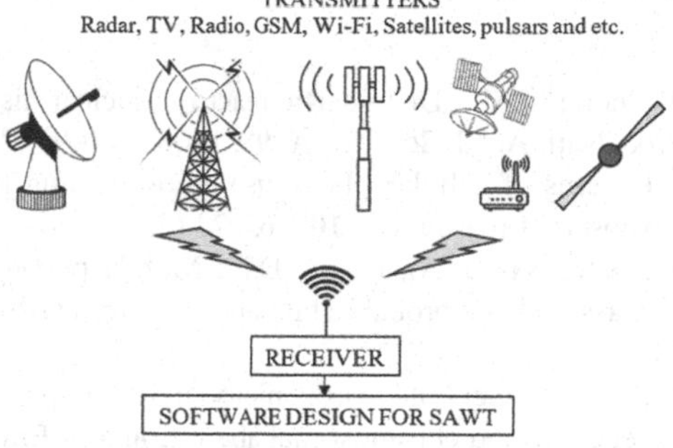

Fig. 3. The SAWT model

5 Conclusions

Enterprise modeling is featuring business processes, stakeholders, and so on. With regard to stakeholders who are humans, we apply business rules and regulations, and we expect those stakeholders to stick to certain public values. Nevertheless, most current enterprise models fail to explicitly focus on the safety of such stakeholders – for example, their exposure to electromagnetic pollution can have effects on their health.

To mitigate this, we have proposed a model featuring the secondary application of wireless technology (aiming at reducing the electromagnetic pollution), basing this on studies concerning both electromagnetic waves and fields as well as their effect on the human body. As it concerns enterprise modeling nevertheless, we propose (inspired by the mentioned studies) several recommendations, as follows:

- We argue that metrics are necessary as it concerns electromagnetic pollution – it should be possible to measure whether or not a stakeholder in his or her current location is exposed to unhealthy electromagnetic pollution (going over a certain threshold).
- In our view, sensors should be applied for effectively sensing the electromagnetic pollution.
- Further, the way those issues would be reflected in stakeholders' behaviors may be a matter of business rules, for example: The stakeholder is forbidden to stay in a polluted area or the stakeholder is just informed and it is up to him/her to decide whether to stay in the polluted area or not.
- Broader safety regulations are needed as well, to guarantee that organizations would not "force" stakeholders to get exposed to electromagnetic pollution in the name of fulfilling business goals.

Our future work will focus on implementing such measures, possibly through context-aware systems [36], where the appearance of electromagnetic pollution affecting a stakeholder would bring the system to another context state where mitigation actions are needed.

Acknowledgement. This work is supported by the Bulgarian National Science Fund, Project: KP-06-N 32/4/07.12.2019.

References

1. Hollenbach, D.F., Herndon, J.M.: Deep-earth reactor: nuclear fission, helium, and the geomagnetic field. Proc. Natl. Acad. Sci. U.S.A. **98**, 11085–11090 (2001)
2. Langer, C.E., et al.: Patterns of cellular phone use among young people in 12 countries: implications for RF exposure. Environ. Int. **107**, 65–74 (2017)
3. Morgan, L.L., Miller, A.B., Sasco, A., Davis, D.L.: Mobile phone radiation causes brain tumors and should be classified as a probable human carcinogen (2A) (review). Int. J. Oncol. **46**, 1865–1871 (2015)
4. Kim, J.-Y., et al.: In vitro assessment of clastogenicity of mobile-phone radiation (835 MHz) using the alkaline comet assay and chromosomal aberration test. Environ. Toxicol. **23**, 319–327 (2008)
5. Kim, J.H., Yu, D.H., Huh, Y.H., Lee, E.H., Kim, H.G., Kim, H.R.: Long-term exposure to 835 MHz RF-EMF induces hyperactivity, autophagy and demyelination in the cortical neurons of mice. Sci. Rep. **7**, 41129 (2017)
6. Jiang, D.-P., et al.: Long-term electromagnetic pulse exposure induces Abeta deposition and cognitive dysfunction through oxidative stress and overexpression of APP and BACE1. Brain Res. **1642**, 10–19 (2016)
7. Falzone, N., Huyser, C., Becker, P., Leszczynski, D., Franken, D.R.: The effect of pulsed 900-MHz GSM mobile phone radiation on the acrosome reaction, head morphometry and zona binding of human spermatozoa. Int. J. Androl. **34**, 20–26 (2011)
8. Altun, G., Deniz, Ø.G., Yurt, K.K., Davis, D., Kaplan, S.: Effects of mobile phone exposure on metabolomics in the male and female reproductive systems. Environ. Res. **167**, 700–707 (2018)
9. Kazemi, E., et al.: Effect of 900 MHz electromagnetic radiation on the induction of ROS in human peripheral blood mononuclear cells. J. Biomed. Phys. Eng. **5**, 105–114 (2015)
10. Ohtani, S., et al.: The effects of radio-frequency electromagnetic fields on T cell function during development. J. Radiat. Res. **56**, 467–474 (2015)
11. Kuybulu, A.E., et al.: Effects of long-term pre- and post-natal exposure to 2.45 GHz wireless devices on developing male rat kidney. Ren. Fail. **38**, 571–580 (2016)
12. Türedi, S., Kerimoğlu, G., Mercantepe, T., Odacı, E.: Biochemical and pathological changes in the male rat kidney and bladder following exposure to continuous 900-MHz electromagnetic field on postnatal days 22–59. Int. J. Radiat. Biol. **93**, 990–999 (2017)
13. Gruber, M.J., Palmquist, E., Nordin, S.: Characteristics of perceived electromagnetic hypersensitivity in the general population. Scand. J. Psychol. **59**, 422–427 (2018)
14. Son, Y., et al.: Long-term RF exposure on behavior and cerebral glucose metabolism in 5xFAD mice. Neurosci. Lett. **666**, 64–69 (2018)
15. Jeong, Y.J., et al.: 1950 MHz electromagnetic fields ameliorate aβ pathology in Alzheimer's disease mice. Curr. Alzheimer Res. **12**, 481–492 (2015)
16. Garvanova, M., Shishkov, B., Vladimirov, S.: Mobile devices – effect on human health. In: Shishkov, B. (ed.) Proceedings of the Seventh International Conference on Telecommunications and Remote Sensing (ICTRS 2018), 8–9 October 2018, Barcelona, Spain, pp. 101–104 (2018)
17. Wyde, M.E., et al.: Effect of cell phone radiofrequency radiation on body temperature in rodents: pilot studies of the National Toxicology Program's reverberation chamber exposure system. Bioelectromagnetics **39**, 190–199 (2018)
18. Cherniakov, M., Kubik, M.: Secondary applications of wireless technology (SAWT): the concept. In: European Conference on Wireless Technology, Paris (2000)

19. Kabakchiev, C., Kyovtorov, V., Garvanov, I.: Secondary application wireless technologies increasing the information potential for defense against terrorism. In: Advances and Challenges in Multisensor Data and Information Processing. NATO Security Through Science Series – D: Information and Communication Security, vol. 8, pp. 236–242. IOS press Inc. (2007)
20. Baan, R., et al.: Carcinogenicity of radiofrequency electromagnetic fields. Lancet Oncol. **12**, 624–626 (2011)
21. Frey, A.H.: Headaches from cellular telephones: are they real and what are the implications? Environ. Health Perspect. **106**, 101–103 (1998)
22. Wagner, P., Roschke, J., Mann, K., Hiller, W., Frank, C.: Human sleep under the influence of pulsed radiofrequency electromagnetic fields: a polysomnographic study using standardized conditions. Bioelectromagnetics **19**, 199–202 (1998)
23. Singh, G.: The effects of mobile phone usage on human brain using EEG. Int. J. Comput. Appl. **105**(13), 16–20 (2014). (0975-8887)
24. Abdel-Rassoul, G., et al.: Neurobehavioral effects among inhabitants around mobile phone base stations. Neurotoxicology **28**, 434–440 (2007)
25. Hinrikus, H., Bachmann, M., Lass, J.: Understanding physical mechanism of low-level microwave radiation effect. Int. J. Radiat. Biol. **94**, 877–882 (2018)
26. Volkow, N.D., et al.: Effects of cell phone radiofrequency signal exposure on brain glucose metabolism. JAMA **305**, 808–813 (2011)
27. Wainwright, P.: Thermal effects of radiation from cellular telephones. Phys. Med. Biol. **45**, 2363–2372 (2000)
28. Kabakchiev, C., et al.: Experimental parameter estimation of vehicles GPS shadows by forward scattering systems. In: International Radar Symposium 2017, 28–30 June 2017, Prague, Czech Republic, pp. 1–7 (2017)
29. Kabakchiev, H., et al.: Multi-channel target shadow detection in GPS FSR. Cybern. Inf. Technol. **19**(1), 116–132 (2019)
30. Garvanova, M., Garvanov, I., Kabakchiev, C., Shishkov, B.: Measuring and clustering moving objects. In: ACM International Conference Proceeding Series, 16 September 2019, 8th International Conference on Telecommunications and Remote Sensing (ICTRS 2019), 16–17 September 2019, Rhodes, Greece (2019)
31. Kabakchiev, H., et al.: Feasibility of cosmic object detection using an X-ray FSR system. In: The International Radar Symposium (IRS 2019), 26–28 June 2019, Ulm, Germany, pp. 1–8 (2019)
32. Garvanov, I., Kabakchiev, H., Behar, V., Garvanova, M., Iyinbor, R.: On the modeling of innovative navigation systems. In: Shishkov, B. (ed.) BMSD 2019. LNBIP, vol. 356, pp. 299–306. Springer, Cham (2019). https://doi.org/10.1007/978-3-030-24854-3_23
33. Shishkov, B.: Systems. In: Shishkov, B. (ed.) Designing Enterprise Information Systems. TEES, pp. 27–51. Springer, Cham (2020). https://doi.org/10.1007/978-3-030-22441-7_2
34. Shishkov, B., Mendling, J.: Business process variability and public values. In: Shishkov, B. (ed.) BMSD 2018. LNBIP, vol. 319, pp. 401–411. Springer, Cham (2018). https://doi.org/10.1007/978-3-319-94214-8_31
35. Shishkov, B., Mitrakos, D.: Towards context-aware border security control. In: Proceedings of the 6th International Symposium on Business Modeling and Software Design (BMSD 2016), 20–22 June 2016, Rhodes, Greece. SCITEPRESS (2016)
36. Shishkov, B.: Tuning the behavior of context-aware applications. In: Shishkov, B. (ed.) BMSD 2019. LNBIP, vol. 356, pp. 134–152. Springer, Cham (2019). https://doi.org/10.1007/978-3-030-24854-3_9

Author Index

Printed in the United States
By Bookmasters